CHILD SUPPORT IN AMERICA

The Legal Perspective

by

HARRY D. KRAUSE

Professor of Law
University of Illinois

THE MICHIE COMPANY
Law Publishers
CHARLOTTESVILLE, VIRGINIA

Library of Congress Catalog Card No. 80-85127

ISBN 0-87215-330-4

TABLE OF CONTENTS

TABLE OF CONTENTS

PART II

PATERNITY AND ITS ESTABLISHMENT

PART III

"COOPERATIVE FEDERALISM": BIG BROTHER FINDS THE FATHER

TABLE OF CONTENTS

TABLE OF CONTENTS

PREFACE

In 1934, the American Law Institute's Restatement of the Law of Conflicts characterized support obligations and their enforcement as "of no special interest to other states and since the duty is not imposed primarily for the benefit of an individual, it is not enforceable elsewhere." [1] In theory, this notion was laid to rest by the widespread enactment of the Uniform Reciprocal Enforcement of Support Acts of 1950, 1958 and 1968.[2] In practice, however, American law remained deeply insensitive to the enforcement of child support obligations.

In the last two decades, several social trends merged to change this situation: Increasing rates of divorce, family abandonment and illegitimacy combined to leave unprecedented numbers of children in single parent homes, typically without adequate or any support from the other parent.[3]

The "New Frontier" and the "Great Society" of the "Soaring Sixties" brought new emphasis on welfare programs for the "poor", so many of them children.

---

1. § 458, Comment (a), RESTATEMENT OF THE LAW OF CONFLICT OF LAWS (1934).

2. Appendix A *infra.*

3. In 1977, according to the Bureau of the Census, 18 percent of the children in the United States were living with one parent. This 18 percent represents a doubling of the corresponding proportion in 1960 (up from 9 to 18 percent). In absolute numbers, the increase amounted to a rise from 7.1 million children in 1960 to 11.3 million in 1977. Although the total number of children under age 18 was about the same in both 1960 and 1977, the number living with a separated parent doubled, the number living with a divorced parent tripled, and the number living with a never-married parent grew to seven times as high. In contrast, the number of children living with two parents actually declined by 10 percent.

SENATE COMM. ON FINANCE, STAFF DATA AND MATERIALS ON CHILD SUPPORT, 96th Cong., 1st Sess., CP 96-7 at 4 (March 19, 1979).

Thoughtlessly, the basic eligibility criterion of the Aid to Families with Dependent Children (AFDC) program — absence of a parent, speak "father" — was carried forward from a program originally intended to deal primarily with orphans. Perversely, the aid program began to encourage fathers to leave their needy families to entitle them to state support and, indeed, to make it financially attractive for women to have children.[4]

Riding the constitutional "equality wave", some twenty United States Supreme Court decisions demanded substantial equality for children born out of wedlock, a mandate seeking implementation in terms of support enforcement.

"Family policy", in terms of public vs. private responsibility, came to be discussed as a national concern.[5]

As welfare costs seemed to soar out of control, the federal government moved into the child support vacuum left by the states in their traditional preserve — family law. By 1975, initiatives of the Senate Finance Committee that had extended over several years and bills, had resulted in amendments to the Social Security Act which mandated federal and state cooperation in the nationwide and strict enforcement of parental support obligations.

Today, five years after this legislation was enacted, more than 1300 million dollars are transferred annually under this extension of "cooperative federalism." The Senate Finance Committee reports proudly:

> In the first 47 months of the child support program (August 1975 through June 30, 1979), States have

---

4. JOINT ECONOMIC COMMITTEE, INCOME SECURITY FOR AMERICANS: RECOMMENDATIONS OF THE PUBLIC WELFARE STUDY, 93rd Cong. 2d Sess., at 80 (Joint Committee Print, December 5, 1974). Cf., Janowitz, The Impact of AFDC on Illegitimate Birth Rates, 38 J. MARRIAGE AND THE FAMILY 485 (1976).

5. E.g., Califano, American Families: Trends, Pressures and Recommendations. A Preliminary Report to Governor Jimmy Carter, Jr., (Mimeograph, September 17, 1976).

reported total collections of over $3.6 billion of which $1.6 billion was for AFDC families and $2.0 billion was for families not on welfare, at a total cost of $1.0 billion or 28 cents per dollar collected.

In the first 47 months of the child support enforcement program, 1,573,000 absent parents were located; there were 970,000 support obligations established; and paternity was established by the courts for 323,000 children.

The heavy impact on the court systems of the cities, counties, and States is apparent from statistics showing the tremendous increase in child support activity in these areas since the program's inception in 1976. In fiscal year 1976, 184,000 parents were located. The number of parents located in fiscal year 1978 was 519,000, an increase of 182 percent in 2 years. In fiscal year 1976, 76,000 support obligations were established. The number of support obligations established in fiscal year 1978 was 350,000, an increase of 361 percent in 2 years. In fiscal year 1976, 15,000 paternities were established. The number of paternities established in fiscal year 1978 was 123,000, an increase of 820 percent in just 2 years.[6]

This volume describes, analyzes and evaluates child support enforcement laws and practices, regulations and working procedures at the state and federal levels and their interaction. The establishment of paternity for children born to unmarried parents is given the thorough attention the subject deserves, and detailed information is included on "medical proof" that is increasingly determinative in paternity actions.[7] Thorough references on all topics range from federal and state statutes to ample, primarily very

---

6. SENATE COMM. ON FINANCE, SOCIAL SECURITY DISABILITY AMENDMENTS OF 1979, 96th Cong., 1st Sess., at 66-67 (November 8, 1979).

7. A few of these sections bring up-to-date and elaborate on subjects I dealt with previously in ILLEGITIMACY: LAW AND SOCIAL POLICY (Bobbs-Merrill, 1971).

recent judicial decisions. Use of, as well as reference to, the increasing store of "Information Memoranda" and "Action Transmittals" developed by the Office of Child Support Enforcement (of the HHS, Department of Health and Human Services, formerly HEW) is made. Appendices include the AMA-ABA Guidelines for the use of blood typing in paternity cases, the Uniform Parentage Act, the Uniform Reciprocal Enforcement of Support Act, a survey of capacities and capabilities of American blood-typing laboratories and more.

This volume is intended for the state's attorney, the private attorney, and the judge who deal with child support problems. It is directed also to the many public aid officials who are involved in the "IV-D program" and who need a compact and comprehensible guide to the legal framework in which they operate.

Beyond that, this review also raises a few questions about a surprisingly efficient federal bureaucracy taking hold of a body of state laws that has not grown out of a principled approach. Many of these problems will have occurred to and must be of concern to anyone involved in child support enforcement at any but the most routine levels. This seems a good time to pause and thoroughly review where we stand in this vitally important area of the law — and ask where we should go. Accordingly, the temptation to refine questions and attempt to point toward possible solutions has not been resisted: Suggestions for future improvements are addressed to the HSS's Office of Child Support Enforcement, the appropriate Committees of Congress, and, by no means least, to state legislators.

Urbana, Illinois   HARRY D. KRAUSE
November, 1980

ACKNOWLEDGMENTS

My involvement in the problems dealt with in this volume reaches back fifteen years. In that time, a greater debt of gratitude has accumulated to more individuals and organizations than can be acknowledged here. As I think back, a few individuals, organizations and events stand out.

First, recognition goes to Attorney Adolph Levy of New Orleans who, at the right time, had in hand just the right case — *Levy* (no relation) *v. Louisiana* — with which to take the Equal Protection issue to the United States Supreme Court. Through the help of Professor Norman Dorsen, the ACLU became the financial vehicle by which the case "went up." The NAACP entered *Levy* and *Glona* with a brief *amicus curiae,* and the ACLU continued to show its support with its *amicus* brief in *Labine v. Vincent.*

In 1969, the National Conference of Commissioners on Uniform State Laws appointed a Committee to study a proposed "Uniform Act on Legitimacy" which ultimately became the "Uniform Parentage Act" (Appendix B). Lewis C. Green of St. Louis most ably served as chairman of that committee.

Under the leadership, successively, of Harry Fain, Neva Talley, Felix Infausto, Jacob Isaacs, Ralph Podell, Arnold Gibbs, Harry Cole, Louise Raggio and Henry Foster, the American Bar Association's Section on Family Law encouraged work on the Uniform Parentage Act, as well as on medical-legal guidelines for lawyers, courts and medical experts in disputed paternity cases. Doctors Alexander Wiener, Kenneth Sell, Joseph Miale, Chang Ling Lee, Joseph B. Jerome, and others of the American Medical Association were instrumental in the successful completion of the latter project (Appendix D). Judge Orman Ketcham and Attorneys Harry Fain and Lawrence Stotter helped provide the legal perspective.

ACKNOWLEDGMENTS

William R. Galvin of the Senate Finance Committee Staff has worked untiringly on federal legislation to improve the child support enforcement process and provided much information and encouragement.

The aid of the Department of Health, Education and Welfare through Contract No. OCD-CB-452, which supported early work on blood typing tests in paternity cases, is acknowledged gratefully.

Attorney Louis B. Hays, since its creation the operating director* of the Office of Child Support Enforcement, has generously provided invaluable information on OCSE's operations.

Dean Kenneth Broun of the University of North Carolina Law School, a leading expert on the law of evidence in the United States and, until his assumption of the deanship, Director of the National Institute for Trial Advocacy, substantially wrote the section that deals with technical aspects of the law of evidence (Chapter VI, Section 3).

Herbert Polesky, M.D., formerly president of the American Association of Blood Banks, collaborated on a survey of American laboratory capacities in the blood typing field (Appendix H). Richard H. Walker, M.D., now chairman of the AABB's Committee on Parentage Testing, is carrying forward the inquiry into methods and standards for paternity testing.

Dr. Klavs Henningsen, Director of the Serological Department at the University of Copenhagen, Denmark, summarized for us the experience collected in his pioneering laboratory (Appendix F). Dr. Chang Ling Lee, Director of the Blood Bank at Mount Sinai Hospital, Chicago, was instrumental in bringing "news" from the medical side of the paternity problem to the legal side

---

* Officially, the Commissioner of Social Security is listed as director of OCSE.

ACKNOWLEDGMENTS

(Appendix E). Dr. Konrad Hummel of Freiburg, Germany, forcefully brought the possibilities of statistical calculation of "plausibility of paternity" to American attention. Doctors Patricia A. Tippett, Patrick J. Lincoln and Barbara E. Dodd of London, were important sources for the production of Appendix G, which describes blood typing techniques and their use in the courts in the United Kingdom.

Certainly not least, I wish to acknowledge the effort and help over the years of excellent law students, now successful attorneys, prominently including Daniel King, Richard Pope, William Lynch, Gerd Otte, William Snapp, Robert Carter, Nancy Rink Carter and Shelley Carter-LaRue.

Sincere thanks are due to "my deans," John Cribbet and Peter Hay, for providing a working environment at the College of Law that makes writing nearly a pleasure, as well as to the Center for Advanced Study at the University of Illinois for giving me time to complete the manuscript by means of a half-time appointment in the fall of 1979.

Linda Graham, Janet Sanderson and Margo Moluf, three most able, dedicated and patient secretaries, labored over the years to keep this manuscript in order. Without them, this book would not have been completed.

Finally, I sincerely thank my wife for her support, but the routine acknowledgment, "without Eva's encouragement, this book could not have been written", must be omitted. Actually, I completed the book against her advice — it took too much time for too long! (As usual, she was right.)

Urbana, Illinois   HARRY D. KRAUSE

November, 1980

PART I
CHILD SUPPORT AND ITS ENFORCEMENT

Chapter I

CHILD SUPPORT OBLIGATIONS UNDER STATE LAW

1. Whose Obligation? Whose Right?

The common law seemingly failed to impose on the father a civil obligation to support his child, although the English "poor laws" allowed support to be charged for a "bastard."[1] Blackstone speaks in terms of a natural, voluntary obligation and a fine for non-compliance, but does not clearly state a civil claim.[2] As late as 1953 the Supreme Court of New Jersey had difficulty finding a legally enforceable support obligation running from the father to his child. The need was as basic as medical care, and the case was resolved by reference to "natural law."[3]

Today, statutes are the rule. Curiously, many statutes still fail to state the support obligation directly, but simply assume (and thereby imply) that there is an underlying liability, for instance when providing for reimbursement for welfare expenditures[4] or when allowing "family expenses" to be charged against the property of parents[5] or when imposing criminal liability for nonsupport.[6]

---

1. An Act for Setting the Poor on Work, 1576, 18 Eliz. 1, c. 3 § 7. *See also* 1601, 43 Eliz. 1, c. 2 § 7; R. FOLEY, LAWS RELATING TO THE POOR 51-61 (3d ed. 1751).

2. W. BLACKSTONE, 1 COMMENTARIES ON THE LAWS OF ENGLAND 434-37 (Oxford 1765).

3. Greenspan v. Slate, 12 N.J. 426, 97 A.2d 390 (1953). For a more recent and more enthusiastic endorsement of "natural law" in a welfare reimbursement situation, *see* Division of Family Services v. Clark, 554 P.2d 1310 (Utah 1976).

4. *E.g.*, ILL. REV. STAT. ch. 23, § 10-1 *et seq.* (1977).

5. *E.g.*, ILL. REV. STAT. ch. 40, § 1015 (1977).

6. While some courts have refused to imply a civil support obligation from a criminal nonsupport statute, *e.g.*, James _____ v. Hutton, 373 S.W.2d 167 (Kan. City, Mo. Ct. App. 1963), the civil obligation

In the absence of the father, the mother has been deemed obligated to support her child — nor has she had a practical alternative. With a father present, however, the mother's obligation typically has been held secondary to the father's primary obligation.[7] Only more recently (and not yet universally), an equal obligation of support has been imposed on mothers and fathers, either by statute[8] or by judicial decisions,[9] the latter sometimes based on state

---

typically is imposed as a condition of probation in the criminal proceeding. *See infra* ch. II.1.a, text at note 18.

7. Pendexter v. Pendexter, 363 A.2d 743 (Me. 1976). *See e.g.,* CAL. CIV. CODE § 196 (Supp. 1979); ME. REV. STAT. ANN. tit. 19, § 301 (Cum. Supp. 1978); S.C. CODE § 14-21-820(b) (1976).

8. *E.g.,* Scarpino v. Scarpino, 201 Neb. 564, 270 N.W.2d 913 (1979); *In re* Kenyon, 41 Or. App. 591, 598 P.2d 1225 (1979); *In re* Westby, 30 Or. App. 435, 567 P.2d 145 (1977). *Also, see e.g.,* N.M. STAT. ANN. § 40-5-1 (1978); NEV. REV. STAT. § 126.030 (1957); OR. REV. STAT. §§ 108.040, 109.030 (1953); UNIFORM CIVIL LIABILITY FOR SUPPORT ACT §§ 2, 3 (1954), 9 U.L.A., MATR., FAM. AND HEALTH LAWS 171 (1979) (Designed to promote and facilitate the use of the UNIFORM RECIPROCAL ENFORCEMENT OF SUPPORT ACT, this Act was adopted by California, Maine, and New Hampshire in 1955, and Utah in 1957).

9. Carter v. Carter, 58 App. Div. 2d 438, 397 N.Y.S.2d 88 (1977); Boriak v. Boriak, 541 S.W.2d 237 (Tex. Civ. App. 1976); Hill v. Hill, 40 Ohio App. 2d 1, 317 N.E.2d 250 (1973); Muldrow v. Muldrow, 61 Cal. App. 3d 327, 132 Cal. Rptr. 48 (1976). *Cf.,* Stanley v. Nuzzo, 160 N.J. Super. 436, 390 A.2d 158 (1978); Tilmon v. Tilmon, 74 Ill. App. 3d 111, 391 N.E.2d 1086, 1089 (1979):

> [T]he courts have approached the problem of joint support on a realistic and flexible basis, having regard for the actual needs and abilities of the respective parties in maintaining a proper amount of support for the child — the approach being one of preventing injustice and assuring continuity and adequate support for the child, rather than that of establishing a mathematical formula based entirely on net annual income.
>
> The untraditional idea that the mother, as well as the father — even where she is a non-custodial parent — may be obliged to contribute to the support of the minor children of the couple evolved from practical considerations. It greatly enlarged the basis of the minor's support in an economy where many women have incomes from wages or salaries.

equal rights amendments [10] or on equal protection reasoning under the Fourteenth Amendment of the United States Constitution.[11] This trend may be reflected in the increase to five percent by 1978 (from one or two percent in 1976) in the proportion of *mothers* among fugitive parents.[12]

Where a joint and equal obligation has been imposed, it is shared in accordance with the parents' respective abilities to pay, render services or other relevant circumstances.[13] Of course, so long as the cultural tradition of awarding child custody on divorce to the mother remains resistant to change and so long as mothers and not fathers continue to be the primary custodians of out-of-wedlock-children, equality in the support obligation will continue to mean that the typical father's obligation is fulfilled by paying dollars and the mother's by rendering personal care. Resistance to change runs deep. In 1976, a federal court opined as follows:

> The stability of the family is essential to the stability of the nation. Traditionally, the father has been the breadwinner. The present state of society provides no basis for a departure from this tradition. Placing primary responsibility for support upon the father is both rational and constitutional. Perhaps at another time or generation when women have achieved economic equality in a realistic rather than idealistic

---

10. *See* Shapera v. Levitt, 394 A.2d 1011 (Pa. Super. 1978); Comment, *Equal Rights Provisions: The Experience Under State Constitutions,* 65 CAL. L. REV. 1086 (1977).

11. Carole K. v. Arnold K., 85 Misc. 2d 643, 380 N.Y.S.2d 593 (1976); A.H. v. W.B.McD., — F. Supp. — [5 F.L.R. 2556] (D. Minn. 1979); but *cf.,* Jones v. Jones, 355 So. 2d 354 (Ala. 1978). Concerning the constitutional requirement of equal duty to pay alimony *see* Orr v. Orr, 440 U.S. 268, 99 S. Ct. 1102, 58 L. Ed. 2d 253 (1979).

12. U.S. NEWS AND WORLD REPORT, February 12, 1979, at 50.

13. *See* CONN. GEN. STAT. ANN. § 46b-84(a) (Supp. 1979).

sense this question may bear constitutional cognizance and should be viewed in the perspective of the experience of that future time. Now is not the time. This is the time for judicial restraint on this question, otherwise in our zeal for change we risk a distortion and overextension of constitutional principles to a domestic relations principle which has been basic to our way of life.[14]

In the long run, as the incidence of custodial awards to fathers increases and the ability of women to earn meaningful incomes improves, money support judgments against mothers will increase and will no longer merit the news notices they attract today.[15]

As the child support obligation comes to be shared more equally by father and mother, the question of whether they may compromise their respective obligations, in a separation agreement for instance, will become increasingly important. The rule is that such contracts bind neither the child[16] nor the public.[17] Nevertheless, a contractual settlement between father and mother allocating or even waiving the support duty may be effective between the parents themselves and define their

---

14. Conley v. Sweeney, 2 F.L.R. 2455 (N.D. Ohio 1976).

15. *E.g.*, 4 F.L.R. 2208 (1978); 5 F.L.R. 2049 (1979). Generally, *see* Annot., *Mother's Duty to Pay Child Support*, 98 A.L.R.3d 1149 (1980).

16. *E.g.*, Knox v. Remick, 371 Mass. 433, 358 N.E.2d 432 (1976); Ebel v. Brown, 70 Mich. App. 705, 246 N.W.2d 379 (1976); Clayton v. Muth, 144 N.J. Super. 491, 366 A.2d 354 (1976). *Cf.*, Henry v. Russell, 19 Wash. App. 409, 576 P.2d 908 (1978); Mayfield v. Kentucky, 546 S.W.2d 433 (Ky. 1977); McIntyre v. McIntyre, — Misc. 2d —, — N.Y.S.2d — [5 F.L.R. 2289] (Fam. Ct. 1979).

17. State v. Gulley, 570 P.2d 127 (Utah 1977); State *ex rel.* Fabian, 116 N.H. 516, 363 A.2d 1007 (1976); Lizotte v. Lizotte, 15 Wash. App. 622, 551 P.2d 137 (1976). *Contra:* Harder v. Towns, 1 Kan. App. 667, 573 P.2d 625 (1977). *See also* Bergen County Welfare Bd. v. Cueman, 164 N.J. Super 401, 396 A.2d 620 (1979).

relative shares of the total duty.[18] If the primary obligor defaults, however, the child (or public) again has recourse to the other parent.

Mirroring the parental obligation to render support, subsidiary support obligations may in some instances ascend the ladder of descent by the operation of "relative responsibility" laws. Children may be held liable to support their indigent parents.[19] In turn, grandparents might be held for the support of indigent grandchildren.[20] Not long ago, support obligations extended "sideways" to siblings

---

18. *E.g.,* Boden v. Boden, 42 N.Y.2d 210, 397 N.Y.S.2d 701, 366 N.E.2d 791 (1977); Everett v. Everett, 57 Cal. App. 3d 236, 129 Cal. Rptr. 8 (1976). *But cf.* Rome v. Beach, 87 Misc. 2d 197, 384 N.Y.S.2d 688 (1976). Consideration for the waiver of support rights may be found in various ways. For instance, in Barlett v. Barlett, 70 Ill. App. 3d 661, 389 N.E.2d 15 (1979), the father agreed to waive visitation rights in exchange for the remarried mother's and stepfather's agreement to waive child support. The court found expressly that the children had *not* been deprived of "material needs or parental guidance." An attempted "settlement" prior to the conception of the child, however, was held to violate public policy in Fournier v. Lopez, second unpublished opinion, *see* 5 F.L.R. 2582 (1979):

> She asked Lopez to father her child. Lopez told her he could not afford the financial responsibility. Fournier promised him that if he would allow her to have the baby, she would raise it herself and assume all financial responsibility for its upbringing. Thereupon the parties orally agreed that Lopez would father the child and Fournier would be solely responsible for its support.
> As stated in *Marvin,* if sexual acts form an inseparable part of the consideration for the agreement, the agreement is invalid. In the present case, the expressed consideration for the agreement was the sexual services of respondent. Without these services there would not have been an agreement. The contract is invalid.

19. *E.g.,* Cal. Civ. Code § 206 (Supp. 1979); Or. Rev. Stat. § 109.010 (1953); Vt. Stat. Ann. tit. 33, § 931 (1959); Va. Code § 20-88 (1975).

20. *E.g.,* Ariz. Rev. Stat. § 12-850 (1956). (Where the putative mother or father is a minor, the grandparents may be liable in an amount not to exceed five hundred dollars). *Contra,* Cal. Civ. Code § 208.5 (Supp. 1979). (Grandparents not liable for support of minor child's children).

7

and "up" to grandparents. Today, however, relative responsibility statutes are on the decline and are invoked primarily — and then rarely and softly — where support reimbursement is sought from children of welfare-receiving parents.[21]

With varying degrees of success, support has sometimes been sought from stepfathers, even if they had not legally adopted the children in question. Such attempts have failed when challenged, if the statute failed to provide a support liability of general applicability and imposed the stepparent obligation only where welfare payments were being made to the children.[22] Statutes or decisions of general applicability, however, do not seem vulnerable.[23] For instance, Iowa's Supreme Court decided in 1972 that Iowa had long recognized that "if a stepparent is living with his stepchildren (in loco parentis), he is obligated to support them."[24] Of course, since that obligation ends when the stepfather moves out (or the mother dies),[25] it is not a significant factor in terms of *enforcement*. On the other hand, whether there is a legal obligation or not, stepparent

---

21. Hospital Services, Inc. v. Brooks, 229 N.W.2d 69 (N.D. 1975); Swoap v. Superior Court of Sacramento County, 10 Cal. 3d 490, 111 Cal. Rptr. 136, 516 P.2d 840 (1973).

22. *In re* Slochowsky, 67 A.D. 926, — N.Y.S.2d — (1979); Application of Slochowsky, 73 Misc. 2d 563, 342 N.Y.S.2d 525 (1973). *See also* Hammond v. Secretary of H.E.W., 475 F. Supp. 675 (D. Colo. 1979).

23. *See* DEL. CODE ANN. tit. 13, § 501(b) (Cum. Supp. 1978); Archibald v. Whaland, 555 F.2d 1061 (1st Cir. 1977). *Cf.,* STAFF OF SENATE COMMITTEE ON FINANCE, 96TH CONG., 1ST SESS., FINANCE COMMITTEE REPORT FOR FISCAL YEAR 1980, 39 (Comm. Print 1979). (In calculating a child's AFDC benefits, the agency may not consider a stepparent's income unless that stepparent is legally responsible for the children under State law.)

24. Kelley v. Iowa Dept. of Social Servs., 197 N.W.2d 192 (Iowa 1972).

25. *In re* Kaiser, 93 Misc. 2d 36, 402 N.Y.S.2d 171 (1978).

support does play an important *de facto* role in functioning second families. In line with this reality, an unemployed Massachusetts man was granted a dependency allowance in connection with his unemployment benefits for stepchildren who were in fact dependent on him, but whom he was not legally obligated to support.[26]

The other side of the question "Whose Obligation?" is "To Whom Is the Obligation Owed?". In principle, of course, the support obligation runs to the child. In practice, on the other hand, the child usually is by the very definition of the support obligation (which runs to the age of majority) of an age where it is unable to sue. Another person, typically the custodial parent (and that usually means the mother), will bring the action, receive the award and exercise broad discretion concerning its use. Most statutes spell out nothing very clearly. South Carolina says "any interested persons may file a petition to the court requesting the court to order persons legally chargeable to provide support as required by law." [27] It might be added that the welfare authorities, if they have rendered support to the child, frequently are specifically listed as permissible plaintiffs in support actions.[28] Beyond that, several states are formulating procedures for intervention by the welfare authorities in divorce proceedings to help assure that adequate child support orders are awarded in the first

---

26. Roush v. Director of Unemployment Sec., — Mass. —, 79 Mass. Adv. Sh. 732, 837 N.E.2d 126 (1979).

27. S.C. CODE § 14-21-840 (1976).

28. In illegitimacy cases, welfare authorities initiate a disproportionately higher number of support cases, ranging in some localities beyond 50% of all paternity actions filed. *See infra* ch. V. 1; A.H. v. W.B. McD., — F. Supp. — [5 F.L.R. 2556] (D. Minn. 1979). *See also, e.g.,* ARIZ. REV. STAT. § 12-2456 (1956); COLO. REV. STAT. § 14-7-102 (1973); N.D. CENT. CODE § 14-08.1-01 (Supp. 1977).

place.[29] Finally, third parties who have furnished child support may sue for reimbursement.[30]

2. Criteria for Setting Support Levels.

Today, civil child support obligations generally are statutory. The extent of the obligation, however, remains largely undefined, especially in the ongoing marriage. This is due to a deliberate reluctance of the courts to involve themselves in the day-to-day operation of the functioning family,[31] unless and until the situation is so bad that "child neglect" laws are offended and furnish the basis of intervention.[32] Moreover, as soon as a dispute over support reaches the stage where litigation is contemplated, the family typically is defunct, or close to it. The context of the litigation, whether divorce, separation or paternity proceeding, determines the extent of the obligation. Even in these contexts few *clear* answers appear. The court's discretion regarding the amount of child support usually reigns supreme, the basic and often the only criteria being the needs of the child and the father's (and perhaps the mother's and the child's) ability to earn.[33]

---

29. *E.g.*, R.I. GEN. LAWS § 15-13-2 (Cum. Supp. 1978); VT. ST. ANN., VT. RULES OF CIVIL PROCEDURE, RULE 80(b) (Cum. Supp. 1979). Both states' procedures are described in Office of Child Support Enforcement, Department of H.E.W., OCSE-IM-78-15 (June 7, 1979). *Cf.*, Wason v. Wason, 83 Mich. App. 364, 268 N.W.2d 405 (1978).

30. *E.g.*, CAL. CIV. CODE § 207 (1954): "If a parent neglects to provide articles necessary for his child who is under his charge, according to his circumstances, a third person may in good faith supply such necessaries, and recover the reasonable value thereof from the parent." Similarly, IND. CODE ANN. § 34-4-1-5 (1973); IOWA CODE ANN. § 675.4 (1950); N.M. STAT. ANN. § 40-5-4 (1978).

31. McGuire v. McGuire, 157 Neb. 226, 59 N.W.2d 336 (1953); Goldstein v. Goldstein, — Pa. Super. Ct. —, 413 A.2d 721 (1979).

32. *See* S. Fox, JUVENILE COURTS IN A NUTSHELL 49-56 (2d ed. 1977).

33. *E.g.*, ARIZ. REV. STAT. § 12-2451 (1956); DEL. CODE ANN. tit. 13, § 514 (Cum. Supp. 1978); ME. REV. STAT. ANN. tit. 19, § 752 (Cum. Supp. 1978); N.C. GEN. STAT. § 50-13.4(c) (1976).

Section 15(e) of the Uniform Parentage Act summarizes factors commonly used by the courts in the exercise of their broad discretion:

> In determining the amount to be paid by a parent for support of the child and the period during which the duty of support is owed, a court enforcing the obligation of support shall consider all relevant facts, including (1) the needs of the child; (2) the standard of living and circumstances of the parents; (3) the relative financial means of the parents; (4) the earning ability of the parents; (5) the need and capacity of the child for education, including higher education; (6) the age of the child; (7) the financial resources and the earning ability of the child; (8) the responsibility of the parents for the support of others; and (9) the value of services contributed by the custodial parent.[34]

The Uniform Marriage and Divorce Act contains a similar listing.[35]

In contrast to these "common-sense" factors, which put some ground under the court's otherwise unbridled discretion, theoreticians have sought to develop principled methods of defining child support obligations.[36] Reducing flexibility still further, legislation was introduced in 1977 in Oregon that would have established a uniform, fixed

---

34. 9A U.L.A., MATR., FAM. AND HEALTH LAWS 588 (1979). *See* Appendix B, *infra* for full text of Act.

35. § 309, 9A U.L.A., MATR., FAM. AND HEALTH LAWS 167 (1979). Many states have enacted variants of similar specificity. *See, e.g.,* MO. ANN. STAT. § 452.340 (1977); N.M. STAT. ANN. § 40-5-2 (1978); OR. REV. STAT. § 107.105 (1977); WIS. STAT. ANN. § 247.25 (Cum. Supp. 1979).

36. *E.g., see* White & Stone, *Consumer Unit Scaling as an Aid in Equitably Determining Need Under Maintenance and Child Support Decrees,* 13 FAM. L.Q. 231, 234 (1979). This is an interesting attempt to put "econometrics" to use, but the effects on taxes and work incentives are not adequately considered. *See also infra* ch. X. 3, and White & Stone, *A Study of Alimony and Child Support Rulings with Some Recommendations,* 10 FAM. L.Q. 75 (1976).

schedule of child support payments, based on net income. While that bill did not pass, the proposal is an indication of growing concern and movement on this issue. A few court systems have taken the initiative and have set specific guidelines for support situations that are somewhat reminiscent of income tax tables.[37] Tables are used more

---

37. The Superior Court of San Francisco County, California, and the Broward County Court of Florida furnish two examples. In each case the guidelines apply to temporary support levels and are not binding on the courts in determining long-range support obligations. The following extracts from the tables illustrate ranges of support deemed appropriate (published at 1 FAM. ADVOCATE 38-39 (1979)):

San Francisco County Superior Court of California

Guidelines for Temporary Support Orders

Net Monthly Income*	Spouse and 1 Child**	Spouse and 2 Children	Spouse and 3 Children	Child Support (per child) Only
$ 400	$ 100	$ 100	$ 100	$ 50—$ 75
800	400	425	450	100—125
1,400	700	800	850	125—175
2,000	1,000	1,100	1,150	150-250

Above 2000 court will exercise discretion.
Special consideration is given for handicapped spouse or children.

---

    * Income is considered "net" after compulsory deductions such as income tax, FICA and any standard deductions which are for the benefit of the family.

    ** Where both spouses are employed, if one's income is 60% or more of the other's, no spousal support; if less than 60%, one-half of the supported spouse's net earnings (after child care expenses) should be deducted from this figure to determine the guideline for temporary spousal support. Other columns would be adjusted.

12

commonly when welfare reimbursement is at issue, in connection with extended support obligations owed

Broward County Court of Florida
Family Support Schedule

DEPENDENTS

Average Wkly Take-Home Pay*	One	Two**	Three	Four	Five	Six or More
$ 30.00	7.50	7.50	7.50	7.50	7.50	7.50
$ 40.00	10.00	15.00	15.00	15.00	15.00	15.00
$ 50.00	12.50	20.00	25.00	25.00	25.00	25.00
$100.00	22.00	32.00	42.00	50.00	50.00	50.00
$110.00	23.00	35.00	45.00	55.00	55.00	55.00
$120.00	24.00	36.00	48.00	60.00	60.00	60.00
$130.00	25.00	38.00	51.00	64.00	65.00	65.00
$140.00	26.00	40.00	54.00	68.00	70.00	70.00
$150.00	27.00	42.00	57.00	72.00	75.00	75.00
$200.00	32.00	52.00	72.00	92.00	100.00	100.00
$210.00	33.00	54.00	75.00	96.00	105.00	105.00
$220.00	34.00	56.00	78.00	100.00	110.00	110.00
$230.00	35.00	58.00	81.00	104.00	115.00	115.00
$240.00	36.00	60.00	84.00	108.00	120.00	120.00
$250.00***	37.00	62.00	87.00	112.00	125.00	125.00

* Average weekly take-home pay is defined as the gross wages or income of the chargeable party less deductions for appropriate withholding taxes and social security.

** The above chart assumes that the custodial parent is employed. In the event that the custodial parent is not employed she (he) shall be counted as two (2) dependents.

*** The Court shall consider extraordinary medical, educational, or dental expenses, large amounts of assets, substantial income of the custodial parent, or other factors which are unusual in nature in determining the amount of support to be paid; and upon finding these unusual factors, modify the amounts suggested accordingly.

See Bair, *How Much Temporary Support is Enough?*, 1 FAM. ADVOCATE 41-42 (1979), for a temporary support formula recommended by the A.B.A. Section on Family Law.

relatives.[38] Inflation, of course, raises serious problems with any fixed-amount guidelines or judgments.

In many places, however, judges do not look kindly at such restraint on their wisdom. To illustrate, Judge Sweet of the Court of Common Pleas of Pennsylvania's Washington County is reported to have commented on the "Scale of Suggested Minimum Contributions for Support by Absent Parents" [39] by calling

> ... it far too rigid. You will have to make so many exceptions, he maintained, that soon you will have no rule. The ideal judge in these matters, Sweet said, uses a common law, rather than a Napoleonic Code, approach .... [— a method he called analogous to bracketing in artillery practice.] What you really should do is read Superior Court cases on the subject, he said. As for the new guidelines, Sweet speculated, they are so inconsistent with the Superior Court cases that judges will not be able to make much use of them. 'While I get my money from the IV-D program I get my law from the superior court' is the phrase you should bear in mind.
>
> As for such things as percentages, Sweet explained, we judges all seem to agree that you cannot give a wife without children more than one third of the husband's

---

38. *E.g.,* Swoap v. Superior Court of Sacramento County, 10 Cal. 3d 490, 111 Cal. Rptr. 136, 516 P.2d 840 (1973). Regarding "relative responsibility," Illinois instructs:

> The standard and the rules shall take into account the buying and consumption patterns of self supporting persons of modest income, present or future contingencies having direct bearing on maintenance of the relative's self-support status and fulfillment of his obligations to his immediate family, and any unusual or exceptional circumstances including estrangement or other personal or social factors, that have a bearing on family relationships and the relative's ability to meet his support obligations.

ILL. ANN. STAT. ch. 23, § 10-3 (Cum. Supp. 1979).

39. Promulgated by the Pennsylvania Child Support Program under PA. STAT. ANN. tit. 62, § 432.6(b) (Supp. 1978). *See* 3 F.L.R. 3101-04 (1977). *See also infra* ch. X 3.

income when setting *pendente lite* amounts or approving a separation agreement. It is also something of a rule that an order for support of wife and child cannot exceed 50 percent of the husband's income....

Judge Sweet said that he had about 50 more cases that seem to refute the positions taken by the guidelines, and he could not find support for the guidelines in the appellate cases. Certainly, Sweet said, 'a judge should not put out a table unless he wraps his table in so much precatory language and leaves so much room for exceptions that the table is in no way controlling.' ... 'For a judge there is no substitute for reading cases,' he said, 'for a support officer there is no substitute for experience.' [40]

The national picture thus remains one of great diversity, divergence and confusion. Basic questions are: what are necessities (a horse?,[41] higher education?),[42] how should the child's "need" be defined once necessities are taken care of (*i.e.*, to what extent is the child entitled to share in the parent's high standard of living)?,[43] what is the father's "ability to pay" if he chooses not to work or is "underemployed?",[44] and finally, must the child's assets be considered in fixing the parental duty of support? [45] As generously concluded by an Illinois Appellate Court, the bottom line is that a father must retain enough to live on after making support payments. A $100 per week child support payment was reversed where the father had a

---

40. 3 F.L.R. 2425 (1977).

41. Yes: Alford v. Alford, 364 So. 2d 1255 (Fla. Dist. Ct. App. 1978).

42. *See infra* text at notes 110-120.

43. Tilmon v. Tilmon, 74 Ill. App. 3d 111, 391 N.E.2d 1086 (1979).

44. If the father's avoidance of employment seems deliberate, his earning *capacity* will be used as the basis for assessing child support. *E.g.,* In re Lipman, — Cal. App. 3d —, — Cal. Rptr. — [5 F.L.R. 2409] (1979), where a board-certified psychiatrist chose to work only 20 hours per month. *See infra* text at notes 71-78.

45. No: Gold v. Gold, 96 Misc. 2d 481, 409 N.Y.S.2d 114 (1978).

take-home pay of $165 per week and a car payment that would have left him with only $32.50 weekly for gasoline, rent, food and all other expenses.[46] At the "welfare level," token awards such as $10 per week have been the rule, although the new federal involvement may change this custom.[47]

Another recent case provided a different dimension: A judgment requiring a father earning approximately $40,000 per year to pay $100 per month in child support was overturned as a gross abuse of discretion because "a parent's duty to support does not necessarily end with the furnishing of mere necessities; a minor child is entitled to be maintained in a style and condition consonant with his parents' position in society." The court disregarded the fact that the father's *combined* alimony and child support payment amounted to $816 per month, *i.e* , $9792 per year.[48] As anyone familiar with taxation will surmise, the payment probably was arranged in this manner so as to qualify the (larger) alimony payment as an income tax deduction. This follows from the *Lester*[49] rule which, in short, holds that when there is a combined alimony and child support award, only amounts specifically so designated are viewed as child support (non-deductible), whereas the rest is regarded as alimony (deductible). Thus, where the payor's and the recipient's marginal income tax rates differ measurably, it will be advantageous to concentrate deductible items in the return of the person in the higher tax bracket and have the income taxed at the other party's lower rate.

---

46. Gray v. Gray, 39 Ill. App. 3d 675, 349 N.E.2d 926 (1976).

47. A detailed tabulation of child support awards at the welfare level in 1973 is provided in SENATE COMMITTEE ON FINANCE, 94th Cong., 1st Sess., CHILD SUPPORT, DATA AND MATERIALS, 170-71 (1975).

48. Ames v. Ames, 59 Cal. App. 3d 234, 130 Cal. Rptr. 435 (1976).

49. Lester v. Commissioner, 366 U.S. 299, 81 S. Ct. 1343, 6 L. Ed. 2d 306 (1961).

The teaching of this case is that it often will not suffice to look at the child support award alone. Tax aspects and other considerations may, and indeed should, play an important role within the ample room to maneuver permitted by the federal tax laws and the law pertaining to separation agreements.[50] This may mean in a given case that alimony or even property awards to the mother should have a decisive bearing when the "adequacy" of child support is judged. Unfortunately, tax considerations have not *openly* played the role that they obviously merit in shaping support awards. As perhaps illustrated by the case discussed above, this possible oversight of tax considerations has created the risk that if a large amount is designated as alimony (to obtain the tax benefit) and only a small amount is listed as child support, a court may not be willing to recognize the obvious and may increase child support without correspondingly decreasing alimony. Attempts to provide in separation agreements for automatic interdependence of such adjustments have not always succeeded.[51] Recent holdings [52] and even some statutes [53] have moved in the direction of greater tax consciousness. Obviously, more sensible tax laws would offer a preferable route, but that is

50. For a summary, *see* H. KRAUSE, FAMILY LAW IN A NUTSHELL 355-60 (1977). For detail, *see* F. Sander & H. Gutman, *Tax Aspects of Divorce and Separation,* 95 TAX MANAGEMENT PORTFOLIOS (3rd ed. 1975).

51. Pellman v. Pellman, 88 Misc. 2d 251, 387 N.Y.S.2d 348, *aff'd in part,* 59 A.D. 371, 399 N.Y.S.2d 277 (1977). *Cf.,* Salmon v. Commissioner, ¶ 75, 126 T.C.M. (P-H 1975).

52. Kruger v. Kruger, 73 N.J. 464, 375 A.2d 659 (1977); Wetzel v. Wetzel, 34 Wisc. 2d 665, 150 N.W.2d 482 (1967); Stotlar v. Stotlar, 5 Ill. App. 3d 790, 365 N.E.2d 1097 (1977). *Cf.,* Newman v. Commissioner, 68 T.C. 494 (1977). The Minnesota Supreme Court, in contrast, ruled in 1979 that a trial judge in a divorce action need *not* consider the *future* capital gains tax consequences of a property distribution because these were regarded as "too speculative." Aaron v. Aaron, — Minn. —, 281 N.W.2d 150 (1979).

53. One example is WIS. STAT. ANN. § 247.25(1)(h) (Cum. Supp. 1979).

not within the courts' control. However, courts *can* accommodate their holdings to existing law.

One last question is whether the court's extensive power to compel evidence concerning the father's financial situation covers the father's tax return or whether that is privileged.[54] The weight of authority would find no problem here and disclosure would be required, although with safeguards concerning "irrelevant" information, such as income data relating to the father's current wife.[55] Whether that information is wholly and always irrelevant may be disputed. For instance, by reducing the support needs of his new family, the father's current wife's earnings may improve the father's ability to support his earlier family.

3. Modifiability of the Support Obligation.

Support orders and child support obligations agreed upon in separation agreements[56] generally remain modifiable to respond to a significant change in circumstances, whether that change be in terms of the parent's ability to pay or the child's need.[57] Scant authority to the contrary may all but be ignored.[58] As in the case of defining the initial award, statutory guidelines defining a "significant change in circumstances" generally are

---

54. Annot., 70 A.L.R.2d 240 (1960) (1978 Supp.).

55. DeGraaff v. DeGraaff, 163 N.J. Super. 578, 395 A.2d 525 (1978).

56. An obligation undertaken in a separation agreement stands on the same footing as a decree, if incorporated in the court's decree. *See* H. KRAUSE, FAMILY LAW IN A NUTSHELL 382-83 (1977). *In re* Corbin, 591 P.2d 1046 (Colo. App. 1979). Concerning the parents' power to contract regarding their respective child support obligations, *see supra* text at notes 16-18.

57. Concurrence of both conditions may be required and proof of only one, i.e., the father's ability to pay, may be inadequate. *In re* Boyce, 68 A.D. 2d 862, — N.Y.S.2d — (1979).

58. Yarborough v. Yarborough, 290 U.S. 202, 54 S. Ct. 181, 78 L. Ed. 269 (1933).

lacking, nor would they be easily conceived.[59] Again, judicial discretion reigns nearly supreme.[60] In an effort to tidy up the resulting uncertainty — which often leads to unwarranted harassment of the supporting parent by the custodial parent and wasteful use of court facilities [61] — the Uniform Marriage and Divorce Act requires "a showing of changed circumstances so substantial and continuing as to make the terms [previously set] unconscionable."[62] Whether this language will produce significantly greater certainty remains open. As a legal term of art, the word "unconscionable" has had a long and checkered history. An interesting innovation was recently enacted in Rhode Island where any child support order must now be reconsidered *de novo* in the event the child becomes a recipient of public assistance.[63]

A common question is what effect should be given the father's creation of a new family, in terms of a modification of the amount of child support, upward or downward.

---

59. A weak try is made by Arizona, which expressly requires "changed circumstance which is substantial and continuing." ARIZ. REV. STAT. ANN. § 12-2453 (1956).

60. *See, e.g.,* N.C. GEN. STAT. § 50-13.7 (1976); N.M. STAT. ANN. § 40-5-19 (1978); WYO. STAT. § 20-2-113 (1977).

61. Consider Judge Wilner's lament in Rand v. Rand, 40 Md. App. 550, 551, 392 A.2d 1149, 1150 (1978):

> An announcer for a soap opera would bill this proceeding as yet another episode in the continuing saga of the Rand family — the eternal, endless quest by Florence Rand to maximize the contribution of her former husband Robert toward the support of their daughter Virginia, and the equally determined effort by Robert to pay as little as he must. Unfortunately, this is not a soap opera. Real people are involved; and, for the fourth time in less than seven years an appellate court of this State is called upon to resolve the post-marital financial disputes between these warring parties. Would only that Virginia have had the benefit of the fortune invested in this seemingly interminable litigation.

62. § 316(a), 9A U.L.A., MATR., FAM. AND HEALTH LAWS 183 (1979).

63. R.I. GEN. LAWS § 15-13-3 (Cum. Supp. 1978).

Traditionally, the courts have taken the position that the father's prior child support obligations take absolute precedence over the needs of his new family.[64] They have disregarded the father's plea that his new responsibilities are a "change of circumstances" justifying a reduction in a prior child support award or at least averting an increase.[65] More recently, however, some courts have considered the interests of both families and have attempted a fair apportionment.[66] This approach seems more realistic. Arguably, the balance of social interest (though not necessarily individual equity) might even weigh in favor of the father's current family because that family might founder if earlier obligations were enforced beyond the father's reasonably available means — with the possible result of two families drawing welfare payments rather than one. Whatever the *policy,* current equal protection reasoning makes it difficult to defend blanket discrimination in favor of or against the children of one or the other marriage or, for that matter, nonmarital children.[67] In competition with each other for their father's

---

64. Rowley v. Rowley, 232 Or. 285, 375 P.2d 84 (1962); Beddoes v. Beddoes, 155 Colo. 115, 393 P.2d 1 (1964); Germer v. Germer, 17 Utah 2d 393, 412 P.2d 922 (1966); Annot., 89 A.L.R.2d 106 (1963). A variation on the theme occurs if the needs of the children of a second marriage conflict with a prior wife's claim for alimony. *See* Besaw v. Besaw, 89 Wis. 2d 417, 279 N.W.2d 192 (1979).

65. State *ex rel.* State of New York v. Hasbun, 27 Or. App. 423, 556 P.2d 166 (1976); Gilmore v. Gilmore, — N.C. App. —, 257 S.E.2d 116 (1979).

66. Emanuel v. Emanuel, — F. Supp. —, [5 F.L.R. 2156] (D.V.I. 1978); Dodson v. Dodson, 461 P.2d 937 (Okla. 1969); Edwards v. Edwards, 125 Ill. App. 2d 91, 259 N.E.2d 820 (1976); Berg v. Berg, 116 R.I. 607, 359 A.2d 354 (1976).

67. Gomez v. Perez, 409 U.S. 535, 93 S. Ct. 872, 35 L. Ed. 2d 56 (1973). *See also* Wiesenfeld v. State of New York, 474 F. Supp. 1141 (S.D.N.Y. 1979) and *cf.,* Zablocki v. Redhail, 434 U.S. 374, 68 S. Ct. 673, 54 L. Ed. 2d 618 (1978).

support, all children should stand on an equal footing and have equal legal claims.[68]

It should be emphasized, however, that increased earnings are not invariably a sound indication of increased ability to pay. Judge Sweet of the Court of Common Pleas of Washington County in Pennsylvania cautions:

> that when a husband finds that two families cannot live as cheaply as one did, he has to go out and get a part-time job or do overtime so as to make ends meet. To hold that this necessarily should lead to an increase in the child support order is circular and very destructive.[69]

Conversely, the issue has been raised whether the father's support obligation should be reduced if his ex-wife remarries and his children receive some support from the mother's new husband. A Pennsylvania father was granted no reduction in support payments after his ex-wife married a judge of the court in which the support hearing was held — he was, however, granted a change of venue.[70]

One fascinating issue that has been litigated time and again concerns the question of the father's freedom to change his occupation or professional status for one less lucrative or to quit work altogether. May the father use a voluntary change in earnings as the basis for a reduction in his obligation? Holdings have been diverse. "Good faith"

---

68. *But cf.,* Kuwajinski v. Kuwajinski, 71 Ill. 2d 563, 376 N.E.2d 1382 (1978), where a statute according the child of divorced parents a qualified right to higher education was upheld although the child of the functioning family has no comparable enforceable claim. *See infra* text at notes 110-120.

69. 3 F.L.R. 2425 (1977).

70. Armor v. Armor, — Pa. Super. Ct. —, 398 A.2d 173 (1978). *But see* Fuller v. Fuller, 89 Cal. App. 3d 405, 152 Cal. Rptr. 467 (1979), which considered the income of a disabled father's girlfriend insofar as it reduced his expenses and thus affected his ability to pay.

has played an important, but not always decisive role. For instance, a reduction in payments was granted a successful, salaried construction worker who became a practitioner of law, whereby his income was reduced by half,[71] to a police officer who wanted to become an aviation pilot,[72] as well as to a physician who decided to train to become a psychiatrist,[73] but not to one who sold his practice to accept a low-paid residency,[74] or to a father who left a $25,000 a year position to go into a business for which he had no experience.[75] A psychologist who wished to enter private practice (at about $15,000 per year) and leave two jobs (at about $25,000 per year) successfully resisted upward modification of his support obligation.[76] Upward modification was resisted unsuccessfully by a machinist who had changed his name to "Krishna Venta" and founded a religious society which paid all his expenses including child support previously ordered, but paid him no salary.[77] Another father remarried, had a child in his second marriage, decided to babysit for the child and quit his $24,000 a year job. Then he sought to escape his support obligation, but found only partial sympathy. The District of Columbia Court of Appeals valued his "babysitting services" at $400 a month and reduced his support obligation from $350 to $200 a month.[78]

A related, more common and thus more serious problem

---

71. McQuiddy v. McQuiddy, 238 Pa. Super. Ct. 390, 358 A.2d 102 (1976).

72. In re Batten, 23 Or. App. 620, 543 P.2d 33 (1975).

73. Lynn v. Lynn, 153 N.J. Super. 337, 379 A.2d 1046 (1977).

74. Kohn v. Kohn, 21 Ill. App. 3d 117, 315 N.E.2d 52 (1974).

75. Commonwealth v. Carlton, — Pa. Super. Ct. —, 395 A.2d 950 (1978).

76. In re Donna L.P., 4 F.L.R. 2223 (N.Y. Fam. Ct. 1978).

77. Pencovic v. Pencovic, 45 Cal. 2d 97, 287 P.2d 501 (1955).

78. Freeman v. Freeman, 397 A.2d 554 (D.C. 1979).

arising out of the rigidity of support judgments is that arrears typically continue to accrue even when the father loses his employment involuntarily. For modification, most jurisdictions require a specific application and, before allowing modification, many courts require a change that is "more or less permanent rather than temporary." [79] Temporary unemployment thus may not warrant relief. [80] In consequence of this unfortunate rule, fathers have been subjected to criminal proceedings for failure to comply with child support obligation that stemmed from better times. For instance, a father who had earned $235 per week, but now was down to $95 per week out of which he could not pay $70 per week support, was ordered to jail for 90 days. Fortunately, the appellate court reversed. [81] Aside from the human aspect, such cases involve a senseless waste of scarce and expensive judicial resources. It is encouraging that, in several Michigan counties, "Friend of the Court" offices help unemployed fathers find employment, sometimes through the CETA program. [82]

Support judgments with automatic adjustment clauses

---

79. Curley v. Curley, 588 P.2d 289 (Alaska 1979).

80. Burdack v. Burdack, 371 So. 2d 528 (Fla. Dist. Ct. App. 1979). A father's union having been on strike for fourteen weeks with no strike benefits, resulting in a $4,000 loss of income to the father, was not such a substantial change in his circumstances as would support a reduction in child support payments. *Cf.,* Glass v. Peitchall, 42 Ill. App. 3d 240, 243, 355 N.E.2d 750, 754 (1976):

> We believe, however, that there should be a different application of the good faith rule where involuntariness is shown. For example, it appears to us that child support payments may properly be abated or reduced where an inability to pay results from involuntary loss of employment, but we think that such relief should be temporary in nature in the sense that the petitioning party should be required within a reasonable time to establish that continued unemployment was in good faith, i.e., was the result of mental or physical disability or unsuccessful attempts to obtain other employment.

81. *In re* Mistriel, 54 App. Div. 945, 388 N.Y.S.2d 338 (1976).

82. 3 F.L.R. 2699 (1977).

(to take into account temporary fluctuations in income) are rare, as are automatic child support escalator clauses (linked, for instance, to the father's income, inflation or the child's foreseeably increasing needs, based on increasing age). Of course, such clauses run the risk of overemphasizing one side of the support equation. On the paying parent's side, an adjustment clause geared to decreases in income will avoid the accrual of large arrears — with interest! — that very likely will never be paid. On the other hand, an *increase* in the supporting parent's income does not *necessarily* entitle the child to more support, nor does an income decrease necessarily signal inability to pay, as when the obligated parent has assets. In rare cases involving automatic adjustment clauses, courts have not favored them [83] and have remained jealous of their discretion in this area.

---

83. *E.g.,* Stanaway v. Stanaway, 70 Mich. App. 294, 245 N.W.2d 723 (1976); *cf.,* Hagbloom v. Hagbloom, 71 Mich. App. 257, 247 N.W.2d 373 (1976); Moore v. Moore, 173 Conn. 120, —, 376 A.2d 1085, 1087 (1977):

> The mere fact of inflation, although it may be judicially noticed without affording an opportunity to be heard, is not sufficient ground for increasing an order of support. It must also be shown that inflation (a) has substantially increased the necessary expenses of the children and (b) has not increased the necessary expenses of the parent against whom the order is entered to a point which renders him unable to pay increased support. There was no such finding in this case. The court merely stated that it 'considered the data set forth in the financial affidavits of the parties.' Such a finding could not have been made on the basis of those affidavits alone. They show that the wife's expenses decreased while her income increased, whereas the husband's expenses increased more than did his income. While it is possible that the husband's expenses were greater than necessary and the wife's income was inadequate to provide properly for the children, there was no finding to this effect. (Footnote omitted.)

See also Wilcox v. Wilcox, 242 Ga. 598, 250 S.E.2d 465 (1978), in which the Georgia Supreme Court reversed an order requiring 15% of the father's net earnings to be paid to each child. *But see In re* Mahalingham, 21 Wash. App. 228, 584 P.2d 971 (1978) which upheld the use of a clause calling for $200.00 child support, plus 20 percent of any net increase in

Despite all justified doubt, however, some intelligent use can be made of automatic adjustment clauses. Clearly ascertainable, objective events such as inflation (measured by the Federal Consumer Price Index) and income fluctuations (evidenced by the supporting parent's income tax return or, for quicker response, his employer's wage data) could be assigned clearly defined consequences in terms of support to be rendered. If this were done in *presumptive,* not conclusive, terms, the "average" case would take care of itself. In the less usual case, the party to whom compliance with the automatic adjustment clause would bring inequities should shoulder the burden of proof (and take the initiative of invoking the court) to obtain an appropriate modification. This approach would go some distance toward the important goal of reducing the frequent, expensive and wasteful recourse to the courts that our present system invites.

Of course, with or without adjustment clauses it would be desirable if there were, if necessary in the family's circumstances, a more efficient (near-automatic) method of recourse to the AFDC program, or if we could develop a broader concept of unemployment benefits. Such a concept would more fully integrate child support elements and take up an appropriate portion of any support deficit caused by

---

salary, plus 10 percent of any net income from other sources against a challenge that it related only to the father's ability to pay and ignored the child's need as well as the other parent's ability to help support the child. In Branstad v. Branstad, 400 N.E.2d 167 (Ind. App. 1980) the Court cited *Mahalingham* and approved an escalator clause linking the amount of child support to the Consumer Price Index "because the provision (1) gives due regard to the actual needs of the child, (2) uses readily obtainable objective information, (3) requires only a simple calculation, (4) results in judicial economy, (5) reduces expenses for attorney fees, and (6) in no way infringes upon the rights of either the custodial parent or the non-custodial parent to petition the court for modification of the decree due to a substantial and continuing change of circumstances."

the obligated parent's temporary or longer-term inability to pay.

The important question of whether, in an appropriate case, modification should be allowed *retrospectively* (and thus wipe out or reduce accumulated arrearages) has been answered variously. While the finality of a judgment and accrued installments must be given due consideration, the better view permits the elimination of "impossible" arrearages. Many courts do eliminate such arrearages under specific or general statutes.[84] Other courts steadfastly refuse to consider retroactive modification.[85] A

84.

[T]he Supreme Court of Oregon interpreted a statute authorizing Oregon courts to "set aside, alter or modify" the provisions of a divorce decree as authorization to cancel overdue support installments. The court found the presence of the phrase "to set aside" to be a specific source of authorization for a divorce court to modify its decrees retrospectively. The court also found the phrase synonymous with the words "to annul, to make void," suggesting that the cancellation of overdue support payments was an authorized setting aside of a decree. This Court adopts the court's reasoning, and concludes that 16 V.I.C. § 110 makes alimony and support payments of a divorce decree subject to retrospective change or cancellations.

This court, in adopting an interpretation favoring retrospective modifications of support obligations, emphasizes that such an interpretation is to be applied only when the court finds it equitable to adjust the responsibilities of divorced parties brought about by substantial changes in circumstances that follow the divorce. The discretionary power to cancel arrearages should be exercised cautiously. Emanuel v. Emanuel, — F. Supp. —, —, [5 F.L.R. 2156] (D.V.I. 1978).

85. Ferry v. Ferry, 201 Neb. 595, 599-600, 271 N.W.2d 450, 453-54 (1978): "This court has often held: where a divorce decree provides for the payment of stipulated sums monthly for the support of a minor child or children, contingent only upon a subsequent order of the court, such payments became vested in the payee as they accrue. The courts are without authority to reduce the amounts of such accrued payments." Accord, Jahn v. Jahn, — Ind. App. —, 385 N.E.2d 488 (1979); Gomez v. Gomez, — N.M. —, 587 P.2d 963 (1978). *See also* Sistare v. Sistare, 218 U.S. 1, 30 S. Ct. 682, 54 L. Ed. 905 (1910) (dictum); Worthley v. Worthley,

related question is whether the obligated parent's support liability can be discharged in bankruptcy. As to future support, the answer clearly should be and is "no." "Normal" support arrears also are not dischargeable, and are thus elevated to a preferred level. In a departure from the past, however, the Bankruptcy Reform Act of 1978 does permit the discharge of child support obligations that have been *assigned* to the welfare authorities.[86] Legislation to change this provision has been proposed.[87]

---

44 Cal. 2d 465, 283 P.2d 19 (1955) (dictum); Gamble v. Gamble, 258 A.2d 261 (D.C. 1969); Robertson v. Cason, 203 So. 2d 743 (La. Ct. App. 1967).

86. 11 U.S.C. § 523(a)(5)(A) (1978). OCSE-AT-79-8 (October 9, 1979) explains:

> Public law 95-598 signed by the President on November 6, 1978, immediately repealed Section 456(b) of the Social Security Act (the Act) which expressly prohibited bankruptcy discharge of child support obligations assigned to the State under Section 402(a)(26) of the Act.
>
> Further, effective October 1, 1979, P.L. 95-598 repealed the existing bankruptcy law and replaced it with new revised bankruptcy provisions. Insofar as child support is concerned, the new bankruptcy provisions exempt from discharge only those unassigned child support obligations owed to a spouse, former spouse or child established in connection with a separation agreement, divorce decree or property settlement agreement. Thus, it is clear that after October 1, 1979, past debts owed by absent parents on child support obligations assigned to the State or those established by administrative procedure or court order not arising on a divorce decree, separation agreement or property settlement agreement may be discharged in bankruptcy. The IV-D agency will then be in the same position as any other creditor in the bankruptcy court.
>
> IV-D agencies should weigh the costs of a bankruptcy court appearance against the amount that is likely to be recovered before making such an appearance. It should also be noted that an absent parent's current child support obligation is not affected by a bankruptcy action and should still be appropriately enforced.
>
> Legislation to reverse or lessen the impact of these provisions on the Child Support Enforcement program is pending in both the House and Senate.

87. 96th Cong. 1st Sess., H.R. 3491; H.R. 3492 (April 5, 1979). In 1979, the A.B.A.'s Section on Family Law considered proposing a resolution to

Finally, it should be emphasized that many or most courts do not view child support orders as self-reducing or self-terminating: for instance when the father takes over custody [88] or when some or all children reach majority or are emancipated,[89] or where social security benefits are paid to the children.[90] If the order is not terminated by the court, the liability may continue to accrue and contempt may lie for nonpayment.[91] Controversy also centers on the question of whether a support-delinquent father's arrears should be credited with voluntary payments made to or on

---

the A.B.A.'s House of Delegates urging Congress to repeal the appropriate sections, reasoning as follows:

> In an effort to clarify the bankruptcy laws and carry the "clean sweep" concept of bankruptcy to an extreme conclusion, Congress permitted discharge of such assigned sums. In so doing, it failed to realize the analogy to ordinary debts did not apply, that these were statutory debts like taxes and punitive damages. In carrying the "clean sweep" concept to this extreme conclusion it failed to recognize that from the debtors' side this concept is not being as fully applied, there being numerous exemptions for real and personal property. It also failed to consider the time consuming and judicially burdensome method by which the bankruptcy can be frustrated, by a modification upward of future payments. Congress also failed to consider the numerous state court devices for relief from hardship caused by support burdens. Finally, because of drafting failures it threatens to also permit discharge of substantial sums owed the custodial parent and threatens to dismantle the protective shield from abuse by absent parents that the welfare assignment concept provides the custodial parent and child.

88. Weber v. Weber, 203 Neb. 528, 279 N.W.2d 379, (1979); Tyler v. Tyler, — A.2d — [5 F.L.R. 2227] (D.C. Super. Ct. 1978). *But see* Brady v. Brady, 592 P.2d 865 (Kan. 1979).

89. Ferry v. Ferry, 201 Neb. 495, 271 N.W.2d 450 (1978); Tilley v. Tilley, 30 N.C. App. 581, 227 S.E.2d 640 (1976). *But see* Brady v. Brady, 592 P.2d 865 (Kan. 1979).

90. Oatley v. Oatley, 387 N.E.2d 245 (Ohio App. 1977); Joachim v. Joachim, 57 App. Div. 546, 393 N.Y.S.2d 63, *appeal dismissed,* 42 N.Y.2d 1011, 368 N.E.2d 285, 398 N.Y.S.2d 535, *cert. denied,* 434 U.S. 1066, 98 S. Ct. 1242, 55 L. Ed. 2d 767 (1978).

91. Calcagno v. Calcagno, 391 A.2d 79 (R.I. 1978).

behalf of his children, especially during visitation or vacations.[92]

4. Duration of the Support Obligation.

a. *The Child's Minority, Emancipation and Higher Education.*

The typical statute defines the parental support obligation in terms of the child's minority, although some are phrased in terms of specific ages.[93] Minority, while defined for centuries to end at age 21,[94] recently was shortened to end upon attaining age 18 — a world-wide movement that has reached most states by now.[95] Emancipation or adoption of the child by a third party, when effected in accordance with applicable law, also ends the parental support obligation.[96] With the shift to the 18-year age of majority, the incidence and with it the importance of emancipation has been substantially reduced, although it still is litigated occasionally.[97] Child

---

92. Goodson v. Goodson, 32 N.C. App. 76, 231 S.E.2d 178 (1977). *See* Annot., 47 A.L.R.3d 1031 (1973).

93. *E.g.,* DEL. CODE ANN. tit. 13, § 501 (Supp. 1978): "(a) The duty to support a child under the age of 18 years, whether born in or out of wedlock, rests primarily upon his parents." FLA. STAT. ANN. § 61.13 (Cum. Supp. 1979); N.M. STAT. ANN. § 40-5-1 (1978): "The father and mother of a child born out of wedlock are jointly and severally liable for the support of the child until he reaches the age of majority." *C.f.,* COLO. REV. STAT. § 14-6-10 (1973) (provides criminal liability for nonsupport of children under sixteen years of age).

94. 1 W. BLACKSTONE, COMMENTARIES ON THE LAWS OF ENGLAND 463-64 (1765).

95. *See* WALD, CHILDREN'S RIGHTS: A FRAMEWORK FOR ANALYSIS, 12 U.C.D.L. Rev. 255, 267 (1979).

96. *E.g.,* IND. CODE ANN. § 31-4-1-19 (Cum. Supp. 1979); NEV. REV. STAT. § 126.060 (1957); N.M. REV. STAT. § 40-5-5 (1978). *See* H. KRAUSE, FAMILY LAW IN A NUTSHELL 182-84 (1977).

97. *E.g., In re* Fetters, 41 Colo. App. 281, 584 P.2d 104 (1978) involved a 16-year old daughter who had married without parental consent by

support liability typically does *not* terminate when a child is institutionalized.[98] Statutes discriminating in matters of support between boys (sometimes to age 21) and girls (to age 18) have been struck down as violating the Equal Protection Clause.[99]

The recent change in the age of majority has resulted in numerous holdings that the parental support obligation now terminates at age 18.[100] Where the support statute speaks in terms of "minority," this result is clearly correct. Less clear has been the status of support obligations defined in terms of "minority" that date back to the time when minority extended to 21 years of age under: (1) support decrees issued previously,[101] (2) separation agreements that were incorporated into support decrees previously issued,[102] and (3) child support agreements standing independently of court decrees.[103] Some courts have refused

---

falsifying her age. The court held that the marriage though voidable had emancipated her, ending the father's support obligation. After annulment of the marriage, the mother succeeded in reinstating the father's support duty, though not for the period during which the voidable marriage had been in effect.

98. *E.g.,* COLO. REV. STAT. § 14-7-101 (1973); Mo. ANN. STAT. § 211.241 (1962).

99. Stanton v. Stanton, 429 U.S. 501, 97 S. Ct. 717, 50 L. Ed. 2d 723 (1977); Stanton v. Stanton, 421 U.S. 7, 95 S. Ct. 1373, 43 L. Ed. 2d 688 (1975).

100. Chrestenson v. Chrestenson, — Mont. —, 589 P.2d 148 (1979); Wilcox v. Wilcox, 242 Ga. 598, 250 S.E.2d 465 (1978), Speer v. Quinlan, 96 Idaho 119, 525 P.2d 314 (1974); Phelps v. Phelps, 85 N.M. 62, 509 P.2d 254 (1973); Beaudry v. Beaudry, 132 Vt. 53, 312 A.2d 922 (1973).

101. *E.g.,* Wiker v. Wiker, — Utah —, — P.2d — [5 F.L.R. 2302] (1978); Orlandella v. Orlandella, 370 Mass. 225, 347 N.E.2d 665 (1976). *See also* Ganschow v. Ganschow, 14 Cal. 3d 150, 170 Cal. Rptr. 865, 534 P.2d 705 (1975) and Wodicka v. Wodicka, 17 Cal. 2d 181, 130 Cal. Rptr. 515, 550 P.2d 1051 (1976).

102. *E.g.,* Paul v. Paul, 214 Va. 651, 203 S.E.2d 123 (1974); Manes v. Manes, 370 Mass. 235, 347 N.E.2d 668 (1976).

103. *C.f.,* Mack v. Mack, 217 Va. 534, 229 S.E.2d 895 (1976); Harding

enforcement after age 18 because "minority," as used in the agreement or decree, is understood to mean minority as of the time of the attempted enforcement of the order.[104] Others have reached the opposite result and have held that the word "minority" must be understood in the sense that it had when the agreement was entered into or when the support order was made. These courts have accordingly extended the support obligation to age 21.[105] A few states deal with this problem specifically, as does Kansas in providing that

> any order requiring either parent or both parents to pay for the support of any child until the age of majority shall terminate when such child attains the age of

---

v. Harding, 46 N.C. App. 62, — S.E.2d — (1980); Manes v. Manes, 370 Mass. 225, 347 N.E.2d 668 (1976) (dictum).

104. *See* Meredith v. Meredith, 216 Va. 636, 222 S.E.2d 511 (1976); Katz v. Katz, 41 Md. App. 142, 395 A.2d 1220 (1979). A surprising result was reached by the Connecticut Supreme Court in Hunter v. Hunter, — Conn. —, — A.2d — [5 F.L.R. 2550] (1979), which involved a divorce judgment incorporating a separation agreement that called for support until age 21 and specifically covered college expenses. Not only was the support duty held terminated when the child reached 18, but the following statute, enacted *after* the child reached 18 years of age, was held not to be applicable "retroactively":

> If the agreement is in writing and provides for the care, education, maintenance or support of a child beyond the age of eighteen, it may also be incorporated or otherwise made a part of any such order and shall be enforceable to the same extent as any other provision of such order or decree, notwithstanding the provisions of [the minority statute].

CONN. GEN. STAT. § 46b-66 (Cum. Supp. 1978). The dissent would have held that "[t]he purpose and effect of this statute is simply to provide that certain contractual rights, rights created by the parties themselves, are now enforceable by contempt proceedings."

105. *E.g.,* Paul v. Paul, 214 Va. 651, 203 S.E.2d 123 (1974) (agreement); Hastings v. Hastings, 114 N.H. 778, 328 A.2d 782 (1974) (agreement); Nokes v. Nokes, 47 Ohio St. 2d 1, 351 N.E.2d 194 (1976) (decree). A summary of the divided authority is provided by *In re* Harpess, — Iowa —, 251 N.W.2d 212 (1977) (decree).

eighteen (18) years, unless by prior written agreement approved by the court such parent or parents specifically agreed to pay such support beyond the time such child attains the age of eighteen (18).[106]

If a trend may be discerned, it appears that an *agreement* speaking of "minority" or "majority" is more likely to be interpreted in terms of the age of majority at the time it was made than is a *court order* for support.[107] No special problems are raised by support orders covering nonmarital children, and good reasons abound to apply this developing law in the context of "illegitimacy."

These cases, of course, deal with a transitional problem. Support and paternity orders entered, and agreements or settlements made after the shift in the age of majority, must be interpreted in accordance with the new law. A more interesting question is raised by what new law may develop — specifically, whether and to what extent statutes or courts will begin to impose support obligations extending beyond minority.

Traditional laws had extended the parental support obligation to incompetent adult children or those otherwise in need of support and unable to provide for their own livelihood.[108] A problem now being encountered more often

---

106. KAN. STAT. ANN. § 60-1610 (Cum. Supp. 1978).

107. *See* Gazale v. Gazale, 219 Va. 775, 250 S.E.2d 365 (1979) and *cf.,* Mack v. Mack, 217 Va. 534, 229 S.E.2d 895 (1978).

108. *E.g.,* Feinberg v. Diamant, — Mass. —, 79 Mass. Adv. Sh. 1321, 389 N.E.2d 998 (1979); McCarthy v. McCarthy, 301 Minn. 270, 222 N.W.2d 331 (1974). The Arkansas Supreme Court may have pushed this salutary doctrine beyond reasonable limits, when a father was ordered to continue support payments during the *higher* education of his brain-damaged child. The dissent observed acidly:

"The son, himself, testified that he was in good physical condition, and that he could do any kind of job requiring hard or light physical labor. . . . One of the old adages of the hills where I grew up was the saying that 'there's no fool like an educated fool'." Elkins v. Elkins, 262 Ark. 63, 65-70, 553 S.W.2d 34, 35-37 (1977).

concerns the child below or above majority age, perhaps pregnant or having her own child, who has left home and seeks or has received welfare aid. Should the parent be required to support the "child" and grandchild and reimburse the welfare authorities for aid rendered? Should the "child's" application be denied, or should welfare be paid without recourse to the recipient's parents? On the basis of recent decisions one may predict that (grand)parental responsibility in this context will decline.[109]

The opposite trend may be foreseen regarding the question of whether the law should allow for the continued education of the "non-child" who, at 18 years of age, may barely have completed high school. In the past few decades, higher education increasingly has come to be perceived as "necessary." Accordingly, an obligation to provide a college education increasingly has been enforced up to the age of majority.[110] There had not been much need to deal with education *past* majority, because college would be completed or nearly completed by the time the student reached 21 years of age, and graduate or professional training was rarely classified as "necessary." In 1967, Illinois was one of the first states to provide in its *divorce* statute that "after the children have attained majority age, the court has jurisdiction to order payments for their support for educational purposes only."[111] This amendment responded to court decisions which had imposed such an

---

109. Devino v. Nebraska Dept. of Public Welfare, 2 F.L.R. 2526 (D. Neb. 1976); Parker v. Stage, 43 N.Y.2d 128, 371 N.E.2d 513, 400 N.Y.S.2d 794 (1977); St. Lawrence County Dept. of Soc. Serv. v. Menard, 86 Misc. 2d 126, 381 N.Y.S.2d 939 (1975).

110. *E.g.,* Charlton v. Charlton, 397 Mich. 84, 243 N.W.2d 261 (1976). *But cf.* Kaplan v. Wallshein, 57 A.D. 828, 394 N.Y.S.2d 439 (1977). *See generally:* Veron, *Parental Support of Post-Majority Children in College,* 17 J. Fam. L. 645 (1978-79).

111. Ill. Rev. Stat., ch. 40 § 19 (1973). *See* Hight v. Hight, 5 Ill. App. 3d 991, 284 N.E.2d 679 (1972).

obligation without specific authority.[112] In 1978, after a statutory change, the Supreme Court of Illinois discussed the question of the special status of the child of divorced parents at length, perhaps setting a national example:

> According to plaintiff, sections 503(d) and 513 permit a dissolution order to require divorced parents to allocate funds for the education of their children beyond the children's minority, and he points out that such burden is not imposed upon nondivorced parents. Defendant's first line of response is that nondivorced parents do have a coextensive legal obligation to provide for the education of their children beyond the minority of the children, He refers to the following statutory obligation which applies to nondivorced parents:
>
> > The expenses of the family and of the education of the children shall be chargeable upon the property of both husband and wife, or of either of them, in favor of creditors therefor, and in relation thereto they may be sued jointly or separately.' (Ill.Rev.Stat.1977, ch. 40, par. 1015.)
>
> This court has not had occasion to consider whether the above-cited provision obligates nondivorced parents to fund the education of their majority aged children, and we have no occasion to do so here. Rather we find that the imposition of such an obligation upon divorced parents is reasonably related to a legitimate legislative purpose.
>
> It cannot be overemphasized that a divorce, by its nature, has a major economic and personal impact on the lives of those involved. That the legislature is cognizant of this is evident by the fact that an express purpose of the Act is to "mitigate the potential harm to the spouses and their children caused by the process of legal dissolution of marriage." (Ill.Rev.Stat.1977, ch. 40, par. 102(4).) Commonly, a divorce means that the

---

112. Crane v. Crane, 45 Ill. App. 2d 316, 196 N.E.2d 27 (1964); *cf.,* Strum v. Strum, 22 Ill. App. 3d 147, 317 N.E.2d 62 (1974); Hight v. Hight, 5 Ill. App. 3d 991, 284 N.E.2d 679 (1972).

spouses will go their separate ways, live independent lives, and accrue additional expenses which they would not have had had the family remained united. Unfortunately, it is not the isolated exception that noncustodial divorced parents, because of such additional expenses or because of a loss of concern for children who are no longer in their immediate care and custody, or out of animosity directed at the custodial spouse, cannot be relied upon to voluntarily support the children of the earlier marriage to the extent they would have had they not divorced. One appellate court stated in ordering a divorced parent to contribute to the college education of his noncustodial child:

> In a normal household, parents ... direct their children as to when and how they should work or study. That is on the assumption of a normal family relationship, where parental love and moral obligation dictate what is best for the children. Under such circumstances, natural pride in the attainments of a child ... would demand of parents provision for a college education, even at a sacrifice.
>
> When we turn to divorce parents — a disrupted family — society cannot count on normal protection for the child, and it is here that equity takes control to mitigate the hardship that may befall children of divorced parents. Maitzen v. Maitzen (1959), 24 Ill.App.2d 32, 38.

We might point out to plaintiff that sections 503(d) and 513 do not mandate that divorced parents must provide their children of majority age with funds for education in all cases. It is certainly a legitimate legislative purpose to minimize any economic and educational disadvantages to children of divorced parents. If parents could have been expected to provide an education for their child of majority age absent divorce, it is not unreasonable for the legislature to furnish a means for providing that they do so after they have been divorced. We have no hesitation, therefore, in concluding that it is reasonably related to that legitimate purpose for the legislature to permit the trial court, in its sound discretion, to compel divorced parents to educate their children to the same extent as might reasonably be expected of nondivorced parents. [Citation omitted]. Sections 503(d) and 513 do not violate the equal protection guarantees of the Federal and State constitutions.[113]

It is difficult to predict the future. Yet more movement in this area seems likely, because a college education is becoming a normal aspiration and the opportunity for students to "work their way through college" seems to have decreased.[114] Already a "non-child" [115] has won a suit for higher education as a third party beneficiary under a separation agreement.[116] The South Carolina Supreme Court granted college support on the basis of a statute permitting post-majority support in "exceptional

---

113. Kuwajinski v. Kuwajinski, 71 Ill. 2d 563, 578-80, 376 N.E.2d 1382, 1389-90 (1978). *Accord,* Childers v. Childers, 89 Wash. 2d 592, 575 P.2d 201 (1978). *See* Veron, *Parental Support of Post-Majority Children in College,* 17 J. Fam. L. 645, 668-78 (1978-79). *Cf.,* Kelsey v. Panarelli, — Mass. App. Ct. —, 77 Mass. App. Ct. Adv. Sh. 818, 363 N.E.2d 1363 (1977).

114. We believe we need not labor the point that today, with rare exceptions, a college education is indispensable for success in obtaining and holding a reasonably well-paid and secure position. Another result of present conditions is that, again with rare exceptions, no one's education is completed at age eighteen, nor in practically all professions, until well after twenty-one. In the case before us, the children's welfare and the likelihood that they will soon have to assist in supporting their ailing mother demand that they be afforded what was once a luxury but has now become a necessity. French v. French, 117 N.H. 696, 700, 378 A.2d 1127, 1129 (1977).

115. Plaintiff had left college, married, and been self-sufficient for eighteen months. Upon his return to college, he sued his father for tuition and living expenses.

116. Bethune v. Bethune, 46 N.Y.2d 897, 387 N.E.2d 614 (1979) (reversing appellate division and reinstating trial court's judgment).

circumstances." [117] The following statute recently was passed in Massachusetts:

> The court may make appropriate order of maintenance, support and education of any child who has attained age eighteen but who has not attained age twenty-one and who is domiciled in the home of a parent, and is principally dependent upon said parent for maintenance. [118]

Fascinating questions arise if a positive answer is given to the "adult child's" demand for parentally furnished higher education: Since parental "custody" ends at majority, the decision to attend college may have to be separated from the traditional right of the custodial parent to make that decision. Divorced parents thus could be confronted with the adult student's own decision to attend college. Given that, however, what justification remains to limit this decision-making power to (adult) children of divorced marriages? At that point, the same right logically should extend to adult offspring of undivorced parents.

The next question will be whether the parent's provision of financial means for post-majority education should give the parent the right to control the type or extent of the "non-child's" education? Should the provision of financial support effect a sort of "reverse emancipation" and give the paying parent a reasonable say in (if not control over) the application of his or her money? It would appear that some accommodation between the interests of the child and the parent must be contemplated. To achieve a fair balance, traditional doctrine dealing with this conflict should remain largely applicable, such as expressed in the New

---

117. Risinger v. Risinger, 273 S.C. 36, 253 S.E.2d 652 (1979); similarly Locke v. Locke, — Iowa —, 246 N.W.2d 246 (1976). *But see* Winikoff v. Winikoff, 339 So. 2d 262 (Fla. App. 1976); Phillips v. Phillips, 339 So. 2d 1299 (La. App. 1976).

118. MASS. ANN. LAWS ch. 208, § 28 (Supp. 1977).

York case defining a paying father's control over his daughter's "lifestyle" while attending college,[119] and the Vermont decision holding that a (not overly affluent) father need pay only the "reasonable" cost of his daughter's education, requiring her to seek less expensive alternatives (state schools) to the expensive schools to which she had applied.[120]

b. *Death of Parent or Child.*

Traditionally, and still typically, the parental support obligation ends at the parent's or the child's death.[121] In the absence of a will, the intestacy laws provide a portion of the parent's estate for each legitimate child.[122] Specific statutes in several states, including the Uniform Parentage Act, and since 1977, the case of *Trimble v. Gordon,*[123] provide equally for nonmarital children,[124] although the question of what formalities state law may require concerning the establishment of the unmarried

---

119. Roe v. Doe, 29 N.Y.2d 188, 272 N.E.2d 567, 324 N.Y.S.2d 71 (1971).

120. Austin v. Sicillano, 137 Vt. 115, 400 A.2d 981 (1979). *But cf.,* Flatley v. Flatley, 42 Ill. App. 3d 494, 356 N.E.2d 155 (1976).

121. Some parents litigate over their liability to pay for the child's funeral expenses. *In re* Terrell, 48 Ohio App. 2d 352, 357 N.E.2d 1113 (1977).

122. The "typical" solution is codified in UNIFORM PROBATE CODE § 2-103, 8 U.L.A. ESTATE, PROBATE & REL. LAWS 88 (Supp. 1979).

123. 430 U.S. 762, 97 S. Ct. 1459, 52 L. Ed. 2d 31 (1977). *See infra* ch. IV. 2, text at note 47.

124. *E.g.,* UNIFORM PROBATE CODE, § 2-109(2), 8 U.L.A. ESTATE PROBATE & REL. LAWS 90 (Supp. 1979); ALASKA STAT. § 13.11.045(2) (1972); ARIZ. REV. STAT. ANN. § 14-2109(2) (1974); COLO. REV. STAT. § 15-11-109(1)(b) (1973); IDAHO CODE § 15-2-109 (Supp. 1977); MONT. REV. CODE ANN. § 91A-2-109 (1976); NEB. REV. STAT. § 30-2309(2) (1974); UTAH CODE ANN. § 75-2-109 (b) (1977).

father's identity has not yet been resolved fairly for the nonmarital child.[125]

By will, a parent has full power to disinherit even a minor, dependent child, legitimate or not, and leave it without any means whatever.[126] "Pretermitted heir

---

125. *In re* Lalli, 439 U.S. 259, 99 S. Ct. 518, 50 L. Ed. 2d 503 (1978) permits a state to insist that the unmarried father's identity have been established during his lifetime in a formal paternity proceeding. Specifically, the following statute, N.Y. EST., POWERS & TRUSTS LAW § 4-1.2(a) (1965), was upheld:

> An illegitimate child is the legitimate child of his father so that he and his issue inherit from his father if a court of competent jurisdiction has, during the lifetime of the father, made an order of filiation declaring paternity in a proceeding instituted during the pregnancy of the mother or within two years from the birth of the child.
>
> The existence of an agreement obligating the father to support the illegitimate child does not qualify such child or his issue to inherit from the father in the absence of an order of filiation made as prescribed by [the preceding] subparagraph.

This denies intestate succession to many children whose paternity is clear, although it was not established formally during the father's lifetime. The Uniform Probate Code, by contrast, provides that:

> ... a person born out of wedlock ... is also a child of the father if: (i) the natural parents participated in a marriage ceremony before or after the birth of the child, even though the attempted marriage is void; (ii) or the paternity is established by an adjudication before the death of the father or is established thereafter by clear and convincing proof, except that the paternity established under subparagraph (ii) is ineffective to qualify the father or his kindred to inherit from or through the child unless the father has openly treated the child as his, and has not refused to support the child.

UNIFORM PROBATE CODE, § 2-109, 8 U.L.A. ESTATE, PROBATE & REL. LAWS 90 (Supp. 1979). The Probate Code's requirement of "clear and convincing proof" was upheld in C.L.W. v. M.J., 254 N.W.2d 446 (N.D. 1977). *See generally* H. KRAUSE, ILLEGITIMACY LAW AND SOCIAL POLICY 87-95, 151-52 (1971).

126. *See* H. KRAUSE, FAMILY LAW: CASES AND MATERIALS, 480-83 (1976).

statutes" provide protection only against unintentional disinheritance and typically apply "if a testator omits to provide in his will for any of his children, whether born before or after the testator's death, or for the issue of a deceased child, whether born before or after the testator's death." In that case, "they shall take the same share of his estate which they would have taken if he had died intestate, unless they have been provided for by the testator in his lifetime or unless it appears that the omission was intentional and not occasioned by accident or mistake . . . ." [127] Accordingly, if a wealthy father whose wife has predeceased him dies with a will that disinherits his small children, they will not receive a cent.

At the opposite extreme stands the civil law which does not permit a parent to deprive even an adult child of inheritance, except in a few specific situations. Based on French law, Louisiana defines "just causes for which parents may disinherit their children" as including physical violence towards the parent, refusal to support a parent when in need, refusal "to ransom them, when detained in captivity", and "if a son or daughter, being a minor, marries without the consent of his or her parents," and a few other grounds. To protect the child's rights, the parent's power to make donations *inter vivos* is restricted.[128]

The common law rule is based on the superficially sensible notion that death ends all. The civil law rule has feudal antecedents and is designed to hold the estate within the family. Today both legal regimes conflict with common sense. At the minimum, the common law should not permit

---

127. Mass. Gen. Laws Ann. ch. 191, § 20 (Supp. 1977). From a policy standpoint it would seem defensible to limit the application of these statutes to legitimate children and some courts have done so. *See* Hanson v. Markham, — Mass. —, 76 Mass. Adv. Sh. 2504, 356 N.E.2d 702 (1976). Whether this will emerge as the general rule, however, is another question.

128. La. Civ. Code Ann. art. 1621, 1493 (1952).

a parent to deprive a minor child of necessary support, and the civil law should not restrict the parent's power of disposition over money he or she has earned, once the children are of age and not in need. A compromise between these extremes would produce a sensible solution. For instance, regarding assets the parent inherited from his or her family, a' rule keeping such assets in the family may seem reasonable, although a restriction on alienability for a period spanning generations would be in conflict with the rule against perpetuities. Regarding the minor child, a sensible regulation would require the parent's estate to provide support during minority. The latter was attempted in a draft of the Uniform Parentage Act, but the relevant provision was not accepted by the Commissioners on Uniform State Laws. It provided that a child's support until the age of majority would be enforceable against the parent's estate in the amount not exceeding the share the disinherited child would have received if the parent had died intestate.[129]

There is some movement away from the common law rule. Rare provisions allow the State to claim child support against a parent's estate if the child becomes a welfare

---

129. The 1971 draft version of the UNIFORM LEGITIMACY ACT (now the UNIFORM PARENTAGE ACT) contained the following provision:

§ 21(b) If the father has disinherited his child or by will or otherwise has left his child an amount or property totaling less than the child's distributive share would have been if the father had died intestate, and the father's liquidated obligation to support his child shall be enforceable against his estate. The child's recovery shall not exceed the amount that would have been allotted to or on behalf of such child as his distributive share had the father died intestate, and the court shall take into consideration benefits received and to be received by the child under Federal and State laws or private survivorship plans or insurance by reason of the death of his father.

See also Krause, Bringing the Bastard Into the Great Society — A Proposed Uniform Act on Legitimacy, 44 TEX. L. REV. 829, 840 § 19(b) (1966).

burden.[130] A few states make special provision regarding the father's post-death liability for the support of children born out of wedlock.[131] In connection with *divorce,* however, more rapid progress is being made. The Uniform Marriage and Divorce Act provides that, *unless otherwise provided in the decree or agreed in writing,* "when a parent obligated to pay support dies, the amount of support may be modified, removed, or commuted to a lump sum payment, to the extent just and appropriate to the circumstances." [132] The Supreme Court of Colorado relied on this provision to uphold a court order which, to secure a divorcing father's "post-mortem" support liability, had required him to take out life insurance.[133] The Kentucky Court of Appeals held that a support obligation undertaken in the parents'

---

130. *E.g.,* CAL. CIV. CODE § 205 (Cum. Supp. 1979); N.D. CENT. CODE § 14-09-12 (1971).

131. IDAHO CODE § 7-1105 (1979):

> If a parent of a child born out of wedlock dies, an order of support or a judicially approved settlement made prior to that parent's death shall be enforceable as a claim against the deceased parent's estate in an amount to be determined by the probate court not greater than is provided in the order of settlement, having regard to the age of the child, the ability of the surviving parent to support and educate it, the amount of property left by the deceased parent, and the number, age and financial condition of those other persons legally entitled to support by the deceased parent during his or her lifetime.

See also IND. CODE ANN. § 31-4-1-7 (1973); NEV. REV. STAT. § 126.070 (1957). In McKamey v. Watkins, 257 Ind. 195, 273 N.E.2d 542 (1971), a *legitimate* child *failed* to obtain support from its father's estate.

132. § 316(c), 9A U.L.A. MATR., FAM. & HEALTH LAWS 183 (1979).

133. *In re* Icke, 189 Colo. 319, 540 P.2d 1076 (1976). *Cf.,* Finley-Wheeler v. Rofinot, 276 Or. 865, 556 P.2d 952 (1976), in which the Oregon Supreme Court held that the father's obligation to maintain life insurance, absent a specific agreement, terminated on the daughter's attaining majority. Other courts have "finessed" the problem by viewing the payment of life insurance premiums as support *currently* rendered. See also Easley v. John Hancock Mutual Life Ins. Co., 403 Mich. 521, 271 N.W.2d 513 (1978), which allowed a nonmarital child to participate in life insurance proceeds "left" by the deceased father.

separation agreement survives the father's death, even (or especially) in the face of a specific disinheritance clause in his will.[134] In 1978, a new Illinois provision for post-death support [135] applying only to children of divorced parents, survived an Equal Protection challenge in the Illinois Supreme Court against the argument that it unfairly discriminated against children of married parents and in favor of children of divorced parents.[136]

In 1979, the Idaho Supreme Court observed:

> Today many states follow this common law approach and hold that upon the death of a parent who has been ordered to make payments for the support of a child, the order terminates automatically with respect to payments which would have accrued after death. * * * These jurisdictions reason that if a court desires to impose a greater duty than that in existence at common law, there must be express language in an agreement or decree so providing. . . .
> These same jurisdictions consider it illogical to impose a child support obligation on a parent's estate

---

134. Herring v. Moore, 561 S.W.2d 96 (Ky. App. 1977).

135. ILL. REV. STAT. ch. 40, § 510(c) (1977).

136. Kuwajinski v. Kuwajinski, 71 Ill. 2d 563, 581-82, 376 N.E.2d 1382, 1390-91 (1978):

> In effect, a child of a nondivorced parent has some indirect security against the possible loss of support due to disinheritance. The dependent child of a divorced parent has no similar protection because a surviving divorced spouse is not entitled to a forced share of a former spouse's estate. It is against the background of this inequity that section 510(c) was conceived. . . .
> Second, while it is comparatively rare for a nondivorced parent to leave a spouse and their children out of a will, it is not so uncommon for a divorced parent to do so. [Citation omitted.] A divorced parent may establish a new family which may command primary allegiance in a subsequent will. The well-being of children of a former marriage may seem more remote to a noncustodial parent than the well-being of those children over whom that same parent has immediate care and custody. In addition, the divorced parent may harbor animosity toward a former spouse, which disposition might obscure the natural tendency to provide in a will for their mutual children. These are reasonable assumptions for the legislature to have made.

since the effect would be to circumvent in part the long established right of the testator to make an unrestricted disposition of his estate. Such an obligation, they argue, invests children of divorced parents, as opposed to children of families where no divorce has occurred, with a preferred status akin to a mandatory right to inherit from a deceased parent, at least to the extent of assured support to and until they attain their majority. Such an obligation would therefore disrupt the general theory of inheritance and interfere with the common rules governing descent and distribution of estates.

With the increased incidence of divorce in our society, other jurisdictions have questioned the propriety of applying the common law doctrine to present day situations. This is because when parents obtain a divorce and one parent takes custody of the children, the likelihood of an embittered or disinterested parent disinheriting a child in the other spouse's custody increases. While it is true that the common law doctrine in effect permits a parent to disinherit a child, there is no great danger that a parent would exercise this arbitrary right so long as the family unit remained intact.

Because of the greater likelihood of a divorced father leaving a child without financial protection or security, these jurisdictions have held that the death of the husband does not discharge or terminate an order in a divorce decree or provision in a property settlement agreement obligating the husband to pay a certain sum periodically for the support of a minor unless a contrary intention is clearly expressed. These jurisdictions acknowledge the need for striking a balance between infringing upon the parent's right to disinherit his/her child (the strongest argument in favor of non-survival) against the protection to be afforded the minor children of divorced parents (the strongest argument in favor of survival.) Invariably, and not unpredictably, these courts consider the latter more important than the former.[137]

---

137. [Citations omitted]. *In re* Brown, 100 Idaho 300, 597 P.2d 23 (1979).

5. Different Rules for Illegitimates?

In terms of support entitlement vis-à-vis its father, the nonmarital child generally has fared worse than the "legitimate" child, at least under the law which was in effect prior to *Gomez v. Perez*.[138] Unjustifiably, much pre-*Gomez* law remains on the books and, worse, still is applied in the courts of many states. On the other hand, many states now provide equality for illegitimate children in one way or another, often by holding that a judgment in a paternity action establishes equality in support matters.[139] Many statutes state expressly that the mother must assist in providing support,[140] sometimes only if the father cannot be reached.[141] The contest between the father's and mother's responsibility for a nonmarital child reached a sort of climax when an unmarried father attempted to escape child support liability with the "proximate cause" argument that he had counseled the mother to have an abortion and had offered to pay for the abortion. The Alabama Supreme

138. 409 U.S. 535, 93 S. Ct. 872, 35 L. Ed. 2d 56 (1973). *See* detailed discussion in ch. IV.

139. *E.g.,* ALA. CODE tit. 26, § 12-4 (1975); ILL. ANN. STAT. ch. 106 ¾, § 52 (Supp. 1978); ME. REV. STAT. ANN. tit. 19 § 271 (Cum. Supp. 1978); MISS. CODE ANN. § 93-9-7 (1972); NEB. REV. STAT. § 13-107 (1977); N.H. REV. STAT. ANN. § 168-A:1 (1977); N.C. GEN. STAT. § 49-15 (1976); OR. REV. STAT. § 109.060 (1977); UTAH CODE ANN. § 78-45a-1 (1977). *Cf.,* ARIZ. REV. STAT. § 8-601 (Cum. Supp. 1979). Several states provided equality long before *Gomez, see* H. KRAUSE, ILLEGITIMACY: LAW AND SOCIAL POLICY 24, 297-306 (1971).

140. *E.g.,* GA. CODE ANN. § 74-202 (Cum. Supp. 1979); ILL. ANN. STAT. ch. 106 ¾, § 60 (Supp. 1978); IOWA CODE ANN. § 675.1 (1950); MD. CODE ANN. art. 16, 66H (Cum. Supp. 1978); MISS. CODE ANN. 93-9-35 (1972); NEV. REV. STAT. § 126.030 (1957); N.M. STAT. ANN. § 40-5-1 (1978). In A.H. v. W.B.McD., — F. Supp. — (D. Minn. 1979), [5 F.L.R. 2556] a law holding *only* the father of a child born out of wedlock liable for its support was struck down under the Equal Protection Clause.

141. NEB. REV. STAT. § 13-108 (1977).

45

Court rejected the father's claim,[142] and, in another case, so did the Maryland Court of Appeals.[143] That climax was eclipsed when a California man attempted to escape child support liability on the basis of a pre-conception contract with the mother, who had asked him to father the child as a favor. The contract purported to absolve the father from any child support liability, but was held invalid by the California Court of Appeals.[144]

The source of the father's duty of support typically remains a "bastardy act" or "paternity statute." [145] Under

---

142. Harris v. State, — Ala. —, 356 So. 2d 623 (1978). *Cf.,* Troppi v. Scarf, 31 Mich. App. 240, 187 N.W.2d 511 (1971) which, in a situation involving the failure of birth control by fault of the pharmacist-defendant, allowed tort recovery for "wrongful life" and rejected the defendant's argument that the mother should have secured an abortion or placed the child for adoption.

143. Dorsey v. English, 283 Md. 522, 528-29, 390 A.2d 1133, 1138 (1978):

> Dorsey next attacks Maryland's paternity statute ... as unconstitutional. He claims that there is no rational basis to treat him, the father, in the same way the mother is treated because the nexus between the act of intercourse and the birth of the child was broken by the mother's independent decision to bring the fetus to full term. He relies on three cases, Roe v. Wade, 410 U.S. 113, 93 S. Ct. 705, 35 L. Ed. 2d 147 (1973); Bellotti v. Baird, 428 U.S. 132, 96 S. Ct. 2857, 49 L. Ed. 2d 844 (1976) and Planned Parenthood of Missouri v. Danforth, 428 U.S. 52, 96 S. Ct. 2831, 49 L. Ed. 2d 788 (1976), which upheld the right of the mother of an unborn child to choose to abort it without consulting the father. Thus, he claims his role in the birth of the child has become so attenuated that his circumstance is dissimilar from the mother and the statute treats him unequally.
>
> Dorsey's assertion of unequal treatment is specious. His voluntary act of intercourse with English carried with it the risk that she would become pregnant and bear a child. She did and the statute holds him and her equally responsible for its support. The statute meets the test and he must meet his obligation thereunder.

See also Levy & Duncan, *The Impact of Roe v. Wade on Paternal Support Statutes,* 10 FAM. L.Q. 179 (1976).

144. Fournier v. Lopez, second unpublished opinion, *see* 5 F.L.R. 2582 (1979).

145. *See infra* ch. V.

support statutes specifically relating to nonmarital children, the level of support at which the child must be maintained is generally left to the court's discretion.[146] Sometimes it is specifically fixed by the statute.[147] Sometimes it is fixed rather vaguely, as in the 1977 North Carolina statute that gives the nonmarital child a right to "adequate" support,[148] or that of Tennessee which speaks in terms of "necessary support",[149] or in that of Idaho, which requires a "fair and reasonable sum." [150] *Gomez* and many earlier legislative enactments now should cover the child's entire minority in all states,[151] and in a few states, liability

---

146. CONN. GEN. STAT. ANN. § 52-442 (1960); DEL. CODE tit. 13, § 514 (Supp. 1977); D.C. CODE ANN. § 16-2349 (1967); FLA. STAT. ANN. § 742.041 (Supp. 1978); IOWA CODE ANN. § 675.25 (1950); KAN. STAT. § 38-1106 (1973); KY. REV. STAT. § 406.121 (1972); ME. REV. STAT. tit. 19, §§ 275, 281 (Supp. 1977); MD. ANN. CODE art. 16, § 66H (Supp. 1977); NEV. REV. STAT. § 126.230 (1973); N.J. STAT. ANN. § 9:17-12 (1976); N.M. STAT. ANN. § 40-5-15 (1978); N.Y. DOM. REL. LAW §§ 33, 34 (1977); N.C. GEN. STAT. § 49-7 (1977); OHIO REV. CODE ANN. § 3111.17 (Supp. 1977); R.I. GEN. LAWS § 15-8-10 (1970); TENN. CODE ANN. § 36-223 (1977); UTAH CODE ANN. § 77-60-7 (1953); VT. STAT. ANN. tit. 15, § 339 (1974); W.VA. CODE § 48-7-4 (1976).

147. FLA. STAT. ANN. § 742.041 (Cum. Supp. 1978):

(1) The court shall order the defendant to pay montly for the care and support of such child the following amounts:
(a) From date of birth to 6th birthday — $40 per month.
(b) From 6th birthday to 12th birthday — $60 per month.
(c) From 12th birthday to 15th birthday — $90 per month.
(d) From 15th birthday to 18th birthday — $110 per month.
(2) Such amounts may be increased or reduced by the judge in his discretion depending upon the circumstances and ability of the defendant.

148. N.C. GEN. STAT. § 49-2 (Supp. 1977).

149. TENN. CODE ANN. § 36-223 (1977).

150. IDAHO CODE § 7-1121 (1979). *Cf.,* UTAH CODE ANN. § 77-60-7 (1978) (a reasonable sum).

151. *E.g.,* COLO. REV. STAT. § 19-6-105 (1974) (or until 21 at court's discretion); CONN. GEN. STAT. ANN. § 46b-171 (Cum. Supp. 1978); DEL. CODE tit. 13, § 1305 (1974); FLA. STAT. ANN. § 742.041 (Supp. 1978); GA.

for educational purposes even may extend beyond minority.[152] Sex discrimination is not unheard of, in that the support obligation for a girl may be shorter than that for a boy.[153] Such statutes, however, clearly are unconstitutional under recent Supreme Court cases.[154] In the pre-*Gomez* past, some states had extended support rights no further than the period of time the child was likely to be unable to support itself,[155] or to a period not exceeding, for instance, six years.[156]

The amount of time *prior* to judgment for which support and similar payments may be awarded ranges from the proportion of expenses already incurred as the court deems just,[157] to six, four, three, two or one years preceding the

---

CODE ANN. § 74-202 (1973); MICH. STAT. ANN. § 25.497 (1974); N.Y. DOM. REL. LAW § 2 (1977); OHIO REV. CODE ANN. § 3111.17 (Supp. 1977); R.I. GEN. LAWS § 15-8-10 (1970); TENN. CODE ANN. § 36-229 (1977); UTAH CODE ANN. § 77-60-7 (1953); WIS. STAT. ANN. § 52.37 (Supp. 1977); W. VA. CODE § 48-7-4 (1976). *But cf.,* ARK. STAT. ANN. § 34-706 (1962) (age 16); IOWA CODE ANN. § 675.25 (1950) (age 16); N.M. STAT. ANN. § 22-4-16 (1954) (age 16).

152. *E.g.,* IDAHO CODE § 7-1121 (1979).

153. *E.g.,* NEV. REV. STAT. § 126.230(2) (1957): "The judgment shall be for annual amounts, equal or varying, having regard to the obligation of the father under NRS 126.030, as the court directs, until the child, if male, reaches the age of 21 years or, if female reaches the age of 18 years."

154. Stanton v. Stanton, 429 U.S. 501, 97 S. Ct. 717, 50 L. Ed. 2d 723 (1977); Stanton v. Stanton, 421 U.S. 7, 95 S. Ct. 1373, 43 L. Ed. 2d 688 (1975).

155. *E.g.,* LA. CIV. CODE ANN. art. 243 (1952); VT. STAT. ANN. tit. 15, § 339 (1974).

156. MASS. ANN. LAWS ch. 273, § 5 (Cum. Supp. 1978).

157. *E.g.,* MICH. STAT. ANN. § 25.497 (1974). THE UNIFORM PARENTAGE ACT § 15(d), 9A U.L.A., MATR., FAM. AND HEALTH LAWS 608 (1979) similarly gives the court discretionary power over the amount of the father's past liabilities: "The court may limit the father's liability for past support of the child to the proportion of the expenses already incurred that the court deems just." This provision resembles the general rule

action.[158] In a few states, the support obligation extends beyond the father's death, sometimes with the provision that the child cannot take more than if he had been an heir.[159]

It must be re-emphasized that to the extent statutes or court decisions still differentiate between children on the basis of their parents' marital status, they are either invalid or subject to severe doubt under current U.S. Supreme Court doctrine. Moreover, many courts have "judicially amended" their state's paternity statutes.[160] Even so, the

---

governing obligations of parents towards legitimate children: The parent has a continuing obligation to support the child. No statute of limitation, not even the doctrine of laches, typically bars collection on behalf of a minor child. *E.g.,* Perez v. Singh, 21 Cal. App. 3d 870, 97 Cal. Rptr. 920 (1971); but *cf.,* Amie v. Superior Court, — Cal. App. 3d —, — Cal. Rptr. —, (1980) [6 F.L.R. 2166] excerpted *infra* in ch. VIII, note 117. *See* also *infra* ch. V. 5.

158. ME. REV. STAT. ANN. tit. 19, § 273 (Cum. Supp. 1978). This statute is Maine's variation on § 3 of the UNIFORM ACT ON PATERNITY. That, now officially withdrawn uniform law, proposed; "The father's liabilities for past education and necessary support are limited to a period of four years next preceding the commencement of an action." 9A U.L.A. MATR., FAM. AND HEALTH LAWS 631 (1979). Utah adopted this provision, UTAH CODE ANN. § 78-45a-3 (1977). Other states adopted the language, but *reduced* the period of the father's liability. KY. REV. STAT. § 406.031(1) (Cum. Supp. 1978) (three years); MISS. CODE ANN. § 93-9-11 (1972) (one year). New Hampshire omitted this provision when it adopted the UNIFORM ACT ON PATERNITY. Iowa has a similar provision, limiting the father's obligation to two years unless a previous written demand was served upon him. IOWA CODE ANN. § 675.3 (Cum. Supp. 1978); Jensen v. Voshell, 193 N.W.2d 86, 59 A.L.R.3d 678 (Iowa 1971).

159. IND. CODE ANN. § 31-4-1-7 (1973) (support, not more than heir); MD. ANN. CODE art. 16, § 16J(c) (Supp. 1977) (child remains limited to one half the sum a legitimate child would receive); NEV. REV. STAT. § 126.070 (1973) (no limit, left to discretion of the court); S.D. COMP. LAWS ANN. § 25-8-33 (1976) (no limit, left to discretion of the court); WYO. STAT. ANN. § 14-64 (1965) (no limit, left to discretion of the court).

160. *E.g.,* Boyles v. Brown, 69 Mich. App. 480, 245 N.W.2d 100 (1976); State v. Booth, 15 Wash. App. 804, 551 P.2d 1403 (1976).

Arkansas Supreme Court held in 1978 that a judgment, requiring the father of a nonmarital child to pay the amount of $10 monthly until the child reached 16 years of age, could not be modified by the court for lack of an appropriate statute, although a support judgment entered in a divorce action could be modified, if necessary.[161] The opposite result was reached in New York and Washington, on the basis of *Gomez*.[162]

---

161. Carter v. Clausen, 263 Ark. 344, 565 S.W.2d 17 (1978).
162. Shan F. v. Francis F., 88 Misc. 2d 165, 387 N.Y.S.2d 593 (1976); State v. Booth, 15 Wash. App. 804, 551 P.2d 1403 (1976).

Chapter II

ENFORCEMENT REMEDIES UNDER STATE LAW

1. In-State Enforcement.

Child support obligations are difficult to enforce in the *ongoing* family. Parental autonomy reigns all but supreme. As previously indicated, the courts are most reluctant to interfere in family affairs, whether the issue be spousal or child support, or any other matter deemed the parties' business.[1] Where the default is gross, the child neglect laws will apply and provide a (typically drastic) remedy.[2] Short of that, an effective vehicle is a suit by a merchant or other person or agency who has furnished "necessaries" for the child's support, (with some flexibility attending the definition of necessaries).[3] Only when the parents live apart, whether by reason of divorce or separation, or if they have remained unmarried, will a court readily define and impose *specific* support obligations.

The support obligation may be enforced through criminal provisions which make it a misdemeanor to default on support obligations, or through the criminal or civil contempt power of the court. In any given case, the criminal penalty or either form of contempt or all three sanctions may apply, depending on the circumstances, the applicable

---

1. *See* McGuire v. McGuire, 157 Neb. 226, 59 N.W.2d 336 (1953).

2. *E.g.,* Commonwealth *ex rel.* Glenn v. Glenn, 208 Pa. Super. Ct. 206, 222 A.2d 465 (1966). *See* S. Fox, Juvenile Courts in a Nutshell 49-56 (2d ed. 1977).

3. Greenspan v. Slate, 12 N.J. 426, 97 A.2d 390 (1953) (support obligation based on "natural law"). Alternatively, the court may imply a promise by the parent to pay for the necessary items that a third party furnished. *See, e.g.,* Watkins v. Medical and Dental Finance Bureau, Inc., 101 Ariz. 580, 422 P.2d 696 (1967) (support obligation to provide necessities to child, but father held not liable).

statutes, and the desired consequences.[4] Although the three enforcement methods are theoretically quite distinct, courts often are trapped by superficial similarities such as the fact that jail may be imposed for civil as well as criminal contempt and, of course, in a criminal prosecution. To add to the potential confusion, the criminal penalty may be (and often is) suspended on condition that (and so long as) support payments are made; just as the civil contempt penalty will be lifted upon compliance. A clear distinction between the contempt remedies and the criminal prosecution for nonsupport is that the former must be predicated on a pre-existing court order, whereas the latter lies when there is noncompliance with a support obligation, not necessarily court-imposed or previously reduced to judgment. Beyond that, a criminal nonsupport prosecution is an action brought by the *State* to vindicate its own interests and, at least in theory, is not available at the behest or option of the support claimant.[5]

In neither type of contempt action, nor in criminal nonsupport prosecutions, have the courts viewed imprisonment resulting from failure to comply with a judicially imposed support obligation as a revival of "debtor's prison."[6] Nor has forcing (by threat of

---

4. *See* Chambers, *Men Who Know They Are Watched: Some Benefits and Costs of Jailing for Nonpayment of Support*, 75 MICH. L. REV. 900, 902 (1977). Professor Chambers' findings support the conclusion that payment of support can be improved by the imposition of jail sentences, if that sanction is coupled with a "well organized and visible system of other efforts to collect."

5. *See, e.g.*, S. v. D., 410 U.S. 614, 93 S. Ct. 1146, 35 L. Ed. 2d 536 (1973).

6. See Gillis v. Gillis, 243 Ga. 1, 252 S.E.2d 434 (1979); Bradley v. Superior Court, 48 Cal. 2d 509, 310 P.2d 634 (1957); Martin v. People, 69 Colo. 60, 168 P. 1171 (1917); Rich v. People, 66 Ill. 513 (1873); *In re* McLemore, 515 S.W.2d 356 (Tex. Civ. App. 1974). *Cf.,* Comment, *Constitutional Law — Cruel and Unusual Punishment — Imprisonment*

imprisonment) an unwilling, unemployed father to seek work been viewed as a violation of the Thirteenth (anti-slavery) Amendment.[7] In an isolated Ohio case, a "quasi criminal" paternity statute was held unconstitutional on the ground that it discriminated on the basis of wealth.[8] In accordance with common practice, the statute provided for imprisonment of putative fathers who failed to give security for support and for release of putative fathers upon payment of support. Of course, the United States Supreme Court has never held poverty to be a suspect class under the Equal Protection Clause[9] and it may thus be doubted that this Ohio case has national significance.

The question of whether there is a right to counsel in support enforcement actions depends to some extent on the type of proceeding involved. The general answer is negative. The detailed discussion of this issue in connection with the paternity action furnishes valid analogies.[10]

a. *Criminal Nonsupport*

Statutes commonly define nonsupport of a minor[11] child as a criminal offense. While details vary from state to state, most provide that a parent who willfully fails to

---

for *Failure to Support Illegitimate Child*, 24 IOWA L. REV. 602 (1939); *Comment, Enforcement of Maintenance and Support Orders by Contempt Proceedings — Imprisonment for Debt*, 42 MO. L. REV. 325 (1977); Walker v. Stokes, 54 Ohio App. 2d 119, 375 N.E.2d 1258 (1977).

7. Commonwealth v. Pouliot, 292 Mass. 229, 198 N.E. 256 (1935).

8. Walker v. Stokes, 54 Ohio App. 2d 119, 375 N.E.2d 1258 (1977).

9. *See* San Antonio Ind. School Dist. v. Rodriguez, 411 U.S. 1, 93 S. Ct. 1278, 36 L. Ed. 2d 16 (1973).

10. *Infra* ch. V. 7.

11. The age of majority now is 18 in most states. Some statutes specifically require a parent to support a child only until the age of 16 years (*e.g.,* COLO. REV. STAT. § 14-6-101 (1978); MASS. ANN. LAWS ch. 273,

support his minor child is guilty of a misdemeanor,[12] although in some states and under certain conditions, the offense may be a felony.[13] While many traditional criminal nonsupport statutes on the books still provide only for the *father's* criminal liability, when challenged, courts have held such statutes unconstitutional.[14] In consequence, California's statute, as well as the statutes of an increasing number of other states, now provides that both parents may be prosecuted for defaulting on their support liability.[15]

In the drafting stages of the federal child support enforcement legislation, imposition of federal criminal liability on "support fugitives" was seriously considered. Probably for good, these proposals were rejected.

---

§ 1 (Supp. 1978); Mo. REV. STAT. § 559.353 (Supp. 1978)). More typically, the obligation is set to end at 18 years of age (*e.g.,* ALA. CODE tit. 30, § 4-51 (1975); CONN. GEN. STAT. § 46b-215(a) (Cum. Supp. 1979); DEL. CODE tit. 13, § 521 (Cum. Supp. 1978); ME. REV. STAT. tit. 19, § 481 (Cum. Supp. 1978); MD. ANN. CODE art. 27, § 88 (1978); N.C. GEN. STAT. § 49-2 (1977); W. VA. CODE § 48-8-1 (1976)). While ARK. STAT. ANN. § 41-2405 (1977) requires support for a legitimate child for 18 years and for an illegitimate child for 16 years only, this distinction would appear to be unconstitutional. *See* Gomez v. Perez, 409 U.S. 535, 93 S. Ct. 872, 35 L. Ed. 2d 56 (1973).

12. *See, e.g.,* ALA. CODE tit. 30 § 4-51 (1975); CAL. PENAL CODE § 270 (Supp. 1979); ILL. REV. STAT. ch. 68, § 24 (1978); MASS. ANN. LAWS ch. 273, §§ 1, 15 (Cum. Supp. 1978); W. VA. CODE § 48-8-1 (1976).

13. *E.g.,* ARIZ. REV. STAT. § 12-2458 (Supp. 1978); COLO. REV. STAT. § 14-6-101(1) (1977); KAN. STAT. ANN. § 21-3605(1)(g) (1977); MISS. CODE ANN. § 97-5-3 (1972).

14. Cotton v. Municipal Court, 59 Cal. App. 3d 601, 130 Cal. Rptr. 876, (1976). CAL. PENAL CODE § 270 (Supp. 1979) now provides for liability of "parents." *Cf.,* MASS. ANN. LAWS ch. 273, § 15 (Cum. Supp. 1978) which still speaks exclusively of the father's liability for nonsupport of an *illegitimate* child.

15. CAL. PENAL CODE § 270 (Supp. 1979). *See also* Mo. REV. STAT. § 559.350 (Supp. 1978); N.C. GEN. STAT. § 49-2 (Supp. 1977); VA. CODE § 20-61 (Cum. Supp. 1978); W. VA. CODE § 48-8-1 (1978).

Nonsupport is "bad," but seems out of line as a federal crime.[16]

Under state law, the penalty for criminal nonsupport may be a fine or imprisonment or both.[17] The common practice is for courts to enter support orders and to suspend the criminal penalty on condition of compliance with the support obligation and, possibly, to post bond.[18] Upon

---

16. The proposed section (§ 461(a)) would have provided:

> Any individual who is the parent of any child or children and who is under a legal duty to provide for the support and maintenance of such child or children (as required under the law of the State where such child or children reside) but fails to perform such duty and has left, deserted, or abandoned such child or children and such child or children receive assistance payments to provide for their support and maintenance which are funded in whole or in part from funds appropriated therefor by the Federal Government shall, upon conviction, be penalized in an amount equal to 50 percent of the residual monetary obligation owed to the United States, or fined not more than $1,000, or imprisoned for not more than one year, or any combination of these three penalties.

H.R. 1, 92d Cong., 2d Sess. PROPOSED AMENDMENTS TO THE SOCIAL SECURITY ACT: REPORT OF THE SENATE COMM. ON FINANCE ON H.R. 1, 92d Cong., 2d Sess. 859 (1972).

17. *E.g.,* ALA. CODE tit. 30 § 4-51 (1975) (maximum of $100 and/or 1 year in jail or at hard labor); ARIZ. REV. STAT. § 12-2458 (1977) ($1000 and/or 1 year); CAL. PENAL CODE § 270 (1979) ($1000 and/or 1 year); DEL. CODE ANN. tit. 13, § 521 (Cum. Supp. 1978) ($500 and/or six months); MINN. STAT. § 609.375 (Cum. Supp. 1978) ($300 and/or 90 days if nonsupport continued 90 days or less and up to 5 years if nonsupport continued in excess of 90 days); MISS. CODE ANN. § 97-5-3 ($500 and/or 2 years); ME. REV. STAT. ANN. tit. 19, § 481 (Cum. Supp. 1978) ($300 and eleven months, but $500 and 2 years, if the offense is "of a high and aggravated nature"). W. VA. CODE § 48-8-1 (1978). *See also* Law v. State, 238 Ala. 428, 191 So. 803 (1939); Smith v. State, 156 Tenn. 599, 4 S.W.2d 351 (1928); State v. Moran, 99 Conn. 115, 121 A. 277 (1923); State v. Latham, 136 Tenn. 30, 188 S.W. 534 (1916); Burton v. Commonwealth, 109 Va. 800, 63 S.E. 464 (1909).

18. ALA. CODE tit. 30 § 4-59 (1975) (court may suspend sentence and impose condition of fulfilling support duty); CAL. PENAL CODE § 270(b) (Supp. 1979) (judge may suspend sentence on condition of payment of

failure of the parent to comply, the court may revoke the suspension and impose the sentence.[19] In this manner, the *criminal* prosecution produces the desired *civil* effect, *i.e.*, fulfillment of the support obligation.

Nonsupport is a criminal offense only if it is willful.[20] In this context, "willfulness" has been defined as "a deliberate or perverse design, malice, or an intentional or deliberate breach" of the duty of support,[21] or as nonpayment "without

---

support); KAN. STAT. § 21-3605(c) (1977) (court may release defendant on probation provided that the defendant appears in court periodically and complies with the order of support); MD. ANN. CODE art. 27, § 88(b) (Cum. Supp. 1979) (court may release defendant on probation provided that defendant complies with support order); VA. CODE § 20-72 (1975) (court may require bond with, or without, surety in such sum as the court may order). *See further* CONN. GEN. STAT. ANN. § 46b-177 (Cum. Supp. 1978):

> The complainant shall not be required to pay or give security for the support of the defendant during his confinement in a community correctional center, nor shall such defendant be discharged from imprisonment by reason of payment or security not being made or given for his support, but the jailer shall furnish such support and may recover the cost of the same from such defendant, or, in case of his inability to pay such cost, from the town where he belongs; and, if he belongs to no town in this state, such cost shall be paid by the state.

See generally, S. RUBIN, THE LAW OF CRIMINAL CORRECTION 201 (1963).

19. *E.g.,* Ex Parte Boyd, 73 Okla. Crim. 441, 122 P.2d 162 (1942); Bohannan v. State, 271 P.2d 739 (Okla. Crim. 1954). *E.g.,* ALA. CODE tit. 30 § 4-63 (1975).

20. *E.g.,* ARIZ. REV. STAT. § 12-2457 (Supp. 1978); ME. REV. STAT. ANN. tit. 19, § 481 (Cum. Supp. 1978); NEV. REV. STAT. § 13-116 (Supp. 1978). *See* Burris v. State, — Ind. App. —, 382 N.E.2d 963 (1978); Moreno v. Superior Court of Pima County, 3 Ariz. App. 361, 414 P.2d 749 (1966). Normally, the state must prove willfulness as an element of the crime of nonsupport. Johnson v. State, 22 Ala. App. 160, 113 So. 480 (1927); State v. Peek, 266 N.C. 639, 146 S.E.2d 827 (1966); State v. Chambers, 238 N.C. 373, 78 S.E.2d 209 (1953); State v. Stiles, 228 N.C. 137, 44 S.E.2d 728 (1947).

21. Burris v. State, — Ind. App. —, 382 N.E.2d 963 (1978).

just cause or excuse."[22] Although some courts have held that carelessness or neglect does not constitute willfulness,[23] other courts have equated little more than proof of neglect with proof of willfulness. For instance, evidence that a parent earned a regular salary but made no support payments has been held to prove willful nonsupport.[24] Moreover, some statutes provide that nonpayment of support is presumptive or *prima facie* evidence of willfulness.[25] Sternly, North Carolina warns:

> [If a] husband neglects applying himself to some honest calling for the support of himself and family, and is found sauntering about, endeavoring to maintain himself by gaming or other undue means, or is a common frequenter of drinking houses, or is a known common drunkard, [this] shall be presumptive evidence that such abandonment and neglect is willful.[26]

Criminal liability also may be based on partial compliance with a support order,[27] unless the circumstances negate an

---

22. People v. Green, 178 Colo. 77, 495 P.2d 549 (1972). *See also* State v. Chambers, 238 N.C. 373, 78 S.E.2d 209 (1953); State v. Russell, 73 Wash. 2d 903, 442 P.2d 988 (1968); Upton v. State, 36 Ala. App. 94, 52 So. 2d 820 (1951); Gallegos v. People, 161 Colo. 158, 420 P.2d 409 (1966).

23. *E.g.,* Burris v. State, — Ind. App. —, 382 N.E.2d 963 (1978); State v. Hayden, 224 N.C. 779, 32 S.E.2d 333 (1944); Bohannan v. State, 271 P.2d 739 (Okla. Crim. 1954).

24. Gallegos v. People, 161 Colo. 158, 420 P.2d 409 (1966).

25. *E.g.,* Ariz. Rev. Stat. § 12-2458(B) (Supp. 1978); Cal. Penal Code (Supp. 1979); N.M. Stat. Ann. § 40-5-20 (1978); Vt. Stat. Ann. tit. 15 § 207 (Cum. Supp. 1979). *See also* People v. Temple, 20 Cal. App. 3d 540, 97 Cal. Rptr. 794 (1971); Bohannon v. State, 271 P.2d 739 (Okla. Crim. 1954); State v. Godines, 9 Wash. App. 55, 510 P.2d 835 (1973).

26. N.C. Gen. Stat. § 14-323 (1977).

27. *E.g.,* State v. Tanner, 224 La. 374, 69 So. 2d 505 (1953); State v. Brodie, 206 Iowa 1340, 222 N.W. 23 (1928); Edwards v. State, 85 Okla. Crim. 285, 187 P.2d 248 (1947).

57

inference of willful nonsupport.[28]

The defendant may defend himself by proof that through no fault of his own, he lacks the financial means to support the child.[29] The Iowa Supreme Court accepts the following "excuses":

> [I]nability on the part of the defendant to make such provision for his minor children because of lack of funds or property or lack of employment, poor health, sickness, unemployment not occasioned by his own act, inability to secure employment, or any other means preventing the defendant from making such provision, through no fault of his own.[30]

But it is no excuse that defendant has lost custody of the child,[31] or that the custodial parent is interfering with or denying the support obligor's visitation rights.[32]

As a prerequisite to prosecution, some statutes require that the child be in "destitute or necessitous circumstances," [33] or in danger of becoming a public burden.[34] This raises the question of whether a parent can be found guilty of criminal nonsupport if the other parent or a

---

28. *E.g.,* Barrow v. State, 87 Ga. App. 572, 74 S.E.2d 467 (1953); Bohannon v. State, 271 P.2d 739 (Okla. Crim. 1954).

29. *See* People v. Cressay, 2 Cal. 3d 836, 471 P.2d 19, 87 Cal. Rptr. 699 (1970); People v. Norton, 47 Cal. App. 2d 139, 117 P.2d 402 (1941); Cox v. Commonwealth, 280 Ky. 94, 132 S.W.2d 739 (1939).

30. State v. Greer, 259 Iowa 367, 371, 144 N.W.2d 322, 325 (1966). *See also* People v. Green, 178 Colo. 77, 495 P.2d 549 (1972); State v. Russell, 73 Wash. 2d 903, 442 P.2d 988 (1968).

31. *See* MASS. ANN. LAWS ch. 273 § 8 (Cum. Supp. 1978).

32. *Cf., Infra,* text at notes 74-76.

33. *E.g.,* ALA. CODE tit. 30, § 4-51 (1975); ME. REV. STAT. ANN. tit. 19, § 481 (Cum. Supp. 1978). *See* Rouse v. State, 43 Ala. App. 171, 184 So. 2d 839 (1966); Cox v. Commonwealth, 280 Ky. 94, 132 S.W.2d 739 (1939); State v. Constable, 90 W. Va. 515, 112 S.E. 410 (1922).

34. *See* McCullers v. State, 26 Ala. App. 314, 159 So. 273 (1935); State v. Karagavoorian, 32 R.I., 477, 79 A. 1111 (1911); *Cf.,* Brown v. State, 122 Ga. 568, 50 S.E. 378 (1905).

third person has relieved the child's necessitous condition. An Alabama court has ruled that noncompliance with a support decree is not of sufficient public interest to justify a criminal sanction so long as there is no danger of the child becoming a public charge. Accordingly, a parent in default on a support obligation was not jailed for criminal nonsupport because the children were receiving support from other sources and were not in "necessitous circumstances." [35] A contempt proceeding was seen as the appropriate means of enforcing compliance. Other courts have upheld convictions for criminal nonsupport even though the immediate need of the child or children in question had been relieved by others.[36]

In a number of states, criminal nonsupport statutes are expressly applicable to illegitimate as well as legitimate children.[37] Others simply refer to "children" and have been interpreted either to apply to legitimate children only or equally to illegitimate children.[38] Only the latter interpretation should be considered proper under recent U.S. Supreme Court decisions, although the U.S. Supreme Court failed to rise to a tailor-made occasion to make a pronouncement on this point when a mother challenged the criminal nonsupport statute of Texas which was enforced only with regard to legitimate children. The Court decided

---

35. *In re* Turner, — Ala. —, 349 So. 2d 605 (1977).

36. Archer v. State, 214 Miss. 742, 59 So. 2d 339 (1952). *Cf.,* Smith v. State, 156 Tenn. 599, 4 S.W.2d 351 (1928); State v. Latham, 136 Tenn. 30, 188 S.W. 534 (1916).

37. *E.g.,* Nev. Rev. Stat. § 126.300 (1957); Mo. Rev. Stat. § 559.353 (Supp. 1978).

38. *E.g.,* Cal. Penal Code § 270 (Supp. 1979) ("The provisions of this section are applicable whether the parents of such child are or were ever married or divorced...."); Del. Code Ann. tit. 13, § 521 (Cum. Supp. 1978) ("whether such child was born in or out of wedlock"); Kan. Stat. Ann. § 21-3605(1)(b) (" 'child' means ... a child born out of wedlock").

the case on the basis of the mother's lack of standing to seek enforcement of a criminal statute.[39]

One matter complicates the case of a child born out of wedlock: Since the question of paternity is an essential incident to a criminal nonsupport prosecution, paternity must be established as a prerequisite to conviction.[40] While the nearly conclusive presumption of legitimacy that applies to the child born in wedlock would usually provide the equivalent of proof of paternity beyond a reasonable doubt, no such aid to proof appears in the case of the nonmarital child. Of course, if paternity is proved simply as one element of the crime of nonsupport, paternity would be established in conformity with the standards of proof in criminal law and no problem appears.[41] If, on the other hand, a *civil* paternity judgment was rendered previously and the prosecution concerns the father's default on his civil obligation, a serious issue of due process arises. Since perhaps the larger number of *criminal* prosecutions for nonsupport of an illegitimate child are based on earlier *civil* adjudications of paternity, the issue is far from academic. Obviously, it will do the defendant little good to have the right to representation by counsel and other constitutional protections in the criminal nonsupport action (the fact of nonsupport typically being very simple to prove beyond a reasonable doubt) when he had no counsel and no other protections in the civil proceeding which decided the much more complex issue of

---

39. S. v. D., 410 U.S. 614, 93 S. Ct. 1146, 35 L. Ed. 2d 536 (1973).

40. *But cf.,* CAL. PENAL CODE § 270 (Supp. 1979) which allows prosecution of the father for nonsupport without his obligation having been established first in a civil action. *See also* MASS. GEN. LAWS ch. 273, § 15 (Cum. Supp. 1978); Commonwealth *ex rel.* Miller v. Dillworth, 204 Pa. Super. Ct. 420, 205 A.2d 111 (1964); Annot., 30 A.L.R. 1075 (1924); State v. Ellis, 262 N.C. 446, 137 S.E.2d 840 (1964).

41. *See* State v. Clay, W. Va. , 236 S.E.2d 230 (1977); State v. Brown, 446 S.W.2d 498 (Mo. App. 1969); State v. Coffey, 3 N.C. App. 133, 164 S.E.2d 39 (1968).

paternity by a mere preponderance of the evidence. Accordingly, it may be argued that the constitutional guaranty of due process should not allow a civil adjudication of paternity to govern the imposition of criminal penalties for nonsupport.[42]

It seems clear that the defendant should be given full opportunity to challenge the civil paternity judgment in the criminal nonsupport proceeding — if it is to be admissible at all — and that he should have the right to insist that his paternity be shown beyond a reasonable doubt. Disregarding this reasoning, some courts have held that, once paternity has been established in a civil action, it need not be relitigated in a subsequent criminal prosecution for nonsupport.[43]

b. *Contempt of Court.*

The duty of support may be enforced through the contempt power of the court.[44] Most courts hold that past due installments of child support become final judgments as

---

42. An interesting criminal nonsupport statute recognizing this problem, but hardly solving it satisfactorily is W. Va. Code § 48-8-5 (1978) which provides:

> No other or greater evidence shall be required to prove the marriage of such husband and wife, or that the defendant is the father or that the alleged mother is the mother of such child or children, than is or shall be required to prove such facts in a civil action.

43. *E.g.,* State v. Jones, 220 La. 381, 56 So. 2d 724 (1951); State v. Sims, 220 La. 532, 57 So. 2d 177 (1952). *See* State v. Schwartz, 137 Ohio St. 371, 374-76, 30 N.E.2d 551, 552-53 (1940); Comment, *Criminal Liability for Nonsupport of an Illegitimate Child,* 12 La. L. Rev. 301, 303-04 (1952).

44. *E.g.,* Ind. Stat. Ann. § 31-6-7-15 (Cum. Supp. 1979); Md. Code Ann. art. 16, § 66J (1973); Minn. Stat. Ann. § 257.262 (Cum. Supp. 1979); Miss. Code Ann. § 93-9-33 (1972); Neb. Rev. Stat. § 13-106 (1977); Pa. Stat. Ann. tit. 42, § 6749 (Supp. 1979); Tex. Fam. Code Ann. § 14.09 (1975); Utah Code Ann. § 77-60-8 (1978).

they accrue,[45] and most statutes which provide for contempt proceedings as a method of support enforcement allow institution of the proceedings at any time after default.[46] An Indiana Court, on the other hand — notwithstanding a statute providing that support payments are enforceable through contempt proceedings [47] — held that support payments must be reduced to a second judgment before proceeding with civil contempt enforcement.[48] Similarly, a South Dakota court held that a judgment must be entered for past due installments before payment of the arrearages will be enforced.[49]

Civil and criminal contempt are theoretically quite distinguishable. In practice, however, "the effort to establish such a line of demarcation is shrouded in hopeless confusion." [50] One reason for the confusion is that the nature of the underlying suit does not necessarily determine the nature of the contempt.[51]

---

45. *E.g.,* Glodis v. Glodis, 115 R.I. 370, 346 A.2d 123 (1975); Masse v. Masse, 112 R.I. 599, 313 A.2d 642 (1974); Ediger v. Ediger, 206 Kan. 447, 479 P.2d 823 (1971); Schaffer v. District Ct., 172 Colo. 43, 470 P.2d 18 (1970); Osborne v. Osborne, 57 Ala. App. 204, 326 So. 2d 766 (1976); Rogers v. Rogers, 505 S.W.2d 138 (Mo. App. 1974).

46. *E.g.,* NEB. REV. STAT. § 42-358 (1978); MISS. CODE ANN. § 93-9-33 (1972).

47. IND. STAT. ANN. § 31-1-11.5-17(a) (Cum. Supp. 1979).

48. Kuhn v. Kuhn, — Ind. App. —, 361 N.E.2d 919 (1977). *Also see* Owens v. Owens, — Ind. App. —, 354 N.E.2d 350 (1976).

49. Loree v. Pearson, 88 S.D. 330, 219 N.W.2d 615 (1974).

50. People v. Keener, 559 P.2d 243, 248 (Colo. App. 1976), quoting from Mainland v. People, 111 Colo. 198, 139 P.2d 366 (1943). *See, e.g.,* Meranto v. Meranto, 366 Mass. 720, 323 N.E.2d 723 (1975). OR. REV. STAT. § 33.010 (1975) attempts to define civil and criminal contempt by giving examples.

51. *For example,* IOWA CODE ANN. § 675.37 (Cum. Supp. 1978) provides that a father who fails to comply with a support order "shall be punished by the court in the same manner and to the same extent as is provided by law for a contempt of such court in any other suit or

The two types of contempt differ in purpose.[52] The civil contempt power of the court is invoked to aid an offended party who seeks private or personal relief through compelling the contemnor to do something which he or she has refused or failed to do.[53] The offended party initiates the contempt proceedings. Resulting imprisonment for civil contempt is coercive or remedial in nature.[54] It is imposed for an *indefinite* period, to terminate upon compliance with the order, thus leaving the contemnor "the key to his cell." [55] Civil contempt secures for a private litigant the benefit to which he is entitled under a court order. Most courts therefore hold that the ability of the defaulter to

---

proceeding cognizable by such court." *See also* Houle and Dubose, *The Nonsupport Contempt Hearing: Constitutional and Statutory Requirements,* 14 N.H.B.J. 165 (1973).

52. *See* Southern Ry. Co. v. Lanham, 403 F.2d 119 (5th Cir.), *reh. denied,* 408 F.2d 348 (5th Cir. 1968); Kramer v. Kelly, — Pa. Super. —, 401 A.2d 799 (1979).

53. *E.g.,* Allen v. Smith, 126 Vt. 546, 237 A.2d 354 (1967); Demetree v. State, 89 So. 2d 498 (Fla. 1956); Blankenship v. Commonwealth, 260 Mass. 369, 157 N.E. 693 (1927); *Ex parte* Clark, 208 Mo. 121, 106 S.W. 990, 996 (1907); Sullivan v. Sullivan, 16 Ill. App. 3d 549, 306 N.E.2d 604 (1973).

54. *See* Barrett v. Barrett, 470 Pa. 253, 368 A.2d 616 (1977); Faircloth v. Faircloth, 321 So. 2d 87 (Fla. App. 1975), *aff'd,* 339 So. 2d 650 (Fla. 1976). Under some rules of civil procedure, a person may be held in civil contempt by either a punitive order or a remedial order. Marshall v. Marshall, 551 P.2d 709 (Colo. 1976).

55. *E.g.,* Johnson v. Johnson, — Pa. Super. Ct. —, 413 A.2d 1115 (1979) (A civil contemnor carries "the keys to his prison in his own pocket." The husband had two options to purge himself of the contempt charge, either to pay the support arrearage outright, or to appoint a master to sell some property owned by the parties in order to raise the necessary funds.) *In re* Nevitt, 117 F. 448, 461 (8th Cir. 1902) (a civil contemnor "carries the key of his prison in his own pocket"). *See also* Houle and Dubose, *The Nonsupport Contempt Hearing: Constitutional and Statutory Requirements,* 14 N.H.B.J. 165, 167 (1973); Southern Ry. Co. v. Lanham, 403 F.2d 119 (5th Cir.), *reh. denied,* 408 F.2d 348 (5th Cir. 1968).

purge himself of contempt though compliance with the court order is such an essential element of civil contempt that a court exceeds its authority if it imposes a sentence of definite duration.[56]

Contempt of court for failure to make child support payments typically is characterized as civil in nature.[57] Illinois courts have held that contempt proceedings to enforce compliance with support orders are civil because the contemnor's actions only incidentally involve the dignity of the court.[58] Some courts have even held that criminal contempt may never be invoked for failure to make support payments or to enforce any other domestic obligation.[59]

The essence of civil contempt for nonpayment of child support is willful violation or refusal to comply with a court order.[60] Although a parent may have failed to support his child, he cannot be held for contempt unless the nonsupport

---

56. *E.g.,* McDaniel v. McDaniel, 256 Md. 684, 262 A.2d 52 (1970); Allen v. Smith, 126 Vt. 546, 237 A.2d 354 (1967); Sword v. Sword, 59 Mich. App. 730, 229 N.W.2d 907 (1975), *aff'd,* 399 Mich. 367, 249 N.W.2d 88 (1976); Sullivan v. Sullivan, 16 Ill. App. 3d 549, 306 N.E.2d 604 (1973); Weinstein v. Heimberg, — Tenn. App. —, 490 S.W.2d 692 (1972).

57. *E.g.,* Md. Code Ann. art. 16, § 66J (1973); Minn. Stat. Ann. § 257.262 (Cum. Supp. 1979); Pa. Stat. Ann. tit. 42, § 6749 (Supp. 1979). *See also* Gailand v. Gailand, 30 Md. App. 45, 350 A.2d 716 (1976); Gonzalez v. Gonzalez, 532 S.W.2d 382 (Tex. Civ. App. 1975); Sullivan v. Sullivan, 16 Ill. App. 3d 549, 306 N.E.2d 604 (1973).

58. *See* Sullivan v. Sullivan, 16 Ill. App. 3d 549, 306 N.E.2d 604 (1973).

59. State *ex rel.* McCurley v. Hanna, 535 S.W.2d 107 (Mo. 1976); Weinstein v. Heimberg, — Tenn. App. —, 490 S.W.2d 692 (1972); Gonzalez v. Gonzalez, 532 S.W.2d 382 (Tex. Civ. App. 1975).

60. *E.g.,* N.C. Gen. Stat. § 50-13.3 (1976); Utah Code Ann. § 77-60-11 (1978). *See also* Canada v. Hatfield, 258 S.E.2d 440 (W. Va. 1979); Crowder v. Crowder, 236 Ga. 612, 225 S.E.2d 16 (1976); Lord v. Lord, 231 Ga. 164, 200 S.E.2d 759 (1973); Stacy v. Speanbury, 53 App. Div. 984, 385 N.Y.S.2d 875 (1976); Ellingwood v. Ellingwood, 25 Ill. App. 3d 587, 325 N.E.2d 571 (1975).

violates a court order.[61] (He might, however, be guilty of criminal nonsupport.)

Proof of nonpayment alone is not adequate proof of willful violation of the support order,[62] although it is generally held that plaintiff makes out a *prima facie* case by presenting the order and proof of nonpayment.[63] Accordingly, the Iowa judge who sought to avoid the expense and trouble of possible contempt proceedings by ordering in a divorce decree that the husband deliver to the wife a quitclaim deed to the family home in case of his "substantial failure" to render support was *not* upheld.[64] If the defendant can show (typically as an affirmative defense [65]) that his (her) nonpayment is due to inability to pay, willfulness is lacking and contempt may not be found.[66] A judgment that is due, however, remains

---

61. Wellington v. Wellington, 158 Ind. App. 649, 304 N.E.2d 347 (1973); Young v. Superior Ct., 105 Cal. App. 2d 65, 233 P.2d 39 (1951).

62. *E.g.,* Lord v. Lord, 231 Ga. 164, 200 S.E.2d 759 (1973); Stacy v. Speanbury, 53 App. Div. 984, 385 N.Y.S.2d 875 (1976); Ellingwood v. Ellingwood, 25 Ill. App. 3d 587, 325 N.E.2d 571 (1975).

63. Redick v. Redick, 266 S.C. 241, 222 S.E.2d 758 (1976); Brown v. Brown, 114 R.I. 117, 329 A.2d 200 (1974); Svehaug v. Svehaug, 16 Or. App. 151, 517 P.2d 1073 (1974).

64. *In re* Florke, 270 N.W.2d 643 (Iowa 1978).

65. *E.g.,* Flynn v. Flynn, 330 So. 2d 782 (Fla. Dist. Ct. App. 1976); Roberts v. Roberts, 328 So. 2d 461 (Fla. Dist. Ct. App. 1976); Garland v. Garland, 30 Md. App. 45, 350 A.2d 716 (1976); Svehaug v. Svehaug, 16 Or. App. 151, 517 P.2d 1073 (1974); Slagle v. Slagle, 155 Ind. App. 304, 292 N.E.2d 624 (1973).

66. *See, e.g.,* UTAH CODE ANN. § 77-60-8 (1978); Barrett v. Barrett, 470 Pa. 253, 368 A.2d 616 (1977); Spabile v. Hunt, 134 Vt. 332, 360 A.2d 51, Marshall v. Marshall, 191 Colo. 65, 551 P.2d 709 (1976); State *ex rel.* Stanhope v. Pratt, 533 S.W.2d 567 (Mo. 1976); Malec v. Malec, 196 Neb. 533, 244 N.W.2d 82 (1976); Sword v. Sword, 59 Mich. App. 730, 229 N.W.2d 907 (1975), *aff'd,* 399 Mich. 367, 249 N.W.2d 88 (1976); Sodones v. Sodones, 366 Mass. 121, 314 N.E.2d 906 (1974); Halverson v. Halverson, 189 Neb. 489, 203 N.W.2d 452 (1973); Fint v. Johnson, 229

enforceable by contempt even if circumstances have changed to warrant modification. The change in circumstances (such as an improvement in the mother's financial situation) must be pleaded in a modification proceeding and constitutes no defense to a contempt action.[67] Similarly, making payments directly to children (instead of to the mother) may be a dangerous practice,[68] although in particularly appealing circumstances (such as where the mother has failed to apply child support to the children and has not complained of payments made directly to the children), some courts will credit the father with such payments, if the mother later seeks to enforce "arrears." [69] Inability is no excuse, if the defendant has voluntarily brought the disability upon himself.[70] For example, the defendant must make a reasonable effort to comply with a support order and may not plead inability if he has remained unemployed voluntarily.[71] And a trial court's finding that "defendant's offer to pay $5,125 in pennies and

---

Ga. 188, 190 S.E.2d 32 (1972); *Ex parte* Rohleder, 424 S.W.2d 891 (Tex. 1967); Ainslie v. Ainslie, — Mass. App. Ct. —, 78 Mass. App. Adv. Sh. 1111, 382 N.E.2d 747 (1978); Teefey v. Teefey, 533 S.W.2d 563 (Mo. App. 1976); *Ex parte* Stringer, 546 S.W.2d 837 (Tex. Civ. App. 1976); *Ex parte* McCrary, 538 2 (Tex. Civ. App. 1976); State *ex rel.* Bigley v. Bigley, 20 Or. App. 220, 531 P.2d 296 (1975); Bennett v. Bennett, 21 N.C. App. 390 (1974).

67. Kight v. Kight, 242 Ga. 563, 250 S.E.2d 451 (1979).

68. *See* Jahn v. Jahn, — Ind. App. —, 385 N.E.2d 488 (1979) (Father ordered to pay support to mother even during periods when the children were with him). *See also* ch. I, note 92.

69. *E.g.,* McCrady v. Mahon, — N.H. —, 400 A.2d 1173 (1979).

70. *Ex parte* Dean, 517 S.W.2d 365 (Tex. Civ. App. 1974).

71. Huchteman v. Huchteman, 557 P.2d 427 (Okla. 1976); Faircloth v. Faircloth, 339 So. 2d 650 (Fla. 1976); Sword v. Sword, 399 Mich. 367, 249 N.W.2d 88 (1976); Weinland v. Weinland, 286 Minn. 303, 175 N.W.2d 506 (1970); Butler v. Butler, 80 Mich. App. 696, 265 N.W.2d 17 (1978); Prestwood v. Hambrick, 306 So. 2d 82 (Miss. 1975); Dunne v. Amerigan, 354 Mass. 368, 237 N.E.2d 689 (1968).

dollar bills amounted to contempt" was upheld by the Georgia Supreme Court.[72] In determining a defendant's ability to comply with a support order, courts consider the amount of his income, the amount of arrears, the proportion of income diverted to other uses, the defendant's physical ability to perform work, and defendant's attempts to make support payments.[73]

Though frequently litigated, the custodial parent's denial of (or interference with) visitation rights generally is no excuse for nonpayment of support and is no defense to a contempt charge.[74] To assert visitation rights, the support obligor's remedy is to have the custodial parent held in contempt.[75] A reasonable middle ground is held by courts which order the child support payments made into a special account for the benefit of the children (for instance, an account in the father's name as custodian for his children under the Uniform Gifts to Minors Act).[76]

In contrast to the civil remedial purpose of civil contempt, the purpose of criminal contempt is to punish a person for conduct which is offensive to the public or disrespectful to

---

72. Davis v. Davis, 243 Ga. 421, 254 S.E.2d 370 (1979).

73. Halverson v. Halverson, 189 Neb. 489, 203 N.W.2d 452 (1973); Bullmer v. Bullmer, 28 Ill. App. 3d 406, 328 N.E.2d 622 (1975); Svehaug v. Svehaug, 16 Or. App. 151, 517 P.2d 1073 (1974); State v. Sizemore, 12 Or. App. 482, 506 P.2d 502 (1973); Slagle v. Slagle, 155 Ind. App. 304, 292 N.E.2d 624 (1973).

74. E.g., Kemp v. Kemp, 42 Md. App. 53, 399 A.2d 923 (1979); Stancill v. Stancill, 41 Md. App. 335, 397 A.2d 218 (1979); Hagstrom v. Smith, 148 Ga. App. 18, 251 S.E.2d 27 (1978); Hester v. Hester, 59 Tenn. App. 613, 443 S.W.2d 28 (1968). Contra, Hudson v. Hudson, 97 Misc. 2d 558, 412 N.Y.S.2d 242 (1979).

75. Cf., Prestwood v. Hambrick, 308 So. 2d 82 (Miss. 1975). (Mother's contempt conviction for child's refusal to visit father reversed because she attempted to uphold visitation arrangement).

76. Nasti v. Nasti, — Misc. 2d —, — N.Y.S.2d — [5 F.L.R. 2468] (Sup. Ct. 1979).

the court's authority.[77] Accordingly, courts impose sentences of definite duration, typically without provision for conditional release.[78] To constitute criminal contempt, the contemnor's actions must exceed mere nonpayment of money in violation of a court order and must involve a willful defiance of the authority of the court with an element of "contumacy" or some distinctive criminal feature.[79] Actions which interfere with or manipulate the judicial process, such as perjury, also may be punished by criminal contempt.[80]

If criminal contempt is sought to be imposed, courts must provide the procedural safeguards applicable in any criminal proceeding.[81] For example, a criminal contemnor is entitled to notice, a reasonable opportunity to defend, assistance of counsel.[82] Proof must be beyond a reasonable doubt. The privilege against self-incrimination also applies. A civil contemnor is entitled to far fewer safeguards.[83] An excerpt from a Michigan case instructs on the procedural differences between civil and criminal contempt:

> Some jurisdictions, it is true, have extended the right to appointed counsel and jury trial to indigent

---

77. Ainslie v. Ainslie, — Mass. App. Ct. —, 78 Mass. App. Adv. Sh. 1122, 382 N.E.2d 747 (1978).

78. *See* Demetree v. State, 89 So. 2d 498 (Fla. 1956).

79. Ainslie v. Ainslie, — Mass. App. Ct. —, 78 Mass. App. Adv. Sh. 1122, 382 N.E.2d 747 (1978).

80. *See* Blankenship v. Commonwealth, 260 Mass. 369, 157 N.E. 693 (1927).

81. *E.g.*, Borden v. Borden, 67 Mich. App. 45, 239 N.W.2d 757 (1976); Barrett v. Barrett, 470 Pa. 253, 368 A.2d 616 (1977).

82. *E.g.*, *Ex parte* Stringer, 546 S.W.2d 837 (Tex. Civ. App. 1976).

83. *E.g.*, Faircloth v. Faircloth, 321 So. 2d 87 (Fla. Dist. Ct. App. 1975), *aff'd*, 339 So. 2d 650 (Fla. 1976), which held that there is no right to counsel in a civil contempt case. *But see* Public Defender Agency v. Superior Ct., 534 P.2d 947 (Alaska 1975), which held that the state statute providing public representation encompasses violations of support obligations.

defendants in non-support or other civil contempt cases. Such an extension, however, is unnecessary. The defendant in a true civil contempt proceeding has no need of the ritual of a full-scale criminal trial, for he may end his imprisonment at any moment by merely complying with the court's order, or may convince the court after a short period of confinement that he will comply. His ability to secure his freedom at any time eliminates the necessity for the elaborate and costly proceedings involved in a criminal jury trial. Furthermore, the state, representing the people, has a substantial interest in the efficiency of proceedings designed to secure support for minor children. To require a pitched battle over the relatively simple issue of disobedience of a support order could lead to a further breakdown of the administration of justice in our courts as expenses and delays increase. Already the circuit courts handle thousand of support cases each year; in some circuits most of them are on a weekly "Fathers' Day" devoted exclusively to domestic relations cases. If each of these support cases were handled like a criminal trial, the burden on the courts would be staggering, which is of concern to many persons involved in trials.

The problems which would arise from making support cases criminal cases would be of both a legal and practical nature. In order to determine whether defendants are entitled to appointed counsel, for example, a trial court must hold an indigency hearing. This procedure in itself will cause delay, confusion, and inconvenience. In addition, it will place courts and defendants in an awkward legal situation. This is so because the subject of inquiry at an indigency hearing may involve matters which are the subject of inquiry at the contempt hearing proper, viz., the financial resources of the defendant. In order to establish the procedural fact of indigency, the court must address the merits of the case and the defendant must risk the compromise of his privilege against self-incrimination in order to establish his right to appointed counsel. The whole process would certainly be confusing. . . .

69

If an attorney must be appointed and a jury trial granted at support hearings because coercive confinement may result therefrom, and thus present the aspect of a criminal case, then all the ritual of GCR 1963, 785 should be required. Self-incrimination must be prevented and any time the Friend of the Court "duns" the delinquent for support money, such delinquent should be advised of his right to remain silent, otherwise an incriminating response to the dun would be inadmissible.

The trial court knows not the facts when presented with the petition for hearing on a Friend of the Court complaint, except as to the amount of the arrearage, unless he has previously had the delinquent on prior occasions on the same problem. This knowledge may prevent a bench hearing on the issue before the judge possessed of such knowledge. Trial judges in Michigan are now disqualified from conducting a felony bench trial if the judge was required to read a portion of a preliminary transcript as a result of a motion filed in the case. We may look forward to disqualification if the judge conducted an indigency hearing, or the delinquent was a periodic recipient of an order to show cause.

Other respects of a contempt hearing would necessarily change if it were to be treated as a criminal prosecution or criminal proceeding. In absence of the use of the delinquent defendant's own testimony or admission, the court would turn to the information obtained by the Friend of the Court, e. g., a recent discharge or quitting of employment. Yet, by virtue of the Sixth Amendment right to confrontation, much information would be inadmissible at the hearing, and the court could not inquire of the delinquent the truth of that matter. Further, the complainant's burden of proof would rise to "beyond a reasonable doubt" from a preponderance of evidence.

A likely consequence of the extension to defendants of the criminal procedure in these matters would result in the horrible plea bargaining process now prevailing in criminal cases and the consequence of such. An accommodation will be reached as is done in criminal cases because of delays and the clogging of court calendars. Once the word is passed to delinquents that they are entitled to an attorney and a jury at the expense of the taxpayers, and that they have the protection of the criminal procedure, it can safely be predicted, as it was by many when wholesale plea bargaining arrived, that the support payments will decrease just as the crime rate increased. The courts will lose the only tool available to coerce parents to provide support for their children.

Should we be required to adopt the criminal procedure in these cases, it would follow that, in the event there is a finding adverse to the delinquent and sanctions of any nature are imposed upon him, the court would be required to render legal advice immediately thereafter as to the right to appeal and an attorney to assist in such, at public expense. . . .

In 1973 about 54,000 divorce cases were disposed of by circuit courts, which includes those cases dismissed after filing. In the same year, there were about 20,000 criminal cases disposed of by the circuit courts of Michigan. . . . Of the 54,000 divorce cases disposed of in 1973, it can be safely estimated 25,000 support cases are added to the thousands of files of the Friend of the Court each year and there remain until all children are 18 years of age. This should indicate the magnitude of a problem to be created by classifying this type of proceeding as a criminal prosecution. The Constitution was established not only to insure justice to the individual but also to all the people and to promote the general welfare of the people.[84]

One should take issue with the Michigan Court's cynical view of the criminal process. Beyond that, serious questions must be raised concerning the practice of jailing defaulting

---

84. Sword v. Sword, 59 Mich. App. 730, 737-43, 229 N.W.2d 907, 910-12 (1975), *aff'd,* 399 Mich. 367, 249 N.W.2d 88 (1976). (Footnotes and citations omitted).

parents for *civil* contempt.[85] It seems appropriate that some courts have extended the safeguards of criminal procedure to civil contempt proceedings because of the risk of imprisonment in these proceedings.[86] The indication is compelling that support enforcement should stay on the civil side of the courts and make better use of truly "civil" remedies.[87]

Certainly, civil contempt incarceration for nonpayment of support may be overly harsh and counterproductive in some circumstances. In one publicized case, a once prosperous home builder served five years and five months in a Vermont prison for failing to pay $2,550 for support of his wife and nine children — without having had a jury trial or the benefit of other constitutional safeguards applicable to accused criminals. While in jail, Mr. Chicoine lost his livelihood, suffered several heart attacks and cost the state between $10,000 and $14,000 to maintain. His family — on welfare — cost $6,900 per year. His wife often visited him in prison and said "there's not one night we didn't pray for him." On release from jail, the state told him that unless he paid an additional $22,000 to his wife covering the period

---

85. *See* Houle and Dubose, *The Nonsupport Contempt Hearing: Constitutional and Statutory Requirements,* 14 N.H.B.J. 165 (1973); Soifer, *Parental Autonomy, Family Rights and the Illegitimate: A Constitutional Commentary,* 7 CONN. L. REV. 1, 25-29 (1974). Soifer explores due process considerations involved in contempt actions labeled "civil" and suggests that the nature of civil contempt prosecutions compels due process rights such as appointment of counsel.

86. Page v. Page, 235 Ga. 131, 218 S.E.2d 859 (1975) (Privilege against self-incrimination available to civil contemnor). Henkel v. Bradshaw, 483 F. Supp. 1386 (9th Cir. 1973) (father who had been convicted of civil contempt by a state court brought a civil rights action in federal court to challenge the state court's refusal to appoint counsel. Although the federal court abstained, it indicated that appointment of counsel for an indigent may be constitutionally required in civil contempt cases).

87. *Infra* text at notes 93-124.

during which he was in jail, he would be re-imprisoned! If he might have been able to pay the original amount when the tragedy started, now he certainly could not pay that or the arrears accrued in the interim.[88]

These questions involve the judicial contempt power generally and its potential abuse. The problem extends far beyond support enforcement and this is not the place to dwell on it — suffice it to say that, in 1976, a three-judge federal court in New York voided contempt procedures for support enforcement on the ground that they violated due process guarantees.[89] New York had permitted the jailing of non-complying persons solely on the basis of a creditor affidavit of service and an *ex parte* proceeding, with a hearing to be held within ninety days of incarceration. The Court held that contempt could properly be found only in a hearing with counsel and both parties present and after notice appropriate to the serious nature of the case. The Court's further order enjoining the enforcement scheme was subsequently stayed by Justice Marshall. While the controversy was of national importance (New York's stricken procedures were not unique), the U.S. Supreme Court subsequently defused the case. It held that the District Court had erred in enjoining the state procedures on the technical ground that, although they had had an

---

88. *See* TIME, March 5, 1973, p. 70, col. 3; N.Y. TIMES, March 25, 1973. *Cf.,* Ellingwood v. Ellingwood, 25 Ill. App. 3d 587, 323 N.E.2d 571 (1975) in which a mother who had silently accepted reduced support payments for sixteen years was held not estopped from collecting the unpaid balance with interest.

89. Vail v. Quinlan, 406 F. Supp. 951 (S.D.N.Y. 1976) *rev'd sub nom.* Juidice v. Vail, 430 U.S. 327, 97 S. Ct. 1211, 51 L. Ed. 2d 376 (1977). *See also* Darbonne v. Darbonne, 85 Misc. 2d 267, 379 N.Y.S.2d 350 (Sup. Ct. 1976).

opportunity to do so, appellants had not presented their federal claim in the state proceeding.[90]

In response to the District Court's opinion, New York amended its contempt statute to require personal service of an order to show cause (including a warning of potential imprisonment) before a defendant may be imprisoned for contempt.[91] Moreover, New York law now provides that indigents in contempt proceedings must be provided with appointed counsel and must be advised of this right.[92]

c. Preventive Remedies: Bond, Attachment, Lien, Garnishment.

In addition to statutes enforcing child support through contempt proceedings or through criminal prosecutions *after* default, statutes commonly authorize the court to require security, such as a bond, to attach wages, or to create a lien on the obligor's property to prevent default.[93] These devices help assure compliance with the support order instead of imposing a penalty when it is too late, after the default has occurred.

Under some statutes, with the issuance of the support order, the court may create a lien on the obligor's property for the benefit of his (or her) child.[94] In a number of states

---

90. Juidice v. Vail, 430 U.S. 327, 97 S. Ct. 1211, 51 L. Ed. 2d 376 (1977).

91. N.Y. FAM. CT. ACT § 454 (Supp. 1978). State v. Sherwood, 94 Misc. 2d 372, 404 N.Y.S.2d 818 (1978). *See also* MD. CODE ANN. art. 16, § 66J (1973); S.C. CODE § 14-21-860 (1976).

92. N.Y. FAM. CT. ACT § 262(a)(vi) (1975).

93. *E.g.,* ARIZ. REV. STAT § 12-2455 (1977); N.M. STAT ANN. (1978). *See also* Box v. McKnight, 215 So. 2d 409 (Miss. 1968); Davis v. Davis, 206 Va. 381, 143 S.E.2d 835 (1965); Caldwell v. Caldwell, 5 Wis. 2d 146, 92 N.W.2d 356 (1958); Robin v. Robin, 45 Ill. App. 3d 365, 359 N.E.2d 809 (1977); Black v. Miller, 219 So. 2d 106 (Fla. App. 1969); Imbrie v. Imbrie, 94 Ill. App. 2d 60, 235 N.E.2d 381 (1968).

94. *E.g.,* Bailey v. Bailey, 86 Nev. 483, 471 P.2d 220 (1970); Tsoufakis

a lien arises upon default.[95] In the absence of a specific statute, there is disagreement as to whether a court may impose a lien to secure *future* installments of child support.[96]

Commonly, especially in paternity actions,[97] support obligors are asked to furnish security in the form of a bond or otherwise.[98] Many statutes provide the court with discretionary power to order such security, and courts may exercise this power at the time the support order is issued, when an order is modified, or upon default. Some courts will impose a bond only after a default has occurred, as in a contempt proceeding for the nonpayment of support.[99] Refusal to furnish security may be punishable by contempt.[100]

---

v. Tsoufakis, 14 Utah 2d 273, 382 P.2d 412 (1963); Voss v. Voss, 91 Idaho 17, 415 P.2d 303 (1966); Longbotham v. Longbotham, 119 Minn. 139, 137 N.W.387 (1912); Myler v. Myler, 137 Ind. App. 605, 210 N.E.2d 446 (1965); Loomis v. Loomis, 181 Cal. App. 2d 345, 5 Cal. Rptr. 550 (1960). *See also In re* Gentile, 69 Ill. App. 3d 297, 387 N.E.2d 979 (1979) (Court's imposition of trust on father's property to guarantee enforcement of child support upheld).

95. *See* FLA. STAT. ANN. § 742.08 (1964) (a judgment of default on support constitutes a lien on all property); Rouse v. Rouse, 313 So. 2d 458 (Fla. App. 1975). *Cf.,* ME. REV. STAT. ANN. tit. 19 § 503 (Cum. Supp. 1978) (lien attaches when order is filed with clerk and registrar of deeds); N.M. REV. STAT. § 40-5-17 (1978) (lien arises when the judgment is filed).

96. *See* Annot., 59 A.L.R.2d 656 (1958).

97. *E.g.,* CONN. GEN. STAT. ANN. § 46b-178 (Cum. Supp. 1978); NEB. REV. STAT. § 13-106 (1978); OKLA. STAT. ANN. tit. 10 § 73 (1966). *Cf.,* N.J. STAT. ANN. tit. 9, § 17-28 (1976) (court may employ all remedies if the reputed father *absconds*).

98. *E.g.,* Imbrie v. Imbrie, 94 Ill. App. 2d 60, 236 N.E.2d 381 (1968); MINN. STAT. ANN. § 518.24 (Supp. 1979); NEB. REV. STAT. § 42-358.05 (1978); N.Y. FAM. CT. ACT, § 471 (McKinney 1975).

99. Wheeler v. Wheeler, 193 Neb. 615, 228 N.W.2d 594 (1975).

100. NEB. REV. STAT. § 13-106 (1978); Hayes v. Towles, 95 Idaho 208, 506 P.2d 105 (1973).

In some jurisdictions (and this is the "wave of the future"), courts monitor compliance with a support order by requiring payments to be made directly to the clerk of the court, to be disbursed by the court to the child's custodian.[101] Any default thus comes to the attention of the court immediately. In addition, child support enforcement may be monitored by periodic meetings between the obligor and a support officer to encourage compliance in a supervised setting.[102]

The most effective method of enforcing child support payments is assignment of the obligor's wages.[103] A general policy of wage assignment in support cases would prevent most instances of default, avoid sequential enforcement proceedings in the courts, and prevent the accrual of unmanageable arrears. In a number of states, the court is *required* to order a wage assignment whenever it is shown that support payments have not been made.[104] Although default often is a precondition to wage assignment,[105] in a number of states the court may order wage assignment at any time, even when the support decree is initially issued.[106]

---

101. *E.g.,* Mo. Rev. Stat. § 452.350 (1974).

102. Kingsley v. Kingsley, 343 A.2d 597 (Del. 1975); Del. Code Ann. tit. 13, § 513 (Supp. 1978); Minn. Stat. Ann. 518.24 (1977); Neb. Rev. Stat. § 42-358.05 (1978).

103. *E.g.,* Alaska Stat. § 47.23.060(c) (1977); Ariz. Rev. Stat. § 12-2454(A) (1977); Cal. Civil Code § 4701(a) (Supp. 1979); Ind. Code § 31-1-11.5-13(e)(2) (1976); Minn. Stat. Ann. § 518.611 (Supp. 1979); Mo. Rev. Stat. § 452.350 (1974).

104. Roberts v. Roberts, 26 Or. App. 777, 554 P.2d 570 (1977). Cal. Civil Code § 4701(b) (Supp. 1979) requires the court to issue a wage assignment order if support is in default for two months or more.

105. *E.g.,* Conn. Gen. Stat. Ann. § 17-324 (Supp. 1978); Mich. Comp. Laws § 552.203 (1970); Minn. Stat. Ann. § 518.611 (Supp. 1977).

106. *E.g.,* Ariz. Rev. Stat. § 12-2455 (1977); Cal. Civ. Code § 4701(a) (Supp. 1979); Fla. Stat. § 61.12(2) (1977); Wis. Stat. § 247.265 (1973).

Assignment orders usually are binding on the defaulting parent's employer two weeks after the employer receives notice of the assignment.[107] Employers who have received notice of an obligation to assign wages may be punished for contempt if they fail to comply with the court's order.[108] In some cases, subsequent employers, as well as the obligor's current employer, may be bound by the wage assignment order.[109] A continuing order of this type presents obvious problems of administration and supervision, as the support obligor may fail to advise the court of a change in employment, and the court will have difficulty locating and notifying subsequent employers.

Wage assignment statutes usually do not provide for employer compensation or reimbursement, although some states allow the employer to deduct one dollar in each payment period in which an assignment is made.[110] Because the wage assignment order places upon the employer a burdensome and costly obligation, possibly under threat of contempt, an employer may be tempted to terminate his involvement simply by discharging the employee. To protect employees against this risk, many wage assignment statutes impose a duty on the employer not to retaliate against employees whose wages are attached.[111] Although most such statutes merely state (without specifying a penalty) that the employer shall not

---

107. *E.g.*, ARIZ. REV. STAT. § 12-2454 (1977); MO. REV. STAT. § 452.350 (1974).

108. *E.g.*, ILL. REV. STAT. ch. 40, § 706 (1977).

109. *E.g.*, CAL. CIV. CODE § 4701(a) (Supp. 1979); ILL. ANN. STAT. ch. 40, § 706 (Supp. 1978).

110. *E.g.*, ALASKA STAT. § 47.23.070(a) (1958); ARIZ. REV. STAT. § 12-2454(e) (1977); CAL. CIV. CODE § 4701(a) (Supp. 1979); MO. REV. STAT. § 452.345 (1974).

111. *E.g.*, ALASKA STAT. § 47.23.070(c) (1958); ARIZ. REV. STAT. § 12-2454(k) (1977); CAL. CIV. CODE § 4701(c) (Supp. 1979); ME. REV. STAT. ANN. tit. 19, § 510 (Cum. Supp. 1978).

discharge an employee whose wages are attached, a few states subject employers to a possible fine or imprisonment or civil liability. For instance, Delaware law provides that an employer may be fined a maximum of $1000 or imprisoned for up to 90 days or both for the first offense and fined a maximum of $5000 or imprisoned up to one year, or both, for subsequent offenses.[112] An employer who wrongfully discharges an employee also may be civilly liable to the employee for damages, reinstatement, attorney's fees, and costs.[113]

A good statute would define permissible maximum limits for wage assignments, but "a good statute is hard to find." [114]

It also should set priorities, such as giving precedence to support obligations over the claims of other creditors. In addition to any tangible property the obligor may have, debts due him may be subject to attachment.[115] Beyond that, it has been held that neither the anti-assignment provision of an obligor's pension fund,[116] nor even that of the Employee Retirement Income Security Act (ERISA) preclude a court from attaching these funds to secure a

---

112. DEL. CODE ANN. tit. 13, § 516(d) (Supp. 1978).

113. ARIZ. REV. STAT. § 12-2454(k) (1977).

114. *Cf.,* — Op. Att'y Gen. — (Or. 1979) [Op. No. 7677]. The Oregon Attorney General explains that the limitation on garnishment of wages, OR. REV. STAT. § 23.185(1)(B), does *not* apply to wage assignments for child support, OR. REV. STAT. § 23.777. The Attorney General stressed that "the garnishment exemption provision should serve as a shield for the wage earner and his or her dependent, not as a sword to be used by the wage earner against those dependents." *See also* Brown v. Tubbs, 2 Kan. App. 2d 522, 582 P.2d 1165 (1978) (Wage garnishment for past-due child support falls within exception to statutory restriction on garnishment, order of unrestricted wage garnishment affirmed).

115. *E.g.,* IOWA CODE ANN. § 675.17 (Supp. 1979).

116. *In re* Aurora G., 98 Misc. 2d 695, — N.Y.S.2d — (Fam. Ct. 1979).

support obligation.[117] In contrast, a California court held Railroad Retirement Act benefits exempt from garnishment to satisfy the recipient's child support obligations.[118]

Since 1975, the federal child support enforcement statute has provided for governmental cooperation in support enforcement through attachment of funds due the obligor. Previously existing "sovereign immunity" was waived and wage assignments ordered by state courts now are enforceable against the United States government.[119] However, not all is well with state garnishment laws. Serious consideration should be given the development of federal standards which prevent the utilization of overly oppressive state laws in connection with the IV-D program. The Senate Finance Committee explains and comments:

> *Limitation on percentage of wages subject to legal process.* — There is no limit in Federal law on the percentage of wages or other employment-related income which may be garnisheed for child support or alimony under court order. Many States allow garnishment of 100 percent of earnings and others

---

117. *See, e.g.,* Cartledge v. Miller, 457 F. Supp. 1146 (S.D.N.Y. 1978); Operating Engineers Local #428 v. Zambarsky, — F. Supp. — [5 F.L.R. 2654] (D. Ariz. 1979); Commonwealth v. Magrini, — Pa. Super. Ct. —, 398 A.2d 179 (1979); Ward v. Ward, 164 N.J. Super. 354, 396 A.2d 365 (1978). *Cf.,* CAL. CIV. CODE § 4701(g) (Supp. 1979).

118. Carter v. Carter, 82 Cal. App. 3d 249, 146 Cal. Rptr. 848 (1978). *Cf.,* Hisquierdo v. Hisquierdo, 439 U.S. 572, 99 S. Ct. 802, 59 L. Ed. 2d 1 (1979) which held that Railroad Retirement Act benefits accrued during marriage are not community property, and are not subject to division on divorce.

119. *See infra* ch. VIII 3.f; Annot. 44 A.L.R. Fed. 494 (1979); CAL. CIV. CODE § 4701(d) (Cum. Supp. 1978) specifically provides that the United States government is an "employer" within the meaning of wage assignment provisions.

provide that 100 percent of wages may be subject to wage assignment. Because of the arrearages that have resulted through incomplete payments (or no payments) of child support and alimony orders, the wages or the annuities of a number of people have been garnisheed at 100 percent for periods of many months and even years. This has sometimes caused the second families of the fathers in those cases to face financial ruin. It would be of questionable equity to place a limit on section 459 which affects only Federal employees and do nothing for other persons faced with financial ruin which cannot be avoided even under the bankruptcy provisions since both child support and alimony are exempt from bankruptcy. To provide equal treatment to all persons who are subject to garnishment under State laws, including persons affected by section 459, the committee amendment would, therefore, modify the provisions of the Consumer Credit Protection Act (15 USC 1673(b)) which now permit 100 percent of earnings and other employment-related income to be garnisheed for child support and alimony, by setting a limit of 50 percent on the amount which is subject to garnishment for child support and alimony for a person supporting a second family and 60 percent for a person who is not — plus an additional 5 percent in each situation if there are outstanding arrearages over twelve weeks old.

The Consumer Credit Protection Act would also be modified to cover garnishment provided under State administrative procedures, as well as under court orders for child support. The administrative procedures would have to be established by State law, afford substantial due process, and be subject to judicial review. At present, the Act refers only to garnishment under court orders. However, in recent years, the legislatures of at least six States — Florida, Georgia, Maine, Utah, Virginia and Washington — have enacted legislation providing for the use of certain administrative procedures for the enforcement of support for financially dependent minor children. States have enacted these laws generally because they have found existing common law and statutory remedies to be insufficiently effective and efficient. These procedures are clearly included in the definition of "legal process" for purposes of section 459 of the Social Security Act. In the view of the committee, these procedures are equally appropriate for inclusion under title III of the Consumer Credit Protection Act and will make the two laws consistent.[120]

d. *The Case Against Arrears.*

Some of the difficulty in child support enforcement lies less with the unavailability of remedies than with their utilization. If the objective is the procurement of child support, it would rarely be productive to fine the defaulting parent, thereby making him less able to comply with his support obligation. Jailing a defaulting parent, whether for contempt of court based on noncompliance with a support order, or in consequence of a criminal prosecution of nonsupport, may be equally destructive of the ends of support enforcement. In the individual case, imprisonment typically will cost the state more than it would cost to pay the deficient support to the family. Worse, while in jail, the defaulting parent will be unable to earn. Still worse, he may lose a job he might have had or impair any prospect of finding work. Of course, as common sense and careful

---

120. SENATE COMM. ON FINANCE, 94th Cong., 2d Sess., REPORT ON CHILD SUPPORT AMENDMENTS, No. 94-1350 at 1, 9-10 (1976).

studies [121] indicate, though these "remedies" are valuable enough as threats, they only "self-destruct" with application. Even "enlightened" variations, such as week-end jailings, seem barbaric when measured against the typical nonsupport offense which is serious, but does not rank with violent crime. It would appear that the flagrantly deliberate support refuser is the exception, not the rule. The more typical defaulter defaults "by default" — because it is so tempting to default. Historically, enforcement has been lax and, once money is in anyone's hands, it tends to spend itself. For a third category of support defaulters, nonpayment is the most accessible reaction to arbitrary or even "impossible" awards imposed by judges who exercise too much discretion with too little judgment.

The first category of offenders should be dealt with harshly, with existing remedies. The second category could be reduced to insignificance, if the money simply were not made available to the obligor. That could readily be achieved by mandatory wage deductions. The third category should be eliminated by sensible law reform.

Overlapping all these categories, however, is the problem of arrears. Even if the initial order may have been reasonable, it is the overwhelming accumulation of unpaid past support that persuades many a basically willing father to flee from responsibilities that have become unrealistic. Careful monitoring of compliance is at least a partial answer. Many local systems are now requiring that all

---

121. *See generally,* D. CHAMBERS, MAKING FATHERS PAY (1979). This interesting empirical study involving Michigan was published after this manuscript was completed and thus can only be referenced here. The main finding is that a well-organized and visible enforcement system, coupled with a firm jailing policy for nonsupport, significantly increases child support collections. Chambers, *Men Who Know They Are Watched: Some Benefits and Costs of Jailing for Nonpayment of Support,* 75 MICH. L. REV. 900 (1977).

support payments be made to the clerk of the court or some other official who, in turn, disburses the funds to the proper recipients. Outstanding support orders may be "computerized" so that defaults are detected without delay and can be pursued while there still is hope of collection. Unfortunately, more than that is wrong with the system. While law reform initiatives at the state level would be the appropriate route, experience teaches that this is an area in which we need not expect much from the states without hard prodding. Despite underlying concerns about further erosion of state sovereignty, it is a good thing that, at least within the context of the federal enforcement program, state laws and procedures have become amenable to change. It is time to consider whether, within the context of the federal program, federal standards should not define a rational framework for state law and judicial discretion in setting and enforcing support obligations.[122]

If two major steps were taken, much of what now is obviously wrong with the "arrears problem" would be cured: First, in appropriate cases, *retroactive* modification of accumulated arrears should be allowed, and indiscriminate enforcement of arrears should not.[123]

Second, *flexible* child support obligations should be imposed that are geared directly to the fluctuating earnings with which so much of our population (though not the judges) lives. This should be effectively coupled with "preventive" enforcement, as by automatic deduction from paychecks. Judgments for fixed amounts of support that

---

122. *See infra* ch. X. 3.

123. *See, e.g.,* Ellingwood v. Ellingwood, 25 Ill. App. 3d 587, 325 N.E.2d 347 (1973) (a mother's silent acceptance of reduced payments does not estop her from enforcing unpaid support after 16 years); Schmidt v. Forehan, 549 S.W.2d 320 (Ky. App. 1977) (Wife waited nearly 25 years before enforcing delinquent child support); Smith v. Smith, 168 Ohio St. 447, 156 N.E.2d 113 (1959) (14 years' delay).

require a specific court order for downward modification in case of unemployment or reduced earnings should become the exception.[124] True, this will bring with it problems of employer cooperation, but what is the burden of administering one more deduction, when the employer now deducts for income taxes, social security, health and pension plans, United Funds, credit unions and more! True, wage assignment presents potential questions relating to infringement of personal liberty and invasion of privacy, especially if the parent does not have a history of default. But what is the greater evil?

In short, timely, regular and automatic support enforcement mechanisms must prevent the accumulation of arrearages that ultimately become impossible to pay.

2. Interstate Enforcement

In our mobile society, the father, mother and child may have important contacts with several states. This may involve the laws of several states in the case, or the law of conflicts may require that the law of one state be chosen. Complex issues of jurisdiction and choice of law thus may have to be resolved.

a. *Out-of-State Action to Enforce Support Obligation.*

In the context of interstate enforcement of support, the objective is to obtain a judgment that is entitled to "full faith and credit" in all states. Obtaining such a judgment is not difficult, if it is feasible to bring the action at the obligor's place of residence or if personal jurisdiction over the obligor can be obtained in a forum that is convenient for the obligee, perhaps under a "long-arm" statute. Often, however, an out-of-state support action must be considered.

---

124. *See supra* ch. I, text at notes 79-84.

In that event, the question of jurisdiction arises even before there can be any question of choice of law.

Support actions, and, by the weight of authority, paternity actions, are *in personam* proceedings.[125] This means that the father may be sued wherever he can be found, *but only where he can be found.*[126] So-called "long-arm" statutes, however, have substantially increased the definition of where the father may be reached.[127]

In considering the validity of jurisdiction asserted under such statutes, it is crucial to examine whether the constitutional "minimum contacts" requirement is satisfied.[128] In *Kulko v. California Superior Court,*[129] a California resident had attempted to sue her nonresident ex-husband for increased child support. The alleged basis of jurisdiction was the defendant's act of sending his daughter

---

125. R. LEFLAR, THE LAW OF THE CONFLICTS OF LAWS 594-95 (1959) [hereinafter cited as LEFLAR]; P. Hay, Dissolution of Marriage and Its Consequences (draft manuscript circulated by the author, to be included in a forthcoming handbook on conflicts of laws) [hereinafter cited as HAY].

126. *See* Hartford v. Superior Court, 47 Cal. 2d 447, 304 P.2d 1 (1956) (discussed by LEFLAR at 595); *see also* Rich v. Rich, 93 Misc. 2d 409, 402 N.Y.S.2d 767 (1978) (discussed by Hay at § IV B, n. 196a). *Cf.,* Pelak v. Karpa, 146 Conn. 370, 151 A.2d 333 (1959) which allowed a non-resident mother to maintain an action against a non-resident father to the extent of his assets within the forum state. Hexter v. Hexter, — Ind. App. —, 386 N.E.2d 1006 (1979) which properly distinguished enforcement of an existing judgment from adjudicating the underlying controversy and allowed the mother to enforce Ohio judgments for child support and arrearages to the extent of the father's property in Indiana.

127. *See generally,* Levy, *Asserting Jurisdiction over Nonresident Putative Fathers in Paternity Actions,* 45 U. CINN. L. REV. 207 (1976); Annot., 76 A.L.R.3d 708 (1977).

128. *See* Kulko v. California Superior Ct., 436 U.S. 84, 98 S. Ct. 1690, 56 L. Ed. 2d 132 (1978); International Shoe Co. v. Washington, 326 U.S. 310, 66 S. Ct. 154, 90 L. Ed. 95 (1945).

129. 436 U.S. 84, 98 S. Ct. 1690, 56 L. Ed. 2d 132 (1978).

to California to live with her mother. The Court held that this act did *not* meet the constitutional requirement that the defendant have "minimum contacts" with the forum. The case is so important in this context (and broader conclusions are sufficiently speculative) that it must speak for itself:

> In reaching its result, the California Supreme Court did not rely on appellant's glancing presence in the State some 13 years before the events that led to this controversy, nor could it have. Appellant has been in California on only two occasions, once in 1959 for a three-day military stopover on his way to Korea, and again in 1960 for a 24-hour stopover on his return from Korean service. To hold such temporary visits to a State a basis for the assertion of *in personam* jurisdiction over unrelated actions arising in the future would make a mockery of the limitations on state jurisdiction imposed by the Fourteenth Amendment. Nor did the California court rely on the fact that appellant was actually married in California on one of his two brief visits. We agree that where two New York domiciliaries, for reasons of convenience, marry in the State of California and thereafter spend their entire married life in New York, the fact of their California marriage by itself cannot support a California court's exercise of jurisdiction over a spouse who remains a New York resident in an action relating to child support.
>
> Finally, in holding that personal jurisdiction existed, the court below carefully disclaimed reliance on the fact that appellant had agreed at the time of separation to allow his children to live with their mother three months a year and that he had sent them to California each year pursuant to this agreement. As was noted below, to find personal jurisdiction in a State on this basis, merely because the mother was residing there, would discourage parents from entering into reasonable visitation agreements. Moreover, it could arbitrarily subject one parent to suit in any State of the Union where the other parent chose to spend time

while having custody of their offspring pursuant to a separation agreement. . . .

The "purposeful act" that the California Supreme Court believed did warrant the exercise of personal jurisdiction over appellant in California was his "actively and fully consent[ing] to Ilsa living in California for the school year . . . and . . . sen[ding] her to California for that purpose." We cannot accept the proposition that appellant's acquiescence in Ilsa's desire to live with her mother conferred jurisdiction over appellant in the California courts in this action. A father who agrees, in the interests of family harmony and his children's preferences, to allow them to spend more time in California than was required under a separation agreement can hardly be said to have "purposefully availed himself" of the "benefits and protection" of California's laws. See Shaffer v. Heitner, 433 U.S., at 216.

. . . .

The circumstances in this case clearly render "unreasonable" California's assertion of personal jurisdiction. There is no claim that appellant has visited physical injury on either property or persons within the State of California. The cause of action herein asserted arises, not from the defendant's commercial transactions in interstate commerce, but rather from his personal, domestic relations. It thus cannot be said that appellant has sought a commercial benefit from solicitation of business from a resident of California that could reasonably render him liable to suit in state court; appellant's activities cannot fairly be analogized to an insurer's sending an insurance contract and premium notices into the State to an insured resident of the State. Furthermore, the controversy between the parties arises from a separation that occurred in the State of New York; appellee Horn seeks modification of a contract that was negotiated in New York and that she flew to New York to sign. [T]he instant action involves an agreement that was entered into with virtually no connection with the forum State.

Finally, basic considerations of fairness point decisively in favor of appellant's State of domicile as the proper forum for adjudication of this case, whatever the merits of appellee's underlying claim. *It is appellant who has remained in the State of the marital domicile, whereas it is appellee who has moved across the continent.* Cf. May v. Anderson, 345 U.S. 528, 534-535, n. 8 (1953). Appellant has at all times resided in New York State, and, until the separation and appellee's move to California, his entire family resided there as well. As noted above, appellant did no more than acquiesce in the stated preference of one of his children to live with her mother in California. This single act is surely not one that a reasonable parent would expect to result in the substantial financial burden and personal strain of litigating a child-support suit in a forum 3,000 miles away, and we therefore see no basis on which it can be said that appellant could reasonably have anticipated being "haled before a [California] court," Shaffer v. Heitner, 433 U.S., at 216. To make jurisdiction in a case such as this turn on whether appellant bought his daughter her ticket or instead unsuccessfully sought to prevent her departure would impose an unreasonable burden on family relations, and one wholly unjustified by the "quality and nature" of appellant's activities in or relating to the State of California. International Shoe Co. v. Washington, 326 U.S. at 319.

In seeking to justify the burden that would be imposed on appellant were the exercise of *in personam* jurisdiction in California sustained, appellee argues that California has substantial interests in protecting the welfare of its minor residents and in promoting to the fullest extent possible a healthy and supportive family environment in which the children of the State are to be raised. These interests are unquestionably important. But while the presence of the children and one parent in California arguably might favor application of California law in a lawsuit in New York, the fact that California may be the " 'center of gravity' " for choice of law purposes does not mean that California has personal jurisdiction over the defendant. *And*

> *California has not attempted to assert any particularized interest in trying such cases in its courts by, e.g., enacting a special jurisdictional statute.*
> California's legitimate interest in ensuring the support of children resident in California without unduly disrupting the children's lives, moreover, is already being served by the State's participation in the Uniform Reciprocal Enforcement of Support Act of 1968.[130]

Many existing "long-arm" statutes assert continuing jurisdiction over persons owing support if their marital domicile was in the state.[131] To illustrate, a recent Maryland case [132] held that it had impliedly retained jurisdiction to enter a support decree even though the divorce decree was silent on support. Even after *Kulko,* it would appear that the former marital domicile will continue to qualify in the ordinary case as a fair forum for the nonresident defendant.[133]

---

130. *Id.* at 92-98, 98 S. Ct. at 1697-1700, 56 L. Ed. 2d at 141-45 (1978). (Emphasis added, citations and footnotes omitted).

131. *E.g.,* S.C. CODE § 14-21-830 (1976).

132. Glading v. Furman, 282 Md. 200, 383 A.2d 398 (1978).

133. *In re* Ash, — Misc. 2d —, — N.Y.S.2d — [5 F.L.R. 2257] (Fam. Ct. 1978), in which a father who had been married in New York and divorced in Mexico, and then lived in California with his children was held subject to the continuing support jurisdiction of the New York courts. In Lontos v. Lontos, 89 Cal. App. 3d 61, 152 Cal. Rptr. 271 (1979) a California court distinguished *Kulko* and found that sufficient "minimal contacts" existed for *in personam* jurisdiction over a non-resident father who had spent 13 of the prior 17 years in California, where California had been the last marital domicile, and where the father still had personal effects and financial interests in California, even though he had left California (originally with his family) and had obtained a divorce in another state. *See also* Mitchim v. Mitchim, 518 S.W.2d 362 (Tex. 1975) for a pre-*Kulko* analysis of minimum contracts" which held that the state of the marital domicile could assert jurisdiction over the then non-resident ex-husband for purposes of awarding alimony. *But cf.,* Hoerler v. Superior Court, 85

In the area of paternity, a few decisions have obtained jurisdiction over out-of-state defendants by applying torts provisions in long-arm statutes.[134] The courts have argued that a "tort" is committed in the state if intercourse in the state results in the birth of a child, or that the failure to support the child constitutes "tortious conduct." To illustrate, in *Poindexter v. Willis,*[135] an Illinois appellate court stated that any breach of duty is a tortious act, and held that the nonresident putative father's failure to support the child is a breach of duty and asserted jurisdiction. Some courts have labeled the Illinois court's reasoning "strained" and "fallacious," [136] but others have followed *Poindexter.* [137] Statutes have followed up on the idea.[138] Prominently, the Uniform Parentage Act provides:

Cal. App. 3d 533, 149 Cal. Rptr. 569 (1978): Although California had been the marital domicile for 14 years, the parties had moved to another state and divorced there. After returning to California, the wife sought support from her now non-resident ex-husband. On the basis of *Kulko,* the Court held that the father had not purposefully availed himself of the benefits of California so that California lacked personal jurisdiction.

134. *E.g.,* ILL. REV. STAT. ch. 110, § 17(1)(b) (1977).

135. 87 Ill. App. 2d 213, 231 N.E.2d 1 (1967).

136. State *ex rel.* Carrington v. Schutts, 217 Kan. 175, 535 P.2d 982 (1975). Oregon v. Bennett, 28 Or. App. 155, 558 P.2d 1281 (1977); A.R.B. v. G.L.P., 180 Colo. 439, 507 P.2d 468 (1973). *See also* Barnhart v. Madvig, 526 S.W.2d 106 (Tenn. 1975); Anonymous v. Anonymous, 49 Misc. 2d 675, 268 N.Y.S.2d 710 (1966). *Cf., In re* People, 30 Colo. App. 603, 498 P.2d 1166 (1972), holding that the fathering of an illegitimate child in and of itself is not a "tortious act" in terms of the long arm statute.

137. *E.g.,* Nelson v. Nelson, 298 Minn. 438, 216 N.W.2d 140 (1974); Gentry v. Davis, 512 S.W.2d 4 (Tenn. 1974); Bebeau v. Berger, 22 Ariz. App. 522, 529 P.2d 234 (1974).

138. *See* KAN. STAT. ANN. § 60-308 (1976), which provides that a person submits to jurisdiction in Kansas by "performing an act of sexual intercourse within the state with a person in this state which results in the conception of a child . . . ."

A person who has sexual intercourse in this State thereby submits to the jurisdiction of the courts of this State as to an action brought under this Act with respect to a child who may have been conceived by that act of intercourse. In addition to any other method provided by [rule or] statute, including [cross reference to "long arm statute"], personal jurisdiction may be acquired by [personal service of summons outside this State or by registered mail with proof of actual receipt] [service in accordance with (citation to "long-arm statute")].[139]

In light of *Kulko,* the Illinois Supreme Court recently considered the issue of support jurisdiction over a nonresident father who had violated a support decree.[140] The Court emphasized that the father derived no "commercial or personal benefit" from his children's presence in Illinois and held that he did not have minimum contacts with Illinois. The Court decided the minimum contacts issue first and thus found it unnecessary to determine whether the failure to pay support would constitute a tortious act within the meaning of Illinois' long-arm statute. *Poindexter* was distinguished on the basis that it involved more significant contacts.

Kulko and the Illinois case noted that the mothers could proceed alternatively under the Uniform Reciprocal Enforcement of Support Act (URESA). This is important, because the availability of URESA as an alternative remedy in interstate support cases may harden the judicial

---

139. UNIFORM PARENTAGE ACT § 8(b), 9A U.L.A. MATR., FAM. AND HEALTH LAWS 598 (1979). Following the *Kulko* decision, this provision might be tightened to express more clearly the "particularized interest" a state has in trying these paternity actions in its own courts, by making it quite clear that it applies only to persons who have sexual intercourse with *residents* of the interested state.

140. Boyer v. Boyer, 73 Ill. 2d 331, 383 N.E.2d 223, 22 Ill. Dec. 747 (1978).

stance on jurisdictional issues under long-arm statutes. It would nevertheless seem to be clear that the principles enunciated in *Kulko* are not limited to situations in which the plaintiff has another convenient route to obtaining support.[141]

The question of choosing the proper law arises after the jurisdictional issue has been resolved against the defendant. Typically that choice will be governed or influenced by Section 7 of the Uniform Reciprocal Enforcement of Support Act which determines the support obligation under "the laws of any state in which the obligor was present during the period for which support is sought." [142]

b. *Out-of-State Support Judgments.*

Once a support judgment has been obtained, problems of out-of-state recognition and enforcement may arise if the obligor's property is in another state or if the obligor has left the state. Decisions of the United States Supreme Court have interpreted the Full Faith and Credit Clause to cover only "final" judgments.[143] The general rule allowing future support payments to be modified presents the problem that support judgments, at least as to amounts to be paid in the future, are *not* final.[144] A support order of

---

141. *See* Bartlett v. Superior Ct. of Santa Barbara, 86 Cal. App. 3d 72, 150 Cal. Rptr. 25 (1978).

142. UNIFORM RECIPROCAL ENFORCEMENT OF SUPPORT ACT § 7, 9A U.L.A. MATR., FAM. AND HEALTH LAWS 672 (1979). The general rule of the law of conflicts is that only the substantive foreign law is applied. The forum court continues to use its own procedural rules. This raises the question of defining "substance" and "procedure," and the result may govern the outcome of the case. *See* A. EHRENZWEIG, CONFLICT OF LAWS 401 (1971).

143. *E.g.,* Sistare v. Sistare, 218 U.S. 1, 30 S. Ct. 682, 54 L. Ed. 905 (1910); Lynde v. Lynde, 181 U.S. 183, 21 S. Ct. 555, 45 L. Ed. 810 (1901).

144. *See* Windham v. Blakeney, 354 So. 2d 786 (Miss. 1978).

a sister state that has been reduced to a money judgment clearly has the requisite finality.[145] Even if accrued installments (arrearages) have not been reduced to a new judgment, full faith and credit is given accrued installments if they are final and not retroactively modifiable where the judgment was rendered.[146] When the court rendering the judgment has discretion to modify arrearages,[147] the Full Faith and Credit Clause does not *require* enforcement by sister states even of accrued installments.[148] Of course,

---

145. Once reduced to judgment, support arrears are enforceable as any other money judgment would be. *See* Aldrich v. Aldrich, 378 U.S. 540, 84 S. Ct. 1687, 12 L. Ed. 2d 1020 (1964); Barber v. Barber, 323 U.S. 77, 65 S. Ct. 137, 89 L. Ed. 82 (1944); Sistare v. Sistare, 218 U.S. 1, 30 S. Ct. 682, 54 L. Ed. 905 (1910); Lynde v. Lynde, 181 U.S. 183, 21 S. Ct. 555, 45 L. Ed. 810 (1901). THE UNIFORM ENFORCEMENT OF FOREIGN JUDGMENTS ACT, 13 U.L.A. CIV. PRO. AND REM. LAWS 2 (Supp. 1979) that has been adopted in twenty-two states provides for a simplified "domestication" procedure for out-of-state judgments. Through registration at the forum in accordance with the Act, a foreign judgment obtains the effect of a forum judgment.

146. *See* Hinds v. Primeaux, 367 So. 2d 925 (Miss. 1979); Catlett v. Catlett, 412 P.2d 942 (Okla. 1966); Clark v. Clark, 380 P.2d 241 (Okla. 1963); Green v. Green, 239 Ala. 407, 195 So. 549 (1940). *See generally* Hay at § IV. B.2.

147. *See* H. CLARK, LAW OF DOMESTIC RELATIONS § 15.2 (1968). *See also* Foster and Freed, *Modification, Recognition and Enforcement of Foreign Alimony Orders,* 11 CAL. W.L. REV. 280, 280-81 (1975).

148. "The older case law required that the claim be final, either reduced to judgment or, as a claim, not subject to retroactive modification before recognizing and enforcing it locally." Hay at § IV. B.2. at 40-41, citing Page v. Page, 189 Mass. 85, 75 N.E. 92 (1905); Levine v. Levine, 95 Or. 94, 187 P. 609 (1920). *See also* Mayer v. Mayer, 154 Mich. 386, 117 N.W. 890 (1908); Bowles v. Bowles, 251 S.W.2d 774 (Tex. Civ. App. 1952). Some recent cases also have adhered to this view. *See* Hay, *supra,* citing Maner v. Maner, 401 F.2d 616 (5th Cir. 1968); Catlett v. Catlett, 412 P.2d 942 (Okla. 1966). *See also* Windham v. Blakeney, 354 So. 2d 786 (Miss. 1978), in which the Mississippi Supreme Court refused to enforce a South Carolina decree which was modifiable as to past due as well as future child support. *But see* Justice Jackson, concurring in Barber v. Barber,

nothing prohibits recognition of a sister state judgment, whether it is modifiable or not. Accordingly, many courts recognize non-final support judgments of sister states on principles of comity, although they will feel free to modify the judgment, giving it the same respect it commanded in the state where rendered.[149] To the extent modification is possible and recognition is not compelled by the Full Faith and Credit Clause, four interests should be considered and balanced: (1) the interest of the state where the decree was rendered in having its decrees respected; (2) the interest of all states in discouraging support obligors from attempting to escape their obligation by fleeing from state to state; (3) the interest of the state where the decree is sought to be enforced (typically the state of the obligor's current residence or domicile) in protecting its residents or domiciliaries. (The obligor may be protected by applying forum law to issues of modification and enforcement); (4) the interest of the state where the support obligation is owed (typically the state of the obligee's current residence or domicile) in having its domiciliaries obtain their due, as well as in avoiding a potential welfare burden.

Authority governing the interstate enforcement of support judgments involving children born in wedlock applies with equal force to judgments involving support of nonmarital children.[150] With respect to the latter, however,

---

323 U.S. 77, 86, 65 S. Ct. 137, 141, 89 L. Ed. 82, 87 (Jackson, J. concurring 1944); Light v. Light, 12 Ill. 2d 502, 147 N.E.2d 34 (1958).

149. *E.g.,* Worthley v. Worthley, 44 Cal. 2d 465, 283 P.2d 19 (1955); Mittenthal v. Mittenthal, 99 Misc. 2d 778, 417 N.Y.S.2d 175 (Sup. Ct. 1979); Light v. Light, 12 Ill. 2d 502, 147 N.E.2d 34 (1958); Pruneau v. Sanders, 25 N.C. App. 510, 214 S.E.2d 288 (1975); Amato v. Sanders, 47 Mich. App. 244, 209 N.W.2d 429 (1973); Garlitz v. Rozar, 8 Ariz. App. 94, 500 P.2d 354 (1972); Johnson v. Johnson, 115 Ga. App. 749, 156 S.E.2d 186 (1967); Salmeri v. Salmeri, 554 P.2d 1244 (Wyo. 1976).

150. *See* H. KRAUSE, ILLEGITIMACY: LAW AND SOCIAL POLICY 51 (1971).

it should be emphasized that a paternity judgment, modifiable though it may be with respect to support, is a *final* judgment in terms of having adjudicated the issue of paternity.[151]

 c. *The Uniform Reciprocal Enforcement of Support Act.*

The complexity and burden of obtaining jurisdiction, recognition and enforcement in child support actions at common law indicates the need for more efficient methods of obtaining support for children in the interstate setting. Fortunately, there is a greatly simplified alternative. The Uniform Reciprocal Enforcement of Support Act [152] (URESA), or an equivalent,[153] has been enacted in every state and territory of the United States.[154] In addition, several states have concluded reciprocal arrangements with foreign countries, such as Canada, the United Kingdom, Australia, and the Republic of South Africa.[155] Under the

---

151. A. EHRENZWEIG, CONFLICT OF LAWS 203, 274-75, 401; Annot., 16 A.L.R.2d 1098 (1951).

152. UNIFORM RECIPROCAL ENFORCEMENT OF SUPPORT ACT (1958) 9A U.L.A. MATR., FAM. AND HEALTH LAWS 747 (1979) [hereinafter referred to as URESA]; UNIFORM RECIPROCAL ENFORCEMENT OF SUPPORT ACT (1968 revision) 9A U.L.A. MATR., FAM. AND HEALTH LAWS 647 (1979) (text is reproduced in Appendix A *infra.*) [hereinafter referred to as RURESA].

153. New York adopted the UNIFORM SUPPORT OF DEPENDENTS LAW, which is substantially similar to URESA in operation and effect. N.Y. DOM. REL. LAW §§ 30-43 (1977).

154. W. BROCKELBANK AND F. INFAUSTO, INTERSTATE ENFORCEMENT OF FAMILY SUPPORT 3, at vii (2d ed. 1971); Fox, *The Uniform Reciprocal Enforcement of Support Act,* 12 FAM. L.Q. 113 (1978).

155. *See* DeHart, *Child Support Enforcement: Reaching Across International Boundaries,* 2 FAM. ADVOCATE 27-29 (1979). In Canada, URESA equivalents have been enacted by Alberta, British Columbia, Manitoba, New Brunswick, Ontario, Saskatchewan, and the Yukon Territories. 5 F.L.R. 2645 (1979).

Act, an action to secure support from an obligor residing in another state may be initiated in one state and tried in another, thereby relieving the support claimant of the burden of leaving the home jurisdiction.[156] The Act originated in 1950, was amended in 1958, and revised substantially in 1968. The pre-1968 versions of the Act were popularly referred to as URESA, whereas the 1968 version is referred to as revised URESA or RURESA. Approximately one-half of the states now have enacted RURESA.[157]

Briefly, the Act provides that the person to whom a duty of support is owed may file a petition in her (or his) own state, called the initiating state. The initiating court then makes a preliminary finding as to whether the petition sets forth sufficient facts indicating that the alleged obligor actually owes a duty of support and that an out-of-state-court (called the "responding court") can obtain jurisdiction over the obligor.[158] There need not be a previous court order fixing the amount of support, if the existence of a support obligation is indicated by the facts. After making a brief, preliminary determination of

156. The objective of the Act "is to aid stationary mothers in exacting child support from peregrinating fathers." *In re* Marriage of Ceganovich, 61 Cal. App. 3d 289, 132 Cal. Rptr. 261 (1976). *See also* Banks v. McMorris, 47 Cal. App. 3d 723, 121 Cal. Rptr. 185 (1975), *cert. denied,* 423 U.S. 871 (1975); Abb v. Crossfield, 23 Md. App. 232, 326 A.2d 234 (1974). *See also* Sellman, *Here's How to Defend Him Against Child Support Collection Proceedings,* 1 FAM. ADVOCATE 33 (1979).

157. The A.B.A. House of Delegates expressed support for RURESA to encourage efforts for its passage in the 24 states where not yet enacted. 65 A.B.A.J. 340 (1979).

158. URESA § 14 at 773; RURESA § 14 at 688. *See* Matter of Proceeding Under Uniform Support of Dependents Law, 92 Misc. 2d 776, 401 N.Y.S.2d 136 (Fam. Ct. 1977). *See also* Bushway v. Riendeau, 137 Vt. 455, 407 A.2d 178 (1979) (RURESA is available whenever *either* party leaves the jurisdiction).

liability, the initiating court certifies and transmits its findings to the responding court having jurisdiction over the obligor, or to an agency in the responding state which will forward the petition to the appropriate court.[159] While RURESA requires that the responding state agency use all available means to locate the obligor,[160] less stringent rules govern locator services in URESA states.[161] The federal child support enforcement act, of course, now offers much more effective means to locate support obligors than had been available before.[162]

Upon receipt of the petition, the responding court dockets the case and notifies the prosecuting attorney whose duty it is to serve the obligor and to prosecute the case diligently.[163] If there is danger that the obligor will flee from the responding court's jurisdiction, he may be arrested or required to post bond.[164] Although the state prosecutor typically represents the obligee in a civil proceeding, URESA does not provide for appointment of counsel for the obligor.

After obtaining jurisdiction over the obligor, the responding court holds a hearing to determine whether a support obligation exists. The duties of support imposed upon an obligor "are those imposed under the laws of any

159. In Maryland, for instance, all URESA petitions are received at the State Bureau of Support Enforcement. This office also provides any follow-up needed for a petition to a Maryland court. 5 F.L.R. 2546 (1979).

160. URESA § 17 at 778; RURESA § 17 at 692.

161. See Fox, The Uniform Reciprocal Enforcement of Support Act, 12 FAM. L.Q. 113 (1978).

162. Infra ch. VIII. 3.c.

163. URESA § 18 at 780; RURESA § 18 at 694.

164. URESA § 16 at 778; RURESA § 16 at 691. See also Sedelmeyer v. Sedelmeyer, 167 N.J. Super. 195, 400 A.2d 571 (1979), where a New Jersey court held that a father, who had been personally served with a petition in New Jersey, could not defeat New Jersey's jurisdiction by moving to another state.

state where the obligor was present for the period during which support is sought." [165] During the hearing, the obligor has an opportunity to present defenses and both parties may submit evidence.[166] After finding a duty of support, the responding court may issue a support order and may subject the obligor's property to the order.[167] The responding court must transmit payments to the initiating court "forthwith." [168]

In general, the responding court's jurisdiction is limited to the support obligation. In most cases, therefore, it has been held that the responding court may not consider collateral issues such as custody or visitation rights and may not condition its support order on the performance of a duty owed by the obligee.[169] This limitation on the

---

165. URESA § 7 at 767; RURESA § 7 at 672. *See* Scott v. Sylvester, 220 Va. 182, — S.E.2d — (1979). *But c.f.,* Chance v. LaPausky, 43 Md. App. 84, 402 A.2d 1329 (1979) (responding court without jurisdiction to impose a support obligation where the original jurisdiction had discharged the respondent of any duty of support in the divorce decree, and that decree had not been appealed).

166. URESA § 21 at 786; RURESA § 20 at 700.

167. URESA § 24 at 789; RURESA § 24 at 713. A proceeding under URESA is an independent action to enforce the support obligation, distinct from a prior or subsequent divorce decree, and the remedies provided in the Act "are in addition to, not in substitution for, any other remedies." URESA § 3 at 763, RURESA § 3 at 659. *See* San Diego v. Elavsky, 58 Ohio St. 2d 81, — N.E.2d — (1979) (The Ohio Supreme Court held that an established URESA order is not automatically modified by a subsequent proceeding in the divorce court); *In re* Burke, 5 F.L.R. 258 (Cal. Ct. App. 1979) (unpublished opinion which held that a prior modification by the divorce court, terminating the father's support obligations, did not bar a subsequent action under another state's RURESA). *See also* Op. Att'y Gen., 5 F.L.R. 2259 (Or. 1979) (Oregon Attorney General states that paying a responding state's support order would only be an offset to, not full satisfaction of, a support order in a greater amount originally issued by a divorce court).

168. URESA § 27 at 792; RURESA § 28 at 732.

169. *E.g.,* Kline v. Kline, 260 Ark. 550, 542 S.W.2d 499 (1976); *In re*

jurisdiction of the responding court enables the parties to participate in the support action without risking the adjudication of peripheral matters.[170] The defense of non-paternity, if there is no judgment establishing paternity and entitled to full faith and credit, has caused courts to disagree on whether paternity may be litigated for the first time in a URESA action. As discussed in a later section, RURESA specificially provides that paternity may be litigated under certain conditions.[171]

Among a variety of other matters, the Act also contains important provisions dealing with criminal enforcement (even allowing the extradition of "support-defendants")[172] and with the registration at the forum of out-of-state support orders.[173]

Moffat, 94 Cal. 3d 724, — Cal. Rptr. — (1979); Brown v. Turnbloom, 89 Mich. App. 162, — N.W.2d — (1979); Grosse v. Grosse, 347 So. 2d 109 (Fla. App. 1977); McDowell v. Orsini, 54 Cal. App. 3d 951, 127 Cal. Rptr. 285 (1976); Pifer v. Pifer, 31 N.C. App. 486, 229 S.W.3d 700 (1976). *But see* Goodwin v. Fayerman, 88 Misc. 2d 690, 389 N.Y.S.2d 527 (1976).

170. Thompson v. Kite, 214 Kan. 700, 522 P.2d 327 (1974).
171. RURESA § 27 at 730, *infra* ch. V. 10.
172. URESA §§ 5, 6 at 764-65; RURESA §§ 5, 6 at 664-69.
173. URESA §§ 34-38 at 797-800; RURESA §§ 36-40 at 741-44.

PART II
PATERNITY AND ITS ESTABLISHMENT

Chapter III

LEGITIMACY AND ILLEGITIMACY

1. The Continued Importance of Old Definitions.

All abandoned children are in the same straits regarding their need for support and to locate an absent parent. The child of unmarried parents, however, struggles against the further obstacle of uncertain paternity and a long (though fortunately nearly lost) tradition of legal discrimination. Within the context of the child support enforcement problem, special emphasis thus must be placed upon those children who, in addition to locating their father and making him pay, must first identify him legally.

In this age of equality, the question might fairly be asked whether a discussion of child support should even be concerned about "legitimacy" and "illegitimacy." The answer is "yes," for several reasons. Most rules regarding child support were fashioned at a time when legitimacy was the precondition to full support entitlement and illegitimate paternity had only limited legal consequences. True, by U.S. Supreme Court doctrine, distinctions between "legitimate" and "illegitimate" children should no longer be maintainable, but many state statutes have not yet been adapted to this view. Distinctions on the basis of legitimacy, however unconstitutional, continue to be made. Since an expanding definition of "legitimacy" neatly eliminates the problem by definitional fiat, "legitimacy" remains alive at least as a definitional shortcut in favor of the child. By the grant of legitimacy, all questions as to the applicability and validity of possibly unconstitutional discriminatory statutes are removed at one stroke.

Moreover, the facts underlying traditional and expanded definitions of legitimacy retain vitality in terms of identification of the father: the mother's husband, even today, may fairly be assumed to be the father of his wife's

103

child, whereas the paternity of the unmarried mother's child must be established by other means. Even the Uniform Parentage Act, though without moral value judgment and purely on the basis of probability, continues to see the mother's husband as her child's most likely father. That Act cuts more finely than does traditional law (which gives all or nothing). It establishes more or less rebuttable presumptions concerning a number of (more or less) compelling fact situations in which one man may be identified as a promising candidate for paternity.[1]

In short, even though the traditional definition of legitimacy does not sweep as cleanly in current constitutional terms as does the Uniform Parentage Act, it does sweep. Where it sweeps, it all but eliminates the question of paternity and any lingering doubt regarding the fullness of the child's legal rights vis-à-vis its father.

There is still another side to this old coin. With the new role of the federal child support enforcement authorities in establishing support obligations that have never been fixed, the "bastardization" of children who seem "legitimate" may be expected to evolve into an important topic, after long dormancy as a relatively unimportant "middle class" issue. While accurate statistics are lacking, there is no doubt that a considerable number of children receiving support through the AFDC program are not in fact the children of their mothers' husbands. Often, these (nominal) husbands left the mothers years ago and simply disappeared by way of "poor man's divorce". Interest in showing the non-legitimacy of these nominally legitimate children may be expected to explode as soon as the states seriously attempt to enforce support obligations in these cases. A traditional discussion thus remains essential.

2. The Presumption of "Legitimacy."

The definition of legitimacy provides the definition of

---

1. § 4, 9A U.L.A., MATR., FAM. AND HEALTH LAWS 590 (1979).

illegitimacy — a child who is not born legitimate, or legitimated later, is "illegitimate." "Legitimacy" is tied to the parents' marital status at the time of their child's birth.[2] The emphasis is on *birth*,[3] not conception. However, there may be reference to the time of conception to make it totally clear that the child, who was conceived before or during marriage or born during or after its termination [4] (such as within 10 months),[5] is legitimate. Excluded from legitimacy are children born to a married mother under circumstances in which the husband could not have been the father.[6] But such exclusion is made only after appropriate legal steps have been taken. In the interest of stabilizing family

2. Where recognized, common law marriage is the equivalent of ceremonial marriage. The trend toward abolition of common-law marriage, however, has had the negative effect of creating legal illegitimacy where, socially, there may be an intact family. *See* H. KRAUSE, ILLEGITIMACY: LAW AND SOCIAL POLICY 17-18 (1971).

3. *E.g.*, ILL. REV. STAT. ch. 40, § 1351 (1977); LA. CIV. CODE ANN. art. 188 (Supp. 1979); NEB. REV. STAT. § 13-101 (1977).

4. "A child born out of wedlock is a child begotten and born to any woman who was unmarried from the conception to the date of birth of the child." MICH. STAT. ANN. § 25.491 (1974). *See also* ILL. ANN. STAT. ch. 106 3/4, § 51 (Supp. 1978); NEB. REV. STAT. § 13-101 (1977); N.H. REV. STAT. § 458:23 (1968); OHIO REV. CODE ANN. § 3105.13 (1972); S.C. CODE ANN. § 20-3-200 (1977). Legitimacy is presumed until the contrary is shown even in case of divorce for adultery. MICH. COMP. LAWS ANN. § 552.29 (Supp. 1979). Child is legitimate if it is the product of the marriage. GA. CODE ANN. § 39-119 (1969).

5. MONT. REV. CODES ANN. § 61-102 (1970); N.D. CENT. CODE § 14-09-02 (1971); OKLA. STAT. ANN. tit. 10, § 2 (1966); S.D. COMP. LAWS § 25-5.2 (1969). *Cf.*, LA. CIV. CODE ANN. art. 185 (Supp. 1979); P.R. LAWS ANN. tit. 31, § 461 (1968) (both stating 300 days).

6. "Child born out of wedlock ... [means] either a child born to an unmarried woman, or a child which, although born to a married woman, is either alleged or adjudicated not to be the issue of her marriage." WIS. STAT. ANN. § 52.45 (Supp. 1979). Concerning the status of a child conceived by a married woman by means of artificial insemination, *see* H. KRAUSE, ILLEGITIMACY: LAW AND SOCIAL POLICY 18-19 (1971).

relationships, there is universal, world-wide acceptance of a strong presumption of legitimacy in favor of children born in wedlock.[7]

This presumption of legitimacy is rooted in case law but also has found statutory expression. A few American states employ a (nearly) conclusive presumption, all but prohibiting a showing to the contrary.[8] The child's legitimacy may be upheld even if non-paternity can be established absolutely. Thus, a California court held in 1967 that a part Negro child born to a white woman was the legitimate child of the mother's white husband.[9] Despite a temporary weakening in California's position,[10] the strict view was reaffirmed in 1979, when a husband was held liable for the support of his wife's child, although blood tests showed him not to be the father.[11]

In states in which the presumption of legitimacy is

7. H. KRAUSE, CREATION OF RELATIONSHIPS OF KINSHIP, 4 INT. ENCYC. OF COMP. LAW ch. 6 at p. 14-21 (1976).

8. CAL. EVID. CODE § 621 (Cum. Supp. 1979) provides: "Notwithstanding any other provision of law, the issue of a wife cohabiting with her husband, who is not impotent or sterile, is conclusively presumed to be a child of the marriage." See also Annot., 57 A.L.R.2d 729 (1958). Cf., OR. REV. STAT. § 41.350 (1977).

9. Hess v. Whitsitt, 257 Cal. App. 2d 552, 65 Cal. Rptr. 45 (1967). See generally Comment, Presumptions of Legitimacy and Related Problems, 23 So. CAL. L. REV. 538 (1950). Comment, California's Tangled Web: Blood Tests and the Conclusive Presumption of Legitimacy, 20 STAN. L. REV. 754 (1968). Comment, Evidence — Presumption of Legitimacy — Blood Grouping Test Insufficient to Prove Non-Paternity Where Statutory Presumption is Conclusive, 16 RUTGERS L. REV. 767 (1962).

10. In re Lisa R., 13 Cal. 3d 636, 532 P.2d 123, 119 Cal. Rptr. 475 1975); Jackson v. Jackson, 67 Cal. 2d 245, 430 P.2d 89, 60 Cal. Rptr. 649 (1967). See also Hughes v. Hughes, 125 Cal. App. 2d 781, 271 P.2d 172 (1954).

11. People v. Thompson, 89 Cal. App. 3d 193, 152 Cal. Rptr. 478 (1979). Cf., Comment, The Uniform Parentage Act: What Will It Mean for the Putative Father in California, 28 HASTINGS L.J. 191 (1976).

rebuttable, rebuttal is typically difficult. Actual impossibility of the mother's husband's paternity often turns out to be the only way to "bastardize" a child born in wedlock. To show impossibility, proof of non-paternity by a conclusive blood test exclusion suffices,[12] and so may proof of non-access by the husband during the relevant period,[13] or proof of the husband's sterility or impotence,[14] or proof that the alleged duration of pregnancy is highly improbable.[15] Estoppel, however, may tie the hands of a husband who has waited too long to raise the question

---

12. Conn. Gen. Stat. Ann. § 46b-168 (1979); Ill. Ann. Stat. ch. 40 § 1404 (1979); § 4 (Supp. 1978); N.Y. Fam. Ct. Act. § 418 (1975); Pa. Stat. Ann. tit. 28, § 307.4 (Supp. 1969); Utah Code Ann. § 78-45a-10 (1977); Wis. Stat. Ann. § 52.36(3) (Supp. 1979).

See, e.g., Hanson v. Hanson, 249 N.W.2d 452 (Minn. 1977); Simmons v. Simmons, 479 S.W.2d 585 (Ky. 1972); Houghton v. Houghton, 179 Neb. 275, 137 N.W.2d 861 (1965); Beck v. Beck, 153 Colo. 90, 384 P.2d 731 (1963); Retzer v. Retzer, 161 A.2d 469 (D.C. 1960); Shepard v. Shepard, 81 Mich. App. 465, 265 N.W.2d 374 (1978); Moore v. Murray, 63 Misc. 2d 401, 311 N.Y.S.2d 794 (1969); Crouse v. Crouse, 51 Misc. 2d 649, 273 N.Y.S.2d 595 (1966); Oliver v. England, 48 Misc. 2d 335, 264 N.Y.S.2d 999 (1964).

13. Puerto Rico admits no other proof. P.R. Laws Ann. tit. 31, § 461 (1968). Under West Virginia law, where a married woman lives apart from her husband for one year or does not cohabit with him during that year, she may, if she is delivered of child at any time after said year or while such separation continues, bring a paternity action against someone not her husband. W. Va. Code Ann. § 48-7-1 (1976). *See also* Lanford v. Lanford, 151 Colo. 211, 377 P.2d 115 (1962); District of Columbia v. Prather, 207 A.2d 119 (D.C. App. 1965); Peters v. District of Columbia, 84 A.2d 115 (D.C. App. 1951); Feltus v. Bland, 210 So. 2d 388 (La. App. 1968).

14. *See, e.g.,* Iowa Code Ann. § 598.22 (1966).

15. *E.g.,* Rose v. Rose, 16 Ohio App. 2d 123, 242 N.E.2d 677 (1968) (224 days).

regarding his paternity,[16] or of one who knew at the time of marriage that his bride was pregnant by another man.[17]

Some statutes provide that only the husband may question the legitimacy of a child born to his wife. Others limit the action to the husband and wife and their descendants.[18] The Uniform Parentage Act "fine-tunes" the circle of persons authorized to challenge a child's legitimacy

---

16. *E.g.*, Watts v. Watts, 115 N.H. 186, 337 A.2d 350 (1975); *In re* Johnson, 88 Cal. App. 3d 848, — Cal. Rptr. — (1979); Williams v. Holland, 39 N.C. App. 141, 249 S.E.2d 821 (1978); Montelone v. Anita, 60 App. Div. 2d 603, 400 N.Y.S.2d 129 (1977). *Cf.*, Myers v. Myers, 39 N.C. App. 201, 249 S.E.2d 853 (1978).

17. Perkins v. Perkins, 34 Conn. Super. 187, 383 A.2d 634 (1978), discussing a variety of views and citing extensive authority. *Accord,* Burse v. Burse, 48 Ohio App. 2d 244, 356 N.E.2d 755 (1976). *See also* Hall v. Rosen, 50 Ohio St. 2d 135, 140, 363 N.E.2d 725, 728 (1977), where the natural father was relieved of liability after the mother married another man who knew of her pregnancy. The Ohio Supreme Court held:

> By this act of marriage, the man promises not only to shoulder the mantle of a husband, but also of a father, and the woman expresses her reliance upon the promise. . . . The possible harm is not merely the illegitimation of a heretofore legitimate child, but the disruption of the normal psychological and sociological relationship between father and child which is nurtured by support and association. The creation of an invitation to bring support actions against alleged biological fathers, perhaps many years after the fact, portends the possibility of "father-shopping," i.e., seeking support from the most successful of possible candidates. These actions will not only present the problem of the staleness of the evidence, but also the possibility of disrupting other established families by moral disparagement and suddenly increased financial responsibilities.

18. *E.g.*, OKLA. STAT. ANN. tit. 10, § 3 (Cum. Supp. 1979); S.D. COMP. LAWS § 25-5-4 (1976). In Maryland, testimony from other persons must be given as to the fact that husband and mother were living apart, before husband and mother may testify as to nonaccess. MD. ANN. CODE art. 16, § 66F (1973). In Wisconsin the husband and wife may testify, but a "clear and satisfactory preponderance of the evidence" is required to overcome the presumption. WIS. STAT. ANN. § 891.39 (1967).

in accordance with the strength of the *factual basis* of the presumption in the given circumstances.[19]

The presumption of legitimacy is supported further by an ancient rule of evidence, blamed on Lord Mansfield, which prohibits a spouse from testifying regarding his or her child's bastardy.[20] Modern cases, however, tend to reject that rule on the basis that "rules that exclude evidence bearing directly on the truth to be determined ought not to survive without very good cause." [21] Doubt also may be raised regarding the constitutionality of the old rule,[22] as well as regarding statutes allowing only *unmarried* mothers to bring paternity actions.[23]

It is worth noting that the common law has applied the presumption of legitimacy with apparently equal force to a child conceived prior to marriage and born in wedlock,[24] as well as to a child conceived during marriage and born after a divorce,[25] despite the different levels of probability involved in these different situations. This presumption is rooted in judicial reluctance to inquire into the internal affairs of the family and, over the centuries, has saved the status of untold numbers of children born to adulterous

---

19. §§ 4, 6, 9A U.L.A. Matr. & Health Laws 591, 593 (1979), Appendix B. *Cf.,* Borchers v. McCarter, — Mont. —, 592 P.2d 941 (1979).

20. Goodrich v. Moss, 98 Eng. Rep. 1257 (1777). *See* H. Krause, Illegitimacy: Law and Social Policy 119 (1971).

21. Savruk v. Derby, 235 Pa. Super. 560, 344 A.2d 624 (1975); Davis v. Davis, 521 S.W.2d 603 (Tex. 1975); Coffman v. Coffman, — Ariz. App. —, 591 P.2d 1010 (1979).

22. *See* Brown v. Danley, 263 Ark. 480, 566 S.W.2d 385 (1978).

23. Gammon v. Cobb, 335 So. 2d 261 (Fla. 1976).

24. L.A.M. v. M.L.M., — W. Va. —, 250 S.E.2d 40 (1979).

25. L.R.R. v. R.A.R., 378 N.E.2d 855 (Ind. 1978). In Rose v. Rose, 16 Ohio App. 2d 123, 242 N.E.2d 677 (1968), the court held the presumption rebutted on the basis of a blood test exclusion, an improbably short 224 day pregnancy, and evidence associating the mother with other men.

mothers by discouraging husbands from even raising the question.

Even today, the presumption of legitimacy remains soundly based on the rational State interest in stabilizing family relationships. However, there has been some erosion in overly rigid interpretation. Impetus to opening up the question of the legitimacy of children born in wedlock has come from U.S. Supreme Court cases providing broad substantive rights to the illegitimate child.[26] The advent of blood typing evidence has provided means of disproving the husband's paternity that were previously unavailable.[27] As just discussed, "Lord Mansfield's Rule," the restriction on the married mother's testimony regarding her child's bastardy, has been dropped in many states. The presumption also has been attacked from the other side, by a natural father who was prevented from establishing his paternity of his child, born to a married woman. Citing *Stanley*,[28] the Supreme Court of California held in 1975 that "a presumption which precludes to appellant in the instant circumstances a right to offer evidence to prove that he is the father of the minor child is unreasonable, arbitrary and capricious, and a denial of due process." [29] Of course, the circumstances of that case were special, inasmuch as both the presumed father and the mother of the child were dead, so that the Court had no difficulty finding inapplicable the "legitimate" State "policy of not impugning a family unit."

---

26. *See infra* ch. IV. 2. *Cf.,* Gammon v. Cobb, 335 So. 2d 261 (Fla. 1976), holding unconstitutional a statute denying a *married* mother the right to bring a paternity action against the father of her child.

27. *See infra* ch. VI.

28. Stanley v. Illinois, 405 U.S. 645, 92 S. Ct. 1208, 31 L. Ed. 2d 551 (1972). *See infra* ch. IV. 3.

29. *In re* Lisa R., 13 Cal. 3d 636, 532 P.2d 123, 119 Cal. Rptr. 475 (1975).

3. "Legitimation" After Birth.

Beyond this presumption of legitimacy, the law has offered other "definitional" relief to potential illegitimates. A major remedy has come out of an expanding definition of "born in wedlock:" Whereas the offspring of a void or defective marriage, when annulled with retroactive effect, used to be illegitimate, many states long have given legitimate status to the child of nearly any alliance that resembles a formal marriage.[30] A large area of potential illegitimacy was thus eliminated. Covered are the children of parents whose marriage did not meet the test of legality by reason of their failure to comply with formal or substantive requirements, such as health checks, consent of a parent's parents and similar details, or because of the legal disability of a parent, such as a continuing prior marriage (bigamy), consanguinity (incest), nonage, idiocy, or insanity and other impediments. In some jurisdictions the impediments of prior marriage[31] and consanguinity [32] have given the legislators pause, and only the children of

---

30. *E.g.,* ILL. REV. STAT., ch. 40, § 1351 (1979). Despite the long-standing abolition of common-law marriage, Illinois gives legitimacy to the offspring of what would be a common-law marriage, if there were such a thing. ILL. REV. STAT., ch. 40, § 212(c) (1979). *See also* MD. CODE ANN. art. 16, § 27 (1973); TEX. PROB. CODE ANN. § 42 (1956). Other states have provisions of varying breadth, sometimes with exclusions for incestuous or bigamous illegitimates: CAL. CIV. CODE § 4453; DEL. CODE ANN. tit. 13, § 105 (1975); D.C. CODE ANN. §§ 16-907, 16-908 (Cum. Supp. 1978); GA. CODE ANN. § 53-104 (1974); HAWAII REV. STAT. § 338-21 (1976); KAN. GEN. STAT. ANN. § 23-124 (1974); N.H. REV. STAT. ANN. § 458:23 (1968).

31. Offspring of a bigamous "marriage" commonly are considered legitimate as to the party who entered the bigamous marriage in good faith. D.C. CODE ANN. § 16-909 (Cum. Supp. 1978), MASS. ANN. Laws ch. 207, § 17 (Cum. Supp. 1978). *See* Comment, *Domestic Relations — Legitimacy of Issue of Bigamous Marriage,* 22 TENN. L. REV. 1066 (1953).

32. *E.g.,* MISS. CODE ANN. § 93-7-5 (1972); N.H. REV. STAT. ANN. § 457:3 (Supp. 1977).

unions void by reason of "lesser" impediments, such as nonage, "idiocy," or insanity of one or both of the partners are legitimated. Under some statutes, the good faith of the parties may play a decisive role.[33] Still others restrict the child's legitimate status to the partner who was not under an impediment.[34] It is of historical interest that some statutes prohibiting racial intermarriage specifically excluded (or were judicially interpreted to exclude) the issue of such unions from a general legitimation statute.[35]

Statutory provisions legitimating potential illegitimates have operated in a number of other situations. In several states, a judgment in a paternity action, for instance, produces full legitimacy.[36] A number of states offer voluntary legitimation procedures to the unmarried father.[37] Much more common are provisions that automatically or through acknowledgment or recognition on the part of the father, legitimate a nonmarital child upon the marriage of its parents after its birth.[38] A frequently

---

33. LA. CIV. CODE ANN. art. 118 (1952) specifically provides that the children of a void marriage are legitimate if one of the parties acted in good faith. Succession of Jene, 173 So. 2d 857, 860 (La. Ct. App. 1965) defines "good faith" as requiring "only that the party should have no certain knowledge of any impediment to the marriage and should have an honest and reasonable belief that the marriage was valid and that no legal impediment existed at the time of its confection."

34. MASS. ANN. LAWS ch. 207, § 16 (1969). See also Unity v. Belgrade, 76 Me. 419 (1884); 10 AM. JUR. 2d Bastards § 2 (1963).

35. Loving v. Virginia, 388 U.S. 1, 87 S. Ct. 1817, 18 L. Ed. 2d 1010 (1967), held that state law could not forbid marriages solely on the basis of racial classifications. See Wadlington, The Loving Case: Virginia's Anti-Miscegenation Statute in Historical Perspective, 52 VA. L. REV. 1189 (1966).

36. E.g., ALASKA STAT. § 25.20.050 (1977).

37. See infra ch. V. 2.

38. See ALA. CODE tit. 26, § 11-1 (1975); ALASKA STAT. § 25.20.050 (1977); CAL. CIV. CODE § 7004 (Cum. Supp. 1979); DEL. CODE ANN. tit. 13, § 1301 (1975); FLA. STAT. ANN. § 742.091 (Cum. Supp. 1979); LA. CIV.

imposed requirement is the specific acknowledgment of the child by the father. This may have to be in writing,[39] or by open conduct implying recognition.[40]

Where recognized, an informal, common law marriage subsequent to the child's birth may effect legitimation.[41] However, if the child in question is *not* the father's biological child, legitimation cannot be effected in this manner.[42] The effect of a void or voidable marriage *subsequent* to the child's birth is not always clear, although the dual handicap has been overcome where a state had both types of legitimation statutes.[43]

CODE ANN. art. 198, 199 (1952); NEB. REV. STAT. § 13-109 (1977); TENN. CODE ANN. § 36-307 (1977); UTAH CODE ANN. § 77-60-14 (1978).

39. ALASKA STAT. § 25.20.050 (1977); DEL. CODE tit. 13, § 1301 (1975); NEB. REV. STAT. § 13-109 (1977); S.D. COMP. LAWS § 34-25-16 (1976).

40. ALASKA STAT. § 25.20.050 (1977); MO. ANN. STAT. § 474.070 (1951); VT. STAT. ANN. tit. 14, § 554 (1974); VA. CODE ANN. §§ 20-13.1, 64.1-7 (1975).

41. *E.g.,* Kester v. Kester, 106 W. Va. 615, 146 S.E. 625 (1929).

42. The appropriate answer in such a case is adoption. Chatman v. Chatman, 54 Ohio App. 2d 6, 374 N.E.2d 433 (1978).

43. Rivieceio v. Bothan, 27 Cal. 2d 621, 165 P.2d 677 (1946); L. v. L., 92 N.J. Super. 118, 222 A.2d 297 (1966); Carroll v. Carroll, 20 Tex. 732, 746 (1858). *See also* ALASKA STAT. § 13.10.030 (1977).

Chapter IV

THE NEW LAW OF "ILLEGITIMACY"

1. Current Facts and not so Ancient History.

Despite declining birth rates, the problem of illegitimacy remains a national crisis. More than 6 million *minor* children who have been born out of wedlock live in the United States today. More than 468,000 non-marital ("illegitimate") children were added in 1976, 447,000 in 1975, 418,000 in 1974, 407,000 in 1973, 403,000 in 1972, 401,000 in 1971 and 399,000 in 1979, for a total of nearly three million in just these seven years. There has been not only an increase in the absolute number of births out of wedlock, but the rate had accelerated to more than fourteen percent of all births by 1975, five times the 1940 rate,[1] and to 15.5 percent by 1977.[2] In many urban areas illegitimacy has exceeded 50 percent for years and is rising.[3]

The "pill" and liberalized abortion have not fulfilled early expectations that the end of illegitimacy is at hand.[4] On the contrary, although births in general have fallen off, the growing acceptance of "new life-styles," the trend abolishing common law marriage and the reduced social stigma of illegitimacy seem to have combined to produce the highest proportion of out-of-wedlock births on the American record. The resulting problem is compounded by the rapidly increasing number of mothers who opt to keep and raise

---

1. U.S. DEPT. OF COMMERCE, BUREAU OF THE CENSUS, STATISTICAL ABSTRACT OF THE UNITED STATES 65 (1978); CHAMPAIGN-URBANA NEWS GAZETTE, August 11, 1978, 1.

2. NATIONAL CENTER FOR HEALTH STATISTICS, 27 VITAL STATISTICS REPORT NO. 11, at 19 (Advance Sheet, February 5, 1979) cited in Parham v. Hughes, 441 U.S. 347, 99 S. Ct. 1742, 60 L. Ed. 2d 269 (1979).

3. H. KRAUSE, ILLEGITIMACY: LAW AND SOCIAL POLICY 8, 357-59 (1971).

4. In 1975, one legal abortion was performed for every three live births. CHAMPAIGN-URBANA NEWS GAZETTE, August 11, 1978, 1.

these children, rather than give them up for adoptive placement.[5] The incidence of illegitimacy increasingly has a racial dimension. By 1977, the black rate had risen to 51.7 percent,[6] from less than 30 percent in 1967,[7] and compared with the national rate of 15.5 percent.

Aside from the personal problems — even tragedies — for child and mother so often implicit in illegitimacy, the public welfare dimensions of illegitimacy have become alarming.[8] The table that follows shows, by individual states, an increase between 1961 and 1973 from 24.2 to 32.7 percent in nonmarital children as a percentage of the total AFDC load, and a 292 percent increase in nonmarital children receiving AFDC. This is not yet the whole story. The common custom (and, indeed, law)[9] that has a married mother continue to report any birth to her as legitimate even if her husband left her long ago, suggests the probability of a significant *under*statement in official figures of the incidence of out-of-wedlock births, both in absolute terms and in the context of welfare statistics.

5. *See, e.g.,* Johnson, *The Business in Babies,* N.Y. Times Magazine (Aug. 17, 1975, 10).

6. *Supra* note 2.

7. *Supra* note 3.

8. A brief and impressive summary of AFDC history and statistics is given by Galvin, *The Runaway Parents,* 12 Trial 20 (April 1976). *Cf.,* Ooms & Maciocha, Teenage Pregnancy and Family Impact: New Perspectives on Policy, (Family Impact Seminar, George Washington University, June 1979).

9. *Supra* ch. III.2.

NEW LAW OF "ILLEGITIMACY"

TABLE 1—AFDC CHILDREN, BY NUMBER OF PERCENT OF ILLEGITIMATE CHILDREN, 1961 AND 1973 [10]

| | 1961 | | | 1973 | | | Percentage change 1961-73 |
| | Illegitimate | | | Illegitimate | | | |
	Total	Number	Percent	Total	Number	Percent	
Alabama	65,328	17,965	27.5	123,026	64,469	52.4	+259
Alaska	3,244	571	17.6				
Arizona	28,756	*	*	55,151	15,923	28.9	
Arkansas	19,198	3,225	16.8	61,240	23,200	37.9	+819
California	248,342	69,287	27.9	955,999	267,555	27.7	+285
Colorado	25,170	5,059	20.1	76,641	15,814	20.6	+213
Connecticut	28,525	6,646	23.3				
Delaware	7,581	2,987	39.4				
District of Columbia	20,405	8,346	40.9				
Florida	75,644	19,365	25.6	259,295	119,855	45.2	+519
Georgia	47,372	4,785	10.1	246,616	95,455	38.7	+1,895
Guam							
Hawaii	9,011	2,118	23.5				
Idaho	6,712	517	7.7				
Illinois	177,506	64,967	36.6	545,528	199,689	36.6	+207
Indiana	32,914	7,570	23.0	128,622	37,714	29.3	+393
Iowa	26,140	3,450	13.2	52,486	9,356	17.8	+171
Kansas	19,148	2,891	15.1	50,576	12,154	24.0	+320
Kentucky	59,376	12,053	20.3	105,531	31,752	30.1	+163
Louisiana	73,271	17,878	24.4	189,453	88,451	46.7	+395
Maine	14,930	2,045	13.7				
Maryland	37,016	13,363	36.1	162,182	62,060	38.3	+364
Massachusetts							
Michigan	82,655	15,622	18.9	431,548	116,670	27.0	+647
Minnesota	29,487	3,745	12.7	88,481	17,495	19.8	+367
Mississippi	62,434	10,926	17.5	135,248	63,635	47.1	+482
Missouri	79,706	21,919	27.5	177,910	67,367	37.9	+207
Montana	6,090	828	13.6				
Nebraska	9,718	1,429	14.7	29,398	8,066	27.4	+464
Nevada	3,635	1,083	29.8				
New Hampshire	3,302	317	9.6				
New Jersey	52,507	19,113	35.4	296,521	105,009	35.4	+449
New Mexico	21,914	5,588	25.5				
New York	250,990	87,847	35.0	917,679	349,946	38.1	+293
North Carolina	89,001	17,533	19.7	117,543	52,539	44.7	+200
North Dakota	5,128	600	11.7	9,633	1,997	20.7	+233
Ohio	100.894	27,140	26.9	334,969	99,441	29.7	+265
Oklahoma	5,529	13,655	26.5	75,531	21,787	28.8	+60
Oregon							
Pennsylvania	209,162	43,506	20.8	442,660	136,624	30.9	+214
Puerto Rico	179,653	30,182	16.8				
Rhode Island	14,671	2,142	14.6	37,065	6,816	18.4	+218
South Carolina	30,158	3,287	10.9				
South Dakota	8,115	1,777	21.9	16,207	3,526	21.8	+98
Tennessee	62,645	19,733	31.5	141,607	58,983	41.7	+199
Texas	62,250	12,886	20.7	326,332	112,703	34.5	+775
Utah	10,655	1,353	12.7				
Vermont	3,554	551	15.5				
Virgin Islands	820	538	65.6				
Virginia	33,920	9,464	27.9	116,431	49,217	42.3	+420
Washington	43,572	5,054	11.6				
West Virginia	93,507	11,782	12.6	53,201	11,253	21.2	−4
Wisconsin	29,038	5,750	19.8	100,913	27,186	26.9	+373
Wyoming	2,230	399	17.9				
U.S. total	**2,658,529	645,230	24.2	***7,724,938	2,529,846	32.7	+292

* Not reported.
** Excludes Massachusetts, Oregon, and Guam.
*** Excludes Massachusetts and Guam.

10. STAFF OF SENATE COMM. ON FINANCE, 94th Cong., 1st Sess., WAGE GARNISHMENT, ATTACHMENT AND ASSIGNMENT, AND ESTABLISHMENT OF PATERNITY 288 (Comm. Print 1975).

The time has come to adapt our law and legal practice to changing and unchanged social facts — changing in terms of the increasing incidence and acceptability of nonmarital relationships, but unchanged in terms of the child's right to and need of a *legal* relationship with its father.

In the eyes of the common law, the nonmarital child had no parent at all. Although the legal relationship between mother and child had long been equalized by law, most states had continued to discriminate heavily in the substantive relationship between father and nonmarital child. Until the United States Supreme Court intervened, traditional discrimination extended to rights of support, inheritance, custody, name, as well as to claims under father-related welfare statutes, such as workmen's compensation, wrongful death, and various state and federal acts.[11] As reflected in (and formed by) the traditional law, society saw the nonmarital child as the mother's child and all but denied the father's existence. The following excerpt from a judicial opinion rendered in 1961 in Ohio, illustrates the depth of this prejudice: "[T]he Decalog, which is the basis of our moral code, specifically states that the sins of the father may be visited upon the children unto the third and fourth generation, so that the argument against making the children suffer for the mother's wrong can be attacked on ethical grounds." [12]

This sentiment helps explain the law's long disregard for the father's role vis-à-vis his nonmarital child. Today, however, this world-wide [13] tradition has run its course.

11. H. Krause, Illegitimacy: Law and Social Policy, Ch. 1 (1971).

12. *In re* Dake, 180 N.E.2d 646, 649, 87 Ohio Abs. 483, 486, (Juv. Ct. Huron Co., 1961).

13. Chicago Sun-Times, Aug. 18, 1978, p. 42:

A United Nations commission agreed Tuesday on the first international principles giving illegitimate children the same rights and status as those born in wedlock. The draft principles, adopted by the 26-nation subcommission on the Prevention of Discrimination,

Beginning in 1968, the U.S. Supreme Court applied the Equal Protection Clause of the U.S. Constitution to a long series of cases. Today, in nearly all substantive areas of the law, the established principle is that the nonmarital child is entitled to legal equality with the child of married parents. Common law and statutes disadvantaging nonmarital children have been declared unconstitutional, and nearly all remaining discriminatory legislation is under severe constitutional doubt.[14]

2. Equality Achieved?

The first two U.S. Supreme Court cases in which the law of illegitimacy was confronted with the Equal Protection Clause declared Louisiana's wrongful death statute unconstitutional insofar as it did not allow nonmarital children to recover for the wrongful death of their mother (*Levy v. Louisiana*),[15] and denied a mother recovery for the wrongful death of her nonmarital child (*Glona v. American Guarantee & Liability Insurance Co.*).[16] Had the children been born in marriage, recovery would have been allowed in both situations. Over Justice Harlan's vigorous dissenting opinion, Justice Douglas wrote for the majority in *Levy*:

Legitimacy or illegitimacy of birth has no relation to

aim at giving every person born out of wedlock, whether adult or child, the same status as a person born in wedlock. The proposed international principles go to the UN Commission on Human Rights for approval at its meeting next year.

Every person born out of wedlock shall be entitled to legal recognition of his or her maternal and paternal filiation and have the right to bear a surname determined as in the case of a person born in wedlock, the draft says.

Regarding reforms in numerous countries, see H. Krause, *Creation of Relations of Kinship,* 4 INT. ENCYC. COMPARATIVE LAW Ch. 6 (Mohr/Mouton 1976).

14. *See infra* ch. IV.5.
15. 391 U.S. 68, 88 S. Ct. 1509, 20 L. Ed. 2d 436 (1968).
16. 391 U.S. at 73, 88 S. Ct. at 1515, 20 L. Ed. 2d at 441 (1968).

the nature of the wrong allegedly inflicted on the mother. These children, though illegitimate, were dependent on her; she cared for them and nurtured them; they were indeed hers in the biological and in the spiritual sense; in her death they suffered wrong in the sense that any dependent would.

We conclude that it is invidious to discriminate against them when no action, conduct, or demeanor of theirs is possibly relevant to the harm that was done the mother.[17]

Subsequently, state and lower federal courts rendered varying decisions concerning the *father* and child relationship, where discrimination was most common and serious. Concerning the child's right to support and its right to bring a paternity action, more courts applied or extended *Levy* or *Glona*[18] than did not.[19] A similar situation

---

17. 391 U.S. at 72, 88 S. Ct. at 1511, 20 L. Ed. 2d at 439-40 (1968).

18. R. v. R., 431 S.W.2d 152 (Mo. 1968); Storm v. None, 57 Misc. 2d 342, 291 N.Y.S.2d 515 (1968) (extended *Levy* and *Glona* to the illegitimate child's right of support from his father); Trent v. Loru, 57 Misc. 2d 382, 292 N.Y.S.2d 524 (1968) (in light of *Levy* and *Glona*, Uniform Support of Dependents Law must be applied to remove as far as possible the obstacles to equal treatment of the illegitimate child); Munn v. Munn, 168 Colo. 76, 450 P.2d 68 (1969) (father's liability to his illegitimate child may not be greater than or different from his obligation to his legitimate child); Wales v. Gallon, 61 Misc. 2d 681, 306 N.Y.S.2d 614 (1969) (Two-year period of limitation on paternity suit brought by mother held unconstitutional in light of *Levy* and *Glona;* court referred to child's right to have his paternity ascertained, but decided case on basis of the inequality presented by a ten-year period of limitations allowed to welfare authorities); Lucey v. Torrence, 62 Misc. 2d 714, 309 N.Y.S.2d 755 (1970) (citing *Levy* and *Glona,* the court appointed a law guardian to represent an illegitimate child in a paternity action where the natural mother had defaulted and refused to cooperate).

19. Baston v. Sears, 15 Ohio St. 2d 166, 239 N.E.2d 62 (1968) (refused to extend *Levy* and *Glona* to the father's support obligation to the child), overruled by Franklin v. Julian, 30 Ohio St. 2d 228, 234, 283 N.E.2d 813, 817 (1972); Kennelly v. Davis, 221 So. 2d 415 (Fla. 1969), *cert. denied,* 396 U.S. 916, 90 S. Ct. 237, 24 L. Ed. 2d 193 (1969) (married mother not

developed in the area of the child's right of inheritance, with some courts applying or extending *Levy* or *Glona* [20] and others refusing to do so.[21] Existing state statutes that allow a child born out-of-wedlock to inherit under limited conditions, usually pertaining to proof of paternity, generally were upheld.[22] Other cases concerned life

---

permitted to bring paternity suit against natural father because a child born in wedlock is presumed to be the legitimate child of her husband; no violation of equal protection was seen because this situation of an unmarried mother having an illegitimate child was considered to be different from the situation of the married mother); G. v. P., 466 S.W.2d 41 (father of a child born out of wedlock has no civil support liability) *writ refused* Tex. S. Ct. 1971, *rev'd,* Gomez v. Perez, 409 U.S. 535, 93 S. Ct. 872, 35 L. Ed. 2d 56 (1973).

20. *In re* Estate of Jensen, 162 N.W.2d 861 (N.D. 1968) (extended *Levy* to the right of descendants to take through their mother in an intestacy situation).

21. Succession of Vincent, 229 So. 2d 449 (La. 1969), *writ refused,* 255 La. 480 (1970), 231 So. 2d 395 (1970), *aff'd sub. nom.,* Labine v. Vincent, 401 U.S. 532, 91 S. Ct. 1017, 28 L. Ed. 2d 288 (1971); Strahan v. Strahan, 304 F. Supp. 40 (W.D. La. 1969), *aff'd,* 444 F.2d 528 (1971); Succession of Bush, 222 So. 2d 642 (La. Ct. App. 1969) (all refusing to extend *Levy* to the illegitimate child's right to take from his intestate father); *In re* Estate of Caldwell, 247 So. 2d 1 (Fla. 1971) (refused to extend *Levy* and *Glona* to cover intestacy rights of illegitimate offspring in dispute between legitimate and illegitimate collaterals).

22. *In re* Estate of Pakarinen, 287 Minn. 330, 178 N.W.2d 714 (1970), *appeal dismissed,* 402 U.S. 903, 91 S. Ct. 1384, 28 L. Ed. 2d 644 (1971): (discrimination based solely upon illegitimacy is not permissible under *Levy* and *Glona,* but Minnesota statute admitting to intestate succession only those illegitimate children who can produce an attested written declaration of paternity has a rational purpose and therefore is constitutional); Burnett v. Camden, 253 Ind. 354, 254 N.E.2d 199 (1970), *reh. denied,* 253 Ind. 354, 255 N.E.2d 650 (1970), *cert. denied,* 399 U.S. 901, 90 S. Ct. 2202, 26 L. Ed. 2d 556 (1970) (*Levy* and *Glona* distinguished as cases where the question of blood relationship was not at issue, and Indiana statute providing that a child may inherit from putative father only if paternity has been established by law or if the putative father has married the mother of the child and acknowledged the child as his, upheld as not denying equal protection).

insurance proceeds [23] as well as custody, visitation, and adoption.[24] Federal laws came under attack,[25] as did state

---

23. *In re* Estate of R.L.B., 259 So. 2d 206 (Fla. 1972) (life insurance proceeds as sole asset in estate ordered paid to orally acknowledged illegitimate child of decedent father, under a Florida statute requiring such monies — when made payable to the estate — to devolve to the spouse and children. While not specifically mentioning *Levy* or *Glona,* the Court held that requiring the illegitimate child to have been acknowledged by father in writing — as required by another statute applying to inheritance from the father — would "constitute an unconstitutional deprivation of rights").

24. Extending *Levy* or *Glona*: R. v. F., 113 N.J. Super. 396, 410, 273 A.2d 808, 816 (1971) (denying visitation rights to putative father of illegitimate child would deny father and child due process and equal protection). Refusing to extend *Levy* or *Glona:* State *ex rel.* Lewis v. Lutheran Social Services of Wisconsin and Upper Michigan, 47 Wis. 2d 420, 178 N.W.2d 56 (1970). (Failure of Wisconsin statutes to grant parental rights or notice of hearing to putative father prior to termination of parental rights does not violate equal protection clause. *Rev'd on remand,* see Rothstein v. Lutheran Social Services of Wisconsin and Upper Michigan, 405 U.S. 1051, 92 S. Ct. 1488, 31 L. Ed. 2d 786 (1972), State *ex rel.* Lewis v. Lutheran Social Services of Wisconsin and Upper Michigan, 59 Wis. 2d 1, 207 N.W.2d 826 (1973). Vanderlaan v. Vanderlaan, 126 Ill. App. 2d 410, 262 N.E.2d 717 (1970) (father denied visitation rights relating to illegitimate child). *Levy* or *Glona* not discussed. *Remanded,* Vanderlaan v. Vanderlaan, 405 U.S. 1051, 92 S. Ct. 1488, 31 L. Ed. 2d 787 (1972).

25. (1) LONGSHOREMEN'S AND HARBOR WORKER'S COMPENSATION ACT — Ingalls Shipbuilding Corp. v. Neuman, 322 F. Supp. 1229, 1245-47 (S.D. Miss. 1970) (dictum: requiring illegitimates to prove dependency — whereas legitimate children need not — probably would not be "invidious discrimination").

(2) FEDERAL EMPLOYEES GROUP LIFE INSURANCE ACT — Haley v. Metropolitan Life Ins. Co., 434 S.W.2d 7 (Mo. App. 1968) (extended *Levy* and *Glona* to include an illegitimate child in the definition of "child" under the Act.

(3) JONES ACT — Hebert v. Petroleum Pipe Inspectors, Inc., 396 F.2d 237 (5th Cir. 1968) (extended *Levy* to include adulterous illegitimate offspring in the Act's definition of "children").

(4) SERVICEMEN'S GROUP LIFE INSURANCE ACT — Prudential Insurance

compensation laws such as workmen's compensation [26] and wrongful death acts.[27] In sum, while *Levy* and *Glona* did not

---

Company v. Willis, 227 Ga. 619, 182 S.E.2d 420 (1971) (reversed lower court's decision which had treated an acknowledged illegitimate child of a deceased serviceman as a "child" under the Act. Child held not entitled to the proceeds of a serviceman's group life policy. Strong dissent relied on *Levy*). *Accord,* Dobyns v. Prudential Insurance Co., 227 Ga. 253, 179 S.E.2d 915 (1971) (no reference to *Levy* or *Glona*).

(5) COPYRIGHT ACT — Jerry Vogel Music Co. v. Edward B. Marks Music Corp., 425 F.2d 834 (2d Cir. 1969) (refused to extend *Levy* and *Glona* to allow the assignee of deceased copyright holder's illegitimate daughter to claim copyright renewal rights in contest with assignee of deceased copyright holder's wife).

26. Stokes v. Aetna Cas. & Surety Co., 257 La. 424, 242 So. 2d 567 (1970); *but see* Weber v. Aetna Cas. & Surety Co., 406 U.S. 164, 92 S. Ct. 1400, 31 L. Ed. 2d 768 (1972), discussed below. (Illegitimate child is entitled to collect workmen's compensation benefits related to father.)

27. Applying or extending *Levy* or *Glona:* Armijo v. Wesselius, 73 Wash. 2d 716, 440 P.2d 471 (1968) (with reference to the equal protection argument, construed wrongful death statute to include illegitimate children of father within the term "child or children" just before *Levy* and *Glona* were decided); Miles v. City-Parish Government, 219 So. 2d 320 (La. App. 1969) (allowed mother to sue for wrongful death of her illegitimate children); *In re* Estate of Ortiz, 60 Misc. 2d 756, 303 N.Y.S.2d 806 (1969) and *In re* Estate of Perez, 69 Misc. 2d 538, 330 N.Y.S.2d 881 (1972) (illegitimate child whose paternity was not formally established during the father's lifetime is entitled to recover the father's wrongful death; statutory provisions to the contrary are abrogated by *Levy* and *Glona*). *In re* Estate of Ross, 67 Misc. 2d 320, 323 N.Y.S.2d 770 (1971) (under *Levy* and *Glona,* illegitimate child is entitled to recover for father's wrongful death and to be issued letters of administration). Weaks v. Mounter, 88 Nev. 118, 493 P.2d 1307 (1972) (*Levy* and *Glona* require that posthumous illegitimate child be allowed action for father's wrongful death, although father had not acknowledged paternity; dissent acknowledges constitutional equality requirement, but seeks to distinguish *Levy* insofar as proof of maternity usually is clear — whereas proof of paternity usually is not — and fears spurious claims if statutory requirements relating to proof of paternity are not met). *Accord,* Cannon v. Transamerican Freight Lines, 37 Mich. App. 313, 194 N.W.2d 736 (1971); Schmoll v. Creecy, 54 N.J. 194, 254 A.2d 525 (1969) (*Levy* and

meet a unanimous response, many courts considered these decisions to require equality between marital and nonmarital children in their legal relationship with their fathers.

It was a great surprise when, within three years of deciding *Levy* and *Glona,* the U.S. Supreme Court reached a conclusion which seemed to be directly at odds with the earlier ones.[28] *Labine v. Vincent*[29] refused to extend *Levy* to permit a nonmarital child to inherit from her intestate father under Louisiana law, although her father had acknowledged her during his lifetime. The *Labine* case was quickly seized upon by conservative courts to restrict *Levy* and *Glona* narrowly to their own facts, and to refuse to accord the nonmarital child broader constitutional

---

Glona extended to allow illegitimate child wrongful death action for death of his father).

Refusing to apply or extend *Levy* or *Glona:* Sanders v. Tillman, 245 So. 2d 198 (Miss. 1971) (illegitimate child may not recover for the wrongful death of his father where father had not legally acknowledged him during his lifetime; *Levy* and *Glona* distinguished on basis of ease of proving maternity and difficulty of proving paternity); Rogers v. State Farm Mut. Auto Ins. Co., 261 So. 2d 320 (La. Ct. App. 1972) (denial of wrongful death action to illegitimate siblings not a denial of due process and equal protection; *Levy* and *Glona* interpreted as applicable only to the parent-child relationship, involving dependency or at least mutual support obligation). City of West Palm Beach v. Cowart, 241 So. 2d 748 (Fla. App. 1970) (father not allowed an action for the wrongful death of his illegitimate child; *Glona* and *Levy* interpreted as applying to the mother and child relationship only), *rev'd,* 255 So. 2d 673 (Fla. 1971); George v. Bertrand, 217 So. 2d 47 (La. Ct. App. 1968), *writ refused,* 253 La. 647, 219 So. 2d 177 (1969), *cert. denied,* 396 U.S. 974, 90 S. Ct. 439, 24 L. Ed. 2d 443 (1969) (legal husband of mother is presumed to be the father of a child born in wedlock, and father of illegitimate child may not recover for the wrongful death of his son. *Levy* and *Glona* distinguished.

28. *E.g.,* H. KRAUSE, ILLEGITIMACY: LAW AND SOCIAL POLICY vii-ix (1971).

29. 401 U.S. 532, 91 S. Ct. 1017, 28 L. Ed. 2d 288 (1971).

protection in the areas of support [30] and inheritance,[31] as well as Social Security benefits.[32]

The surprise engendered by *Labine* in 1971 was surpassed when the Supreme Court again reversed its position in 1972. In a dramatic departure from *Labine,* the

---

30. Mitchell v. Mitchell, 445 F.2d 722 (D.C. Cir. 1971) (distinguished *Levy* and *Glona* and applied *Labine* to hold that children resulting from a marital relationship were entitled to support before and in preference to an illegitimate child); S. v. D., 335 F. Supp. 804 (N.D. Tex. 1971) (denied declaratory judgment to mother of illegitimate child that Texas support laws unconstitutionally exclude illegitimate children; also denied injunction against state officials to require them to apply support law to cover support for illegitimate children; dissent distinguishes *Labine* and would apply *Levy* and *Glona* to allow action.)

31. *In re* Estate of Hendrix, 68 Misc. 2d 439, 326 N.Y.S.2d 646 (1971) (statute conditioning illegitimate child's right to inherit from father on order of filiation during father's lifetime upheld; *Levy* and *Glona* distinguished and *Labine* held controlling). Similarly, *In re* Estate of Belton, 70 Misc. 2d 814, 335 N.Y.S.2d 177 (1972).

32. Parker v. Secretary of Dept. of HEW, 453 F.2d 850, 852 (5th Cir. 1972) (applied *Labine* to hold that where a reduction of Social Security benefits is required because of a family maximum, benefits payable to an illegitimate child may be reduced first; court held that "any doubt in regard to the legislature's power to distribute rights on basis of status stemming from legitimate or illegitimate birth was resolved by *Labine*"). *Accord,* Garner v. Richardson, 333 F. Supp. 1191, 1197 (N.D. Cal. 1971) ("in view of *Labine,* this Court cannot conclude that any discrimination in favor of legitimate children and against illegitimate children is violative of the principles of equal protection"). Watts v. Veneman, 334 F. Supp. 482 (D.D.C. 1971) (Social Security Act provisions limiting benefits to illegitimate child whose father has acknowledged the child in writing, or who has been ordered by a court to support the child, or who has been judicially decreed to be the father, or who is shown by other evidence to be the child's father and to be living with or contributing to the child's support, held reasonably designed to bar spurious claims and, in light of *Labine,* held not to deny due process). Johnson v. Finch, 350 F. Supp. 945 (N.D. Tex., 1972) (upheld the requirement of the Social Security Act that the wage earner must have been living with his illegitimate children at the time of death to entitle them to receive benefits).

Court held that workmen's compensation benefits related to the death of their father are due dependent, unacknowledged, nonmarital children.[33] The Court said:

> The status of illegitimacy has expressed through the ages society's condemnation of irresponsible liaisons beyond the bonds of marriage. But visiting this condemnation on the head of an infant is illogical and unjust. Moreover, imposing disabilities on the illegitimate child is contrary to the basic concept of our system that legal burdens should bear some relationship to individual responsibility or wrongdoing. Obviously, no child is responsible for his birth and penalizing the illegitimate child is an ineffectual — as well as an unjust — way of deterring the parent. Courts are powerless to prevent the social opprobrium suffered by these hapless children, but the Equal Protection Clause does enable us to strike down discriminatory laws relating to status of birth where — as in this case — the classification is justified by no legitimate state interest, compelling or otherwise.[34]

One of the first cases to apply *Weber* distinguished *Labine,* and enjoined enforcement of provisions of the Social Security Act discriminating against nonmarital children by denying such children benefits where the family award was insufficient to meet maximum payments to wife and marital children.[35] The Court discussed earlier, contrary decisions that had upheld the provisions on the strength of

33. Weber v. Aetna Cas. & Surety Co., 406 U.S. 164, 92 S. Ct. 1400, 31 L. Ed. 2d 768 (1972). The explanation is that the two justices most strongly opposing the new approach to illegitimacy had left the Court just before *Weber* was decided: Justice Harlan had gone on record with his dissent in *Levy* and *Glona,* and Justice Black had authored the majority opinion in *Labine.*

34. 406 U.S. at 175-76, 92 S. Ct. at 1406-07, 31 L. Ed. 2d at 779 (1972).

35. Davis v. Richardson, 342 F. Supp. 588 (D. Conn. 1972). *Accord,* Williams v. Richardson, 347 F. Supp. 544 (W.D.N.C. 1972). *See also* Morris v. Richardson, 346 F. Supp. 494 (N.D. Ga. 1972).

Labine but in the light of *Weber* viewed them as no longer controlling. Other cases followed and dealt with other subjects.[36]

In 1973, the U.S. Supreme Court considered the nonmarital child's substantive right of greatest importance; the right to support. Another "breakthrough" decision held that "once a State posits a judicially enforceable right on behalf of children to needed support from their natural fathers there is no constitutionally sufficient justification for denying such an essential right to a child simply because its natural father has not married its mother."[37] Justices Stewart and Rehnquist dissented on technical grounds. The Court's "dispositive" language, quoted above, did not quite make it clear that *full* equality is required, although one may and probably should read the case that way. Accordingly, some state courts have imposed equality[38] but

---

36. For example, in Butcher v. Pollard, 32 Ohio App. 2d 1, 15, 288 N.E.2d 204, 213 (1972) the Court, looking at *Weber,* held that the word "children" in the beneficiary clause of a life insurance policy "must be construed to mean all offspring, regardless of legitimacy." On the authority of *Levy* and *Weber,* Walker v. Walker, 266 So. 2d 385 (Fla. 1972) held invalid a mother's release of the putative father insofar as it purported to affect the child's rights. Heather v. Delta Drilling Co., 533 P.2d 1211 (Wyo. 1975) was a "late bloomer" covering workmen's compensation.

37. Gomez v. Perez, 409 U.S. 535, 538, 93 S. Ct. 872, 875, 35 L. Ed. 2d 56, 60 (1973). Almost simultaneously, the mother of an illegitimate child sought to compel a local district attorney to bring a criminal prosecution of the child's father for failure to render support. She relied on a Texas statute which had been consistently applied only to fathers of legitimate children and argued that the same remedy should be available in respect of her illegitimate child. The Supreme Court denied the mother's claim on technical grounds related to standing. Linda R.S. v. Richard D., 410 U.S. 614, 93 S. Ct. 1146, 35 L. Ed. 2d 536 (1973).

38. *E.g.,* Huss v. DeMott, 215 Kan. 450, 524 P.2d 743 (1974); State *ex rel.* Carrington v. Schutts, 217 Kan. 175, 535 P.2d 982 (1975).

some have been satisfied with less,[39] and still others may continue to provide more.[40]

Rounding off this phase of its involvement, the U.S. Supreme Court, in *Cahill*,[41] struck down a New Jersey welfare statute which discriminated against illegitimates, with only Justice Rehnquist dissenting. In *Jimenez*, [42] the Court held unconstitutional a provision of the Social Security Act relating to disability benefits because it discriminated between two classes of nonmarital children: (1) those entitled to inherit from the parent under state law, or those who are legitimated under state law or whose illegitimacy is the result of a formal defect in the parents' ceremonial marriage; and (2) those who do not fall into either category. Justice Rehnquist again dissented, calling the Court's opinion a "perplexing three-legged stool."

This series of cases seemed to signal a victorious end to the struggle for the nonmarital child. Since that time, state and lower federal courts have readily granted the nonmarital child relief in a large variety of cases, with

---

39. *See* Ellen N. v. Stuart K., 88 Misc. 2d 280, 387 N.Y.S.2d 367 (1976); Fener v. Fener, 58 A. D. 529, 395 N.Y.S.2d 197 (1977).

40. *Cf.,* McKamey v. Watkins, 257 Ind. 195, 273 N.E.2d 542 (1971).

41. New Jersey Welfare Rights Organization v. Cahill, 411 U.S. 619, 93 S. Ct. 1700, 36 L. Ed. 2d 543 (1973).

42. Jimenez v. Weinberger, 417 U.S. 628, 94 S. Ct. 2496, 41 L. Ed. 2d 363 (1974). *See also* Lucas v. Sec. of HEW, 390 F. Supp. 1310 (D.R.I. 1975), *rev'd,* 427 U.S. 495, 96 S. Ct. 2755, 49 L. Ed. 2d 651 (1976), and *cf.,* Norton v. Weinberger, 364 F. Supp. 1117 (D. Md. 1973), *remanded* for reconsideration in the light of *Jimenez*, 418 U.S. 902, 94 S. Ct. 3191, 41 L. Ed. 2d 1150 (1974), but not changed on reconsideration. The dissent by Judge Winter seems to state the better law, Norton v. Weinberger, 390 F. Supp. 1084 (D. Md. 1975). Final disposition: Norton v. Mathews, 427 U.S. 524, 96 S. Ct. 2771, 49 L. Ed. 2d 672 (1976).

awards ranging from workmen's compensation [43] to social security.[44]

Doubt concerning the Supreme Court's intentions and renewed concern about consistency resurfaced in 1976, when the Court decided *Mathews v. Lucas* [45] adversely to the nonmarital child. The case involved a section of the Social Security Act that conditions a child's eligibility for father-related benefits on its dependency upon the father. Writing for the majority, Justice Blackmun cited administrative convenience and allowed the Act to *presume* dependency with respect to marital and numerous categories of nonmarital children with ascertained paternity, and to leave the task of proving actual dependency to nonmarital children that do not fall into the defined subclasses.[46] Dissenting Justices Stevens, Brennan, and Marshall found *Lucas* too difficult to distinguish from *Jimenez* to warrant a dissimilar holding.

On its narrow facts, this case is not particularly important, although it truly is all but indistinguishable from *Jimenez.* As a "signal," its outer dimensions were sufficiently unclear to give the nonmarital child new cause for concern — at least until 1977.

In 1977, a further change occurred in the Supreme

---

43. Carr v. Campbell Soup Co., 124 N.J. Super. 382, 307 A.2d 126 (1973); Lehigh Foundation, Inc. v. Commonwealth, 39 Pa. Commw. Ct. 416, 395 A.2d 576 (1978); Westinghouse v. Commonwealth, 39 Pa. Commw. Ct. 42, 394 A.2d 1071 (1978).

44. Beaty v. Weinberger, 478 F.2d 300 (5th Cir. 1973).

45. 427 U.S. 495, 96 S. Ct. 2755, 49 L. Ed. 2d 651 (1976); Norton v. Mathews, 427 U.S. 524, 96 S. Ct. 2771, 49 L. Ed. 2d 672 (1976). The *Lucas* trend is followed by Kimbrell v. Mathews, 429 F. Supp. 440 (M.D. La. 1977) (deceased rather than disabled father); *cf.,* Gentry v. U.S., 546 F.2d 343 (U.S. Ct. Cls. 1976).

46. Mathews v. Lucas, 427 U.S. 495, 497-99, 96 S. Ct. 2755, 2758-59, 49 L. Ed. 2d 651, 656-67 (1976).

Judicial Attitude: In *Trimble v. Gordon*,[47] the Court reversed a decision by the Illinois Supreme Court which — fully in accord with *Labine*[48] — had denied the nonmarital child intestate succession rights involving its father. The Court essentially overruled *Labine,* although it did not quite admit that much. Struggling to distinguish the older case, the Court ultimately confessed that "to the extent that our analysis in this case differs from that in *Labine* the more recent analysis controls."[49]

Perplexingly, a companion decision reserved immigration as one area in which discrimination on the basis of illegitimacy will be allowed. *Fiallo v. Bell*[50] held that the immigration laws' preference for foreign-born nonmarital children of female U.S. citizens over children of male U.S. citizens somehow does withstand the test of rationality. Justices Marshall, Brennan and White dissented in no uncertain terms and reached the only consistent (as well as fair) conclusion.[51]

In 1978, the seesawed observer had to contend with a retreat from *Trimble v. Gordon* and a partial resurrection of *Labine. Lalli*[52] upheld a New York statute that conditioned a nonmarital child's right to intestate succession upon its having had its paternity judicially established during the

---

47. 430 U.S. 762, 97 S. Ct. 1459, 52 L. Ed. 2d 31 (1977).

48. Labine v. Vincent, 401 U.S. 532, 91 S. Ct. 1017, 28 L. Ed. 2d 288 (1971).

49. Trimble v. Gordon, 430 U.S. at 776, 97 S. Ct. at 1468, 52 L. Ed. 2d at 43 (1977).

50. 430 U.S. 787, 97 S. Ct. 1473, 52 L. Ed. 2d 50 (1977). *Cf.,* In the Matter of Maloney, Board of Immigration Appeals, — I. & N. Dec. —, (12/21/78) [5 F.L.R. 2319]; In the Matter of Wong, Board of Immigration Appeals, — I. & N. Dec. — (2/6/78) [5 F.L.R. 2320].

51. Fiallo v. Bell, 430 U.S. 800, 97 S. Ct. 1482, 52 L. Ed. 61 (Marshall, J., dissenting, 1977). *See* H. KRAUSE, ILLEGITIMACY: LAW AND SOCIAL POLICY 102-03 (1971).

52. Lalli v. Lalli, 439 U.S. 259, 99 S. Ct. 518, 58 L. Ed. 2d 503 (1978).

father's lifetime. Thus it opened the door to the denial of succession rights to nonmarital children whose paternity is known beyond doubt, but whose paternity had not been formally established in court while the father was alive. Justice Blackmun said:

> I agree with the result the Court has reached and concur in its judgment. I also agree with much that has been said in the plurality opinion. My point of departure, of course, is at the plurality's valiant struggle to distinguish, rather than overrule, *Trimble v. Gordon....*
>
> It seems to me that the Court today gratifyingly reverts to the principles set forth in *Labine v. Vincent.* What Mr. Justice Black said for the Court in *Labine* applied with equal force to the present case and, as four of us thought, to the Illinois situation with which *Trimble* was concerned.
>
> I would overrule *Trimble,* but the Court refrains from doing so on the theory that the result in *Trimble* is justified because of the peculiarities of the Illinois Probate Act there under consideration. This, of course, is an explanation, but, for me, it is an unconvincing one. I therefore must regard *Trimble* as a derelict, explainable only because of the overtones of its appealing facts and offering little precedent for constitutional analysis of State intestate succession laws." [53]

The dissenters — Justices Brennan, White, Marshall and Stevens — cogently observed:

> All interested parties concede that Robert Lalli is the son of Mario Lalli. Mario Lalli supported Robert during his son's youth. Mario Lalli formally acknowledged Robert Lalli as his son. Yet, for want of a judicial order of filiation entered during Mario's lifetime, Robert Lalli is denied his intestate share of his father's estate.

---

53. *Id.,* 439 U.S. at 276-77, 99 S. Ct. at 529, 58 L. Ed. 2d at 516 (Blackmun, J., concurring).

There is no reason to suppose that the injustice of the present case is aberrant. Indeed it is difficult to imagine an instance in which an illegitimate child acknowledged and voluntarily supported by his father, would ever inherit intestate under the New York scheme. Social welfare agencies, busy as they are with errant fathers, are unlikely to bring paternity proceedings against fathers who support their children. Similarly, children who are acknowledged and supported by their father are unlikely to bring paternity proceedings against him. First, they are unlikely to see the need for such adversary proceedings. Second, even if aware of the rule requiring judicial filiation orders, they are likely to fear provoking disharmony by suing their father. For the same reasons, mothers of such illegitimates are unlikely to bring proceedings against the father. Finally, fathers who do not even bother to make out wills (and thus die intestate) are unlikely to take the time to bring formal filiation proceedings. Thus, as a practical matter, by requiring judicial filiation orders entered during the lifetime of the father, the New York statute makes it virtually impossible for acknowledged and freely supported illegitimate children to inherit intestate. . . .

I see no reason to retreat from our decision in *Trimble v. Gordon.* The New York statute on review here, like the Illinois statute in *Trimble,* excludes "forms of proof which do not compromise the State['s] interests." The statute thus discriminates against illegitimates through means not substantially related to the legitimate interests that the statute purports to promote. I would invalidate the statute.[54]

Looking at the *Lalli* facts through a microscope, Justice Powell (joined by Chief Justice Burger and Justice Stewart; Justices Rehnquist and Blackmun concurred in the judgment separately) explained the Court's deviation from

---

54. *Id.,* 439 U.S. at 277-78, 99 S. Ct. at 529-30, 58 L. Ed. 2d at 517-18 [some citations omitted].

132

the *Trimble* rationale by pointing out that the statute involved in *Trimble* did not even allow an adjudication of paternity to create eligibility under the intestacy laws, so that it involved a broader disqualification than that involved in *Lalli:*

> The Illinois statute . . . was constitutionally flawed because, by insisting upon not only an acknowledgment by the father, but also the marriage of the parents, it excluded "at least some significant categories of illegitimate children of intestate men [whose] inheritance rights can be recognized without jeopardizing the orderly settlement of estates or the dependability of titles to property passing under intestacy laws." We concluded that the Equal Protection Clause required that a statute placing exceptional burdens on illegitimate children in the furtherance of proper state objectives must be more "carefully tuned to alternative considerations," . . . quoting *Mathews v. Lucas,* . . . than was true of the broad disqualification in the Illinois law.
>
> Under § 4-1.2 [the New York statute], by contrast, the marital status of the parents is irrelevant. The single requirement at issue here is an evidentiary one — that the paternity of the father be declared in a judicial proceeding sometime before his death. The child need not have been legitimated in order to inherit from his father. Had the appellant in *Trimble* been governed by § 4-1.2, she would have been a distributee of her father's estate.[55]

The distinction sought to be drawn is there, but does not convince. It harks back to Justice Harlan's dissent in *Levy* and *Glona:*

> [F]or many of the same reasons why a State is empowered to require formalities in the first place, a

---

55. *Id.,* 439 U.S. at 266-67, 99 S. Ct. at 523-24, 58 L. Ed. 2d at 510-11 (1978) [citations omitted].

State may choose to simplify a particular proceeding by reliance on formal papers rather than a contest of proof. That suits for wrongful death, actions to determine the heirs of intestates, and the like, must as a constitutional matter deal with every claim of biological paternity or maternity on its merits is an exceedingly odd proposition.[56]

This argument should have failed in *Lalli* as it had failed before: Inheritance should be denied in the absence of proof of paternity, but granted in the presence of proof. It is not rational categorically to exclude *all* proof of paternity other than marriage to the mother, a paternity judgment, or legitimation. This is not to say that some *rational* standard of proof should not be set to prevent frivolous claims or harassment. Justices Harlan and Powell fairly invoked the state interest in "the just and orderly disposition of property at death." And they were correct in emphasizing that, in paternity matters, proof tends to disappear more quickly than in other areas and the potential for fraud and blackmail abounds. However, in cases with facts such as *Lalli*, the disposition of property on the father's death would have been considerably more "just and orderly" had the child's claim been allowed. As Justices Brennan, White, Marshall and Stevens pointed out, "the New York statute

---

56. 391 U.S. at 80-81, 88 S. Ct. at 1518, 20 L. Ed. 2d 446-47 (1968). Justice Powell put the point more politely in *Lalli:*

The primary state goal underlying the challenged aspects of § 4-1.2 is to provide for the just and orderly disposition of property at death. [Footnote 6: The presence in this case of the State's interest in the orderly disposition of a decedent's property at death distinguishes it from others in which that justification for an illegitimacy-based classification was absent.] We long have recognized that this is an area with which the States have an interest of considerable magnitude. This interest is directly implicated in paternal inheritance by illegitimate children because of the peculiar problems of proof that are involved.

439 U.S. at 267, 99 S. Ct. at 24, 58 L. Ed. 2d at 511 (1978) [citation omitted].

makes it virtually impossible for acknowledged and freely supported illegitimate children to inherit intestate."

The flaw in the Court's position is that too much latitude is given the states to draw the range of acceptable proof too narrowly:

> In affirming the judgment below, we do not, of course, restrict a State's freedom to require proof of paternity by means other than a judicial decree. Thus a State may prescribe any formal method of proof, whether it be similar to that provided by § 4-1.2 or some other regularized procedure that would assure the authenticity of the acknowledgment. As we noted in *Trimble*, such a procedure would be sufficient to satisfy the State's interests.[57]

---

57. Lalli v. Lalli, 439 U.S. at 272, 99 S. Ct. at 526, 58 L. Ed. at 513. *See also id.* at 274-75, 99 S. Ct. at 528, 58 L. Ed. 2d at 515 (1978):

The dissent of Mr. Justice BRENNAN would reduce the opinion in *Trimble v. Gordon*, to a simplistic holding that the Constitution *requires* a State, in a case of this kind, to recognize as sufficient any "formal acknowledgment of paternity." This reading of *Trimble* is based on a single phrase lifted from a footnote. *Id.,* at 772, n. 14, 97 S.Ct. at 1466. It ignores both the broad rationale of the Court's opinion and the context in which the note and the phrase relied upon appear. The principle that the footnote elaborates is that the States are free to recognize the problems arising from different forms of proof and to select those forms "carefully tailored to eliminate imprecise and unduly burdensome methods of establishing paternity." *Ibid.* The New York Legislature, with the benefit of the Bennett Commission's study, exercised this judgment when it considered and rejected the possibility of accepting evidence of paternity less formal than a judicial order. Fourth Report of the Temporary State Commission on the Modernization, Revision and Simplification of the Law of Estates, Legis.Doc.1965, No. 19, at 266-267.

The "formal acknowledgment" contemplated by *Trimble* is such as would minimize postdeath litigation, *i. e.,* a regularly prescribed, legally recognized method of acknowledging paternity. See n. 8, *supra.* It is thus plain that footnote 14 in *Trimble* does not sustain the dissenting opinion. Indeed, the document relied upon by the dissent is not an acknowledgment of paternity at all. It is a simple "Certificate of Consent" that was required at the time by New York for the marriage of a minor. It consists of one sentence:

"This is to certify that I, who have hereto subscribed my name, do

Moreover, the Court accepts the paternity action without adequate regard to "real life." The truth is that paternity actions permitted by the states vary widely and all too often flagrantly ignore the best interests of the child — when the action is brought and more importantly, in the context of *Lalli,* when the action is *not* brought. The significant question that should have been addressed — before the Court relied so blindly on state law governing paternity actions — is what the states may and must do to offer the nonmarital child a fair chance to have its paternity established. That question has not yet been considered in any of the cases; although the Court had at least one opportunity to do so.[58]

It comes as no surprise that after *Labine, Trimble* and *Lalli,* state courts have reached widely varying holdings on the same, similar and related inheritance issues,[59]

---

hereby consent that Robert Lalli who is my son and who is under the age of 21 years, shall be united in marriage to Janice Bivens by an [sic] minister of the gospel or other person authorized by law to solemnize marriages. App. A-16.

Mario Lalli's signature to this document was acknowledged by a notary public, but the certificate contains no oath or affirmation as to the truth of its contents. The notary did no more than confirm the identity of Lalli. Because the certificate was executed for the purpose of giving consent to marry, not of proving biological paternity, the meaning of the words "my son" is ambiguous. One can readily imagine that had Robert Lalli's half-brother, who was not Mario's son but who took the surname Lalli and lived as a member of his household, sought permission to marry, Mario might also have referred to him as "my son" on a consent certificate.

The important state interests of safeguarding the accurate and orderly disposition of property at death, emphasized in *Trimble* and reiterated in our opinion today, could be frustrated easily if there were a constitutional rule that any notarized but unsworn statement identifying an individual as a "child" must be accepted as adequate proof of paternity regardless of the context in which the statement was made.

58. S. v. D., 410 U.S. 614, 73 S. Ct. 1146, 35 L. Ed. 2d 536 (1973).

59. (1) Statutes requiring an acknowledgment of paternity by the putative father during his lifetime before the illegitimate child may receive an intestate share of father's estate have been upheld: Mitchell

including the question of whether the omitted nonmarital child has a claim under the state's pretermitted heir statute.[60]

The last illegitimacy case of the October 1978 term was *Califano v. Boles.*[61] Involved were "mother's insurance benefits" which, under the Social Security Act, are available only to divorced wives or widows of deceased wage earners. This provision was upheld against the claim of an unmarried mother, Justice Rehnquist arguing as follows:

> We conclude that the legislation in this case does not have the impact on illegitimates necessary to warrant further inquiry whether § 202(g) is the product of

v. Freuler, 297 N.C. 206, 254 S.E.2d 762 (1979); Outlaw v. Planters Nat. Bank & Trust, 41 N.C. App. 571, 255 S.E.2d 189 (1979).

(2) Some states continue to require that a formal order of filiation have been made during the father's lifetime: Matter of Johnson's Estate, 560 P.2d 962 (Okla. 1977); Matter of Murray's Estate, 90 Misc. 2d 852, 396 N.Y.S.2d 149 (1977).

(3) Other statutes allow various methods of demonstrating paternity, even after the putative father's death: C.L.W. v. M.J., 254 N.W.2d 446 (N.D. 1977); Robinson v. Kolstad, 84 Wis. 579, 267 N.W.2d 886 (1978); *In re* Estate of Blumreich, 84 Wis. 545, 267 N.W.2d 870 (1978).

(4) At least before *Trimble,* some courts flatly held it constitutional for a state to exclude illegitimates from inheriting property from their natural intestate fathers: Rias v. Henderson, 342 So. 2d 737 (Miss. 1977); Murray v. Murray, 549 S.W.2d 839 (Ky. App. 1977); *but cf.,* Pendleton v. Pendleton, 560 S.W.2d 538 (Ky. 1977) (holding the same statute to be violative of the equal protection clause.)

(5) Before and after *Trimble,* more courts, however, held such a blanket exclusion (of illegitimate children from intestate succession, or a requirement that the child's parents had married subsequent to its birth) a violation of equal protection guarantees: Allen v. Califano, 456 F. Supp. 168 (D. Md. 1978); *In re* Succession of Thompson, 367 So. 2d 796 (1979); Rudolph v. Rudolph, 556 S.W.2d 152 (Ky. App. 1977); Matter of Sharp's Estate, 163 N.J. Super. 148, 394 A.2d 381 (1978); Matter of Sharp's Estate, 151 N.J. Super. 579, 377 A.2d 730 (1977).

60. Hanson v. Markham, 371 Mass. 296, 356 N.E.2d 702 (1976).

61. 443 U.S. 282, 99 S. Ct. 2767, 61 L. Ed. 2d 541 (1979).

discriminatory purposes. "Mother's insurance benefits" are distinct from "child's insurance benefits." The latter are benefits paid to the minor children of the deceased wage earner and, as noted, [plaintiff's] son did receive child's insurance benefits. The benefit to a child as a result of the parent or guardian's receipt of mother's insurance benefits is incidental: mother's insurance benefit payments do not vary with the number of children within the recipient's care, they are not available in the foster care context, and they are lost on remarriage or if the surviving parent earns a substantial income — all despite the needs of the child. Thus the focus of *these* benefits is on the economic dilemma of the surviving spouse or former spouse; the child's needs as such are addressed through the separate child's insurance benefits.[62]

Justices Marshall, Brennan, White and Blackmun dissented:

[O]nly by disregarding the clear legislative history, structure, and effect of the Mother's Insurance Benefits Program can the Court characterize dependent spouses, rather than children, as the intended beneficiaries of § 202(g) .... Indeed, the author of today's opinion for the Court concurred separately in *Wiesenfeld* on the ground that an examination of the legislative history and statutory context of § 202(g) "convincingly demonstrates that the *only* purpose of [§ 202(g)] is to make it possible for children of deceased contributing workers to have the personal care and attention of a surviving parent. 420 U.S. at 655 (Rehnquist, J., concurring, emphasis added). That same legislative history and statutory context now persuade the Court that the "animating concern" of § 202(g) is to assist a surviving spouse, and that any benefit to a child is merely "incidental." I cannot agree. ... The constitutional infirmities identified in *Jimenez* are equally evident in this case; that statute, like § 202(g),

---

62. *Id.* 443 U.S. at 294, 99 S. Ct. at 2775, 61 L. Ed. 2d at 551 (1979). [Citations and footnotes omitted, emphasis in original].

was over-inclusive to the extent it aided legitimate children not actually dependent on the insured wage earner, and under-inclusive to the extent it withheld assistance from illegitimate children who were in fact dependent. And here, as in *Jimenez,* it serves no purpose consistent with the aims of the Social Security Act to deny illegitimates all opportunity to establish their dependence and their concomitant right to insurance benefits. See 417 U.S., at 636, 41 L.Ed.2d 363, 94 S.Ct. 2496.

We cannot, of course, expect perfect congruence between legislative ends and means in the administration of a complex statutory scheme. But neither should we give our imprimatur to distinctions needlessly predicated on a disfavored social status, particularly one beyond an individual's power to affect. Although a "blanket and conclusive exclusion" of illegitimate children may be an administratively expedient means of screening for dependence under § 202(g), see *Jimenez v. Weinberger,* 417 U.S. at 636, it is also inaccurate, unjust, and, under this Court's settled precedents, unconstitutional.[63]

This case is not the end of the line.[64]

3. The Unmarried Father and His Child.

The U.S. Supreme Court also had occasion to deal with the converse of the child's right to its father — the father's rights concerning his nonmarital child. Three decisions were rendered in 1972. The leading case gave the father an imprecisely defined interest in his nonmarital child's custody and has caused difficulty with the adoption process in many states.

In *Stanley,*[65] a father who had long lived with the mother

---

63. *Id.* 443 U.S. at 297-306, 99 S. Ct. at 2777-81, 61 L. Ed. 2d at 553-59 (1979). [Footnotes omitted].

64. *Infra* Text at note 111 *et seq.*

65. Stanley v. Illinois, 405 U.S. 645, 92 S. Ct. 1208, 31 L. Ed. 2d 551 (1972).

and his nonmarital children in a *de facto* family unit was held entitled to notice and a hearing in proceedings involving the custody of his children. In *Rothstein*,[66] the Court remanded to the Wisconsin Supreme Court, for decision in the light of *Stanley,* a case involving an unmarried father challenging a completed adoption. In *Vanderlaan,*[67] the Court remanded to an appellate court of Illinois a case involving a father's claim to visitation rights concerning his nonmarital children.

These cases exerted a significant effect on adoptions of children born out of wedlock.[68] Even today, after several U.S. Supreme Court cases on related issues, substantial uncertainty persists concerning the extent of the father's rights in this context. Early, the Supreme Court of Illinois applied *Stanley* to a fact situation involving an alleged father who claimed his nonmarital child from an adoption agency to which the mother had surrendered the child upon birth.[69] The Wisconsin Supreme Court, in deciding the *Rothstein* remand, held that there can be no valid adoption without a valid termination of parental rights of the

---

66. Rothstein v. Lutheran Social Services of Wisconsin and Upper Michigan, 405 U.S. 1051, 92 S. Ct. 1488, 31 L. Ed. 2d 786 (1972).

67. Vanderlaan v. Vanderlaan, 405 U.S. 1051, 92 S. Ct. 1488, 31 L. Ed. 2d 787 (1972).

68. Before *Stanley,* the adoption of a child born out of wedlock was wholly under the mother's control in most states. In several states, however, the unwed father had long been heard on the question of adoption where he had acknowledged the child in some way, where he had adequately contributed to the support of the child, or where paternity had been established by the court. A few states specify that the unmarried father may adopt his child. With respect to the father's right of visitation, specific statutory direction remains scant. Some courts all along would grant visitation in appropriate circumstances. Since *Stanley* and its progeny, more courts have gone this route.

69. People *ex rel.* Slawek v. Covenant Children's Home, 52 Ill. 2d 20, 284 N.E.2d 291 (1972).

unmarried father.[70] Many lower state courts interpreted *Stanley* very broadly, probably too broadly, and the adoption process has become cumbersome. Other courts have taken a more daring approach and have all but read the most inconvenient features of *Stanley* out of the picture.[71] That approach may run the risk of making adoption less secure, although the U.S. Supreme Court has not insisted on clamping down.[72] The crux of the problem remains the (in)famous "Footnote 9" contained in *Stanley:*

> We note in passing that the incremental cost of offering unwed fathers an opportunity for individualized hearings on fitness appears to be minimal. If unwed fathers, in the main, do not care about the disposition of their children, they will not appear to demand hearings. If they do care, under the scheme here held invalid, Illinois would admittedly at some later time have to afford them a properly focused hearing in a custody or adoption proceeding.
> Extending opportunity for hearing to unwed fathers

---

70. State *ex rel.* Rothstein v. Lutheran Social Services of Wisconsin, 59 Wis. 2d 1, 207 N.W.2d 826 (1973).

71. *In re* Adoption of Malpica-Orsini, 36 N.Y.2d 568, 331 N.E.2d 486, 370 N.Y.S.2d 511 (1975).

72. The U.S. Supreme Court dismissed *Malpica, supra* note 71, for alleged want of a substantial federal question, *sub nom.,* Orsini v. Blasi, 423 U.S. 1042, 92 S. Ct. 765, 46 L. Ed. 2d 631 (1977). Later, the Court had second thoughts:

> In Orsini v. Blasi, the Court dismissed an appeal from the New York Court of Appeals challenging the constitutionality of § 111 as applied to an unmarried father whose child had been ordered adopted by a New York Surrogate. In dismissing the appeal, we indicated that a substantial federal question was lacking. This was a ruling on the merits, and therefore is entitled to precedential weight. At the same time, however, our decision not to review fully the questions presented in Orsini v. Blasi is not entitled to the same deference given a ruling after briefing, argument, and written opinion. Insofar as our decision today is inconsistent with our dismissal in *Orsini,* we overrule our prior decision."

Caban v. Mohammed, 441 U.S. 380, 390, 99 S. Ct. 1760, 1767, 60 L. Ed. 2d 297, 306 (1979).

who desire and claim competence to care for their children creates no constitutional or procedural obstacle to foreclosing those unwed fathers who are not so inclined. The Illinois law governing procedure in juvenile cases provides for personal service, notice by certified mail or for notice by publication when personal or certified mail service cannot be had or when notice is directed to unknown respondents under the style of "all whom it may concern." Unwed fathers who do not promptly respond cannot complain if their children are declared wards of the State. Those who do respond retain the burden of proving their fatherhood.[73]

In the scramble to reduce the feared impact of *Stanley* on adoptions, some legislatures let themselves be stampeded into passing more or less inadequate legislation.[74] The Uniform Parentage Act, by contrast, provides a procedure by which the rights of the *disinterested* unmarried father may be terminated with reasonable efficiency.[75] Delay and interference with the adoption process are kept to the minimum consistent with a reasonable interpretation of *Stanley*. The Act focuses on the worrisome case in which the father has not been formally ascertained and the mother seeks to surrender the child for adoption. The court must try to ascertain the identity of the father. But his potential rights may be terminated speedily, if he shows no interest in the child or if a reasonable effort provides no clue to his identity. Publication — to conform with "Footnote 9" — is not required if the court determines that such publication would not be likely to lead to identification of the father.[76]

---

73. 405 U.S. at 657, 92 S. Ct. at 1215-16, 31 L. Ed. 2d at 562 (1972).

74. *See* Freeman, *Remodeling Adoption Statutes after Stanley v. Illinois,* 15 J. FAM. L. 385 (1977).

75. UNIFORM PARENTAGE ACT § 24, 9A U.L.A. MATR., FAM. AND HEALTH LAWS 615-16 (1979).

76. UNIFORM PARENTAGE ACT § 24(e), 9A U.L.A. MATR., FAM. AND HEALTH LAWS 616 (1979).

Since that will be the typical case, the Act allows the vast majority of children to be freed for adoption very quickly. In the case in which the natural father or a man representing himself as the natural father claims custodial rights, the court is given authority to determine custodial rights. As to the determination of "unfitness," the grounds generally applicable would control. Any attempt to single out the unmarried father as unfit without a statement of objective facts probably would be unconstitutional; [77] although a provision phrased in terms of demonstrated "disinterest" within a given, reasonable period of knowledge of birth (30 days in Illinois) [78] would seem to be a sound addition to the more general ground of "abandonment" or "desertion." In a case in which the man alleging himself to be the father is clearly unfit, the court would proceed to terminate his potential parental rights without deciding whether he actually is or is not the father of the child. If, on the other hand, the man alleging himself to be the father and claiming custody is *prima facie* fit to have custody of the child, an action to ascertain paternity is indicated — unless the mother's agreement to a voluntary acknowledgment can be obtained in accordance with the Act.

The application of the *Stanley* case and its progeny still causes difficulties. Many courts and legislatures in many states are taking "Footnote 9" of *Stanley* sufficiently

---

77. *See* Caban v. Mohammed, 441 U.S. 380, 99 S. Ct. 1760, 60 L. Ed. 2d 297 (1979); Quilloin v. Walcott, 434 U.S. 246, 98 S. Ct. 549, 54 L. Ed. 2d 511 (1978); Stanley v. Illinois, 405 U.S. 645, 92 S. Ct. 1208, 31 L. Ed. 2d 551 (1977). If there is a "legal" father, however, the unmarried father's rights may be terminated on the basis of a hearing focusing on the best interests of the child rather than the unmarried father's fitness or unfitness. Matter of Barlow, 404 Mich. 216, 273 N.W.2d 35 (1978), *also In re* Still, 5 F.L.R. 2182 (Cook County Cir. Ct., Ill. 1978).

78. ILL. REV. STAT. ch. 40, § 1507(B)(f) (1977). *See also* ILL. REV. STAT. ch. 37, § 705-94 (1977) regarding the required notice to the putative father.

seriously to require publication in more or less embarrassing terms.[79] Clearer definitions have not yet

---

79. *E.g.,* ILL. REV. STAT. ch. 37, § 705-9.4 (1977). Consider the following sample publications: CHICAGO LAW BULL., February 15, 1978, p. 2:

ADOPTION NOTICE

STATE OF ILLINOIS, COUNTY OF COOK, SS. — In the Circuit Court of Cook County, County Division. In the matter of Petition for the adoption of Jenifer Marie Porter.

Adoption No. 78 CoA 202.

To Unknown father, and All whom it may concern, take notice that a Petition was filed in the Circuit Court of Cook County, Illinois, for the adoption of a child named Jenifer Marie Porter.

Now, therefore, unless you,

Unknown father, and All whom it may concern, file your answer to the Petition in said suit or otherwise file your appearance therein in the said Circuit Court of Cook County, Room 801, Richard J. Daley Center, in the City of Chicago, Illinois, on or before the 17th day of March, 1978, a default may be entered against you at any time after that day and a judgment entered in accordance with the prayer of said Petition.

Dated, Chicago, Illinois, February 15th, 1978.

MORGAN M. FINLEY, Clerk.

Robert E. Cronin, Attorney for Petitioners, One First National Plaza, Chicago, Illinois.

VERO BEACH PRESS JOURNAL, October 11, 1979, p. 6C:

IN THE CIRCUIT COURT
NINETEENTH JUDICIAL CIRCUIT
OF FLORIDA IN AND FOR
INDIAN RIVER COUNTY
CIVIL ACTION

CASE NO. 79-1065

IN RE: THE MATTER OF THE ADOPTION OF: AUBREY LEE ANTONE BY: HOWARD R. BARBER, PETITIONER.

NOTICE OF SUIT—NO PROPERTY

TO: AUBREY A. ANTONE, Natural Father, Residence Unknown.
YOU ARE HEREBY NOTIFIED that an action for ADOPTION OF AUBREY LEE ANTONE, MINOR, has been filed against you and you are required to serve a copy of your written defenses, if any

emerged, despite the decision of several other "father's rights" cases by the U.S. Supreme Court. The situation has

to it, on the plaintiff's attorney, whose name and address is Associated Legal Clinics, Edward J. Kennedy, Attorney, 8500 South Federal Highway, Port St. Lucie, Florida 33452, Telephone: (305) 878-5450 and file the original with the clerk of the above styled court on or before November 5, 1979: otherwise a judgment may be entered against you for the relief demanded in the complaint or petition.

WITNESS my hand and the seal of said Court on September 28, 1979.

> FREDA WRIGHT
> As Clerk of said Court
> -s-Jeanne Hine, Deputy Clerk

(Copy Ct. Ct. Seal)
Oct. 4, 11, 18, 25, 1979.

IN THE JUVENILE & FAMILY
DIVISION OF THE CIRCUIT COURT
IN AND FOR INDIAN RIVER
COUNTY, FLORIDA

CASE NO. 79-558

IN THE INTEREST OF: Baby Boy Moody. Born: August 25, 1979, Dependent Child.
THE STATE OF FLORIDA — TO:
  Unknown father of Baby Boy Moody
  Residence Unknown

NOTICE

You are hereby notified that a Petition under oath, copy of which is delivered to you herewith, has been filed in the above styled Court for the permanent commitment of Baby Boy Moody, a Caucasian male child, born on the 25th day of August, 1979, at Okeechobee, Okeechobee County, State of Florida to the State of Florida, Department of Health and Rehabilitative Services, for subsequent adoption, and you are hereby commanded to be and appear before the Honorable Charles E. Smith, Judge of the Circuit Court in the above Court at: Indian River County Courthouse, Room 232, 14th Avenue, Vero Beach, Florida, at 4:00 P.M. o'clock, on the 2nd day of November, A.D. 1979, and to show cause why said Petition should not be granted.

A response to the above Court is required within 20 days from the date you are served, excluding the day of service. Failure to

145

not been helped by dicta in several Supreme Court cases deciding other issues to the effect that the father and child relationship, as "familial relations," may merit stricter scrutiny than other classifications on the basis of illegitimacy.[80]

Quilloin v. Walcott,[81] in 1978, denied an unmarried father a "veto power" over the adoption of his child. Unfortunately, that case involved sufficiently unusual facts that it did little to clarify the murky situation in which the adoption industry had found itself after *Stanley.* In contrast to the law of most states, the Georgia law involved in *Quilloin* gave the unmarried father an opportunity to legitimate his nonmarital child and thereby gain full parental rights with respect to the child's adoption. However, for eleven years, the father had not availed himself of this opportunity. He had not sought, and did not now seek custody of his child, although he now sought legitimation and visitation rights. Moreover, throughout the period, the father had only "irregularly" supported the child (although the mother had never brought a support action) and the child had been in

---

respond within 20 days, or failure to appear at the hearing shall constitute consent to permanent commitment.

WITNESS my hand as the Clerk of said Court and the Seal thereof, this 2nd day of October A.D., 1979.

FREDA WRIGHT, CLERK

By:-s-Janice M. Randall, Deputy Clerk

Oct. 4, 11, 18, 25, 1979.

See also In re Cecilie, Ann T., — Misc. 2d —, — N.Y.S.2d — [6 F.L.R. 2057] (Surr. Ct. 1978), where the court criticized the needless expense and bother of a technical notice requirement when the putative fathers are simply "fleeting disinterested impregnators." *Cf., In re* "Male F'", 97 Misc. 2d 505, 411 N.Y.S.2d 982 (1978), dealing with the conflict between the requirement of notice to the unmarried father and the need to maintain confidentiality in adoption proceedings.

80. *Infra* text at note 107. See Locke v. Ladd, 119 N.H. 136, 399 A.2d 962 (1979).

81. 434 U.S. 246, 98 S. Ct. 549, 54 L. Ed. 2d 511 (1978).

the mother's custody and had never (as had the children in *Stanley*) been a member of the father's *de facto* family. Finally, and very significantly, the child was now sought to be adopted by the mother's husband.

The Court concluded:

> the result of the adoption in this case is to give full recognition to a family unit already in existence, a result desired by all concerned, except appellant. Whatever might be required in other situations, we cannot say that the State was required in this situation to find anything more than that the adoption, and denial of legitimation, was in the "best interests of the child." [82]

It is difficult to quarrel with *Quilloin*, except in terms of its irrelevance to the vast majority of adoption situations. The Court's time and effort would have been better directed to the open question — all the more open in view of "Footnote 9" of *Stanley* [83] — as to what need be done in the typical adoption case, the case where the mother wishes to place her child for adoption at birth. This was not answered, not even by further dictum or by implication.

Another atypical case, also not answering that basic question, followed soon. Explicitly toying with the issue, Caban v. Mohammed [84] succeeded only in making it far clearer what it did *not* decide than what it did:

> The New York Court of Appeals in In re Malpica-Orsini, [36 N.Y.2d 568], suggested that the requiring of unmarried fathers' consent for adoption would pose a strong impediment for adoption because often it is impossible to locate unwed fathers when adoption proceedings are brought, whereas mothers are more likely to remain with their children. Even if the special difficulties attendant upon locating and

---

82. 434 U.S. at 255, 98 S. Ct. at 555, 54 L. Ed. 2d at 520 (1978).

83. *See* text at note 73, *supra*.

84. 441 U.S. 380, 99 S. Ct. 1760, 60 L. Ed. 2d 297 (1979).

identifying unwed fathers at birth would justify a legislative distinction between mothers and fathers of newborns, [*Because the question is not before us, we express no view whether such difficulties would justify a statute addressed particularly to newborn adoptions, setting forth more stringent requirements concerning the acknowledgment of paternity or a stricter definition of abandonment*] these difficulties need not persist past infancy. When the adoption of an older child is sought, the State's interest in proceeding with adoption cases can be protected by means that do not draw such an inflexible gender-based distinction as that made in § 111. In those cases where the father never has come forward to participate in the rearing of his child, nothing in the Equal Protection Clause precludes the State from withholding from him the privilege of vetoing the adoption of that child. Indeed, under the statute as it now stands the Surrogate may proceed in the absence of consent when the parent whose consent otherwise would be required never has come forward or has abandoned the child." [85]

Caban involved a natural father who had lived with the mother for a period of five years until they separated, their two children going with the mother. For the next two years, the father had contributed to the children's support and had seen them frequently, even after the mother married her present husband who now sought to adopt the children. Emphasizing the *de facto* relationship the natural father had maintained with his children, the Court allowed him to block the adoption.

So far, so good — the *Caban* case may provide a cornerstone for the much-needed definition of parental rights for cohabiting, unmarried couples after they "split up." Not much else can be safely said, except that it is clear today that the difference between an unmarried father who

---

85. 441 U.S. at 392-93, 99 S. Ct. at 1768, 60 L. Ed. 2d at 307 (1979). [Footnote in brackets, emphasis added].

has long lived with the children involved and the man who has not is of constitutional significance.

On another level, however, this seemingly routine case threw a serious curve. Instead of continuing to decide illegitimacy cases on the basis of comparing the relevance of legal distinctions between married and unmarried fathers in their relationship to their children, or between legitimate and illegitimate children in their legal relationship with their fathers, *Caban* foregoes that analysis in a simple footnote.[86] Surprisingly, Justice Powell decided to pursue the case on the more perilous route of sex discrimination. Comparison was made between mothers and fathers and the issue was seen as the rationality of legally distinguishing between them.[87]

Aside from drawing unnecessarily into the context of illegitimacy the many uncertainties the Supreme Court has introduced into the subject of sex discrimination under the 14th Amendment, this new approach to illegitimacy is logically faulty. It pursues the more remote, rather than the nearer comparison, properly employed in all the earlier illegitimacy cases.[88] The child is not and should not be concerned whether its father, for rational legislative purposes, is the equal of its mother. The child is concerned whether its legal position rationally differs from that of its

---

86. 441 U.S. at 393, 99 S. Ct. at 1769, 60 L. Ed. 2d at 308 (1979).

87. Justice Powell may have taken his cue from Judge Fuchsberg of the New York Court of Appeals, dissenting in Orsini v. Blasi, 36 N.Y.2d 568, 591, 331 N.E.2d 486, 502, 370 N.Y.S.2d 511, 533 (1975).

88. In Quilloin v. Walcott, 434 U.S. 246, 253, 98 S. Ct. 549, 553, 54 L. Ed. 2d 511, 518 (1978), the potentiality of the sex-discrimination approach was alluded to by Justice Marshall: "In the last paragraph of his brief, appellant raises the claim that the statutes make gender-based distinctions that violate the Equal Protection Clause. Since this claim was not presented in appellant's Jurisdictional Statement, we do not consider it."

149

legitimate half sibling! [89] Similarly, the unmarried father should be compared with the married father, not with the unmarried mother.

If "sex discrimination" is to be the Court's new approach to illegitimacy, it is fraught with danger for the nonmarital child because mothers *are* different from fathers and will be, at least until the ERA is ratified. If a noticeable distinction between mothers and fathers were the proper touchstone of permissible discrimination in this field, a great variety of distinctions might be justified. Indeed, a few early decisions that did not appreciate *Levy v. Louisiana* distinguished *Levy* on precisely that ground and, for a time and in some places, halted the nonmarital child's progress toward legal equality.[90]

The case of *Parham v. Hughes*,[91] decided on the same day as *Caban,* wove together a number of strands from previous decisions. Instead of being sorted out, however, these strands now seem more tangled than ever. It may be that a solution will have to await the break-up of the unfortunate divisions that lately have so clouded the Supreme Court's line of reasoning in this area — with plurality, concurring and dissenting opinions and, it almost seems, only an occasional majority opinion, and that usually 5:4.

Specifically, *Parham* involved a father's attempt to sue for the wrongful death of his nonmarital child, whom he had supported and with whom he had maintained continuous contact by visitation. He was listed as the child's father on its birth certificate and there was no doubt regarding his paternity. No paternity action, however, had been brought

---

89. Krause, *Legitimate and Illegitimate Offspring of Levy v. Louisiana — First Decisions on Equal Protection and Paternity,* 36 U. CHI. L. REV. 338, 340-41 (1969).

90. *Id.*

91. 441 U.S. 347, 99 S. Ct. 1742, 60 L. Ed. 2d 269 (1979).

to establish his paternity legally (a strand from *Lalli*),[92] nor had he availed himself of the opportunity under Georgia law to legitimate his child (a strand from *Quilloin*).[93] The plurality opinion by Justice Stewart rejected the father's claim on the logical basis — though in direct conflict with *Glona* [94] — that his was not an immutable status (a strand from *Weber*).[95]

The father's claim of sex discrimination also was denied, on the ground that:

> [t]he fact is that mothers and fathers of illegitimate children are not similarly situated. Under Georgia law, only a father can by voluntary unilateral action make an illegitimate child legitimate. Unlike the mother of an illegitimate child whose identity will rarely be in doubt, the identity of the father will frequently be unknown. [Citing *Lalli*] By coming forward with a motion under § 74-103 of the Georgia Code, however, a father can both establish his identity and make his illegitimate child legitimate.[96]

Justice Powell's separate concurrence, by re-emphasizing the gender-based approach he had pioneered in *Caban,* did not improve the situation.[97] Worse, even the four dissenters (Justices White, Brennan, Marshall and Blackmun) chose to view this case primarily in terms of sex discrimination — perhaps to the lasting disadvantage of further

---

92. Lalli v. Lalli, 439 U.S. 259, 99 S. Ct. 518, 58 L. Ed. 2d 503 (1978).

93. Quilloin v. Walcott, 434 U.S. 246, 98 S. Ct. 549, 54 L. Ed. 2d 511 (1979).

94. Glona v. American Guaranty & Liab. Ins. Co., 391 U.S. 73, 88 S. Ct. 1515, 20 L. Ed. 2d 441 (1968).

95. Weber v. Aetna Cas. & Surety Co., 406 U.S. 164, 92 S. Ct. 1400, 31 L. Ed. 2d 768 (1972).

96. 441 U.S. at 355-56, 99 S. Ct. 1747-48, 60 L. Ed. 2d 277 (1979).

97. 441 U.S. at 359, 99 S. Ct. at 1749-50, 60 L. Ed. 2d at 279-80 (Powell, J., concurring, 1979).

constitutional litigation in the area of illegitimacy.[98] Given this lapse, the dissenters' correct analysis of *Glona's* relevance provides only slight consolation:

> Unmarried mothers and those fathers who legitimate their children but remain unmarried presumably also defy the state interest in "the integrity of the family unit." In any event, it is untenable to conclude that denying parents a right to recover when their illegitimate children die will further the asserted state interests. In Glona v. American Guaranty & Liability Insurance Co., 391 U.S. 73, 88 S.Ct. 1515, 20 L.Ed.2d 441 (1968), we were faced with the same argument in the context of an unmarried mother's attempt to recover for her child's death in a State allowing wrongful death suits by parents of legitimate children. Even though that mother — like appellant in this case — had not pursued a statutory procedure whereby she could have unilaterally legitimated her child and thereby become eligible to sue for the child's death, we held that it was impermissible to prevent her from seeking to recover. What we said in *Glona* about unmarried mothers applies equally to unmarried fathers:
>
> "[W]e see no possible rational basis . . . for assuming that if the natural mother is allowed recovery for the wrongful death of her illegitimate child, the cause of illegitimacy will be served. It would, indeed, be farfetched to assume that women have illegitimate children so that they can be compensated in damages for their death." [99]

That *Glona* might and perhaps should originally have been decided differently from *Levy* on precisely the ground exhumed by the majority, *i.e.,* that the parent in question had control over his or her status, is another matter —

---

98. 441 U.S. at 361, 99 S. Ct. at 1750, 60 L. Ed. 2d at 281 (Brennan, J., dissenting, 1979).

99. 441 U.S. at 363, 99 S. Ct. at 1752, 60 L. Ed. 2d at 282 (Brennan, J., dissenting, 1979).

Glona might have, but did not avail itself of that reasoning.[100]

The sorriest aspect of *Parham*, however, is that while it did much to cloud further the line of analysis to be applied in illegitimacy cases, it did little to clarify the law on the limited issue before the court: the father's right to recover for the wrongful death of his nonmarital child. As mentioned in connection with *Quilloin,* not many states offer the father a procedure to legitimate his child. By the Court's specific words, the relevance of *Parham* is limited to these states: "[W]e need not decide whether a statute which completely precluded fathers, as opposed to mothers, of illegitimate children from maintaining a wrongful death action would violate the Equal Protection Clause." [101]

4. Scrutiny, With Teeth or Without?

Mathews v. Lucas [102] was the first decision to speak specifically to one other matter which all preceding U.S. Supreme Court cases had almost teasingly neglected. The question whether, as a legislative criterion, illegitimacy invites "strict scrutiny" [103] had interested this observer even

---

100. *See* Krause, *Legitimate and Illegitimate Offspring of Levy v. Louisiana — First Decisions on Equal Protection and Paternity,* 36 U. CHI. L. REV. 338, 343-44 (1969).

101. 441 U.S. at —, 99 S. Ct. at 1748, 60 L. Ed. 2d at 277 (1979).

102. 427 U.S. 495, 96 S. Ct. 2755, 49 L. Ed. 2d 651 (1976).

103. H. KRAUSE, FAMILY LAW IN A NUTSHELL 19-20 (1976):

The equal protection test is "rationality." Law is subjected to the question whether a given regulation accords with permissible legislative purposes....

Without attempting to be entirely accurate in this short space, the operation of the Equal Protection Clause of the Fourteenth Amendment (which simply states that "no state shall ... deny to any person within its jurisdiction the equal protection of the laws") may be summarized as requiring that legislation must operate equally upon all members of a group that is defined reasonably and in terms of a proper legislative purpose. The courts will examine a legislative scheme "to determine whether it rationally furthers some legitimate, articulated state purpose and therefore does not constitute invidious discrimination" (San Antonio Ind. School Dist.

before *Levy*[104] and was the subject of much concern and debate after.[105] Now it was answered in the negative by Justice Blackmun:

> Appellees do not suggest, nor could they successfully, that strict judicial scrutiny of the statutory classifications is required here because, in regulating entitlement to survivorship benefits, the statute discriminatorily interferes with interests of constitutional fundamentality. *Weinberger v. Salfi,* 422 U.S. 749, 768-770, 95 S.Ct. 2457, 2468-2469, 45 L.Ed.2d 522 (1975), *Dandridge v. Williams,* 397 U.S. 471, 90 S.Ct. 1153, 25 L.Ed.2d 491 (1970).
>
> The Court, of course, has found the privacy of familial relationships to be entitled to procedural due process protections from disruption by the State, whether or not those relationships were legitimized by marriage under state law. *Stanley v. Illinois,* 405 U.S. 645, 92 S.Ct. 1208, 31 L.Ed.2d 551 (1972). But the concerns relevant to that context are only tangential to the analysis here, since the statutory scheme does not interfere in any way with familial relations.[106]

v. Rodriquez, 411 U.S. 1, 93 S. Ct. 1278, 36 L. Ed. 2d 16 (1973)). Over the years, two tests have evolved to which legislation is subjected. If the legislation involves a "mere economic interest", there is the equivalent of a presumption of constitutionality, and the courts will respect almost any reason that might uphold the rationality of the legislation. If, on the other hand, a "fundamental human right" or a "suspect classification" (such as race) is involved, the scrutiny is much stricter, and the legislation will be upheld only if there is a "compelling state interest" in its favor (Shapiro v. Thompson, 394 U.S. 618, 89 S. Ct. 1327, 22 L. Ed. 2d 600 (1969)). Current constitutional theory perceives a blurring of the lines between these tests, and it is suggested that there is and should be a "sliding scale" of values and interests (Nowak, 62 Geo.L.J. 1071 (1974)).

104. Krause, *Equal Protection for the Illegitimate,* 65 MICH. L. REV. 477, 488 (1967).

105. The best of many early discussions is found in *In re* Adoption of Malpica-Orsini, 36 N.Y.2d 568, 311 N.E.2d 486, 370 N.Y.S.2d 511 (1975) (especially Judge Jones' dissent).

106. 427 U.S. at 504, 96 S. Ct. at 2761, 49 L. Ed. 2d at 660 (1976).

The cited authority suggests that this conclusion applies *at least* in the context of welfare laws and probably *not* when custody or other questions involving "familial relations" are at issue.[107] Dissenting in *Trimble v. Gordon,* Justice Rehnquist subsequently tried to summarize Supreme Court doctrine on this important point:

> Illegitimacy, which is involved in this case, has never been held by the Court to be a "suspect classification". Nonetheless, in several opinions of the Court, statements are found which suggest that although illegitimates are not members of a "suspect class," laws which treat them differently from those born in wedlock will receive a more far-reaching scrutiny under the Equal Protection Clause than will other laws regulating economic and social conditions. [Citing *Levy, Glona, Labine, Weber, Gomez, Cahill, Jimenez.* But see *Lucas*]. The Court's opinion today contains language to that effect. In one sense this language is a source of consolation, since it suggests that parts of the Court's analysis used in this case will not be carried over to traditional "rational basis" or "minimum scrutiny" cases. At the same time, though, it is a source of confusion, since the unanswered question remains as to the precise sort of scrutiny to which classifications based on illegitimacy will be subject.[108]

Justice Rehnquist was criticizing the following words of the majority:

> Appellants urge us to hold that classifications based on illegitimacy are "suspect," so that any justifications must survive "strict scrutiny." We considered and rejected a similar argument last Term. . . . As we recognized in *Lucas,* illegitimacy is analogous in many respects to the personal characteristics that have been

---

107. *Cf.,* Roe v. Connecticut, 417 F. Supp. 769 (D. Ala. 1976).

108. 430 U.S. at 781, 97 S. Ct. at 1470-71, 52 L. Ed. 2d at 46 (Rehnquist, J., dissenting, 1977).

held to be suspect when used as the basis of statutory differentiations. We nevertheless concluded that the analogy was not sufficient to require "our most exacting scrutiny." Despite the conclusion that classifications based on illegitimacy fall in a "realm of less than strictest scrutiny," *Lucas* also establishes that the scrutiny *"is not a toothless one,"* a proposition clearly demonstrated by our previous decisions in this area. (Emphasis added).[109]

Dissenting in *Boles,* Justices Marshall, Brennan, White and Blackmun subsequently restated their view as follows:

Statutes that foreclose opportunities solely because of a child's status at birth represent a particularly invidious form of discrimination. Gomez v. Perez, 409 U.S. 535 (1973); Levy v. Louisiana, 391 U.S. 68 (1968). To penalize an illegitimate child for conduct he could not prevent and a status he cannot alter is both "illogical and unjust." Weber v. Aetna Casualty & Surety Co., 406 U.S. at 175. Accordingly, classifications based on legitimacy violate the equal protection requirements of the Fifth Amendment *unless they bear a close and substantial relationship to a permissible governmental interest.* (Emphasis added).[110]

Caveat emptor!

5. Conclusion.

In early 1980, Justice Marshall, seemingly despairing of the mess the Court has made of constitutional argument in these cases, strained to reach a decision favoring a nonmarital child's recovery under the Civil Service Retirement Act on *statutory grounds,* protesting (too

---

109. 430 U.S. at 767, 97 S. Ct. at 1463, 52 L. Ed. 2d at 37 (1977).

110. 443 U.S. at 303-04, 99 S. Ct. at 2780, 61 L. Ed. 2d at 557 (Marshall, J., dissenting, 1979).

156

much!) [111] against use of the equal protection clause [112] —

111. This is neither a complex issue, nor has it been disputed for some time. As the Court itself acknowledges, "The lower federal courts have uniformly held that the 'lived with' requirement violates the equal protection component of the Due Process Clause of the Fifth Amendment. Gentry v. United States, 212 Ct. Cl. 1, 546 F.2d 343 (1976), *rehearing denied,* 212 Ct. Cl. 27, 551 F.2d 852 (1977); Jenkins v. United States Civil Service Comm'n, 460 F. Supp. 611 (D.C. 1978); Proctor v. United States, 448 F. Supp. 418 (D.C. 1977) (three-judge court); Fenny v. United States, 441 F. Supp. 224 (E.D. Mo. 1977); Myers v. Commissioners of Civil Service Commission, Civ. No. 8682 (S.D. Ohio Aug. 8, 1977)." — U.S. —, 100 S. Ct. 895, 899, — L. Ed. 2d —, — (note 3) (1980). Should the public now conclude that these cases *may* have been wrong and that, absent the specific factual constellation of the *Clark* case the "lived with" requirement is possibly back in business? In his concurrence, Justice Powell (joined by Chief Justice Burger) worries: "I believe that the Court errs in assuming that its broad interpretation of the 'lived with' requirement will always avoid constitutional difficulty. The imposition of the "lived with" requirement as a test of actual dependency may be unconstitutional in a case in which a father had always supported, but never lived with, an illegitimate child." — U.S. —, —, 100 S. Ct. 895, 904, — L. Ed. 2d —, — (1980).

112. In U.S. v. Clark, — U.S. —, 100 S. Ct. 895, — L. Ed. 2d — (1980) the Court of Claims had granted the appellee's motion for summary judgment. Ignoring the statutory issue, that Court had granted relief on the authority of one of its earlier decisions which had held that the "lived with" requirement of 5 U.S.C. § 8341(a)(3)(A) unconstitutionally discriminated against illegitimate children. Justice Marshall held that

it is well settled that *this Court will not pass on the constitutionality of an Act of Congress if a construction of the statute is fairly possible by which the question may be avoided....*

Where both a constitutional issue and an issue of statutory construction are raised, we are not, of course, foreclosed from considering the statutory question merely because the lower court failed to address it.... Accordingly, *we turn to the statute to determine whether resolution of the constitutional question is necessary to the disposition of this case....*

If the appellee's construction of the statutory language is correct, the children are entitled to survivors' annuities and *decision of the constitutional question is unnecessary....*

The Government also urges that Congress intended the "lived with"

as though he had just communicated with Justice Oliver

requirement to serve as a means of thwarting fraudulent claims of dependency or parentage, and to promote efficient administration by facilitating the prompt identification of eligibility annuitants. It is evident from the facts of this case, however, that the classification is not narrowly tailored as a means of furthering either goal. As we recognized in Jimenez v. Weinberger, 417 U.S. 628, 636 (1974), the prevention of fraud is a legitimate goal, but it does not necessarily follow "that the blanket and conclusive exclusion of [appellee's] subclass of illegitimates is reasonably related to the prevention of spurious claims." Thus, even if the "lived with" requirement is assumed to serve as a device to prevent fraud or to promote efficient administration, *it raises serious equal protection problems that this Court must seek to avoid by adopting a saving statutory construction not at odds with fundamental legislative purposes.*

In sum, the legislative history of the 1956 amendments provides no direct guidance on the purpose of the "lived with" provision or on whether it was intended to be restricted to children living with the parent at a particular time. The less restrictive construction proposed by the appellee appears fair and reasonable in light of the language, purpose, and history of the enactment, *and it avoids a serious constitutional question. . . .*

Moreover, *the Government's position again unnecessarily raises the equal protection question,* because legitimate children and adopted children were not required to demonstrate that they had received support from the decedent. In the absence of any persuasive evidence to the contrary, therefore, we assume that Congress' failure to alter the "lived with" requirement likewise failed to modify the purpose of that provision as envisioned by the Congress that enacted it.

We conclude that the "lived with" requirement is satisfied when a recognized natural child has lived with the deceased employee in a "regular parent-child relationship," regardless of whether the child was living with the employee at the time of the employee's death. Our consideration of the language and purpose of the statute and of the available legislative history convinces us that this construction is a fair and reasonable reading of the congressional enactment.[10] *Furthermore, the construction is necessary to avoid a serious constitutional question.* [Note 10: We recognize that the Civil Service Commission has interpreted the "lived with" requirement to be a "living with" requirement, although the Government does not inform us whether the agency interpretation was contemporaneous with the 1956 enactment. We do not disregard this evidence of the meaning of the statute. See, e.g., Batterton v. Francis, 432 U.S. 416, 425, n.9 (1977). In view of our analysis of the statute and its legislative history, and *considering the need to avoid unnecessary constitutional adjudication,* however, the agency interpretation would not be decisive even if it were contemporaneous.] [Emphasis added. Some citations and footnotes omitted].

158

Wendell ("the usual last resort of constitutional arguments ...") [113] Holmes, Jr.

In a relatively short span, the U.S. Supreme Court has expended an enormous amount of time and effort on this narrow topic. The Court's engagement is remarkable because it runs counter to the long-standing "hands-off" tradition regarding family law still invoked by Justices Black and Harlan in *Levy* and *Labine*.[114] It is all the more remarkable in view of its heavy schedule. Each case the overburdened Court accepts necessarily involves the rejection of another important subject! Was it really necessary to take on some twenty full-fledged cases to decide the simple proposition that there shall be "hardly any" legal discrimination against the child of unmarried parents? By now, the confusion stirred up by eleven years of Supreme Court vacillation has cost a fortune in wasteful litigation at all levels. Chief Justice Burger's frequent complaints regarding the bar might well be turned around.[115] One well reasoned case at the outset [116] (instead of Justice Douglas' opinion in *Levy*) [117] and *per curiam*

113. Buck v. Bell, 274 U.S. 200, 208, 47 S. Ct. 584, 585, 71 L. Ed. 2d 1000, 1002 (1927).

114. *See,* dissent of Justices Harlan and Black in Levy, 391 U.S. at 76, 88 S. Ct. at 1512, 20 L. Ed. 2d at 444 (Harlan, J., dissenting, 1976). *See also* Justice Black's opinion in *Labine,* 401 U.S. 532, 91 S. Ct. 1017, 28 L. Ed. 2d 288 (1971). *Cf.,* Solomon v. Solomon, 516 F.2d 1018 (3d Cir. 1975). A detailed and thoughtful analysis of this new trend is provided by Burt, *The Constitution of the Family,* 1979 SUPREME COURT REVIEW 329-95. *Also see* Note, *The Constitution and the Family,* 93 HARV. L. REV. 1156-1383 (1980).

115. *E.g.,* 46 U.S.L.W. 2615 (1978); 63 A.B.A.J. 1412 (1977); WASHINGTON POST, August 10, 1978, p. A-11.

116. Review, as an early contender, Justice Brennan's dissent in Labine v. Vincent, 401 U.S. 532, 91 S. Ct. 1017, 28 L. Ed. 2d 288 (1971).

117. Levy v. Louisiana, 391 U.S. 68, 88 S. Ct. 1509, 20 L. Ed. 2d 436 (1968).

decisions in several of the later cases, especially in *Caban* and *Parham,* would have avoided the confusion we now face and made the future more predictable! [118] But however tortuous the road behind or ahead, we may fairly conclude from this "wealth" of decisions that state and federal law may *not* significantly discriminate between children on the basis of their parents' marital status in any significant substantive area.[119]

One question may suggest itself: why would a discourse on child support go into the detail developed in the preceding discussion? Did not *Gomez v. Perez* fix the child support obligation the father owes his nonmarital child? The answer is that the full meaning of *Gomez* in terms of

---

118. Professor Amsterdam has thoughtfully considered the constraints under which the Court must labor. Amsterdam, *Perspectives on the Fourth Amendment,* 58 MINN. L. REV. 349, 350-54 (1974). Portions of his charitable view no doubt apply here. For instance, the departure from the Court of Justices Black and Harlan made possible the Court's departure from *Labine,* both in *Weber* and in *Trimble.* But why *Lalli?* Nor are we dealing with a recent phenomenon, nor one that is limited to the area of illegitimacy. *See* Schwartz, *Foreword — The Supreme Court, October 1977 Term,* 6 HASTINGS CONST. L.Q. 1, 6 (1978):

> Critics of the Supreme Court have directed continuing animadversions against the Court's failure to follow precedent. They repeat the famous charge of Justice Roberts, made in a 1944 dissent, that it is "the present policy of the court freely to disregard and to overrule considered decisions and the rules of law announced in them." The result, said the learned judge, in one of the few bon mots he ever permitted himself while on the bench, is that adjudications of the Supreme Court are brought "into the same class as a restricted railroad ticket, good for this day and train only."

Cf., Greenawalt, *The Enduring Significance of Neutral Principles,* 78 COLUM. L. REV. 982 (1978), Hazard, *The Supreme Court as a Legislature,* 64 CORNELL L. REV. 1 (1978), Berger, *Government by Judiciary: John Hart Ely's "Invitation",* 54 IND. L. J. 277 (1979), Ely, *Constitutional Interpretivism: Its Allure and Impossibility,* 53 IND. L. J. 399 (1978).

119. *See also* Clark, *Constitutional Protection of the Illegitimate Child,* 12 U.C.D.L. REV. 383 (1979).

the likelihood of its implementation, especially in facilitating the establishment of paternity, can only be assessed in the light of the decrease in (or removal of) legal and social prejudice generally. That, in turn, is a corollary of the totality of substantive rights which now make up the nonmarital child's legal relationship with its father. Accordingly, it can hardly be overemphasized — to overcome ingrained tradition to the contrary — that the establishment of paternity now carries a meaning far broader than providing access to support, even if the latter is the initial objective.

So far, state legislatures have made inadequate efforts to enact new laws to conform with the constitutional mandate of equality. This failing is unfortunate, though perhaps forgiveable — in view of the confusing judicial signals. Consequently, the gulf between the abstract constitutional principle and the practical realization of legal equality (between marital and nonmarital children) continues to loom wide. Nowhere is it as wide, however, as in terms of inadequate procedures for ascertaining paternity, the subject so blithely ignored in *Lalli* and *S. v. D.*[120] All gains in substantive rights — prominently including support — will mean little or nothing if these procedures are not improved. Owing largely to deficient and antiquated paternity and child support enforcement statutes, only a fraction of nonmarital children now achieve legal status vis-à-vis their fathers, and collect the support they are owed.

The Uniform Parentage Act, promulgated by the National Conference of Commissioners on Uniform State

---

120. Lalli v. Lalli, 439 U.S. 259, 99 S. Ct. 518, 58 L. Ed. 2d 503 (1978); S. v. D., 410 U.S. 614, 73 S. Ct. 1146, 35 L. Ed. 2d 536 (1973), discussed, *supra* text at notes 52-58, *infra* ch. V, text at note 136; *cf.*, ch. V, text at notes 32-43.

Laws and approved by the American Bar Association in 1973, was developed specifically to fill the legislative void created by the Supreme Court's venture into this arena. By 1980, nine states had adopted the Act and its influence had spread to legislation proposed and enacted in other states. More of that below.[121]

---

121. *See infra* ch. V. 11; Appendix B.

Chapter V

ASCERTAINING THE FATHER OF THE NONMARITAL CHILD

To have meaning, legal rights must be enforceable. In the context of illegitimacy, enforcement of the child's rights first requires identification of its parents. While the fact of birth usually proves the mother and child relationship, proof of paternity is another matter, except in the case of legitimate birth where the presumption that the mother's husband is her child's father makes for legal (if not always factual) certainty.[1]

1. Paternity in the Courts Today.

Current paternity practice dramatizes the need for change. In many areas, conditions still resemble those described in a 1968 report of the Family Study Commission of the State of Illinois:

> The investigation and information obtained by the Commission on paternity law and practice leads to the inescapable conclusion that coercion, corruption, perjury and indifference to the rights of the individual defendant pervade in the day to day practice in this area of judicial proceedings .... Testimony before the Commission revealed that generally defendants appear before judges who have a daily case load of about 140 cases. ... Testimony from the sitting judiciary hearing paternity cases revealed to the Commission that the evidence in most cases consists of an accusation by the woman and a denial by the defendant. Under such circumstances, the judges feel constrained to enter a finding of paternity. Not even the slightest corroborating evidence is required.[2]

---

1. *See supra*, ch. III. 2.

2. Family Study Commission, State of Illinois, Report and Recommendations to the 76th General Assembly 55 (1969).

A survey of a random group of judges (experienced and active in paternity cases) undertaken just before the federal child support enforcement legislation was enacted did not dispel the pessimistic conclusion reached by the Illinois Commission.[3] That survey was conducted at minimal expense. For lack of funding, it did not attempt to obtain a statistically valid sample. Yet some findings are clear:

Public aid departments play a major role in initiating paternity actions, although they themselves bring less than 10 percent of all such actions, partly because of statutory limitations. A majority of the responding judges indicated that 50 percent or more of paternity suits are brought as a result of public aid department pressure on the mother.

The survey results indicated that half of the defendants in paternity cases are employed full-time, one-fourth or fewer are employed part-time and the remainder are unemployed. The employment situation is somewhat better in rural than in urban areas. The median estimates in regard to income of defendants indicate that 25 to 50 percent of the defendants earn less than $5,000 per year, 10 to 15 percent earn between $5,000 and $10,000, and fewer than 10 percent earn more than $10,000. In urban areas approximately 75 percent of the defendants are black, far fewer in rural areas. Fewer than 10 percent are Hispanic-Americans. Of the cases filed, not even one-fourth actually reach the trial stage. Court time needed to resolve paternity cases varies with the circumstances. If uncontested, cases require approximately ten to thirty minutes of court time. A contested paternity trial without a jury takes about two hours. A contested paternity trial with a jury usually requires five to eight hours, but a jury is used in less than 10 percent of all paternity trials. More

---

3. Krause, Snapp, Carter and Rink-Carter, Paternity Cases in the Courts: Judicial Attitudes and Practices (1974-78, unpublished paper).

court time generally is allowed in rural than in urban jurisdictions.

Fewer than half of the defendants in paternity cases have the aid of counsel. While mothers generally can obtain free legal aid in prosecuting paternity actions, few defendants appear to receive similar aid. Most of the responding judges (73%) favored providing counsel to defendants in paternity cases, but a majority of the state's attorneys (63%) opposed this proposal.

Blood tests generally are used for exclusionary purposes only. They are employed in less than 10 percent of the uncontested cases and in 50 percent or less of contested cases. When blood tests are used, the most common practice is to use only the basic ABO, Rh-Hr and MNSs typing systems, although there is some application of other systems which, of course, increases the chance of excluding non-fathers.

A majority of the judges (67%) and state's attorneys (89%) expressed full confidence in the value of blood tests in paternity cases. In states where the judge may order blood tests, most urban judges said they actually order such tests in less than 10 percent of the cases. Rural judges, however, are much more likely to order blood tests. Judges explain that even if they may order tests, there are few sanctions if a defendant refuses to comply. The refusal may not affect the case at all, although in some states the case may be resolved against the defendant on that basis and in others the refusal may be divulged to the jury. If a mother refuses, the case usually is dismissed. The defendant must usually pay for all blood tests, even if he is found to be excluded as a possible father.

Most judges (68%) disapprove of the use of lie detector tests in paternity cases. Accordingly, 76 percent of the judges said that they never use such tests. By contrast, 86 percent of the urban state's attorneys approve of lie detector

165

tests and 78 percent reported that they sometimes use them.

The respondents had the impression that the accused men commit perjury more frequently than do the mothers. A majority of the judges estimated that at least 10 percent of the defendants commit perjury, whereas a majority of the state's attorneys put that percentage at 25 or more. Moreover, 21 percent of the judges and 35 percent of the state's attorneys felt that at least one-half of the defendants commit perjury. On the other hand, a majority of the respondents felt that mothers commit perjury in fewer than 10 percent of all paternity cases, and only 4 percent of the judges and 6 percent of the state's attorneys believed that one-half or more of the mothers lied under oath. There usually is no vigorous follow-up of suspected or discovered perjury. The principal reason given was lack of evidence.

In 50 to 75 percent of paternity cases the defendant admits that he is the father of the child. In 75 to 90 percent of contested paternity cases the defendant is adjudged to be the father. This means that between 87 and 97 percent of all defendants are ultimately determined to be fathers.

Most child support awards in paternity cases range from $10 to $20 per week. Awards in excess of $30 per week seem nearly non-existent.[4] Theoretically the judge determines the amount of support by considering the defendant's financial situation and the needs of the child, but it is clear that many courts regularly provide less child support in paternity suits than they would order in divorce cases. Few courts apply a formula in fixing the support award.

Over 25 percent of urban fathers and 10 percent of rural

4. Detailed national and state-by-state data for 1973 on support payments (not limited to nonmarital children) are provided in SENATE COMM. ON FINANCE, 94th Cong. 1st Sess., CHILD SUPPORT DATA AND MATERIALS 163-70 (Comm. Print 1975).

fathers default on their support payments within one year. Only about one-half of the respondents felt that follow-up on defaults is adequate. When there is a follow-up, the most commonly used sanction is incarceration as a result of a *civil* prosecution for contempt, rather than a criminal prosecution.

A growing number of jurisdictions require fathers to make support payments to the clerk of the court, rather than directly to the mother. Computerization of the payment, disbursement, and follow-up processes has been achieved in several localities.

Disappointingly, a 1977-78 update on the survey just described failed to discover significant "grassroots" change in the wake of the 1975 federal law.[5]

2. Acknowledgment, Legitimation, Declaratory Actions and Admission of Paternity.

The states which have adopted the Uniform Parentage Act and several other states give the father the opportunity to accept responsibility for his nonmarital child by voluntary acknowledgment or by permitting him to bring a paternity action.[6] Applicable statutes vary from procedures resulting in full legitimation, thus providing equality with legitimate children,[7] to arrangements of

---

5. *Supra* note 3.

6. UNIFORM PARENTAGE ACT § 4(a)(5), 9A U.L.A. MATR., FAM. AND HEALTH LAWS 591 (1979), enacted as COLO. REV. STAT. § 19-6-105(i)(e) (1978); HAW. REV. STAT. § 584-4(a)(5) (1976); MONT. REV. CODE ANN. § 61-305(i)(e) (Cum. Supp. 1977); NEV. REV. STAT. 126.051.1(f), 126.051.2 (1979); N.D. CENT. CODE § 14-17-04 (i)(e) (Supp. 1977); WASH. REV. CODE ANN. § 26.26.040(5) (Supp. 1978). This provision of the Uniform Act was not enacted in California, CAL. CIV. CODE § 7004 (Cum. Supp. 1979), or Wyoming, WYO. STAT. ANN. § 14-2-102 (1977). *Infra* Appendix B.

7. UNIFORM PARENTAGE ACT § 2, 9A U.L.A., MATR., FAM. AND HEALTH LAWS 588 (1979). Other representative legitimation statutes are ALA. CODE § 26-11-2 (1975); ME. REV. STAT. ANN. tit. 18, § 1003 (1965); MICH.

"partial" legitimation (usually in support and inheritance matters), and may go no further than the judgment in the traditional paternity action.[8] The admission of a nonmarital child into the family, or other acts or events tending to show voluntary acceptance by the father of his child, accomplishes legitimation in some states.[9] Current Supreme Court doctrine casts doubt on any attempt, statutory or contractual, to limit the effect of an acknowledgment to anything less than the full rights of a legitimate child.[10]

A declaratory action to establish paternity offers an interesting alternative both to acknowledgment and to the regular paternity action. Such an action may be allowed under a general statute authorizing declaratory judgments. Specific statutes that authorize the declaration of family relationships are rare, although they may gain broader acceptance with the Uniform Parentage Act.[11]

COMP. LAWS ANN. § 702.83 (Supp. 1978); N.C. GEN. STAT. § 49-11 (1976); N.H. REV. STAT. ANN. § 460:29 discussed in Locke v. Ladd, 119 N.H. 136, 399 A.2d 962 (1979); TENN. CODE ANN. § 36-302 (1977); TEX. FAM. CODE ANN. tit. 2, § 13.21 (Cum. Supp. 1978). *See also* Parham v. Hughes, 441 U.S. 347, 99 S. Ct. 1742, 60 L. Ed. 2d 269 (1979) and Quilloin v. Walcott, 434 U.S. 246, 98 S. Ct. 549, 54 L. Ed. 2d 511 (1978), both involving GA. CODE ANN. § 74-103 (1973).

   8. CONN. GEN. STAT. ANN. § 46b-172 (Cum. Supp. 1979); OR. REV. STAT. § 109.092 (1977); VA. CODE § 20.61.1 (Cum. Supp. 1978).

   9. UNIFORM PARENTAGE ACT § 4(a)(4), 9A U.L.A. MATR., FAM. AND HEALTH LAWS 591 (1979). *See also* ME. REV. STAT. ANN. tit. 18, § 1003 (1965); NEB. REV. STAT. § 13-109 (1977).

   10. *But cf.*, Lalli v. Lalli, 439 U.S. 259, 99 S. Ct. 518, 58 L. Ed. 2d 503 (1978).

   11. UNIFORM PARENTAGE ACT § 6, 9A U.L.A. MATR., FAM. AND HEALTH LAWS 593 (1979), enacted as CAL. CIV. CODE § 7006 (Cum. Supp. 1979); COLO. REV. STAT. § 19-6-107 (1978); HAW. REV. STAT. § 584-6 (1976); MONT. REV. CODE ANN. § 61-307 (Cum. Supp. 1977); N.D. CENT. CODE § 14-17-05 (Supp. 1977); WASH. REV. CODE ANN. § 26.26.060 (Supp. 1978); WYO. STAT. ANN. § 14-2-107 (1977).

Even when the jurisdiction's statutes do not provide the father a ready means of legitimating or otherwise recognizing or acknowledging his nonmarital child, a voluntary admission of paternity suffices to determine paternity when entered as a judgment either in a paternity action or in an equivalent procedural setting.

The great majority of cases in which paternity is established, including even initially disputed cases, are ultimately (and often quickly) settled by the man's admission of paternity.

However, this seemingly innocuous matter of voluntary admission of paternity has taken on somewhat doubtful dimensions in connection with the federal child support enforcement program. As will be detailed, that program has resulted in far greater emphasis on the establishment of paternity than seemed thinkable only a few years ago. Welfare workers as well as states' attorneys have become deeply involved. Actual or perceived pressures can be brought to bear on a man named by the mother as the father of her child, resulting in an admission of paternity with an open-ended liability for child support. A few courts are now waking up to the potential for abuse and imposition in these cases and are giving such "confessions" careful scrutiny. A leading California case graphically describes the manner in which courts throughout the nation are dealing with paternity cases. It speaks for itself, alerting concerned parties (including states' attorneys and welfare workers) to the potential for abuse and imposition:

> Prior to August 2, 1977, Viola Gonzales applied for welfare benefits from the County of Ventura. She informed the county employees that she was pregnant and that Rudy Castro, Jr. was the father of her unborn child. The Family Support Division of the Office of the District Attorney of Ventura County wrote a letter to

Mr. Castro requesting that he come into the Ventura County District Attorney's office to discuss the matter. On August 2, defendant came to the office in response to the letter and spoke to Juanita J. Hickman, a family support officer of the office of the district attorney.

Ms. Hickman asked defendant if he was the father of the child and defendant stated that there were some doubts in his mind but "more than likely I am the father." Ms. Hickman explained to defendant his options. She explained that if he wished to agree to paternity of the unborn child, he could enter into an agreement of paternity with the district attorney's office which would be filed with the court and which would result in a judgment of paternity and an order that he pay child support. She told him that if he was not sure he was the father, the office would file a civil paternity action, serve him with summons and complaint, and he would have thirty days within which to file an answer and have a trial on the issue. She also explained that if he did nothing after the summons and complaint were served upon him, a judgment by default would be entered against him, resulting in an order requiring him to pay child support.

She told him that Ms. Gonzales had nothing to do with bringing the action except that she had accepted welfare assistance and that any money paid by defendant for the support of the child would be used to reimburse the county for the welfare assistance expended for the child. Defendant agreed to sign the agreement for judgment. He read and signed the agreement prepared by Ms. Hickman and was provided with a copy of the agreement.

The agreement was filed with the Ventura County Superior Court on August 11, 1977. The agreement contains the following provisions:

"It is hereby agreed by plaintiff, through C. STANLEY TROM, District Attorney for the County of Ventura, and Rudy Castro, Jr., defendant, that the following facts are true and that a judgment be entered against the defendant in accordance with this agreement.

"1. Defendant acknowledges that the District Attorney of Ventura County does not represent him and that he understands that he has had an opportunity to have an attorney advise and represent him in this matter.

"2. Defendant understands that a judgment for child support will be entered against him based upon this agreement.

"3. The defendant is the father of: unborn child of Viola Gonzales, due to be born December 1977.

"4. The defendant agrees to pay $125.00 per child per month commencing on Sept. 1, 1977, and on the same date each month thereafter until termination by operation of law or further order of court."

In addition, the agreement provides for payment of a $2.50 processing service charge per month, a mode of payment and address to which payments are to be mailed, a requirement that defendant keep the district attorney's office apprised of his address, and an acknowledgment that if defendant should become two months in arrears in child support payments, his wages shall be assigned.

On August 11, 1977, judgment for child support by agreement was entered by the Ventura County Superior Court. In that judgment, the court decrees that defendant is the father of the unborn child of Viola Gonzales and orders defendant to pay the sum of $125 per month child support "until termination by operation of law or further order of court."

On February 9, 1978, defendant moved to set aside the agreement and the judgment entered thereon pursuant to Code of Civil Procedure section 473. Defendant's motion was supported by his declaration that at the time he visited the district attorney's office, he had serious doubts that he was the father of the child; that he was aware that the district attorney prosecutes criminal cases and feared that he could be sent to jail for refusal to sign the agreement; that he did not realize that he was giving up his right to trial by

171

jury on the issue of paternity, his right to discovery, and his right to a blood test. He further stated that he was not aware that by signing the agreement he was agreeing to support an unborn child until the child reached the age of 18 years.

Defendant averred that he did not sign the agreement freely and voluntarily but as the result of coercion and duress, nor did he understand the nature and consequences of the document.

Opposition to the motion to set aside the judgment was supported by a declaration executed by Juanita Hickman setting forth the information she had provided to defendant and the explanation she had given him concerning his options. The contents of her declaration are as previously summarized in the summary of the facts. Her declaration concludes:

"At no time was Mr. Castro threatened in any fashion nor were any promises made to him to induce him to enter into this agreement. I made every attempt to explain to him his options to his satisfaction and answer his questions. There was no mention of any criminal action in any respect during our conversation nor was there any mention of the possibility of any jail sentence being imposed."

Defendant's motion to set aside the judgment was denied, and this appeal followed.

. . .

Respondent argues that the waiver by defendant in this case was knowing and voluntary and makes reference to the declaration of Juanita Hickman concerning her conversation with defendant. We recognize that we must resolve any factual dispute between appellant and respondent in favor of respondent. However, our inquiry here must be not whether this defendant knowingly and intelligently and voluntarily waived his right to notice and hearing, but whether the statute makes provision for such waiver. The [California Supreme Court in *Isbell* v. *County of Sonoma*] at page 65, 145 Cal.Rptr. at page 369-70, 577 P.2d at page 189-190 summarized its

172

holding as follows: "Because the California statutes provide insufficient safeguards to assure that the debtor in fact executed a voluntary, knowing, and intelligent waiver, ... we conclude that the confession of judgment procedure established in sections 1132 through 1134 violates the due process clause of the Fourteenth Amendment."

In the instant case, the statute under consideration makes no provision for protection of the due process rights of the noncustodial parent, nor does it address the issue of the manner in which defendant shall be permitted to waive those rights. The only provision with respect to information which must be provided to the defendant is the following sentence: "Prior to entering into this agreement, the noncustodial parent shall be informed that a judgment will be entered based on the agreement." (Welf. & Inst.Code, § 11476.1.) Glaringly absent from the provisions is any requirement that the defendant be informed that he has a right to trial on the issues of paternity and his obligation to support the minor child.

Waiver of constitutional rights is never presumed. (*D. H. Overmyer Co. v. Frick Co.* (1972) 405 U.S. 174, 186, 92 S.Ct. 775, 31 L.Ed.2d 124.) Yet, in the instant case, we are called upon to presume that a defendant knowingly, intelligently, and voluntarily waived his right to notice and an opportunity to be heard when the statute contains no requirement that he even be made aware of those rights.

Nor does the document executed by defendant reflect such a knowing and voluntary waiver. The court is instructed to enter judgment based on the agreement. However, the required waiver of due process rights could not be apparent to the court on the face of the document executed herein. No mention is made in the agreement of an understanding on the part of defendant that he has a right to a trial on the issue of paternity and child support and that he is freely giving up that right.

In *Isbell, supra*, the Supreme Court concluded that the confessions of judgment executed therein demonstrated neither the voluntary character of any waiver of due process rights nor that such waiver was knowing or intelligent. The court observed the disparity of bargaining power between the creditor who prepared the agreement, in that case the County of Sonoma, and the debtor. The court observed that the drastic nature of the document which resulted in the debtor's advance waiver of all possible defenses and of the right to be notified of the existence of the proceeding against him, strongly implied overreaching on the part of the creditor and precluded the indulgence in a presumption that the execution of the document by the debtor was voluntary. (*Isbell v. County of Sonoma, supra,* 21 Cal.3d at pp. 69-70, 145 Cal.Rptr. 368, 577 P.2d 188.)

In the instant case the agreement was entered into between a lay person and an employee of the office of the district attorney. The declaration of defendant that at the time of the discussion with Ms. Hickman he believed that he could be sent to jail for refusal to sign the agreement and believed that refusal to sign the agreement would result in "dire consequences," is, of course, uncontradicted in the record and eminently reasonable. It is common knowledge that the district attorney's office prosecutes criminal cases. We would be blinding ourselves to reality if we were to presume that an agreement such as the one in the case at bar were voluntarily executed in the absence of some express evidence of that fact. As stated in *Isbell,* at page 70, 145 Cal.Rptr. at page 373, 577 P.2d at page 193, "[A] court presented only with the verified confession of judgment cannot assume the voluntariness of any waiver of due process rights implicit in that confession."

By the same token, the mere fact that the defendant read and executed the agreement does not demonstrate that he knowingly and intelligently waived the rights lost by that execution. Absent an express statement in the agreement setting forth the rights to which defendant is entitled and stating that he understands those rights and knowingly waives them, we must " 'indulge every reasonable presumption against waiver' of fundamental constitutional rights."

(*Johnson v. Zerbst* (1938) 304 U.S. 458, 464, 58 S.Ct. 1019, 1023, 82 L.Ed. 1461.)

Finally, the statute makes no provision for any prejudgment judicial determination on the issue of waiver. The statute directs that once an agreement for judgment has been filed, "The court shall enter judgment thereon without action." Similar language in the Confession of Judgment statutes was found infirm because it did "not provide for a case by case determination of the validity of the debtor's waiver." (*Isbell, supra,* 21 Cal.3d at p. 71, 145 Cal.Rptr. at p. 374, 577 P.2d at p. 194.)

Code of Civil Procedure section 1134 directs the *court clerk* to enter judgment upon the filing of a written confession. Welfare and Institutions Code section 11476.1 directs that the judgment shall be entered by the *court.* However, neither statute requires or provides an opportunity for a judicial determination of the validity of any constitutional waivers. Respondent seeks to persuade us that the analogy drawn between confessions of judgment and agreements for judgment is erroneous. Respondent contends that the fact that defendant is informed that judgment will be entered based on the agreement, that he is informed that he has the right to consult an attorney, and that he is provided with a cooy of the agreement, serve to distinguish the two documents. But we believe that the position of the parties in this case, and the direct and collateral consequences of the execution of an agreement for judgment concerning paternity and child support, demand even closer constitutional scrutiny.

Defendant was informed that if he signed the agreement for judgment, he would be obligated to pay $125 per month child support until termination by operation of law or further order of court. He was also advised that the money was to be paid to the county, not to Ms. Gonzales, as reimbursement so long as she was accepting welfare benefits. He was further advised that if at any time he became two months in arrears in child support payments, his wages could be assigned. However, he was not advised that he could be subject to criminal prosecution for failure to support the child as ordered. On the contrary, Ms. Hickman's declaration states: "There was no mention of any criminal action in any respect during our conversation nor was there any mention of the possibility of any jail sentence being imposed." In fact, Penal Code section 270 provides that the failure to support one's child is a misdemeanor punishable by fine and/or incarceration.

Of additional concern is the fact that the explanation given to the defendant and the agreement which he signed imply that the obligation assumed is only to the County of Ventura so long as the mother of the minor child is receiving welfare aid. However, it is not unlikely that were such aid to terminate, the mother would seek child support payments directly from defendant. The execution of the agreement by defendant, admitting paternity, and the existence of a judgment establishing paternity, would be admissible as evidence on that issue in any subsequent support action. (See *Salas v. Cortez* (1979) 24 Cal.3d 22, p. 29, 154 Cal. Rptr. 529, 593 P.2d 226; Pen.Code, § 270e.)

. . .

What we view as a trend toward providing protection against the entry of judgments without notice, where due process rights may not have been waived, is properly followed in this case. The judgment here will deprive defendant of personal property and may deprive him of his freedom. Any statute authorizing the entry of a judgment under such circumstances must contain adequate safeguards to assure that defendant's rights to due process are properly waived.

Therefore, an agreement for judgment or a judgment entered pursuant to Welfare and Institutions Code section 11476.1 is constitutionally defective.[12]

3. Settlements and Compromises.

A settlement regarding *uncertain* paternity stands on a very different footing than does a contractual attempt to

---

12. County of Ventura v. Castro, 93 Cal. App. 3d 462, 156 Cal. Rptr. 66 (1979).

compromise or waive parental support obligations.[13] In the case of uncertain paternity, the issue that is compromised is not *what* support is owed the child. The settlement rests on the uncertainty of being able to establish paternity in court, *i.e., whether* any obligation exists at all. In these circumstances, a fair settlement should stand, assuming the child was represented effectively.[14]

As envisaged by the Uniform Parentage Act, the key to the validity of such agreements is careful scrutiny by an outsider charged with safeguarding the best interests of the child. Someone other than the mother should represent the child [15] and all such agreements should require court approval on the basis of a non-public pre-trial hearing. Such a hearing should bring out all available facts and circumstances that are relevant to the settlement, particularly evidence tending to allow an estimate as to the degree of difficulty with which paternity could be established in court.[16]

Under traditional state laws, binding settlements may be made by simple contract between mother and putative father. In the past, some statutes prescribed pitifully inadequate minimum terms for a settlement.[17] Statutes often require that settlements and compromises be officially

---

13. *See supra* ch. I. 1 text at notes 16-18.

14. For considerable detail, *see* the excellent analysis by Havighurst, *Settlement of Paternity Claims,* 1976 ARIZ. ST. L.J. 461 (1976).

15. UNIFORM PARENTAGE ACT § 9, 9A U.L.A., MATR., FAM. AND HEALTH LAWS 599 (1979).

16. *Id.* at § 13(a)(2). 9A U.L.A., MATR., FAM. AND HEALTH LAWS 604 (1979).

17. *See* Haag v. Barnes, 9 N.Y.2d 554, 175 N.E.2d 441, 216 N.Y.S.2d 65 (1961).

approved, either by a court [18] or by the state's attorney.[19] Even then, the settlement may not stand up against subsequent challenge by welfare (AFDC) authorities.[20] Traditionally, the child was bound by the settlement even though not represented.[21] This followed from statutes which allowed only the mother to bring the paternity action.[22] The requirement of official approval, where applicable, was intended to compensate for this shortcoming. More recent statutes provide that the child must be a party to a settlement with the putative father.[23] While there has been no major litigation questioning settlements between mother and putative father on constitutional grounds,[24] cases dealing with the

---

18. In Oregon, the judge may make such compromise or arrangement with the putative father as the judge deems just and equitable. OR. REV. STAT. § 109.220 (1977). *See also* IDAHO CODE § 7-1106 (1979); IOWA CODE ANN. § 675.30 (1950); NEB. REV. STAT. §§ 13-104, 13-110 (1977); OKLA. STAT. ANN. tit. 10, § 85 (1966); UTAH CODE ANN. § 78-45A-13 (1977).

19. MD. ANN. CODE art 16, § 66L (1973). *Cf.,* Petit v. Ratner, 92 Nev. 421, 551 P.2d 426 (1976).

20. State of Maine Dept. of Human Resources v. Webster, 398 A.2d 792 (Me. 1979). *Cf.,* IND. CODE ANN. § 31-4-1-25 (1973).

21. *See, e.g., In re* Paternity, 33 Ohio Op. 2d 299, 211 N.E.2d 894 (1965), in which the nonmarital child unsuccessfully attempted to upset a compromise agreement between the putative father and its mother. *But see* ABC v. XYZ, 50 Misc. 2d 792, 271 N.Y.S.2d 781 (1966) in which an agreement between mother and putative father which specifically denied paternity but nevertheless allowed child support, was held not to bar the child's later action to have paternity determined. The action was held barred, however, by the statute of limitations.

22. *Infra* ch. V. 4.

23. *E.g.,* TEX. FAM. CODE ANN. tit. 2, § 13.07 (Cum. Supp. 1979).

24. *Cf.,* Bacon v. Bacon, 46 N.Y.2d 477, 386 N.E.2d 1327, 414 N.Y.S.2d 307 (1979), in which the New York Court of Appeals upheld a statute allowing a settlement between the mother and the putative father on the ground that the statute is substantially related to the "permissible state interest" in encouraging putative fathers to settle claims.

applicability of statutes of limitation furnish some analogy.[25]

It also should be mentioned that a settlement of sorts occurs if the mother and putative father marry, inasmuch as marriage extinguishes the paternity claim in many states.[26] Since the parents' marriage is not always and inevitably tied in with legitimation of the child, the child again may be the loser.[27]

4. Bringing the Paternity Action.

Traditionally, the paternity action has been of limited scope. The primary and often sole objective has been to charge the father with a limited duty to support his nonmarital child. The principal purpose has been to help the welfare authorities on whom will fall the burden of supporting the child if the father cannot be held responsible. Several states had for some time allowed their courts to confer legitimate status on the child in the paternity proceeding or to award inheritance rights in addition to support.[28] In several others the concept of illegitimacy was abolished by statute long before the U.S. Supreme Court began to apply the Equal Protection Clause.[29] In those states, a paternity judgment

---

25. *See infra* ch. V.5.

26. The statute may attempt to bar the action even if the mother marries someone other than the putative father. *See* Franklin v. Julian, 30 Ohio St. 2d 228, 283 N.E.2d 813 (1972).

27. *See supra* ch. III. 3.

28. ALASKA STAT. § 25.20.050(a) (1977); IDAHO CODE § 7-1104 (1978); TENN. CODE ANN. § 36-234 (1977); TEX. FAM. CODE ANN. tit. 2, § 13.09 (Cum. Supp. 1978).

29. ARIZ. REV. STAT. ANN. § 8-601 (Supp. 1979); OR. REV. STAT. § 109.060 (1977). While Arizona and Oregon are the pace setting "equality states," California, Colorado, Hawaii, Minnesota, Montana, Nevada, North Dakota, Washington and Wyoming have followed suit by adopting the UNIFORM PARENTAGE ACT, 9A U.L.A. MATR., FAM. AND HEALTH LAWS 579 (1979). Appendix B *infra*.

automatically produces the full range of filial rights against the father. Today, Supreme Court doctrine would seem to require the same result in *all* states, regardless of specific statutes.

Under traditional paternity statutes that remain in effect in many states, only the mother or a public authority is authorized to bring the paternity action, and the child (unless the mother is dead) has no claim on its own. Nor may the father bring a paternity action to establish his paternity.[30] Relics, such as the West Virginia statute next quoted, survive in quantity:

Any unmarried woman may go before a justice of the county in which she resides and accuse any person of being the father of a bastard child of which she has been delivered. Such justice shall examine her under oath, and reduce her examination to writing and sign it. On such examination, unless the child be three years old or upwards, the justice shall issue a warrant, directed to the sheriff of, or a constable in, any county where the accused may be, requiring him to be apprehended and taken before a justice of the county in which he may be found; and it shall be the duty of such justice to require the accused to enter into a recognizance, with one or more good securities, in a sum not less than five hundred nor more than one thousand dollars, conditioned for his appearance at the next term of the circuit court or any other court of record having jurisdiction of the county in which such warrant issued, to answer such charge, and to abide by and perform the order of the court in relation thereto. If a married woman live separate and apart from her husband for the space of one year or more, and shall not at any time

---

30. *E.g.*, Conn. Gen. Stat. Ann. §§ 46b-160, 46b-162 (Cum. Supp. 1979); Fla. Stat. Ann. § 742.011 (Supp. 1978); Ind. Code Ann. § 31-4-1-9 (Cum. Supp. 1979); Neb. Rev. Stat. § 13-113 (1977); Tenn. Code Ann. § 36-224 (1977). *See generally,* H. Krause, Illegitimacy: Law and Social Policy 112-15 (1971).

during such separation, cohabit with such husband she may, if she be delivered of a child at any time after such one year, and while such separation continues, accuse any person, other than her husband, of being the father of such child, in like manner, and the same proceedings shall thereupon be had, as if she were an unmarried woman.[31]

On the more logical premise that the substantive rights involved in the father and child relationship belong to the child and to the father, the Uniform Parentage Act gives both the child and the father an opportunity to establish their relationship.[32] Even in some states other than those in which the Uniform Parentage Act is in effect, the child,[33] the father,[34] or both[35] may bring the paternity action. Of course, if the child is truly represented adequately in a paternity action brought by its mother, guardian, or even by the welfare authorities, the distinction is academic. As a practical matter, the most important question is whether a mother who (as the natural guardian of the child) chooses *not* to bring the action or who settles on terms she thought acceptable to *her* should be allowed to bind the child. It is at least arguable that the primacy of the child's rights

31. W. VA. CODE ANN. § 48-7-1 (1976).

32. UNIFORM PARENTAGE ACT §§ 6, 9, 9A U.L.A. MATR., FAM. AND HEALTH LAWS 593, 599 (1979).

33. *E.g.,* MINN. STAT. ANN. § 257.253 (Cum. Supp. 1979); MISS. CODE ANN. § 93-9-9 (1972); UTAH CODE ANN. § 78-45a-2 (1977).

34. *E.g.,* N.M. REV. STAT. ANN. § 40-5-7 (1978); OR. REV. STAT. § 109.125 (1977).

35. *E.g.,* ARIZ. REV. STAT. ANN. § 12-843 (1956); IDAHO CODE § 7-1110 (1978); KY. REV. STAT. § 406.021 (Supp. 1976); ME. REV. STAT. tit. 19, § 272 (Supp. 1978); MINN. STAT. ANN. § 257.252 (Supp. 1978); MISS. CODE ANN. § 93-9-9 (1972); NEB. REV. STAT. § 13-111 (1977); N.H. REV. STAT. ANN. § 168-A:2 (1977); UTAH CODE ANN. § 78-45a-2 (1977). *Cf.,* IOWA CODE ANN. § 675.8 (1950) which provides that "[t]he proceedings may be brought by the mother, *or other interested person . . . .*" (Emphasis added).

under the Equal Protection Clause should mean that the child is not barred if no action was brought at all or if the settlement that was reached is not in the child's best interest. A thought from *Boddie v. Connecticut* (which involved access to state courts in connection with divorce) is relevant: "Due process requires, at a minimum, that absent a countervailing state interest of overriding significance, persons forced to settle their claims of right and duty through the judicial process must be given a meaningful opportunity to be heard."[36] Concerned about these problems, the Uniform Parentage Act perceives a potential conflict of interest between mother and child in regard to these important decisions. It does not permit either parent to represent the child, but mandates that the child be represented independently.[37]

Aside from the unsettled question of the statute of limitations, to be discussed in the next section, the child's constitutional right to bring the paternity action has not yet been litigated directly in the upper judicial echelons. However, in a case involving a child's challenge to a judicial finding of *non*paternity, a California Court of Appeals held as follows:

> In contrast to enforcement of a child's right of a present or past support obligation, the establishment of the parent-child relationship is the most fundamental right a child possesses to be equated in importance with personal liberty and the most basic of constitutional rights. To hold a child bound prospectively by a finding of nonpaternity in a divorce action in which the child was not a party would be to allow the conduct of the

---

36. Boddie v. Connecticut, 401 U.S. 371, 377, 91 S. Ct. 780, 785, 28 L. Ed. 2d 113, 118 (1971).

37. UNIFORM PARENTAGE ACT § 9, 9A U.L.A. MATR., FAM. AND HEALTH LAWS 599 (1979).

mother to foreclose the most fundamental right a child possesses in our system of jurisprudence.[38]

The Ohio Supreme Court has come close to finding that the child has such a right in a holding to the effect that a married mother cannot be prevented from bringing a paternity action, as the Ohio paternity statute had long proscribed, [39] and the Florida Supreme Court has made that point explicit:

> [T]o require that the mother of an illegitimate child be legally unmarried at the time of the child's conception in order to bring suit ... is an unreasonable and invidious discrimination against such child, depriving the child of equal protection of the law.... Assuming, as we clearly must, that the purpose of the statute is to (i) protect the interests of a child illegitimately conceived and (ii) to impose an obligation on the natural father to provide support, it is the relationship between the natural father and the child which should be controlling rather than the marital status of the mother.[40]

Concerning the right of the putative father of a nonmarital child to bring an action to establish his paternity, the Wisconsin Supreme Court concluded that the father "does have the constitutional right to establish, if he can, his natural parentage, to assert parental rights, and [to] a legal forum with due process procedures to establish these rights." [41] The Supreme Court of Maine has held

---

38. Ruddock v. Ohls, 91 Cal. App. 3d 271, 277-78, 154 Cal. Rptr. 87, 91 (1979).

39. Franklin v. Julian, 30 Ohio St. 2d 228, 283 N.E.2d 813 (1972). *See also* Brown v. Danley, 263 Ark. 480, 566 S.W.2d 385 (1978).

40. Gammon v. Cobb, 335 So. 2d 261, 267-68 (Fla. 1976). The related issue of the continued validity of "Lord Mansfield's Rule" is discussed, supra.ch. III. 1, text at notes 20-29; *infra* text at notes 99-100.

41. Slawek v. Stroh, 62 Wis. 2d 295, 304, 215 N.W.2d 9, 15 (1974).

essentially the same.[42] In Florida, on the other hand, several cases have concluded that the father may not sue to establish his paternity, where the mother denies his paternity.[43]

To provide assistance with the practical details of instituting and carrying through a paternity action, in-state and interstate, the federal child support authorities have developed and transmitted to all state agencies a detailed work booklet that provides numerous, often quite useful, forms and checklists.[44]

5. Statutes of Limitations.

State law traditionally has set short periods of limitation for the paternity action, typically one,[45] two,[46]

---

42. Johannesen v. Pfeiffer, 387 A.2d 1113 (Me. 1978).

43. Ford v. Loeffler, 363 So. 2d 23 (Fla. Ct. App. 1978); Perez v. Stevens, 362 S.2d 998 (Fla. Ct. App. 1978), under FLA. STAT. ANN. § 742 (1977). The Florida and U.S. Supreme Courts *denied certiorari* in Perez v. Stevens, 368 So. 2d 1372 (Fla. 1979), and —— U.S. ——, 100 S. Ct. 72, 62 L. Ed. 2d 47 (1979).

44. UNIVERSITY OF SOUTHERN CALIFORNIA, CENTER FOR HEALTH SERVICES RESEARCH, PATERNITY CASE PROCESSING HANDBOOK (1977). Transmitted by HEW/OCSE as OCSE-IM-78-4 (Feb. 9, 1978). Copies may be obtained from Planning and Evaluation Branch, Division of Policy and Planning, Office of Child Support Enforcement, Department of Health, Education and Welfare. *See also* UNIVERSITY OF SOUTHERN CALIFORNIA, CENTER FOR HEALTH SERVICES RESEARCH, PATERNITY DETERMINATION: TECHNIQUES AND PROCEDURES TO ESTABLISH THE PATERNITY OF CHILDREN BORN OUT OF WEDLOCK (1976) and CENTER FOR POLICY RESEARCH, INC., USING BLOOD TESTS TO ESTABLISH PATERNITY (New York, N.Y., 1977).

45. *E.g.*, KAN. STAT. ANN. § 38-1104 (1973); MISS. CODE ANN. § 93-9-11 (1972); TEX. FAM. CODE ANN. tit. 2, § 13.01 (Cum. Supp. 1978).

46. *E.g.*, ALA. CODE § 26-12-7 (1975); N.H. REV. STAT. ANN. § 168-A:12 (Supp. 1977); N.M. STAT. ANN. § 40-5-23 (1978).

three [47] or four [48] years. Recently, Oregon extended its statute from six to ten years.[49] If the putative father has acknowledged paternity, provided support, or left the jurisdiction, several states specifically toll the statute of limitations.[50] Other statutes limit the amount of back support that may be recovered.[51] Several states allow [52] and others forbid [53] the action to be instituted during the mother's pregnancy. Recognition of the primacy of the child's interest in the paternity action is implicit in the provision of the Uniform Parentage Act that preserves the child's right to sue until after majority, unless earlier action was taken on the child's behalf.[54]

---

47. *E.g.*, CONN. STAT. ANN. § 46b-160 (Cum. Supp. 1978); OKLA. STAT. ANN. tit. 10, § 83 (1966); N.C. GEN. STAT. § 49-4 (1976).

48. UTAH CODE § 77-60-15 (1978).

49. OR. REV. STAT. § 109.135 (1977).

50. ALA. CODE § 26-12-7 (1975); IOWA CODE ANN. § 675-33 (1950); MICH. COMP. LAWS ANN. § 722.714 (Supp. 1978); MISS. CODE ANN. § 93-9-9 (1972); N.C. GEN. STAT. § 49-14 (Supp. 1977); TENN. CODE ANN. § 36-224 (1977).

51. *E.g.*, IOWA CODE ANN. § 675.3 (Cum. Supp. 1979); ME. REV. STAT. ANN. tit. 19, § 273 (Cum. Supp. 1978); MINN. STAT. ANN. § 257.255 (Cum. Supp. 1979); UTAH CODE ANN. § 78-45a-3 (1978).

52. D.C. CODE ENCYCL. § 16-2342 (Cum. Supp. 1978); ILL. ANN. STAT. ch. 40 § 1354 (1979); MD. CODE ANN. art. 16, § 66F (1973) which states that while no trial on the merits may be held until after the birth of the child, the court has the power: (1) to order the person alleged to be the father of the child and/or the pregnant woman to give bond in such form and penalty as the court prescribes, conditioned upon their further appearance in the proceedings and their compliance with such orders as may thereafter be passed therein; (2) to increase or decrease any bond which may have been theretofore furnished by the alleged father and/or the pregnant woman; and (3) to conduct such other preliminary proceedings as the court deems just and proper.

53. IDAHO CODE § 7-1107 (1979).

54. UNIFORM PARENTAGE ACT § 7, 9A U.L.A. MATR., FAM. AND HEALTH LAWS 596 (1979). *See* In Interest of W.M.V., 268 N.W.2d 781 (N.D. 1978) in which the North Dakota Supreme Court held that the statute of

Siding with the child, the District of Columbia Superior Court employed the constitutional weapon to strike down a statute of limitations, holding that the State's interest in "preventing stale claims" is subordinate to the support claim of the nonmarital child.[55] Similarly, New Mexico held that since no time limit applies to the legitimate child's claim for support, it would offend the Equal Protection Clause to withhold the same right from illegitimate children by applying New Mexico's two-year statute of limitations.[56]

Another way out of the dilemma was found by Wisconsin and Kansas courts sympathizing with the child. Turning obsolete paternity statutes to the child's advantage, it was held that since the statutory paternity action is the mother's, only the mother is barred by the applicable statute of limitations. The child was held to have a common law right to support, and to have its paternity established. That right was held not to be affected by the period of limitations applicable to the paternity action.[57] On similar reasoning, the District of Columbia allowed a *father* seeking visitation rights to sue after the expiration of the period of limitation for paternity actions.[58]

----

limitations of the UNIFORM PATERNITY ACT, N.D. CENT. CODE § 14-17-06, applied retroactively to children born prior to the effective date of the Act. Among other things, the Court found that such retroactive application did not violate due process because putative fathers have no vested interest in not being made a party to a paternity action.

55. Plowden v. Barbee, —— A.2d —— [5 F.L.R. 2336] (D.C. Super. Fam. Div. 1979).

56. Stringer v. Dudoich, —— N.M. ——, 583 P.2d 462 (1978).

57. Huss v. DeMott, 215 Kan. 450, 524 P.2d 743 (1974); *In re* J.M.S., 4 F.L.R. 2401 (Wis. Cty. Ct. March 22, 1978). *See also* Holden v. Alexander, 39 A.D.2d 476, 336 N.Y.S.2d 649 (1972). *Cf.,* Arsenault v. Carrier, 390 A.2d 1048 (Me. 1978). (By the same reasoning, a child was held not barred by a settlement between mother and putative father.)

58. Felder v. Allsop, 391 A.2d 243 (D.C. 1978).

A contrary view of the constitutionality of short statutes of limitations was taken by the Supreme Courts of Illinois and Iowa, which emphasized the state's interest in the speedy and efficient settlement of claims.[59] The U.S. Supreme Court's reasoning in *Lalli* implies some support for the latter view, but the issue was specifically *not* decided.[60] Moreover, the Iowa Supreme Court withdrew from its prior ruling when it held that Iowa's Uniform Support of Dependents Act provides an alternative method of adjudicating paternity and that, in contrast to an action

---

59. Cessna v. Montgomery, 63 Ill. 2d 71, 344 N.E.2d 447 (1976); State *ex rel.* Krupke v. Witkowski, 256 N.W.2d 216 (Iowa 1977).

60. On similar grounds, *Lalli* upheld a New York statute that denied intestate succession to nonmarital children whose paternity had not been established judicially during the father's lifetime. *Lalli* compounds the problem caused by short statutes of limitation inasmuch as the child whose paternity was not established within the statutory period is forever barred from becoming eligible to take under the intestacy laws. Lalli v. Lalli, 439 U.S. 259, 267, 99 S. Ct. 518, 524, 58 L. Ed. 2d 503, 510-11 (1978):

> Section 4-1.2 requires not only that the order of filiation be made during the lifetime of the father, but that the proceeding in which it is sought be commenced "during the pregnancy of the mother or within two years from the birth of the child." The New York Court of Appeals declined to rule on the constitutionality of the two-year limitation in both of its opinions in this case because appellant concededly had never commenced a paternity proceeding at all. Thus, if the rule that paternity be judicially declared during his father's lifetime were upheld, appellant would lose for failure to comply with that requirement alone. If, on the other hand, appellant prevailed in his argument that his inheritance could not be conditioned on the existence of an order of filiation, the two-year limitation would become irrelevant since the paternity proceeding itself would be unnecessary. *As the New York Court of Appeals has not passed upon the constitutionality of the two-year limitation, that question is not before us.* Our decision today therefore sustains § 4-1.2 under the Equal Protection Clause only with respect to its requirement that a judicial order of filiation be issued during the lifetime of the father of an illegitimate child. [Citations omitted; emphasis added].

under the paternity act, an action under the former statute is *not* barred by *any* statute of limitations.[61]

While the weight of authority thus seems to be swinging in the direction of upholding the nonmarital child's claim against short statutes of limitations, the intelligent solution accommodating all interests would be the enactment of statutes that would mandate in all cases that a paternity action be instituted within a reasonable period after the child's birth.[62]

Quite aside from statutes of limitation, paternity actions seeking support usually are held to die with the father, so that a paternity action against the father's estate typically will not be allowed.[63] This rule is related to the more general rule that support obligations cease upon death.[64] The issue of intestate succession is still another matter.[65]

6. Civil or Criminal Proceeding?

In several states the paternity action still has not evolved from its history in the criminal law.[66] Where the

---

61. State *ex rel.* Andrew v. Cardella, 282 N.W.2d 117 (Iowa 1979). *See also In re* L.B., 179 Colo. 11, 498 P.2d 1157 (1972), *appeal dismissed,* 410 U.S. 976 (1973); *In re* Estate of Hendrix, 68 Misc. 2d 439, 326 N.Y.S.2d 646 (1971); Thompson v. Thompson, 40 Md. App. 256, 390 A.2d 1139 (1978); Texas Dept. of Human Resources v. Chapman, 570 S.W.2d 46 (Tex. Civ. App. 1978).

62. *See infra* ch. V.11, text at notes 148-151.

63. *In re* Henry, 95 Misc. 2d 996, —— N.Y.S.2d —— (Fam. Ct. 1978). *Cf.,* UNIFORM PROBATE CODE § 3-803, 8 U.L.A. EST., PROB. AND REL. LAWS 457 (1972).

64. K.K. v. Estate of M.F., 145 N.J. Super. 250, 367 A.2d 466 (Juv. and Dom. Rel. Ct. 1976); *In re* Henry, —— Misc. 2d ——, —— N.Y.S.2d —— [5 F.L.R. 2008] (Fam. Ct. 1978); Annot., 58 A.L.R.3d 188 (1974). *See supra* ch. I.4.b.

65. *Supra,* ch. I.4.b., text at notes 126-128.

66. G.L. v. S.D., 382 A.2d 252 (Del. 1977); Davis v. Misiano, —— Mass. ——, 77 Mass. Adv. Sh. 1792, 366 N.E.2d 752 (1977); Matthews v. Cuff, 254 Pa. Super. Ct. 65, 385 A.2d 526 (1978).

action remains "criminal," the usual safeguards attending a criminal prosecution are applicable, but are not always applied. Accordingly, proof must be beyond a reasonable doubt, the prohibition on double jeopardy may be invoked and, among other things, the defendant will have a right to free counsel and, presumably, a free record on appeal.[67] The criminal process also may provide blood test at public expense,[68] whereas such tests would typically have to be paid for by the parties in a civil action.[69] Even in states which have a civil paternity action, criminal procedure may become involved if the initial prosecution of the putative father may be brought under a criminal nonsupport statute.[70]

In most states, however, the paternity action is viewed exclusively as a civil proceeding.[71] The chief consequence of this is that proof of paternity need measure no higher than a "preponderance of the evidence" and other safeguards of the criminal process do not apply to protect the alleged father.[72] Nevertheless, whatever the form of the action, most states will allow the alleged father a jury trial on the

---

67. *See* Reynolds v. Kimmons, 569 P.2d 799 (Alaska 1977); G.L. v. S.D., 382 A.2d 252 (Del. 1977); Artibee v. Cheboygan Circuit Judge, 397 Mich. 54, 243 N.W.2d 248 (1976); McDaniel v. Jackson, 78 Mich. App. 218, 259 N.W.2d 563 (1977).

68. *E.g.,* Walker v. Stokes, 45 Ohio App. 2d 275, 344 N.E.2d 159 (1975).

69. *But see* Franklin v. Colorado Tenth Judicial District, 571 P.2d 1072 (Colo. 1977); Lurry v. Mills, 152 N.J. Super. 127 (1977). *See also* Artibee v. Cheboygan Circuit Judge, 397 Mich. 54, 243 N.W.2d 248 (1976), and *infra* ch. X.5, text at notes 65-69.

70. State v. Clay, 236 S.E.2d 230 (W. Va. 1976).

71. *E.g.,* Neb. Rev. Stat. § 13-111 (1977); N.M. Stat. Ann. § 40-5-9 (1978).

72. *E.g.,* Montgomery v. Watts, 135 Vt. 464, 380 A.2d 75 (1977); Huntington v. Crowley, 64 Cal. 2d 647, 414 P.2d 382, 51 Cal. Rptr. 254 (1966); Fulmore v. Deveaux, 3 Conn. Cir. Ct. 553, 220 A.2d 462 (1966).

issue of paternity,[73] even where filiation proceedings are
"for all purposes . . . deemed suits in equity." [74] A number of
states employ hybrid proceedings that try to have the best
(and sometimes get the worst) of the civil and criminal
law.[75] In those states, a common approach is to require that
proof, in what otherwise remains a civil proceeding, be
"clear and satisfactory" or "to the entire satisfaction of the
court" or "beyond a reasonable doubt," whatever this may
mean in practical application.[76]

Since the establishment of the child's *civil* relationship
with its father is involved, serious doubts must be expressed
as to the constitutionality of statutes which still deal with
the establishment of paternity as a criminal matter as well
as those civil paternity statutes that raise the requirement
of proof to a level higher than that required for other civil

---

73. *E.g.*, Conn. Gen. Stat. Ann. § 52-438 (Supp. 1979); Md. Ann. Code
art. 16, § 66F (1973); Mich. Comp. Laws Ann. § 722.715 (1968); Miss.
Code Ann. § 93-9-15 (1972); N.J. Stat. Ann. § 9:17-20 (1976). *Contra,*
Idaho Code § 7-1114 (1979). *Cf.,* Uniform Parentage Act § 14(d),
Comment, 9A U.L.A. Matr., Fam. and Health Laws 606 (1979).

74. Or. Rev. Stat. § 109.135 (1977).

75. *E.g.*, Utah Code Ann. § 77-60-1 (1978) describes a "bastardy"
proceeding that is criminal in form and prosecuted by the state, but
which is civil nonetheless. State v. Reese, 43 Utah 447, 135 P. 270 (1913).
See also Walker v. Stokes, 54 Ohio App. 2d 119, 375 N.E.2d 1258 (1977);
Mathews v. Cuff, 254 Pa. Super. Ct. 65, 385 A.2d 526 (1978). *Cf.,* Ala.
Code § 26-12-1 (1975).

76. *See* N.C. Gen. Stat. § 49-14 (1976, Supp. 1977); Wis. Stat. Ann.
§ 52.355 (Supp. 1979). *See also* "HH" v. "II", 31 N.Y.2d 154, 286 N.E.2d
717, 335 N.Y.S.2d 274 (1972), *appeal dismissed,* 409 U.S. 1121 (1973);
"RR" v. "SS", 40 A. D. 2d 908, 337 N.Y.S.2d 840 (1972). While New York's
special burden of proof must be met in an action *against* the alleged
father, a man alleging himself to be the father need prove his paternity
by only a preponderance of the evidence. Jaynes v. Tulla, — A. D. 2d
—, 416 N.Y.S.2d 357 (1979).

actions.[77] The Uniform Parentage Act makes it quite clear that the action is civil and recommends against the use of even a civil jury.[78]

7. Right to Counsel — Putative Father, Child and Mother.

The landmark decisions involving counsel for indigents involve *criminal* proceedings.[79] The prevailing rule remains that no free counsel (other than what might be available through legal aid services) need be provided for indigents in civil actions.[80] Paternity actions are civil actions in most states as they should be. Logically, but regrettably, the alleged father's right to counsel in

---

77. *See* H. Krause, Illegitimacy: Law and Social Policy 110-11 (1971). *But* consider the comments of Justices Brennan, White, Marshall and Stevens, dissenting in Lalli v. Lalli, 439 U.S. 259, 278-79, 99 S. Ct. 518, 530, 58 L. Ed. 2d 503, 518 (Brennan, J., dissenting, 1978).

> But even if my confidence in the accuracy of formal public acknowledgments of paternity were unfounded, New York has available less drastic means of screening out fraudulent claims of paternity. In addition to requiring formal acknowledgements of paternity, New York might require illegitimates to prove paternity by an elevated standard of proof, e.g., clear and convincing evidence, or even beyond a reasonable doubt. Certainly here, where there is no factual dispute as to the relationship between Robert and Mario Lalli, there is no justification for denying Robert Lalli his intestate share.

78. Uniform Parentage Act § 14, 9A U.L.A. Matr., Fam. and Health Laws 606 (1979).

79. Gideon v. Wainwright, 372 U.S. 335, 83 S. Ct. 792, 9 L. Ed. 2d 799 (1963); Argersinger v. Hamlin, 407 U.S. 25, 92 S. Ct. 2006, 32 L. Ed. 2d 530 (1972); Scott v. Illinois, 440 U.S. 367, 99 S. Ct. 1158, 59 L. Ed. 2d 383 (1979). *See generally,* J. Nowak, R. Rotunda, J. Young, Constitutional Law chs. 13 and 16 (1978).

80. *In re* Smiley, 36 N.Y.2d 433, 330 N.E.2d 369 N.Y.S.2d 87 (1975) (divorce); Miller v. Gordon, 58 A. D. 2d 1027, 397 N.Y.S.2d 500 (1977) (paternity); Ford v. Herndon, 62 Cal. App. 3d 492, 133 Cal. Rptr. 111 (1976) (paternity).

paternity proceedings has often turned on the question whether the paternity action is criminal or civil in nature. It is ironic that the anachronistic — and possibly unconstitutional — criminal paternity action should have provided this beneficial result. Of course, since actual imprisonment is the test for applicability of the Sixth and Fourteenth Amendments to the right of counsel [81] and imprisonment is not the primary goal of even a *criminal* paternity case, the analogy may be less useful than some courts seem to have thought.

On the plaintiff's side, the state has long championed the mother's cause and that of the child by providing representation.[82] By contrast, the idea of providing counsel for indigent *defendants* in *civil* paternity proceedings is relatively new. Recent supreme court decisions in Michigan and Alaska illustrate one attempted solution which leans on the criminal past of the paternity action. In Michigan, the majority viewed the action as "quasi-criminal" in nature and derived from that a right to counsel for an indigent defendant. The dissent considered the action to be primarily civil and came out against a right to counsel.[83] The Supreme Court of Alaska discussed the problem in similar terms and reached the same result.[84] Emphasis was placed on the fact that an increasing number of courts have allowed the parent a right of counsel in proceedings to terminate parental rights. The Alaska court also recognized the great zeal of the federally-sponsored support enforcement drive, which makes it highly desirable that alleged fathers be provided legal advice.

---

81. Re-emphasized in Scott v. Illinois, 440 U.S. 367, 99 S. Ct. 1158, 1162, 59 L. Ed. 2d 383 (1979).

82. *E.g.*, KAN. STAT. ANN. § 38-1103 (1973).

83. Artibee v. Cheboygan Circuit Judge, 397 Mich. 54, 243 N.W.2d 248 (1976).

84. Reynolds v. Kimmons, 569 P.2d 799 (Alaska 1977).

In 1979, the Minnesota Supreme Court faced the problem squarely. Concerning a paternity action which is "unequivocally established [to be] civil in nature," the Minnesota Court held that

> [P]ursuant to our supervisory power to ensure the fair administration of justice, [we hold that] counsel must be provided indigent defendants where the complainant is represented by the county attorney. We hold that counsel is required, not because we are constitutionally compelled to do so, but because, given the present adversary nature of paternity adjudications, there is no better method available to us to protect the important interests involved.[85]

The California Supreme Court persuaded itself on similar policy grounds to single out child support actions brought by the State.[86] It held it a violation of due process *not* to

---

85. Hepfel v. Bashaw, — Minn. —, —, 279 N.W.2d 342, 346 (1979). Endorsing the UNIFORM PARENTAGE ACT and recommending that it be enacted by the legislature, the Court continued:

> In our view, improvements in this approach by which paternity is determined are long overdue. In recent years the right of illegitimate children to equal treatment under the law has been increasingly recognized. The right to equal protection is meaningless if the initial determination of paternity is not made with care and precision. Because the child's right to inheritance, workers' compensation benefits, and insurance proceeds flow from an adjudication of paternity and because of the increasing recognition of the rights of an illegitimate child to equal treatment under the law, it must now be accepted that the child's interest in an accurate determination of paternity at least equals that of the putative father. Moreover, since the adjudicated father may also assert rights to custody superior to the rights of any person except the mother, and must give consent before the child can be adopted, the child's interests may arguably exceed those of the putative father. (Citations omitted)

86. Salas v. Cortez, 24 Cal. 3d 22, 593 P.2d 226, 154 Cal. Rptr. 529 (1979), *cert. denied,* — U.S. —, — S. Ct. —, 62 L. Ed. 2d 136 (1979).

provide counsel in a civil paternity action when that action is brought by the State:

> It is argued that if appellants are entitled to court-appointed counsel, then counsel would have to be appointed for indigent defendants in every civil case. However, the present cases are not ordinary civil actions. Unlike other civil actions, even those in which the state is a party, in these cases the full power of the state is pitted against an indigent person in an adjudication of the existence of a fundamental biological relationship entailing serious financial, legal and moral obligations. Thus, appellants' entitlement to counsel turns on whether the state has a compelling interest that would justify its insistence on denying appellants a fair opportunity to defend.

> The state's interest in denying counsel to indigent paternity defendants is largely financial. Respondents argue it will require a greater expenditure of public funds if indigent defendants, as well as plaintiffs, are represented at public expense. In addition, it may become more difficult to identify potential fathers and establish paternity if defendants have the full benefits of the adversary system. However, the state has no legitimate interest in incorrectly ascribing parentage and imposing the obligations of fatherhood on someone other than the child's actual father. Appointment of counsel for indigent defendants will make the fact-finding process in paternity cases more accurate, thereby furthering the state's *legitimate* interests in securing support for dependent children.

> Accordingly, this court holds that in proceedings to determine paternity in which the state appears as a party or appears on behalf of a mother or child, indigent defendants are constitutionally entitled to appointed counsel.[87]

---

87. 24 Cal. 3d at 32-34, 593 P.2d at 233-34,154 Cal. Rptr. at 536-37 [citations omitted].

A somewhat different situation arises when a minor is alleged to be the father and is sued. Here the appointment of a guardian *ad litem* would appear to be mandatory. On the ground that the minor putative father was not represented at his paternity trial by a guardian *ad litem,* the California Court of Appeals voided a judgment entered against him because he had not appeared at the trial, nor did he know or consult with the attorney who purported to represent him in the proceeding.[88]

Whether the *child* should have a right to counsel (and the possible need for appointment of a guardian *ad litem*) raises still other problems. Typically, the child has not been represented by separate counsel. The mother or the welfare authorities who bring the action have been seen as representing the child's interests,[89] and it has been assumed that the child's interests will be represented effectively.[90] This assumption has rested on the tradition that the paternity action is the mother's, not the child's right — a tradition that now is constitutionally suspect. More acceptable support may be drawn from the mother's position as the child's natural guardian. Nevertheless, there may be a conflict of interest between the mother and the child. To guard against that, the Uniform Parentage Act insists that the mother *not* be seen as the automatic

---

88. Jeffrey S. II v. Jeffrey S., 76 Cal. App. 3d 65, 142 Cal. Rptr. 625 (1977).

89. *But see* TEX. FAM. CODE ANN. tit. 2, § 1307 (Cum. Supp. 1978), which provides that a child must be a party to a settlement agreement with the alleged father, and requires appointment of a guardian *ad litem* to represent the child in the settlement agreement.

90. *But see* Everett v. Everett, 57 Cal. App. 3d 65, 129 Cal. Rptr. 8 (1976) which held that the child was not bound by its mother's allegedly collusive suit against the putative father. The preclusion of the child's claim by a paternity action brought by another person is discussed in Comment, *Privity, Preclusion, and the Parent-Child Relationship,* 1977 B.Y.U.L. REV. 612.

guardian of the child's interest in the paternity action.[91] A further concern is the potential conflict of interest between a welfare authority prosecuting a support or paternity claim and the persons entitled to support.[92]

One thing is very clear: The problem of separate representation for the child in paternity litigation is much less serious than the problem of representation in the decision of whether the action should be brought at all — especially considering the confusion currently clouding the validity of short statutes of limitations on paternity actions.[93]

8. Proof.

An open admission by the father in court,[94] or a statement from the father under oath,[95] is adequate

---

91. UNIFORM PARENTAGE ACT § 9, 9A U.L.A., MATR., FAM. AND HEALTH LAWS 599 (1979).

92. Gibson v. Johnson, 3 Fam. L. Rptr. 2096 (Or. Cir. Ct. 1976).

93. *Supra* ch. V. 5. Especially text at notes 55-61.

94. *E.g.,* KY. REV. STAT. ANN. § 406.021 (Supp. 1976); MICH. COMP. LAWS ANN. § 722.717 (1968). But *cf.,* County of Ventura v. Castro, 93 Cal. App. 3d 462, 156 Cal. Rptr. 66 (1979), discussed *supra* text at note 12 (admission *not* in court).

95. *E.g.,* VA. CODE § 64.1-5.2(G) (Supp. 1978). More unusually, Virginia lists specific types of evidence that are admissible in various paternity actions and excludes all other proof. VA. CODE § 64.1-5.2 (Supp. 1978), states that for purposes of descent and distribution evidence of paternity must not only be clear and convincing but limited to the following:

1. That he cohabited openly with the mother during all of the ten months immediately prior to the time the child was born;
2. That he gave consent to a physician or other person, not including the mother, charged with the responsibility of securing information for the preparation of a birth record that his name be used as the father of the child upon the birth records of the child;
3. That he allowed by a general course of conduct the common use of his surname by the child;
4. That he claimed the child as his child on any statement, tax

evidence of paternity in many states. Many states no longer require corroboration of the mother's testimony.[96] Perhaps too often, the mother's statement alone may go very far,[97] even after her death.[98] Many states have discarded "Lord Mansfield's rule." [99] In those that still follow it, a married mother is not allowed to testify as to the illegitimacy of her child.[100]

Proof that the mother has had sexual relations (at the critical time), with a man or men other than the putative father, is a traditional and (due to frequent perjury)

---

return or other document filed and signed by him with any local, State or federal government or any agency thereof;

5. That he admitted before any court having jurisdiction to try and dispose of the same that he is the father of the child; or

6. That he voluntarily admitted paternity in writing, under oath.

VA. CODE § 20-61.1 (Supp. 1978), the criminal nonsupport statute, allows evidence of paternity only by the first four factors listed above and, of course, the standard for conviction is proof of paternity beyond a reasonable doubt.

96. Vander Werf v. Anderson, 86 S.D. 321, 195 N.W.2d 145 (1972). District of Columbia v. Stovall, 253 A.2d 541 (D.C. 1969); Collins v. Wise, 156 Ind. App. 424, 296 N.E.2d 887 (1973); Kimble v. Keefer, 11 Md. App. 48, 272 A.2d 668 (1971). *Contra,* Wade v. Hicks, 191 Neb. 847, 218 N.W.2d 222 (1974).

97. *See* State *ex rel.* Brajdic v. Seber, 53 Wis. 2d 446, 193 N.W.2d 43 (1972); Solomon v. Fenton, 144 Ind. App. 100, 244 N.E.2d 228 (1967). *See also* Salisbury v. Conroy, — Misc. 2d —, — N.Y.S.2d — [5 F.L.R. 2585] (Fam. Ct. 1979) (where the respondent refuses to testify, the court may draw the "strongest inference possible" from the petitioner's evidence).

98. MISS. CODE ANN. § 93-9-71 (1972).

99. *E.g.,* VT. STAT. ANN. tit. 15, § 207 (Cum. Supp. 1979); VA. CODE § 20-82 (1975). *See* Davis v. Davis, 521 S.W.2d 603 (Tex. 1975).

100. Fox v. Hohenshelt, 275 Or. 91, 549 P.2d 1117 (1976); Note, *Prohibiting Nonaccess Testimony by Spouses: Does Lord Mansfield's Rule Protect Illegitimates?,* 75 MICH. L. REV. 1457 (1977). *See supra* ch. III. 1, text at notes 20-29.

potentially vicious defense to a paternity charge.[101] Such evidence may still bar the action absolutely, to the extreme that not even blood tests would be permissible to determine whether the other man is excluded as a possible father.[102] This should not be confused with evidence of the mother's or the alleged father's general unchastity or promiscuity, which may be admissible to raise doubt regarding credibility, but would not be conclusive.[103] Nor with the opportunity given in some states to bring in rebuttable evidence of the "good" character of the accused *man*.[104]

The Uniform Parentage Act seeks to end wide-spread abuse of this defense by providing that evidence offered by the alleged father with respect to the possible paternity of another man is admissible only if combined with blood test results showing that man to be a possible father. In addition, if the other man is subject to the jurisdiction of the court, he is made a defendant in the action.[105]

---

101. Leonard v. Hogan, 32 Or. App. 89, 573 P.2d 328 (1978); *cf.,* Huntingdon v. Crowley, 64 Cal. 2d 647, 414 P.2d 382, 51 Cal. Rptr. 254 (1966). Reversing an acquittal in paternity suit, finding error in the instruction that the jury *must* find for the defendant if it determined that the mother had a *mere* association or opportunity to have sexual relations with other men.) *See* Sass, *The Defense of Multiple Access in Paternity Suits: A Comparative Analysis,* 51 TUL. L. REV. 468 (1977). A statutory illustration is N.Y. FAM. CT. ACT § 531 (McKinney Cum. Supp. 1979).

102. Yarmark v. Strickland, 193 So. 2d 212 (Fla. App. 1966). *But see* Linda W.W. v. William XX, — A.D.2d —, 415 N.Y.S.2d 275 (1979).

103. *See* South Carolina Dept. of Soc. Serv. v. Brown, 272 S.C. 568, 253 S.E.2d 100 (1979); Price v. Sampson, 205 So. 2d 642 (Miss. 1968); State *ex rel* Brown v. Middleton, 259 Iowa 1140, 147 N.W.2d 40 (1966); State v. Crittenden, 29 Wis. 2d 413, 139 N.W.2d 94 (1966); *In re* Sales (Buys), 4 F.L.R. 2493 (N.Y. Fam. Ct. 1978); Thirdgill v. Williams, 17 Or. App. 509, 522 P.2d 911 (1974).

104. *E.g.,* CONN. GEN. STAT. ANN. § 46b-167 (Cum. Supp. 1978).

105. UNIFORM PARENTAGE ACT § 14(c), 9A U.L.A., MATR., FAM. AND HEALTH LAWS 606 (1979).

Scientific and quasi-scientific evidence that may be relevant and admissible in paternity cases ranges from blood typing tests which are discussed quite fully below,[106] to questions regarding sterility,[107] physical resemblance,[108]

---

106. *Infra* ch. VI.

107. H. KRAUSE, ILLEGITIMACY: LAW AND SOCIAL POLICY 143-44 (1971).

108. *Id.* at 137-39. A recent case highlighting this problematical area is Dorsey v. English, 283 Md. 522, 524-25, 527, 390 A.2d 1133, 1135-37 (1978) which held:

> "At the request of the State's Attorney, who represented English, the trial court permitted the child to be exhibited to the jury and allowed English to direct the jury's attention to points of resemblance between Kevyn and Dorsey, specifically that they both had unusually shaped ears and eyebrows, gaps in their teeth and the "same cheeks." The jury returned a verdict finding Dorsey to be "most likely" Kevyn's father. The propriety of exhibiting a child before a jury and permitting them to consider its resemblance to the alleged father as evidence of paternity presents an issue of first impression in Maryland. We note, however, that there is a sharp conflict of authority among our sister states which basically follow four approaches in resolving this issue.
>
> Some states never permit exhibition of a child. *See, e. g., Cook v. State,* 172 Tenn. 42, 109 S.W.2d 98 (1937). The reason that such a basis for comparison between a child and a putative father is speculative and tends to be prejudicial to the father. Other states allow the exhibition of the child without qualification, apparently based on the assumption that such evidence is inherently trustworthy. *See e. g., Nimmo v. Sims,* 178 Ark. 1052, 13 S.W.2d 304 (1929). A third group allows exhibition of a child, provided a preliminary showing is made to insure that the evidence has some probative value. Most of this latter group have adopted some variation of the rule suggested by Professor Wigmore that "the sound rule is to admit the fact of similarity of specific traits, *however presented,* provided the child is in the opinion of the trial court old enough to possess settled features or other corporal indications." J. Wigmore, *Evidence,* § 166, at 627 (3rd ed. 1940). *See Flores v. State,* 72 Fla. 302, 73 So. 234 (1916); *Hall v. Centolanza,* 28 N.J.Super. 391, 101 A.2d 44 (1953); *State v. Powers,* 75 S.D. 209, 62 N.W.2d 764 (1954); *State v. Anderson,* 63 Utah 171, 224 P. 442 (1924); *Lohsen v. Lawson,* 106 Vt. 481, 174 A. 861 (1934). These states give the trial judge discretion in making a preliminary determination based on two factors, age and specificity, in order to limit the exhibition of children to those who are sufficiently mature so that a comparison of the child and an adult will be reliable. Exhibition is permitted only respecting those traits for which testimony has been admitted.

duration of pregnancy[109] and polygraph tests.[110]

9. Judgment.

The judgment in a paternity action normally includes an order against the father for the support of the child,[111] and may go as far as legitimating the child.[112] Periodic support payments are the rule,[113] but lump-sum

---

The fourth approach is to leave the question of admissibility of resemblance evidence entirely to the sound discretion of the trial court.

In the instant case English pointed out specific areas of resemblance between her son, Kevyn, and Dorsey, both of whom were present in the courtroom. Under these circumstances, the jury had ample opportunity to make a comparison and to weigh the probative force and reliability of the testimony of the witnesses. We are persuaded that, under the circumstances of this case, the trial court properly admitted English's testimony.... *See also* Joseph v. State, 149 Ga. App. 296, 254 S.E.2d 383 (1979) (Not error to demonstrate to the jury the child's physical ressemblance to the respondent); State *ex rel.* Plourde v. Magee, 26 Or. App. 505, 552 P.2d 1341 (1976) (Doubt expressed, but exhibition of child to jury permitted). *Generally* Annot., 55 A.L.R.3d 1087 (1974).

109. H. KRAUSE, ILLEGITIMACY: LAW AND SOCIAL POLICY 139-43 (1971). A recent case holding a 306-day pregnancy "not ... medically impossible" is Hude v. Vannest, 75 Mich. App. 490, 255 N.W.2d 659 (1977). The odds against a 301-day pregnancy have been stated as 31,000:1 and the odds against a 310-day pregnancy as 3,400,000:1. *See* Levy, *Letter to the Editor,* 149 J.A.M.A. 1052 (1952).

110. H. KRAUSE, ILLEGITIMACY: LAW AND SOCIAL POLICY 144-48 (1971). *See also* DEPT. OF HEALTH, EDUCATION AND WELFARE, OFFICE OF CHILD SUPPORT ENFORCEMENT, PATERNITY DETERMINATION: TECHNIQUES AND PROCEDURES TO ESTABLISH THE PATERNITY OF CHILDREN BORN OUT OF WEDLOCK (Condensed Report of University of Southern California, Center for Health Sciences Research under HEW Grant #18-P-90263/9-01), April 30, 1976, at 20-22, 27-28.

111. *Supra* ch. I. 5.

112. *Id.*

113. *E.g.,* NEB. REV. STAT. § 13-106 (1977); N.H. REV. STAT. ANN. § 168-A:6 (1977); N.M. STAT. ANN. § 40-5-75 (1978); UTAH CODE ANN. § 78-45a-11 (1977).

settlements may be permissible.[114] Usually, in addition to the child's support, the cost of the mother's confinement,[115] sometimes including maintenance, and other expenses incurred by her in connection with her pregnancy are allowed,[116] as are the expenses of prosecuting the paternity

---

114. For example, Ohio provides that support is to be paid weekly until the child is 18 years old, OHIO REV. CODE ANN. § 3111.17 (Page Supp. 1978), but lump-sum settlements are permissible if accepted as full payment by the mother. OHIO REV. CODE ANN. § 3111.07 (Page 1953).

115. *E.g.*, MINN. STAT. ANN. § 257.251 (Cum. Supp. 1979).

116. N.Y. FAM. CT. ACT § 514 (1972) provides: "The father is liable to pay the reasonable expenses of the mother's confinement and recovery and such reasonable expenses in connection with her pregnancy as the court in its discretion may deem proper." In Anonymous v. Anonymous, 48 Misc. 2d 794, 265 N.Y.S.2d 827 (1965), the court construed this provision to include the cost of necessary psychiatric care, if a patently clear causal relationship exists between the need for psychotherapy and the pregnancy, confinement, and recovery. Relics, such as ARK. STAT. ANN. § 34-706 (Cum. Supp. 1979), survive:

> If it is found by the court that the accused is the father of the child, the court, shall render judgment against him for the lying-in expenses in favor of the mother, or person who incurred the same, if required or claimed, for a sum not less than twenty-five dollars ($25.00), and if the same shall not be paid upon the rendition of such judgment, together with all costs which may be adjudged against him in said case, then the court shall have the power to commit the accused person to jail until the same shall be paid, with all costs; and, if claimed by the mother, the court or judge shall give judgment for a monthly sum of not less than ten dollars ($10.00) per month for every month from the birth of the child until it shall attain the age of sixteen (16) years, and shall further order that the father enter into bond to the State of Arkansas in the penal sum of five hundred dollars ($500.00), with good and sufficient security, conditioned to be void if such person or his executors or administrators shall indemnify each county in this State from all costs and expenses for the maintenance or otherwise of such child while under the age of sixteen (16) years, and for the payment of the monthly dues that may be adjudged as aforesaid, which bonds shall be approved by the judge and an entry made on the record of the conditions and the securities thereon. Provided, however, that the court may at any time, enlarge, diminish, or vacate any order or judgment in the proceedings under this Act as justice may require and on such notice to the defendant as the Court may prescribe.

action, often including counsel fees.[117] In connection with a paternity judgment, the usual remedies (such as wage garnishment, imposition of a trust, lien or requirement of other security or bond and more) facilitating enforcement of child support apply. Appropriate details may be incorporated into the judgment.[118]

10. Interstate Adjudication of Paternity Under (R) URESA.

URESA offers an efficient and economical method for the interstate enforcement of support for nonmarital children. Yet for a variety of reasons the Act has not been used to its fullest potential in that context. In cases in which paternity has been determined previously and the duty of support established, the obligation may, of course, be enforced in an URESA proceeding. The more interesting question is whether paternity may be established for the first time in a URESA proceeding. The pre-1968 versions of URESA do not specifically provide that courts may make the initial determination of paternity in the URESA proceeding, but neither is it ruled out. This silence, coupled with the general reluctance of courts to litigate under URESA any matters other than the narrow issue of support, has caused some courts to refuse to determine paternity in URESA proceedings.[119] They have required a prior

---

See also DEL. CODE ANN. tit. 13, § 504 (Cum. Supp. 1978); FLA. STAT. ANN. § 742.031 (1964); KAN. STAT. § 38-1106 (1973); N.H. STAT. ANN. § 168-A:6 (1977).

117. *E.g.,* ARIZ. REV. STAT. § 12-849 (1956); MD. ANN. CODE art. 16, § 66H (1973).

118. *See supra* ch. II. *also see* KAN. STAT. § 38-1106 (1973); N.H. STAT. ANN. § 168-A:4 (1977); OKLA. STAT. ANN. tit. 10, § 78 (1966); UTAH CODE ANN. § 78-45a-5 (1977).

119. URESA is discussed *supra* ch. II. 2. c. *See generally,* Levy, *Asserting Jurisdiction over Nonresident Putative Fathers in Paternity Actions,* 45 U. CINN. L. REV. 207 (1976); Annot., 81 A.L.R.3d 1175 (1977).

adjudication of paternity.[120] Under that interpretation, URESA provides little of value to the mother of a nonmarital child whose paternity has not been established. If she must first obtain a judgment of paternity by going to a court having personal jurisdiction over the putative father, the support obligation may as well (and will be) imposed and enforced in that proceeding.[121]

Many other courts have held to the contrary. To illustrate, in a recent URESA case, the District of Columbia Court of Appeals held that the responding court must determine whether a putative father owes a duty of support and that such a determination properly includes an adjudication of paternity.[122] The Tennessee Supreme Court said that "[u]nder the [URESA] statute, the duty of support need not be the result of court action; but may be any duty imposable by law." [123] The Oregon Supreme Court similarly

---

120. Courts in Ohio and Colorado, for example, refused to interpret URESA to allow the determination of paternity. Nye v. District Court for County of Adams, 168 Colo. 272, 450 P.2d 669 (1969); Aguilar v. Holcomb, 155 Colo. 530, 395 P.2d 998 (1964); Smith v. Smith, 11 Ohio Misc. 25, 224 N.E.2d 925 (1965). Subsequently, both Ohio and Colorado enacted RURESA, including § 27, thereby rendering the prior decisions obsolete. In New York, the Uniform Support of Dependents Law is unavailable in cases in which paternity is an issue. Spong v. Eckelberger, 89 Misc. 2d 1008, 393 N.Y.S.2d 164 (1977).

121. See Chapman v. Sutton, 4 F.L.R. 2707 (D.C. 1978); Clarkston v. Bridge, 273 Or. 68, 539 P.2d 1094 (1975); Yetter v. Commeau, 84 Wash. 2d 155, 524 P.2d 901 (1974); Sardonis v. Sardonis, 106 R.I. 469, 261 A.2d 22 (1970); Brown v. Thomas, 221 Tenn. 319, 426 S.W.2d 496 (1968); M. v. W., 352 Mass. 704, 227 N.E.2d 469 (1967); Guerra v. DeLuna, 526 S.W.2d 225 (Tex. Civ. App. 1975). See also 10 Am. Jur., Trials 682 (1965), and W. Brockelbank and F. Infausto, Interstate Enforcement of Family Support 62-63 (2d ed. 1971).

122. Chapman v. Sutton, 4 F.L.R. 2707 (D.C. 1978).

123. Brown v. Thomas, 221 Tenn. 319, 323, 426 S.W.2d 496, 498 (1968).

held that URESA authorizes both the initial determination of and the enforcement of duties of support.[124] A Kansas court dismissed a non-URESA paternity action against a nonresident defendant for lack of personal jurisdiction, but suggested, in dictum, that the mother could proceed under URESA to obtain a paternity and support judgment.[125] Somewhat relevant is the North Carolina case which allowed the defendant to relitigate the issue of paternity during a URESA proceeding because the prior paternity judgment was invalid for lack of personal jurisdiction.[126] Beyond that, a court may refuse to recognize a prior criminal conviction for failure to support an illegitimate child as conclusive on the issue of paternity in a civil URESA action.[127]

To resolve this problem, RURESA (the 1968 version) provides that the responding court, under certain conditions, may adjudicate the issue of paternity for the first time, as follows:

> Section 27. Paternity. If the obligor asserts as a defense that he is not the father of the child for whom support is sought and it appears to the court that the defense is not frivolous, and if both of the parties are present at the hearing or the proof required in the case indicates that the presence of either or both of the parties is not necessary, the court may adjudicate the paternity issue. Otherwise the court may adjourn the hearing until the paternity issue has been adjudicated.[128]

By 1978, RURESA had been enacted in twenty-five

---

124. Clarkston v. Bridge, 273 Or. 68, 539 P.2d 1094 (1975).

125. Carrington v. Schutts, 217 Kan. 175, 535 P.2d 982 (1975).

126. Brondum v. Cox, 292 N.C. 192, 232 S.E.2d 687 (1977).

127. Smith v. Burden, 31 N.C. App. 145, 228 S.E.2d 662 (1976).

128. UNIFORM RECIPROCAL ENFORCEMENT OF SUPPORT ACT § 27 (1968 revision) 9A U.L.A. MATR., FAM. AND HEALTH LAWS 730 (1979) [hereinafter cited as RURESA].

states,[129] but scant use appears to have been made of this Section.[130] When it becomes better known, and especially where it may be combined with the Uniform Parentage Act,[131] this section should go a long way toward facilitating the interstate enforcement of support obligations arising from nonmarital paternity. It should be noted, however, that the requirement that either or both parties be present, unless the presence of either or both is not necessary, severely limits the potential effect of the section. To require the mother to be present at the paternity hearing inevitably destroys the primary advantage of the Act—the ability to obtain enforcement while she remains in her home state. Accordingly, the Section provides relief only in cases in which the mother's presence is "not necessary," and that would be the rare paternity case. One commentator complains that "the presence of § 27 in RURESA is a step toward improvement, but it may prove to be so narrowly drafted that it forecloses the possibility of a paternity determination by its very terms."[132]

Whatever the shortcomings of RURESA in this context, it probably represents an improvement over URESA interpretations allowing the adjudication of paternity. Since Section 27 no more than reflects basic mandates of due process; there would seem to be little room for further

---

129. For a detailed listing, see Fox, *The Uniform Reciprocal Enforcement of Support Act,* 12 FAM.L.Q. 113, 134-45 (1978), reprinted in 4 F.L.R. 4017, 4024-26 (1978).

130. *Cf.,* Nickle v. Guarascio, 28 Utah 2d 425, 503 P.2d 861 (1972) (court upheld determination of paternity in URESA case, but did not address § 27 specifically).

131. 9A U.L.A. MATR., FAM. AND HEALTH LAWS 587 (1979). The UNIFORM PARENTAGE ACT was proposed in 1973 and has been adopted in nine states. Appendix B.

132. Fox, *The Uniform Reciprocal Enforcement of Support Act,* 12 FAM.L.Q. 113, 127, 4 F.L.R. 4017, 4022 (1978).

"improvement". After all, the initial adjudication of paternity is a very serious matter. Moreover, the relatively small number of reported cases in which courts have refused to adjudicate paternity under the unrevised Act does not necessarily reflect widespread acceptance of the broader interpretation of URESA. More likely, in states requiring a prior adjudication of paternity, cases not meeting this requirement simply are not filed. For example, when a California resident attempted to use URESA to obtain support from the putative father of her nonmarital child, a Florida resident, the state's attorney in Florida refused to file the case as a URESA action because Florida interprets URESA to preclude actions in which paternity has not been determined previously.[133] In a subsequent California action involving the same parties, the California Court held that it did not have personal jurisdiction over the defendant and therefore could not determine either paternity or the existence of a support obligation.[134] Discussing the plaintiff's unsuccessful attempt to use URESA, the California Court assumed that URESA does not apply to cases in which paternity is at issue and indicated that the plaintiff's only course of action would be to sue the defendant in Florida, without the aid of URESA.

11. Reform in Reach: The Uniform Parentage Act.

It fairly may be said that the typical state's paternity statute is not yet history, but should no longer be law. Unless state law makes fair provision for the child to find its father, the Supreme Court's talk about equality will

---

133. *See* Bartlett v. Superior Ct. of Santa Barbara, 86 Cal. App. 3d 72, 74, 150 Cal. Rptr. 25, 26 (1978), in which the court discussed the history of the case.

134. *Id.* at 77, 150 Cal. Rptr. at 28 (1978). Relying on *Kulko*, the Court refused to require the father to defend the suit in California. *See supra* ch. II. 2. a, text at notes 129-141.

have been an academic exercise.[135] Accordingly, inquiry cannot be avoided as to what is the permissible range of state regulation of procedures for the ascertainment of paternity. A second question is whether the State should initiate an action to establish paternity if the mother fails to do so.

Cases, as yet, have not come to grips with these questions in depth. Similarly, too few legislatures have reviewed their paternity statutes to see what amendments are needed to conform to the new situation. In S. v. D.,[136] the U.S. Supreme Court itself missed an opportunity to speak out on this subject when it refused to compel enforcement of a criminal nonsupport statute against the father of a nonmarital child, although the Act in question was routinely enforced against fathers of legitimate children. While the case was (technically correctly) decided on the narrow issue of the mother's lack of standing, the Court might have provided guidance to the courts regarding the right to bring paternity actions. Accordingly, no "hard law" exists on this vital problem.

In several other cases that were more or less remotely related to the issue of ascertainment of paternity, such as *Trimble*,[137] *Lalli*,[138] *Quilloin*,[139] *Parham*[140] and *Caban*,[141]

---

135. Improvement is taking place under the influence of the IV-D program. Nationwide, the number of cases in which paternity has been established has moved upward rapidly in recent years. In 1976 the estimated figure was 14,790, but in 1977 the figure was 89,386, and in 1978, 110,726. STAFF OF SENATE COMM. ON FINANCE, 96th Cong., 1st Sess., DATA AND MATERIALS ON CHILD SUPPORT 7 (Comm. Print 1979).

136. 410 U.S. 614, 93 S. Ct. 1146, 35 L. Ed. 2d 536 (1973).

137. Trimble v. Gordon, 430 U.S. 762, 97 S. Ct. 1459, 52 L. Ed. 2d 31 (1977).

138. Lalli v. Lalli, 439 U.S. 259, 99 S. Ct. 518, 50 L. Ed. 2d 503 (1978).

139. Quilloin v. Walcott, 434 U.S. 246, 98 S. Ct. 549, 54 L. Ed. 2d 511 (1978).

140. Parham v. Hughes, 441 U.S. 347, 99 S. Ct. 1742, 60 L. Ed. 2d 269 (1979).

141. Caban v. Mohammed, 441 U.S. 380, 99 S. Ct. 1760, 60 L. Ed. 2d 297 (1979).

the U.S. Supreme Court accepted existing state processes without question. For instance, in *Lalli* no inquiry was directed at the possible unconstitutionality of New York's paternity statute which, among other doubtful aspects, still requires evidence well beyond the level required in other civil actions.[142] In *Quilloin* and *Parham,* the Court did not question the procedure by which the unmarried father may legitimate his child in Georgia,[143] nor was recognition given the fact that a considerable number of states do *not* give unmarried fathers any opportunity to legitimate their children.[144] Thus the Court left open the question of whether state laws dealing with adoption *(Quilloin)* or wrongful death *(Parham),* would be upheld or struck down in the absence of a procedure for legitimation.

Given the substantive legal equality mandated by the U.S. Supreme Court — and with or without Supreme Court direction on how to go about achieving it — fundamental reform of the paternity action has become the most pressing task in the area of illegitimacy. Reform is needed, as much to facilitate finding a responsible father for the nonmarital child, as to protect the possibly great number of men who are falsely accused of paternity in vigorous pursuit of the federal child support enforcement program.[145]

Reform must come on two levels: A new procedural framework for the paternity action must improve the quality and the volume of adjudication. More efficient and speedier proceedings must provide fuller safeguards for falsely accused men. Within that new framework and to achieve both objectives, medical evidence must play a central role.[146]

---

142. *Supra* text at notes 75-78; ch. I, note 125; ch. IV, text at notes 52-58.

143. GA. CODE ANN. § 74-103 (1973).

144. *Supra* ch. V. 2.

145. *Infra* ch. X. 5.

146. *Infra* ch. VI.

The Uniform Parentage Act was developed specifically in response to the U.S. Supreme Court decisions securing the nonmarital child's substantive rights. It was adopted by the National Conference of Commissioners on Uniform State Laws in 1973, and approved by the American Bar Association in 1974.[147] It sets out a framework in which traditional paternity practice is superseded by a more efficient and constitutionally sound procedure. The central goal is fairness to the child as well as to the accused man.

The Uniform Parentage Act abandons the concept of illegitimacy. All children are equal in terms of their relationship with their parents. An elaborate network of presumptions identifies circumstances in which it is more likely than not that a particular man is the child's father, thus reducing the need for litigation. These presumptions cover the basic situation in which the parents are married, the case in which the man and the child's mother have attempted to marry prior to the child's birth but the marriage is void or voidable, the case where the man and the child's mother have married or attempted to marry after the child's birth and the father has given some additional indication of recognizing the child, the case where the man receives the child into his home and openly holds it out as his own and, finally, the case where the man acknowledges his paternity of the child in a formal writing without objection from the mother. Specifically defined interested parties, in some circumstances limited to the mother, her husband and the child, may bring a formal action to affirm or disaffirm any of the formal presumptions.

A proceeding to establish paternity is available when no circumstances exist that presumptively identify the probable father. The first stage of that proceeding is an informal (pre-trial) hearing before a judge or referee who is

---

147. *See* Appendix B *infra.*

not bound by formal rules of evidence and who renders no binding judgment. Instead, on the basis of all the evidence, including blood tests, the judge or referee makes a recommendation to the parties concerning settlement. The recommended settlement may involve dismissal of the action, the voluntary acknowledgement of the child by the putative father, or may be a compromise which does not establish paternity but fixes a specific economic obligation. If all parties accept the recommendation made to them, judgment is entered accordingly. If they do not, the matter is set for trial. It is expected that wide-scale use of sophisticated blood typing evidence in these "administrative" (pre-trial) proceedings will greatly stimulate acceptance of recommended settlements so that relatively few cases will need to be tried in court.

Patterned after Minnesota law,[148] a provision in a draft of the Uniform Parentage Act (that would have had appropriate public authorities bring a paternity action at a reasonably early point in time if the mother had failed to sue) was *not* included in the final version.[149] A renewed effort to propose such legislation is needed to alleviate the effect of a few recent state court cases upholding short statutes of limitations on paternity actions against the nonmarital child's constitutional claim.[150] Such legislation is also needed in view of the United States Supreme Court's

---

148. MINN. STAT. ANN. § 257.33 (1965).

149. The OFFICIAL COMMENT to § 7 of the UNIFORM PARENTAGE ACT quotes the omitted section:

If a child has no presumed father under Section 4 and the action to determine the existence of the father and child relationship has not been brought and proceedings to adopt the child have not been instituted within [1] year after the child's birth, an action to determine the existence of the relationship shall be brought promptly on behalf of the child by the [appropriate state agency].

9A U.L.A. MATR., FAM. & HEALTH LAWS 596-97 (1979).

150. *Supra* ch. V. 5.

reliance on the state-offered paternity action, expressed in *Lalli*.[151] As a practical matter, it should be noted that the rapidly increasing involvement of the AFDC authorities in child support enforcement, at least at the welfare level, has brought the "automatic paternity action" closer to reality.

By 1980, the Uniform Parentage Act had been enacted in nine states [152] and had left its mark on reform legislation in others.[153] Important courts have prodded their legislatures to adopt the Act.[154] In the face of the vast need for reform, however, the rate of progress so far achieved is too slow. Opposition in several states has clearly been traceable to the Act's concern for the falsely accused man. It is clear, however, that the protections there provided are no more than a necessary corollary of ascertaining paternity for the benefit of the child. Not even the child is served fairly if a biological stranger is tagged as its father.

A strong stimulus to the implementation of necessary reforms should come from the federal child support enforcement legislation enacted in 1975. Even before that

---

151. *Supra* ch. IV. 2, text at note 58.

152. 9A U.L.A. Matr., Fam. & Health Laws 579 (1979), enacted as Cal. Civ. Code §§ 7000 through 7018 (Cum. Supp. 1979); Colo. Rev. Stat. §§ 19-6-101 through 19-6-129 (1978); Haw. Rev. Stat. §§ 584-1 through 584-26 (1976); Minn. Laws 1980, ch. 589; Mont. Rev. Code Ann. §§ 61-301 through 61-334 (Cum. Supp. 1977); Nev. Rev. Stat. 126.031-126.231 (1979); N.D. Cent. Code §§ 14-17-01 through 14-17-26 (Supp. 1977); Wash. Rev. Code Ann. §§ 26.26.010 through 26.26.905 (Supp. 1978); Wyo. Stat. Ann. §§ 14-2-101 through 14-2-120 (1977). *See* Comment, *Washington's Parentage Act: A Step Forward for Children's Rights,* 12 Gonzaga L. Rev. 455 (1977); Note, *The Uniform Parentage Act: What It Will Mean for the Putative Father in California,* 28 Hastings L.J. 191 (1976). In 1980, the Act was pending in the legislatures of Delaware, Florida, Idaho, Kansas, New Jersey and Ohio.

153. *See, e.g.,* D.C. Code Encycl. §§ 16-908, 16-909 (Cum. Supp. 1978).

154. Hepfel v. Bashaw, — Minn. —, —, 279 N.W.2d 342, 348 (1979).

legislation was enacted, the Senate Finance Committee repeatedly recommended that "in evaluating state child support programs, the Secretary [of HEW] should take into account the Uniform Parentage Act." [155] H.E.W.'s Office of Child Support Enforcement, however, has not yet used its influence to move the Act toward wider adoption.[156]

---

155. S. Rep. No. 553, 93rd Cong., 1st Sess. (1973); accompanying H.R. Rep. No. 3153, 93rd Cong., 1st Sess. (1973) at 45; S. Rep. 1356, 93rd Cong., 2d Sess. (1974), accompanying H.R. Rep. 17045, 93rd Cong., 2d Sess. (1974) at 47-48.

156. OCSE-IM-79-9 (May 8, 1979) at p. 17, lists the Uniform Parentage Act as an item on the "Information Sharing Index" prepared by the National Child Support Enforcement Reference Center.

Chapter VI

PATERNITY: OF BLOOD AND SCIENCE.

1. From Opinion to Fact.

An extraordinary confluence of social and legal events have given blood typing work unprecedented importance. By fortunate coincidence, these events are occurring at a time when scientific capabilities in this area are incomparably better than ever before.

These events include, first, the unprecedented increase in births out of wedlock.[1]

Second, since 1968, the United States Supreme Court has decided about twenty illegitimacy cases.[2] By now, these decisions have provided all but complete substantive legal equality for nonmarital children, as a matter of *federal* (constitutional) law, whereas, under pre-existing *state* laws, those children typically had only limited rights of support and usually no rights of inheritance, even if their paternity was established.[3]

Third, the stunning increase in the nonmarital birth rate has brought a corresponding increase in the cost of the AFDC program.[4]

Fourth, motivated primarily by its interest in alleviating the AFDC cost burden, the federal government has become actively concerned about lagging, or indeed, lacking, child support enforcement. Since 1975, comprehensive federal support enforcement legislation has provided for federal assistance to state programs to establish paternity, among other things.[5]

---

1. *Supra* ch. IV.1.

2. *Supra* ch. IV.2-.5.

3. *See,* generally, H. KRAUSE, ILLEGITIMACY: LAW AND SOCIAL POLICY 1-42 (1971).

4. *Supra* ch. IV.1, table at note 10 and *infra* ch. VIII, note 2.

5. *Infra* Part III.

Unfortunately, state legislatures and state courts have remained far behind these developments and have barely begun to adapt the decision-making process to available blood typing science and technology. Much of this lag is due to an information and communication gap between the legal and medical professions, a gap which only recent efforts have sought to bridge.[6]

The scientific fact is that blood typing in its various forms now is capable of establishing non-paternity in the vast majority of cases (95-99%) in which the man named by the mother actually is not the father. Beyond that, significant statistical evidence may be derived in many circumstances from blood tests and may indicate persuasive probabilities (or improbabilities) of paternity. With *further* scientific advances, especially in the HLA sector, the time may come (*but has not yet arrived*) when the father of the child can be identified positively through medical expertise.

Lawyers and judges, however, are not at all certain of their ground in this complex and rapidly changing area. The old saying that "maternity is a matter of fact whereas paternity is a matter of opinion" retains too much vitality. As recently as 1974, a survey found that fully 11 percent of judges *never* use blood typing evidence in the solution of disputed paternity cases, whereas only 7.6 percent use such evidence in all cases. Only 62 percent of the judges surveyed had full confidence in the value of blood tests, whereas 24 percent did not, with the rest qualifying their responses variously.[7] To understand this better, one must remember

---

6. Joint AMA-ABA Guidelines: *Present Status of Serologic Testing in Problems of Disputed Parentage,* 10 FAM.L.Q. 247-85 (1976). *Infra.*

Appendix D. Not only has there been an information gap, but the literature most readily accessible to *lawyers* has not always carried the most expert and reliable information.

7. Krause, Snapp, Carter and Rink-Carter, Paternity Cases in the Courts: Judicial Attitudes and Practices (1974-78, unpublished paper).

the (in)famous case involving Charlie Chaplin.[8] There a jury chose to disregard blood test results which excluded Mr. Chaplin; instead, the jurors held him to be the father. And one should know that as recently as 1974 the North Carolina Supreme Court went the same route.[9] Nevertheless, the smug confidence with which commentators excoriate cases which disregard blood typing evidence is not always justified. There has been a great deal of poor work in this area, and the chance of error (indeed, the likelihood of error) is considerable if blood grouping tests are conducted inexpertly. One expert cautions, "there has been an unfortunate tendency to assume that these tests can be done by any blood bank or laboratory where clinical blood grouping tests are carried out . . . . This false belief has been fostered by the ready availability commercially of the antisera needed for conducting such examinations. This has led individuals with little or no experience in the field to accept the assignment from a court to conduct these examinations . . . ." [10] Specific case studies make a convincing case in favor of stringent quality control of blood grouping tests. The same expert reports that, while checking blood test reports as an independent expert in a sizable series of cases, he found one-third of them to be in error! [11] Lawyers and courts have not been adequately

---

8. Berry v. Chaplin, 74 Cal. App. 2d 652, 169 P.2d 442 (1946).

9. State v. Camp, 286 N.C. 148, 209 S.E.2d 754 (1974). The North Carolina statute was amended in 1975 to provide that blood tests excluding paternity be given conclusive effect. N. C. GEN. STAT. § 8-50.1 (1977).

10. Wiener, *Blood Grouping Tests in Disputed Parentage: Qualifications of Experts,* 13 ACTA GENETICAE MEDICAE ET GEMELLOLOGIAE 340 (1964).

11. *See* Wiener, *Foreword,* L. SUSSMAN, BLOOD GROUPING TESTS — MEDICO-LEGAL USES, ix (1968). Inasmuch as a re-check was requested in the first place, it may be assumed that the sample was skewed. But the problem nevertheless is real and serious; even if the error rate does not

warned to insist on full assurance that blood typing tests have been conducted in accordance with the highest standards of care and expertise. From both the medical and legal professions we need the will to adopt a more responsible, knowledgeable, reliable and cost-effective approach to blood typing in disputed paternity cases.

It *is* clear — but not generally understood — that the possibility of error could be all but eliminated if appropriate medical procedures were agreed upon and then (required to be) followed. On the scientific level, we need a definitive statement clarifying which tests now are scientifically wholly reliable and can thus be considered useful for testing. Beyond that, a judgment must be made on the practicality of any given testing system. This would involve an interdependent evaluation of the ease of performing the tests reliably (*i.e.*, low chance of technical error); the value of each system for exclusionary purposes (*i.e.*, what percentage of randomly selected men will a given test exclude?); the availability of reliable testing reagents needed for the particular test; and the cost of the specific test relative to its value for producing an exclusion. On the basis of this information, sets or "batteries" of tests should be administered in stages. A first, relatively less expensive, battery of tests that might give an average 70 percent chance of exclusion should be run routinely in all cases. If no exclusion is reached at that stage, an additional set of tests should bring the cumulative (average) exclusion rate of non-fathers to 90 percent or above. A cost-conscious and result-oriented analysis built on the factors listed above would determine the optimal composition of tests at each level. Obviously, the presence or absence of specific expertise or the availability or unavailability of specific

---

reach 30 percent in a "normal" sample. *See also* Wiener, *Problems and Pitfalls in Blood Grouping Tests for Non-Parentage,* 15 J. FOR. MED. 106, 126 (1968).

sera in a specific laboratory might make different compositions of reliable tests optimal at either stage.

On the technical level, scientifically sound standard laboratory procedures and safety standards should be prescribed for the execution of paternity tests. This phase would cover technical typing procedures, control the requisite quality and freshness of anti-sera and other testing agents, and govern the proper identification of the samples throughout the testing process. Finally, we need agreement on necessary qualifications for blood typing experts and laboratories, enforced by accreditation through a reliable private or governmental agency.

This proposal is not all fantasy. Nor is it futuristic speculation. Detailed recommendations concerning most of these matters are the subject of a joint report of committees of the American Medical Association and the Amercian Bar Association issued in 1976.[12] While these guidelines are being welcomed in the courts, an organized effort must be directed toward wider implementation.[13]

2. The Weight of Blood Tests in the Courts.

This section highlights the interplay of law and science in terms of the fundamental substantive question of what weight, under present law, a court will (or must) give to blood test evidence. Subsequent sections will carefully consider equally important *technical* aspects of the law of evidence regarding the admissibility of blood tests in court.

The question concerning the evidentiary effect of blood test evidence breaks down into four subsidiary questions. While these should be distinguished carefully, their interrelationship also need be recognized: (1) What is the

---

12. *Infra* Appendix D.
13. *E.g.,* Hepfel v. Bashaw, — Minn. —, —, 279 N.W.2d 342, 347 (1979). *Infra* ch. X.5.

weight and effect of blood typing evidence once it has been admitted by the court; (2) may the test results be used only for exclusionary or also for inclusionary purposes; (3) what is the validity of the specific test that is involved, in terms of its acceptability to the court; (4) was proper expertise employed in the performance and evaluation of the test?

For the record, let us remind ourselves that state law applies. Fifty states, the District of Columbia and assorted other U.S. jurisdictions have provided a broad range of legal opinion in answer to any of these questions. Through the federal child support enforcement legislation of 1975, however, federal influence is beginning to be felt. It ultimately will have a unifying, and should have a modernizing influence.[14]

a. Blood Tests As "Exclusionary" Evidence.

The first question — the weight and effect to be given to blood test evidence in disputed paternity cases — has been dealt with in some states expressly by statute, while in others it has been left to the courts.[15] Whether the blood typing evidence comes into court under a statute or by judicial discretion, the weight that it will be accorded may differ. On the basis of older cases that have not yet been overruled, a few states may still leave the matter at allowing even exclusionary results to be given no more than the same weight as any other evidence — thus, at least theoretically, permitting a jury to overrule a clear exclusion.[16] In 1974, for instance, the North Carolina

---

14. See infra ch. X.5.

15. E.g., Groulx v. Groulx, 98 N.H. 481, 103 A.2d 188 (1954). See also Annot. 46 A.L.R.2d 1000 (1956).

16. E.g., Jordan v. Davis, 143 Me. 185, 57 A.2d 209 (1948); Ross v. Marx, 24 N.J. Super. 25, 93 A.2d 597 (1952). Cf., Commonwealth v. Hunscick, 182 Pa. Super. Ct. 639, 128 A.2d 169 (1956); Cortese v. Cortese, 10 N.J. Super. 152, 76 A.2d 717 (1950).

Supreme Court upheld a jury which had determined a man
to be the father although his paternity was clearly excluded
on the basis of blood tests on the (nearly foolproof) ABO
system.[17] After this embarrassing experience, North
Carolina enacted a statute that makes a definite exclusion
conclusive.[18] A somewhat better informed group of states
holds that, even though test results excluding paternity are
not conclusive, they should be given considerable weight.[19]
In the "fully informed" states the rule is that a blood
grouping test which excludes paternity is conclusive,[20] if
conducted properly.

  b. *Blood Tests as "Probability" Evidence.*
  The three views just discussed concern exclusionary

  17. State v. Camp, 286 N.C. 148, 209 S.E.2d 754 (1975).
  18. N.C. GEN. STAT. ANN. § 8-50.1 (Cum. Supp. 1977).
  19. Prochnow v. Prochnow, 274 Wisc. 491, 80 N.W.2d 278 (1957); State
ex rel. Dolloff v. Sargent, 100 N.H. 29, 118 A.2d 596 (1955); State v. H.L.,
61 N.J. Super. 432, 161 A.2d 273 (1960); State *ex rel.* Steiger v. Gray, 3
Ohio Op. 2d 394, 145 N.E.2d 162, 76 Ohio L. Abs. 394 (1957). *Contra* Beck
v. Beck, 153 Colo. 90, 384 P.2d 731 (1963) (and cases cited therein);
Commonwealth v. Gromo, 190 Pa. Super. Ct. 519, 154 A.2d 417 (1959).
  20. *E.g.,* TEX. FAM. CODE § 13.05(a) (Cum. Supp. 1978) requires
dismissal with prejudice of a paternity action predicated on the results
of blood tests showing that the respondent is not the natural father of the
child in question. In the Interest of B.M.N., 570 S.W.2d 493 (Tex. Civ.
App. 1978); Hanson v. Hanson, 311 Minn. 388, 249 N.W.2d 452 (1976);
Commonwealth v. D'Avella, 339 Mass. 642, 162 N.E.2d 19 (1959);
Houghton v. Houghton, 179 Neb. 275, 137 N.W.2d 861 (1965); *In re*
Schneider, 72 Misc. 2d 423, 339 N.Y.S.2d 52 (1972); State *ex rel.* Lyons
v. DeValk, 47 Wisc. 2d 200, 177 N.W.2d 106 (1970). Illustrative of this
rule is Anonymous v. Anonymous, 1 A. D. 2d 312, 316, 150 N.Y.S.2d 344,
348 (1956), which states:

  Reason and logic, as well as a recognition of the modern advances in
  science, compel a determination that the presumption of legitimacy
  is not conclusive but rebuttable. The probative value of the results
  of skillfully conducted blood grouping tests has been widely accepted.
  The tests of course will be relevant only if they show
  noncompatibility.... If so, such evidence should be deemed
  conclusive as to nonpaternity.

evidence and a large number of states permit *only* such evidence to be introduced.[21] To complicate the picture further, the admissibility (and if admissible, the weight) of statistical evidence attempting to show probability or likelihood of paternity remains in much greater dispute. What is meant by "probability" or "likelihood" of paternity?

It stands to reason that as more and more reliable blood typing tests (for exclusions) become available and are applied, certain positive inferences become attractive. The question is what does it really mean if: (1) the blood tests run on the alleged father would exclude, say, 95% of the general population as possible fathers of the "average" child and this alleged father is not excluded; (2) the tests run on the mother and the child show that, say, 95% of the general population of men would be excluded as possible fathers, and the tests run on the alleged father show that he is not excluded; (3) the tests run on the alleged father, the mother and the child show that *this* alleged father (given his genetic make-up and focusing on that part of the child's genetic make-up that must stem from its father because the mother could not have passed on what she does not have) is, say, 20 times more likely to have fathered the child than a man picked at random out of the general population?

---

21. *E.g.,* ALA. CODE § 26-12-5 (1975); ARK. STAT. ANN. § 34-705.1 (1962); CONN. GEN. STAT. ANN. § 46b-168 (Cum. Supp. 1978); MD. ANN. CODE art. 16, § 66G (Cum. Supp. 1978); TENN. CODE ANN. § 36-228 (1977); W. VA. CODE § 48-7-8 (1976). *See* State *ex rel.* Isham v. Mullally, 15 Wisc. 2d 249, 112 N.W.2d 701 (1961); Hurd v. State, 125 Ga. App. 353, 187 S.E.2d 545 (1972); People *ex rel.* Bucaro v. Johnson, 8 Ill. App. 2d 618, 291 N.E.2d 9 (1972); Carpenter v. Goodall, 144 Ind. App. 134, 244 N.E.2d 673 (1969); Foglio v. Foglio, 13 Misc. 2d 767, 176 N.Y.S.2d 43 (1958). *See also* Robertson v. Apucco, 170 Conn. 367, 365 A.2d 824, *cert. den.,* 429 U.S. 852 (1976); People *ex rel.* Alexander v. Kelly, 20 App. Div. 2d 740, 246 N.Y.S.2d 877 (1964); Torino v. Cruz, 82 Misc. 2d 684, 369 N.Y.S.2d 291 (1975). *Accord,* State *ex rel.* Campbell v. Johnson, — Iowa App. —, 285 N.W.2d 766 (1979).

It is quite obvious that some sort of positive inference can be drawn from such results. What is not so obvious, however, is how the weight of that inference might be properly or most appropriately expressed in a percentage statement of probability of paternity. Not helping the situation, many physicians who are experts in blood typing confess outright to being insufficiently conversant with mathematics to work effectively with complex statistical formulae. (Worse, some do not "confess", do not understand and do the work anyway). This being so, we can assume with confidence that the typical judge, lawyer or jury (who have less reason to be conversant with the mathematics of statistics and probability) may *never* fully understand what is involved. The courts will have to operate on faith. But whom or what to believe? Already, some of the calculations of probability that have been accepted by some courts obviously abuse common sense. And, so far, a drawn-out dispute among medical experts has not finally resolved what data base is to be employed, what conclusions fairly may be drawn, how these should be communicated to the court and what weight they may be given there.

To deal with the last point first, considerable dispute surrounds the very idea of using statistical estimates in the adjudication of individual cases, whether the issue be paternity, criminal guilt or whatever. Professors Broun and Kelly have stated the case in favor of admissibility:

> The relatively weak probative force of percentage statements when compared with assertions of artificial certainty exists only up to a point. A particularly high statement of probability or improbability will have as much if not more probative force than a mere indication of probability or even medical certainty. For example, a cross-examiner blindly seeking to force a witness into a percentage statement of probability would be devastated if the expert answered, "Permanent disability would occur in 999 out of a thousand such cases." It is therefore not surprising to find that in most

221

reported cases in which a probability statement has been offered into evidence to show the likelihood of occurrence of a past event that statement was one of an extremely high or low probability. . . .

Despite the fact that the law generally recognizes probability theory, simple probability statements that are neither very high nor very low are significantly undervalued in the litigation process. There is little the courts can do to bolster the persuasive value of such statements before the jury. The adversary system carries its own safeguards here. In dealing with the admissibility and sufficiency of evidence, however, the law should reassess the value of mathematical estimates. The disproportionate treatment given to nonastronomical statements of mathematical fact can only result from the apparent fact that not only average jurors but the courts themselves commendably strive for absolute certainty. Perhaps the courts should set their sights lower and recognize that, in many instances where a scientifically supported statement of mathematical probability can be made, that statement will be as close to absolute certainty as we are ever going to get.[22]

Other authorities have taken a more jaundiced view of such evidence, the leading exponent being Professor Tribe:

[T]he very mystery that surrounds mathematical arguments — the relative obscurity that makes them at once impenetrable by the layman and impressive to him — creates a continuing risk that he will give such

---

22. Broun and Kelly, *Playing the Percentages and the Law of Evidence, 1970* U. ILL. L.F. 23, 37-38 (1970). *See also* the important exchange between Professors Tribe, Finkelstein and Fairly: Tribe, *A Further Critique of Mathematical Proof,* 84 HARV. L. REV. 1810 (1971); Finkelstein and Fairly, *A Comment on "Trial by Mathematics",* 84 HARV. L. REV. 1801 (1971); Tribe, *Trial by Mathematics: Precision and Ritual in the Legal Process,* 84 HARV. L. REV. 1329 (1971); Finkelstein and Fairly, *A Bayesian Approach to Identification Evidence,* 83 HARV. L. REV. 489 (1970).

arguments a credence they may not deserve and a weight they cannot logically claim.

The California Supreme Court recently perceived this danger when it warned that "[m]athematics, a veritable sorcerer in our computerized society, while assisting the trier of fact in the search for truth, must not [be allowed to] cast a spell over him." The court ruled improper a prosecutor's misconceived attempt to link an accused interracial couple with a robbery by using probability theory. The victim of the robbery, an elderly woman, had testified that she saw her assailant, a young woman with blond hair, run from the scene. One of the victim's neighbors had testified that he saw a Caucasian woman, with her hair in a dark blond ponytail, run from the scene of the crime and enter a yellow automobile driven by a male Negro wearing a mustache and beard. Several days later, officers arrested a couple that seemed to match these descriptions . . . .

In an effort to bolster the identification of the defendants as the perpetrators of the crime, the prosecutor called a college mathematics instructor to establish that, if the robbery was indeed committed by a Caucasian woman with a blond ponytail accompanied by a Negro with a beard and mustache and driving a yellow car, there was an overwhelming probability that the accused couple were guilty because they matched this detailed description.

The witness first testified to the "product rule" of probability theory, according to which the probability of the joint occurrence of a number of mutually independent events equals the product of the individual probabilities of each of the events. Without presenting any supporting statistical evidence, the prosecutor had the witness assume specific probability factors for each of the six characteristics allegedly shared by the defendants and the guilty couple.*

---

*

Characteristic	Assumed Probability of its Occurrence
1. Partly yellow automobile	1/10
2. Man with mustache	1/4

Applying the product rule to the assumed factors, the prosecutor concluded that there was but one chance in twelve million that any couple chosen at random would possess the characteristics in question, and asked the jury to infer that there was therefore but one chance in twelve million of the defendants' innocence.

The jury convicted but the California Supreme Court reversed, holding the mathematical testimony and the prosecutor's associated argument inadmissible on four separate grounds. First, the record was devoid of any empirical evidence to support the individual probabilities assumed by the prosecutor.

Second, even if the assumed probabilities were themselves correct, their multiplication under the product rule presupposed the independence of the factors they measured — a presupposition for which no proof was presented, and which was plainly false. If two or more events tend to occur together, the chances of their separate occurrence obviously cannot be multiplied to yield the chance of their joint occurrence. For example, if every tenth man is black and bearded, and if every fourth man wears a mustache, it may nonetheless be true that most bearded black men wear mustaches, so that nearly one man in ten — not one in forty — will be a black man with a beard *and* a mustache.

Third, even if the product rule could properly be applied to conclude that there was but one chance in twelve million that a randomly chosen couple would possess the six features in question, there would remain a substantial possibility that the guilty couple did not in fact possess all of those characteristics — either because the prosecution's witnesses were mistaken or lying, or because the guilty couple was somehow disguised. "Traditionally," the court reasoned, "the jury weighs such risks in evaluating the

---

3. Girl with ponytail	1/10
4. Girl with blond hair	1/3
5. Negro man with beard	1/10
6. Interracial couple in car	1/1000

credibility and probative value of trial testimony," but
— finding itself unable to quantify these possibilities of
error or falsification — the jury would be forced to
exclude such risks from any effort to assign a number
to the probability of guilt or innocence and would be
tempted to accord disproportionate weight to the
prosecution's computations.

Fourth, and entirely apart from the first three
objections, the prosecutor erroneously equated the
probability that a randomly chosen couple would
possess the incriminating characteristics, with the
probability that any given couple possessing those
characteristics would be innocent. After all, if the
suspect population contained, for example, twenty-four
million couples, and if there were a probability of one
in twelve million that a couple chosen at random from
the suspect population would possess the six
characteristics in question, then one could well expect
to find two such couples in the suspect population, and
there would be a probability of approximately one in
two — not one in twelve million — that any given
couple possessing the six characteristics would be
innocent. The court quite reasonably thought that few
defense attorneys, and fewer jurors, could be expected
to comprehend these basic flaws in the prosecution's
analysis. Under the circumstances, the court
concluded, this "trial by mathematics" so distorted the
jury's role and so disadvantaged defense counsel as to
constitute a miscarriage of justice.[23]

Several of the concerns identified by Professor Tribe are
transferable into the context of blood typing evidence *not*
showing an exclusion. Others are not. Noting one basic
distinction, a California appellate court held:

In reversing the conviction in *Collins,* the
[California] Supreme Court "established restrictions on

---

23. Tribe, *Trial by Mathematics: Precision and Ritual in the Legal
Process,* 84 HARV. L. REV. 1329, 1334-38, 1393 (1971). (Copyright © 1971
by the Harvard Law Review Assn., reprinted with permission).

the assignment of numerical values to the probability of encountering a given set of circumstances in a random population, and the use to which such coefficients might be put." [Citations omitted.] The HLA test interpretations are not based on arbitrarily assigned numerical probability values or on a statistical theory unsupported by the evidence. Instead, they are based upon objectively ascertainable data and a statistical theory based upon scientific research and experiment.[24]

Nevertheless, many statutes and courts have simply (but too radically) transferred their unease with statistical evidence into the fixed conclusion that blood typing evidence is admissible only if a clear exclusion is shown.[25] This approach, if the phrase be permitted, throws out the baby with the bathwater. As pointed out above, *some* sort of positive inference may rationally be drawn in certain circumstances. *We need only learn how to quantify that inference properly and how to communicate it to the court without risk of misunderstanding.* Already, a number of states have specific statutory provisions covering the admissibility of "probability" evidence in paternity cases. Such statutes prominently include the Uniform Parentage Act which provides as follows:[26]

Evidence relating to paternity may include: . . .
blood test results, weighted in accordance with evidence, if available, of the statistical probability of the alleged father's paternity;
medical or anthropological evidence relating to the alleged father's paternity of the child based on tests performed by experts. If a man has been identified as a possible father of the child, the court may, and upon

24. Cramer v. Morrison, 88 Cal. App. 3d 884, 153 Cal. Rptr. 865, 871-72 (1979).

25. *Supra* note 21.

26. UNIFORM PARENTAGE ACT § 12, 9A U.L.A. MATR., FAM. AND HEALTH LAWS 602 (1979). *Infra* Appendix B.

request of a party shall, require the child, the mother,
and the man to submit to appropriate tests; and
   all other evidence relevant to the issue of paternity of
the child.

By 1980, nine states had enacted the Act, California,
however, without this provision.[27]

Before that, the 1957 version of the Uniform Act on Blood
Tests to Determine Paternity provided that "if the experts
conclude that the blood tests show the possibility of the
alleged father's paternity, admission of this evidence is
within the discretion of the court depending upon the
infrequency of the blood type". By 1979, nine states had
enacted the Act, several, however, without that provision.[28]

In 1979, North Carolina enacted the nation's most
detailed provision on the subject:

> Whereas, the medical state of the art was formerly
> such that blood tests made in paternity cases could only
> be used to exclude a putative parent from the class of
> persons potentially capable of being the biological
> parent; however, a recent breakthrough in medical
> science now enables extended factor blood tests to show
> the inclusionary probability that a putative parent is
> the biological parent of a child; and . . . .
>
> Whereas, the availability of inclusionary in addition
> to exclusionary results of extended factor blood tests
> promotes the use of objective medical evidence in
> parentage matters by plaintiffs as well as defendants
> and thereby facilitates the plaintiffs' ability to fairly
> and accurately meet their burden of proof; and . . . .
>
> In the trial of any civil action in which the question
> of parentage arises, the court before whom the matter
> may be brought, upon motion of the plaintiff,
> alleged-parent defendant, or other interested party,
> shall order that the alleged-parent defendant, the
> known natural parent, and the child submit to any

27. 9A U.L.A. Matr., Fam. and Health Laws 579 (1979).
28. 9 U.L.A. Matr., Fam. and Health Laws 382 (Supp. 1976).

blood tests and comparisons which have been developed and adapted for purposes of establishing or disproving parentage and which are reasonably accessible to the alleged-parent defendant, the known natural parent, and the child. The results of those blood tests and comparisons, including the statistical likelihood of the alleged-parent's parentage, if available, shall be admitted in evidence when offered by a duly qualified, licensed practicing physician, duly qualified immunologist, duly qualified geneticist, or other qualified person. Upon receipt of a motion and the entry of an order under the provisions of this subsection, the court shall proceed as follows:

Where the issue of parentage is to be decided by a jury, where the results of those blood tests and comparisons are not shown to be inconsistent with the results of any other blood tests and comparisons, and where the results of those blood tests and comparisons indicate that the alleged-parent defendant cannot be the natural parent of the child, the jury shall be instructed that if they believe that the witness presenting the results testified truthfully as to those results, and if they believe that the tests and comparisons were conducted properly, then it will be their duty to decide that the alleged-parent defendant is not the natural parent.[29]

In the absence of a specific statute or binding precedent, of course, any court is free to admit into evidence *anything* that is considered relevant and useful. Accordingly, progressive (but often inadequately informed and therefore sometimes gullible) courts have been increasingly willing to admit "probability evidence" regarding paternity.[30] This

---

29. General Assembly of North Carolina, Session 1979, ch. 576, Senate Bill 230, effective May 16, 1979, amending G.S. 8-50.1, G.S. 49-7.2 and other relevant statutes.

30. *See* Malvasi v. Malvasi, 167 N.J. Super. 513, 401 A.2d 279 (1979); Broadwater v. Broadwater, 247 Md. 607, 233 A.2d 782 (1967); Cramer v. Morrison, 88 Cal. App. 3d 873, 153 Cal. Rptr. 865 (1979). *Cf.,* Livermore v. Livermore, 233 Iowa 1155, 11 N.W.2d 389 (1943).

development gives as much reason for concern as it is cause for optimism. Optimism is justified because it is clear that there is *some* positive inference just waiting to be drawn. Concern is justified, on the other hand, over the considerable confusion and disagreement that continues to surround this subject, even as displayed in the preamble to the North Carolina statute quoted above. But if the lawyers are confused, their confusion is due in substantial measure to disagreement that still exists in the medical community.[31] Several more or less different methods are used to calculate probabilities, and while each may have its "pros" and "cons" and may be *mathematically* accurate, different premises underlie different methods and these premises rarely are communicated effectively to the courts.

The AMA-ABA Guidelines suggest use of the following formula:

---

31. K. HUMMEL, BIOSTATISTICAL OPINION OF PARENTAGE BASED UPON THE RESULTS OF BLOOD GROUP TESTS (1971); Walker, *Probability in the Analysis of Paternity Test Results,* in H. SILVER and A. BARNES, PATERNITY TESTING 69-135 (Am. Assc. of Blood Banks, 1978); Lee, *Estimation of Likelihood of Paternity,* in H. POLESKY, PATERNITY TESTING 28 (Am. Soc. of Clinical Pathologists, 1975); Beautyman, *Paternity Actions — A Matter of Opinion or a Trial of the Blood?,* — J. LEGAL MED. 17, 20-21 (1976). *Cf.,* Wiener and Socha, *Methods Available for Solving Medico-legal Problems of Disputed Parentage,* 21 J. FOR. SCIENCES 42, 61-63 (1976); Letters to the Editor, Langaney & Pison, *Probability of Paternity: Useless,* 27 AM. J. HUMAN GENETICS 558 (1975); Valentris, *Statistical Evidence in Paternity Cases: Imperative,* 28 AM. J. HUMAN GENETICS 620 (1976); Salmon & Brocteur, *Probability of Paternity,* 28 AM. J. HUMAN GENETICS 622 (1976); Chakraborty & Schull, 28 AM. J. HUMAN GENETICS 615 (1976). *See further,* Forrest, *The Legal Implications of HLA Testing for Paternity,* 16 J. FAM. L. 537 (1977-78); Terasaki, *Resolution by HLA Testing of 1000 Paternity Cases Not Excluded by ABO Testing,* 16 J. FAM. L. 543 (1978); Jaffee, *Comment on the Judicial Use of HLA Paternity Test Results and Other Statistical Evidence: A Response to Terasaki,* 17 J. FAM. L. 457 (1979).

In "one-man" cases Hummel has proposed the application of the equation of Essen-Möller. The plausibility of paternity, W, is calculated from:

$$W = \cfrac{1}{1 + \cfrac{(Y_1}{(X_1} \cdot \cfrac{Y_2}{X_2} \cdot \cfrac{Y_3}{X_3} \cdots \begin{matrix})\\)\end{matrix}}$$

Where Y is the frequency of various blood group phenotypes of men among the normal male population and X is the frequency of corresponding phenotypes of true fathers in the given mother-child combination.

The calculation can be carried out from tables of genotype frequencies, but Hummel has prepared tables based on logarithms which facilitate the estimation of probability of paternity.

Example: In a given child-mother-putative father combination the putative father is not excluded. The phenotypes are:

Child: A_1; Rh_0rh (cDe/cde); NN; K^+; Fy(a+)
Mother: A_1; Rh_0rh (cDe/cde); MN; K^-; Fy(a-)
Man: A_1; Rh_1rh (Cde/cde); MN; K^+, Fy(a+)

Calculation (using tables of Hummel)

1. $\Sigma \ \log \dfrac{Y}{X}$ + 10 for the blood group systems tested:

A-B-O	9.8739
Rh	9.9477
MN	9.9604
K	8.8865
Fy	9.8176
	48.4861

2. Subtract 10 (n-1), when n = number of systems used

48.4861
-40.0000
8.4861

3. Value for W = about 97 percent [32]

Dr. Polesky explains further:

The basis of these calculations is as follows:
1. for each independent genetic system, the child has both a paternal and maternal gene.
2. the true father must have all the genes needed to account for the paternal markers in the child.
3. one can estimate the chance of a sperm from the alleged man carrying the needed genes. This value is labeled as "X". Assume a genetic system with two alleles (alternate forms of the gene at a specific chromosomal location) a & b. If the paternal contribution to the child is a, then all the sperm of a man who is (a + b -; aa) will carry a (X = 1.0); half the sperm of a man who is (a + b +; ab) will carry a (X = 0.5).
4. there is data on the frequency of the genes in the random population (defined as unrelated individuals of an appropriate racial background). The frequency of the paternal contribution in the random population is labeled as "Y" and represents the likelihood of a man other than the accused contributing the gene to the child.

To compute the *paternity index* (PI) the ratio of X (likelihood of gene a from the accused) to Y (likelihood of gene a from the random population) is determined. [When a is frequent (eg Y = 0.80) if the accused is (a + b -; aa) then $\frac{X}{Y} = \frac{1.0}{0.8} = 1.25$ or if the accused is (a + b +; ab) then $\frac{X}{Y} = \frac{0.5}{0.8} = 0.625$.

When a is rare (eg Y = 0.08) then $\frac{X}{Y}$ is 12.5 or 5.25.]

This value is calculated for each genetic system taking into account the mother-child pair, the alleged father's genetic makeup and the frequency in random man. Since the true father must have all the appropriate

---

32. Joint A.M.A.-A.B.A. Guidelines: *Present Status of Serologic Testing in Problems of Disputed Parentage,* 10 Fam. L.Q. 247, 261 (1976). *See infra* Appendix D.

genes the PI $= \dfrac{X^1}{Y^1} \cdot \dfrac{X^2}{Y^2} \cdots \dfrac{X^n}{Y^n}$ where 1, 2 . . . ^{n} are values for each system.

The PI can be converted into a probability value (plausibility of paternity) "W". This is calculated by the formula W $= \dfrac{1}{1 + \dfrac{Y}{X}}$ (100). If the PI $= 19$, W - 95%. *In this case 20 random men would have to be tested to find one who could have fathered the child in question and hence compared to one random man the alleged father is 95% more likely to be the true father. . . .* [A] second individual with access could be the true father; however, statistically this possibility (a second man with the appropriate genes when the PI = 19) can occur only 5% of the time. [Emphasis added] [33]

Professor Hummel criticizes this explanation as follows: "If [this approach] were proper, then the W-value would be nothing other than the probability of exclusion." [*I.e.*, the cumulative probability that a non-father would be excluded by successive blood tests]. Professor Hummel continues:

> Serologists understand the latter very well and want to deal with the whole question of serostatistics on that basis . . . . In reality, a W-value of 95% means that among 100 otherwise equal cases there are 95 in which the alleged father actually is the father, whereas in five cases another man is the child's progenitor. This presupposes that in disputed "one-man cases" as many actual fathers as non-fathers are named, *i.e,* that the *a priori* probability is 0.5.[34]

Basic assumptions underlying this formula have been explained by Professor Hummel as follows:

> Equality before the law requires that if a man denies a child's allegation that he is the child's father, these

---

33. Mimeograph prepared by Minneapolis War Memorial Blood Bank.

34. Letter of March 20, 1980, from Professor Hummel to Harry D. Krause, commenting on a draft of this manuscript.

two claims must be treated as equal. The probability of his being the father is the *same* as that of *not* being a father. Accordingly, in cases involving one man the *a priori* probability of paternity should be 0.5. The legal philosophy behind this *a priori* probability cannot be challenged so long as the legal rights asserted by the child are valued as highly as those defended by the man. Thus far, there have not yet been any court decisions in Germany — nor any signs of such a trend — which treat the opposing interests of the parties in paternity as *unequal* in principle.

The problem of *a priori* probability of paternity can also be dealt with statistically. If a woman claims that a man is the father of her child, and the man denies the allegation, he implies that her statement is false (whether this be intentionally or not does not concern us here). If *all* women were always to name the *actual father* there would be little call for blood group and other opinions; the *a priori* probability would always be 1. If women always claimed that *non*-fathers were the fathers, paternity opinions would be equally superfluous; the *a priori* probability that the man named by the mother is the father would be zero. In *reality*, some of the mothers' statements will be correct and some will be false (intentionally or unintentionally). From the results of our own studies we were able to establish that in ... Europe the percentage of incorrect statements increased from north to south. The percentage of false allegations in Denmark is a little over 10%, in Germany approximately 25%, and in Austria more than 40% .... These figures should serve to illustrate the differences between realistic *a priori* assumptions as to the probability of paternity and that of 0.5; the former always deviate upwards (excluding cases of contested legitimacy). Notwithstanding this evidence we shall disregard a realistic *a priori* probability — except in special cases — and accept *Essen-Möller's* proposal of a normed *a priori* of 0.5. There are telling reasons in legal philosophy for accepting this on the one hand, and on the other hand, in practice judges unconsciously recognize an immediate realistic *a priori* probability

233

and take account of this in their decisions. If the serological expert were also to take account of this *a priori* probability in the W-value it would then be included *twice*, which would falsify the evidence.

Certainly, there are cases where there is a large realistic deviation *downwards* from the normed *a priori* probability of 0.5, and this must be taken into account somehow. Thus, it is conceivable that in cases where the man alleged to be the father *denies cohabitation* (indeed, denies even being acquainted with the mother), the percentage of non-fathers will be greater than 50%. Mothers who lead promiscuous lives have greater difficulty in naming the fathers of their children than do other women. In such cases the percentage of non-fathers may also exceed 50%. Thus far, we do not have any concrete figures for realistic *a priori* probabilities in cases involving contested cohabitation and promiscuity. In such situations the wisest course is to require particularly compelling evidence of paternity, *e.g.*, W = 99.73%.

[T]here are *several* types of *a priori* probability in serostatistics. In one-man cases (filiation cases in which only one man is involved), the child's mother has either named the actual father or not. In Germany the man named by the mother as the father is *not* the father of the child in 25% of all cases. Thus, at least *this* percentage of supposed one-man cases in Germany are, in reality, cases *involving two or more men.* Seen in this way, the realistic *a priori* probability in one-man cases is a direct measure of the willingness of the child's mother to admit to cohabitation with more than one man, or to tell the truth in naming the child's father. In Germany approximately 25% of these mothers simply conceal the fact that they have cohabited with more than one man (cases of actual lying are relatively rare), whereas in the Nordic countries the figure is approximately 10%. If cohabitation with more than one man were *never* concealed, one-man cases could be decided directly in court, *i.e.*, without the necessity of opinions of parentage.

In cases involving *more than one man* there are two types of *a priori* probability. The first gives the frequency with which the real father is among the men included in the opinions. In this case the willingness of the child's mother to provide information plays a large role. The more complete her information about her cohabitants, the greater the probability that a single non-excluded man in a case involving more than one man is in fact the father of the child plaintiff. In Germany at the present one may assume that in more than 80% of cases involving more than one man the real father is included in the blood group opinions. The realistic *a priori* probability for a non-excluded man in a case involving more than one man is, therefore, at least 80%. If it were 100% (which would be the situation if the mother were to disclose all her information), there could not be any doubt that the non-excluded man in a case involving more than one man is the father of the child.

The second type of *a priori* probability in cases involving more than one man is of a different nature. In keeping with legal practice in Germany, the *mother* of an illegitimate child is asked to name the father of her child. If she has cohabited with only one man during the period of conception she is able (if she so wishes) to give the *correct* information. But if she had sexual intercourse with more than one man her information may be misleading. As the number of cohabitants increases so will the percentage of incorrect statements. The man named by the child's mother as the father of her child is formally the "accused" in the case in question; the other men are the "cohabiting witnesses" (or simply the "witnesses"). The actual fathers in such cases will sometimes be the accused and sometimes be among the witnesses. Knowledge of the respective percentages will permit the calculation of an *a priori* probability that, in cases involving more than one man, the "accused" is the father or one of the "witnesses" is. The results of my own studies of two-men cases have revealed that 70% of the actual fathers are 'accused', and 30% are 'witnesses'. Therefore, in a two-men case the *a priori* probability of paternity of an "accused" is more than twice that of a "witness". This B_v/Z_v *a priori* probability has little to do with the willingness of the child's mother to give information or to tell the truth. It has far more to do with the fact that women, even if they cohabit with more than one man during the period of conception, have a sound intuitive feeling of which of the cohabitants is in fact the father of her child.

These two *a priori* probabilities for cases involving *more than one man* are applied in a *normed* form in serostatistical practice — similar to the procedure followed in one-man cases — and generally have the value 0.5. Thus, one assumes: (a) that in every second case involving more than one man the real father is not included in the blood group opinions; (b) that, in two-men cases, the "accused" is just as frequently the father of the child as the "witness" is; and (c) that in cases involving three or more men, each man has an *equal chance* of being the father of the child (even a man who has not been named).

As mentioned above, in serostatistical practice *every* type of *a priori* probability is subject to Bayes' postulate. Norming the *a priori* probabilities affects the results of the W-value obtained for each individual case. We must deal with this in greater detail: The *realistic a priori* probability in *one-man* cases is either 0.5 or greater. Accordingly, the W-value is a fairly accurate or slightly deflated reflection of the correct probability. 1 — W, the probability of error, reflects the actual situation or is a little too high. In Germany, the realistic probability of error is approximately only 1/3 of 1 — W. Hence, if one applies an *a priori* probability of 0.5 in one-man cases, the alleged father will be biostatistically *favored* as a rule. But, as dealt with above, this is not a sufficient cause to either change the *a priori* value of 0.5 or to abandon the use of a normed value completely.

If the exclusion of all men except one changes *cases involving more than one man* into *one-man cases*, the correct probability is always higher than that given by W, for the realistic *a priori* probability is always clearly *above* 0.5. The expectation of error is correspondingly lower than that indicated by 1 — W.

> If two men cannot be excluded from paternity the
> W-value calculated for the *accused* will be too low and
> that for the *witness* too high, as compared with the
> actual situation, because the realistic B/Z *a priori*
> probability is greater than 0.5.[35]

The reader is invited to form his or her own opinion as to
whether (and, if so, as to the most appropriate method by
which) these underlying assumptions should be
individualized in any specific case and related to the
percentage statement of probability of paternity, and how
the end-product is to be communicated to the court. What
is clear is that the typical court is *not* aware of these
assumptions, nor of the potential range of error they might
introduce. It would appear that there is a problem even if
few of these factors weigh heavily in the *typical* case and
even if, in the *majority* of cases, the formula tends to resolve
uncertainties in favor of the men alleged to be fathers.

Another point of some disagreement among scientists is
how properly to define the "random man" with whom the
alleged father is to be compared. The resolution of this issue
involves questions of race and gene frequencies. Clearly,
the possibility of introducing error into probability
calculations by this route is far greater in a multi-ethnic
and multi-racial society such as the United States than it is
in a country with a highly homogeneous population, such
as, for instance, Denmark.[36]

In 1979, the American Association of Blood Banks' *Ad
Hoc* Committee on Parentage Testing sent out three
hypothetical problem cases to a number of reputable,
international experts who routinely engage in calculating
"probability of paternity." The problems gave all facts

---

35. K. Hummel, Paper presented at 8th International Congress of the
Society for Forensic Haemogenetics (Gesellschaft für forensische
Blutgruppenkunde, e.V.), September 23-27, 1979, London.
36. *Infra* Appendix F.

(blood types of alleged father, mother and child, etc.) needed to calculate probability, but did not specify that any particular method be used. The results that returned to the Committee were not reassuring. Although there was reasonable agreement on two of the problem cases, there was considerable disparity on one. As commented by the Committee's chairman, "different logic is being used by some workers in this field." [37] These results raise doubt as to the propriety of the methods employed by some of the respondents and point to disagreement (or even possible misunderstanding on the part of some experts) as to what "probability of paternity" calculations are to show. Above all, the results point up the need for acceptance of a uniform method of calculation, including clear and explicit agreement on (and detailed statement of) all premises and assumptions that underly the computation.

In an experiment throwing further caution on the careless use of probability evidence, Dr. Polesky calculated the probability values for 469 men who had been *excluded* by at least one gene system (*i.e.*, all of them had definitely been determined *not* to be the fathers of the children in question). The calculation proceeded in the normal manner, except that the gene systems in which the exclusions were obtained were omitted from each individual calculation. This experiment resulted in 26% of these *excluded* men having probability values in excess of 95% and only 18% obtaining a probability value of less than 50%.[38]

Thus the confusion is considerable. Still worse, aside from the mystery surrounding the calculation of probability of paternity, many lawyers and judges seem to have come to believe that blood tests can affirmatively establish

---

37. Letter of December 11, 1979, from Richard H. Walker, M.D., to Harry D. Krause.

38. Mimeograph prepared by Minneapolis War Memorial Blood Bank.

paternity. To repeat, *they cannot.* It seems appropriate to remind the judge that it is he or she (and not the blood typing expert) who must determine whether blood typing test results are evidence. And it is the judge who must decide how much weight to give such evidence.

To summarize, a legal mechanism exists in a number of states and is being developed in others for the admission into evidence of this type of circumstantial, "positive evidence" of paternity. At this point, we need be concerned that this transition may be happening faster than the rate at which understanding how properly to calculate this "positive evidence" is penetrating the scientific community. Certainly, the following recommendation transmitted by the federal support enforcement authorities to the states ("developed" by the University of Southern California's Center for Health Services and Research under contract with OCSE) is wrong on the law. On the "facts," it is at best premature and probably worse:

> Blood testing for exclusion, inclusion and probability of paternity is an accurate and effective tool which is acceptable to the judiciary and very useful to IV-D jurisdictions and should be used as integral part of all paternity determination systems.
>
> Due to the reliability and acceptability of blood test results which indicate probability of paternity, state law should provide for the admissibility of such evidence.[39]

Approaching this dangerous ground more cautiously, the A.M.A.-A.B.A. "Guidelines on the Present Status of

---

39. Office of Child Support Enforcement, U.S. Dept. of Health, Education and Welfare, Summary of Conclusions and Recommendations, Research Report on "Techniques and Procedures to Establish the Paternity of Children Born Out of Wedlock". In IM-77-6 (1976), OCSE recommended:

The maximum benefit from this study will be obtained through distribution to operating offices throughout your State.

Serologic Testing in Problems of Parentage" contain the following *caveat* — while explaining the widely accepted system of statistical calculation described above:

> The difficulty judges, juries, and lawyers may experience in interpreting statistical evidence correctly, and possible due process issues under the 14th Amendment of the U.S. Constitution arising in the light of the assumptions just discussed, raise questions regarding the indiscriminate use of such evidence .... [T]he matter should be studied further and appropriate safeguards need be developed to guard against possible misinterpretation of calculations of "likelihood of paternity." [40]

The further study (*i.e.*, identifying and agreeing on the proper method of calculation, defining the exact meaning of the result of the calculation with full statement of all

---

40. Joint A.M.A.-A.B.A. Guidelines: *Present Status of Serologic Testing in Problems of Disputed Parentage* 10 FAM. L.Q. 247, 260-263 (1976). *Infra* Appendix D. These guidelines have advanced far beyond a 1957 report of an A.M.A. committee which counseled:

> ... routine medicolegal applications of blood grouping be restricted at present to tests for the four blood groups O, A, B and AB of the A-B-O system; the three types M, N, and MN of the M-N-S system; and factors Rh, rh', rh'', and hr' of the Rh-Hr system. Tests for additional factors and systems are considered insufficiently established for routine use at present, although they may provide evidence in particular selected cases. Such evidence should be submitted in a separate letter not part of the standard report and should be presented with proper caution. Similarly, the value of rare combinations of groups providing indication of paternity, in contrast to the conventional use of the tests to establish only non-paternity, should be recognized in unusual cases but should be treated with caution in a separate communication not part of the definitive report. The question of qualification of experts remains a difficult and unsolved problem requiring serious study. [Emphasis added.]

Committee on Medicolegal Problems, Medicolegal Applications of Blood Grouping Tests, 164 J.A.M.A. 2036 (1957). *See also* Committee on Medicolegal Problems, Medicolegal Application of Blood Grouping Tests, 149 J.A.M.A. 699, 706 (1952).

premises) recommended by the "Guidelines"[41] has begun under the auspices of a special committee of the American Association of Blood Banks.[42]

In the meantime, it is comforting that the higher and higher probabilities of excluding falsely accused men that are being obtained by use of ever more sophisticated tests will have the natural consequence that the statistical probability of *inclusion* will be called for in less cases. In that sense, the problems surrounding the proper and precise calculation of the probability of paternity are becoming somewhat less important. With the skewed sample of doubtful cases submitted to today's laboratories, however, the typical experience is that exclusions are found in only about one-quarter of the cases submitted for analysis. This means that the great majority of blood tests that are carried out produce seemingly inconclusive results. This, of course, is the natural result of the fact that the man named as the father actually *is* the father in many or most cases. But in *which* cases?

Along with the other relevant evidence, probability evidence will help decide that question. Rather than tell a man that he cannot be excluded as a possible father, would it not be much more likely to enlist his voluntary cooperation (and indeed make him feel better) if (based on the non-excluding but not at all inconclusive blood tests) he could be told that there is a probability of, say, 99.8% that he is actually the father? But first we must agree on how to do the calculation properly and how to bring it into court without risk of misunderstanding.

---

41. Joint A.M.A.-A.B.A. Guidelines: *Present Status of Serologic Testing in Problems of Disputed Parentage,* 10 Fam. L. Q. 247,283 (1976). Appendix D.

42. Committee on Parentage Testing of the American Association of Blood Banks, Dr. Richard Walker, Chairman.

c. *Admissibility of Specific Tests.*

There do not seem to be statutes which say specifically that, for instance, only the ABO, MNS, and Rh systems are acceptable, although these remain the three basic systems. Nor should a statute attempt to freeze scientific progress at any given point in time. New developments in this area are occurring too fast to make that a profitable means of achieving certainty in the courts. Some authority, but not much, may nevertheless be obtained from court decisions. For instance, the recently developed HLA testing system has been accepted in California and New Jersey courts [43] and other individual cases accepting or rejecting specific systems could be cited.[44]

Broadly speaking, however, all evidence "having any tendency in reason to prove or disprove any disputed fact that is of consequence to the determination of the action" is admissible.[45] Translated into the context of the acceptability of *any* specific system of blood typing, the general rule thus requires that the system that is sought to be introduced as evidence be *scientifically reliable.* In the case of newer systems, this means that they must be properly and specifically proved to the court, whereas in the case of well established systems (such as ABO, MNS, Rh

---

43. *E.g.,* Cramer v. Morrison, 88 Cal. App. 3d 873, 153 Cal. Rptr. 865 (1979); Malvasi v. Malvasi, 167 N.J. Super. 513, 401 A.2d 279 (1979); County of Fresno v. Superior Ct. of Fresno County, 92 Cal. App. 3d 133, 154 Cal. Rptr. 660 (1979).

44. *E.g.,* Groulx v. Groulx, 98 N.H. 481, 103 A.2d 188 (1954), accepting an anti-S grouping test. In 1966, the Supreme Court of California rejected a now acceptable system. Huntingdon v. Crowley, 64 Cal. 2d 647, 650 414 P.2d 382, 385, 51 Cal. Rptr. 254, 257 (1966):

"It may well be, of course, that some day in the near or distant future the Kell-Cellano test will achieve the same degree of acceptance as the present standard blood tests. In that event the courts will welcome their use as an aid in our never-ending pursuit of the truth."

45. Cal. Evid. Code Ann. § 210 (1966).

and more) "judicial notice" should be taken and specific proof of scientific acceptance not be required.

The leading statement on the subject remains the following:

> Just when a scientific principle or discovery crosses the line between the experimental and demonstrable stages is difficult to define ... while courts will go a long way in admitting expert testimony deduced from a well-recognized scientific principle or discovery, the thing from which the deduction is made must be sufficiently established to have gained general acceptance in the particular field in which it belongs.[46]

By the late sixties — in relation to blood typing evidence — it was readily apparent that this answer was at least inefficient and probably inadequate.[47] Courts were left as much at the mercy of "experts" who did or did not know what they were talking about as they remained victims of legislation that had not been updated to reflect modern scientific capabilities. Indeed, justified uncertainty regarding scientific capabilities may be the basis for the relatively low credibility our judges tended to accord blood typing evidence. The A.M.A.-A.B.A. Guidelines set out to correct this situation. As more and more courts look to them for needed guidance, they are becoming increasingly influential.

d. *Reliability of the Blood Typing Facility and Expert.*

The last question in this section goes to the conduct of the tests in terms of their proper scientific execution. An Arizona court has said about all that need be said:

---

46. Frye v. U.S., 293 F.2d 1013, 1014 (D.C. Cir. 1923).

47. *Cf.,* Note, *Frye Standard of "General Acceptance" for Admissibility of Scientific Evidence Rejected in Favor of Balancing Test,* 64 CORNELL L. REV. 875 (1979).

Is, then, evidence of *properly conducted* blood grouping tests which excluded the husband as the father of his wife's child clear and convincing? In our opinion, such evidence is not only clear and convincing, but is conclusive of the question. To hold otherwise would be tantamount to this court, by judicial decree, declaring the laws of motion and gravity to be repealed.

This does not mean that courts should abdicate their traditional role as seekers of truth to the laboratories of scientists and medical experts. The key words in reaching this decision are "properly conducted." In order for a particular blood grouping test to reach the pinnacle of infallibility to which we have elevated it, there must be a close scrutiny of the soundness of the scientific procedures followed and a sharp delving into the skill of the supervising expert. Mistakes can occur through difficulty in the laboratory's obtaining proper anti-serum of a sufficient strength and classification; mistakes may arise as to some individuals from the presence in their blood serum of blocking antibodies which may be present because of transfusions or pregnancy; mistakes may develop through failure to follow testing methods recommended by manufacturers of the anti-serum employed; mistakes may occur through failure of the laboratory technician to observe the clumping process, either through lack of skill or inattention; further mistakes may occur, especially in the Rh grouping test, because of lack of skill of the individual conducting the test. These problems and others must stand the bright light of judicial inquiry. While the transmission of blood groupings may be a natural law, the manner in which these blood groupings are determined is subject to the human frailties inherent in all human conduct. When the trier of fact has satisfied itself by clear and convincing evidence of the qualifications of the expert and that the procedures under which the tests were obtained were proper, then and only then, may the stamp of conclusiveness be placed upon them. If there is no evidence, over which reasonable men may differ, to impugn the integrity of these tests, the court should grant the appropriate relief without submission of the question to the jury.[48]

How then may these technical problems be minimized? How may the court satisfy itself that the laboratory or expert reporting test results to the court has indeed followed proper procedures? The hard way — in terms of excessive expense and unfulfillable demands on the time of experts and courts — is the traditional way: In each *individual* case, the expert executing the tests — and not infrequently, the expert re-checking the tests — will testify as to the scientific acceptability of the systems used, the chain of custody involving the blood samples, the specific test results and their meaning in the context of the specific case and be subject to cross examination on all these issues.[49]

To minimize these costs and thereby make "state-of-the-art" paternity testing a practical option in the

---

48. Anonymous v. Anonymous, 10 Ariz. App. 496, 500, 460 P.2d 32, 35-36 (1969) (Emphasis in original, citations omitted). Pitfalls in testing, leading to conflicting expert opinions, were graphically at issue in Torino v. Cruz, 82 Misc. 2d 684, 369 N.Y.S.2d 291 (1975). *See also infra* note 49 and ch. VI.4.

49.
It is submitted that in a search for the truth our modern procedure should be to admit the blood tests and also admit a searching cross-examination, because, as with any other item that may be taken or sent to a laboratory for examination, there is always a possibility of error. Such matters as (1) although not a great possibility, the containers could have been mislabeled; (2) the failure to see the agglutenation, particularly if it is weak; (3) proper control of temperatures; (4) use of too concentrated or diluted an antiserum, or red cell suspension solution; (5) allowing too much or too little time for the reaction to occur; (6) too much or too little centrifugal force which is required in some tests; (7) the deterioration or contamination of antiserums; (8) deterioration of blood tested, especially if it has been stored too long or exposed to extreme hot or cold; (9) chemical solutions in which the agglutenation takes place being improper for the specific anti-serum; and (10) biological errors in using rare groupings of blood and lack of information on these types. Plaintiff's brief in Jackson v. Jackson, 67 Cal. 2d 245, 250, 430 P.2d 289, 292, 60 Cal. Rptr. 649, 652 (Burke, J., dissenting, 1967).

large, even vast, number of paternity cases contemplated by current federal law, it appears that the certification of centralized, specialized, approved and audited blood typing laboratories provides the only practical alternative. In view of the importance of this point and the fact that federal legislation has already come close to this subject, this point is developed more thoroughly below.[50] The other point — how a central, "mass-production" testing laboratory may effectively "produce" and "package" its evidence in a manner that will minimize procedural problems of introducing such evidence and provide sorely needed confidence to the courts that what they are accepting is indeed reliable information — is dealt with after a review of applicable aspects of the law of evidence.

3. Producing Blood Tests in the Courts: The Law of Evidence.*

If more adequate judicial *understanding* of blood typing evidence is essential to fairness in paternity actions, it is equally essential to provide effective *means* to produce that evidence. What now follows is an investigation, first of the *legal* implications of authorizing the courts to order blood tests and second, of centralizing blood typing tests in specialized blood typing centers. Appropriate legal procedures must be devised for the courts to obtain reliable evidence and for that evidence to be introduced. With regard to the latter, the "packaging" of the evidence must be good enough to permit the average judge, (who, of course, is not an expert in the evaluation of scientific evidence), to understand what the evidence means in the particular case and what weight he should give it. In addition, the law of evidence poses certain obstacles that may impede the admissibility of blood tests which means that appropriate

---

50. *Infra* ch. X.5.

* Principal Author: Kenneth S. Broun

adjustments in the rules of evidence should be considered to facilitate the introduction of properly conducted tests.

Naturally, the best way to deal with the question of the admissibility of blood typing tests (and the earlier question of whether tests are to be run), is by way of stipulation. If the parties stipulate as to the taking of the tests and the admissibility of the laboratory's report, no significant technical problems involving the law of evidence arise. As a matter of practice, much of the blood typing evidence now entering the courts comes in on that basis. It also should be noted that some of the difficulties in finding experts willing to testify in court (and the associated, high costs) can be reduced through the use of depositions. This leaves, however, a large number of cases in which an appropriate stipulation cannot be obtained or in which a depositionis not an available or reasonable alternative. What follows relates primarily to those situations.

The range of questions extends from the procedures that should govern the taking of the blood sample to the laboratory's report back to the court. How can that whole process be standardized and, (insofar as possible), mechanized so as to provide maximum efficiency? With regard to the taking of the sample, the chief question concerns whether, under what circumstances and by what sanctions, the court may order the parties to submit to blood tests against their will. With regard to the transmission of the sample to the laboratory, the important issue is that the "chain of custody" be properly maintained. Concerning the laboratory's report to the court, the key question is whether an opportunity to cross examine the "expert" can be denied the parties or, if not, what procedures will as a practical matter minimize the incidence of cross examination. Obviously, along with the prohibitive expense that would be involved, the shortage of qualified experts would make it impossible for the expert who performed the test to appear at each trial for cross examination. Nor, indeed, would any one expert perform all the tests relating to a particular blood sample or set of samples in a sophisticated laboratory. Instead, the laboratories find it more economical to specialize their personnel so that several technicians handle the various tests.

a. *The Court's Power to Order the Parties to Undergo Blood Tests: Of Privacy and the Constitution.*

If blood tests in paternity actions are to be an effective evidentiary tool, the courts must be able to compel all necessary persons — the alleged father, the mother and the child — to submit to the taking of blood samples. Is there a constitutional impediment to such orders?

The U.S. Supreme Court has not dealt explicitly with the question of compulsory blood tests in paternity actions. It has, however, considered such tests in criminal cases, where constitutional issues usually are taken even more seriously than in civil cases. In *Breithaupt v. Abram,*[51] a blood sample was taken from the defendant while he was unconscious as the result of an automobile accident. The results of a blood-alcohol test were introduced in the "involuntary manslaughter" trial that arose from the accident. Petitioning for *habeas corpus,* the defendant claimed that the admission at his trial of the results of the involuntary blood test had deprived him of his liberty without due process of law within the meaning of the Fourteenth Amendment. The Supreme Court rejected his arguments. Following the doctrine of that time (*i.e.,* that the Fourteenth Amendment does *not* extend Fourth and Fifth Amendment rights to a defendant in a state court prosecution), the Court rejected the claim that the test violated the privilege against self-incrimination or

---

51. 352 U.S. 432, 77 S. Ct. 408, 1 L. Ed. 2d 448 (1957).

constituted an unreasonable search and seizure. More significantly, especially in the light of the later extension of Fourteenth Amendment protections, the Court held that the conduct of the police in taking the blood sample did not offend due process. Unlike the forcible use of a stomach pump (found unconstitutional in *Rochin v. California*),[52] the Court found nothing "brutal" or "offensive" in the taking of a sample of blood when done under the protective eye of a physician. The Court noted:

> The blood test procedure has become routine in our everyday life. It is a ritual for those going into the military service as well as those applying for marriage licenses. Many colleges require such tests before permitting entrance and literally millions of us have voluntarily gone through the same, though a longer, routine in becoming blood donors. Likewise, we note that a majority of our States have either enacted statutes in some form authorizing tests of this nature or permit findings so obtained to be admitted in evidence. We therefore conclude that a blood test taken by a skilled technician is not such conduct that shocks the conscience.[53]

The issue of compelled blood tests again came before the Court in *Schmerber v. California*,[54] an appeal from a conviction for driving while under the influence of intoxicating liquor. By this time the guarantees of the Fourth and Fifth Amendments had been extended to defendants in state courts.[55] Nevertheless, relying upon *Breithaupt*, the Court again upheld the constitutionality of

---

52. 342 U.S. 165, 72 S. Ct. 205, 96 L. Ed. 183 (1952).

53. Breithaupt v. Abram, 352 U.S. 432, 436-37, 77 S. Ct. 408, 410-11, 1 L. Ed. 2d 448, 451-52 (1957) (citation omitted).

54. 384 U.S. 757, 86 S. Ct. 1826, 16 L. Ed. 2d 908 (1966).

55. *See, e.g.,* Malloy v. Hogan, 378 U.S. 1, 84 S. Ct. 1489, 12 L. Ed. 2d 653 (1964) and Mapp v. Ohio, 367 U.S. 643, 81 S. Ct. 1278, 6 L. Ed. 2d 575 (1961).

the test and rejected the notion that the taking of the sample offended due process. Also rejected was the argument that the taking of blood violated the petitioner's privilege against self-incrimination, because the taking did not involve evidence of "a testimonial or communicative nature" and therefore was not within the privilege.[56] While the taking of blood falls within the "broadly conceived reach of a search and seizure under the Fourth Amendment," there was nothing unreasonable about the conduct of the authorities in this instance. The attempt to secure evidence of blood alcohol content was appropriate and incident to the petitioner's arrest. And the test chosen to measure the blood-alcohol level was reasonable and performed in a reasonable manner. Rephrasing the dictum in *Breithaupt,* the Court noted that the blood was taken by a physician in a hospital environment according to accepted medical practices and that such common tests involve, for most people, virtually no risk, trauma, or pain.[57]

The holding of the *Schmerber* case is echoed by courts that have dealt with blood tests in *criminal* cases both before and after *Schmerber.*[58] Not surprisingly, courts dealing with paternity cases that usually are *civil* in nature have had even less trouble approving compulsory tests. The questions of "self-incrimination" and "search and seizure"

---

56. The petitioner also claimed that he had been denied the right to assistance of counsel in that he had been compelled to submit to the test despite an objection made on the advice of counsel. The Court noted that, since petitioner was not entitled to assert the privilege, "he has no greater right because counsel erroneously advised him that he could assert it." 384 U.S. at 766, 86 S. Ct. at 1833, 16 L. Ed. 2d at 917 (1966).

57. Schmerber v. California, 384 U.S. 757, 771, 86 S. Ct. 1826, 1836, 16 L. Ed. 2d 908, 914 (1966). The Court also noted that petitioner "is not one of the few who on grounds of fear, concern for health, or religious scruple might prefer some other means of testing. . ." (*Id.*).

58. *E.g.,* People v. Kemp, 55 Cal. 2d 458, 359 P.2d 913 (1961); State v. McGrew, 25 Ohio App. 2d 175, 268 N.E.2d 286 (1971).

are less significant in civil cases, not only because constitutional guarantees apply less stringently, but also because the testing typically is done under court order. Although in a paternity action there is the possibility of a violation of due process similar in nature to an invasion of privacy as in *Breithaupt* or *Schmerber,* the courts have not found the invasion unreasonable. Where the question of invasion of privacy was raised specifically, (in *Anthony v. Anthony* which upheld compulsory blood tests in New Jersey despite earlier authority to the contrary), the court responded:

> The pin prick of a blood grouping test is hardly more substantial than the ignominy of the fingerprinting process under an accusation of crime. A pin prick, and a more painful one, is authorized by R.S. 18:14-52, N.J.S.A., which permits school boards to exclude from attendance unvaccinated children, and which has been held constitutional . . . I believe that the health of our judicial system, depending as it does on the finding of truth so that justice may be done is of equal importance with the physical health of the community. I cannot believe that a blood grouping test made by skilled physicians constitutes the mythical nose of the camel under the tent which will be followed by such extreme measures as the trepanning of the skull of a witness.[59]

Numerous courts have approved and enforced statutes providing for court-ordered blood tests.[60] Others have interpreted general rules providing for physical examination as including blood-grouping tests.[61] Several

---

59. 9 N.J. Super. 411, 417, 74 A.2d 919, 921-22 (1950). *Accord,* Beckwith v. Beckwith, 355 A.2d 537 (D.C. 1976).

60. *E.g.,* Rider v. Rider, 110 Ga. App. 382, 138 S.E.2d 621 (1964); Anonymous v. Anonymous, 1 A.D.2d 312, 150 N.Y.S.2d 344 (1956); Com. *ex rel.* Goldman v. Goldman, 199 Pa. Super Ct. 274, 184 A.2d 351 (1962).

61. *E.g.,* Beach v. Beach, 114 F.2d 479 (D.C. Cir. 1940), which interpreted Fed. R. Civ. P. 35 to permit the court to order a

state courts have held that, even in the absence of a statute, the court has inherent power to order blood tests. For example, in *State ex rel. Evertson v. Cornett*,[62] a divorce action in which the defendant-husband claimed non-paternity of a child born during the marriage, the trial judge had ordered the wife to submit to a blood test but claimed that he had no power to order the non-party child to give a blood sample. The Oklahoma Supreme Court held that, since the tests offered the defendant his only chance to prove non-paternity, it was an abuse of the trial judge's discretion to refuse to order the necessary tests. Relying solely upon the inherent power of the court to order such tests, a writ of mandamus was issued to the trial judge, directing him to order the test.[63]

In another case, *State ex rel. Lyons v. DeValk*,[64] it was held that the denial of a blood test constitutes a deprivation of due process to the party requesting the test, in this case the defendant in a paternity action. Although the child had been placed for adoption without notice to the defendant, the action was continued by the county welfare department, which sought reimbursement for expenses that it had paid. Neither the mother nor the child had appeared for the blood test ordered by the court. The Wisconsin Supreme Court found that the statutory remedy, which simply allowed the disclosure at trial of the complainant's refusal to undergo

---

blood-grouping test as a physical examination. *See also* cases approving the use of blood-grouping tests in immigration cases: Et Min Ng v. Brownell, 258 F.2d 304 (9th Cir. 1958); Yee Szet Foo v. Dulles, 18 F.R.D. 237 (S.D.N.Y. 1955). By a 1970 amendment, Rule 35 now specifically refers to blood-grouping tests.

62. 391 P.2d 277 (Okla. 1964).

63. For other cases holding that there is an inherent power in the court to order blood tests, *see* People v. Bynon, 146 Cal. App. 2d 7, 303 P.2d 75 (1956); Bowden v. State, 137 So. 2d 621 (Fla. App. 1962). *See also* Zavaleta v. Zavaleta, 43 Ill. App. 3d 1017, 358 N.E.2d 13 (1976).

64. 47 Wis. 2d 200, 177 N.W.2d 106 (1970).

tests, was insufficient under these circumstances. The trial court's dismissal of the action was affirmed.

Other problems that the courts have encountered with regard to ordering blood tests do not reach the constitutional level. For example, there is divided opinion as to whether, when the child is not actually a party to the case, a guardian *ad litem* need be appointed before the test can be ordered. A few courts have said that such an appointment is necessary,[65] but in the light of the mother's duty and interest in protecting the child and the harmless nature of the test, the better view goes to the contrary.[66] One court has balked at forcing the defendant in a paternity action to submit to a blood test, even though he had already submitted to one test that had excluded the possibility of his being the father of the child. However, that case turned not upon the constitutionality of compelling the father to submit to the test, but on the meaning of the statute directing the court to order the tests.[67] There also has been reluctance, now on the wane, to order and admit blood tests where the alleged father is the husband and the child was born during the marriage.[68] Again, the admissibility of

---

65. *E.g.,* Mestichelli v. Mestichelli, 44 Misc. 2d 707, 255 N.Y.S.2d 185 (1964).

66. *E.g.,* State *ex rel.* Evertson v. Cornett, 391 P.2d 277 (Okla. 1964). *See also* Beckwith v. Beckwith, 355 A.2d 537 (D.C. 1976) (mother had adequately represented child's interests under the circumstances.)

67. People *ex rel.* Hawthorne v. Hamilton, 9 Ill. App. 3d 551, 292 N.E.2d 563 (1973). *Contra,* on similar facts: Commonwealth v. Potts, 220 Pa. Super Ct. 152, 286 A.2d 663 (1971).

68. Compare Commonwealth v. O'Brien, 390 Pa. 551, 135 A.2d 451 (1957), refusing to order a blood test in an action for support of children born in wedlock, with Commonwealth v. Goldman, 199 Pa. Super Ct. 274, 184 A.2d 351 (1962), interpreting the UNIFORM ACT OF BLOOD TESTS TO DETERMINE PATERNITY, adopted by Pennsylvania in 1961, as applicable to such cases. *See also* discussion in Wright v. Wright, 281 N.C. 159, 188 S.E.2d 317 (1972) (authorizing blood tests to be considered in rebuttal of the presumption of legitimacy), and *supra* ch. III.2.

tests in these instances has not involved constitutional questions, but the scope of statutory authority and the strength and nature of the presumption of legitimacy covering children born to married mothers.

One important question remains at least partially unanswered. If the person ordered by the court to submit to the test refuses to comply, what can the court do? The mildest method of "enforcement" is to permit or require evidence of the party's refusal to appear for the test to be introduced in evidence. A number of state statutes provide for that now.[69] Although easy and clearly constitutional, this sanction, at least as applied against the refusing party, probably has little deterrent effect in most cases. Another possibility, authorized in several states, is to permit the court to resolve the issue against the party refusing the test.[70] In most instances, the threat of this sanction should be sufficient to coerce the reluctant party to appear.[71]

---

69. *E.g.,* ALA. CODE § 26-12-5 (1977); ARK. STAT. ANN. § 34-705.1 (1962); WIS. STAT. ANN. § 52.36 (1978). *But see* ILL. ANN. STAT. ch. 40 § 1401 (1979) which provides that the court may order all parties to undergo blood tests, but then defeats itself by providing no sanction for refusal and adding the following provision: "If the defendant refuses to submit to such test, such fact shall not be disclosed upon the trial."

70. *E.g.,* IDAHO CODE ANN. § 7-1114 (1979); ME. REV. STAT. tit. 19, § 277 (Cum. Supp. 1978). THE UNIFORM ACT ON BLOOD TESTS TO DETERMINE PATERNITY § 1 provides: "If any party refuses to submit to such tests, the court *may resolve the question of paternity of a child against such party,* or enforce its order if the rights of others and the interests of justice so require." (Emphasis added). *See also* Rider v. Rider, 10 Ga. App. 382, 138 S.E.2d 621 (1964).

71. In almost all cases a failure to appear for a blood test would justify a presumption of an admission of want of merit in the asserted claim within the meaning of Hammond Packing Co. v. Arkansas, 212 U.S. 322 (1909), the case which provides the basis for similar sanctions for failures to comply with discovery orders under Fed. R. Civ. P. 37 (b). *See* discussion and cases cited in 4A Moore's Federal Practice ¶ 37.03 (2.1) (1974).

However, neither sanction fully protects the rights of the child who seeks his actual father.[72]

Concerning the question of the court's power to order blood tests and possible sanctions, Texas recently provided as follows:

> When the respondent appears in a paternity suit, the court shall order the mother, alleged father, and child to submit to the taking of blood for the purpose of one or more blood tests. ... An order issued under this section is enforceable by contempt, except that if the petitioner is the mother or the alleged father and refuses to submit to the blood test, the court shall dismiss the suit. If the respondent is the mother or the alleged father and refuses to submit to the blood test, the fact of refusal may be introduced as evidence as provided in Section 13.06(d) of this code.

> Evidence of a refusal by the respondent to submit to a blood test is admissible to show only that the alleged father is not precluded from being the father of the child.[73]

The Texas statute makes a courageous start in facing up to the necessity of blood tests and the need for the contempt sanction, but utterly fails to carry through. To protect the interests of the child and those of other parties, it does appear that the only fully effective sanction is the court's contempt power. So far, no case has directly addressed the question of the constitutionality of the exercise of the contempt power to force a person to submit to a blood test.

---

72. There are other cases in which the sanction of dismissal will not be adequate. For example, in State *ex rel.* Lyons v. Devalk, 47 Wis. 2d 200, 177 N.W.2d 106 (1970), the original plaintiff was the mother of the child, but she had given up the child for adoption and thus had no ongoing interest in the case. The loser, in consequence of the court's dismissal of the action, was the county department of welfare, which had sought reimbursement for its expenses.

73. TEX. FAM. CODE ANN. § 13.02(a),(b); § 13.06(d) (Supp. 1978).

It is possible that an obstacle to such action may be raised by Federal Rule of Civil Procedure 37(b) and cases interpreting that rule. The rule provides for various possible sanctions in the event that a party fails to comply with discovery orders. For example, the court may order the taking of designated facts as established, prevent a party from introducing evidence, strike a pleading, or order the dismissal of any action.[74] Furthermore, while most refusals to comply with discovery may subject the recalcitrant party to contempt proceedings, failures to obey orders under Rule 35 for physical or mental examination, including blood testing, are specifically exempt from contempt treatment.[75] No explanation for this exception is given in any of the Advisory Committee's comments.[76] Interestingly, however, in *Sibbach v. Wilson & Co.*,[77] the Supreme Court, in upholding the power of the federal court to order a physical

---

74. FED. R. CIV. P. 37(b)(2)(A), (B) and (C).

75. FED. R. CIV. P. 37(b)(2)(D).

76. *See* discussion in Barnet, *Compulsory Medical Examination under the Federal Rule,* 41 VA. L. REV. 1059, 1078, where the author states that the Federal Rules reject the penalty "because it is superfluous." He continues:

> The principle of mutuality, which motivates the Rule, requires no more than exclusion of plaintiff's medical evidence or dismissal of his case. The law should recognize a right in an individual to the sanctity of his person as long as he challenges no one else by making claims based on his physical condition. If he is deprived of the right to prosecute such claims, there is little reason to compel him to submit to the court's order. The affront to the dignity of the court is not so serious as to require sending a party to jail for failure to take an examination no longer needed. The exclusion of imprisonment as a sanction was undoubtedly designed to convince the critics of the Rule that the examination provisions were not unduly harsh. There appears to be no constitutional basis for its elimination.

The author's reasoning with regard to the absence of need for the power would not seem applicable to blood-grouping tests in paternity actions, where the child's or the public's interest may provide a valid reason to compel submission to the court's order.

77. 312 U.S. 1, 61 S. Ct. 422, 85 L. Ed. 479 (1941).

examination under Rule 35, specifically noted that the contempt citation ordered by the trial court was not provided for under Rule 37. In connection with the argument that ordering a party to submit to a blood test offends the right to freedom from invasion of the person, the Court noted that such an argument ignores "the fact that, as we hold, no invasion of freedom from personal restraint attaches to refusal so to comply with its provisions." [78] The dictum of the Court in the *Sibbach* case is puzzling. An order compelling a physical examination either does or does not constitute an offensive invasion of the person, completely apart from the question of what sanction is imposed for non-compliance. Sanctions other than contempt, such as dismissal of a claim (implicitly approved in *Sibbach),* can in certain circumstances be even more coercive than a jail sentence.[79] On the other hand, "personal restraint" may occur from the violation of such a simple order as one compelling the production of a document.

On balance, the important question concerns the constitutionality of an order compelling the blood test or other examination. If such an order is constitutional — and we have concluded that it is[79.1] — there would seem to be no valid reason why a contempt citation for failure to obey

---

78. *Id.,* at 14, 61 S. Ct. at 426, 85 L. Ed. at 485.

79. "The contempt sanction, though wicked-sounding, is not nearly as drastic a sanction as dismissal. It only leads to a fine or a possible jail sentence — its use does not result in the termination of a litigant's cause of action." Waterman, *An Appellate Judge's Approach When Reviewing District Court Sanctions Imposed for the Purpose of Insuring Compliance with Pretrial Orders,* 29 F.R.D. 420, 423 (1961).

79.1. The Supreme Court of Washington essentially confirmed this conclusion, upholding the Uniform Parentage Act and its blood test requirement against challenge on privacy as well as First and Fourth Amendment grounds. Washington v. Meacham, Supreme Court of Washington, June 19, 1980, excerpted at 6 F.L.R. 2623 (1980).

it should offend constitutional guarantees. Obviously, a specific punishment arising from a finding of contempt might be so severe as to be constitutionally offensive in and of itself. However, the severity of the punishment is an entirely different question from the exercise by a court of its fundamental contempt powers. Since orders for blood tests are constitutionally permissible, contempt citations arising out of refusals to comply with such tests should be equally valid, if no unduly severe punishment is imposed. The conclusion seems inevitable that the Court spoke without due consideration in *Sibbach* and that, at least with regard to simple procedures such as blood group testing, there is no constitutional compulsion to exempt non-compliance with orders for such tests from the contempt sanctions.

In conclusion, blood tests can provide important and often conclusive evidence in paternity actions. All that is needed for such tests is a small sample of blood taken by a harmless and practically painless procedure. Most of us have learned to live with blood tests in our ordinary health affairs. Admittedly, there may be persons for whom, whether for physical or religious reasons, the taking of a blood sample may not be the simple and harmless procedure that it is for most. Such persons can be excluded from the testing procedure without destroying the power of the courts to order such tests for the vast majority of the population.[80] As a practical matter, one might guess, such persons would not frequently be parties to paternity actions. Aside from this limited exception, however, there is no constitutional reason why such tests cannot or should not be ordered, or why failures to submit to such tests when ordered should not subject the recalcitrant party to having the action

---

80. On the question of excusing persons, on religious grounds, from clearly valid exercises of state power, *see, e.g.,* Wisconsin v. Yoder, 406 U.S. 205, 92 S. Ct. 1526, 32 L. Ed. 2d 15 (1972).

resolved against him or her, or to a citation for contempt of court.

b. *Of Hearsay and Exceptions.*

The evidentiary requirements for the admission of results of blood tests in paternity cases are logical and do not differ in kind from the requirements for the introduction of proof of any scientific test. The crucial questions relate to authentication and hearsay. Was the thing tested the same thing, in substantially the same form, that is involved in the case at bar? Is the person who did the testing available for cross examination with regard to his or her methods, competence, and conclusions? Applied to blood tests, the questions translate: Was the blood tested the blood of the child, the mother, and the alleged father? Did the blood remain in proper condition until the time of the test so that the results of the tests can be trusted? Did the person administering the test use proper scientific procedures and approved reagents? Did he or she have the scientific knowledge to interpret the test correctly?

The need for answers to these questions has led the courts to ask for the establishment of a "chain of custody" relating to the blood sample through "live testimony" [81] and for the appearance in court of the person or persons doing the testing.[82] This may have been feasible when the incidence

---

81. *E.g.*, Madden v. Madden, 160 Cal. App. 2d 422, 325 P.2d 538 (1958); People v. Sansalone, 208 Misc. 491, 146 N.Y.S.2d 359 (1955).

82. *E.g.*, United States *ex rel.* Lee Kum Hoy v. Shaughnessy, 115 F. Supp. 302 (S.D.N.Y. 1953); Nicks v. Nicks, 51 Tenn. App. 520, 369 S.W.2d 909 (1962). Two examples at opposite ends of the spectrum are MD. CODE. ANN. art. 16, § 66H (Cum. Supp. 1978), which provides: "When the tests are admitted in evidence, the laboratory technicians who made them are subject to cross-examination by all parties to the proceedings"; and ARK. STAT. ANN. § 34-705.2 (1962) which provides:

A written report by the State Medical Examiner, certified by an affidavit duly subscribed and sworn by him before a Notary Public,

of blood typing was low, when only few tests were known and one expert performed them, and when the sample was taken by the tester himself. In terms of modern testing capabilities and procedures, however, these days are over. Samples are and should be taken at a place convenient for the parties, they may be mailed by the sample taker to the testing laboratory, and the complexity of modern testing is such that only specialized laboratories can offer a full range of tests reliably.[83]

Accordingly, it is no longer feasible in many of the cases involving this "better evidence" to establish, by live testimony, the possession of the sample at all points along its route from the subject to the laboratory to the courtroom. Typically, not all handlers or testers are available. Even if they were, such proof would be quite expensive, often prohibitively so. Thus it is encouraging that, despite their clear preference for a complete chain of custody and live testimony, modern courts often have been lenient in their receipt of blood test evidence. The common practice of the courts now appears to be to permit the introduction of blood tests, even though each person who has handled the blood does not testify, provided the court is assured that sound and regular procedures have been followed by the agency or agencies obtaining and testing the blood. Similarly, the appearance in court of the person or persons who tested the blood may not be required where the scientific propriety and regularity of the testing procedures have been established.

---

showing the results of the blood tests performed by him, may be introduced in evidence in illegitimacy actions without calling the State Medical Examiner as a witness. If either party shall desire to question the State Medical Examiner in those cases where he has performed blood tests and filed his report, that party shall have him subpoenaed within reasonable time after his report has been filed and prior to trial.

83. *Infra* text at notes 111-116, and ch. X.5.

Examples of this realistic view include *Brown v. Commonwealth*[84] and *State v. McFarland*,[85] which held that the testimony of each person involved in the chain was not essential if the blood had been handled only by persons under the supervision of the witness testifying to the test results. In *Wooley v. Hafner's Wagon Wheel, Inc.*,[86] the Illinois Supreme Court refused to find significant an obvious gap in the chain of custody of the blood tested in that the persons who had handled the blood had not been identified. The Court stated that, in civil cases, the test for the admission of blood typing results into evidence is not as stringent as in criminal cases, noting:

> In our opinion, in a civil case, the foundation laid for introduction of evidence of a blood analysis need not preclude every possibility of a doubt as to the identity of the specimen or the possibility of a change of condition in the blood. If the routine and procedures of a laboratory are shown by the evidence as having been commonly accepted by the medical profession, and the business of the laboratory is the securing, handling and analysis of blood specimens, amongst other types of specimens, those routines and procedures ought to be acceptable to the courts.[87]

Several courts have in effect dispensed with the requirement that a witness be presented for cross

---

84. 449 S.W.2d 738 (Ky. 1969) (involuntary manslaughter prosecution; person actually making the blood-alcohol analysis did not testify).

85. 88 Idaho 527, 401 P.2d 824 (1965) (drunk driving prosecution). *See also* Piester v. State, 161 Tex. Crim. 436, 277 S.W.2d 723 (1955) (drunk driving prosecution; blood test admissible despite period of time in which it was left unguarded in a laboratory refrigerator); Abrego v. State, 157 Tex. Crim. 264, 248 S.W.2d 490 (1952) (murder prosecution; blood-alcohol test admissible where blood sample mailed to chemist).

86. 22 Ill. 2d 413, 176 N.E.2d 757 (1961) (wrongful death case).

87. *Id.*, at 418; 176 N.E.2d at 760. *See also* Note, 110 U. PA. L. REV. 895 (1962).

examination by holding that reports of blood tests, in various situations, come within either the business or official records exceptions to the hearsay rule. In a personal injury case, a court held that a hospital record containing an entry showing the result of a blood test for intoxication was admissible as a business record under the "federal shopbook rule." [88] *Wheeler v. United States* [89] held that the report of a bacteriologist noting the presence of sperm in vaginal smears taken from the prosecuting witness in a rape case was similarly admissible under the same federal statute. In a wrongful death case, the Florida Supreme Court held that a report of blood alcohol content made by a laboratory technician employed by the State Board of Health was admissible under the "public records" exception to the hearsay rule.[90] The Court reasoned that

> [p]ersons hired by a governmental agency to perform chemical tests will be presumed to have been properly qualified and to have skillfully performed their duties unless contradictory testimony is offered. Public records are made as matter of routine and preserved in the interest of general welfare. The investigation is impersonal to those charged with the duty of making it. The prime object is to determine the facts by using acceptable methods and to preserve those facts in the interest of the state for its use and the use of its citizens. There is little likelihood of or reason for fabrication and no purpose to be served by it.[91]

In at least one instance a court has relied upon another exception to the hearsay rule to admit the report of a blood test in a paternity case without requiring the tester's

---

88. Thomas v. Hogan, 308 F.2d 355 (4th Cir. 1962) ("Shopbook rule" codified at 23 U.S.C. § 1732). *Accord,* Kissinger v. Frankhouser, 308 F.2d 348 (4th Cir. 1962).

89. 211 F.2d 19 (D.C. Cir. 1953), *cert. denied,* 347 U.S. 1019 (1954).

90. Smith v. Mott, 100 So. 2d 173 (Fla. 1957).

91. *Id.,* at 176.

testimony. In a divorce case [92] in which paternity was at issue, a pathologist testified with regard to the results of a blood test. He stated that the actual testing of the blood specimens had been done by hospital technicians working under his supervision. Plaintiff objected on the ground that, in light of the defendant's failure to produce the technicians, an adequate foundation had not been laid for the admission of the tests. The Nebraska Supreme Court held that the objection had been properly overruled, and that the reports were admissible under the Nebraska version of the "Uniform Composite Reports as Evidence Act." That statute provides, in essence, that an expert may testify to his conclusions even though the conclusions are based wholly or partly upon written information furnished by the cooperation of several persons acting for a common purpose. [93]

The Federal Rules of Evidence are now in force in the federal courts and have been adopted in several states. Admission of blood test reports should be facilitated under Rule 803(6), which provides for the admissibility of records of a regularly conducted activity as an exception to the hearsay rule. The proponent simply must show that the record was made at or near the time of the analysis, based on information supplied by the laboratory personnel performing the tests, and that the record was made and kept in the course of the laboratory's regular business. [94] The rule specifically provides that the record may contain "opinions" or "diagnoses." In contrast to prior law in many

---

92. Houghton v. Houghton, 179 Neb. 275, 137 N.W.2d 861 (1965).

93. NEB. REV. STAT. §§ 25-12,115, 25-12,119 (1951). For a brief discussion of this statute, see 3 Wigmore, *Evidence* § 752(a) (CHADBOURN REV. 1970).

94. The testimony may be given by the custodian of records, or any other person knowledgeable about the record and the record-keeping activity.

jurisdictions, the record will not automatically be excluded if prepared for purposes of litigation.[95] Exclusion will occur only when the trial judge finds that the "source of information or the method or circumstances of preparation indicated lack of trustworthiness."[96] If the laboratory conditions are carefully maintained and set procedures are followed, there would be no good reason for a judge to exclude these reports as untrustworthy.

If the testing laboratory is a public institution, the records will also be admissible under Rule 803(8), which provides for the admission of public records and reports. Both "matters observed pursuant to duty imposed by law" and, in civil actions and against the government in criminal cases, "factual findings resulting from an investigation made pursuant to authority granted by law," are admissible. Again, the only *caveat* involves circumstances indicating a lack of trustworthiness. The advantage in proceeding under the public records exceptions (Rule

---

95. *See, e.g.,* Palmer v. Hoffman, 318 U.S. 109, 63 S. Ct. 477, 87 L. Ed. 645 (1943).

96. FED. R. EVID. 803(6). Although courts operating under the Federal Rules might still exclude speculative opinions, such as some psychiatric diagnoses, as was the case under earlier, more restrictive rules, *see, e.g.,* United States v. Bohle, 445 F.2d 54 (7th Cir. 1971), chemical analyses, such as blood tests, presented little difficulty even under those rules, *see, e.g.,* Thomas v. Hogan, 308 F.2d 355 (4th Cir. 1962). Judge Jack B. Weinstein writes:

> Statements by professionals, such as doctors, expressing their opinion on a relevant matter, should be excluded only in rare instances, particularly if the expert is independent of any party and especially if the reports have been made available to the other side through discovery so that rebuttal evidence can be prepared.

Weinstein, EVIDENCE ¶ 803(b) [05], 803-167 (1977). Admissibility is aided further by FED. R. EVID. 703 which provides that an expert may base his opinion upon facts or data "of a type reasonably relied upon by experts in the particular field in forming opinions or inferences upon the subject."

803(8), as opposed to Rule 803(6) discussed above, would be the absence of a requirement in Rule 803(8) that the record be made at or near the time of the event. Since, in the case of blood tests, the record should and usually would be made reasonably contemporaneously with the analysis, the difference between the two sections would seem to be academic.

In cases in which courts have held results of blood tests to be inadmissible, there typically were serious gaps in the chain of custody and the scientific validity of the tests was not established. To illustrate, in *Madden v. Madden*,[97] a divorce case in which the legitimacy of a child was at issue, the only testimony was that of a physician who testified that, in view of the blood types of the samples tested, the defendant could not be the father of the child in question. The physician had not drawn the blood. No connection was made between the blood drawn and the blood examined. There was no evidence as to the identity of the person who drew the blood or concerning the length of time between the drawing of the blood and the tests.[98] The Court held that the blood test had been admitted erroneously because "there was a complete lack of identification of the blood tested."

In *United States ex rel. Lee Kum Hoy v. Shaughnessy*[99] the Court considered the validity of a hearing in which the hearing officer relied upon documentary evidence concerning the results of blood tests in excluding from the country persons who claimed to be children of U.S. citizens. The Court held that the officer's reliance upon the naked documents infected the hearing with a degree of unfairness which amounted to a denial of due process of law, noting:

---

97. 160 Cal. App. 2d 422, 325 P.2d 538 (1958).

98. *See also* McGowan v. City of Los Angeles, 100 Cal. App. 2d 386, 223 P.2d 862 (1950), relied upon by the court in *Madden* and involving a failure of identification of blood used in a blood-alcohol test.

99. 115 F. Supp. 302 (S.D.N.Y. 1953).

In effect, relators were confronted with pieces of paper purporting to give test results and yet were not afforded an opportunity to examine beyond the face of these pieces of paper before they were admitted in evidence. The reports of the blood tests put in evidence do not show who performed the tests. They only contain indecipherable monograms. Not knowing who performed the tests, relators were unable to examine into qualifications of the testers, a matter of considerable importance according to both of the articles referred to above. Likewise, relators had no opportunity to learn what techniques or procedures were employed in these tests which is also of no little importance. More than that they could not determine whether any danger of confusion or substitution of samples or testing serums existed during the handling of the samples and the making of the tests.[100]

In conclusion, if appropriate standard procedures are set up and followed carefully, reports of blood test results emanating from centralized and specialized blood typing laboratories should be more than adequate to meet the objections to blood test evidence raised in cases such as *Madden* and *Lee Kum Hoy*. As outlined in a following section, the blood should be accounted for from the moment it leaves the subject until the moment the test is completed.

---

100. *Id.,* at 308. Other cases in which courts have found gross violations of the chain of custody requirement include People v. Sansalone, 208 Misc. 491, 146 N.Y.S.2d 359 (1955) (gap in chain of custody during which a change in condition could have occurred); Nicks v. Nicks, 51 Tenn. App. 520, 369 S.W.2d 909 (1962) (divorce case involving paternity of a child in which the blood test considered by the trial judge had not been introduced in evidence). *See also* Greenwood v. United States, 97 F. Supp. 996 (D. Ky. 1951); Hawkins v. Jackson, 97 Ga. App. 525, 103 S.E.2d 634 (1958); Pearce v. Gunter, 238 So. 2d 534 (La. App. 1970); People v. Wyner, 207 Misc. 673, 142 N.Y.S.2d 393 (1955); Fletcher v. Walters, 246 Or. 362, 425 P.2d 539 (1967); Pomainville v. Bicknell, 118 Vt. 328, 109 A.2d 342 (1954); Newton v. City of Richmond, 198 Va. 869, 96 S.E.2d 775 (1957).

The established, specialized expertise of the laboratories in this kind of scientific testing should satisfy questions with regard to the qualifications of the testers and validity of their procedures. Elaborate checks should be part of the regular laboratory procedure so that any danger of confusion or substitution of samples or testing sera will be negligible. The only significant problem is the absence of live testimony from the tester or other persons in the chain of custody. As noted above, however, not all courts have required such testimony; some hold that either the business or the official records exception to the hearsay rule applies, and at least one other has stated that, in a civil case, evidence of scientifically sound laboratory procedures will substitute for live testimony without reference to any particular hearsay exception.[101]

It is clear, however, that the practicality of centralized and specialized laboratories would be enhanced substantially if there could be full confidence that the test results are admissible in court, without the absurd possibility that all of the laboratory's testers might have to appear in court to authenticate each test. This confidence could be engendered by the enactment of statutes which provide that the results of blood tests can be admitted into evidence (when otherwise admissible) if they bear the certification of the director of an "approved" laboratory stating that the test was conducted in his laboratory in accordance with procedures established by some appropriate certifying or monitoring authority (such as OCSE). Such statutes would have ample precedent. Exceptions to the hearsay rule exist or may be created when the evidence sought to be introduced, although technically hearsay, is needed to promote the search for truth and is

---

101. Wooley v. Hafner's Wagon Wheel, Inc., 22 Ill. 2d 413, 176 N.E.2d 757 (1961).

trustworthy. In the case of blood tests performed at specialized and centralized laboratories, the admission of documentary evidence is clearly necessary. The trustworthiness of results could be insured by designing the certifying procedures and the required form of reports to answer any reasonable questions that might be posed by a cross examiner.

It should be emphasized that evidence admissible under a hearsay rule exception is only *admissible*: it is not conclusive. The detailed laboratory reports with regard to the tests will be available to counsel for both sides. If the party seeking to challenge the report elects to do so, he would have the option of calling under subpoena any of the regional laboratory's employees who were involved with the tests. Thus, the admission of these reports would merely result in placing the burden of going forward with evidence of inaccuracy on the party contesting the reported result, instead of requiring the proponent of the test to present live testimony supporting it. The need for fewer, specialized laboratories, the prohibitive expense of requiring that the blood testers appear in court in each case, and the trustworthiness of the test results more than justify this shifted burden.

As a practical matter, experts indicate that even today it is relatively rare for parties to a paternity action to go to the expense of calling as a witness a recognized blood typing expert who has performed routine tests. Moreover, rather than attempting to challenge the credibility of one set of blood typing results, it may be cheaper and more effective to have the same tests rerun in another laboratory. Indeed, it may be sensible to draft a new statute relating to the admissibility of laboratory reports in terms of permitting an initial challenge only by way of an independent retest in another recognized laboratory.

268

c. *Constitutional Considerations Relating to Admissibility.*

In a criminal case, the admission of blood test results without the presentation of a witness who can be cross-examined about those results arguably raises a question of the application of the Sixth Amendment's confrontation clause. However, in the great majority of states, paternity actions are not (and, in the others, should not be) criminal actions.[102] Only one civil case has stated that the introduction of documentary evidence relating to blood test results violates the Constitution. As discussed above, in *United States ex rel. Lee Kum Hoy v. Shaughnessy,*[103] the U.S. District Court for the Southern District of New York held that an administrative hearing violated due process of law when exclusion from the country was ordered on the basis of documentary evidence of blood tests which purported to establish that the relators were not in fact the children of U.S. citizens. It seems probable, however, that the holding of the *Lee Kum Hoy* case should be limited strictly to its facts. Not only was there no testimony with regard to the tests, but the documentary evidence was difficult to decipher, incomplete, and inconsistent in some respects. Perhaps even more significantly, the administration of the blood test in and of itself raised serious constitutional doubts in the circumstances of that case, since such tests apparently were administered only to Chinese.[104]

---

102. *Supra* ch. V.6.

103. 115 F. Supp. 302 (S.D.N.Y. 1953).

104. The question of racial discrimination in the administration of the tests was taken to the U.S. Supreme Court as the result of an appeal from another order in the same proceedings that gave rise to the case discussed in the text. The Supreme Court refused to pass upon the question when assured by the Solicitor General that the tests were, at the time of the appeal, being applied in all cases, irrespective of race. United States *ex*

Even in criminal cases, courts have not had difficulty with the constitutional questions raised by the introduction of documentary blood test evidence. For example, in *Kay v. United States*,[105] the Fourth Circuit Court of Appeals upheld a Virginia statute providing for the admissibility in criminal proceedings of a certificate issued by the office of the state's chief medical examiner showing the results of a blood-alcohol test.[106] The statute was upheld over an objection that its introduction denied the right of confrontation to the accused. The Court stated: "The alcoholic content of the blood, the evidentiary fact sought to be proved by the certificate may be accurately determined by well recognized chemical procedures. It is an objective fact, not a mere expression of opinion, and its proof by introduction of the certificate violates no constitutional right of the defendant." [107] Other courts have upheld similar statutes in criminal cases.[108]

---

rel. Lee Kum Hoy v. Murff, 355 U.S. 169, 78 S. Ct. 203, 2 L. Ed. 2d 177 (1957).

105. 255 F.2d 476 (4th Cir. 1958).

106. VA. CODE § 18.1-56 (1960). While this statute was replaced by § 18.2-268 in 1975 and amended in 1977, the present statute still permits the admission in evidence of the certificate.

107. Kay v. United States, 255 F.2d 476, 481 (4th Cir. 1958). Interestingly, later cases held that the Virginia statute was intended to apply only in criminal cases, so that the certificate was not admissible in civil actions. Russell v. Hammond, 200 Va. 600, 106 S.E.2d 626 (1959); Brooks v. Hufham, 202 Va. 488, 106 S.E.2d 631 (1959). *But see,* Robertson v. Commonwealth, 211 Va. 62, 175 S.E.2d 260 (1970) (medical examiner's report admissible under statute in rape case, overruling *Russell* and *Brooks* in regard to admissibility of post-mortem examinations).

108. *See* State v. Torello, 103 Conn. 511, 131 A. 429 (1925) (statute providing for admissibility of certificate of alcoholic content of "moonshine"); Commonwealth v. Slavski, 245 Mass. 405, 140 N.E. 465 (1923) (same).

Although the U.S. Supreme Court has not dealt directly with the question involved, a recent opinion which deals with the introduction of similar evidence in an administrative hearing gives a good indication of how the issue might be resolved. In *Richardson v. Perales* [109] the Court held not only that a physician's report had been properly admitted into evidence in a hearing on a claim for Social Security benefits, but also that the report might constitute substantial evidence upon which the hearing officer could base his decision, despite the existence of live testimony to the contrary. The Court recognized the hearsay nature of the evidence but noted both its probable reliability and the need for the report in light of the busy schedule of doctors. In reaching its conclusion, the Court noted with apparent approval decisions by two Court of Appeals in civil cases where physicians' reports were held to be admissible under either the official records or the business records exceptions to the hearsay rule. [110]

In conclusion, it is conceivable that there could be tests of blood which deviate so far from the scientific and evidentiary norms governing the analysis and identification of blood that the introduction of documentary evidence relating to such tests would violate due process. However, as long as recognized and regular scientific procedures are followed, the courts have not found (nor should there be) constitutional limitations on the admissibility of blood test results, despite the absence of an opportunity to cross-examine the person doing the actual testing.

---

109. 402 U.S. 389, 91 S. Ct. 1420, 28 L. Ed. 2d 842 (1971).
110. Long v. United States, 59 F.2d 602 (4th Cir. 1932); White v. Zutell, 263 F.2d 613 (2d Cir. 1959).

4. Recommended Safeguards and Procedures in the Processing of Blood Typing Evidence.

To satisfy the requirements of the law of evidence just discussed and to assure that blood test results may be used with complete confidence, standard procedures — including forms — should be developed to facilitate the introduction of the blood typing evidence into the courts. These forms must document the full series of events relating to the blood testing procedures, beginning with the court's order that samples be taken and that tests be made, and ending with the laboratory's report of its conclusions back to the court. While there may be advantages to having the series of events documented on a single form, one form may become too bulky, and it may be more convenient to develop several, or at least two, interrelated forms. While many of the suggestions summarized below have already found their way into the AMA-ABA Guidelines[111] and similar suggestions have been detailed elsewhere,[112] a quick review of basic considerations may be useful in this space.

a. *From Court to Laboratory.*

The court's initial order that samples be drawn and blood tests made should identify the court, the case, and the parties. The form should direct the named parties to present themselves on or by a certain date for the taking of blood samples at the office of a stated physician or laboratory, preferably one designated for that purpose by an accrediting agency. No serious "accreditation" formalities

---

111. *A.M.A.-A.B.A. Guidelines: Present Status of Serologic Testing in Problems of Disputed Parentage,* 10 Fam. L.Q. 247 (1976). *Infra* Appendix D.

112. H. Silver, Introduction, in H. Silver and A. Barnes, Paternity. Testing ix-xi (Am. Assoc. of Blood Banks, 1978). Polesky, *Parentage Testing* 1979, 10 Laboratory Medicine 601-06 (1979).

would be necessary *at this stage.* The purpose of "designation" merely would be to assure that reasonable standards are maintained in the simple task of drawing the samples, and that the "designated" physician or laboratory may be relied upon to comply with the identification and shipping formalities described below. Each party who has been ordered to have a blood sample taken should be given his or her individual copy of the form, which would prominently show his or her name. The form should contain relevant technical information for the "sample taker," specifically, the quantity of blood to draw, a statement that no anti-coagulants may be used, and instructions ensuring the preservation of the testing characteristics of the sample, as well as how the sample is to be labeled, dated, packaged, and shipped to a specific testing laboratory, the address of which also should be stated on the form. The sample should be shipped as soon as practicable after it is drawn. "Registration" or "certified mail" to establish the "chain of custody" from the sample taker to the laboratory may be necessary. In appropriate cases, priority mail and special delivery service may avoid delays.

As to the proper identification of the subjects, the case of all parties appearing together to have their blood samples drawn is ideal insofar as it permits establishing the identity of at least the man and the woman by confrontation. From a psychological standpoint, however, confrontation may not be as ideal. It is thus more likely and possibly preferable that the parties will appear at different times to have their samples drawn. This procedure raises no serious difficulty, if the "sample taker" is instructed to and does take specific steps to identify the party whose blood sample is taken, since each party would have his or her copy of the court's order relating to the blood tests and that copy would prominently display the party's name. Fingerprints (or, in the case of the child, a footprint) may be a useful device, as may be a "Polaroid" portrait taken when the sample is taken, if used in combination with some documentary evidence of the person's name, such as a driver's license.

The form should end with a certification by the sample taker to the effect that he or she took the sample from the person identified and discussed the person's relevant medical history (recent transfusions, etc.) with him or her. There also should be a certification by the person whose sample is being taken to the effect that he or she is aware of the penalties for misrepresentation of any relevant fact related to the blood tests (such as identity or medical history). Such a penalty might be imposed by a new statute or under a general statute relating to the falsification of evidence; it might be based on contempt of court or on perjury if, as may be desirable, the certification is to be given under oath and before a notary.[113]

---

113. The form of certification used in West Germany is worth being considered. In translation, it provides as follows:

DOCUMENTATION

CONCERNING THE TAKING OF BLOOD SAMPLES AND PROOF
OF IDENTITY

In the matter of _____ vs. _____

Court _____

File Number _____

On _____ (date) appeared here upon request:
   1. Mr./Mrs. _____

born _____ (date) at _____
(place) resident at _____ official identity
card with photograph, issued by _____ on _____
(date) No. _____ Expires on _____ (date)
distinguishing marks (e.g., scars, skin color) _____
   2. Child _____ born _____ (date) at
_____ (place) resident at _____
Identity   card/birth   certificate   _____

274

Finally, the form should provide for the parties' own consent to the taking of the blood sample. While the court's

distinguishing marks (e.g., skin color) _____

Space for finger (foot) print (left thumb; in the case of children, left foot)

I hereby certify by my signature:
1. That I am the person named under #1.
2. That the child brought with me is the child named _____ under #2.
3. That labels filled in with the correct names were attached to the corresponding blood vials in my presence.
4. That I — and the child — have/has not received a transfusion of blood or of ingredients of blood within the last 3 months.
5. That I — and the child — to the best of my knowledge do/does not suffer from a disease of the blood or of blood producing organs.

Only if applicable
6. That a photograph was made of me which I signed with my name.

_____
Signature

I have examined the identity of the person(s) described above in the following manner:

I have
1. examined the identity card and/or the birth certificate and have entered/had someone else enter/in this form the information contained therein.
2. had this form signed in my presence.
3. made the fingerprint.
4. made a photograph. yes/no
5. Confrontation yes/no with _____
_____
_____
_____
_____.

_____
Signature of the physician

275

order that blood samples be drawn should make the parties' own consent unnecessary, such a provision would help overcome possible difficulty.[114] Consent would of course be essential if the sample were to be drawn without the compulsion of a court order.

b. *In the Laboratory and Back to the Court.*

Once received by the laboratory, standardized and carefully detailed internal control procedures must assure that the identity of each sample and, in the legal sense, the "chain of custody" are maintained. The latter requires that adequate records document that the prescribed procedures were followed; *i.e.,* appropriate worksheets should accompany each sample at all times. Presumably, in the interest of efficiency, internal testing procedures would be specialized by various systems or groups of systems, so that not just one but a number of technicians would be involved with the testing of any one sample. Each sample should be processed as it is received, and the three or more worksheets relating to each case ultimately would meet in one file. Together they would be ready for evaluation by a specialist — or indeed, a computer might be programmed to print out the appropriate medical conclusions following from given man-woman-child blood constellations.

After evaluating the test results, the laboratory should report back to the court. If only one form is used, space for the laboratory's report should be left at the end of the court's order that went along with the parties to the sample taker and thence to the laboratory. To avoid too bulky a form, however, the laboratory probably should use a separate form for its report to the court and attach that form to the court's form that was transmitted along with the sample.

---

114. *Supra* ch. VI. 3.a.

The laboratory's report should detail the medical conclusions reached as to exclusion or non-exclusion of the man or men named as the father or as a possible father. It should explain what testing systems were used and the results with respect to each system. In case no exclusion is shown, the report, if appropriate in the circumstances of the case, also should state conclusions as to the probability of paternity, *detailing precisely what method was used in determining that probability.* (In view of the variety of systems that are being used to compute various kinds of probability, specificity is an indispensable requirement in this connection).[115] It also would be advisable for the form to contain a description of the laboratory's internal working procedures, *e.g.,* a statement to the effect that the tests were completed twice and independently by different technicians using different batches of testing agents, and that no discrepancies were found. Statements also should be made concerning other information that formerly might have become the subject of cross examination.[116] In addition, it might be useful to print on the back of the laboratory's report form, or on an additional sheet, basic information for consideration by the court and the attorneys as to the value and reliability of given testing systems. Giving such information has proved to be of value in Danish practice.

Finally, the form should contain a certification by the director of the laboratory to the effect that he or she is charged with the general supervision of the operation of the laboratory; that the laboratory is operated in compliance with applicable regulations of an accrediting agency; and that he or she certifies all statements made on the report to be accurate to the best of his or her knowledge.

The use of forms developed in accordance with these

---

115. *Supra* ch. VI. 2.b.
116. *See* especially *supra* text at note 48 and material in note 49.

guidelines will go far to assure that no unnecessary errors creep into the test results, whether by mistaken identification when the sample is taken or by poor handling or inadequate testing at any later stage. At the same time, such forms will greatly facilitate the introduction of the test results into evidence and reduce or eliminate the need for "live" testimony. In broad outline, the AMA-ABA Guidelines address themselves to some of these questions.

PART III

"COOPERATIVE FEDERALISM": BIG BROTHER FINDS THE FATHER

Chapter VII

CROSSROADS 1974

1. Chaos In Child Support.

In 1974, child support enforcement lay in shambles.[1] Inadequate laws were producing low returns at prohibitive expense. Studies of the subject, even those commissioned by the federal government, met with apathy.[2] Aggravating the practical neglect was ideological dislike of support enforcement that sprang from the spreading notion that the State, rather than absent fathers, should support abandoned children by means of the AFDC program. What feeble attempts there were to bring deserting fathers to accept responsibility were discounted with the argument that the funds thus collected would not benefit the children, because collections would be offset against AFDC

---

1. A landmark article, about twenty years ahead of its time, is Foster, *Dependent Children and the Law,* 18 U. PITT. L. REV. 579 (1957). *See further* D. CHAMBERS, MAKING FATHERS PAY (1979); Weitzman, *Legal Regulation of Marriage: Tradition and Change,* 62 CAL. L. REV. 1169, 1195 (1974), citing and summarizing several sources; J. CASSETTY, CHILD SUPPORT AND PUBLIC POLICY: SECURING SUPPORT FROM ABSENT FATHERS (1978); Johnson, *Growing Pains in Child Support,* ILLINOIS ISSUES 7 (April 1978) and Johnson, *Divorce, Alimony, Support and Custody: A Survey of Judges' Attitudes in One State (Illinois),* 3 F.L.R. 4001 (1976), describing the findings of a detailed field study; WINSTON & FORSHER, NONSUPPORT OF LEGITIMATE CHILDREN BY AFFLUENT FATHER AS A CAUSE OF POVERTY AND WELFARE DEPENDENCE (Rand Corporation, 1971).

2. A detailed study published by H.E.W. in 1960 carefully analyzed comprehensive 1955 data relevant to absent father child support, actual and potential. S. Kaplan, *Support From Absent Fathers of Children Receiving ADC,* 1955 PUBLIC ASSISTANCE REPORT No. 41, U.S. Dept. of H.E.W., Soc. Sec. Admin., Bureau of Public Assistance (1960), especially pp. 4-5, 11-26, 31-40. *See also* COMPTROLLER GENERAL OF THE UNITED STATES, REPORT TO THE COMMITTEE ON WAYS AND MEANS, COLLECTION OF CHILD SUPPORT UNDER THE PROGRAM OF AID TO FAMILIES WITH DEPENDENT CHILDREN (March 13, 1972).

entitlements.[3] In Congress, the Senate Finance Committee, chaired by Senator Long, had concerned itself with child support legislation since the early 1970s (especially in connection with "H.R. 1"). On several occasions, the Senate passed significant child support amendments which failed in the House. Representative Martha Griffiths chaired the influential Subcommittee on Fiscal Policy of the Joint Economic Committee which developed and published the most comprehensive and thoughtful series of analyses of the welfare system in print.[4] In her effort to stimulate Congressional interest in child support enforcement,[5] she described the situation graphically:[6]

> Over 12 million American children — almost one child out of every five — does not live with both parents. Most of these children live with their mothers and of those, about half live in poverty. I suspect that many children in one-parent families are being supported on incomes far below those of their absent parents. . . .
> Eighty percent of AFDC children have absent parents, and almost one-third of these children are covered by support orders or agreements. However, although these orders represent findings that the parents are able to pay, few are obeyed. The Federal

---

3. *E.g.*, Stack & Semmel, *The Concept of the Family in the Poor Black Community,* in STUDIES IN PUBLIC WELFARE, PAPER NO. 12 (Part II), JOINT ECONOMIC COMMITTEE, 93d Cong. 1st Sess., at 275, 293-94 (1973). *See also infra* ch. X.6.

4. STUDIES IN PUBLIC WELFARE, JOINT ECONOMIC COMMITTEE, 92d and 93d Cong., Papers No. 1-15 and "*Recommendations*" (1973-74).

5. Earlier federal efforts in this area are detailed in Note (Stewart), *Interstate Enforcement of Support Orders: Necessity and Feasibility of Federal Legislation,* 48 CORNELL L.Q. 541 (1963).

6. 120 CONG. REC. 38196-98 (Dec. 4, 1974). Concrete proposals based on Representative Griffith's interest are summarized in JOINT ECONOMIC COMMITTEE, 93d Cong., 2d Sess., REPORT OF SUBCOMMITTEE ON FISCAL POLICY, INCOME SECURITY FOR AMERICANS RECOMMENDATIONS OF THE PUBLIC WELFARE STUDY 94-96 (1974).

Government has an obligation to enforce these court orders.

The major obstacle to enacting effective child support legislation always has been uncertainty about absent parents' incomes. Congress long has known that parents absent from welfare families pay little toward their children's support. However, Congress never has known how much those absent parents could pay. As chairman of the Subcommittee on Fiscal Policy, I asked the General Accounting Office to find out.

In telling you the results of this investigation, I shall be telling you about absent welfare parents who earn $10,000, $15,000, $20,000 a year and pay almost nothing in child support. I shall also be telling you about absent parents who earn $3,000, $4,000, $5,000 a year and pay as much as they can. . . .

In its investigation, the GAO drew two samples of AFDC families. One sample included 500 families with absent parents who were under support order or agreement; the other included 1,000 families with absent parents who were not. Both samples were drawn from seven different States. . . .

Three- and four-quarter incomes were obtained for 149 absent parents under support order or agreement. Of these parents, 26 percent earned from $6,000 to $9,000; 24 percent earned from $9,000 to $12,000; 13 percent earned from $12,000 to $15,000; and 5 percent earned $15,000 or more. Median earnings were $8,200. . . .

Out of median earnings of $712 a month, these parents had been ordered or had agreed to make a median family monthly child support payment of $95, or $50 per child. Few actually paid the full amount. The financial circumstances of the welfare families these parents left behind were considerably different. Although almost half of the mothers worked outside the home, the families lived on a median monthly cash income of $288, $211 of which came from welfare.

In light of absent parents' incomes, many of the support amounts ordered or agreed upon seemed surprisingly small. For example, of the 28 absent parents from one California county, 4 with incomes between $12,000 and $14,000 had been ordered to pay these monthly amounts: $40 for one child, $45 for 1 child, $80 for 2 children, and $100 for 3. Per child, this is little more than a dollar a day. The families of these four absent parents were receiving monthly welfare checks of $239 to $314. None of the four fathers was known to have a large non-welfare family to support. Yet only one was paying the amount he owed. Payments from the other three were few and far between.

A fifth absent parent in the same California group had been ordered to pay child support of $50 a month, although he earned $21,000 a year. He also was in arrears.

A sixth, whose wife and three children lived on monthly welfare payments of $295, had agreed to pay monthly child support of $25. That is 27 cents a day per child. He was not paying the full amount. Yet he sent $50 a week to his credit union savings account. He could afford to. Last year he earned almost $17,000.

In addition to being small, support amounts were not clearly related to absent parents' incomes. Among the 149 parents, those earning over $12,000 were almost as likely as those earning under $6,000 to have per child support amounts less than $50 a month.

Numerous inconsistencies in support amounts appeared in each county. For example, of two Pennsylvania fathers with two welfare children each, one father earned $5,200 a year and was expected to pay monthly child support of $172; the other earned $11,600 but was expected to pay only $69. Of two Washington fathers with two welfare children each, one earned $10,000 and had been ordered to pay monthly child support of $200; the other earned $17,000 but had been ordered to pay only half as much. Inequities of this kind were not hard to find.

Of course, debate about the fairness of support amounts may be largely academic, since relatively few appear to be paid. Only about a quarter of our 149 absent parents were paying 90 percent or more of the amount ordered or agreed upon. Of the rest, about half were making partial payments and half were paying hardly anything at all.

If it is puzzling how support amounts are set, it is even more puzzling which ones are paid. We found no clear, consistent relationship between compliance with support orders and absent parents' incomes. Eighty-one percent of the parents earning less than $6,000 were not substantially complying with their support orders or agreements — but neither were 66 percent of those earning between $6,000 and $12,000, or 70 percent of those earning $12,000 or more. . . .

The widespread noncompliance with support obligations must be blamed in part on weak enforcement action. Of those of our 149 parents who were not in substantial compliance with their support orders, 30 percent had not been the subject of enforcement action. That is, the enforcement agency had not even tried to contact them. Over time, parents were more than twice as likely to have their support amounts decreased, than increased, and few were ordered to pay arrears.

2. Opposition to Child Support Enforcement.

Even before the federal child support enforcement legislation was passed in 1975, strong opposition was brought to bear against it. To illustrate, the influential League of Women Voters testified:

The League is not opposed to child support; but we want constructive programs that reinforce and strengthen family life. We believe this bill has little in it that is constructive to offer and much that is unjustifiable.

We urge the members of the Finance Committee to reject the proposals in S. 2081 for child support and establishment of paternity for these reasons:

(1) The tremendous human and financial resources required to carry out the program as proposed could and should be used to strengthen family life and the welfare program in more constructive ways;

(2) The proposal discriminates against AFDC recipients, most of whose family heads are women, and deepens the separation of people living in poverty;

(3) The proposed new federal system of administration would make an already complex AFDC system a costly hydraheaded monstrosity;

(4) The coercive policies it proposes smack of an Orwellian violation of individual rights and excessive invasion of privacy;

(5) The proposed new federal system of enforcing child support and paternity determination would be available to nonwelfare families as well as to AFDC recipients. Jurisdiction of this committee therefore, seems questionable.[7]

Quite probably, the legislation ultimately was successful only because it was coupled with social service amendments which spelled financial advantages for many of the opponents of support enforcement. President Ford demonstrated the opposition's influence even while signing the Act:

The second element of this bill involves the collection of child support payments from absent parents. I strongly agree with the objectives of this legislation.

In pursuit of this objective, however, certain provisions of this legislation go too far by injecting the Federal Government into domestic relations. Specifically, provisions for use of the Federal courts, the tax collection procedures of the Internal Revenue Service, and excessive audit requirements are an undesirable and unnecessary intrusion of the Federal Government into domestic relations. They are also an undesirable addition to the workload of the Federal courts, the IRS and the Department of Health, Education, and Welfare Audit Agency. Further, the establishment of a parent locator service in the

---

7. *Statement of Mrs. Kenneth Greenawalt, LWVUS, Hearing on S. 1842, S. 2081 Before Committee on Finance, U.S. Senate,* 93d Cong., 1st Sess., (September 25, 1973).

Department of Health, Education, and Welfare with access to all Federal records raises serious privacy and administrative issues. I believe that these defects should be corrected in the next Congress, and I will propose legislation to do so.[8]

Having achieved passage of the social services portions of the Act, the lobby quickly and quite optimistically turned against the child support enforcement provisions of the new law. Sweeping amendments were proposed in Congress. Some passed the House,[9] but only a few became effective on August 1, 1975.[10] Most of these were minor and technical or concerned the extension of deadlines for implementation. One amendment, however, seriously threatened the program by diluting the requirement that the mother cooperate in the ascertainment of paternity.[11]

The *Family Law Reporter* described these developments:

> The ACLU fully endorsed the proposal of H.R. 8598 to repeal the Child Support Act's authorization of IRS mechanisms to collect child support obligations, but it urged that certain other provisions of the bill represented improvements that were not fully satisfactory. For instance, while the House proposal would cut down on the number of state officials allowed access to state welfare files, ACLU would like to see the access provision, Sec. 101(c)(2) of P.L. 93-647 simply repealed. Also, though H.R. 8598 would allow parent

8. 11 WEEKLY COMPILATION OF PRESIDENTIAL DOCUMENTS 20 (Jan. 13, 1975).

9. 94th Cong., 1st Sess., H.R. 8598, passed by the House of Representatives by a vote of 357 to 37. For the House debate on this *see* CONG. REC. H 7149 (July 21, 1975). *See also* WAYS AND MEANS COMMITTEE, HOUSE OF REPRESENTATIVES 94th Cong., 1st Sess., REPORT No. 94-368 (July 17, 1975).

10. Pub. L. No. 94-98, 94th Cong., 1st Sess. H.R. 7710 (Aug. 9, 1975), 89 STAT. 433 (1975).

11. *Infra* ch. IX.2-5.

287

locator service access to fewer government agency files, it would require only the filing of a support petition rather than the existence of a state court support order, as a precondition of allowing parent locator service access to IRS files. ACLU in its concern for privacy also urges the deletion of Sec. 101(c) (5)(C), which conditions AFDC eligibility upon furnishing the state welfare agency with one's Social Security Number. Finding fault also with the vagueness of the same section in its failure to define the "cooperation" required of an AFDC applicant in establishing paternity and enforcing support obligations, the ACLU would like to see "cooperation" specifically defined by statute. On this point it offered to the Senators the full text of a proposed amendment drafted by the Center on Social Welfare Policy and Law in New York City.[12]

In the face of the chaotic conditions on the child support enforcement scene — the problem was not limited to welfare recipients but wreaked equal or, due to the absence of ameliorative AFDC, even greater havoc at the lower end of the middle class scale — the ACLU's emphasis on the mother's privacy and welfare rights seemed misplaced. This observer agrees that privacy is a basic concern,[13] especially in the welfare context where arbitrary abuse of helpless

---

12. 1 F.L.R. 2671-72 (Aug. 12, 1975); *See also* Bernet, *The Child Support Provisions: Comments on the New Federal Law,* 9 FAM. L.Q. 491, 517-21 (1975). The A.C.L.U. sent the following letter to all U.S. senators, July 23, 1975:

P.L. 93-647, Social Services Amendments of 1974, authorized a substantial invasion of the privacy of welfare recipients . . . . [T]he bill passed by the House, H.R. 8598, makes certain changes in AFDC law. Although the bill would reduce the harm occasioned by P.L. 93-647, the American Civil Liberties Union does not believe that the privacy of welfare recipients has been adequately protected.

13. *See* Krause, *The Right to Privacy in Germany — Pointers for American Legislation?* 1965 DUKE L.J. 481, 516-17 (1965); Krause & Marcus, *Privacy,* in J. HAZARD & W. WAGNER, LAW IN THE U.S.A. IN THE BICENTENNIAL ERA 377-92, and in 26 AM. J. COMP. L. (Supp. 1978).

recipients is always a possibility.[14] In this instance, however, the issue of privacy seems to have served, conveniently and seductively, as camouflage. The serious issue of the *mother's* privacy is dealt with in detail and disposed of below.[15] The question as to whether the *father* has a right to privacy that allows him to evade this most elementary human obligation (assuming due process in enforcement) is almost too silly to require discussion. The *child*, if indeed it has any interest in privacy in this context, has a far greater interest in knowing its father's identity and whereabouts.

It is a more serious matter that the very existence of a federal data bank able to pinpoint the location of the great majority of the population may invite abuse or, in any event, use by other governmental agencies for purposes unrelated to child support enforcement. To date, attempts to extend the availability of the parent locator service to other objectives have been turned back.[16] Legislation proposed so

---

14. *See especially*, REPORT, THE PRIVACY PROTECTION STUDY COMMISSION [created by the Privacy Act of 1974], PERSONAL PRIVACY IN AN INFORMATION SOCIETY, (pp. 445-86) (ch. 11 The Citizen as Beneficiary of Government Assistance) (July 1977). *Also see* Note (DeBoice), *Due Process and the Path of Progress*, 1979 U. ILL. L.F. 469.

15. *Infra* ch. IX.

16. *See infra* ch. VIII, text at notes 90-95. An early attempt to bring the parent locator system to bear in a related area was contained in "anti-child-snatching" legislation proposed by Senators Wallop, Thurmond, Kennedy, McGovern, Cranston, Simpson, Hayakawa, Riegle and DeConcini. This legislation would have allowed the States and Federal Government to utilize the parent locator system to locate parents who violate custody determinations and parents who "kidnap" their children. S. 105, 96th CONG. 1ST SESS., 125 CONG. REC. No. 5 (1979): "The parent locating system has been established in all 50 States and 4 territories as well as in the Federal Government. It has proven to be very successful in locating parents in nonsupport cases and should prove to be equally effective in child custody and parental kidnapping cases." *See also* H.R. 1290, H.R. 3654, 96th Cong., 1st Sess. (1979). At the state level,

far primarily concerned child custody disputes. But what are the merits of commercial creditors and what about the needs of the criminal justice system? Whether the pressures to expand use of the locator system can be resisted in the long run is an unanswered question. It is worth noting, however, that all efforts to develop a general, national identification system have been rejected by Congress, despite many costly pressures seemingly militating in favor of such a system.[17]

Aside from this broader concern, key opposition to child support enforcement came from several other sources:

There were those who questioned whether child support enforcement remains "relevant" in a society that has come to rely on government to take care of the "poor." The following comments summarize this attitude:

> ... it is not the status of illegitimacy which most harms poor children but the resulting denial of government benefits. Illegitimacy carries little stigma in many poor communities and continuing social relationships often exist between illegitimate fathers and children, even if these do not conform to middle class patterns. . . .
> Professor Krause . . . errs in suggesting that poor illegitimate children can be benefited by a systematic effort to force their fathers to pay support. First, such a program would not create more stable families. Rather, the effect would be to encourage fathers to desert their illegitimate children entirely. Second, many children would not benefit financially even if

---

extensions to custody disputes of state parent locator systems are also being discussed. *See* Law Scope, 65 A.B.A.J. 175 (1979). In the long run, it does seem likely that more far-reaching and less family-related attempts to (ab)use the parent locator service may be expected at both the federal and state levels.

17. Krause & Marcus, Privacy, in J. HAZARD & W. WAGNER, LAW IN THE U.S.A. IN THE BICENTENNIAL ERA 377, and in 26 AM. J. COMP. L. (1978 Supp.).

fathers did pay, since the support payments would be deducted from any welfare benefits.[18]

On a more philosophical level, Professors Cooper and Dodyk question the continued validity of consanguinity as the legal nexus for the child support obligation:

> Though consanguinity has been traditionally recognized as an acceptable basis for the allocation of support costs, that criterion is markedly discordant with the ability-to-pay notions which determine so much of the modern allocation of public costs. Particularly where an extended net of liable relatives is recognized under state law, the wisdom of departing from the normal general-revenue tax base may be questioned. Indeed, even where one is dealing with the relation of father to son, one finds the reports replete with cases in which the biological nexus is paralleled by no ties of familiarity, affection or support, — cases which raise grave doubt as to the ultimate significance of simple blood relationship for the problems at hand.
> Moreover, whatever the conclusions one may reach on such matters, one must contend with the fact that reluctance to precipitate enforcement of support obligations causes many applicants to refrain from seeking public assistance. The aversion to trenching upon the already stretched resources of another household has caused many, particularly among the elderly, to prefer private penury to public assistance. Whatever the gain derived from reliance upon support obligations, its cost is some degree of frustration of the central purpose of public assistance.[19]

It is an unfortunate coincidence that the American welfare crisis suffers from the complicating factor that the problem of child abandonment, parental non-support and illegitimacy runs perilously close to the problem of racial

---

18. Gray, *Book Review,* 46 N.Y.L. REV. 1228, 1233 (1971).

19. G. COOPER & P. DODYK, INCOME MAINTENANCE 285 (1973).

discrimination.[20] In consequence, issues have become obscured and objectivity has been lost. Well-meaning people have suggested seriously that the black "subculture" does not lend itself to white notions of "middle class" social responsibility.[21] For a time, "matriarchal subculture" theories seemed to provide "scientific" support for the victims of this view. Recent research, however, raises doubt that a true matriarchal culture exists in the black community.[22] The cited evidence merely may reflect the

---

20. *See* H. KRAUSE, ILLEGITIMACY: LAW AND SOCIAL POLICY 257-65 (1971).

21. *See especially,* Gans, *The Negro Family: Reflections on the Moynihan Report,* COMMONWEAL, Oct. 15, 1965, reprinted in M. PAULSEN, FAMILY LAW AND POVERTY 1159, 1162-63 (1969).

22. *See especially,* Gutman, *The Black Family Reconsidered,* NEW YORK TIMES, September 22, 1976, p. 39, col. 2 (Sept. 23, p. 41, col. 1; Sept. 24, p. 25.):

> The litany defining the poor urban black family in 1976 is familiar: Sustained by a "culture of poverty" that emphasizes resignation and helplessness, it is "deviant," "matriarchal," "broken," "unstable," and "pathological." Relatively few households contain nuclear families: a husband and wife and their children. Men are "emasculated." "Illegitimacy" thrives among women. Rootless children mature without aspirations.
>
> Such views often describe all the poor, white and black. But for poor blacks this alleged "culture" retains a tenacious hold because of the legacy of slavery. It all began with the supposed inability of slaves to sustain durable families. . . .
>
> Fresh historical evidence is reason to discard this misreading of the lower-class Afro-American historical experience. Most slave field hands and common laborers did not live in "maternal families." Evidence left by thousands of ex-slaves in 1865 and 1866 indicates the following:
>
> Depending upon their location, between three-fourths and five-sixths of ex-slave households contained either a married couple or two parents and their children. Among thousands of ex-slaves registering marriages, about one in four had lived with the same mate for 10 to 19 years, and another one in five for 20 or more years. These were not the experiences of the "favored few." About nine in ten describing their families and marriages had been slave field hands and common laborers.

best possible adaptation to an economic situation in which the black male was unable (rather than disinclined) to perform his economic paternal role.[23] For instance, one study involving a primarily black sample showed that, far from being disinterested or irresponsible, many unmarried fathers voluntarily aid their illegitimate children. Specifically, about 64 percent of the mothers studied had received some financial aid from the putative father at some time within eighteen months after the child's birth:

> At any one point in time, about 43 percent of the group were being aided by the putative father, and for about 24 percent the putative father was the main source of support for the mother and baby, while for about 15 percent he was the sole source of support.... The father's own employment status was a key factor in this

---

23. *See, e.g.,* Parker and Kleiner, *Social and Psychological Dimensions of the Family Role Performance of the Negro Male,* 31 J. MARRIAGE AND THE FAMILY 500, 506 (1969). Greenleigh Assoc., Inc., *A Study of the Aid to Dependent Children Program of Cook County, Illinois,* (in abridged form) in F. HARPER AND J. SKOLNICK, PROBLEMS OF THE FAMILY, 286, 292 (rev. ed. 1962): "All but a few felt great guilt at having illegitimate children. Contrary to much of the literature on the subject of Negro cultural patterns, these mothers did not accept illegitimacy as a normal way of life. They resented their status and recognized the handicaps." *Cf.,* Billingsley, *Black Family Structure: Myths and Realities,* 93d CONG. 1st Sess., JOINT ECONOMIC COMMITTEE, STUDIES IN PUBLIC WELFARE PAPER No. 12 (Part II) at pp. 306-19 (Dec. 3, 1973) (*also see,* other contributions in that volume and in Part I (Nov. 4, 1973); Blood and Wolfe, *Negro-White Differences in Blue-Collar Marriages in a Northern Metropolis,* 48 SOCIAL FORCES 59 (1969); Aldous, *Wives' Employment Status and Lower-Class Men as Husband-Fathers: Support for the Moynihan Thesis,* 31 J. MARRIAGE AND FAMILY 469 (1969); Allen, *The Search for Applicable Theories of Black Family Life,* 40 J. MARRIAGE AND THE FAMILY 117 (1978); Goode, *Illegitimacy, Anomie, and Cultural Penetration,* 26 AM. SOC. REV. 910 (1961); Chilman, *Child-Rearing and Family Relationship Patterns of the Very Poor,* 3 WELFARE IN REVIEW 9 (1965); W. KEPHART, THE FAMILY, SOCIETY AND THE INDIVIDUAL, 206-11 (1966); T. SOWELL, RACE AND ECONOMICS (1975).

role as a source of support: employment was usually associated with contribution and unemployment with lack of contribution.[24]

Even if a better case *could* be made to support subculture theories that relegate black fathers to lower levels of social responsibility, it should not be made. In practice such theories help perpetuate the lack of self-sufficient family structures that has been the legacy of economic deprivation. To the extent non-responsibility is excused, even justified, rather than merely explained, these theories help perpetuate a *status quo* in which the black father is encouraged *not* to stand up for his child. Certainly, on the question of ability to pay, times have changed. By the mid-1970's, black men had found employment opportunities that previously were closed to them,[25] and black income continues to move up.[26] The nation must hope that the long-term effects of recent economic disruptions, including the rapid increase in the minimum wage and its brutal effect on teenage unemployment [27] will not undo this most important social development since Emancipation.[28] *But*

---

24. *Sauber, The Role of the Unmarried Father,* 4 WELFARE IN REVIEW 15, 17 (1966).

25. TIME June 17, 1974, pp. 19-28; U.S. DEPT. OF COMMERCE, BUREAU OF THE CENSUS, STATISTICAL ABSTRACT OF THE UNITED STATES 56 (1974), p. 345. A detailed analysis is provided by B. WATTENBERG, THE REAL AMERICA 124-51 (1974).

26. *See,* DEPT. OF COMMERCE, BUREAU OF THE CENSUS, SOCIAL INDICATORS 1976 at 404-07, 453-54 (December, 1977). 1978 Census Bureau figures show a 6 percent increase in *real income* (after inflation) over 1977. C-U NEWS GAZETTE, Nov. 25, 1979, p. A-9.

27. *E.g.,* Welch, *The Rising Impact of Minimum Wages,* 2 REGULATION 28 (Nov./Dec. 1978).

28.

Unemployment rose to 7.1 per cent in August as joblessness among blacks returned to the peak recession levels of two years ago, bringing new political and economic problems for President

beyond all that, it must be emphasized that the child support enforcement problem is at least as much (and probably more) a "white" as a "black" problem, a middle class as a poverty problem. Opposition to the enforcement program on the basis of race or even poverty mistakes its target by a wide margin.

Other opponents have reached for the same result from the opposite side of the political spectrum. Even in the context of parental responsibility, some people really do feel that it "is a traditional liberty for Americans to pull up stakes, leave and start a new life elsewhere, free of earlier responsibilities," as a successful California lawyer put it to this writer recently. This quaint misapplication of pioneer philosophy remains a surprisingly powerful obstacle to fair and effective child support enforcement. Ironically, this vision of a right to migrate to instant *in*dependence from personal obligations is the mirror image of the constitutional right to instant (welfare) *de*pendence, also through migration, that was pronounced in 1969 when the U.S. Supreme Court struck down welfare residence

---

Carter.... The new report prompted Carter to meet with Labor Secretary Ray Marshall and his chief economic adviser to order them to find out why minority joblessness is rising and to recommend solutions. Powell said Carter was "very deeply concerned" about what Powell termed "a rather outstanding jump" in joblessness among blacks.... Jobless rates were up for black men, from 10.1 to 11.7 per cent, and for black women, up from 10.9 to 12.2 percent. The rate for black teenagers, age 16 to 19, edged down from 40.7 to 40.4 percent. But earlier this week, the government reported joblessness among all black youths age 16 to 21, was at an all-time summer high of 34.8 per cent.

DAILY ILLINI, Sept. 3, 1977, p. 1. *See also* Singer, *The Problem of Being Young, Black and Unemployed,* NATIONAL JOURNAL, Sept. 16, 1978, pp. 1456-1461; Malabre, *Joblessness Among Young Blacks Keeps Right on Rising,* THE WALL STREET JOURNAL, February 1, 1979, p. 36.

requirements as interfering with the right to "migrate, resettle, find a new job, and start a new life." [29]

Some women receiving AFDC oppose child support enforcement because it tends to eliminate voluntary contributions by the father that sometimes are not reported to the AFDC authorities.[30]

Many mothers (and lawyers and social workers trained to identify with them instead of with the children) [31] oppose child support enforcement for somewhat the opposite reason: They shun further contact with the father. The

---

29. Shapiro v. Thompson, 394 U.S. 618, 629, 89 S. Ct. 1322, 1328, 22 L. Ed. 2d 600, 612 (1969).

30. *See, e.g.,* Stack & Semmel, *The Concept of the Family in the Poor Black Community, in Studies in Public Welfare,* PAPER No. 12 (PART II), 93d CONG. 1st SESS., JOINT ECONOMIC COMMITTEE 275, 295 (1973).

31.

It is to the danger or threats to the freedom and dignity of the individual that the recent literature of the lawyers has turned. A good way to discuss the issues is to examine the work of Professor Charles Reich. His three articles — *Midnight Welfare Searches and the Social Security Act,* [72 YALE L.J. 1347 (1963)]; *The New Property* [73 YALE L.J. 733 (1964)], and *Individual Rights and Social Welfare: The Emerging Legal Issues* [74 YALE L.J. 1245 (1965)] — have received a great deal of attention. They purport to define some of the more important issues, and suggest how we should solve them. Much new legal research adopts Reich's analysis and approach.

Handler, *Controlling Official Behavior in Welfare Administration,* 54 CALIF. L. REV. 479, 480-81 (1966), *in* THE LAW OF THE POOR, 155, 156-57 (J. tenBroek ed. 1966). *Cf.,* Handler & Hollingsworth, *Stigma, Privacy, and other Attitudes of Welfare Recipients,* 22 STAN L. REV. 1 (1969); Bendich, *Privacy, Poverty and the Constitution,* 54 CALIF. L. REV. 407 (1966). Kronich, *An Assessment of Research Knowledge Concerning the Unmarried Mother,* in THE UNWED MOTHER, 233-51 (R. Roberts ed. 1966). *See also* Vincent, *Unmarried Fathers and the Mores: "Sexual Exploiter" as an Ex Post Facto Label,* 25 AM. SOC. REV. 40 (1960): "Unmarried fathers are, so to say, half the biological cause of illegitimacy, yet the ratio of studies of them to studies of unwed mothers is approximately 1:25." Vincent, *Teenage Unwed Mothers in American Society,* 22 J. SOC.

mothers' personal reasons, however, rarely outweigh the child's interest in support.[32] It might be noted here that the National Organization of Women (N.O.W.) has favored the federal child support enforcement legislation from the beginning.[33]

The Joint Economic Committee of Congress reports that "[S]ome observers assert that prosecutors, judges and

---

ISSUES 22, 28-29 (1966); Herzog, *Unmarried Mothers: Some Questions to Be Answered and Some Answers to Be Questioned,* 41 CHILD WELFARE 339 (1962); L. YOUNG, OUT OF WEDLOCK (1954).

32. H. KRAUSE, ILLEGITIMACY: LAW AND SOCIAL POLICY 294-95 (1971):

Unfortunately, in this explosive context the central issues have become obfuscated. Well-intentioned people have lavished disproportionate effort on the welfare mother. "Middle class" notions of "rights" have been transferred into contexts in which middle class values do not govern conduct. While reprehensible activities of welfare bureaucrats have come under just scrutiny, they usually have been attacked with the objective of eliminating interference with the welfare mother rather than with the objective of transforming a negative interference with the welfare mother into a positive influence for the child. This preoccupation with the mother is reflected in the bulk of current illegitimacy literature and in the activities of social assistance groups. Why? Perhaps because the *white* illegitimacy problem, to the extent it is a public concern, is primarily a "mother problem." The white child typically ceases to be of public concern through adoption, legitimation, or acceptance into the mother's well-off family. As discussed above, however, the factual dimensions of the black illegitimacy problem are different. The realities of the inner city are such that the psychologically and socially fatal situation of the illegitimate welfare child wholly overshadows the mother's concerns.

This is not to downgrade the "mother aspect" of the illegitimacy problem. An important social value lies in safeguarding the privacy and dignity of the welfare mother. She surely has a right to what limited happiness she can pursue in her condition. All too often, however, the practice has been to allow the welfare mother to consign her child to a life not only without means but without hope of acquiring the tools to become a productive member of society. For too long, the child has been overlooked as a factor in the social equation. The law must recognize the child as a legal person who is in a direct relationship with society and who is not a chattel of his mother. Whether or not society owes adults a living, the child is owed a chance.

33. 1 F.L.R. 2162 (1975).

legislators exhibit a 'pro-male bias' against enforcement. Others say that some lawyers and officials 'are actually hostile to the concept of fathers' responsibility for children,' and that many are bored with child support cases." [34]

Finally, eminent psychologists and psychiatrists have gone on record to the effect that a nonmarital child's experience in finding out the identity of a "bad" father may be so traumatic that, for this reason alone, paternity should not be investigated.[35] This may be the case in specific circumstances, but surely in few. Moreover, who stands ready to protect the nonmarital child of the "bad" mother or the legitimate child with an "undesirable" parent? Until applied to a specific case, the "psychological" argument is worthless. In any specific case, however, protection may be provided by a two-stage inquiry: At the first stage, the mother would be required to tell all she knows. At the second stage, the investigator or judge would make an impartial decision as to whether the establishment of paternity is in the *child's* best interest.[36] A similar procedure is provided in the Uniform Parentage Act.[37]

3. In Defense of Child Support Enforcement.

In the long run (but as a long deceased economist is said to have put it, "in the long run, we'll all be dead"), the state

---

34. JOINT ECONOMIC COMMITTEE, REPORT OF SUBCOMMITTEE ON FISCAL POLICY, INCOME SECURITY FOR AMERICANS: RECOMMENDATIONS OF THE PUBLIC WELFARE STUDY 95, 93d CONG. 2d SESS. (1974), citing *e.g.,* Nagel and Weitzman, *Women as Litigants,* 23 HASTINGS L.J. 171, 191 (1971).

35. Affidavit of Dr. Edward Zigler, Apr. 30, 1974, rec. at 125-28, Doe v. Norton, 365 F. Supp. 65 (D.Conn. 1973). *Cf.,* Deposition of Dr. A.J. Solnit, rec. at 62-71.

36. In extreme cases involving primarily the mother's best interest, *e.g.,* conception by rape, the child's best interest would coincide with the mother's in not pursuing the father.

37. *Supra* ch. V. 11, text at note 147 and *infra* Appendix B (§ 10).

may have to take a more active role in supporting the rearing of children. Indeed, government does just that in democratic Western European welfare states where the two most burdensome aspects of child support — health and higher education — are accepted as primarily social, more than individual responsibilities. Even the duties of providing sustenance and personal care are tempered by "children's allowances" of varying generosity and through subsidized day care arrangements.[38]

In a few decades, our society may conclude that the enforcement of individual parental child support obligations, at least at "full support" levels, is no longer good social policy. Reproduction rates may drop to levels endangering our economy and social security system,[39] and rigorous child support enforcement may then turn out to be a deterrent to having children. Given easy birth control and access to abortion, even now increasing numbers of married and unmarried couples choose to remain childless or limit reproduction under the "compulsion" resulting from both parties' pursuit of individual careers.[40] The popular image of the child seems to have evolved from that of a working

---

38. A comparative analysis of the interrelationship between private and public sources of support, with particular reference to West Germany, France, England, and Sweden is found in M. GLENDON, STATE, LAW AND FAMILY 272-79, 323-27 (1977). *See also* A. MYRDAL, NATION AND FAMILY ch. XVIII, pp. 327-38 (1941, 1968); J. EEKELAAR, FAMILY LAW AND SOCIAL POLICY 256-65, 197-99 (1978); S. KAMERMAN & A. KAHN, Eds., FAMILY POLICY: GOVERNMENT AND FAMILIES IN FOURTEEN COUNTRIES (1978); M. RHEINSTEIN, MARRIAGE STABILITY, DIVORCE AND THE LAW 425-26 (1972).

39. Hyatt, *Population Figures Suggest Problems for Public Policy*, WALL STREET JOURNAL, Jan. 12, 1979, reporting on the findings of the House of Representatives' Select Committee on Population.

40.

The [government] report shows that in 1976, about 30.2 percent of couples with wives aged 15 to 44 said they were physically unable to

asset on the farm and security for old age, to that of a post-Spockian, TV-addicted nightmare in his younger years and, potentially, an ungrateful, drug-culture drop-out later. Even if all goes well, the costs have become staggering: The financial alternative to each middle-class child is a sizable yacht. Before more than a decade of inflation, the 1968 "Rockefeller Commission" estimated child-raising cost at $100,000, from birth through college.[41] Moreover, these calculations included only a conservative estimate of the loss of the mother's earnings, did not speak of the less quantifiable but nonetheless real value of the mother's economic independence from her husband and did not compensate the mother for her probable difficulty in entering a future job market, if she forgoes employment until the youngest of a series of children gets by without her care. While it goes without question that career access and rewards for women must equal those of men, an inevitable corollary of the current emphasis in that direction is that the relative rewards of child-rearing are declining correspondingly.[42] Quite aside from "fairness," women now *need* the economic alternatives they have never had before:

------

have children. This increase of 6 percentage points from 1973 is due primarily to a dramatic increase in surgical sterilization among white couples, the report says. Figures show that about 29.1 percent of white couples in 1976 were sterile as a result of surgery, compared to 23.1 percent in 1973. The percent of black couples that were sterile as a result of surgery was 21.7 percent in 1976, compared to 20.8 percent in 1973. . . . Figures in the report show that 19.3 percent of all couples had surgery for contraceptive reasons. In 9.6 percent of the couples, the woman had the surgery, and in 9.7 percent of the couples, it was the man. The report shows that 22.3 percent of all fertile couples in 1976 used the oral contraceptive pill, compared to 25.1 percent in 1973.

DAILY ILLINI, Aug. 23, 1978, p. 27.

41. COMMISSION ON POPULATION GROWTH AND THE AMERICAN FUTURE [Rockefeller Commission], REPORT at 81 (1972).

42. More than one-half of all mothers with children under 18 years of age now work outside the home. By 1990, the proportion of working

the cultural movement to easy divorce has raised the economic risk of choosing the home over a career to nearly unacceptable levels — and thus has raised the "opportunity cost" of child-rearing.

Meanwhile, out in the "real world," the mother's childless sister has been building up social security credits which ultimately will have to be earned and paid — by none other than the *mother's children.* Under our current scheme the mother, on the other hand, will not have earned any social security entitlement in her own right.[43]

Surely the time is approaching when rational women will choose careers over raising children — unless their economic security is assured by society at large. Society may soon have to decide that parenting is a socially worthy career and not just private folly. Ultimately, mothers and fathers may have to be compensated for their "parenting services" — financed, perhaps, by means of a "privilege tax" on those who choose not to accept the social responsibility of bearing, rearing and supporting children.

Before we need go that far, we should assure (re)entry into the job market for mothers whose children have grown. (The analogy to returning veterans and the preferences traditionally accorded them is not far-fetched). One way to help in that direction would be to legislate encouragement of part-time work for mothers that ultimately will lead to full-time employment, as her children become more

---

mothers is expected to be two-thirds. DAILY ILLINI, Sept. 25, 1979, p. 11, col. 1.

43. A "derivative" benefit, based on her husband's earnings record, is provided for widows and to divorced women, if divorce occurs after more than ten years of marriage (twenty years until January, 1979). *See* Dept. of H.E.W., Report of the H.E.W. Task Force on the Treatment of Women Under Social Security (mimeograph, Feb., 1978), responding to the Congressional mandate expressed in the 1977 Social Security Amendments, P.L. 95-216, § 341.

self-sufficient. Minimally, current tax law follies must be reconsidered: The emphasis in granting tax relief should be placed on *children* (whose presence seriously affects the income tax criterion of "ability to pay," but who are all but ignored in the current tax schedule) and not on *marriage* alone (which usually has no negative effect on tax-paying ability and may often enhance it).[44]

Modest beginnings have been made in European countries which allow mothers and wives some contributory and non-contributory social security credits.[45] Some proposals even suggest that mothers be paid for the job of child raising.[46] While these ideas may be ahead of our place and time, the next generation will have to consider similar and broader legislation — when unreasonable over-concern with overpopulation in America is replaced by more legitimate concern about maintaining an adequate working population — to keep the economy alive (in general) and (in particular) to fund social security and other income transfer programs for the retired, disabled and poor. When that time comes, the enforcement of individual (parental) support obligations may no longer make sense. But that time has not yet come.

For now, knowledge of the identity of and financial access to both parents remains a necessary and fundamental human right of each child. If a child's parents have neglected or declined to comply with the formalities of the husband-wife laws, it follows that the parent-child laws

---

44. *See generally* Bittker, *Federal Income Taxation and the Family,* 27 STANFORD L. REV. 1389 (1975).

45. *See* Dept. of H.E.W., Report of the H.E.W. Task Force on the Treatment of Women under Social Security, Appendix E: Foreign Social Security Systems 121-30, *see especially* p. 129 (France) (mimeograph, Feb. 1978).

46. DIE ZEIT, Feb. 14, 1975, p. 22, proposals of D. Rollmann, MdB, (West Germany).

must be adapted to that omission. Parentage is a question of fact, not of sexual morality. As long as there is no socially acceptable alternative (large-scale communal child rearing?) to a family-centered, two-parent culture, as long as we continue to think in terms of the primacy of the individual rather than in terms of collective responsibility, as long as many quasi-welfare programs remain on an "earned-by-the-parent" (rather than "need-of-the-child") basis, as long as the welfare system remains a stop-gap measure to alleviate only extreme deprivation — for just that long parental responsibility remains "relevant" and must take over where the sphere of public welfare ends; for that long each child is entitled to and needs the help of *both* parents.

There is another perspective. Whatever philosophical position one may hold on child abandonment and illegitimacy, the practicalities are that the social system has a choice on this issue only so long as the rate of welfare dependency remains small. So long as abandoned children represent only a small fraction of all children, society can take care of their immediate financial problems. After that rate reaches a certain level, public funds will be inadequate to deal with the problem. In large part, our welfare crisis resulted from the large fatherless child population. It seems clear, however, that any welfare system must break down — if child abandonment and illegitimacy increase too far. At some point, individual support obligations must be enforced, or the social system must be changed to provide state support for all children. Any other model would result in increasing numbers of parents refusing to marry, simply because they would find themselves unwilling or unable to take care of their own children after paying the taxes needed to support the children of others. This is not hyperbole.

Sweden has passed these crossroads. After experiencing a significant drop in the marriage rate, it is approaching an

303

illegitimacy rate of twenty percent of all births. To deal with that, a mandatory paternity action is instituted in nearly all cases of nonmarital birth in which the father does not voluntarily acknowledge the child — and fathers are thus determined for approximately 95 percent of all nonmarital children. The threat of the mandatory paternity action so effectively encourages voluntary acknowledgment that court action is required only in some twenty percent of all cases. Once paternity is established, clearly defined but rationally limited support obligations are enforced as an essential supplement to comprehensive social services.[47] Since Sweden's tax rates are far higher than those in the United States, no other course was open. It is ironic that so many Americans (given America's tradition of individualism) should have come to view illegitimacy and child abandonment as a public welfare problem. It is instructive that socialist Sweden has opted for individual, parental (though rationally limited) responsibility for child support.

A psychological nuance is of interest. The Scandinavian countries have made it a point to view social assistance to mothers with dependent children as an *advance* on the father's support obligation which then is enforced by the State and, to the extent not enforceable, is assumed by the State.[48] The difference between that and our system *as it*

---

47. *See* H. Krause, *Creation of Relationships of Kinship,* 4 INT. ENCYC. OF COMP. L. Ch. 6 §§ 15-16 (1976).

48. A. Agell, Maintenance and Social Benefits, Report From a Field Study, University of Uppsala, Faculty of Law (mimeograph, May 1978) pp. 4-5:

According to a special Act on Maintenance Advance the child is also guaranteed that a maintenance allowance will in fact be paid to it. The maintenance advance has in effect been constructed to fulfill a double purpose. *On the one hand it is, as is indicated by its name, an advance on the maintenance allowance in case the maintenance debtor does not pay the maintenance allowance which has been imposed on him in a judgment or in an agreement.* The maintenance

now stands is largely one of semantics — but so important: Much of the confusion of thought of the opposition to our child support enforcement effort is due to confusion of the identity of the primary obligor. The long-continued operation of the AFDC program without recourse to fathers had conveyed the impression that the primary obligor is the State, so that the sudden interest in pursuit of the father was viewed as punitive, arbitrary, even vindictive. AFDC assistance had come to be seen as the norm, and parental support as the exception — all the less useful insofar as it did not improve the financial condition of the children because offset against AFDC. The Scandinavian idea of subordinating social assistance to the father's primary obligation has not only kept their priorities straight, but has avoided the public indignation that continues to plague the AFDC program here.

None of this is to reject fair criticism of our new child support enforcement program. Serious and specific concerns continue with regard to the mother's duty to cooperate in the location or ascertainment of the father,[49] to "cost-benefit" questions,[50] to inadequate state laws defining the level of support obligations [51] and providing the means

---

advance, the payment of which in 1975 was handled by the child welfare committee in the municipality, is limited to an index regulated amount of at present (May 1978) 420 crowns per month and child. In January 1975 it amounted to 300 crowns. If the child receives a maintenance advance from the community the maintenance debtor has to pay the fixed maintenance allowance to the community and no longer directly to the child. On the other hand the maintenance advance is a guarantee that the child will receive an allowance of a certain amount even if the fixed maintenance allowance is paid punctually to the child's custodian. If the fixed maintenance allowance is lower than the maintenance advance the community will pay the difference up to this amount as a so-called supplementary allowance to the child. (Emphasis added).

49. *Infra* ch. IX, especially ch. IX. 5.

50. *Infra* ch. X. 2.

51. *Supra* ch. I. 2, 3 and *infra* ch. X. 3.

305

of enforcement.[52] Outdated paternity procedures [53] also cause continued concern, as much in terms of their inutility for establishing paternity efficiently and decently as in terms of their failure to provide adequate protection for falsely accused men.[54]

Most importantly, it is *not* proposed that men who are not in a fair position to contribute to their children be deprived of their means of livelihood and the "pursuit of happiness." A well-administered support enforcement program must make critical decisions regarding "ability to pay." [55] Even if some of these decisions have yet to be made, it is clear that all too many "support fugitives" do *not* have primarily a problem of inability to pay.[56]

Finally, there is another important consideration. Increasingly, our society is turning from wealth in the form of disposable assets to wealth (or at least well-being) in terms of social "entitlements." A man may have little cash, but he may be well off in terms of entitlements designed to secure his obligations to his family. The rights in question range from life insurance policies to survivors benefits under the Social Security Act and myriad private schemes, and include veteran's benefits, health insurance plans, workmen's compensation, and claims under wrongful death acts. In other words, even if a father is not in a position to make an immediate financial contribution, locating him, ascertaining his paternity and fixing his responsibility ultimately may turn into a valuable asset for his child.

---

52. *Supra* ch. II.
53. *Supra* chs. V, VI.
54. *Infra* ch. X. 5.
55. *Infra* ch. X. 3.
56. *See* C. Jones, N. Gordon, I. Sawhill, Child Support Payments in the United States, Working Paper 992-03, The Urban Institute, Washington, D.C. 47-48 (Oct. 1, 1976) and *supra* text at note 6; *infra* ch. X, note 21.

Chapter VIII

THE FEDERALIZATION OF CHILD SUPPORT ENFORCEMENT

1. Public Law No. 93-647, Regulations and Directives.

The states' failure to accept responsibility commensurate with their sovereignty in the field of domestic relations had brought on the chaotic situation deplored by Representative Griffiths.[1] Federal attention was attracted to this area by the towering costs of the AFDC program.[2] Left to themselves, the states had failed their children and their taxpayers. Given these conditions, even the most ardent supporters of states' rights and autonomy should not have resented the resulting federal intrusion.

For several years, legislation had been pending in Congress (and various bills had passed the Senate)[3] to

---

1. *Supra* ch. VII.1.

2. AFDC costs, in billions, came to $7.6 in fiscal 1973 ($4.2 federal and $3.4 state); $10.7 in fiscal 1976 ($5.8 federal and $4.9 state); and $11.7 in fiscal 1977 ($6.4 federal and $5.3 state). In addition, considerable portions of other welfare costs were attributable to the AFDC program. For instance, total food stamps expenditures in 1973 were $2.2; in 1976 they had reached $5.9. Medicaid expenditures totalled $9.1 in 1973 and had risen to $17.1 by 1977. *See* SENATE COMM. ON FINANCE, STAFF DATA AND MATERIALS ON PUBLIC WELFARE PROGRAMS, 95th Cong. 2d Sess. at 3 (1978). *See also supra* ch. IV.1, Table at note 10.

3. Including H.R. 1, Title IV, Part C § 451 *et seq.* 92d Cong., 2d Sess., (1971); S. 2081 § 451 *et seq.*, 93rd Cong., 1st Sess., (1973); H.R. 3153 § 151 *et seq.* 93rd Cong., 1st Sess., (1973); H.R. 17045 § 151 *et seq.*, 93rd Cong., 2d Sess. (1974). *See also* Comment, *Federal Law and the Enforcement of Child Support Orders,* 4 N.Y. REV. OF L. AND SOC. CHANGE, 23, 25-26 (1976); Bernet, *The Child Support Provisions: Comments on the New Federal Law,* 9 FAM. L.Q. 491, 495-96 (1975).

bring the resources of the federal government to bear on the lax and inadequate child support enforcement that had become the rule in most states. The strong federal interest derived from, and continues to center on, the burgeoning cost of the Aid to Families with Dependent Children (AFDC) program. Amendments in 1950 and 1968 to the Social Security Act that required HEW to encourage the states to improve their child support enforcement systems, had had no visible success.[4]

Congress finally moved to strengthen enforcement of child support obligations across the nation — thereby, it was hoped, reducing the cost of AFDC programs significantly. Effective August 1, 1975, sweeping amendments changed the AFDC Title of the Social Security Act, and a new Child Support Title (IV-D) was added.[5] A broad base of regulations was soon developed to implement the new legislation.[6]

Even under this federal initiative, state authority and state laws remain the primary vehicles for the establishment of paternity and child support collection.

------

4. Social Security Act, § 402(a)(10), effective July 1, 1952, 64 Stat. 550 (1950), §§ 402(a)(21), (22), 410, 42 U.S.C.A. § 602(a) (21), (22) (1974). *See also* H. KRAUSE, ILLEGITIMACY: LAW AND SOCIAL POLICY 274-79 (1971). Galvin, *The Runaway Parents,* TRIAL 20 (April 1976). A 1972 government study lauded the child support enforcement program of the State of Washington, but found serious weaknesses in the three other states studied. Comptroller General of the United States REPORT TO THE COMMITTEE ON WAYS AND MEANS, COLLECTION OF CHILD SUPPORT UNDER THE PROGRAM OF AID TO FAMILIES WITH DEPENDENT CHILDREN (March 13, 1972).

5. 42 U.S.C.A. §§ 651-662 (Supp. 1979). The primary enactment was Pub. L. No. 93-647, § 101, 88 Stat. 2337, 2351-60 (1975). The originally intended effective date of July 1, 1975, was changed to August 1, 1975, by P.L. 94-46, § 2.

6. *See* 45 C.F.R. §§ 232.1-232.49, 301.0-305.50 (1978).

What is new is that the federal government has become an active stimulator, overseer and financier of state collection systems.[7] Each state enforcement agency — now commonly

---

7. 42 U.S.C.A. § 652 (Supp. 1979) provides:

... (a) The Secretary shall establish, within the Department of Health, Education, and Welfare a separate organizational unit, under the direction of a designee of the Secretary, who shall report directly to the Secretary and who shall —

(1) establish such standards for State programs for locating absent parents, establishing paternity, and obtaining child support as he determines to be necessary to assure that such programs will be effective;

(2) establish minimum organizational and staffing requirements for State units engaged in carrying out such programs under plans approved under this part;

(3) review and approve State plans for such programs;

(4) evaluate the implementation of State programs established pursuant to such plan, conduct such audits of State programs established under the plan approved under this part as may be necessary to assure their conformity with the requirements of this part, and, not less often than annually, conduct a complete audit of the programs established under such plan in each State and determine for the purposes of the penalty provision of section 403(h) whether the actual operation of such programs in each state conforms to the requirements of this part;

(5) assist States in establishing adequate reporting procedures and maintain records of the operations of programs established pursuant to this part in each State;

(6) maintain records of all amounts collected and disbursed under programs established pursuant to the provisions of this part and of the costs incurred in collecting such amounts;

(7) provide technical assistance to the States to help them establish effective systems for collecting child support and establishing paternity;

(8) receive applications from States for permission to utilize the courts of the United States to enforce court orders for support against absent parents and, upon a finding that (A) another State has not undertaken to enforce the court order of the originating State against the absent parent within a reasonable time, and (B) that utilization of the Federal courts is the only reasonable method of enforcing such order, approve such applications;

(9) operate the Parent Locator Service established by section 453; and

(10) not later than June 30 of each year beginning after December 31, 1975, submit to the Congress a report on all activities undertaken pursuant to the provisions of this part.

known as a "IV-D Agency," reflecting its statutory location — must meet standards imposed by HEW's Office of Child Support Enforcement (OCSE) or lose 5 percent of its federal AFDC funding. If, on the other hand, the enforcement program meets federal standards, the state receives 75 percent of the program's cost from HEW.

In summary, the amendments impose on state AFDC programs the additional function of acting as intake agencies for child support enforcement programs, and require them to collect data. Specific new rules include the following: state AFDC agencies must use the social security numbers of all AFDC applicants as identification; the AFDC agency must notify the state child support enforcement agency whenever it grants benefits to deserted children and must open its records to support enforcement officials; applicants must assign their right to uncollected child support to the state and must agree to cooperate in locating the absent parent, establishing paternity, obtaining a support judgment if none is outstanding and securing payments. Limited exceptions are authorized to the duty to cooperate, but not to the assignment requirement. In case of an applicant's unjustified failure to cooperate, AFDC benefits are withheld from the applicant, but *not* from the child or children.

Each state IV-D agency maintains a "state parent locator service" equipped to search state and local records for information regarding the whereabouts of an absent parent and may call upon the sophisticated, computerized federal parent locator service based in Washington with access to Social Security, Internal Revenue and vast other federal data resources. Once the absent parent (or alleged parent) is located, the state (if necessary and possible) establishes paternity, obtains a support judgment, and enforces the obligation through either in-state or interstate proceedings

310

(with access to the federal courts as a last resort). All states are bound to cooperate fully with the enforcement efforts of sister states. *In extremis,* HEW may request the Internal Revenue Service to collect outstanding judgments as though they were a tax liability. Finally, anyone with support rights against a federal employee or beneficiary may garnish the absent parent's federal money under a statutory waiver of sovereign immunity.

After collection, the state disburses child support payments, keeping detailed records and reporting to OCSE. To encourage local participation in child support enforcement, a portion of the proceeds is turned over to the collecting unit of local government.

The program also is available to non-AFDC parents who pay an application fee and agree to pay the cost of collection from payments collected for them.

2. The Office of Child Support Enforcement (OCSE).

HEW's Office of Child Support Enforcement (OCSE) [8] is directly responsible for administering the nationwide child support enforcement program.[9] In addition to its

---

8. The Office of Child Support Enforcement formally came into existence on June 10, 1975. 40 Fed. Reg. 27156 (1975).

9. OCSE has published a 1st ANNUAL REPORT TO THE CONGRESS ON THE CHILD SUPPORT ENFORCEMENT PROGRAM (GPO ed. 1976) (hereinafter cited as 1976 REPORT); CHILD SUPPORT ENFORCEMENT: SUPPLEMENTAL REPORT TO THE CONGRESS (GPO ed. 1977) (OCSE-IM-77-15) (hereinafter cited as 1976 SUPP. REPORT); CHILD SUPPORT ENFORCEMENT: 2d ANNUAL REPORT TO THE CONGRESS (GPO ed. 1977) (OCSE-IM-78-1) (hereinafter cited as 1977 REPORT); CHILD SUPPORT ENFORCEMENT: 3d ANNUAL REPORT TO THE CONGRESS (GPO ed. 1978) (OCSE-IM-79-8) (hereinafter cited as 1978 REPORT).

Washington headquarters,[10] OCSE maintains 10 regional offices for liaison with state IV-D agencies. By statute, OCSE establishes organizational, staffing and procedural standards for state IV-D agencies, reviews and approves state plans for implementing IV-D programs, collects detailed financial and operational reports from IV-D agencies, provides technical assistance to the states, audits IV-D programs to determine if monetary sanctions should be imposed for inadequate enforcement efforts, rules on state applications to use federal courts for collection of child support, and operates the federal Parent Locator Service.[11] Approved IV-D programs are operating in all 50 states, the District of Columbia, Puerto Rico, the Virgin Islands, and Guam.[12]

In addition to prescribing initial standards for approval of a IV-D program,[13] OCSE has promulgated extensive regulations covering maintenance of case records,[14]

---

10. OCSE, Department of Health and Human Services, 6110 Executive Boulevard, Suite 900, Rockville, MD 20852, Telephone (301) 443-4442.

11. 42 U.S.C. § 652(a) (1976).

12. Regulations governing start-up of new IV-D agencies appear at 45 C.F.R. §§ 301.0-.15 (1978). In November, 1979, the addresses and telephone numbers of all state IV-D agencies were reported in OCSE-IM-79-15 (November 29, 1979). *See* Appendix I *infra*, for this list.

13. OCSE-AT-75-2 (1975) contains an application and program checklist for certifying new IV-D agencies.

14. The IV-D agency must keep detailed case records for each AFDC and non-AFDC applicant, including contacts with the absent parent, efforts at absent-parent location before application to the federal parent locator service (PLS), a level of child support set by court order or administrative calculation, and efforts at enforcement. 45 C.F.R. § 303.2 (1978).

location of absent parents,[15] establishment of paternity [16] and of support obligations,[17] enforcement of support,[18] and cooperation between states.[19]

So far, OCSE's organizational and staffing requirements for state IV-D programs relate primarily to functional descriptions of enforcement activities, although the regulations do define which activities may be delegated by IV-D agencies, and which may not.[20] State agencies maintain financial records for their operation and

---

15. To locate an absent parent, the agency must search all appropriate sources at the state and local level within 60 days of opening the case file, and then contact either the federal parent locator service (PLS) or IV-D agencies of other states of possible residence if the parent is not located. The in-state search must include social service agencies; relatives, friends, and past employers; the post office; police records; and state welfare, unemployment, income tax and motor vehicle offices. 45 C.F.R. § 303.3 (1978).

16. If paternity is unknown, the IV-D agency must use state legal processes to establish paternity. Laboratories within the state which perform acceptable paternity tests are to be identified for use by courts and law enforcement officials. Determination of paternity need not be undertaken in case of rape, pending adoption, or if otherwise detrimental to the child's interest. 45 C.F.R. § 303.5 (1978). *See also infra* ch. IX.

17. The IV-D agency must use state legal processes to establish a support obligation from the absent parent and review its level periodically. 45 C.F.R. § 303.4 (1978).

18. Once the IV-D agency establishes a support obligation, it must enforce it through either contempt proceedings, garnishment, property attachment, a federal court order, or use of the Internal Revenue Service. 45 C.F.R. § 303.6 (1978).

19. State IV-D agencies must cooperate fully with each other to locate an absent parent, establish paternity, and secure support through legal action. 45 C.F.R. § 303.7 (1978).

20. 45 C.F.R. § 303.20 (1978). Although it may contract for enforcement and collection, the IV-D agency may not delegate financial control of the operation or regular evaluation of its effectiveness. *Id.* at paragraph (d). Additionally, the IV-D agency may not delegate its responsibility to the state AFDC agency. *Id.* at paragraph (e).

313

collections under detailed accounting guidelines and report quarterly to OCSE, which provides forms for revenue collection estimates, actual revenue collections, and expenditures. OCSE summarizes data from these reports in annual reports to Congress, which provide breakdowns on the number of cases processed to collection, cost incurred and revenues generated, the effect of federally supervised support enforcement on the cost of the AFDC program, and information on non-AFDC child support enforcement.[21]

OCSE must conduct annual audits of state enforcement operations to gauge their effectiveness. It has authority to reduce by five percent federal AFDC payments to any state whose enforcement effort does not pass federal muster.[22] While the first such audits have been completed, no penalties had been imposed by the end of 1979.[23] Audit criteria include the program's administrative structure, procedures for obtaining child support — ranging from ascertainment of paternity to disbursement of collections on judgments — and financial and record-keeping policies.[24] The Office also has published summaries of program implementation and characteristics for all 54 IV-D agencies.[25]

A steady stream of "Action Transmittals" and "Information Memoranda" goes out from OCSE to all

---

21. *See* 1976 REPORT, 1976 SUPP. REPORT, 1977 REPORT and 1978 REPORT.

22. 42 U.S.C.A. §§ 652(a)(4), 603(h) (Supp. 1979); 45 C.F.R. §§ 305.10, 305.50, 25.146(d) (1978).

23. Letter of December 26, 1979, from Louis B. Hays, Esq., Deputy Director, OCSE, to Harry D. Krause.

24. 45 C.F.R. §§ 305.20 through 305.50 (1978).

25. 1976 REPORT at 45-96, 97-106; 1976 SUPP. REPORT at 25-134; 1977 REPORT at 30-86; 1978 REPORT at 33-88.

persons and agencies connected with the IV-D program.[26] Beyond that, OCSE has published and disseminated widely a considerable body of material designed to assist state and local programs in their enforcement efforts.[27] Outside organizations, some under contract with the Office, have prepared technical assistance publications including major studies on use of blood tests and comparative procedures and systems to establish paternity,[28] an operational handbook for paternity determination,[29] a guide for determining appropriate levels for child support orders,[30] a

---

26. OCSE-IM-79-2 (1979) (information memorandum) contains a topical list of all information memoranda and action transmittals issued up to its effective date.

27. OCSE-IM-80-4 (April 23, 1980) catalogues materials available from the National Child Support Enforcement Reference Center, OCSE, 6110 Executive Boulevard, Beltway View Building, Room 924, Rockville, MD 20852, telephone (301) 443-5106.

28. USING BLOOD TESTS TO ESTABLISH PATERNITY, CONDENSED REPORT, CENTER FOR POLICY RESEARCH Dept. of HEW, OCSE, IM-77-11 (1977); PATERNITY DETERMINATION: TECHNIQUES AND PROCEDURES TO ESTABLISH THE PATERNITY OF CHILDREN BORN OUT OF WEDLOCK, UNIVERSITY OF SOUTHERN CALIFORNIA CENTER FOR HEALTH SERVICES RESEARCH, OCSE-IM-77-6 (1976); Joint A.M.A.-A.B.A. Guidelines: *Present Status of Serologic Testing in Problems of Disputed Parentage,* 10 FAM. L.Q. 247 (1976); Polesky and Krause, *Blood Typing in Disputed Paternity Cases-Capabilities of American Laboratories,* 10 FAM. L.Q. 287 (1976), 17 TRANSFUSION 521 (1977); H. SILVER & A. BARNES, eds., PATERNITY TESTING (American Assn. of Blood Banks 1978).

29. UNIVERSITY OF SOUTHERN CALIFORNIA CENTER FOR HEALTH SERVICES RESEARCH, PATERNITY CASE PROCESSING HANDBOOK, OCSE-IM-78-4 (1978).

30. M. Sauber and E. Taittonen, *Guide for Determining the Ability of an Absent Parent to Pay Child Support,* OCSE-IM-77-12 (1977) (Research and Program Planning Information Department, Community Council of Greater New York, 225 Park Avenue South, New York, N.Y. 10003).

critique of ten ongoing IV-D operations,[31] training manuals for OCSE central and regional staff and for IV-D record keeping reporting,[32] a "Sampling Manual for OCSE Statistical Reporting Requirements"[33] and a description of a model administrative and reporting system for IV-D agencies.[34] Finally, the Office has sought reports on useful practices from IV-D agencies and has distributed information on specific programs and ideas to all agencies.[35]

---

31. OCSE-IM-77-16 (1977) summarizes recommendations, titled "IV-D Technology Transfer Model." Principal recommendations: (1) State agencies should concentrate on absent-parent location from the office, as more cost-effective than field location. Office efforts should include letters, telephone calls and development of access to state and local records. (2) State agencies should seek legislation to speed case processing through such procedures as automatic payroll deduction for child support payments, and *ex parte* consent judgments. (3) State agencies should direct their limited enforcement resources to new referrals and delinquencies, and then to the potentially most productive cases in the backlog.

32. OCSE WARRANT UNIT PROJECT MANUAL (1978); MICHIGAN TRAINING MANUAL, OCSE-IM-78-14 (1978).

33. OCSE-IM-79-5 (February 16, 1979).

34. MODEL ADMINISTRATIVE AND REPORTING SYSTEM, OCSE-IM-78-17 (1978).

35. One such program, the Massachusetts "Phone Power Project," generated an estimated $15,000 per month in new child support payments by adopting business telephone collection procedures for locating and obtaining support agreements from absent parents. Estimated yearly cost for the trial program was $60,727. OCSE-IM-77-17 (Sept. 9, 1977). The State of Washington's IV-D agency uses a standardized format for cooperative service agreements between the IV-D agency and local government units that regularly assist the state agency and thus become eligible for federal aid. The standardized format saves expenses of negotiation and preparation, clarifies state and local responsibilities and simplifies accounting, reporting, and reimbursement. OCSE-IM-77-1 (1977). The Texas Department of Human Resources has developed a training film and manual for trial of contested

Outside of the federal government, the National District Attorneys Association (NDAA) has developed a Child Support Enforcement Project that publishes a useful newsletter, has held a series of support enforcement training seminars, has produced child support enforcement training materials, and has published an extensive bibliography relating to child support law.[36] Important work is being done by the National Reciprocal and Family Support Enforcement Association.[37] The Eastern Regional Conference on Uniform Reciprocal Enforcement of Support, the American Public Welfare Association and various other organizations have sponsored conferences on child support. Many aspects of the program have been studied by private and public agencies.[38]

---

paternity proceedings. OCSE-IM-78-2 (1978). The State of Oregon can intercept state tax refunds owed an absent parent and apply the amount to child support arrearages owed the IV-D agency for past AFDC payments, OCSE-IM-78-13 (1978). The State of Wisconsin amended its divorce laws to ease collection of child support. 1977 Wis. Laws 597-616, OCSE-IM-78-16 (1978). The State of Utah manages enforcement cases through individualized teams. OCSE-IM-78-30 (1978).

36. The project terminated in 1980. Its NEWSLETTER contained reports on various IV-D projects and procedures. Each issue included a section on recent legal developments. Training materials included tape cassettes on child support enforcement, covering developing a case, URESA, garnishment, liens, the criminal process, orders and judgments, cross examination, the UNIFORM MARRIAGE AND DIVORCE ACT, the IV-D office, and collection procedures and general administrative problems. NDAA also developed a book out of a previous child support enforcement training seminar, including forms. Most of these materials are still available and inquiries may be addressed to NDAA Publications, 666 N Lake Shore Dr., Suite 1432, Chicago, Illinois 60611, (312) 944-4610.

37. "NRFSEA," 503 E. 15th St. A., Des Moines, IA 50316, (515) 262-6807. *See, e.g.,* NRFSEA News, Vol. 4, Special Edition, March 1979.

38. The National Conference of State Legislatures' *A Legislator's Guide to Child Support Enforcement,* represents a useful idea. (OCSE Contract No. 600-79-0043, available for $5.00 from the Conference). *See also* HEW, SOCIAL AND REHAB. SERV., ABSENT PARENT CHILD SUPPORT,

In 1979, the National Institute for Child Support Enforcement [39] (funded by OCSE) became active on a broad range of educational, training and technical assistance projects. One of the Institute's early goals is the development of model forms that may be used by the state programs.[40]

3. The Operation of the Child Support Enforcement Program.

a. *Collection for AFDC-Dependents.*

The primary purpose of the national IV-D program is to reduce public aid expenditures by requiring absent parents to contribute to the support of their children who receive AFDC. The IV-D program thus is normally invoked with the initial application for aid by deserted parents with children — whether the children are legitimate or illegitimate, and whether or not a support judgment is outstanding.

As a condition of eligibility for aid, all new AFDC applicants and current recipients must furnish their and their dependents' social security numbers to the AFDC agency, to be used as principal identifiers in program administration.[41] If an applicant or recipient does not have a number, the AFDC agency will help obtain one. The agency may not delay processing the case if the applicant or recipient makes a good-faith effort to obtain and furnish the number to the agency.[42] The purpose of this requirement is

---

COST-BENEFIT ANALYSIS (Contract. No. SRS-7456, submitted December, 1975). Arthur Young also sponsored several training seminars early in the program.

39. 6110 Executive Blvd., Suite 250, Rockville Md. 20852, (301) 984-9160.

40. Letter of December 26, 1979, from Louis B. Hays, Esq., Deputy Director, OCSE, to Harry D. Krause.

41. 42 U.S.C.A. § 602(a)(25) (Supp. 1979), 45 C.F.R. § 232.10 (1978).

42. 45 C.F.R. § 232.10(c), (d) (1978).

to reduce the incidence of fraud,[43] but it has been attacked

---

43. "U.S. Welfare Commissioner Robert B. Carlsen said 'the requirement will make it more difficult for welfare mothers to apply for public assistance for children who don't exist and assist state agencies in keeping track of the fathers of welfare children.'" MIAMI HERALD, July 1, 1975, at 3A.

"More difficult," yes, but this requirement will be no "cure-all." It remains so easy to obtain a social security number that the issuance of multiple or false cards to ineligible persons undoubtedly continues at a high rate. Criminal penalties are rarely enforced and remain mild. *See* 20 C.F.R. § 422.108 (1978). Applications continue to be accepted by mail and the quality and quantity of required personal identification, is minimal. *See* 20 C.F.R. § 422.107 (1978): "Applicants for social security numbers are required to submit such evidence as the Secretary may regard as convincing of their age, citizenship, or alien status and true identity."

Detailed advice contained in an official HEW pamphlet (SSA 75-10064) supports concern regarding the reliability of identification by Social Security number:

> *If you were born in the United States:* A variety of documents can be submitted as evidence of your age, identity, and citizenship. Examples of these documents are included in the two lists [below]. If possible, please submit one document from each list.
> *Evidence of age and citizenship:* A birth certificate or church record of birth of baptism is preferred as proof of your age and place of birth. If neither of these records is readily available, please furnish one of the documents listed below which shows your date of birth or age: School record, Church record, State [or] Federal census record, Insurance policy, Marriage record, Military discharge papers, Delayed birth certificate, Draft card, U.S. passport, Any other record which shows your age or date of birth.
> *Evidence of identity:* Driver's license, State identity card, Voter's registration, School identification card, Work badge or building pass, Draft card or military ID, U.S. passport or U.S. identity card, Credit card if your signature is shown, Library card with signature, Any other document which shows either your signature or photograph.

Of course, this laxity may be explained in terms of the history of the social security identification number. Originally it had no function other than to *benefit* the claimant, so that it was wholly in the claimant's interest to provide correct information to ensure that his or her earnings record would be properly reflected on his or her account. Given the seemingly inevitable national move to the social security number as a universal identifier (on income tax returns, driver's license, college student

on privacy grounds.[44]

As a further condition of eligibility, the applicant, on behalf of the children for whom welfare is sought, must assign to the state any rights of support owed by a deserting

identification and now in the child support enforcement program), a new look at the verification procedures on issuance of the numbers is obviously needed. Washington has recognized the problem, but has not produced an effective remedy:

> The Attorney General explained how illegal schemes are carried out: "A man of 25 checks old newspaper obituaries of about the time of his birth to learn of a child's death. What the man is seeking is to have a birth certificate whose age will about match his own and — ideally — also match such physical characteristics as race and color of hair and eyes. He then requests a copy of the child's birth certificate — either in person or in writing. For a tiny fee, he can obtain it — and often it is even mailed to him.
> "Let's assume the birth certificate is for a John J. Smith. The offender then uses it to obtain a driver's license in that name. And then uses both to get credit cards and other gold-plated credentials. He may use this approach to acquire several new identities. . . ."
> The Advisory Committee will pinpoint the extent of the problem, develop plans and possibly draft proposed new statutes. Finally, it will assist state and local governments in combatting this menace. One suggestion has been to computerize the records of all vital statistics bureaus nationwide to facilitate interstate cooperation.
> Attorney General Saxbe noted how fraudulent identification credentials are used by narcotics peddlers, persons passing counterfeit checks and securities, bank swindlers, and persons involved in social security and welfare frauds. He also explained how illegal aliens insulate themselves from authorities and settle into new jobs and new lives through the use of false credentials.
> He stressed that "birth certificates are the foundation upon which the bulk of the false identification empire is built," and that the federal government is going to do something about it. (1 F.L.R. 2069 (Nov. 26, 1974)).

44. *See* Arthur v. Washington State Dept. of Social and Health Svcs., 19 Wash. App. 542, 576 P.2d 921 (1978):

> We hold that by the terms of 42 U.S.C. § 602(a)(25), Arthur's children are "recipients" of aid and, as such, are required to have social security numbers.
> We also hold that Arthur has not sustained the burden of establishing that the requirement of social security numbers for his minor children is a constitutionally impermissible invasion of their right of privacy. At the administrative hearing, Arthur stated that

parent.[45] Through this assignment, the obligation becomes one that is owed by the absent parent to the state and the

he refused to obtain social security numbers for his children because he did not want his children raised in a police state atmosphere and he anticipated his children's resentment when they became of age.

Arthur asserts that his concerns are within an area of family relationships, child rearing and education which has been judicially recognized as fundamental to and implicit in concepts of ordered liberty....

The holding in Chambers v. Klein, 419 F.Supp. 569 (D.N.J. 1976) supports the Department on both statutory and constitutional grounds.

We agree with the reasoning in Chambers v. Klein that requiring social security numbers for children receiving aid does not violate any constitutionally protected right of privacy. By the enactment of the Privacy Act of 1974, Public Law 93-579, 88 Stat. 1896, the Congress has circumscribed the use of social security numbers. Section 7 of the Privacy Act provides: Sec. 7(a)(1) it shall be unlawful for any Federal, State or local government agency to deny to any individual any right, benefit, or privilege provided by law because of such individual's refusal to disclose his social security account number, (2) the provisions of paragraph (1) of this subsection shall not apply with respect to — (A) any disclosure which is required by Federal statute, or (B) the disclosure of a social security number to any Federal, State, or local agency maintaining a system of records in existence and operating before January 1, 1975, if such disclosure was required under statute or regulation adopted prior to such date to verify the identity of an individual. (b) Any Federal, State, or local government agency which requests an individual to disclose his social security account number shall inform that individual whether that disclosure is mandatory or voluntary, by what statutory or other authority such number is solicited, and what uses will be made of it.

The enactment reflects congressional concern that some uses of social security numbers might violate an individual's right of privacy. But, it is the use, not the requirement, that poses the threat. We believe we can properly judicially notice that the complexities of modern society justify a governmental requirement for a precise method of individual identification. A name affords neither precision nor permanence. A social security number does. We hold that 42 U.S.C. § 602(a)(25) requires the furnishing of social security numbers for Arthur's children and that the requirement does not violate their constitutional right of privacy.

45. 42 U.S.C.A. § 602(a)(26) (Supp. 1979), 45 C.F.R. § 232.11 (1978). Simmons v. Simmons, 72 Cal. App.3d 212, 139 Cal. Rptr. 832 (1977). Persons receiving AFDC prior to enactment of the child support

state may collect it through all available legal processes.[46] Following the assignment, the mother must cooperate with the state in identifying the father and establishing paternity if the children are illegitimate, or by helping the authorities to locate her absent husband.[47] According to OCSE regulations, "cooperation" means that the mother must furnish the aid authorities with all information she possesses concerning the absent father, and must appear and testify under oath as a witness in court or in other proceedings when necessary.[48] Limited exceptions are provided, if it is determined that her cooperation would not be in the best interests of the child.[49] An applicant who refuses to assign support rights or who does not agree to cooperate in securing support payments will be denied AFDC payments for herself, but not for her children. In such a case, the children's assistance will be furnished through a system of vendor or protective payments.[50] As discussed more fully below, a 1977 statutory amendment authorizes similar conditions to be imposed on applicants for medicaid payment eligibility.[51]

Once the applicant has assigned her (children's) support rights to the state, the AFDC agency must promptly inform the IV-D agency of the applicant's situation, as necessary in the circumstances of the case. The IV-D agency then must

---

enforcement program were required to make assignments no later than at the time of their next redetermination of eligibility. 45 C.F.R. § 232.11(a)(4) (1978).

46. 42 U.S.C.A. § 656 (Supp. 1979).

47. 42 U.S.C.A. § 602(a)(26), 45 C.F.R. § 232.12 (1978).

48. 45 C.F.R. § 232.12(b) (1978).

49. *See infra* ch. IX.

50. 42 U.S.C.A. § 606(f) (Supp. 1979), 45 C.F.R. §§ 232.11(a)(2), 232.12(d), 233.90(b)(4)(i), (ii), 232.11(a)(3), 232.12(e), 234.60(a)(13) (1978).

51. *Infra* text at note 138.

promptly begin its efforts to locate the parent, establish paternity, and secure support.[52]

b. *Collection for Claimants Not Receiving or Applying for Public Aid.*

The resources of the child support enforcement program also are available to a person not eligible for AFDC who is owed child support by an absent parent.[53] Enforcement procedures for non-AFDC claimants are identical to those for "welfare parents," except that the non-welfare parent must contact the state IV-D agency directly. Many of the procedures detailed below are thus bypassed. Since no public aid payments are to be reimbursed, support rights are not assigned to the state. Instead, a small application fee is assessed and an agreement made to allow the IV-D program to deduct and retain certain enforcement costs from support payments collected for the non-AFDC child.[54]

In 1977, OCSE statistics indicated that almost precisely one-half of all support collections by all state IV-D agencies

---

52. 42 U.S.C.A. § 602(a)(11) (Supp. 1979), 45 C.F.R. § 235.70 (1978); 42 U.S.C.A. § 654(4) (Supp. 1979), 45 C.F.R. § 302.31 (1978). Prompt notice means written notification, including a copy of the AFDC case record, within two working days of the time aid payments are made. The AFDC agency need not wait for aid payments to begin, but may make referrals upon application for aid. 45 C.F.R. § 235.70(a) (1978). With OCSE approval, the State of Washington's IV-D agency takes referrals from AFDC by telephone. OCSE-IM-79-1 (1979).

53. 42 U.S.C.A. §§ 653(b), (c)(3), 654(6) (Supp. 1979); 45 C.F.R. § 302.33(a) (1978).

54. The application fee, if a flat dollar amount, must not exceed $20; and if based on the applicant's income according to a sliding scale, must not discourage needy applicants. 45 C.F.R. § 302.33(b). Upon obtaining support payments, recovery of large initial costs may be prorated. *Id.* at (c). The IV-D agency must establish offices in every political subdivision of the state to receive applications for support enforcement. OCSE-AT-76-9 (1976).

were on behalf of non-AFDC claimants.[55] Individual state reports, however, remained highly diverse on this aspect of the program. In 1977, collections for non-AFDC support claimants ranged from zero in Guam, Hawaii, Massachusetts, Mississippi, Missouri, New Hampshire, Rhode Island, Virginia and West Virginia, to more than 50 percent of all collections under the program in Alaska, California, Connecticut, Delaware, Louisiana, Nevada, New Jersey, New York, Oregon, Pennsylvania, Puerto Rico and Tennessee.[56] The states that do not yet produce significant non-AFDC collections are under considerable pressure from OCSE to improve their performance, as the law mandates clearly that non-AFDC collections *must* be provided.[57] In fiscal year 1979, non-AFDC collections amounted to $736,000,000 (up from $441,000,000 in 1977) and exceeded AFDC-related collections ($596,000,000) by approximately $140,000,000. Only New Hampshire still reported no non-AFDC collections, although several other states remained significantly below the national norm. Showing what an effort will do, Hawaii moved up from zero non-AFDC collections in 1978 to non-AFDC collections exceeding AFDC-related collections in 1979.[58] Although there can be no question that some portion of the non-AFDC (and even of the AFDC-related) collections represents amounts that would have been collected without the federal

---

55. From Aug. 1, 1975, through March 31, 1977, state IV-D agencies collected $979.6 million in support payments; of that, $542.1 million was for AFDC parents, and $437.5 million was for non-AFDC parents. S. Rep. No. 95-573, 95th Cong., 1st Sess. at 93 (1977).

56. Senate Comm. on Finance, Staff Data and Materials on Public Welfare Programs, 95th Cong., 2d Sess. at 32-33 (1978).

57. 42 U.S.C.A. § 654(6) (Supp. 1979).

58. Dept. of HEW, OCSE, CHILD SUPPORT ENFORCEMENT, 4TH ANNUAL REPORT TO THE CONGRESS FOR THE PERIOD ENDING Sept. 30, 1979, at 97-98 (Dec. 31, 1979).

program (so that it becomes difficult to gauge the net benefit of the program), there is little doubt that the greater portion of non-AFDC collections represents "new money," that is to say, funds that would not have been collected under traditional procedures.

Extending the collection processes to non-AFDC claimants serves the immediate social purpose of significantly reducing the risk of such claimants soon or ever becoming AFDC recipients. Beyond that, however, the extension of the support collection process to non-AFDC claimants helps remedy serious support enforcement problems faced by middle class families.[59]

Initially experimental and subject to yearly renewal through Congressional authorization of funding,[60] the non-AFDC funding features of the program expired in 1979 amid great controversy. The Senate Finance Committee summarized the problem as it stood in 1979:

> The original statute provided Federal matching of 75 percent for services to AFDC families on a permanent basis. Matching for non-AFDC families was provided for only 1 year, to allow the committee an opportunity to observe the implementation of this feature of the program. Federal matching was twice extended by the Congress. The last 1-year extension expired September 30, 1978.
>
> During the 95th Congress the committee reported, and the Senate passed, an amendment to the child support law which would authorize Federal matching for services to nonrecipients on a permanent basis. In reporting this amendment, the committee stated:

---

59. The Senate Finance Committee staff estimated that, during fiscal 1979, the program will serve 760,000 AFDC families and 500,000 non-AFDC families. SENATE COMM. ON FINANCE, FISCAL YEAR 1979 FINANCE COMM. REPORT, 95th Cong., 2d Sess. at 30 (Comm. Print 1978).

60. P.L. 93-647, 93d Cong. (H.R. 17045), Jan. 4, 1975, 42 U.S.C. 654, 655, § 454(b) and 455; P.L. 94-365, § 3, 90 Stat. 990 (1976); P.L. 95-59, § 4, 91 Stat. 255 (1977); P.L. 95-482 (Continuing Resolution).

The committee believes that the existing programs of required services for non-AFDC families may flounder if Federal financing for the services is allowed to terminate. It also believes that States will be more willing to develop and expand the programs if they are convinced that Federal financing will be continued. In addition, it seems reasonable and fair to assist in the financing of a State program which is mandated by Federal law. The committee notes in particular that States which do not have an effective program for non-AFDC families are subject to a penalty provision which requires a reduction in Federal matching for AFDC of 5 percent if a State is found as the result of a Federal audit to have failed to have an effective child support program. For these reasons, the committee amendment would provide for Federal matching for services to non-AFDC families on a permanent basis.

The committee amendment was agreed to by the House of Representatives in the final days of the Congress. However, the bill to which the amendment was added failed to enactment in the final rush of business. Despite this lapse, Federal matching has been allowed to continue in 1979 under the authority of an HEW continuing resolution. Upon an interpretation by HEW's General Counsel, the States were informed that their programs would continue to be eligible for Federal funding, although at a rate not in excess of the amounts claimed for 1978. In an Action Transmittal to the States, dated November 29, 1978, the Office of Child Support Enforcement stated:

The Labor-HEW Appropriations Act for fiscal year 1979, Public Law 95-480, does not include funds for "unauthorized" programs which expired at the end of fiscal year 1978. However, section 101(a) of Public Law 95-482, the Continuing Resolution does provide funds to continue operation of these programs in fiscal year 1979, and is interpreted as authorizing Federal financial participation in expenditures incurred in providing child support enforcement services to non-AFDC recipients under section 454(6) of the Social Secuirity Act at a rate not to exceed the current (fiscal year 1978) rate.

As a result of this interpretation the States are

continuing their programs for non-AFDC recipients although they are subject to the limit on the amount of funding.[61]

On April 6, 1979, OCSE informed the state agencies administering the program that "In an opinion dated March 28, 1979 the Comptroller General of the United States held that, absent specific legislation repealing or delaying the effective date of the prohibition clause of section 455 (a) of the Social Security Act, Federal funding is not available for expenditures made under section 454(6) of the Act." [62]

Political maneuvering continued, as reported by the Washington Post:

> [Senator] Long wants the reimbursement extended permanently, retroactive to last Oct. 1 and has tacked such a provision onto a minor bill giving state legislators a tax break on living expenses while state legislatures are in session.
>
> Corman and Ullman, however, have refused to go along with this. They know, as Long [h]as repeatedly said, the most recently yesterday, that Long dislikes the president's $5.5 billion welfare revision bill and he has reservations about some of the child-welfare provisions. He believes the welfare bill provisions would encourage people to go on welfare instead of seeking to get off.
>
> Corman and Ullman fear that Long will block or delay these measures, particularly the $5.5 billion welfare bill. So they have in effect offered him a deal: They have offered to put an authorization for "fleeing fathers" reimbursements for fiscal 1979 in the state

---

61. SENATE COMM. ON FINANCE, STAFF DATA AND MATERIALS ON CHILD SUPPORT, 96th Cong., 1st Sess. at 5-6 (Comm. Print 96-7, 1979). *See* 45 C.F.R. § 304.20(a)(4) and 42 U.S.C.A. §§ 654(6), 655(a) for the authorizing legislation and regulations that expired October 1st, 1978. *See further*, Senate Comm on Finance, Adoption Assistance and Child Welfare Act of 1979, 96th Cong., 1st Sess. at 77-78 (Report No. 96-336, 1979).

62. OCSE-AT-79-1 (1979).

legislator bill, if he will in effect agree to the big welfare bill.

As an inducement to take up the $5.5 billion bill, a permanent extension of the reimbursements beyond fiscal 1979 has been written into the welfare measure.

House sources say this is the way Corman and Ullman are playing hardball against a master of the game who has done the same kind of thing to them repeatedly in past years.

The states, meanwhile, have been continuing their outlays on Nab-a-Dad in expectation of full federal reimbursement of their administrative costs, but in order to make sure they get the money they went to court two weeks ago.[63]

In August, 1979, in response to legal action filed by thirteen states, Judge Greene of the District of Columbia ruled as follows:

> ... Plaintiffs have demonstrated a substantial likelihood of success on the ultimate merits of this lawsuit in two respects.
>
> First, an opinion of the Comptroller General dated March 28, 1979, has concluded that a congressional prohibition in an authorization act on federal funding for services to non-AFDC recipients under Title IV-D precludes further disbursement to the states with respect to that program. However, it is quite likely that the Comptroller General is in error. By a rather peculiar and unusual circumstance, although there is presently no authorization legislation for the non-AFDC part of the Title IV-D program, the necessary funds have actually been appropriated by a Joint Resolution of the Congress. Moreover, that Resolution represents but the latest chapter in a congressional history of continuously providing federal funds for such services. While, to be sure, an appropriation does not validly subsist without a prior legislative authorization, there is a substantial probability that ultimately it will be determined that

---

63. THE WASHINGTON POST, July 28, 1979, p. A4.

the appropriation act repealed by implication the ban contained in the authorization legislation, thus validating the expenditure of funds. . . .

On the equities, it is clear that, absent a preliminary injunction, plaintiffs and numerous beneficiaries will suffer irreparable harm. If the disputed funds are recouped by HEW immediately, some, perhaps most, of the states will be forced to dismantle part of their enforcement machinery, and they will have to restrict child support enforcement services, not only to non-AFDC recipients but, due to the substantial cuts in funds, to AFDC families as well. As a result, program beneficiaries not now on welfare may have to resort to welfare in order to subsist, the present program will be disrupted, services will be reduced, and experienced staffs will be dissipated. Child support that might have been collected during the period of reduced funding will be unavailable until the administrative review process is completed, and much of it will never be collected. These injuries obviously could not be remedied by simply returning the recouped funds to the states at some subsequent time if the plaintiff states should subsequently prevail either in the administrative or the judicial forums.

HEW, on the other hand, will suffer little or no harm if the states are permitted to retain the funds while the legal disputes are winding their way through the appropriate channels. HEW has conceded that, should it ultimately prevail, it will have no difficulty recouping these funds in full. There is no reason why it needs to have these monies now — lying idle — only to return them to the states in the event that it does not prevail (and after the damage to the substantive programs and their intended beneficiaries has been done).

Finally, the public interest favors having the Title IV-D program go forward.[64]

Legislation passed in December, 1979, extended the federal financial participation feature from (retroactively)

---

64. Louisiana v. Califano, Jr., Civil Action 79-1836, filed 8/8/79.

October 1, 1978, to March 31, 1980.[65] In June, 1980, the non-AFDC funding feature was finally made permanent.[66]

c. Locating the Absent Parent.

If the mother does not request a "good-cause exception," or if the AFDC agency denies a claimed exception, or if the AFDC agency grants an exception but decides that enforcement may proceed without active participation by the mother, then the AFDC agency must inform the IV-D agency promptly that an unsatisfied support obligation exists.[67] Upon receipt of the applicant's case information from the AFDC agency, the IV-D agency must immediately establish its own case record. This record begins with the AFDC referral documents and may grow to include information on contacts with the mother and absent parent, and a description of all parent locator and support enforcement activities.[68] The IV-D agency must establish a similar record for non-AFDC parents who apply for assistance in obtaining child support.[69]

If the absent parent's location is not known, the IV-D agency must attempt to find him through the statutorily mandated state and federal parent locator services.[70] The

---

65. Pub. L. No. 96-178, 93 Stat. 1295 (Jan. 2, 1980), amending 42 U.S.C.A. § 655.

66. Infra ch. X. 8.

67. 42 U.S.C.A. § 602(a)(11) (Supp. 1979), 45 C.F.R. § 235.70 (1978). See infra ch. IX.

68. 45 C.F.R. § 303.2 (1978).

69. Id. The non-AFDC applicant applies for IV-D enforcement directly to the IV-D agency. 45 C.F.R. § 303.33(a) (1978). The state IV-D plan must provide offices in each political subdivision of the state at which non-AFDC parents may apply for enforcement services; this function may be delegated to other governmental offices under 45 C.F.R. §§ 302.12(a)(2), 303.20(c)(1), (d) (1978). OCSE-AT-76-9 (June 9, 1976).

70. 45 C.F.R. § 303.3 (1978), 42 U.S.C.A. §§ 653(a), 654(8) (Supp. 1979). If the mother requests a good-cause exception to her duty to

combined federal-state locator services are available not only to IV-D agencies, but also to courts and custodians of unsupported children.[71] In all requests, except those by private custodians, the IV-D agency may request aid from the Federal Parent Locator Service at the same time it begins a state search. When a private custodian makes the request, the IV-D agency must first exhaust state locator services before requesting a federal search.[72]

The state Parent Locator Service must have a central office and also may maintain local offices.[73] Within 60 days of AFDC referral or non-AFDC application, the state locator service must inquire into all appropriate state and local sources that might possess information on the whereabouts of the absent parent.[74] At the state level, these sources include employment,[75] unemployment, public assistance, income tax and motor vehicle offices, as well as criminal-record repositories.[76] At the local level, sources include personnel of state or local assistance, food stamp and social services programs, relatives, friends and past employers of the absent parent, financial references, the telephone company and post office, as well as police, union and fraternal organization records.[77] However, if the

---

cooperate, the IV-D agency must delay location activities, as part of its support securement activities, until the AFDC agency informs it that no exception will be granted. See 45 C.F.R. § 302.31(b)(2) (1978).

71. 42 U.S.C.A. § 653(c) (Supp. 1979), 45 C.F.R. § 302.35(c) (1978).

72. 45 C.F.R. §§ 302.35(c), 303.3(a), (e); OCSE-AT-78-16 (1978); 1978 REPORT at 17. The requirement that state locator services be exhausted before private custodians may make a request for location is statutory. 42 U.S.C.A. § 653(f) (Supp. 1979).

73. 45 C.F.R. § 302.35(b) (1978).

74. 45 C.F.R. § 303.3(d) (1978).

75. 29 U.S.C. § 49b(a) (1976).

76. 45 C.F.R. § 303.3(c) (1978).

77. 45 C.F.R. § 303.3(a) (1978).

deserted parent is unable to provide the absent parent's social security number, the locator service need search only sources that are not keyed to social security number identification.[78] To improve the locator process, the locator service may enter into cooperative agreements with courts and law enforcement officials.[79] If the state locator efforts prove fruitless and there is a reasonable belief that the absent parent is residing in another state, the initiating state must refer the case to the appropriate sister state IV-D agency, which is required to cooperate fully and must provide location efforts identical to those of the initiating state.[80]

A state IV-D agency *may*, but need not, initiate a federal search as soon as it begins a state search. If, however, the state locator service or sister state services cannot locate the absent parent after diligent and reasonable effort, the agency *must* request a search by the federal parent locator service maintained by OCSE.[81] The federal service accepts requests only for the state IV-D central office and up to two state field offices, on behalf of AFDC referrals, non-AFDC applicants, and courts of competent jurisdiction.[82]

While IV-D agencies may request a search with

---

78. OCSE-AT-77-15 (1977).

79. 45 C.F.R. § 302.34(1978). Costing guidelines for IV-D services purchased from public agencies or obtained through cooperative agreements appear at OCSE-AT-75-6 (1975).

80. 45 C.F.R. §§ 303.3(f), 303.7, 302.36(b) (1978).

81. 42 U.S.C.A. § 654(8)(B) (Supp. 1979); 45 C.F.R. §§ 303.3(e), 302.70(b), 302.35(c) (1978).

82. 42 U.S.C.A. §§ 653(d) (Supp. 1979); 45 C.F.R. §§ 302.70(a), 302.35(c), (d) (1978). If the federal parent locator service is used for non-AFDC parents, the state IV-D agency must collect a fee and reimburse OCSE. 42 U.S.C.A. § 653(e)(2) (Supp. 1979), 45 C.F.R. § 302.35(e) (1978).

information provided on written forms, punch cards or magnetic tape,[83] OCSE is strongly encouraging the expansion of a direct-transmission computer terminal network for federal locator requests.[84] By mid-1978, more than one-half of the states were "hooked" into the computer network and more have been added since. Under this system,[85] the federal parent locator service compiles all search requests and, once weekly, disseminates all requests to the Social Security Administration, the Internal Revenue Service, the Veterans Administration, the Department of Defense, the Department of Transportation (Coast Guard), the National Personnel Records Center, the General Services Administration, and the Immigration and Naturalization Service.[86] These agencies report the results of their internal searches to the federal parent locator service, which updates its answers to state requests as information from the federal agencies' searches comes in. If they have computer access to the federal data bank, the states may call up and view the responses to their search requests at any time.

---

83. 1976 REPORT at 29. OCSE-AT-76-3 (1976) details procedures for states requesting information from the federal parent locator service.

84. 1976 REPORT at 24. In September, 1976, OCSE issued a Federal Parent Locator Service Terminal User's Manual as an attachment to OCSE-IM-76-11 (1976). OCSE is developing a comprehensive State User Guide which consolidates all previous directions on the operation of the system. In late 1979, this guide was expected to be available in early 1980. OCSE-IM-79-16 (1979).

85. *See* "Terminal User's Manual" at 2-4 (OCSE-IM-76-11 (1976)).

86. 1978 REPORT at 16; OCSE-IM-78-19 (1978). By statute, federal agencies must disclose information sought by the federal parent locator service, unless disclosure would "contravene the national policy or security interests of the United States or the confidentiality of census dat[a]." 42 U.S.C.A. § 653(b), (e) (1)-(2) (Supp. 1979). Another statute specifically authorizes the Internal Revenue Service to disclose tax return information for IV-D purposes. 26 U.S.C.A. & 6103(1)(b) (Supp. 1979).

Although the federal parent locator service keys its search to the absent parent's social security number, in some circumstances, state IV-D agencies may request a federal search even if the social security number is unknown.[87] If the state can provide the absent parent's name, birth date, the parent's father's name, and the parent's mother's maiden name,[88] a computer search will be made for the social security number itself, followed automatically by an address search. With less than all of this information, the federal parent locator service may in some cases provide a manual social security number search.[89]

As a federal agency subject to the Privacy Act of 1974,[90] OCSE has promulgated an extensive series of regulations

---

87. 45 C.F.R. § 302.70 (c)(2) (1978).

88. OCSE-AT-77-15 (1977).

89. The IV-D agency must supply either: 1) the complete name of one parent and the first name of the other parent, plus the complete birth date, or 2) the first name of both parents, the complete birth date, and the complete place of birth, or 3) the complete name of one parent with a different surname than the absent parent, plus the complete birth date and complete place of birth. OCSE-AT-77-15 (1977).

90. 5 U.S.C.A. § 552a, especially 552a(e) (1977). The impact of that Act and others in the context of child support enforcement was discussed by William Galvin of the Senate Finance Committee Staff at the 27th Annual Conference on Child Support Enforcement as reported in 4 NRFSEA NEWS at 29-30 (Special edition, March, 1979):

The Privacy Act of 1974 affects federal government agencies and government contractors. The term government contractor, the term agency, was kicked around for almost a year before they decided what that meant. It has an interrelationship with the Freedom of Information Act. The only exception to that is relating to social security numbers. Section seven was put in as an after-thought when someone on the Finance Committee saw what the rest of the law did. Section seven gives the federal government the authority to statutorily provides for exemptions to the Act. . . .

The Privacy Act has two sections exempting various agencies. One of them is 3J and the other 3K. Any files maintained by Central

and directives to safeguard the information on absent parents collected by the enforcement program. The IV-D agencies may request information on absent parents only

Intelligence Agency are exempt from most of the systems of records or maintained by an agency or component thereof that performs as its principal function any activity pertaining to the enforcement of criminal laws, including police efforts to prevent, control or reduce crime and the activities of prosecutors, courts, correctional, probation, pardon or parole authorities. So, it is very broad. 3K is not that broad, but there are additions to that. So, if you look at Sections 3J or 3K you will find out.

There are at the present time five acts relating to privacy. The first one is the Fair Credit Reporting Act of 1970. It is Public Law 903-321. That regulates information about bill paying habits and credit. That has been updated. It is 15 USC 1681 and if you are in child support you know we have utilized that particular Act, a different section thereof, to put a limit on the amount of garnishments under court orders.

The next one is the Crime Control Act of 1973. That is Public Law 93-83. That Act was almost updated in this last Congress. If it had been, the Federal Parent Locator Services would have had to accept as a priority equal to child support at state level to accept anything on runaway parents and custody of children. It would have had a damaging affect on the system. Fortunately, we were able to stop it. It got through the Senate as a floor amendment.

The third one is the Family Educational Rights and Privacy Act of 1974, Public Law 93-380.

The fourth is the Privacy Act itself of 1974, Public Law 93-579.

The last one is the Tax Reform Act of 1976, Public Law 94-455. There is a feature in that law that affects child support. . . .

We had our first problem with the Privacy Act very early. We ran into the refusal of the Social Security Agency which comes under HEW and, by the way, HEW at the time of the enactment of the law was totally against the law. Their refusals were based on the Privacy Act, they did not want to release the social security number of the absent parent to the FPLS or to the SPLS. The position of Social Security was that there was no specific authority in the IV-D legislation authorizing the release of the number and it was not compatible with the purpose for which the information was originally collected. That is almost a direct quote, if not a direct quote, from the Privacy Act. The staff of the Committee knew that the IV-D language is identical to the language in prior law by which the social security number had been released. And they had been released routinely to states and localities since 1958. There were authorized forms with SRS and all. However, their counter argument in Social Security was that it had never been authorized and if any number had been released, it was improper.

We went to their archives and collected all their information and showed they were releasing the number and that did not persuade

through a referral signed by the state IV-D director who
thereby attests that the search is solely for the purpose of

---

them, so what we did is, in spite of all their proof, I guess that was
about the first of April, it took another three months before they
would release the number. Fortunately, we had a chairman who did
not go along with that. He insisted that the SSA release the number
and about that time the Department of Justice found that the release
did fall under the routine use and agency concept in the Privacy Act.
It was then resolved, HEW decided the FPLS could obtain the
information on an inter-agency need to know basis, which is
provided in Section 3B1 of the Act and then release it to the states
on a routine use basis, which is provided in Section 3B3 of the Act.

Section 7 of the Act, exempts from the restrictions demands for an
individual's social security number that are mandated by a statute
or regulation adopted prior to January 1, 1975. This Act was not one
of the most publicized Acts in the world. Most of the states did not
know what was happening. The Section 7 was supposed to have
provided only a moratorium for demands of an individual's social
security number by a government agency where the individual was
required to comply. The Finance Committee in response to state
agencies and IV-D agencies recommended to the Congress that they
authorize, pursuant to Section 7A2, exemption authority,
compulsory divulgence of the number, and this became enacted into
Public Law 94-455. It provides that upon written request by the
Secretary of HEW, the Secretary of the Treasury may disclose
information returns filed pursuant to Chapter 61 of the Internal
Revenue Code for the purpose of disclosure of Federal return
information, the federal, state and local child support enforcement
agencies. This is return information from the master files of the
Internal Revenue Service relating to the address, filing status,
amount and nature of income, the number of dependents reported on
any return filed by or with respect to any individual with respect to
whom child support obligations also ought to be established or
enforced pursuant to provisions of Part D of the Act and with respect
to any individual to whom such support obligations are owing. And,
second, from the return itself on any individual relating to the
amount of such individual's gross income or consisting of the names
and addresses of payors of such income and the names of any
dependents reported on such income, but only if such return
information is not reasonably available from any other source. That
is restricted to the extent that it is necessary in establishing and
collecting child support obligations from and locating individuals
owing such obligations.

Under the strict disclosure provisions each state agency or local
agency in the state supervised system that wants to receive that
information has to meet the disclosure requirements of the Internal
Revenue Service. Eighteen states have signed up for that. They have
received a total of 2,203 requests for Type 1 information. . . .

establishing paternity or securing support, and that the confidentiality of the information will be maintained by appropriate safeguards.[91] Information obtained through the locator service is subject to the nondisclosure regulations of the AFDC program. These generally prohibit any disclosure that is not directly necessary for administering federally supported welfare and related programs or for official investigations and proceedings connected with the programs.[92] Similar nondisclosure requirements apply to information collected solely by effort of the IV-D agency or through the federal parent locator service.[93] Finally, data processing through the federal parent locator service is subject to extensive administrative protection. Federal parent locator service personnel must sign a nondisclosure oath, all address-request data must be

---

The final report of the Privacy Commission mentions the enactment of Section 1211 of the Tax Reform Act in relation to Section 7 of the Act, but discloses only in one of the separate appendices that a month prior to date Congress effectively nullified the routine use concept of Section 7. In September of 1976 Congress amended the enabling legislation of the Veteran's Administration to require that the head of any federal department or agency provide such information to the administrator as he may request for purposes of verifying other information with respect thereto. That is about as broad as you can get a request.

91. 45 C.F.R. § 302.70(d) (1978).

92. 42 U.S.C.A. § 602(a) (9) (Supp. 1979), 45 C.F.R. § 205.50 (1978). States may enact legislation granting public access to AFDC financial records on payments and disbursements, provided that names may not be used for commercial or political purposes. 45 C.F.R. § 205.50(e) (1978). 42 U.S.C. § 602(a) (9) prohibits disclosure "to any committee or a legislative body, of any information which identifies by name or address any such applicant or recipient." HEW has interpreted this language to mean that AFDC agencies may disclose such information to legislative bodies and committees when the groups certify they will use the information only for permissible purposes described in 42 U.S.C.A. § 602(a) (9) and 45 C.F.R. § 205.50(a) (1) (i) (A)-(C). SRS-AT-76-38 (1976).

93. 45 C.F.R. §§ 302.18, 302.70(d) (1978).

inventoried and accounted for, and operational control is vested in a single manager.[94] State computer access to the federal data bank is limited to information concerning individual state requests only, and the information can be retrieved by only a limited number of IV-D staff members.[95]

d. *Securing the Support Obligation: State Procedures, Federal Courts and the Internal Revenue Service.*

When the AFDC agency has located the deserting parent, it must use all available state legal procedures to establish paternity, obtain a support judgment in an appropriate amount, and enforce the support obligation.[96] Although the IV-D agency may undertake these activities directly, it also may enter into agreements with other agencies to secure and enforce child support obligations.[97]

---

94. OCSE-AT-76-3, Attachment A at 2-3 (Feb. 13, 1976).

95. "Terminal User's Manual" at 3 (OCSE-IM-76-11 (1976)).

96. 42 U.S.C.A. § 654(4) (Cum. Supp. 1979); 45 C.F.R. §§ 302.31, 302.50, 303.4, 303.5, 303.6 (1978). When there is no court order covering the amount of the support obligation, 45 C.F.R. § 302.53 specifies the criteria the IV-D agency should take into account in determining a support level. The regulation provides that, at a minimum, the absent parent should make payments for the unsupported child "on an equitable basis in comparison with any other minor children of the absent parent." *Id.* § 302.53(8)(b). For a critique of existing support-determination procedures, *supra* ch. I. 2. *Infra* ch. X. 3.

97. 42 U.S.C.A. § 654(7) (Supp. 1979); 45 C.F.R. § 302.34 (1978). Many states provide standardized forms for cooperative agreements with local prosecutors to enforce support obligations. *E.g.*, ILLINOIS TITLE IV-D STATE PLAN, available from State of Illinois, Department of Public Aid, 316 S. Second, Springfield, IL 62762; MINNESOTA COUNTY ATTORNEYS COUNCIL IV-D CHILD SUPPORT ENFORCEMENT PROGRAM PLAN OF COOPERATION, available from National District Attorneys Association Child Support Enforcement Project, 1900 L Street, N.W., Suite 607, Washington, D.C. 20036.

If the deserting parent resides in another state, the IV-D agency must attempt to secure support through cooperative legal procedures, primarily under the Uniform Reciprocal Enforcement of Support Act.[98] It must similarly cooperate with sister state IV-D agencies in collecting support obligations owed by its residents.[99]

If all efforts to obtain support from a deserting parent residing in another state have failed, the IV-D agency may request approval from HEW to obtain federal court jurisdiction as a last resort.[100] Ultimately, this may overcome the traditional abstinence many federal courts still maintain on family law issues, even when all technical grounds for federal jurisdiction are fulfilled.[101] By late 1979, however, federal courts had not yet been used to enforce support orders.[102] In contrast, available procedures to use the collection machinery of the Internal Revenue

---

98. *Supra* chs. II. 2. c, V. 10.

99. 45 C.F.R. §§ 302.36, 303.7 (1978).

100. 42 U.S.C.A. § 660 (1976) grants federal jurisdiction to any IV-D child support action certified by the Secretary of HEW. Under 42 U.S.C.A. § 652(a)(8) (Supp. 1979) and 45 C.F.R. § 302.72 (1978) the IV-D agency may apply to OCSE for certification when (1) its child support order has not been enforced within 60 days of receipt by the sister state; (2) after the 60-day period, it notifies the sister state IV-D agency that it plans to apply to HEW for certification of federal jurisdiction and (3) use of federal court is "the only reasonable method of enforcing such order." 42 U.S.C.A. § 652(a)(8)(B), (Supp. 1979); 45 C.F.R. § 302.72(a)(1), (b)(3), (a)(2) (1978). HEW will certify only actions originating with a IV-D agency. OCSE-AT-76-1 (1976).

101. *E.g.*, Solomon v. Solomon, 516 F.2d 1018 (3rd Cir. 1975), relying on dictum in Barber v. Barber, 62 U.S. 582, 16 L. Ed. 226 (1859), and citing numerous cases. *See* H. KRAUSE, FAMILY LAW IN A NUTSHELL 6 (1977).

102. Letter of December 26, 1979, from Louis B. Hays, Esq., Deputy Director, OCSE, to Harry D. Krause.

Service [103] had been used with moderate success.[104]

e. *Disbursing Collections.*

When the IV-D agency has taken responsibility for obtaining or enforcing a child support obligation, the deserting parent is ordered to pay the obligation to the IV-D agency rather than to his deserted family.[105] The IV-D agency informs the AFDC agency each month of the amount the deserting parent has paid toward his obligation.[106] The AFDC agency then determines whether the support payment is sufficient to disqualify the deserted parent for continued AFDC assistance.[107]

If the AFDC agency makes a determination of

---

103. 42 U.S.C.A. § 652(b) (Supp. 1979), 26 U.S.C.A. 6305 (Supp. 1979). HEW may certify to the IRS only those cases in which there is a court order of support and the IV-D agency has made "diligent and reasonable" efforts to collect the support. 42 U.S.C.A. § 652(b) (Supp. 1979); 45 C.F.R. § 302.71(a)(1), (a)(4) (1978). The IV-D agency must possess a reasonable belief that the deserting parent possesses assets sufficient to satisfy the delinquency; the delinquency must be for at least $75 and also equal three months of unpaid support; and the IV-D agency must provide the deserting parent's name, social security number, last known address and place of employment. 45 C.F.R. § 302.71 (1978). The IV-D agency must reimburse the IRS for collection efforts, whether or not successful. 45 C.F.R. § 302.71(a)(3) (1978), OCSE-AT-76-2 (1976). For IRS regulations on collection procedures, *see* 26 C.F.R. § 301.6305-1 (1979).

104. Letter of December 26, 1979, from Louis B. Hays, Deputy Director, OCSE, to Harry D. Krause: "For Fiscal Years 1976 through 1979, 500 cases have been certified to the Internal Revenue Service for collection of 2.5 million dollars. Fifty thousand dollars has been collected to date."

105. 42 U.S.C.A. § 654(5) (Supp. 1979), 45 C.F.R. § 302.32(a) (1978).

106. The calculation of any deficiency will be based directly on the court order, if the order provides for monthly payments. If not, the IV-D agency determines the equivalent monthly amount. OCSE-AT-76-5 at 1 (1976). *See* 45 C.F.R. § 302.51(a) (1978).

107. 45 C.F.R. § 302.32(b) (1978).

ineligibility, the IV-D agency will pay the support obligation directly to the child's parent, guardian or caretaker relative,[108] and continue to make collections from the deserting parent and disbursements to the deserted parent for up to five months after the last AFDC assistance payment was made. During this period, the IV-D agency retains any applicable arrearage payments as reimbursement for AFDC benefits that were provided the deserted parent in the past.[109] Independently of the five-months period of continued enforcement and for so long as the federal and state governments remain unreimbursed for past AFDC assistance rendered,[110] the IV-D agency may continue to collect arrearages from the deserting parent. The deserted parent, on the other hand, has the option of continuing collection of monthly support payments through the IV-D agency even after AFDC eligibility ends.[111]

If the AFDC agency determines that AFDC eligibility continues, the IV-D agency simply retains the support payment to offset the mother's receipt of current AFDC assistance.[112] It also retains arrearage payments until the state and federal governments have been reimbursed fully

---

108. *Id.* at § 302.38 (1978). The parent may continue to receive AFDC assistance pending a hearing on termination of benefits. 45 C.F.R. § 302.31(b), (c) (1978); OCSE-AT-76-5 at 13 (1976).

109. 42 U.S.C.A. § 657 (Supp. 1979); 45 C.F.R. § 302.51(e)(1), (b)(2) (1978); OCSE-IM-77-22 (1977). The IV-D agency must give priority to current collections. 45 C.F.R. § 302.51(f)(4) (1978).

110. 45 C.F.R. § 302.51(f) (1978).

111. 42 U.S.C.A. § 657(c)(2) (Supp. 1979); 45 C.F.R. § 302.51(e)(2) (1978).

112. 42 U.S.C.A. § 657(b)(1) (Supp. 1979); 45 C.F.R. § 302.51(b)(2) (1978). For the transitional period between August 1, 1975, and September 30, 1976, 40 percent of the first $50 collected monthly were paid to the mother over and above her AFDC benefit level, to induce her cooperation. 45 C.F.R. § 302.51(b)(1) (1978).

for past AFDC assistance.[113] Once fully reimbursed, the IV-D agency turns any additional arrearage payments over to the family.[114]

This leads to the question whether, once a court order fixes a support level, that order defines the extent of the father's obligation to reimburse the state for AFDC payments made to his family. To illustrate, if a court fixes $100 as the father's monthly payment and AFDC in the amount of $250 a month is rendered to the family, does the father accrue any obligation to reimburse the state for the $150 in aid provided in excess of the $100 support order? The answer is that the reimbursement of public assistance is limited to the amount of the order. OCSE amplifies:

> [T]here are cases in which the IV-D agency can collect unreimbursed assistance payments. The custodial parent applies for public assistance, receives a grant of $250, there is a court order for $100 and an arrearage of $5000. The IV-D agency begins to collect the $100 court-ordered support, leaving $150 of unreimbursed public assistance each month. Six months later, the IV-D agency's successful enforcement efforts have resulted in an extra $125 a month to be collected to reduce the arrearages. This $125 can be used to reimburse the previously unreimbursed $150 in assistance payments.[115]

The situation turns a little less clear if there is *no* support order outstanding and aid is rendered the family. Under

---

113. 42 U.S.C.A. § 657(b)(3) (Supp. 1978); 45 C.F.R. § 302.51(b)(4) (1978). Thus, any payments larger than the monthly support obligation are considered reimbursement for past assistance and not income to the mother, so long as the state and federal governments remain unreimbursed. OCSE-AT-76-5 at 11 (March 11, 1976).

114. 45 C.F.R. § 302.51(b)(5) (1978). The question of how collections are disbursed is covered in OCSE-AT-76-5 (1976). *Also see infra* ch. X. 6.

115. Letter of December 26, 1979, from Louis B. Hays, Esq., Deputy Director, OCSE, to Harry D. Krause.

these circumstances, does the father's liability accrue in the amount of the aid provided? It would seem that it does.[116] True, this example is rather theoretical insofar as most fathers have trouble enough keeping up with current payments and what current payments they can make are, often enough, inadequate to reimburse current aid. The problem may be worth pursuing nevertheless: What of the case of the man who (because of illness or whatever) could not support his family for a period of, say, two years, had no judgment rendered against him because of the apparent worthlessness of such a judgment, and who now recovers and finds a well-paid job, say, as a plumber? Of course, the first result of these events will be that a support judgment will be obtained (or the father will render support voluntarily) so that his family will leave the aid rolls. What, however, of the money paid the family during the two years aid was rendered, assuming that the father now earns quite enough to be capable of reimbursing for that aid?

Does it make sense to exempt him from liability — as current law would — if he had the foresight to have entered against himself a token judgment for, say, $10 per month while he lay ill, but hold him liable for reimbursement if no judgment was ever obtained? In the latter case, the answer rests on state law which typically does *not* bar claims for past support, although awards for past support would be more closely scrutinized by judges. Some state laws seem to require reimbursement for welfare expenditures without qualification, and others do not.[117]

---

116. *See* 45 C.F.R. § 302.51 (1979).

117. *But see* Amie v. Superior Court, 99 Cal. App. 3d 421, 160 Cal. Rptr. 271, 272-74 (1980) in which a county sought reimbursement from a father for fifteen years of public assistance rendered his now fifteen year old daughter. The Court held:

In short, this is an area which is not all that clear on the law, which is at least potentially subject to abuse, and

---

The county maintains that there is no statute of limitations in regard to its action or, if a limitations period exists, it does not run while the child is a minor.

Although the county insists that the right to obtain reimbursement for support furnished to a child is well-established and of ancient origin, we have found no case in which a noncustodial parent has been required to reimburse another for support furnished to a child in the absence of an order or agreement. It is established that "a mother cannot claim reimbursement for money paid out in support of a child prior to an order of the court directing the father to pay support to meet the current needs of the child." (Bierl v. McMahon (1969) 270 Cal. App. 2d 97, 105.) . . . In the present action, the county admitted in its complaint that there is no existing order for the support of the minor child. Under Civil Code section 207, a third party furnishing necessities to a child may obtain reimbursement from a parent, but only if the parent has custody of the child. . . . Petitioner has apparently never had custody of Lorina.

The county has argued that its right of action is derived, by way of assignment or subrogation, from the child's right of action against her parent for support. . . . As the child's minority would toll the statute of limitations in an action commenced by her . . . the county maintains that the statute likewise is tolled as to its action.

Although a minor child may sue in his own name for support . . . we are not aware of any case in which a child has attempted to obtain reimbursement from a noncustodial parent for past support. Furthermore, the disability of a minor which tolls the statute of limitations is personal and may not be transferred by assignment or subrogation. . . . Assignment destroys the purpose of the tolling provision for minors. . . .

Here, the county seeks reimbursement for itself, not for Lorina; the county does not suffer the burdens of minority and therefore has no claim to its benefits. . . .

The county has also relied on the general rule that "[t]he obligation of a father to support his child, whether legitimate or illegitimate, is a continuing duty against which the statute of limitations does not run during the time the child needs such support." (Perez v. Singh (1971) 21 Cal. App. 3d 870, 872, citing Fernandez v. Aburrea (1919) 42 Cal. App. 131, 132.) . . .

[E]xamination of the cases stating this rule indicates that in each case the issue was the child's right to present and future support, not reimbursement for support furnished before the action was brought. By stressing the continuing nature of the parent's duty to support the child until adulthood, the rule invokes the familiar principle that each breach of a continuing duty gives rise to a new cause of action. . . . The statute runs against each new cause of action from the date of breach. . . .

344

concerning which OCSE would be well advised to formulate a sensible policy.

f. Garnishment of Federal Payments.

The child support enforcement program includes an enforcement provision that is applicable to all persons owing child support and receiving federal funds, whether or not their deserted spouses have invoked IV-D enforcement. If the person owing support is a federal employee or receives federal benefits, the United States has waived sovereign immunity for garnishment proceedings against that person's salary or benefits.[118] The waiver applies to District of Columbia employees and allows the deserted parent to recover attorneys' fees as a part of the support obligation.[119] Certain withholdings are exempt from garnishment [120] and, through concurrent amendments to the Consumer Credit Protection Act, the amount of periodic federal

---

The Legislature has decided that a limitations period of three years (or four years where hospital care has been provided) is a reasonable length of time to allow for an action by a county to recover the cost of various welfare benefits, where such recovery is authorized by statute. We see no reason why the same should not be true of an action by a county to obtain reimbursement for public assistance furnished for the support of a child.

118. 42 U.S.C.A. §§ 659, 661-662 (Supp. 1979). One state court has held that a § 659 garnishment action will lie for collection of support accruing before the effective date of the statute. Pellerin v. Pellerin, 534 S.W. 2d 767 (Ark. 1976). An interim list of federal agency offices to contact for garnishment appears in OCSE-IM-77-20 (1977) and in the NDAA CHILD SUPPORT ENFORCEMENT PROJECT NEWSLETTER, No. 14 November/December 1977.

119. 42 U.S.C.A. §§ 659, 662(b) (Supp. 1979).

120. Exceptions include money owed by the deserting parent to the United States; legally ordered deductions such as fines; federal, state and local income tax withholdings; health insurance premiums; life insurance premiums; and retirement contributions. 42 U.S.C.A. § 662(g) (Supp. 1979).

payments the deserted parent may garnish is limited to a maximum of 65 percent.[121]

Plaintiffs seeking to garnish an absent parent's federal funds have encountered two areas of procedural uncertainty. First, should garnishment actions be brought in a state or federal court? Most federal courts considering garnishment actions have expressed considerable unwillingness to involve themselves in family law questions. Their approach has been to hold that the federal statute merely waives sovereign immunity but does not create a federal cause of action. Then they have sent the garnishment action to state courts.[122] Plaintiffs who have filed suit in state courts, on the other hand, have found

---

121. The statute limits garnishment against *all* United States residents, for child support purposes, to 50 percent of disposable earnings for current support when the individual is supporting another family, and to 60 percent for current support when the individual is not supporting another family. The statute raises the limits to 55 and 65 percent, respectively, when the garnishment is for support that is more than 12 weeks in arrears. 15 U.S.C.A. § 1673(b) (Supp. 1979). Previously, the Consumer Credit Protection Act had placed no limitation on garnishment for child support. This lack of *any* limit on garnishment drew some sharp criticism from the Senate Finance Committee in 1976:

> It has come to the committee's attention that some States allow up to 100 percent of disposable earnings to be garnished for purposes of child support and alimony. Although the committee believes that a family's rights to support sometimes must be enforced by using the garnishment process, it does not believe that this process should be used in such a way so as to cause the financial ruin of the parent or of his second family, if a second family exists.

S. Rep. No. 94-1350, 94th Cong., 2d Sess. 3 (1976). State-law garnishment limitations still apply, however, if they limit garnishment *more* strictly than does the Federal Act. 15 U.S.C.A. § 1677 (1979). *See* infra note 125.

122. *E.g.*, Diaz v. Diaz, 568 F.2d 1061 (4th Cir. 1977), in which a wife sued in federal court to garnish her husband's federal retirement and disability benefits. The District Court dismissed the suit, saying the wife should first have obtained a state support judgment. The Fourth Circuit Court of Appeals held that the District Court should have abstained. *But*

THE FEDERALIZATION OF CHILD SUPPORT ENFORCEMENT

themselves the targets of attempts by the United States, as third party defendant-garnishee, to remove their actions to federal courts. Some federal courts then have refused to find removal jurisdiction and have ordered the garnishment action back into state courts,[123] whereas others have asserted jurisdiction and rendered decisions on the merits of the case.[124]

---

see Overman v. United States, 563 F.2d 1287 (8th Cir. 1977) in which the plaintiff's wife brought a § 659 garnishment action, and plaintiff sued to enjoin the garnishment by attacking the underlying divorce decree as fraudulently procured. The District Court dismissed the action for failure to join the wife as an indispensable party. The Eighth Circuit Court of Appeals held that the District Court should have dismissed for failure to state a claim on which relief could be granted, because § 659 did not waive federal sovereign immunity against injunctions. The Court asserted jurisdiction to dismiss the United States as a defendant, and held that the dispute over the underlying divorce decree was subject to remand to a state court. Significantly, the Court noted in *Overman* that the federal abstention doctrine would not affect federal jurisdiction under 42 U.S.C.A. § 660, which grants federal jurisdiction in any child support proceeding certified by HEW. 563 F.2d 1287, 1292. *Accord,* Bolling v. Howland, 398 F. Supp. 1313 (M.D. Tenn. 1975).

123. Wilhelm v. United States Dept. of Air Force Accounting, 418 F. Supp. 162 (S.D. Tex. 1976); Golightly v. Golightly, 410 F. Supp. 861 (D. Neb. 1976); Morrison v. Morrison, 408 F. Supp. 315 (N.D. Tex. 1976); Popple v. United States, 416 F. Supp. 1227 (W.D.N.Y. 1976); Bolling v. Howland, 398 F. Supp. 1313 (M.D. Tenn. 1975).

124. In Williams v. Williams, 427 F. Supp. 557 (D. Md. 1976), the Court agreed that no statute grants original jurisdiction to federal garnishment actions for child support, but found removal jurisdiction under 28 U.S.C.A. § 1442(a)(1), which allows removal to a federal court of civil actions in which a federal official or agent is a party. Courts which have reached decisions on the merits following removal of the action from state courts include Murray v. Murray, 558 F.2d 1340 (8th Cir. 1977); Marin v. Hatfield, 546 F.2d 1231 (5th Cir. 1977); Kelley v. Kelley, 425 F. Supp. 181 (W.D. La. 1977); Watson v. Watson, 424 F. Supp. 866 (E.D.N.C. 1976); Evans v. Evans, 429 F. Supp. 580 (W.D. Okla. 1976); Samples v. Samples, 414 F. Supp. 773 (W.D. Okla. 1976); Crane v. Crane, 417 F. Supp. 38 (E.D. Okla. 1976).

The second area of uncertainty involves the applicability of state law to garnishment actions. Several courts have held that state law controls the amount of money the plaintiff may garnish if it is more restrictive than federal law and that state law controls whether the plaintiff may garnish the deserting parent's salary or benefits at all, despite the waiver of federal sovereign immunity.[125] Virtually all of these cases were decided under an earlier version of the federal statute, however, and the amended version has imposed a more pervasive federal presence in garnishment actions.[126] Thus, the extent to which state garnishment laws are preempted remains unsettled.[127]

---

125. In Evans v. Evans, 429 F. Supp. 580 (W.D. Okla. 1976), Samples v. Samples, 414 F. Supp. 773 (W.D. Okla. 1976), and Willhite v. Willhite, 546, P.2d 612 (Okla. 1976), the courts held that state limitations on garnishment control federal limitations when the state limitations are more restrictive. These decisions follow the directives of 15 U.S.C.A. § 1677 (1974). *But see* Murray v. Murray, 558 F.2d 1340 (8th Cir. 1977), in which the Court indicated that federal garnishment of attorneys fees, as part of a state judgment, was controlled by the federal definition of child support contained in 42 U.S.C.A. § 662(a)-(b); and Elmwood v. Elmwood, 245 N.C. 168, 244 S.E.2d 668 (1978), holding garnishability of certain disability payments a matter controlled by federal law.

Federal courts usually have dismissed garnishment actions when the deserted mother seeks to garnish, under a divorce decree, her vested right in community property as alimony or child support. Marin v. Hatfield, 546 F.2d 1231 (5th Cir. 1977); Kelley v. Kelley, 425 F. Supp. 181 (W.D. La. 1977); Watson v. Watson, 424 F. Supp. 866 (E.D.N.C. 1976). In Crane v. Crane, 417 F. Supp. 38 (E.D. Okla. 1976), the Court dismissed a garnishment action removed to it from state court because the amount had not been reduced to judgment as required by Oklahoma law.

126. The requirements apply to service of process, the duty of federal branches to prescribe garnishment regulations, the definition of child support, the types of federal remuneration and benefits that may be garnished, and exemption of certain payments from garnishment. 42 U.S.C.A. §§ 659(b)-(f), 661, 662(b), (f)-(g) (Supp. 1979).

127. *Cf.,* Murray v. Murray, 558 F.2d 1340 (8th Cir. 1977). *See generally,* 44 A.L.R. Fed. 494 (1979).

Detailed guidelines seeking to answer questions just raised and explaining the procedures to be followed in the garnishment of the pay of military personnel have been issued by the U.S. Army, Air Force, Navy and Marine Corps.[128]

g. *Federal Financial Assistance to State and Local Agencies.*

In order to encourage active enforcement efforts, units of local government that assist the IV-D agency in child support enforcement receive incentive payments based on the amount of support they generate. These incentive payments are made by the IV-D agency out of the federal share of child support payments applied to reimburse the state and federal governments for current or past AFDC assistance provided the deserted parent.[129] With respect to non-AFDC enforcement, local units are not eligible for incentive payments.[130] Similarly, if the support payments have caused the AFDC agency to remove the deserted parent from the AFDC rolls, the local unit receives incentive payments for collection of arrearages, but only for those accrued during the period of assignment.[131]

To qualify for incentive payments, the local unit must take steps to secure support by obtaining or enforcing a court or administrative support order. Merely locating an absent parent, case investigation, or routine collection service does not make a local unit eligible to receive

---

128. Collected by OCSE and transmitted as OCSE-IM-79-14 (October 18, 1979).

129. 42 U.S.C.A. § 658(a) (Supp. 1979); 45 C.F.R. § 302.52(b) (1978).

130. 42 U.S.C.A. § 658(a) (Supp. 1979); 45 C.F.R. § 302.52(a) (1978).

131. OCSE-AT-76-5 at 36 (1976); 45 C.F.R. § 302.51(f) (1978).

incentive payments.[132] When support enforcement involves more than one local unit (for instance, if the deserting parent has moved from the county to another state in which IV-D enforcement is initiated), the incentive payment in almost every case goes to the locality that secures support in response to a request for enforcement assistance.[133]

The federal government reimburses the state IV-D agency for 75 percent of the agency's operational expenses. The matching funds apply to cases of AFDC enforcement on a permanent basis.[134] As just discussed in detail, matching funds for non-AFDC enforcement initially were made available only on a temporary basis and remained controversial until 1980.[135]

The 75 percent federal matching covers expenses necessary for IV-D administration, securing support, operating the state parent locator service, specialized

---

132. OCSE-AT-75-5 (1975). OCSE has, however, drawn a fine distinction in cases where the local unit, such as a court clerk's office, collects all payments in the locality *and* the local prosecutor agrees to enforce all delinquent obligations. In such a case, the local unit will receive an incentive payment based on all payments collected by the clerk, even though no enforcement is necessary. On the other hand, if the IV-D agency handles all collections in the locality, and the local prosecutor agrees to enforce all delinquent obligations, the locality will receive incentive payments only for cases where the prosecutor affirmatively enforces a delinquency. OCSE-AT-76-22 (1976).

133. In cases involving several local jurisdictions, OCSE has statutory authority to allocate the incentive payment. 42 U.S.C.A. § 658 (Supp. 1979); 45 C.F.R. § 302.52(3) (1978). In cases of intrastate enforcement, the entire incentive payment goes to the locality responding to a request for enforcement. The same holds true for cases of interstate enforcement, unless another locality has provided assistance to the responding locality. In this case, the two localities allocate the payment between themselves. OCSE-AT-76-23 (1976).

134. 42 U.S.C.A. § 655 (Supp. 1979).

135. *See supra* text at notes. 60-66 and *infra* ch. X.7.

training for court and law enforcement personnel, as well as the cost of cooperative agreements and purchased services.[136] For the time being, eligible expenses do *not* include judicial salaries that are related to an increased volume of child support enforcement proceedings.[137]

h. *Medical Support Enforcement: Reimbursement for "Medicaid."*

Under a law passed in 1977,[138] the federal enforcement mechanism also may be engaged in collecting reimbursement for medical support rendered under the Medicaid program. The relevant amendments to the Social Security Act were buried in "An Act to strengthen the capability of the Government to detect, prosecute, and punish fraudulent activities under the medicare and medicaid programs, *and for other purposes.*[139] The amendments authorize state Medicaid agencies to establish programs of medical support enforcement directed to recovering from support obligors at least some of the immense sums now expended on Medicaid for dependent children and eligible parents — typically the children's mothers. Detailed regulations prepared jointly by the Office of Child Support Enforcement and the Health Care

---

136. 45 C.F.R. §§ 304.20, 304.21, 304.22 (1978).

137. 45 C.F.R. § 304.21(b) (1978). Judicial salaries would have been eligible for 75 percent federal matching under provisions of H.R. 7200. *See* S. Rep. No. 95-573, 95th Cong., 1st Sess. 11, 187-88 (1977). *See also infra* ch. X, text at notes 17-19.

138. P.L. 95-142, October 25, 1977, 91 Stat. 1196-97. 42 U.S.C.A. § 1396K (Supp. 1979).

139. P.L. 95-142 at Preamble.

Financing Administration flesh out the structure of the enforcement program.[140]

The statute authorizes state Medicaid agencies to require Medicaid applicants and recipients, as a condition of eligibility, to assign to the State their rights to medical care support, including any other third-party liability for medical care, such as insurance policies.[141] The regulations emphasize immediate restoration of the individual's future right of support as soon as their Medicaid eligibility ends, "using whatever method is least burdensome to the individual." [142]

The statute authorizes the agency to require an applicant or recipient to cooperate with the state in establishing paternity, or otherwise enforcing the obligation. The required extent of cooperation mirrors that required in IV-D enforcement: Non-cooperation is excused only for "good cause."[143] The statute also allows incentive payments to the agency of 15 percent of the amount of medical support collected.[144]

The program calls for state Medicaid (Title XIX) agencies to make agreements with other state agencies or law enforcement officials for collection of the assigned

---

140. These regulations were proposed in August, 1978, and were finally adopted by the agencies involved in February 1980. 43 Fed. Reg. 38,668 (1978); 45 Fed. Reg. 8982 (1980); at 42 C.F.R. §§ 433, 435, 436 and 45 C.F.R. §§ 302, 304, and 306 (1980).

141. 42 U.S.C.A. § 1396K(1)(A) (Supp. 1979).

142. 45 Fed. Reg. 8982 (1980); 42 C.F.R. § 433.149 (1980).

143. 42 C.F.R. § 433.147(c)(1) (1980). *See infra* ch. IX.

144. 42 U.S.C.A. § 1396B(p)(1). The regulations prohibit federal payment for medical assistance to a Medicaid recipient who is covered by a private health insurance policy having a "Medicaid Exclusion" provision. 42 C.F.R. § 433.140(a)(3) (1980).

claims.[145] The collection is enforced by remedies available under state law. The proposed regulations anticipate that in ordinary circumstances the Title XIX agency will enter into a cooperative arrangement with the state IV-D agency. The collection effort thus would be facilitated by IV-D agency expertise, as well as by the use of the federal and state parent locator services. The state IV-D agency, however, must assure that there will be no decrease in basic child support enforcement as a result of the new responsibilities and "must obtain additional personnel and resources to carry out these new responsibilities." [146] Finally, the IV-D agency must keep the collected funds segregated. Funds collected on behalf of the AFDC program may not be transferred to the Medicaid program. Specifically, "no portion of any amounts collected which represent a support obligation assigned under § 232.11 of this title may be used to satisfy a medical support obligation unless the court or administrative order requires a specific amount for medical support." [147]

---

145. 43 Fed. Reg. 38,669 (1978) (to be codified at 42 C.F.R. § 450.33).

146. The preamble to the proposed regulations expressed concern about the possible dilution of IV-D resources through this added responsibility. 43 Fed. Reg. 38,670 (1978).

147. 45 C.F.R. 302.50(e) (1980). The regulations leave unclear precisely what this provision means to do. Is it simply intended to protect the AFDC reimbursement process, to ensure that funds are not diverted for Medicaid reimbursement before all claims arising from the provision of public aid are satisified? Some of the language in the regulations and statements by OCSE policy-makers support this view. *See* discussion *infra* ch. X.6, text after note 93. On the other hand, the provision also may be read to protect fathers from open-ended liability for Medicaid reimbursement that might accrue in the absence of a specific support order covering medical needs. The problem is analogous to whether the father *not* under a court order incurs open-ended reimbursement liability for AFDC assistance provided his family, assuming he later becomes able to pay. *See supra* text at notes 116-117.

Chapter IX

THE MOTHER'S COOPERATION IN
ASCERTAINING AND LOCATING
THE ABSENT FATHER

The mother's cooperation in identifying her child's father
or revealing his whereabouts is, of course, the indispensable
starting point of child support enforcement and the
establishment of paternity. At issue and in potential
conflict are the mother's right to "privacy" and the child's
right to know its father. The latter follows directly from the
U.S Supreme Court cases which require equality in the
father-child relationship without regard to legitimacy or
illegitimacy,[1] and the former may be inferred from various
U.S. Supreme Court cases involving marital and sexual
privacy.[2] While it is obvious that equal protection for the
child born out of wedlock cannot be achieved without
knowing who the father is — and that requires active efforts
to find him — there remains popular [3] and professional [4]

---

1. *Supra* ch. IV.

2. *E.g.,* Griswold v. Connecticut, 381 U.S. 479, 85 S. Ct. 1678, 14 L. Ed.
2d 510 (1965); Eisenstadt v. Baird, 405 U.S. 438, 92 S. Ct. 1029, 31 L. Ed.
2d 349 (1972); Roe v. Wade, 410 U.S. 113, 93 S. Ct. 705, 35 L. Ed. 2d 147
(1973). *See also* Poulin, *Illegitimacy and Family Privacy: A Note on
Maternal Cooperation in Paternity Suits,* 70 N.W.L. REV. 910 (1976).

3.
> DEAR ABBY: Our daughter, a 21-year-old working girl, is pregnant.
> She isn't going with anyone steady and doesn't want to get married
> right now. . . . Our daughter will be getting help from welfare. Does
> that mean she has to tell them who the father is? She would rather
> not. Also, does she have to put the father's name on the baby's birth
> certificate?
>
> GRANNY-TO-BE
>
> DEAR GRANNY: . . . tell her to ignore the people who ask who the
> baby's father is. That's her business. And her secret.

CHAMPAIGN-URBANA NEWS-GAZETTE, March 11, 1976, p. 24.

4. *E.g.,* Soifer, *Parental Autonomy, Family Rights and the
Illegitimate: A Constitutional Commentary,* 7 CONN. L. REV. 1 (1974);

hostility against attempts to go to the best source of the relevant information, the mother.

The current controversy is *not* limited to the federal support enforcement legislation. That legislation *requires* the mother to cooperate but applies only the mildest possible sanction — denial to the mother *not* of her children's AFDC benefits, but *only of her own,* in case of her refusal. At least as importantly, the issue extends to state statutes requiring the mother to cooperate under penalty. Finally, the controversy extends to the powers of the courts. In the last case, the question simply is whether the mother can or should be required to testify as a witness in the paternity action and whether the usual sanctions applied to recalcitrant witnesses extend to her.

This observer's view remains unchanged:

> Serious hardships will be avoided if the court is given discretion in evaluating whether pursuit of the child's father would be in the child's best interest. If that decision is positive, however, there is no reason why the uncooperative mother should not be subject to all the usual remedies applied to reluctant witnesses. Insofar as the interests of her child are concerned, the uncooperative mother would be neither more nor less than a hostile witness holding the key to the child's case. In short, the mother should be subject to a statutory duty to name the father, if that information is necessary to allow the decision whether a paternity action should be brought. If a case actually is brought, the mother should be required to testify. Of course, no harm would be done — and some good would result — if the proceeding to determine paternity would remain largely confidential.[5]

Disanto & Podolski, *The Right to Privacy and Trilateral Balancing — Implications for the Family,* 13 FAM. L.Q. 183, 191-98 (1979). *Also see supra* ch. VII. 2.

5. H. KRAUSE, ILLEGITIMACY: LAW AND SOCIAL POLICY 120 (1971).

This position has found expression in the Uniform Parentage Act,[6] which safeguards the *child's* best interests against the indiscriminate establishment of paternity (§ 13(a)) and provides for confidentiality (§ 20), but does hold the mother accountable as a witness (§ 14(a)), on penalty of civil contempt (§ 10(b)). Appropriate immunity is provided to protect the mother from possible criminal prosecution under state "fornication," "adultery" and similar statutes (§ 10(b)). This essentially equates the mother's position in the paternity proceeding with that of any other witness who, subject to narrow constitutional limitations,[7] may be compelled to tell all he or she knows, if the information is relevant to a legal proceeding.

1. The Mother as a Witness.

Some current paternity statutes specifically permit the parties to be witnesses,[8] some require them to testify,[9] and others provide that they may not be compelled to testify.[10] Where the paternity action itself remains a criminal proceeding (and the mother may be punishable), or if the state views fornication or adultery as a crime, the privilege against self-incrimination will be available, unless there is an appropriate immunity statute.[11] In some states the mother's statement alone may be adequate evidence of

---

6. 9A U.L.A. Matr., Fam. and Health Laws 587 (1979). *See* Appendix B *infra.*

7. Especially as expressed in the 5th Amendment, *see infra* text at notes 111-138.

8. *E.g.,* COLO. REV. STAT. ANN. § 19-6-104 (1973); N.M. STAT. ANN. § 40-5-11 (1978); N.Y. FAM. CT. ACT § 531 (Supp. 1978); UTAH CODE ANN. § 77-60-5 (1978).

9. *E.g.,* WIS. STAT. ANN. § 891.39 (1966); WYO. STAT. ANN. § 14-2-108 (1977).

10. *E.g.,* N.Y. FAM. CT. ACT § 531 (Supp. 1978).

11. *E.g.,* N.C. GEN. STAT. § 49-6 (1976). CONN. GEN. STAT. ANN. 46b-165-66 (Supp. 1978) protects both the mother and the putative father. *See infra* text at note 111.

paternity.[12] Other states require corroboration of the mother's testimony.[13] In the decreasing number of states that still follow it, "Lord Mansfield's rule" altogether disallows a *married* mother's testimony as to the illegitimacy of a child born to her during marriage.[14]

Situations in which the mother does not wish to bring a paternity action or cases in which she actively opposes prosecution, raise the question of how the mother's cooperation can be enforced — and whether, when and how it should be enforced. A set of cases ante-dating the federal child support enforcement initiative had concluded that the Social Security Act, before the 1975 amendments, did *not* require the mother to cooperate. In consequence, important constitutional issues relating primarily to the contest between the mother's right to privacy and her child's right to access to its father were not settled at that time, although touched upon in several cases.[15]

Under a state law, a federal court in Connecticut has squarely faced the constitutional issue. Connecticut's requirement that the mother divulge the name of the father of her illegitimate child, under penalty of contempt ($200 and/or a year's imprisonment), was challenged. In a

---

12. *E.g.,* Solomon v. Fenton, 144 Ind. App. 100, 244 N.E.2d 228 (1969); District of Columbia v. Stovall, 253 A.2d 541 (D.C. 1969); Collins v. Wise, 156 Ind. App. 424, 296 N.E.2d 887 (1973); Kimble v. Kiefer, 11 Md. App. 48, 272 A.2d 668 (1971); Vander Werf v. Anderson, 86 S.D. 321, 195 N.W.2d 145 (1972).

13. *E.g.,* Wade v. Hicks, 191 Neb. 847, 218 N.W.2d 222 (1974).

14. *Supra* chs. III. 2, IV. 4.

15. *E.g.,* Doe v. Shapiro, 302 F. Supp. 761 (D. Conn. 1969), *appeal dismissed,* 396 U.S. 488, *rehearing denied,* 397 U.S. 970 (1970). *See* discussion in Comment, *The Social Services Amendments of 1974: Constitutionality of Conditioning AFDC Grant Eligibility on Disclosure of Paternity of Illegitimate Child,* 64 GEO. L. J. 947, 948 (1976).

detailed opinion, the Court held that the statute requiring the mother's cooperation

> . . . rationally furthers a legitimate articulated state purpose in establishing the paternity of children born out of wedlock and securing support for them; that it does not invidiously discriminate against any of the plaintiffs in violation of the equal protection clause of the fourteenth amendment; that its operation does not constitute an unwarranted invasion of privacy; and that it violates no rights guaranteed by the Constitution.[16]

In reaching that holding, the Court carefully dealt with numerous contentions and made its most telling point when it rejected the plaintiffs' argument that the statute must be subjected to strict judicial scrutiny on the ground that it adversely affects a "suspect class" — illegitimate children. Judge Blumenfeld said:

> Instead of operating to the disadvantage of children born out of wedlock the statute operates to their benefit. The statute imposes no additional burden upon them. To the contrary, the statute under consideration operates prophylactically against the adverse differential treatment which the unwed mothers would impose on their children. Indeed, if the legislature were to enact a law protecting the "right" of unwed mothers to exclude their children from the benefit of paternal support, it would be struck down.[17]

Concerning the mother's responsibility to testify, the court invoked the U.S. Supreme Court,[18] to the effect that

> [t]he power of government to compel persons to testify in court or before grand juries and other governmental agencies is firmly established in

---

16. Doe v. Norton, 365 F. Supp. 65, 84 (D. Conn. 1973).

17. *Id.* at 79 [footnotes omitted].

18. Kastigar v. United States, 406 U.S. 441, 443-44, 92 S. Ct. 1653, 1655, 32 L. Ed. 2d 212, 216 (1972).

Anglo-American jurisprudence. The power with respect to courts was established by statute in England as early as 1562, and Lord Bacon observed in 1612 that all subjects owed the King their "knowledge and discovery." While it is not clear when grand juries first resorted to compulsory process to secure the attendance and testimony of witnesses, the general common law principle that "the public has a right to every man's evidence" was considered an "indubitable certainty" which "cannot be denied" by 1742. The power to compel testimony, and the corresponding duty to testify, are recognized in the Sixth Amendment requirements that an accused be confronted with the witnesses against him, and have compulsory process for obtaining witnesses in his favor. The first Congress recognized the testimonial duty in the Judiciary Act of 1789, which provided for compulsory attendance of witnesses in the federal courts. Mr. Justice White noted the importance of this essential power of government in his concurring opinion in Murphy v. Waterfront Comm'n, 378 U.S. 52, 93-94, 84 S. Ct. 1594, (1611) 12 L. Ed. 2d 678, 704 (1964):

> Among the necessary and most important of the powers of the States as well as the Federal Government to assure the effective functioning of government in an ordered society is the broad power to compel residents to testify in court or before grand juries or agencies. Such testimony constitutes one of the Government's primary sources of information. [Citations and footnotes omitted.]

Judge Blumenfeld continued, stating:

> As a broad proposition, this power extends to and includes with particular pertinence, those situations in which the testimony sought to be elicited may prove embarrassing, or otherwise impinges upon the sensitivities of the witness whose testimony is sought. As a noted commentator has stated:
>
> "[T]he sacrifice may be of his privacy [or] of the

360

knowledge which he would preferably keep to himself because of the disagreeable consequences of disclosure. This inconvenience which he may suffer, in consequence of his testimony, by way of enmity or disgrace or ridicule or other disfavorable action of fellow members of the community, is also a contribution which he makes in payment of his duties to society in its function of executing justice. ... When the course of justice requires the investigation of the truth no man has any knowledge that is rightly private." 8 WIGMORE, EVIDENCE § 2192 at 72 (McNaughton rev. 1961). [Footnote omitted.]

The privilege asserted by the unwed mothers has its closest analogy to the marital privilege sometimes afforded to husband and wife. But that privilege has no roots in the Constitution.

Furthermore, the privilege to withhold information asserted here concerns a relationship at least one step removed from that of husband and wife. Whatever merit there may be in the argument that a privilege in the wife not to testify against her husband preserves a marital relationship, the "policy of the privilege applies only to these who profess to maintain toward each other the legal relationship of husband and wife." 8 WIGMORE, EVIDENCE, § 2230 (McNaughton rev. 1961).

The relationship which these unwed mothers seek to protect from disclosure is emphatically different. There is no privilege to withhold the testimony of a mere paramour or witness. *Id.* In the absence of any legal relationship the alleged "right" of these plaintiffs to refuse to answer the inquiries directed by the statute is devoid of any elements that comprise a jural interest.

But even if we ignored the character of the relationship urged to merit such protection and equated it with the more durable one of legal husband and wife, the disclosure required of these plaintiffs would not invade any "zone of privacy." Viewed from the perspective of the class denied the privilege of remaining silent the "embarrassing" information has in large part been widely disclosed before any inquiries are made. Furthermore, the inquiry focuses on identity of the father, not on the mother's misconduct. The question asked of the unwed mother is, "Who is the father of your child?" The object of the inquiry is to enforce a familial monetary obligation, not to interfere with personal privacy. There is no intrusion into the home nor any participation in interpersonal decisions among its occupants, even to the extent held permissible in Wyman v. James, 400 U.S. 309, 91 S. Ct. 381, 27 L. Ed. 2d 408 (1971). The statute does not forbid an unwed mother to have a man in the house or even in her bedroom. Compare King v. Smith, 392 U.S. 309, 88 S. Ct. 2128, 20 L. Ed. 2d 1118. The only restriction it imposes upon either the unwed mother or the biological father to do as they please or make any decisions they wish in whatever relationship they desire to maintain is that the father satisfy his legal obligation to support his own child and that the mother provide what information she possesses useful toward that end.[19]

Judge Blumenfeld also answered those who point to the problems that would result if a mother, in consequence of her refusal to testify, were to be separated from her child: [20]

The incarceration of an unwed mother for contempt, or for any other unlawful behavior, may work to the disadvantage of her child. Yet no one would be heard to argue that motherhood per se provides an absolute defense to the imposition of undesired but otherwise lawful sanctions simply because that mother's child might suffer from the separation resulting from her incarceration. . . .

Throughout this case, the plaintiffs have argued as if the touchstone of our inquiry was whether the expected advantages to the state from the statute were

19. Doe v. Norton, 365 F. Supp. 65, 75-78 (D. Conn. 1973). (Some citations and footnotes omitted.)

20. *E.g.,* Soifer, *Parental Autonomy, Family Rights and the Illegitimate: A Constitutional Commentary,* 7 CONN. L. REV. 1 (1974).

outweighed by the harmful effects to the families affected by its enforcement. But even if the task of balancing these competing values was for the judiciary, rather than for the legislature, we would not find any basis for depriving the state of this traditional method of compelling witnesses to give answers to the inquiries under the statute. In holding that the policy favoring the right of the state to have every person's testimony may be enforced by imprisoning the witness who refuses to answer, the Court has recently held that there is no exception for one who is reluctant to testify, either for his own behalf or to shield another because of the adverse effect which such testimony might have on his future relationship with the person who is the object of the inquiry. See Branzburg v. Hayes, *supra,* 408 U.S. 665, 92 S. Ct. 2646, 33 L. Ed. 2d 626. The exposure of the plaintiffs in this case to imprisonment for contempt does not constitute an unacceptable sacrifice of competing policy interests nor contravene the Act.[21]

On first review, the U.S. Supreme Court seemed to fail to understand the importance of this issue to the success or failure of the federal child support enforcement legislation. Avoiding a stand, the Court considered that the new legislation — although it does require parents to cooperate with state efforts to locate and obtain support from absent parents as a condition of eligibility for AFDC assistance — does not provide punitive sanctions comparable to those provided by the Connecticut law. On that basis, the judgment was vacated and remanded "for further consideration in light of Pub. L. 93-647." [22] Since the federal

---

21. Doe v. Norton, 365 F. Supp. 65, 83 (D. Conn. 1973). This decision was followed quickly by a similar holding in Burdick v. Miech, 385 F. Supp. 927 (E.D. Wis. 1974).

22. Roe v. Norton, 422 U.S. 391, 393, 95 S. Ct. 2221, 2222, 45 L. Ed. 2d 268, 271 (1975). *See also* Lascaris v. Shirley, 420 U.S. 730, 95 S. Ct. 1190, 43 L. Ed. 2d 583 (1975) which involved an action to enjoin enforcement of provisions of the New York social services law requiring the mother's cooperation in the ascertainment of paternity. The Court

legislation has no direct bearing on the duty to testify in court as a witness in pending cases, imposed by court or under a state statute, Judge Blumenfeld, quite fairly, saw no reason to change his earlier views, just detailed. On remand, he "adhered to the conclusions reached in our former opinion." [23] This second time, the Supreme Court let the ruling stand,[24] perhaps indicating tacit approval.

2. The "Good Cause Exception" to the Mother's Statutory Duty to Cooperate Is Enacted.

Critics of enforcing the mother's cooperation in ascertaining paternity and locating an absent father envisioned two major threats to the well-being of children receiving AFDC. First, they argued that a deserting father might retaliate against his family — physically or by threat — if he viewed state enforcement efforts as the product of the mother's cooperation. Second, it was argued that in at least some cases the mother's revelation of the illegitimacy of her children would come as an unpleasant surprise to her children and her associates, from whom the mother may have hidden the "stigma" of illegitimacy. These concerns and continuing debate over the privacy arguments disposed of by Judge Blumenfeld in *Doe v. Norton*,[25] have made the statutory provision conditioning the mother's AFDC benefits on compliance with her statutory duty to cooperate into one of the most controversial elements of the whole program.[26] Even those who opposed the Act for other

---

held that the conflict between this requirement and prior federal law had been resolved by the Social Services Amendments of 1974.

23. Doe v. Maher, 414 F. Supp. 1368, 1381 (D. Conn. 1976).

24. Doe v. Maher, 432 U.S. 526, 97 S. Ct. 2474, 53 L. Ed. 2d 526 (1977).

25. *Supra* text at notes 16-21.

26. *E.g.,* Comment (Altman), *The Social Services Amendments of 1974: Constitutionality of Conditioning AFDC Grant Eligibility on Disclosure of Paternity of Illegitimate Child,* 64 GEO. L. J. 947 (1976).

reasons rallied to this cause as it promised a potential "loophole" as big as the whole program.

Less than a year after enacting the basic enforcement scheme, Congress added the following exception to the mother's duty to cooperate:

> unless (in either case) such applicant or recipient is found to have good cause for refusing to cooperate as determined by the State agency in accordance with standards prescribed by the Secretary, which standards shall take into consideration the best interests of the child on whose behalf aid is claimed.[27]

Congressional debate on this amendment was pointed: [28]

> *Mr. Bauman:* Would the gentleman tell me when it would be in the best interest of a child not to seek out the parent or when it would be in the best interest of the child not to seek the parents' financial support? That seems to be a contradiction of terms.
>
> *Mr. Vander Jagt:* With regard to the specific question that the gentleman asked, I have difficulty thinking of an instance when locating an absent father would not be in the best interest of the child.
> Conversely, though, I believe that if there were an instance when it would not be in the best interest of the child, since that interest is so paramount, we should permit an option.
> There might be an instance, for example when a child might be in danger of physical harm or when it might be advisable to shield information from the child. There might be such cases, and when those cases arise, we would provide for them.
>
> *Mr. Bauman:* If the gentleman will yield further, I readily agree that there are perhaps individual instances when a great many people would just as soon not know their parents, or at least their ancestry; but

---

27. 42 U.S.C.A. § 602(a)(26)(B)(1970 Supp. V).
28. Cong. Rec. 23698 (July 21, 1975).

we are talking about U.S. taxpayers in this instance, and when I read Section 7 of the bill it appears there is a wide-open loophole for professional welfarists to claim blanket amnesty when people refuse to cooperate in finding the father. The welfare mother is asked, "Who is the father of this child?" and this bill allows her to refuse to respond. The alternative would be for the taxpayer to pay the bill, and the welfare mother can say, "I refuse to cooperate because in the best interest of the child I do not want to tell who the father is."

That seems to me to be a wide-open loophole. . . .

That, I think, is unreasonable when the average taxpayer has his own children to support.

Mr. Vander Jagt: Mr. Speaker, I think the gentleman from Maryland has a very valid point that needs to be made and needs to be remade. I would disagree with the gentleman from Maryland only on his statement of the size of that loophole.

The gentleman calls this a wide-open loophole. I call it a loophole which is only about the size of the eye of a needle. The section does require that the mother cooperate with the authorities in locating the whereabouts of the father. The exception to that is when such cooperation would not be in the best interests of the child, and the State agency would make that determination. I think those cases would be very minimal.

Mr. Speaker, I would, therefore, call this an eye-of-the-needle loophole rather than a wide-open loophole, as my friend, the gentleman from Maryland, describes it.

Mr. Bauman: Mr. Speaker, if my biblical friend will yield once more, I am sure he will recall that it was a camel that was alleged to pass through the eye of a needle. If this bill is passed, I can just see whole herds of camels galloping through this one.[29]

---

29. The House Committee did not do much to clarify the intended scope of the exception:

The committee's concern extends to situations in which the

3. A Controversial Regulation Takes Shape.

The vague statutory terms of what has come to be
called the "good cause exception" left HEW with the
difficult task of prescribing standards for AFDC agencies to
determine when and whether to grant an exception to the
mother's duty to cooperate. These standards — eventually
adopted as a final regulation after two sets of proposed
regulations [30] — were the object of serious conflict between
representatives of prosecutors on the one hand, and those of
welfare recipients on the other. After the second proposal
had taken effect as an interim regulation for several months
in 1978, Senator Russell Long, Chairman of the Senate
Finance Committee and the major Congressional moving
force behind the child support enforcement legislation,
stepped into the fray. Several changes in the interim
regulation were negotiated at the highest levels of HEW,
and these changes were reflected in the final regulation
that was issued late in 1978.

These often angry conflicts — foreshadowed in the biting
Congressional debate — produced significant differences
between the first proposal and the final regulation. HEW
still insists that its commentary on the interim regulation
is to be read together with the final regulation and final
commentary "for a complete understanding" of the final
regulation.[31] Some knowledge of the forces at work in the

---

tracking down of the absent parent might subject the child or mother
to a substantial danger of physical harm or of undue harassment.
The committee did not feel that the subject had been sufficiently
covered in regulations developed by the Department of HEW. At the
same time, it does not intend that cooperation will be broadly waived
because of a philosophy that the collection of child support does not
generally serve the best interests of a child. Its concern is with
individual families where a significant hardship is likely if the
provisions of part D of title IV are enforced. H.R. Rep. No. 94-368,
94th Cong., 1st Sess. Child Support Program Improvements, to
accompany H.R. 8598 at 7 (July 17, 1975).

30. 45 C.F.R. § 232.40-.49 (1979).

31. 43 Fed. Reg. at 45,742 (preamble to final regulation).

development of the final regulation thus is necessary to appreciate fully its intended application.

To start at the beginning — in August, 1976, HEW responded to Congress' statutory directive with a proposed regulation based on the premise that, in balancing the protection of the child against the integrity of the child support enforcement program, the mother should be afforded the "good cause exception" in only a limited number of cases. Exceptions were limited to situations where cooperation would be "likely to result in substantial danger, physical harm, or undue harassment" to the child or mother; to cases where the child was conceived through forcible rape or incest; and to cases where the mother was releasing, or considering releasing, the child for adoption.[32] The proposal required the AFDC agency to inform the mother of her option to claim a good cause exception, and required the objecting mother to provide enough competent evidence, supplemented when necessary by an AFDC investigation, to establish the likelihood that an exception applied. It also required the AFDC agency to determine independently whether support enforcement could proceed safely without the mother's cooperation, and allowed the mother to receive AFDC payments pending determination of her "good cause" claim, so long as she provided either substantial evidence of danger, or enough information to allow an agency investigation into her unsubstantiated claim. Finally, the proposal directed the AFDC agency to inform IV-D prosecutors promptly whenever it decided to grant a good cause exception.[33]

---

32. 41 Fed. Reg. 34,300 (1976); (there to be codified as 45 C.F.R. § 232.13), *id.* at 24,299, col. 2 (preamble to first proposal). The standard of substantial danger, physical harm or undue harassment follows the report of the House committee that drafted the child-support legislation.

33. 41 Fed. Reg. 34,300-01 (1976) (there to be codified as 45 C.F.R. § 232.13(b), (c), (h)-(j)).

HEW received approximately 1,700 comments concerning the proposed regulation.[34] All but 200 were from private citizens who overwhelmingly opposed the exception. Among few positive voices, the American Bar Association favored adoption of the first proposal, with reservations regarding its effectiveness.[35] Prosecutors criticized the proposal as allowing too many loopholes and burdening enforcement efforts unreasonably. Legal service and welfare rights groups, on the other hand, considered the first proposal insensitive to legitimate concerns of welfare mothers and children.

The interim regulation, which was in effect from March

---

34. 43 Fed. Reg. 2171 (1978) (preamble to interim regulation).

35.

The American Bar Association's House of Delegates, at its [1977] midyear meeting, adopted a resolution by the Section of Family Law that supports HEW's regulations under the Child Support Enforcement Act which define "good cause" ... Professor Henry H. Foster, Jr., chairman of the Family Law Section, recommended that the American Bar Association support the regulations ... [but] added ... that the Section is concerned that the program not be compromised by a mechanism which will provide an "open invitation for refusals to cooperate." The Section urged that circumstances under which enforcement of paternity proceedings would not be in the best interest of the child be specifically defined. Also, he reported that there are some conditions relating to "good cause" determinations which are "somewhat vague and might invite spurious claims." The Section will seek clarification of those provisions, Foster said.

The Section was also concerned, Foster said, that the investigative burden in verifying "good cause" claims could prove onerous to agencies' limited resources unless specific guidelines describing the extent and intensity of investigation required are adopted. In a case where no reprisals could be expected if a caretaker relative does not cooperate and where the welfare of the child would not be threatened, the Section recommended that action by the enforcement agency alone would be proper. It supports the provision in the proposed regulations that would permit this. Finally, Foster stated, the Section supports the principle that existence of a small number of instances where non-cooperation will be justified should not be construed to tie the hands of state and local officials or to justify non-cooperation by parties involved in child support and paternity proceedings which are brought outside the scope of Title IV. [3 F.L.R. 2295 (1977)].

17, 1978, until the final regulation took effect on December 4, 1978,[36] retained most of the original proposal. It extended the "good cause exception" to emotional harm, as well as physical harm. It emphasized that the primary consideration must be the possibility of harm to the child, and that harm to the mother should be considered only to the extent that it probably would affect the child. An AFDC investigation into every claim for which the mother did not furnish documentation was mandated, and IV-D prosecutors were granted an advisory role in good cause determinations.[37]

Shortly after the interim regulation took effect, Senator Long brought several specific objections to the attention of Secretary of HEW Califano. A serious problem was seen in the provisions allowing aid to be paid to the mother pending determination of a claimed exception and requiring IV-D prosecutors to suspend enforcement while a good cause claim was pending. In the Senator's view, these provisions were inconsistent with the "good cause" statute.[38] Further criticisms were that no time limit governed receipt of aid pending determination, that the AFDC agency had too much discretion in deciding what amount of evidence would support a claim, that the required notice was too technical and thus raised the specter of frivolous appeals on technical grounds, that the help to be rendered by the AFDC agency in the applicant's effort to substantiate her claim needed express limitation, and that the exception involving physical or emotional harm should apply only in serious cases.[39]

---

36. 43 Fed. Reg. 45, 742, col. 1 (1978).

37. *See generally* 43 Fed. Reg. 2171-78 (1978).

38. *See* Memorandum to Senator Long from Douglas Hester, Senate Office of the Legislative Counsel, March 21, 1978, taking the position that the benefits of an exception could result only after an exception was granted.

39. *See* Memorandum to Senator Long from Douglas Hester, Senate Office of the Legislative Counsel, March 21, 1978.

Five days after the interim regulation took effect, Senator Long and Secretary Califano reached a written agreement stating that the interim regulation would be "clarified" by HEW and that a third and final regulation would be promulgated, to take effect after review by the Senator's Committee.[40] On April 5, 1978, HEW issued its "clarification" which subjected good cause determinations to the general 45-day deadline required for eligibility determinations, emphasized that unsubstantiated claims would not support a good cause exception, limited AFDC help to an applicant trying to document her case, and confirmed that physical or emotional harm need be serious in order to support an exception.[41] These clarifications became part of the final regulation. On the other hand, the final regulation retains the "aid pending" provision, as well as the requirement that IV-D suspend enforcement when a mother claims a good cause exception.[42]

40. Agreement of March 21, 1978, between Senator Long and Secretary Califano. This agreement was confirmed in an HEW press release dated April 12, 1978, which detailed aspects of the dispute, scheduled a public hearing for May 5, 1978, and asked for comments from "anyone" on the following principal points at issue:

— Should AFDC applicants receive financial assistance pending the determination of good cause?
— Should the regulation require that anticipated physical and emotional harm to mother and/or child be of a serious nature?
— Should applicants be required to corroborate their claims with additional evidence, such as supporting written statements?
— Is the proposed notice to applicants concerning "good cause" excessive or overly technical?
— How much should State agencies be required to do in assisting applicants in locating documentary evidence?

41. OCSE-AT-78-8 (April 5, 1978). Both this transmittal and a portion of Secretary Califano's press release, pursuant to the agreement with Senator Long, were published in the Federal Register. 43 Fed. Reg. 15,424-26, 15,457 (1978).

42. The AFDC agency must promptly inform the IV-D agency whenever "good cause" is claimed. By corresponding regulation, IV-D

4. The Final Regulation: "Good Cause" For Refusal to Cooperate.

a. *Notice and Claim.*

Before requiring cooperation, the AFDC agency must notify the applicant [43] in writing that exceptional circumstances may allow an exception to her duty to cooperate with prosecutors who seek to enforce support against the father. Both the applicant and the AFDC agency must certify that the applicant was given and did receive such notice, and a certified copy of the notice becomes part of the individual case file.[44] States have the option of providing a single, comprehensive notice on all major facets of the good cause exception, or they may provide an initial, general notice, to be followed by a more detailed explanation of "good cause" procedures if an applicant requests one.[45] States using a two-stage notice must furnish the applicant a more detailed explanation of the good cause exception upon request, "promptly without the applicant or recipient having to reschedule a follow-up appointment or endure unnecessary delays." [46] A model

---

must then suspend enforcement until it receives a green light from AFDC. 45 C.F.R. §§ 232.45, 302.31 (1979).

43. Or current recipient, in case of conversion to the enforcement system.

44. 45 C.F.R. § 232.40(b) (1) (i)-(iii) (1979).

45. 45 C.F.R. § 232.40 (b) (2)-(3) (1979). The two-part notice first appeared in the final regulation, after critics of the interim regulation charged that a contemplated model notice was too complex. (Some prosecutors opposed a notice requirement altogether on the ground that it would encourage spurious claims). 43 Fed. Reg. 2175, col. 3 (1978) (preamble to interim regulation). Critics of the one-part notice cited two disadvantages. First, administration would be unnecessarily cumbersome and costly if only a minority of applicants would want to claim an exception. Second, the notice would add to the burdensome amount of paper given to applicants and might be incomprehensible. 43 Fed. Reg. 45,743, col. 1 (1978) (preamble to final regulation).

46. 43 Fed. Reg. 45,743 (1978) (preamble to final regulation); 45 C.F.R. § 232.40(b)(2)(ii) (1979).

two-stage notice appears as an appendix to the notice regulation. The unified notice must contain all the relevant information contained in the two-part notice.[47]

---

47. 45 C.F.R. § 232.40(b) (3)-(4), Appendix A (1979).

NOTICE OF REQUIREMENT TO COOPERATE AND RIGHT TO CLAIM GOOD CAUSE FOR REFUSAL TO COOPERATE IN CHILD SUPPORT ENFORCEMENT

BENEFITS OF CHILD SUPPORT ENFORCEMENT

Your cooperation in the child support enforcement process may be of value to you and your child because it might result in the following benefits:

Finding the absent parent;

Legally establishing your child's paternity;

The possibility that support payments might be higher than your welfare grant; and

The possibility that you and your children may obtain rights to future social security, veterans, or other government benefits.

WHAT IS MEANT BY COOPERATION?

The law requires you to cooperate with the welfare and child support agencies to get any support owed to you and any of the children for whom you want AFDC, unless you have good cause for not cooperating.

In cooperating with the welfare or child support agency, you may be asked to do one or more of the following things:

Name the parent of any child applying for or receiving AFDC, and give information you have to help find the parent;

Help determine legally who the father is if your child was born out of wedlock;

Give help to obtain money owed to you or the children receiving AFDC; and

Pay to the State any money which is given directly to you by the absent parent (you will continue to get your full AFDC grant from the State).

You may be required to come to the welfare office, child support office, or court to sign papers or give necessary information.

WHAT IS MEANT BY GOOD CAUSE?

You may have good cause not to cooperate in the State's efforts to collect child support. You may be excused from cooperating if you believe that cooperation would not be in the best interest of your child, and if you can provide evidence to support this claim.

373

b. *Grounds for Exception.*

The statutory basis for granting a good cause

_____

IF YOU DO NOT COOPERATE AND YOU DO NOT HAVE GOOD CAUSE

You will be ineligible for AFDC.

Your children will still be eligible for AFDC for their own needs. Your children's grant will go to another person, called a "protective payee."

HOW AND WHEN YOU MAY CLAIM GOOD CAUSE

If you want to claim good cause, you must tell a worker that you think you have good cause. You can do this at any time you believe you have good cause not to cooperate.

If you claim "good cause" you must be given another notice. This second notice will explain the circumstances under which the Welfare Agency may find good cause, and the type of evidence or other information the Welfare Agency needs to decide your claim. You may also ask for this second notice to help you decide whether or not to claim good cause.

I have read this notice concerning my right to claim good cause for refusing to cooperate.

. . . .
(Signature of applicant/recipient)

. . . .
(Date)

I have provided the applicant/recipient with a copy of this notice.

. . . .
(Signature of Worker)

. . . .
(Date)

SECOND NOTICE OF RIGHT TO CLAIM GOOD CAUSE FOR REFUSAL TO COOPERATE IN CHILD SUPPORT ENFORCEMENT

GOOD CAUSE CIRCUMSTANCES

You may claim to have good cause for refusing to cooperate if you believe that such cooperation would not be in the best interests of your child. The following are circumstances under which the Welfare

374

exception to the duty to cooperate is consideration of "the

Agency may determine that you have good cause for refusing to cooperate:

Cooperation is anticipated to result in serious physical or emotional harm to the child;

Cooperation is anticipated to result in physical or emotional harm to you which is so serious it reduces your ability to care for the child adequately;

The child was born after forcible rape or incest;

Court proceedings are going on for adoption of the child; or

You are working with an agency helping you to decide whether to place the child for adoption.

PROVING GOOD CAUSE

It is your responsibility to:

Provide the Welfare Agency with the evidence needed to determine whether you have good cause for refusing to cooperate. (If your reason for claiming good cause is your fear of physical harm and it is impossible to obtain evidence, the Welfare Agency may still be able to make a good cause determination after an investigation of your claim.)

Give the necessary evidence to the agency within 20 days after claiming good cause. The Welfare Agency will give you more time only if it determines that more than 20 days are required because of the difficulty in obtaining the evidence.

The Welfare Agency may:

Decide your claim based on the evidence which you give to the agency, or

Decide to conduct an investigation to further verify your claim. If the Welfare Agency decides an investigation is needed, you may be required to give information, such as the absent parent's name and address, to help the investigation. The agency will not contact the absent parent without first telling you.

NOTE. — If you are an applicant for assistance, you will not receive your share of the grant until you have given the agency the evidence needed to support your claim, and, if requested, the information needed to permit an investigation of your claim.

EXAMPLES OF ACCEPTABLE EVIDENCE

The following are examples of acceptable kinds of evidence the Welfare Agency can use in determining if good cause exists.

If you need help in getting a copy of any of the documents, ask the Welfare Agency. The Welfare Agency will give you reasonable assistance which is needed to help you obtain the necessary documents to support your claim.

Birth certificates, or medical or law enforcement records, which

375

best interests of the child on whose behalf aid is claimed." [48]

indicate that the child was conceived as the result of incest or forcible rape;

Court documents or other records which indicate that legal proceedings for adoption are pending in court;

Court, medical, criminal, child protective services, social services, psychological, or law enforcement records which indicate that the alleged or absent father might inflict physical or emotional harm on you or the child;

Medical records which indicate emotional health history and present health status of you or the child for whom support would be sought; or written statements from a mental health professional indicating a diagnosis or prognosis concerning the emotional health of you or the child;

A written statement from a public or private agency confirming that you are being assisted in resolving the issue of whether to keep or give up the child for adoption; and

Sworn statements from individuals, including friends, neighbors, clergymen, social workers, and medical professionals who might have knowledge of the circumstances providing the basis of your good cause claim.

CHILD SUPPORT AGENCY PARTICIPATION AND ENFORCEMENT

The Child Support Enforcement Agency may review the Welfare Agency's findings and the basis for a good cause determination in your case. If you request a hearing regarding this issue of good cause for refusing to cooperate, the Child Support Enforcement Agency may participate in that hearing.

The Notice must include one of the following statements, as applicable depending on the State plan option chosen. See § 232.49. *Option 1.*

If you are found to have good cause for not cooperating, the Child Support Enforcement Agency may attempt to establish paternity or collect support only if the Welfare Agency determines that this can

---

48. 42 U.S.C.A. § 602 (A) (26) (B) (1970). OCSE took the position that the "best interest of the child" is the *only* basis for excusing cooperation and rejected the possibility of weighing the child's best interests (including its interest in obtaining support and a paternity judgment) against other considerations, (perhaps mental distress to the mother without any effect on the child). 43 Fed. Reg. 2171 (1978) (preamble to interim regulation). Thus, all consequences of cooperation are judged solely by their probable effect *on the child,* although "it is also clear that many different and competing considerations may be in the child's best interests." *Id.*

The final regulation defines several narrow circumstances as exceptions that are *potentially* in the best interest of the child. Briefly, these are threat of physical harm to the child, or to the mother so that it affects her ability to care for the child. Similar provision is made for emotional harm. Further exceptions apply if conception was by rape or incest or if there is a possibility that the child will be adopted, thus promising to eliminate the claim for AFDC.[49]

HEW stresses that the grant of a good cause exception should be a rare occurrence and that granting the exception on grounds of emotional harm should be the rarest occurrence of all. HEW expects the most frequently used exception to be that relating to physical harm.[50] Whether that exception will be granted will depend primarily on the AFDC agency's assessment of the character and behavior of the father.[51] The threat of physical harm must be serious

---

be done without risk to you or your child. This will not be done without first telling you.

Option 2.

If you are found to have good cause for not cooperating, the Child Support Enforcement Agency will not attempt to establish paternity or collect support.

I have read this notice concerning my right to claim good cause for refusing to cooperate.

. . . .
(Signature of applicant/recipient)

. . . .
(Date)

I have provided the applicant/recipient with a copy of this notice.

. . . .
(Signature of worker)

. . . .
(Date)

49. 45 C.F.R. § 232.42(a)(1)-(2) (1979).
50. 43 Fed. Reg. 2172 (1978) (preamble to interim regulation).
51. *Id.* at 2175 (1978) (preamble to interim regulation).

and, if directed at the mother rather than at the child, must reduce her "capacity to care for the child adequately." [52] Plausible situations in which this exception would apply include the case of the battered woman whose partner threatens abuse if he is named or prosecuted, the woman who has escaped from the father of her children and who is afraid to reveal his whereabouts, and the case of the violent, unstable man who does not know that he is the father of the child in question. [53]

As in the case of the exception for physical harm, asserted *emotional* harm must be serious and, if claimed in respect of the mother, must affect the children. [54] Because of the subjective nature of emotional harm (which may depend on an assessment of the character and behavior of the entire family), the harm must be demonstrable and must substantially affect the individual's functioning, although it need not be "lasting." [55] The final regulation requires the AFDC agency to weigh the following factors in deciding whether to grant an exception for emotional harm: the relevant individual's present emotional state and history of emotional health; the intensity and probable duration of the emotional impairment; the degree of cooperation required;

---

52. 45 C.F.R. §§ 232.43(a)(1) (iii), 232.43(b) (1979).
53. 43 Fed. Reg. 45, 743 (1978) (preamble to final regulation).
54. 45 C.F.R. § 232.42(a)(1)(ii),(iv),(b) (1979).
55. 45 C.F.R. § 232.42(b) (1979). According to its preamble, the final regulation requires

> the emotional impairment to be demonstrable and to have the observable consequence of substantially impairing the individual's functioning. However, the definition does not, as some commenters requested, require that the emotional harm be "lasting." Serious emotional harm is itself a strict good cause standard, and the Department wants to avoid the implication of an additional durational test which would have precluded serious impairments that were not likely to continue indefinitely. 43 Fed. Reg. at 45, 743, col. 3. *See also* 43 Fed. Reg. 2175, col. 1-2 (1978) (preamble to interim regulation).

and the extent of the child's involvement in the paternity or enforcement proceedings.[56]

Probably the strongest case for applying the emotional harm exception is when the child has been conceived by forcible rape or incest; indeed, the regulations particularize this as an independent ground.[57] Other plausible examples include a father of harmful character (such as a drug addict, criminal or psychotic individual), a father who has harmed the child in the past, a nonmarital child who does not know it is "illegitimate," particularly if it has accepted a stepfather and cooperation would produce potentially harmful ties with the previously unknown biological father.[58]

Finally, AFDC may excuse cooperation, but need not do so automatically, if the child is the subject of pending adoption proceedings, or where the mother is considering placing the child for adoption and is in contact with a social agency to help her resolve the question. In the latter case, however, the suspension of enforcement will not continue for more than three months.[59]

c. *Standards for Granting the Exception.*

The claimant has the burden of establishing circumstances sufficient to grant a good cause exception.[60]

---

56. 45 C.F.R. § 232.42(c) (1979).

57. 45 C.F.R. § 232.42(a)(2)(i) (1979).

58. 43 Fed. Reg. at 45, 743, col. 3 (1978) (preamble to final regulation). *See also* 43 Fed. Reg. 2175 (1978) (preamble to interim regulation).

59. 45 C.F.R. § 232.42(a) (2)(ii)(iii) (1979). This and the exception for rape or incest mirror 45 C.F.R. § 303.5(b) (1979) of the regulations which was in effect well before the good cause exception came into existence: "The IV-D agency need not attempt to establish paternity in any case involving incest or forcible rape, or in any case in which legal proceedings for adoption are pending, if, in the opinion of the IV-D agency, it would not be in the best interests of the child to establish paternity."

60. The burden includes alleging sufficient circumstances to invoke a ground for exception, corroborating the allegations and, if requested,

Regarding physical or emotional harm, the claimant must provide proof sufficient to establish reasonable anticipation of resulting harm.[61] The regulations reject a standard approaching a technical burden of proof and provide little objective guidance for the case worker or applicant.[62] Although neither the final regulation nor the relevant commentary expressly say so, it seems probable that HEW envisions a largely *ad hoc* balancing of every relevant benefit and detriment to coercing cooperation in any given case, with considerable respect accorded the judgment of the AFDC supervisory personnel who grant or deny exceptions.[63] It is clear, in any event, that proof "beyond a reasonable doubt" or "by clear and convincing evidence" is not required and that proof similar to a "preponderance of the evidence," will support a good cause exception.[64] After all, if harm is more likely to occur than not, a reasonable person would anticipate trouble. Beyond the simple

---

providing enough information (including the name and address of the absent parent) to allow AFDC to conduct its own corroborating investigation. 45 C.F.R. § 232.406(c) (1979).

61. 45 C.F.R. § 232.42(a)(1) (1979).

62. *See* 43 Fed. Reg. 2173-74 (1978) (preamble to interim regulation).

63. *Id.* The standards are designed to excuse cooperation where the physical or emotional harm resulting from activities necessary to establish paternity or enforce support surpass the physical, emotional and financial benefits derived from those activities.... Congress intended that cooperation be excused only in those relatively few cases where potential harm exceeds those benefits. *Id.* at 2172. *See also* 43 Fed. Reg. 45,742, col. 3 (1978) (preamble to final regulations); *cf., Id.* at 45,748 45 C.F.R. § 232.40(b)(2)(i)(A) (1979) (notice to applicant must include statement of benefits of enforcement).

64. According to the final regulation's preamble, 43 Fed. Reg. 45,745 (1978): "[S]ome commenters were dissatisfied with 'reasonably anticipated to result,' and suggested alternatives (such as 'proves beyond a reasonable doubt,' and 'shows by clear and convincing proof'), the Department rejected the alternatives. The Department finds 'reasonably anticipated to result in' a sufficiently stringent test."

probability of some harm occurring, the seriousness of the threatened harm, both objectively and in terms of its likely impact on the target, of course, is an important factor. In cases of more serious threatened harm, there is less need for demonstration of probable occurrence to establish "good cause." [65] Some review is possible on appeal.[66]

The standard for granting an exception based on the claim that conception of the child was by forcible rape or incest offers more tangible criteria, but still nothing wholly definitive. Specifically, once the AFDC agency has determined that one of those circumstances "exists," it may grant an exception if it "believes" that cooperation would be "detrimental" to the child in that particular case.[67] This standard leaves some room for interpretation,[68] although comments to the intermediate regulation indicate that, in a case of conception by rape or incest, the AFDC agency should refuse a good cause exception in only the rarest cases.[69] Of course, as discussed below, the AFDC agency

---

65. "Reasonable anticipation" replaced the standard of "likely to result" that was suggested in the first proposed regulation. 41 Fed. Reg. 34,300 (1976). HEW did not wish to create too technical a burden of proof. 43 Fed. Reg. 45,745 (1978). *Cf.,* 43 Fed. Reg. 2173-74 (1978).

66. The final regulation requires AFDC supervisors to review all grants of good cause exceptions. 45 C.F.R. § 232.43(f)(3) (1979). Federal regulations require a fair hearing for all AFDC applicants or recipients denied financial assistance, with a right to an administrative appeal. 45 C.F.R. §§ 205.10(a)(1), (5); 220.11 (1977). These regulations cover uncooperative mothers denied a good-cause exception. *See* 43 Fed. Reg. 45,745 (1978) (preamble to final regulation).

67. 45 C.F.R. § 232.42 (a)(2) (1979).

68. The regulation requires only that the AFDC agency "believe" cooperation would be detrimental to the child's best interest. It seems safe to say the belief should be reasonable, so that the AFDC agency *may,* at the lower end, grant the exception if there is a *reasonable* possibility of the harm occurring.

69. 43 Fed. Reg. 2172 (1978).

need not take at face value an uncorroborated assertion that the child was conceived by forcible rape or incest.

Least problematical is the standard for granting the good cause exception in case of a pending or proposed adoption. Assuming an adoption proceeding is pending or the mother contemplates adoption in good faith (subject to the three-months time limit), it is difficult to imagine that the IV-D agency would want to go after the father before this matter is settled. Adoption, after all, will create an entirely new set of support rights and obligations and, in most cases, remove the child from AFDC eligibility.[70]

d. *Evidence of "Good Cause."*

As a general rule, the claimant of a good cause exception must provide evidence corroborating the asserted grounds within twenty days of asserting the claim. If the claimant does not provide corroboration, the AFDC agency will deny the exception.[71] Examples of corroborative evidence are birth certificates, court documents, medical, law enforcement or other official records, or sworn statements from neighbors or acquaintances (but not from the applicant herself).[72] If requested, the claimant must supply the putative or absent father's name and address, if known, to permit the agency to verify her good cause claim.[73] Upon the claimant's request, the AFDC agency will help by advising how relevant documents may be obtained

---

70. Concerning "subsidized adoption", *see* H. KRAUSE, CASES AND MATERIALS ON FAMILY LAW 668-69 (1976).

71. 45 C.F.R. §§ 232.40 (c) (1)(ii), (2), 232.43 (a)-(b) (1979). The AFDC agency may extend the 20-day deadline if necessary. *Id.*

72. 45 C.F.R. § 232.43(c)(1)-(6) (1979). Because the list of evidence is exemplary, state or local AFDC agencies may accept other documents similar to those specified in the final regulation. 43 Fed. Reg. at 45,745 (1978) (preamble to final regulation).

73. 45 C.F.R. §§ 232.40(c)(iii), 232.43(g) (1979).

and assist in obtaining documents that the claimant is not reasonably able to obtain without assistance.[74]

An exception to the corroboration requirement is made when the applicant grounds her claim on threat of physical harm and cannot corroborate her assertion by documentary evidence. In such cases, the AFDC agency will investigate and grant the exception if "satisfied" that the claimant "has good cause for refusing to cooperate." [75]

In other cases, the AFDC agency may — but need not — launch its own investigation if the applicant's statement, together with the corroborative evidence "do not provide [a] sufficient basis for making a determination".[76] If the AFDC agency believes that contact with the father (from whom support would be sought) is necessary to establish the good cause claim, the regulations provide the mother the safeguard of first being notified so as to enable her to present additional corroborative evidence (to make contact with the father unnecessary), to withdraw her application for aid altogether or to have the good cause claim denied.[77] If the claimant chooses to have her claim denied, she may

---

74. 45 C.F.R. § 232.43(e) (1979). *See also* 43 Fed. Reg. 45,745 (preamble to final regulation).

75. 45 C.F.R. § 232.43(f) (1979). HEW has indicated that exceptions should rarely be granted under this procedure, which seems to make an AFDC investigation more mandatory than discretionary. *See* 43 Fed. Reg. 45,744 (1973) (preamble to final regulation).

76. 45 C.F.R. § 232.43(g) (1979). This is a substantial change from the interim regulation, which required an AFDC investigation in almost every case (43 Fed. Reg. 45,744 (1978), preamble to final regulation) and may reduce the danger that good cause claims will slow down the child support enforcement program. Of course, the AFDC agency retains authority to require the claimant to submit more evidence at any time, although it must specify the evidence desired and possibly help the applicant obtain it. *Id.* at 75, 749 [to be codified in 45 C.F.R. § 232.43(d), (e) (1979), 43 Fed. Reg. 75,745 (1978) (preamble to final regulation).

77. 45 C.F.R. § 232.43(h) (1979). *See also* 43 Fed. Reg. 2174 (1978) (preamble to interim regulation).

nevertheless appeal the denial under applicable federal regulations.[78]

For a claim based on emotional harm, the AFDC agency may condition the grant of an exception on the claimant's submission to examination by a mental health professional (psychiatrist, psychologist, psychiatric social worker, who would be available under the Medicaid or social services program). HEW has indicated that a mental examination should not be required where the claimant provides clear documentation of a serious emotional condition. However, in less clear cases the claimant's duty to furnish more evidence on request, together with her duty to assist an investigation into her claim, would allow denial of the claim if she refuses to submit to an examination.[79]

e. *The Role of IV-D in "Good Cause" Determinations.*

The statute places responsibility for determining good cause exceptions with the AFDC agency.[80] HEW takes the position, however, that the statute does not preclude all involvement by agencies other than AFDC in a pending claim for exception.[81] Thus, the final regulation allows the IV-D enforcement agency an opportunity "to review and comment" on good cause determinations, make recommendations to the AFDC agency and participate in any appellate hearings.[82] This provision ensures that parties whose bias typically would be in favor of enforcement will be heard in good cause determinations.

An optional provision of the regulation permits a state plan to provide that the IV-D agency may enforce a child

---

78. *Id.* at 75,745 (preamble to final regulation). The appeal is taken under 45 C.F.R. § 205.10 (1977).

79. 43 Fed. Reg. 45,744 (1978) (preamble to final regulation); 45 C.F.R. § 232.40(c)(1) (1979).

80. 42 U.S.C.A. § 602(a)(26)(B) (Supp. 1979).

81. 43 Fed. Reg. 2173 (1978) (preamble to interim regulation).

82. 45 C.F.R. § 232.44 (1979).

support obligation against an absent father, even though a good cause exception has been granted and the mother does not cooperate. In that event, enforcement may proceed only when a separate, written determination has been made that enforcement will not risk harm to the child or caretaker relative and the applicant has been given an opportunity to withdraw her application for aid. The IV-D agency must be given an opportunity to review and comment on the proposed determination and the IV-D recommendation must be considered by the AFDC agency.[83]

f. *Provision of Aid Pending Determination of Exception.*

The AFDC agency may not deny, delay or stop payments to a new applicant or current recipient who claims a good cause exception, if the claimant specifies facts constituting grounds for an exception, corroborates the facts, and provides information for an AFDC investigation if requested by the agency.[84] Under *Goldberg v. Kelly,*[85] of

---

83. 45 C.F.R. § 232.49, 45 C.F.R. § 232.44(b) (1979); *see* 43 Fed. Reg. 45,747 (1978) (preamble to final regulation).

84. 45 C.F.R. 232.46 (1979). Despite technical objections that the statute allows AFDC benefits only to those found to have good cause, HEW decided to allow aid pending a good-cause determination. HEW stated that to disallow aid pending a determination would cause unnecessary hardship to children and would be inconsistent with congressional intent. 43 Fed. Reg. 45,747 (1978) (preamble to final regulation).

85. 397 U.S. 254, 261-62, 264,90 S. Ct. 1011, 1017, 1018, 25 L. Ed. 2d 287, 295, 296-297 (1970). Although *Goldberg* contains language that might permit extending the hearing requirement to the denial of a new application for benefits, it has not been so extended. But *cf.,* Griffeth v. Detrich, 603 F.2d 118 (9th Cir. 1979), *cert. denied,* Peer v. Griffeth, —— U.S. ——, 100 S. Ct. 1348, 64 L. Ed. 2d 247 (1980), Justice Rehnquist, dissenting. According to the *Goldberg* majority, "the crucial factor . . . is that termination of aid pending resolution of a controversy over eligibility may deprive an *eligible* recipient of the very means by which to live while he waits." 397 U.S. at 264, 90 S. Ct. at 1018, 25 L. Ed. 2d

course, current recipients have the right to a hearing that meets carefully and specifically delineated standards of due process, before their payments are terminated. While HEW has indicated that it will distinguish between current recipients and new applicants in terms of the hearings offered them (apparently proposing to interpret the *Goldberg* holding narrowly),[86] this assertion is relatively unimportant in light of existing HEW regulations which offer a fair hearing or appeal to any new applicant denied payments under the AFDC program.[87]

g. *Determination of "Good Cause."*

The AFDC agency must make a good cause determination within "a State established time-standard that does not exceed 45 days from the day the good cause claim is made." If the exception is denied, the applicant must be notified and given the choice between cooperating, withdrawing the application for assistance or having her case closed, or losing her benefits and having her children's benefits paid to a protective payee.[88]

h. *Records,   Periodic   Review,   Privacy   and Confidentiality.*

HEW requires AFDC agencies to retain statistics on good cause claims and grants, case-file records on receipt of

at 297 (emphasis in original). In *Goldberg,* the Court balanced the cost to the state against the interests of the individual recipient in uninterrupted receipt of welfare payments. *Id.* at 264-66, 90 S. Ct. at 1019, 25 L. Ed. 2d at 297-98. One commentator acidly concluded that the Court "must have used the term 'eligible' recipient to mean 'determined-to-be-eligible' by the welfare bureaucracy." *B. Brudno, Poverty, Inequality, and the Law* 751 (1976). For an overview of *Goldberg's* effect on lower courts, together with an exposition on due process in administrative hearings, *see* Friendly, *Some Kind of Hearing,* 123 U. PA. L. REV. 1299, 1304 (1975).

86. 43 Fed. Reg. 2172 (1978) (preamble to interim regulation).

87. 45 C.F.R. §§ 205.10(1), (5), 220.11 (1977).

88. 45 C.F.R. § 232.41 (d) (1979).

notice for claiming good cause, and the agency's findings, basis for determination and determination of a denied exception.[89] If the agency grants an exception based on circumstances that might change in time, periodic reviews must be conducted at least as often as welfare eligibility is redetermined.[90]

HEW has expressed awareness that information supplied by the applicant and obtained by the IV-D enforcement agency might be used in a proceeding wholly outside the IV-D support enforcement program.[91] This possibility seemed enhanced by HEW commentary to its interim good cause regulation, to the effect that the grant of a good cause exception does not preclude proceedings based solely on state law.[92] However, the current regulations clarify that the protected status of AFDC information, together with the ability of the applicant to withdraw her application, will provide protection against violations of privacy and confidentiality involving the applicant.[93]

It is not quite clear, however, whether those safeguards — stopping short of absolute immunity which HEW in any event could not grant — suffice to remove the possibility that a mother of an illegitimate child may claim a constitutional privilege against self-incrimination, on the ground that the information she is asked to supply might subject her to prosecution for a crime defined by state law, such as adultery or fornication.[94]

---

89. 45 C.F.R. §§ 232.41(b), 232.48 (1979).

90. 45 C.F.R. § 232.47 (1979), 43 Fed. Reg. 45,746 (1978) (preamble to final regulation).

91. *Id.* (preamble to final regulation).

92. 43 Fed. Reg. 2176 (1978).

93. 43 Fed. Reg. 45,746 (1978) (preamble to final regulation).

94. *Infra* text at notes 111-138.

5. A Summary Appraisal.

It is difficult to fault the basic thrust of the "good cause" exception to the cooperation requirement. Indeed, it is difficult to imagine that a sensible prosecutor would pursue fathers in the type of situations that are covered by the "good cause" exception, *even in the absence of a statutory provision and regulations on this subject,* and even in the presence of the cooperation requirement as originally expressed in the legislation.

As a practical matter, therefore, this law and regulation bring in line the *unreasonable* prosecutor who might have found encouragement in the unqualified cooperation requirement of the original legislation. To achieve that end, however, the regulations "unleash" the unreasonable mother. The significant question these regulations raise thus goes to the proper balance between these two problems. It may well turn out that these regulations pose a greater threat to the efficacy of the enforcement program than can be justified in terms of the evil they seek to remedy. That threat is not so much the chance that AFDC agencies might be tempted to indiscriminately grant "good cause" exceptions simply to reduce their administrative burden, but the more realistic possibility that the detailed, complex and potentially expensive fact-finding and appeals procedures may overburden already understaffed AFDC agencies, *if many mothers claim exceptions.* OCSE writes:

> Department policy regarding *Kelly v. Goldberg*[95] hearings in good cause situations is that the applicant [or] recipient has the right for a fair hearing and that there will be no denial, suspension, or termination of aid pending the final determination. The applicant [or] recipient may request a hearing if IV-A decides that

---

95. 397 U.S. 254, 90 S. Ct. 1011, 25 L. Ed. 2d 287 (1970).

good cause does not exist and begins to terminate AFDC payments.[96]

If a significant backlog of good-cause determinations develops at AFDC offices, enforcement efforts might bog down because the IV-D agency may not begin enforcement activity until it receives a green light from the AFDC agency.[97] Beyond that, there is the policy question of how many dollars should be spent on administration of this exception that otherwise would be available for aid. Potentially serious "cost-benefit" issues raise their head.[98] So far, however, it appears that no major obstruction to the support enforcement program has come through this channel. OCSE reports optimistically that

> in Fiscal Year 1978, 28 States reported 10,454 cases in which the custodial parent refused to cooperate and 22 states reported 455 cases in which good cause was found. Fiscal Year 1979 figures will be available shortly. Our perception of the cooperation issue is that it is not a major problem in the states.[99]

---

96. Letter of December 26, 1979, from Louis B. Hays, Esq., Deputy Director, OCSE, to Harry D. Krause.

97. 45 C.F.R. § 232.45. According to the interim regulation's official commentary:

> Several Legal Service Organizations and NWRO pointed out that if the prompt notice was provided by the IV-A agency prior to the applicant or recipient's claim of good cause, the IV-D agency could be proceeding against the absent parent at the same time the IV-A agency is making a good cause determination. To avoid this situation, the final regulation ... requires the IV-A agency to promptly notify the IV-D agency when good cause is claimed in any case for which prompt notice has already been furnished. The final regulation also adds a new requirement that IV-A promptly notify the IV-D agency of a final determination that good cause does not exist. The corresponding Title IV-D regulation (45 C.F.R. 302.31(b)) prohibits the IV-D agency from proceedings with enforcement until notified by IV-A of the final determination. 43 Fed. Reg. 2173.

98. *Infra* ch. X.2.

99. Letter of December 26, 1979, from Louis B. Hays, Esq., Deputy Director, OCSE, to Harry D. Krause.

The figures for fiscal year 1979 show a total of 13,349 refusals to cooperate "for any reason" and 1,358 findings of "good cause." However, only 25 jurisdictions reported and 29 did not. Even so, the 1979 figures show surprising discrepancies between states. For instance, Illinois reported 4,842 refusals to cooperate and 13 findings of good cause, followed by Arizona with 1,551 refusals and 14 findings of good cause, Michigan with no report on claims but reporting 131 determinations of good cause, Ohio with 174 refusals to cooperate, but 253 findings of good cause, Utah with 35 claims and 20 findings of good cause and Missouri with 22:22. In short, the results are very inconclusive and OCSE's optimism may be premature. The figures certainly are very poorly reported. They do seem to indicate, however, that there are substantial differences from state to state in the administration of the "exception." [100]

As a matter of principle, criticism may be directed at the very core of the good cause exception — the threat of physical harm. If this exception (as seems clear) refers to the risk of criminal assault by the father, it seems peculiar, if not unique, to have the law prescribe that a legal right will be waived in the face of threatened criminal reprisals. Certainly, no *court* would exempt a father from paying child support if he threatened or inflicted harm. Instead, he would be subjected to the court's contempt power and the full force of the criminal law, if need be. Nor has Congress waived enforcement of taxes, if a taxpayer threatens harm to the IRS! Far-fetched as it seems, the analogy bears some relationship to the issue at hand, since it is the taxpaying public that must make up each dollar lost through non-enforcement! Indeed, the question arises whether these regulations might not encourage some men to resort to threats and violence to escape their support liability. Or

---

100. U.S. DEPT. OF HEW, OCSE, 4thANNUAL REPORT TO THE CONGRESS FOR THE PERIOD ENDING SEPTEMBER 30, 1979 at 119 (1979).

might the regulations encourage the mother to allege that the most violent man on the block happens to be the father of her child? If, for fear of angering him, it is determined in either case that the man should not be contacted, where would that leave the program?

These comments are not intended to belittle the special problems inherent in attempting to deal effectively with family violence — ranging from spouse battering to child abuse — recently the target of much federal and state-level attention.[101] We are dealing here, however, with a rather different situation. The parties are physically separated and no social interest remains in preserving "family harmony." Unless we stand ready to admit to social anarchy, the criminal law (if necessary, with appropriate amendments) should offer protection.

Considerable critical publicity has resulted from misunderstandings regarding the purpose and nature of the support enforcement program in general and of the cooperation requirement in particular. Some of the trouble has been caused by inept handling of this sensitive issue by state enforcement agencies. A headline in the *St. Louis Post Dispatch* proclaimed: "Unwed Mothers Asked to Detail Sex Lives" and the accompanying article criticized state efforts to determine paternity by use of a questionnaire that included the following questions:[102]

> When did you first have sexual intercourse with him?
> How often did you have intercourse with him?
> When did you have the intercourse which you believe resulted in this pregnancy? Where?

---

101. *See, e.g.,* 1978 CONG. QUARTERLY 5-6 (May 27, 1978); Bruno v. Codd, 90 Misc. 2d 1047, 396 N.Y.S.2d 974 (1977); H. KRAUSE, CASES AND MATERIALS ON FAMILY LAW 196 (1976) and 1978 Supp. 24-29 (1978).

102. ST. LOUIS POST DISPATCH, May 14, 1978, p. 1, cont'd. May 15, 1978, p. 1-16C.

Date of last menstrual period (before the pregnancy)?
Did you or the alleged father use any preventatives or preventative methods?

Name of preventative or method used?
While you were associating with the father of this child, were you having sexual intercourse with anyone else?
Who? When?
Did you have sexual intercourse with anyone else 90 days prior to the conception of this child? Who? When?
Are you married?
Were you living with your husband when you became pregnant?

Similar flaps developed in several other states. Nationwide, a survey run by OCSE [103] turned up remarkably insensitive or irrelevant questions that were posed quite indiscriminately:

Texas: Did the absent parent climax? How many times? Circumstances leading up to each occasion.
Puerto Rico: Where did the absent parent climax?
Monroe County, New York: Date, hour and place of each and every act of sexual intercourse with respondent.
Philadelphia, Pennsylvania: What compensation the woman received for the act of sexual intercourse?
Indiana: Since child was born, has mother had sexual relations with any other men except defendant?

The resulting publicity was given attention at the highest levels of HEW. The situation was particularly delicate as the publicity arose at the very time the disputed regulations governing the mother's cooperation were under final consideration. A working group was convened by OCSE in August, 1978. Overcoming its reluctance to involve itself in details of local administration of state programs, OCSE is

_____

103. Informal summary prepared by OCSE for use by working group, August, 1978.

establishing standards to reduce or minimize the potential for violation of privacy.[104]

Some of the "choicer" questions truly were good material for headlines. However, the real problem is more one of tact and confidentiality than of substance. When *any* paternity action reaches a lawyer, intimate detail regarding the sexual relationship between the mother and the alleged father *must* be investigated. This investigation has nothing to do with "welfare status." A set of questions recommended by a leading practice guide for lawyers contains more searching and intimate questions than those that were highlighted in the press.[105] The key to an intelligent solution of the problem is in the manner and circumstances in which the relevant information is elicited, the use to which it is put, and the confidentiality that is maintained. Since these inquiries are preliminary to a legal action to enforce child support, the matter properly belongs under the supervision of a lawyer (although shortage of legal personnel may dictate that the preliminary information is elicited by a lawyer-supervised and properly instructed non-lawyer), instead of being dealt with as a part of the AFDC eligibility determination by social case workers.

Unfortunately, the opposing forces allow little middle ground in this crucial area. As a practical matter, it is quite obvious that no matter what sanctions the law provides to enforce the mother's cooperation, enforcement will be stymied and effective coercion of the mother will be all but impossible, if the mother simply claims a loss of memory.[106]

---

104. To be published in 1980. Letter of December 26, 1979, from Louis B. Hays, Esq., Deputy Director OCSE, to Harry D. Krause.

105. 10 Am. Jur. Trials 666 (1965).

106. A very practical consideration has a basic human aspect. Many women and children receiving full benefits under the AFDC program do in fact receive some support from the fathers of their children in the forms of "presents" in kind or in cash. Judges tell of fathers who, confronted with evidence of such payments, argue with moral conviction

Her good will and voluntary collaboration thus are the proper goals for which to strive. In this connection it is particularly unfortunate that the limited "disregard" of the father's contribution (that directly benefitted the mother and her child over and above the AFDC benefit) was discontinued so early in the program. It seems plausible that the mother will be more forthcoming with information concerning the father's whereabouts or identity, and that the father will be more cooperative in making his contributions, if both have the knowledge that their children will live better with the father's contribution than without.[107]

We need the will to recognize and compromise between (1) the primacy of the child's right to know its father, (2) the child's interest (in rare, specific cases) in not having its father's identity established, and (3) the mother's self-interest that may control a particularly unusual case. Naturally deriving from this compromise will be attitudes that favor ascertainment of paternity where that is sensible. Proper counseling of the mother concerning the importance of providing her child legal access to the father is more humane and effective than are threats and coercion. The detailed "notice" prescribed in the final Regulation begins to look in that direction.[108] The rest of the Regulation (as required by the statute) may create an administrative nightmare by threading these cases through the Congressman's "eye of a needle" and still allow "whole herds of camels to gallop through."[109]

---

that *their* children could not be expected to get by on the inadequate money provided by the AFDC program. Other fathers are cajoled by the mother into making "voluntary" payments on threat of exposure of their paternity or whereabouts to the welfare authorities. While no reliable statistics document this problem, it may be significant.

107. *See infra* ch. X. 6.
108. *Supra* note 47.
109. *Supra* text at note 29.

A sensible social consensus and compromise has been achieved in Sweden, where the out-of-wedlock birth rate exceeds twenty percent. Beginning in the early stages of prenatal care, social workers impress upon the mother how important — psychologically, in terms of child support and father-derived social benefits — it is that her child have a known father. In consequence, mothers cooperate willingly. Official resort to laws requiring maternal cooperation in the ascertainment of paternity is exceedingly rare. Previously existing legal sanctions have been dropped, and the mother's cooperation is readily excused if it would do her serious psychological harm. Despite that potential "loophole," paternity is determined in approximately 95 percent of out-of-wedlock births. We, too, should ultimately go the voluntary route, but this will be possible only when all concerned agree that child support enforcement is as much a social imperative as it is the child's birthright. Until then, a reasonable level of compulsion will remain necessary.

As discussed earlier, the problem of requiring the mother's cooperation in the location or ascertainment of the father extends into the judicial process and is not limited to the IV-D program. The latter applies only the mildest possible sanction — denial to the mother not of her children's AFDC benefits, but only of her own. The courts, by contrast, have at their disposal the full range of the contempt arsenal. It should be reemphasized that the federal law and regulations do not now control or affect state law or state court processes regarding the mother's cooperation in locating or identifying an absent father. However, North Carolina illustrates how both remedies may be brought together in a potent combination.[110] A good

---

110. N.C. GEN. STAT. tit. 110, art. 9, § 110-131:

   (a) If a parent of any dependent child receiving public assistance fails or refuses to cooperate with the county in locating and securing

case may be made for a more active stance on the part of OCSE to encourage the enactment of more effective state laws on this subject that will be consistent with the joint federal and state goal — better child support enforcement, with due respect for the legitimate interests of all parties involved.

6. The Fifth Amendment as Grounds for Refusal to Cooperate?

A potentially serious issue arises in connection with the "cooperation requirement" in general and the preliminary paternity investigation in particular. The "Good Cause Regulations" have not squarely faced the problem of how to deal with the mother's refusal to cooperate if she claims that cooperation may incriminate her under state criminal statutes punishing "fornication," "adultery" or "bastardy." In a significant number of states, such statutes continue to apply to the conduct about which information is sought and thus may entitle the mother to invoke the Fifth Amendment and refuse to incriminate herself. While it is well known that such "sex crime" statutes are honored mainly in disregard, it also is true that where these statutes remain on the books, prosecutions are

---

support from a nonsupporting responsible parent, this parent may be cited to appear before any judge of the district court and compelled to disclose such information under oath and/or may be declared ineligible for public assistance by the county department of social services for as long as he fails to cooperate.

(b) Any parent who, having been cited to appear before a judge of the district court pursuant to subsection (a), fails or refuses to appear or fails or refuses to provide the information requested may be found to be in contempt of said court and may be fined not more than one hundred dollars ($100.00) or imprisoned not more than six months or both.

(c) Any parent who is declared ineligible for public assistance by the county department of social services shall have his needs excluded from consideration in determining the amount of the grant, and the needs of the remaining family members shall be met in the form of a protective payment in accordance with G.S. 108-50.

396

at least a technical possibility.[111] While such statutes may be subject to attack under rapidly expanding constitutional rights to sexual privacy [112] and, indeed, already have been held unconstitutional in state courts,[113] none of this detracts from the central point that there is a Fifth Amendment claim to refuse to testify, at least until and unless immunity is granted or the use of the information is appropriately restricted.[114]

The Fifth Amendment holds that no person "shall be compelled in any criminal case to be a witness against himself...." Although early decisions interpreted this privilege against self-incrimination to extend only to defendants in criminal cases, the privilege now extends to persons who are not defendants and who are testifying in proceedings other than criminal.[115] Professor McCormick

111. The argument that the mother's sexual indiscretion (or "crime") is evident from the openly available facts that the child exists and that the mother is not married (so that information regarding the identity of the father really does not disclose anything new), does *not* dispose of the Fifth Amendment problem. The identity of the father may constitute evidence that the "sex crime" was "adultery" or "bigamy" rather than "fornication." Moreover, crucial factual elements of the "crime" may be implicit in testimony disclosing the identity of the father, *e.g.,* the "open and notorious" conduct that some statutes require for a prosecution. See also Grant v. State, 83 Wis. 2d 77, 264 N.W.2d 587 (1978) quoted in text at note 118, *infra.*

112. *See* H. KRAUSE, CASES AND MATERIALS ON FAMILY LAW 265-77 (1976).

113. State v. Saunders, 75 N.J. 200, 381 A.2d 333 (1977). *See also* Note, *Fornication, Cohabitation and the Constitution,* 77 MICH. L. REV. 252 (1978).

114. *See, e.g.,* Kastigar v. U.S., 406 U.S. 441, 92 S. Ct. 1653, 32 L. Ed. 2d 212 (1972). It may offer some comfort that a "Miranda warning" need not be given, inasmuch as the interrogation is not custodial. *See* J. ISRAEL & W. LaFAVE, CRIMINAL PROCEDURE IN A NUTSHELL 213-15 (2d ed. 1975); Beckwith v. U.S., 425 U.S. 341, 96 S. Ct. 1612, 48 L. Ed. 2d 1 (1976); Oregon v. Mathiason, 429 U.S. 492, 97 S. Ct. 711, 50 L. Ed. 2d 714 (1977).

115. McCormick, EVIDENCE, § 116 (2d ed. 1972).

notes four limitations: first, the privilege protects only against criminal liability; second, the danger of incrimination must be real and appreciable; third, the compelled activity must be testimonial in nature; and fourth, the compulsion must be legal compulsion, or compulsion authorized by law.[116] McCormick finds further that the prevailing judicial attitude holds "almost any conceivable danger is real and appreciable." [117]

In a Fifth Amendment challenge to the duty of the mother of an illegitimate child to cooperate with enforcement authorities, the primary questions therefore are the following:

(1) Is the danger of prosecution for the crime of "fornication," "bastardy" or "adultery" real and appreciable?

(2) Is the administration of the support enforcement program a proceeding in which the mother may raise the privilege?

(3) Does the denial of AFDC benefits to the mother, which is the sanction for refusal to cooperate, amount to legal compulsion?

The Wisconsin Supreme Court has provided most of the answers while upholding a mother's Fifth Amendment right not to disclose the father of her illegitimate child because of fear of prosecution:

> In May, 1974, the Milwaukee County corporation counsel obtained an order for an examination of Sheila Grant in county court concerning the paternity of her child. This examination is authorized by sec. 52.24, Stats., which provides that "[i]f any woman bears a child out of wedlock which is or is likely to become a public charge," and if the corporation counsel believes

---

116. *Id.,* §§ 121, 123 through 25.
117. *Id.,* § 123.

it to be in the best interests of the child, he shall apply to any court which "shall thereupon examine such woman on oath respecting the father of such child, the time when and the place where such child was begotten and such other circumstances as he deems necessary;....."

During the examination, the Milwaukee corporation counsel asked her: "The law presumes you became pregnant sometime between July 13th and September 11, 1972, during that period of time, with whom, if with any man did you have sexual intercourse?" Sheila Grant responded: "I refuse to answer on the grounds that it might tend to incriminate me." The court cleared the courtroom of all uninterested persons; and after hearing oral argument, the court ruled that Sheila Grant did not have a privilege against self-incrimination in a statutory paternity proceeding. The court ordered her to answer; and when she did not, the court found her in contempt of court and sentenced her to imprisonment of ten days in the county jail, or until such time as she expressed a willingness to answer the corporation counsel's question. The court stayed this sentence pending appeal....

We hold that, in refusing to reveal the identity of a partner to sexual intercourse during the period of conception, Sheila Grant appropriately asserted her privilege against self-incrimination. We hold further that neither the restrictions on access to this testimony nor the immunity statutes provide a basis for compelling her to testify when she asserted her privilege concerning incriminating testimony.

The right against self-incrimination is a fundamental right guaranteed by both art. I, sec. 8, Wis.Const., and by the U.S. Const., amend. V, which is made applicable to the states by reason of the due process clause of the fourteenth amendment. The fact that a paternity proceeding authorized by Ch. 52, Stats., is characterized as civil has no bearing on whether a witness in such a proceeding has a privilege against self-incrimination. The privilege extends to all court proceedings, civil and criminal. *Kastigar v.*

United States, 406 U.S. 441, 444, 92 S.Ct. 1653, 32 L.Ed.2d 212 (1972); *In re Gault,* 387 U.S. 1, 44, 87 S.Ct. 1428, 18 L.Ed.2d 527 (1967). The privilege against self-incrimination exists whenever a witness has a real and appreciable apprehension that the information requested could be used against him in a criminal proceeding. *Murphy v. Waterfront Commission of New York Harbor,* 378 U.S. 52, 94, 82 S.Ct. 146, 7 L.Ed.2d 91 (1964); *Mason v. United States,* 244 U.S. 362, 366, 37 S.Ct. 621, 61 L.Ed. 1198 (1917); *Blau v. United States,* 340 U.S. 159, 161, 71 S.Ct. 223, 95 L.Ed. 170 (1950). It extends not only to testimony which would support a conviction but also to evidence which would furnish a link in a chain of evidence necessary to prosecution. *Hoffman v. United States,* 341 U.S. 479, 486, 71 S.Ct. 814, 95 L.Ed. 1118 (1951).

Sheila Grant contends that testifying concerning a specific occasion of sexual intercourse could elicit information which could be used against her in a prosecution for any one of several crimes contained in Ch. 944, Stats., crimes against sexual morality. The corporation counsel does not deny that admissions of sexual intercourse and cohabitation out of wedlock are incriminating. Indeed, it is evident that they are. *See: United States v. Matlock,* 415 U.S. 164, 94 S.Ct. 988, 39 L.Ed.2d 242 (1974), (because cohabitation out of wedlock is a crime in Wisconsin, statements admitting cohabitation out of wedlock are against the declarant's penal interest); *Poplowski v. State ex rel. Lewandowski,* 194 Wis. 385, 216 N.W. 488 (1927), (in a paternity proceeding the trial court's right, if not its duty, was to instruct the witness of his right not to answer a question intended to elicit an admission of sexual intercourse with the prosecutrix); *See also: State v. Robbins,* 318 A.2d 51 (Me. 1974); *Commonwealth v. Carrera,* 424 Pa. 551, 227 A.2d 627 (1967). But Milwaukee County does argue that: (1) because few if any prosecutions under Ch. 944, Stats., are based on information obtained from paternity suits; and (2) because of the restrictions on access to the testimony, the likelihood of prosecution is too remote to give rise to the privilege.

The fear of self-incrimination must be "real and appreciable," "not merely [an] imaginary possibility of danger." *Mason v. United States, supra.* This danger should be appraised "with reference to the ordinary operation of law in the ordinary course of things — not a danger of an imaginary or unsubstantial character, having reference to some extraordinary and barely possible contingency, so improbable that no reasonable man would suffer it to influence his conduct." *Id.* 244 U.S. at 366, 37 S.Ct. at 622. *Accord: Blau v. United States, supra.* . . .

The Court has liberally construed the privilege in favor of the right which it was intended to protect. *Hoffman v. United States, supra* at 486, 71 S.Ct. 814. In *Hoffman,* the Court stated:

'To sustain the privilege, it need only be evident from the implications of the question, in the setting in which it is asked, that a responsive answer to the question . . . might be dangerous because injurious disclosure could result.' *Id.* at 486-87, 71 S.Ct. at 818.

In the present case it is clear that Sheila Grant's testimony concerning specific occasions of sexual intercourse would admit critical elements of a crime. Most if not all of Ch. 944, Stats., crimes require the state to name the defendant's victim or partner in the crime. Thus evidence of the child's birth alone would have been insufficient to support a criminal charge. But by supplying the names of a partner to sexual intercourse during the period of conception, Sheila Grant would have furnished evidence of most if not all of the elements of several Ch. 944 crimes and under *Hoffman v. United States, supra,* would have furnished a link in a chain of evidence necessary for prosecution. Despite the fact that it may be less than probable that Sheila Grant will be prosecuted with evidence compelled in a sec. 52.24, Stats., proceeding, her fear of self-incrimination is sufficiently real and appreciable to be a valid exercise of her right.

The corporation counsel also contends that restrictions on access to Sheila Grant's testimony afford sufficient protection from criminal prosecution. . . .

A distinction must be made between restrictions on access which protect the individual's privacy interest and restrictions which protect the individual from criminal prosecution. In this case it appears that the restrictions contained in secs. 52.27, 52.35, and 52.42, Stats., are intended to protect privacy rather than to grant immunity from criminal prosecution. These statutes apply equally to the privacy of the mother of the illegitimate child as well as the privacy of the putative father, yet the putative father has been expressly held to have a privilege against self-incrimination in paternity cases. Moreover, in other instances involving the adjudication of paternity and parental rights and responsibilities, the legislature has directly dealt with the problem of self-incriminatory testimony. *See, e.g.,* sec. 52.10(21), Stats., authorizing immunity under the revised Uniform Reciprocal Enforcement of Support Act; the Uniform Desertion and Nonsupport Act, sec. 52.05(6), Stats., where the statutory language clearly refers to the possibility of incriminating evidence by stating that "neither [the husband nor the wife] shall be compelled to give evidence incriminating himself or herself." The fact that other statutes address the incrimination issue directly suggests that the restrictions on access to testimony under secs. 52.27, 52.35, and 52.42, Stats., secure only the individual's privacy interest.

In ruling that appellant did not have a privilege against self-incrimination, the court below relied on *In Re Cager,* 251 Md. 473, 248 A.2d 384 (1968). In *In Re Cager* the Maryland Court of Appeals ruled that the state attorney could not use information obtained from the state department of public welfare in a child neglect prosecution. The *Cager Case* differs from the facts of the present case in two significant ways. First, the *Cager Case* raised no fifth amendment issue. Since none of the defendants had refused to provide information to the welfare department and asserted a fifth amendment privilege, the question of whether the state could compel the defendants to provide incriminating evidence never arose. Second, the

Maryland statute, under which the state had obtained the information, differs from sec. 52.24, Stats., in that it expressly restricts the use of the information. By contrast, secs. 52.21 — 52.45, Stats., do not contain a use restriction on information obtained under sec. 52.24, Stats.; they merely provide access restrictions. Once a district attorney obtains access, through direct inquiry under sec. 52.24 or a court order under sec. 52.42, Stats., he is not prohibited by the statutes from using the testimony itself or other evidence derived from the testimony in a criminal prosecution. Thus the privacy restrictions in Ch. 52, Stats., cannot substitute for a grant of immunity and do not make the danger of prosecution so remote that the privilege cannot be asserted. . . .

Of course, the privilege can be replaced by a sufficient grant of immunity. *Kastigar v. United States, supra*. However, no immunity statute is applicable here. Although sec. 891.39(2), Stats., provides immunity to a married woman who answers questions concerning the paternity of her child born out of wedlock, Sheila Grant testified that she has never been married. The general immunity statute, sec. 972.08(1), Stats., applies only to an assertion of the privilege in a criminal hearing or trial. Sec. 52.45, Stats., states that sec. 52.24 is "a civil special proceeding" and shall be conducted "according to the provisions of these statutes with respect to civil actions and civil proceedings in courts of record, as far as applicable except as otherwise provided in this chapter." In establishing a civil construction for proceedings under Ch. 52, Stats., the legislature presumably acted with the existing statutes in mind, including the general criminal immunity statute, and thereby manifested an intent to make the general criminal immunity statute inapplicable. The power to grant immunity is a legislative power and not an inherent power of either the prosecutor or the court. *Elam v. State,* 50 Wis.2d 383, 392, 393, 184 N.W.2d 176 (1971). Therefore, until the legislature enacts an immunity statute which applies to all witnesses testifying under sec. 52.24, Stats., the county court cannot compel Sheila Grant to answer incriminating questions about the circumstances in which her child was conceived. Her refusal to testify was a proper exercise of her constitutional right, and accordingly the judgment of contempt must be reversed.[118]

It would seem clear that a state IV-D agency investigation constitutes the type of state action in which individuals may assert protection afforded by the Bill of Rights. An administrative investigatory proceeding was held capable of raising Fifth Amendment considerations even in the last century.[119] More recently, the Supreme Court has stated that the privilege against self-incrimination is "as broad as the mischief against which it seeks to guard," [120] and "the scope of the privilege is comprehensive.... The privilege can be claimed in any proceeding, be it criminal or civil, administrative or judicial, investigatory or adjudicatory...." [121]

There remains the question whether the sanction for refusal to cooperate (that is, withdrawal of, or ineligibility for, AFDC) constitutes "legal compulsion." For many years, potential sanctions that would trigger the privilege were

---

118. Grant v. State, 83 Wis. 2d 77, 78-89, 264 N.W.2d 587, 589-94 (1978) (Some footnotes and citations omitted). *See* Commonwealth v. Carrera, 424 Pa. 551, A.2d 627 (1967) (in an abortion prosecution, the witness, upon whom defendant had performed an abortion, had "reasonable cause" to apprehend a danger of self-incrimination for fornication or adultery). United States *ex rel.* Berberian v. Cliff, 300 F. Supp. 8 (E.D. Pa. 1969) (woman who had only requested the defendant to perform an abortion held entitled to Fifth Amendment protection because of possible prosecution for fornication).

119. Interstate Commerce Commission v. Brimson, 154 U.S. 447, 14 S. Ct. 1125, 38 L. Ed. 1047 (1894).

120. Miranda v. Arizona, 384 U.S. 436, 460, 86 S. Ct. 1602, 1620, 16 L. Ed. 2d 694, 715 (1966).

121. *In re* Gault, 387 U.S. 1, 47-48, 87 S. Ct. 1428, 1454, 18 L. Ed. 2d 527, 557 (1967).

the standard forms of legal compulsion, such as contempt of court.[122] Today, the applicable standard seems to be "potent sanctions." With this, the Supreme Court has increased considerably the probability that denial of aid to the uncooperative mother would indeed be held to constitute compulsion for purposes of the privilege against self-incrimination. In *Lefkowitz v. Turley*,[123] a public contractor claimed the privilege before a grand jury investigating corruption in public contracting. A New York statute then automatically cancelled all state contracts held by him and barred him for five years from performing future public contracts. The Court held that the imposition of such a substantial economic burden constituted compulsion, even though the bar on future contracts did not affect an enforceable property right. The Court expanded this holding in *Lefkowitz v. Cunningham*,[124] in which the grand jury was investigating the defendant's conduct as an office-holder in the New York Democratic Party. Upon his refusal to testify, another statute automatically deprived the defendant of his party offices and activated a five year ban on future office holding. The Court held that the denial of potential renumeration from future party positions was a "potent sanction" constituting compulsion. To draw the analogy to welfare, it would seem that the denial of a welfare applicant's "very means by which to live," [125] would qualify as a "potent sanction" under the *Lefkowitz* cases and thus constitute "compulsion."

In addition to a challenge to the duty to cooperate based solely on the privilege against self-incrimination, a Fifth-Amendment/Equal-Protection challenge might

---

122. 8 J. WIGMORE, EVIDENCE § 2252 (3d ed. 1940).

123. 414 U.S. 70, 94 S. Ct. 316, 38 L. Ed. 2d 274 (1973).

124. 431 U.S. 801, 97 S. Ct. 2132, 53 L. Ed. 2d 1 (1977).

125. Goldberg v. Kelly, 397 U.S. 254, 264, 90 S. Ct. 1011, 1018, 25 L. Ed. 2d 287, 297 (1970).

possibly be mounted under *Shapiro v. Thompson.*[126] *Shapiro* holds that the State may not penalize the exercise of a constitutionally protected fundamental right by withholding welfare payments. Although the statutory right to receive welfare is not a right that is subject to "strict scrutiny" under the Equal Protection Clause,[127] the right to interstate migration is, and *Shapiro* invalidated laws that denied welfare assistance to persons who did not meet residence requirements. The Court held further that the state's interest in preserving public funds is not a "compelling state interest" and cannot justify classifications that burden constitutionally protected interests.[128] If analogous reasoning were applied to the duty to cooperate, the conclusion might be that the State cannot penalize, by withholding welfare benefits, a mother's exercise of her right to refuse to incriminate herself.[129]

Although the Fifth Amendment privileges an individual not to incriminate him- or herself, the state may nevertheless compel testimony by granting immunity from prosecution or by assuring that the information cannot be used in a prosecution.[130] Translated into the child support

---

126. 394 U.S. 618, 89 S. Ct. 1322, 22 L. Ed. 2d 600 (1969). *See also, e.g.,* Memorial Hospital v. Maricopa County, 415 U.S. 250, 94 S. Ct. 1076, 39 L. Ed. 2d 306 (1974).

127. Dandridge v. Williams, 397 U.S. 471, 90 S. Ct. 1153, 25 L. Ed. 2d 491 (1970).

128. Shapiro v. Thompson, 394 U.S. 618, 638, 89 S. Ct. 1322, 1333, 22 L. Ed. 600, 617 (1969).

129. But *cf.,* Beal v. Doe, 432 U.S. 438, 97 S. Ct. 2366, 53 L. Ed. 2d 464 (1977); Poelker v. Doe, 432 U.S. 519, 97 S. Ct. 2391, 53 L. Ed. 2d 528 (1977) (abortion funding); Harris v. McRae, — U.S. —, 100 S. Ct. 2671, — L. Ed. 2d — (1980) and Williams v. Zbaraz, — U.S. —, 100 S. Ct. 2694, — L. Ed. 2d — (1980) ("Hyde Amendment"); Wyman v. James, 400 U.S. 309, 91 S. Ct. 381, 27 L. Ed. 2d 408 (1971) (AFDC home visit) upheld (against 4th Amendment challenge).

130. *E.g.,* Ullman v. U.S., 350 U.S. 422, 76 S. Ct. 497, 100 L. Ed. 511 (1956).

enforcement context, the Fifth Amendment affects the mother's duty to cooperate only if the state has the capability to use the information, directly or indirectly, to prosecute the mother for her "sex crime." Thus the next question is whether protection provided by existing law suffices to rule out the Fifth Amendment claim.

Concerning the welfare applicant's privacy, the Social Security Act sets out the following requirements for state plans under the AFDC program: [131]

> A State plan for aid and services to needy families with children must ... provide safeguards which restrict the use or disclosure of information concerning applicants or recipients to purposes directly connected with (A) the administration of the plan of the State approved under this part ... (B) any investigation, prosecution, or criminal or civil proceeding, conducted in connection with the administration of any such plan or program, and (C) the administration of any other Federal or federally assisted program which provides assistance, in cash or in kind, or services, directly to individuals on the basis of need; and the safeguards so provided shall prohibit disclosure, to any committee or a legislative body, of any information which identifies by name or address any such applicant or recipient.

Federal regulations reiterate, and supplement these statutory provisions:

> A state plan must provide that ... pursuant to state statute which imposes legal sanctions ....
> Types of information to be safeguarded include but are not limited to ... information related to the social ... conditions or circumstances of a particular individual ... [and] agency evaluation of information about a particular individual ....
> In the event of the issuance of a subpoena for the case record or for any agency representative to testify

---

131. 42 U.S.C.A. § 602(a)(9) (1980 Supp.).

concerning an applicant or recipient, the court's attention is called, through proper channels to the statutory provisions and the policies or rules and regulations against disclosure of information.[132]

The final regulation covering the "good cause exception" to the mother's duty to cooperate in the location or ascertainment of the absent father, states in its preamble:

[S]ection 402(a)(9) of the Social Security Act requires each State plan under title IV-A of the Social Security Act to provide safeguards restricting the use of disclosure of information concerning applicants or recipients to "purposes directly connected with . . . the plan or program of the State under (among others) part . . . D of this title." Regulations at 45 CFR 205.50 which implement the statutory safeguards require that restrictions on improper uses or disclosures of information must be enacted through State statutes which impose legal sanctions on violators. 45 CFR 302.18 makes the same safeguards applicable to information contained in title IV-D case records. These safeguards should allay fears that IV-D agencies will gain access to the evidence supporting a good cause claim and then use the information for a purpose not directly connected with the IV-D program, e.g., conducting totally State funded paternity or child support enforcement proceedings. Thus, even though the evidence supporting a successful good cause claim may be revealed to the IV-D agency pursuant to § 232.44, IV-D would only be able to use the evidence in a paternity or child support enforcement proceeding conducted pursuant to § 232.49. That regulation conditions the initiation of paternity or support enforcement proceedings following a finding that good cause exists on a IV-A agency determination that the proceedings would not cause harm to the child or caretaker relative if conducted without their participation. The regulation further requires that, if

---

132. 45 C.F.R. § 205.50(a)(2) (a)(2)(iv) (1977). *Also see* 45 C.F.R. § 205.50(a)(1)-(3), (e) (1977).

IV-A approves paternity or support proceedings, the applicant or recipient be notified of the IV-A decision and given an opportunity to withdraw her application or have the case closed. This IV-A review followed by a notice giving the applicant or recipient an opportunity to withdraw her application, or have the case closed should sufficiently protect applicants and recipients from harmful consequences of any IV-D activities that postdate a finding of good cause.[133]

Concern regarding the effectiveness of these confidentiality requirements remains. First, the regulations do not state specifically that a cooperating mother's testimony must be safeguarded to prevent a criminal prosecution by the state. Second, the regulations do not expressly prohibit the derivative use of testimony furnished by the cooperating mother in a criminal prosecution, nor could they do so effectively.[134]

In short, enough doubt may be raised regarding the adequacy of existing federal regulations regarding use-restrictions that it would seem sensible to address the Fifth Amendment problem in the specific context of child support enforcement. The complication is that the potential

---

133. 43 Fed. Reg. 45,746 (1978) (preamble to final "good cause" regulation).

134. In Doe v. Shapiro, 302 F. Supp. 761 (D. Conn. 1969) *appeal dismissed*, 396 U.S. 488 (1970), plaintiffs challenged a state welfare regulation that required AFDC mothers to name the fathers of their illegitimate children or lose benefits. Under then existing federal law, the District Court held that such a condition on aid was not intended by Congress, and thus did not reach plaintiffs' Fifth Amendment challenge to the regulation. In defense to that challenge, the State had argued that Connecticut's confidentiality statute provided adequate immunity from prosecution to welfare mothers, *id.* at 763, and the dissenting opinion (which would have upheld the regulation) found the State's argument persuasive. *Id.* at 771 (Clairie, D.J. dissenting). *See also* Note, *Relative Responsibility in AFDC: Problems Raised by the NOLEO Approach — "If at First You Don't Succeed . . .",* 9 URBAN L. ANN. 203, 222-25 (1975).

threat is from a *state* prosecution, so that *state* legislation is at issue.

The neatest way to deal with the problem, of course, would be to persuade the states to repeal these outdated "sex crime" statutes. In this age of *Marvin*,[135] the lack of zeal on the part of state's attorneys in enforcing these statutes clearly indicates the absence of any real, continuing state interest in the matter. To ask for outright repeal of "morality," however, may be asking for more than can be had from most legislatures at this time. Next best would be the enactment by each state of an appropriate immunity statute. Of course, in many states, immunity statutes now on the books effectively dissolve any Fifth Amendment threat to the support enforcement program. Nevertheless, these statutes vary greatly and only focus partially on the child support enforcement problem.[136]

---

135. Marvin v. Marvin, 18 Cal. 3d 660, 557 P.2d 106, Cal. Rptr. 815 (1977).

136. Many current statutes invite conflicting or strained interpretation. To illustrate, ILL. REV. STAT. ch. 23, § 11-9 (1977) provides: "In any judicial proceeding, except a proceeding directly concerned with the administration of programs provided for in this Code, or in which the applicant or recipient is a party thereto, such records, files, papers and communication, and their contents shall be deemed privileged communications."

As the applicant would of course be a party to any proceeding against her, the stated exception seems to nullify any privilege. Moreover, the Illinois statute permits disclosure to "appropriate law enforcement officials" regarding "the desertion or abandonment by a parent of a child, as a result of which financial aid has been necessitated . . ." or regarding "instances in which a mother under age 18 has a child out of wedlock and is an applicant for or recipient of aid under any Article of this Code." *Id.,* thus apparently allowing derivative use of incriminating testimony that the duty to cooperate might compel from the mother. The next question is whether the following proviso saves the situation: "The provisions of this Section and Section 11-11 as they apply to applicants and recipients of public aid . . . shall be operative only to the extent that

Moreover, many or most such statutes apply to *judicial* proceedings only.

The most effective means of dealing with this threat would be a mandate from OCSE that would encourage the states to enact more specific and comprehensive statutes as part of required compliance with the AFDC program. These immunity statutes should prohibit use in any "sex crime" prosecution of the mother (and, preferably, also the putative father), of evidence, including testimony, developed in the course of support enforcement. The immunity should apply at the very first level of involvement of the AFDC and IV-D agencies (interview and interrogation) and should not be limited to testimony in judicial proceedings. If specific legislative authority is deemed needed for such a condition to federal participation in the state program, OCSE should seek such authority from Congress.[137]

---

they do not conflict with any federal law or regulation governing Federal grants to this State for such programs." *Id.*

If so, the Illinois scheme may provide sufficient protection — if 45 C.F.R. § 205.50 and 42 U.S.C.A. § 602(a)(9) do. In other states, a number of courts have held that, due to the strong federal presence in the AFDC program, state confidentiality statutes must be interpreted in the light of the purpose of federally mandated restrictions. *See e.g.,* Hanson v. Rowe, 18 Ariz. App. 131, 500 P.2d 916 (1972); Triplett v. Bd. of Social Protections, 19 Or. App. 408, 528 P.2d 563 (1974); *In re* Cager, 251 Md. 473, 248 A.2d 384 (1968); Addie W. v. Charles U., 44 A.D. 727, 354 N.Y.S.2d 721 (1974); Paine v. Chick, 50 A.D. 686, 375 N.Y.S.2d 198 (1975).

137. While Congress itself might consider enacting a federal immunity statute, that would seem to go further than necessary or desirable. As stated in a different context:

[S]erious considerations of federalism arise when and to the extent that immunity granted a witness by one state impinges upon the independent power of another state to prosecute him . . . [S]tates may well differ in judgment as to the importance and desirability of prosecuting a particular participant in a wrongdoing. Thus, to deprive a state of the right to prosecute a violation of its criminal law on the basis of another state's grant of immunity would be gravely

411

Lest it be confused what the issue is, the attack here is *not* on the Fifth Amendment right against self-incrimination, nor on the integrity of the enforcement of the criminal laws. The attack is solely upon the (ab)use of the testimonial privilege in *technical* reliance on the *unlikely* event of a state prosecution under a fornication or adultery statute. The disuse of these statutes demonstrates amply that they no longer vindicate significant state interests. The enforcement of child support, by contrast, is not only a legitimate state interest, but a most important one.

---

in derogation of its sovereignty and obstructive of its administration of justice.

But merely to prevent a state from using the text or fruits of coerced testimony that another state has obtained is much less likely to obstruct the normal administration of justice. For the same unwillingness to testify that led the first state to grant immunity would almost always make the testimony of the reluctant witness unavailable to any other government. Thus, the imposition of use immunity upon a second state is not likely to deprive it of anything that it otherwise might have obtained by its independent inquiry. [United States *ex rel.* Catena v. Elias, 449 F.2d 40, 44 (3rd Cir. 1971)].

Chapter X

SECOND THOUGHTS FOR THE SECOND
FIVE YEARS

1. An Early Accounting.

As seen from Washington, the new law is well on its
way to success. Early critics are being convinced of its
viability and most now believe that the near future will
bring greatly increased efficiency and corresponding
results. In 1974 the influential *Washington Post*
characterized the program as "an unwarranted intrusion of
the federal government [into personal lives that] would
yield little while costing a great deal . . . the benefits to be
derived are minimal at best. The dangers are
incalculable." [1] By March, 1978, the *Washington Post* had
been converted:

> Today, no one is sniggering. About 1 million parents
> who otherwise would pay nothing are now making
> payments. And the more than $1 billion anticipated
> this fiscal year in child-support payments obtained for
> welfare mothers or other families where the father has
> disappeared or refuses to support the children is equal
> to about 10 percent of the entire national cost of the Aid
> to Families with Dependent Children program.
> "This program is a success," said Secretary of Health,
> Education and Welfare Joseph A. Califano, Jr., warmly
> praising [Senator] Long for his efforts to get it enacted
> in 1974. . . .
> Califano . . . is enthusiastic about the program. He
> believes the regulations will prevent abuses of privacy.
> He has told aids to shoot for a doubling of the amount
> collected under the program — from $1 billion in fiscal
> 1978 to $2 billion in fiscal 1979.[2]

Only a few negative voices remain. William Haskins of

---

1. Quoted in WASHINGTON POST, March 13, 1978, p. A-1.
2. *Id.*

413

the National Urban League: "If all the money spent tracking down these men and harassing them was spent on counseling and job training, many would come back on their own." Alan Reitman, American Civil Liberties Union: "Use of Social Security records to trace missing parents is an invasion of privacy, since records intended for one purpose are being used for another purpose without the individual's consent." Richard Doyle, Men International: "Most fathers who run away do so in protest against being saddled with excessive child-support payments without being granted adequate visitation rights. I respect a man who refuses to knuckle under to such an unfair system." [3]

Experience is developing rapidly and favorably. The federal parent locator service was initiated in late March, 1975. In its very first year, the new service was able to find addresses for almost 90 percent of the names concerning which the states sought help.[4] During fiscal year 1977, child support enforcement programs yielded IV-D agencies a total of $818 million ($603 million in 1976) composed of $409.5 million for AFDC recipients ($280 million in 1976) plus $408.5 million for non-AFDC claimants ($323.7 million in 1976). The stated cost in 1977 amounted to $258.8 million ($142.6 million in 1976) for an average return of $3.16 for each dollar spent.[5] An additional estimated $21.3 million in

---

3. Quotations in U.S. NEWS AND WORLD REPORT, February 12, 1979, p. 50, *Cf., supra* ch. VII. 2.

4. The federal parent locator service received 152,228 address requests in fiscal 1977. OCSE, CHILD SUPPORT ENFORCEMENT: 2D ANNUAL REPORT TO THE CONGRESS 111-12 (GPO ed. 1977) (hereinafter cited as 1977 REPORT). *See generally id.* at 17-22.

5. SEN. FIN. COM. STAFF DATA AND MATERIALS ON PUBLIC WELFARE PROGRAMS, April 1978, 95th Cong., 2d Sess. (hereinafter cited as 1978 STAFF DATA) at 32-33. *See also* 1977 REPORT at 89, 97. In 1977, top-ranking Michigan collected $64.4 million in support for AFDC families with a return of $4.03 for every $1 expended. Massachusetts, another large-volume state that collected $24.3 million for AFDC

support payments went directly to AFDC families and thereby reduced AFDC assistance payments.[6] The fiscal 1977 program (for both AFDC recipients and non-AFDC applicants) located 341,111 persons (181,504 in 1976), established paternity in 68,263 cases (14,706 in 1976), and

---

families in 1977, leads the cost-benefit field with a return of $6.74 per $1 expended. 1978 STAFF DATA at 34-35. These and the following figures are derived from summaries of statistical reports sent to OCSE by state IV-D agencies regarding total AFDC collections and total state and local expenditures, excluding non-AFDC expenditures. 1977 REPORT at 89, 97. Cost-benefit calculations do not include non-AFDC collections because an unknown portion of these collections presumably would have been made without the new enforcement program.

States with unusually favorable cost-benefit ratios for fiscal 1977 *also* included New Hampshire ($1.9 million collected at $6.06 per $1 expended); Rhode Island ($3.1 million collected at $4.20 per $1 expended); and Iowa ($7.4 million collected at $4.05 per $1 expended). Among states making large collections, Ohio collected $19.5 million at $3.18 per $1 expended; Wisconsin collected $19.4 million at $2.85 per $1 expended; Washington collected $15.6 million at $2.65 per $1 expended; Pennsylvania collected $24.3 million at $1.72 per $1 expended; New Jersey collected $19.9 million at $1.28 per $1 expended; New York collected $44.0 million at $1.06 per $1 expended; and California collected $63.4 million at $1.01 per $1 expended.

States reporting collections at between $3 and $4 per $1 expended include Maine and Wyoming. States making collections at between $2 and $3 per $1 expended include Georgia, Idaho, Indiana and North Dakota. States making collections at between $1 and $2 per $1 expended include Colorado, Connecticut, Delaware, Hawaii, Illinois, Maryland, Minnesota, Mississippi, Nebraska, Oregon, Tennessee, Vermont and Virginia.

Among the jurisdictions with the worst returns in terms of collections per $1 expended in fiscal 1977 were the Virgin Islands, 34 cents; Nevada, 26 cents; Alaska, 22 cents; Guam, 14 cents; Alabama, 8 cents; and Puerto Rico, 2 cents. Other states with collections lower than expenditures were Arizona, Arkansas, District of Columbia, Florida, Kentucky, Louisiana, Montana, New Mexico, North Carolina, Oklahoma, South Carolina, South Dakota, Texas and West Virginia.

6. 1977 REPORT at 92.

established support obligations in 183,073 cases (75,008 in 1976).[7]

Later figures show continuing acceleration. In fiscal year 1979, 480,000 absent parents were located, support obligations were established in more than 300,000 cases, paternity was ascertained in more than 117,000 cases and more than one and one-third billion dollars were collected, composed of $596,739,000 in AFDC collections and $736,520,000 in non-AFDC collections.[8] Interestingly, two originally controversial remedies had not seen much use: By late 1979, Federal court enforcement had not yet been tried and IRS collection had been used sparingly.[9]

In 1977, 20 percent of AFDC families (600,000) were being served by the support enforcement program, and HEW projections in 1978 looked toward 35 percent by 1981.[10] It is difficult to assign precise causes to the recent

7. 1978 STAFF DATA at 36-41; 1977 REPORT at 106.08. OCSE, CHILD SUPPORT ENFORCEMENT: SUPPLEMENTAL REPORT TO THE CONGRESS 154-56 (GPO ed. 1977) (hereinafter cited as 1977 SUPP. REPORT). Somewhat revised 1977 and new 1978 figures are provided in SEN. FIN. COM. STAFF DATA AND MATERIALS ON CHILD SUPPORT C.P. 96-7, March 19, 1979, 96th Cong., 1st Sess. For instance, the fiscal 1977 figure for establishment of paternity was given as 89,386 and for fiscal 1978 as 110,726.

8. U.S. DEPT. OF H.E.W., OFFICE OF CHILD SUPPORT ENFORCEMENT, CHILD SUPPORT ENFORCEMENT, FOURTH ANNUAL REPORT TO THE CONGRESS FOR THE PERIOD ENDING SEPTEMBER 30, 1979 (Dec. 31, 1979) (hereinafter cited as 1979 REPORT).

9. OCSE writes "To date, Federal Courts have not been used by the States to enforce court orders." Letter of December 26, 1979, from Louis B. Hays, Esq., Deputy Director, OCSE, to Harry D. Krause. "For Fiscal Years 1976 through 1979, 500 cases have been certified to the Internal Revenue Service for collection of 2.5 million dollars. Fifty thousand dollars has been collected to date." Id. See also 1979 REPORT at 96.

10. 1978 STAFF DATA at 34. See also MIAMI HERALD, July 20, 1978, p. 23A:

The government announced plans Wednesday to intensify efforts

decline in AFDC recipients [11] — after years of steady and often rapid increases — but OCSE officials need have no doubt that the credit is at least partly theirs. Although in 1979 only 14,000 AFDC cases were reported closed as a result of child support collections, less than one-half of the states reported this figure,[12] so that the actual may be assumed to be much greater, *nor does the figure indicate the number of cases never opened due to non-AFDC child support enforcement!*

In short, the program is off to a running start. By late 1978, 1.2 million missing parents had been located, 1.3 billion dollars had been collected for children on welfare (as compared to about 10.7 billion paid out in aid) and a further 1.5 billion had been collected for children not on public aid.[13] The fledgling OCSE has reason to be proud. It does not detract to note that much of the success just described

---

to track down the missing parents of children on welfare and make them pay child support. Secretary Joseph Califano of the Department of Health, Education and Welfare said he hopes to double the collection rate to $1 billion annually by the end of fiscal 1979. ... He said he was launching 'Project Responsibility.' It will include a new training center in Washington for the federal, state and local officials who enforce the program, a model child support computer system for states, and creation of a clearinghouse to share information on the state programs. ...

The number of missing parents located jumped 32 percent in the first half of fiscal 1978 to 213,000, he said.

11. By November, 1978, the number of AFDC recipients was the lowest since 1971. Between early 1976 and late 1978 the number of recipients decreased by 1.1 million, to 10.3 million. U.S. SEN. COM. ON FINANCE, STAFF DATA AND MATERIALS ON CHILD SUPPORT, 96th Cong., 1st Sess. C.P. 96-7, p. 2-3, 53-57 (March 19, 1979). *See also* MIAMI HERALD, June 18, 1978, p. 30A: The government announced that the over-all cost of the program rose by 1.9 percent, from $10 billion in 1977 to $10.2 billion this year, while the number of persons on the program's rolls were reduced by 2.3 percent. *C.F., supra* ch. VIII. 1, note 2.

12. 1979 REPORT at 101.

13. U.S. NEWS AND WORLD REPORT, February 12, 1979, p. 50.

was achieved in a few states that moved early and efficiently to implement the new program and, indeed, in states that were able to build on successful existing programs.[14] Top-ranked Michigan [15] as well as California, Massachusetts and Washington [16] are models in the latter category. Even now, considerable evidence indicates that only some states are moving ahead at full capacity to implement their share of the joint federal-state task [17] and, in a few states, the new enforcement philosophy is only

---

14.

> As required by law, all of the States now have an approved plan for the operation of a child support enforcement program. However, some States have been slow in fully implementing their programs as a result of a number of factors. Statistics indicate that there is wide variance in the operation of State programs. Looking at collections since the beginning of the program on behalf of AFDC and non-AFDC families, the States reporting the largest amount of collections are Michigan, California, New York and Pennsylvania. . . .
>
> States have varied in the extent to which they are developing and expanding components of the child support program. Nationwide there was a 23 percent increase from fiscal year 1977 to 1978 in the number of cases for which paternity was established (89,000 to 110,000). Twenty seven jurisdictions reported an increase in such cases in that time period, and 24 showed no increase or a decrease. The number of parents located increased between fiscal years 1977 and 1978 for the nation as a whole (430,000 to 454,000). Thirty jurisdictions reported increases in that period.

SEN. COM. ON FINANCE, STAFF DATA AND MATERIALS ON CHILD SUPPORT, REPORT C.P. 96-7 (March 19, 1979) 96th Cong. 1st Sess., p. 6.

15. *See* Chambers, *Men Who Know They Are Watched: Some Benefits and Costs for Jailing for Nonpayment of Support,* 75 MICH. L. REV. 900 (1977). *Also see* WALL STREET JOURNAL, August 25, 1976, p. 28; U.S. NEWS & WORLD REPORT, February 12, 1979, p. 50.

16. *See* DEPT. OF H.E.W., SOC. & REHAB. SERV., "HOW THEY DO IT," CHILD SUPPORT PAYMENTS CONTROL, MASSACHUSETTS, WASHINGTON (SRS) 75-21223 (July 1974). Zumbrun & Parslow, *Absent Parent Child Support: The California Experience,* 8 FAM.L.Q. 329 (1974).

17. *See* 1979 REPORT.

beginning to make itself felt at the local level. *But the very fact that many areas so far have shown little vigor in implementing their programs bodes well for future collection figures: There remains substantial potential that has barely been tapped.*

An essential step that remains to be taken before the program can reach its full potential relates to local staffing. Inadequacy of local funding has been a pervasive problem. In a sort of "Catch 22," it appears that the typical local program is funded only *after* collections are coming in. Many localities still lack the initiative or optimism to provide the "pump-priming" money needed to get their enforcement program under way. Where enforcement efforts have been started, bottlenecks often have been the first visible consequence. The Child Support Enforcement Project of the National District Attorneys Association reports that chief problems are obtaining adequate courtroom time and keeping the detailed records required to qualify for federal reimbursements and incentives. In some jurisdictions overburdened judges have set quotas on the number of child support cases they will hear each month.[18] As collection efforts intensify, this situation will get worse. The states must take a hard and comprehensive look at all aspects of staffing requirements. New judges, assistant state's attorneys and supporting personnel are needed. The states will do what is needed as soon as they come to believe that the broader social and (preferably) even the immediate financial rewards of fair enforcement of child support obligations are worth that investment. Federal help may be on the way:

> During the 95th Congress the [Senate Finance] committee approved several additional amendments to the child support law. A provision was included in H.R.

---

18. *See* 3 F.L.R. 2244-45 (Feb. 15, 1977).

13511 authorizing Federal matching for expenditures for judges and other court personnel which are clearly identifiable and directly related to services performed under the child support enforcement program. The amendment was deleted in conference. The committee also reported as amendments to H.R. 12973 provisions strengthening the child support collection and disbursement requirements; increasing Federal matching (from 75 to 90 percent) for the costs to States and localities of developing new computerized management information systems, expanding or enhancing their existing systems, or utilizing model systems developed by HEW's Office of Child Support Enforcement; extending IRS collection responsibilities to non-AFDC child support enforcement cases. The Senate did not act on these provisions prior to adjournment.[19]

---

19. SEN. COM. ON FINANCE, DATA AND MATERIALS FOR THE FISCAL YEAR 1980 FINANCE COMMITTEE REPORT UNDER THE CONGRESSIONAL BUDGET ACT C.P. 96-3, 96th Cong. 1st Sess., p. 40 (February 1979). *See also* 96th Cong. 1st Sess., S. 1396, explained by Senator Hatfield at CONG. REC. S. 8413 (June 25, 1979):

Mr. Hatfield, Mr. President, earlier this year I introduced S. 941. Today I am introducing for myself, Mr. Leahy and Mr. Packwood an updated version of that amendment to the Social Security Act, which would permit States such as Oregon and Vermont with excellent State programs to retain 15 percent of the support collected on AFDC public assistance cases.

The bill I am introducing would correct an inequity in the child support program that was unforeseen when the program was originally designed. At that time, it appeared that the incentive provisions of title IV-D of the Social Security Act were necessary to encourage local political subdivisions of States with county-administered and State-supervised programs to become actively involved in implementing the program. That goal has been achieved in most of such States.

Unfortunately, the present IV-D incentive system has created a completely unforeseen result by tearing down and eroding away the effectiveness of some State-administered child support programs which were in operation and performing well at the time the IV-D programs started. It has also inhibited the development of some State-administered programs which had not existed previously.

In June, 1980, Congress enacted legislation that realized a number of these goals.[19.1]

So far, OSCE has been lenient in allowing the states time to gear up for the program. Federal audits of state programs ultimately will pin-point problems and help provide

---

My bill would extend the incentive program to those 42 States administered programs which collect child support on their own behalf. The cost would be minimal and the value great since it would provide the funding necessary to enlarge some of those State programs to provide the child support services needed by many of their residents. . . .

At the same time, my amendment would establish performance criteria beginning in fiscal year 1982 to encourage those States — or political subdivisions — without an adequate program to develop one. After all the program would then be over 6 years old and that should be more than enough time for all jurisdictions to have an effective program for child support and determination of paternity programs.

The State or political subdivision, as applicable, would have to meet one of the following performance requirements to be eligible for child support collection incentives after September 30, 1981:

First. The total of the amounts collected on behalf of AFDC families by a State on its own behalf, or by a political subdivision on its own behalf, during any quarter of any fiscal year must equal or exceed the total of the expenditures incurred during such quarter by such State, or by such political division, as the case may be, in collecting such amounts; or

Second. The total of the amount collected on behalf of AFDC families by the State during any quarter or any fiscal year must exceed 3.5 percent of the total expenditures made during that same quarter in the form of money payments for AFDC recipients.

My bill would also provide that, at least 50 percent of the incentives received by the State or political subdivision, as applicable, would be expended to enhance or improve the scope of the State's plan.

To reduce the administrative burden on the States, the States would be authorized to determine the amount of the incentive to which they are entitled on the total amount of collections they made on their behalf during the quarter rather than on a case-by-case basis. There would, however, be no change to the present system of determining the amount of the incentives of the political subdivisions of a State. They would still compute the amount of incentives due a political subdivision on a case-by-case basis.

19.1. *Infra* text at notes 102-106.

solutions, by assistance and by the threat of federal sanctions.[20]

2. "Cost-Benefit" Evaluation — What Cost, What Benefit?

The returns reported by OCSE seem to indicate success. However, what is "success?" A sensible question comes from those who wonder whether child support enforcement is "cost-benefit effective." The basic question goes to the *transfer* costs. As will be shown, few clear answers appear. Only one point seems obvious: Enforcement should cease when too large a percentage of AFDC-related support collections goes to the enforcers rather than to the families concerned. When what is billed as *child* support enforcement turns into an income transfer program from (mostly rather poor) fathers to lawyers, social workers and other enforcement personnel, we shall have overshot the mark.

Despite the obvious legitimacy of the "cost-benefit" question, an unqualified answer is impossible. Even a properly differentiated evaluation is elusive at best. Clearly various studies have (too simplistically) measured dollars

---

20. The Deputy Director of OCSE writes:

The effectiveness audits of State programs for the period January 1, 1977 through September 30, 1977 are completed, final reports have been issued and are available to the public. OCSE recommendations for audit penalties will be made to the Secretary shortly. Final decisions on any penalties will be made by the Secretary and will be released to the public at that time. The field work for the FY-78 program audits is completed for half of the States and interim reports will soon be issued. Administrative cost audits were performed in 16 States and interim reports are to be issued by December 31, 1979. However, these interim reports are not available to the public. In addition, two special reviews have been completed by the Audit Division on undistributed collections in California and New York. The California review is final and available to the public. An interim audit report has been issued for New York and will be finalized in approximately three months. [Letter of December 26, 1979, from Louis B. Hays, Esq., Deputy Director, OCSE, to Harry D. Krause.]

returned against dollars expended in child support enforcement. Aside from occasional anecdotes,[21] the states and OCSE most commonly report results in these terms.[22] An early positive answer to the cost-effectiveness question was produced for HEW by Arthur Young & Company on the basis of such data.[23] OCSE continues to seek similar answers.[24]

---

21. The WASHINGTON POST, Monday, March 13, 1978 p. A-1:

While some fathers are too poor to pay, the program's deputy director, Louis B. Hays, said in an interview that officials have discovered plenty of well-to-do fathers:

In Sacramento, officials in one nonsupport action discovered the father was a retired military officer who was collecting both a pension and a salary from a second job, with a total income of $60,000 a year.

In Michigan, a law student who had divorced his wife years earlier and fallen $5,000 behind on $20-a-month child-support payments was tracked down when his family went on welfare. He had advanced considerably in his profession — he was now a judge.

Also in Michigan, a man who at the time of his divorce was ordered to pay $100-a-month-child support, was $13,000 in arrears. His family went on welfare. He was tracked down and discovered to be an official of an aircraft manufacturing company in California. When he learned that officials were after him, he turned the matter over to his attorney and sent $10,000 as a downpayment on his arrears. "He's now caught up and current in his payments," says Hays.

In Utah, a man in default on monthly payments was found to own half a financial corporation and a fast-food chain. "He's now paying $625 a month and is current in his payments," said Hays.

Hays said that while statistics are still not complete, at least half of the fathers tracked down "have the capacity to pay some reasonable level of child support and some have rather substantial incomes. State officials say some doctors and lawyers making up to $100,000 a year have been evading child support. Not a high percent, but a few hundred.

22. *Supra* note 5.

23. HEW, SOCIAL AND REHABILITATION SERVICE, ABSENT PARENT CHILD SUPPORT: COST BENEFIT ANALYSIS (Executive Summary, submitted by Arthur Young & Co., Dec. 1975, HEW Contract No. SRS-7456); *See also* DETAILED SUMMARY OF FINDINGS, submitted December 1975.

24. 1 CHILD SUPPORT REPORT, No. 10, p. 4 (October 1979):

This month's featured indicator of program effectiveness is the ratio

To be sure, the traditional "dollars spent vs. dollars

of *total* collections to *total* program expenditures for the first and second quarters of FY 79. Both the AFDC and non-AFDC components are included in both the numerator and denominator. The ratios are expressed in terms of collection per dollar of expenditures.

State	Total Collections per Dollar of Total Expenditures 1st & 2nd Qtr. FY 79
1. Michigan	16.97
2. Pennsylvania	13.90
3. Oregon	12.42
4. Delaware	7.76
5. Massachusetts	5.81
6. Hawaii	4.82
7. Connecticut	4.37
8. New Jersey	4.25
9. Wisconsin	4.13
10. Rhode Island	3.68

The ratio on a nationwide basis is 3.71.

See also Welfare Research, Inc., Warrants Demonstration Projects Under HEW Grant (Section 1110, Social Security Act), and *cf.*, Contract Number SRS-74-56 evaluating California data antedating the enactment of Title IV. A complex "decision tree" formula for evaluating the cost-effectiveness of establishing paternity was constructed for OCSE by the University of Southern California's Center for Health Services Research in their report under Grant No. 18-P-90263/9-01. (Report of June 1976, Appendix A and Chapter 4).

Alternatively, the Senate Finance Committee suggests [Senate Comm. on Finance, 96th Cong., 1st Sess., STAFF DATA AND MATERIALS ON CHILD SUPPORT at 6 (Committee Print 96-7 March 19, 1979)]:

[P]erhaps a better way to measure the effectiveness of a State's child support program is to look at AFDC payments. In fiscal year 1978, the State of Utah ranked first by this measure, with collections making up 11.2 percent of their total AFDC payments. Washington was second, with collections equalling 9.5 percent of their payments, Michigan was third with 9.3 percent and New Hampshire was fourth with 9.1 percent. (In the prior year, the four top-ranking States were Washington, Michigan, New Hampshire and Idaho, in that order.)

collected" approach to measuring cost-effectiveness of child

For the United States as a whole the percentage was 4.4 in 1978 (increased from 4.1 percent in 1977). Twenty-six jurisdictions had percentages exceeding the national percentage in 1978.

This is interesting information, but tells nothing about *cost*-effectiveness, as it ignores administrative cost. In 1979, OCSE announced [1 CHILD SUPPORT REPORT 6, July 1, 1979]:

For the first time, OCSE has computed a measure of cost-effectiveness for the AFDC portion of the child support enforcement program. The following table compares AFDC collections to AFDC expenditures for the first and second quarters of Fiscal Year 1979.

State	AFDC collections per dollar of AFDC expenditures first and second quarters FY 1979
1. Michigan	5.76
2. Massachusetts	5.21
3. Pennsylvania	4.20
4. Wisconsin	3.80
5. Rhode Island	3.69
6. Maine	3.33
7. Hawaii	2.98
8. New Hampshire	2.86
9. Iowa	2.86
10. Oregon	2.68

The figures were derived a
The figures were derived as follows: Form OCSE-4134, line 3 (Total AFDC child support collections), divided by Form OCSE-OA 41.17, line 4A(e) (Net expenditures for Federal funding, AFDC).

Neither this nor any other single ranking is the sole measure of program effectiveness. Comparisons should be taken in context with other information in performing any program evaluation.

425

support enforcement programs is tempting, but it is too crude. Specifically, when comparing operating programs that report perhaps quite different cost-benefit ratios, appropriate allowance typically is not (although it obviously should be) made for the "reach" of each program. *Any* program can achieve splendid ratios, if the easy accounts are "skimmed off" and the difficult cases left alone. *Some* of the collections successes reported by the states and OCSE, especially in the non-AFDC collection category, very probably (and presumably unintentionally) involve "skimming" as well as amounts that would have been paid without the program. A proper analysis thus must ask not only what proportion of the total outstanding support debt is sought to be enforced, but also must limit the inquiry to accounts that are in "default." There is no way of developing any of these figures reliably, because there are many levels of "default." Even if we had that data, the information would not be comparable from state to state because of the diversity of substantive support criteria and the exercise of judicial discretion. Beyond that, an intelligent comparison would require information regarding the socio-economic status of the absent parent population. Again, we have no reliable data. It *is* clear, however, that the further away any enforcement program moves from "skimming," the *worse* its ratio will appear to be — despite the obvious fact that the program that penetrates more deeply into the problem is the *better* program. Up to a point!

Any sensible qualitative assessment of a program must define an appropriate point where enforcement is to stop. The most simplistic answer would have enforcement stop

---

The corresponding figures for Fiscal Year 1978 are tabulated by state in Senate Comm. on Finance, 96th Cong., 1st Sess., STAFF DATA AND MATERIALS ON CHILD SUPPORT, Table 13 at 44-45 (Committee Print 96-7, March 19, 1979). *See also* the interesting tabulation in terms of child support collections included in AFDC payments for 1978 and 1977. *Id.*, Tables 14 and 15 at 46-49.

when the marginal cost of collecting an extra dollar of support equals one dollar. As discussed below, this answer is quite wrong. Even if it were correct, however, it would hardly be useful. What factors that reliably define the *marginal* cost of collection could be identified with sufficient precision to guard against "over-enforcement?" Complex questions cloud what proportion of general "overhead" costs (*e.g.,* office expenses, state's attorneys salaries and supporting staff, court support personnel, judicial salaries, building utilization and maintenance, utilities) should be taken into account to arrive at a true picture of the actual cost allocable to the program. Choices range from allocating these costs proportionately between the various functions performed by the offices involved to seeking to identify and "count" only the "marginal costs," *i.e.,* the *additional* funds required to collect the child support dollars.

Even if these problems could be resolved, we still would not have the immediate financial answer to the cost-benefit question. We must resist the temptation of relating the cost of collection solely to the cases actually involved in enforcement! Once establishment of paternity and enforcement of support obligations have become the rule, and as soon as absent parents learn that they cannot escape their support obligations, there will be a substantial increase in the rate of *voluntary* compliance that will not show up in official enforcement statistics. To illustrate, it is not *necessarily* cost-benefit *in*efficient to spend as much as $5 for $1 collected — if the universal certainty of enforcement produces $6 in total payments, $5 rendered voluntarily and $1 enforced. Accordingly, *any* case — even if prosecuted at a cost that is "prohibitive" in terms of only that case — serves an important purpose as a catalyst for zero-cost, voluntary payments in other cases. We probably shall never know what "multiplier" to employ, but it seems probable that, over a period of time, voluntary compliance

427

will gain increasing acceptance. *If the enforcement program is truly successful, voluntary compliance will be the norm.* When that happens, however, the cost-benefit *appearance* of the enforcement program will be very poor indeed!

Above and beyond the arithmetic involving dollars spent versus dollars collected, social value judgments must be factored into the equation. We must look further than support dollars collected and welfare dollars saved when we measure "benefit" and we must think beyond enforcement dollars expended when we measure "cost." Prominently, the interest of other dependents to whom the absent parent may be obligated (*i.e.,* his current family) merit consideration. This involves the complex question of how the "social utility" of an income transfer from "relatively poor" Family No. 2 to "very poor" Family No. 1 may and should be measured. Quite probably, the proper *social* answer may be found by concentrating on the status of the absent parent against whom support enforcement is sought and the needs of his current family. At the extreme, it seems obvious that enforcement of support obligations against a "poor" father should not be so stringent as to result in the production of two welfare families where there was only one. But the proper *social* answer may not be acceptable (nor fair) to the father's "first" dependents.[25]

A final complication goes beyond the immediate question of dollars to be collected: Our society offers as much (or more) in social entitlements and insurance as it does in wealth or current income. Viewed from this perspective, the definition of the child's legal relationship with its father has the function of making the child eligible for social or private insurance entitlements which now range far and wide. They may include survivors' benefits under the Social Security Act or veterans' laws and extend to benefits under private

---

25. *See infra,* text at notes 27-47.

insurance and pension schemes as well as workmen's compensation and wrongful death acts. This "speculative" factor is most difficult to quantify in cost-benefit terms — not only are we comparing present cost with *contingent* future benefits, but many of the benefits in question are themselves transfer payments. To explain: If the alternatives are a child's eligibility for father-related Social Security survivors' benefits or for AFDC, then the potentially substantial expense of removing the child from one public trough and putting it on another may seem wasteful. The child would benefit only to the extent the father-related benefits are greater than the assistance payments, and the taxpayer would be "out" the transfer cost. An important intangible, however, may be the removal of the "welfare stigma."

In conclusion, the political pressure exerted by proponents and opponents of the program to prove statistically that the program works or that it does not work, is all but irresistible and likely to remain so. Mindful of the considerations just outlined, the intelligent observer must be suspicious of *any* attempt to mathematically "prove" that the support enforcement program is "cost-effective," (however attractive or necessary it may be politically to play that game). Both in terms of raw figures as well as in terms of social value judgments, so many relevant factors are unknown and cannot be quantified with any degree of accuracy that a properly differentiated cost-benefit evaluation may be impossible to perform. A significant role must be left to intuition and human(e) judgment. Socially, the most productive approach to "cost-benefit" may ultimately have to weigh the other end of the enforcement equation. "Cost" may be less what it costs to prosecute and collect, than what it "costs" to pay. As discussed in detail below, collection should stop when the burden on the obligated parent becomes greater than may be justified in terms of the benefit received by the "first family" (or by society in terms of reduced welfare dependency).[26]

If a verdict regarding the support enforcement program may be attempted by this observer at this stage, the overall impression is good — even excellent. Enormous progress has been made toward alleviating a serious social problem. However, this verdict is conditional. It relates to what should be seen as the first stage of the program — it is praise for where the program stands five years after the authorizing legislation became effective. This initial period of successfully putting the basic program into place in the field and in Washington, prodding reluctant or indifferent states to cooperate, and improving the mechanics of collecting support at the national, state and local levels, is over. The time has come for a qualitative leap forward. A good program must now become better — not necessarily in dollar-cost-benefit terms, but in cost-benefit terms that reflect more of the underlying social values sought to be realized.

Throughout this volume, numerous proposals suggest specific improvements in state and federal law and, especially, regarding their interaction. There has been discussion of the importance of instituting a reasonable system of deduction of support obligations from wages; of the "case against arrears"; of the potential value (in terms of court costs saved and unconscionable arrears not accrued) of instituting flexible child support obligations that are "self-adjusting" if predefined changes in conditions occur; of the need for reform in the paternity action to provide a more efficient forum for the child as well as to improve the protection of non-fathers falsely named by the mother; of the "good cause exception" to the requirement that the

---

26. *Infra* text at notes 27-47, 74-96.

mother cooperate in support enforcement efforts; and more.

Beyond that, *Congress, OCSE and the states should single out for early attention:* (1) setting a reasonable floor, in terms of the father's ability to pay, below which there will be no support enforcement; (2) enforcing alimony obligations when related to child support; (3) according "due process" to men accused of paternity, especially by responsible utilization of blood typing tests; (4) humanizing the program by giving to the children some portion of the money collected from the father; and (5) permanently extending the full aid of the federal program to support-claimants who are not receiving public aid.

3. Setting Child Support Levels: Of Blood and Turnips.

A cynic may hypothesize that state child support laws, both in terms of substance and enforcement procedures, have been permitted to survive in their present state of disarray, unevenness and consequent unfairness only because they have *not* been enforced with any degree of regularity. Indeed, the seeming irresponsibility of American fathers may at least in part be explained in terms of unrealistic obligations being imposed and sought to be enforced under unrealistic laws.

It seems reasonable to conclude that the federal initiative that now causes the sudden activation of these laws, imposes a corresponding responsibility on the federal authorities to assure that the states develop more sensible, more uniform and more predictable support laws. So far, OCSE has failed to provide leadership regarding this crucial point. OCSE's position is stated as follows: "One of OCSE's goals for Fiscal Year 1980 is to assume a greater role in improving the child support laws in the States. However, our role is to encourage, not mandate, the States to adopt model legislation, and effective enforcement procedures." [27]

But with all reasonable respect for state sovereignty regarding family law, current federal law provides adequate room for OCSE to play an important role in defining standards for acceptable state law on these questions. If OCSE believes that this goal requires more specific federal legislation, it should work toward that. At the very minimum, in the context of OCSE-sponsored support enforcement, federal standards ultimately *must* assure less arbitrary and diverse conceptions of the "needs of the child" and the "father's ability to pay" as well as assuring less counterproductive methods of support enforcement than are now the rule.[28] Affectionate references in OCSE's *Child Support Report* to "Hanging Judge" Ralph H. Ross of Maine do not help promote a sensible climate.[29] Most citizens prefer their judges sitting.

OCSE has limited itself to setting the following guidelines:

> The State plan shall provide as follows:
> (a) There shall be a formula to be utilized by the IV-D agency in determining the amount of the support obligation pursuant to § 302.50 when there is no court order covering the obligation. Such formula must take into consideration the following criteria:
> (1) All earnings, income and resources of the absent parent including real and personal property;
> (2) The earnings potential of the absent parent;
> (3) The reasonable necessities of the absent parent;
> (4) The ability of the absent parent to borrow;
> (5) The needs of the child for whom the support is sought;

---

27. Letter of December 26, 1979 from Louis B. Hays, Esq., Deputy Director, OCSE, to Harry D. Krause.

28. *Supra* chs. I. 2, 3, II. 1.

29. 1 CHILD SUPPORT REPORT 1 (December 1979).

(6) The amount of assistance which would be paid to the child under the full standard of need of the State's IV-A plan;

(7) The existence of other dependents; and

(8) Other reasonable criteria which the State may choose to incorporate.

(b) The formula described in paragraph (2) of this section must be designed to insure, as a minimum, that the child for whom support is sought benefits from the income and resources of the absent parent on an equitable basis in comparison with any other minor children of the absent parent.

(c) The formula described in paragraph (a) of this section shall be utilized to determine the required monthly support obligation, the amount of support obligation arrearage, if any, and the amount to be paid periodically against such arrearage.[30]

By its terms, this formula applies only "when there is no court order covering the obligation," and thus is directed principally to agreements concerning support. It also may influence the formulation of IV-D support claims that are ultimately raised in court.[31] It is quite apparent, however, that this formula provides no significant improvement over typical existing state law.[32] One unusual factor, the absent parent's "ability to borrow," is only in the fewest cases a valid criterion regarding ability to pay support. It may bring forth a payment now, but typically will decrease ability to render support later — with interest!

From the standpoint of sound policy, it should be an important goal of federal involvement to assure that state enforcement efforts will not reach the point of increasing, rather than reducing, social disorganization. This involves manageable, live and let-live, levels of support. In the

---

30. 45 C.F.R. § 302.53(a) (1978).

31. *Cf.,* 45 C.F.R. § 305.50 (1978).

32. *Supra* ch. I. 2.

abstract, the issue is relatively simple. The father must be assured a standard of living that does not impair his earning capacity, his work incentive, nor his ability to provide for himself and his current functioning family, if he has established one. If a "second," current family is in the picture, it would not seem unreasonable to conclude that support enforcement for a "first family" becomes socially counterproductive when it threatens to deprive a "second family" of a realistic basis for economic survival. What is a "realistic" basis for economic and social survival?

Current state law draws no "bottom line" below which support obligations will not be enforced and neither does OCSE's formula. *That* such a line should be set seems clear. *Where* that "bottom line" is to be set is the most important of unanswered questions. Traditional state law, of course, would consider the needs of the prior family first and either ignore or discount the father's new responsibilities.[33] As previously discussed, this approach seems untenable in the light of decisions equalizing the support rights of legitimate and nonmarital children. If discrimination on the basis of illegitimacy is not permissible, discrimination on the basis of priority is equally untenable.[34]

The logical conclusion would be to put all children on an equal footing [35] regardless of priority (although age would figure in terms of need). The support award for children would thus be determined on the basis of full equality of

---

33. *Supra* ch. I. 3.

34. Gomez v. Perez, 409 U.S. 535, 93 S. Ct. 872, 35 L. Ed. 2d 56 (1973); *cf.,* Zablocki v. Redhail, 434 U.S. 374, 98 S. Ct. 673, 54 L. Ed. 2d 618 (1978). Supra ch. IV. 2-5.

35. Recognizing the problem, but begging the answer, OCSE's formula requires that "as a minimum, . . . the child for whom support is sought benefits from the income and resources of the absent parent on an *equitable* basis in comparison with other minor children of the absent parent." (Emphasis added.) 45 C.F.R. § 302.53(b).

each child's claim on the father's resources. The next question, however, is "what resources?" And it seems obvious that the term must be refined to encompass *disposable* resources only. A simplistic formula might define the father's *disposable* resources (those that are to be shared equally by all of his children) as any amount above the federally defined poverty line.[36] With appropriate adjustments for age and special needs (*e.g.,* health), that formula would ratably apportion the father's earnings in excess of the poverty level between his old and his new responsibilities.[37] Most would agree that the "bottom line" below which there should be *no* support enforcement relating to earlier responsibilities hardly could be drawn *lower,* although some welfare officials think in terms of equalizing the father's and his first family's position by exacting money from him until his standard of living resembles that provided under the AFDC program — which even when combined with food stamps does *not* reach the poverty line in any state.[38] Others will wonder whether the

---

36. In April, 1979, the Labor Department redefined the poverty level for a single urban dweller at $3,400 a year. The level rose to $4,500 for a family of two, $6,700 for a family of four and $8,900 for a family of six. The income levels are slightly less for farm families. U.S. NEWS AND WORLD REPORT, April 30, 1979. In 1977, the "poverty line" for a nonfarm family of four was $6,191. U.S. DEPT. OF COMMERCE, BUREAU OF THE CENSUS, STATISTICAL ABSTRACT OF THE UNITED STATES 1978 at 465. In 1978, that level was redefined at $6,662. WALL STREET JOURNAL, Nov. 26, 1979, p. 7.

37. A similar formula was recommended to, but not adopted by, the Senate Finance Committee Staff when a predecessor bill of P.L. 93-647 (H.R. 3153) was under consideration. *See* H. Krause, Review of Part X, Child Support, 92d Cong., 2d Sess., Soc. Sec. Amendments of 1972, Committee on Finance, U.S. Senate, H.R. 1, (unpublished consultant's paper, pp. 52-53 (1972), excerpted at H. KRAUSE, FAMILY LAW: CASES AND MATERIALS 503-504 (1976)).

38. *See* HOUSE COMM. ON WAYS AND MEANS, SOCIAL WELFARE REFORM AMENDMENTS OF 1979, 96th Cong., 1st Sess., Rept. 96-451 Part 1 at 92 (Sept. 20, 1979).

"poverty line" is not too low and whether this approach would provide an acceptable balance between the defunct and the functioning family. To repeat, the social issue is whether the formula creates too much risk of putting a potentially destructive burden on the father's new family.

The inquiry thus turns on the question of whether the analysis of the father's "ability to pay" may give priority to his current responsibilities and arrive at a support duty regarding "outside" responsibilities only after the needs of his current family are satisfied.

Despite the constitutional considerations that favor equality, it would seem to be a permissible, even a "compelling," [39] state purpose first to assure a basis of economic and social survival for the current family before a payment to other dependents is exacted. This argument would seem to permit *some* inequality of support apportionment between "old" and "new" dependents — in favor of the new. The open question is how much?

Under contract with OCSE, the Greater Community Council of New York developed a "Guide for Determining the Ability of an Absent Parent to Pay Child Support." [40] OCSE transmitted this study to state agencies, characteristically without taking a position on it.

The Guide is a sincere attempt to take into account various factors that should be considered in fixing support obligations. Unfortunately, in terms of the compelling need for a *national* policy, the effort all but defeats itself in its own preamble: "In offering the Guide, it is recognized that each state will have its own laws, and its own requirements

---

39. *See, e.g.,* Shapiro v. Thompson, 394 U.S. 618, 89 S. Ct. 1322, 22 L. Ed. 2d 600 (1969).

40. M. Sauber & E. Taittonen, Guide for Determining the Ability of an Absent Parent to Pay Child Support, 1977, (transmitted as OCSE-IM-77-12).

and point of view regarding priority of child support obligations and the determination of equitable amounts of levels of required payments."

The Guide adopts the reasonable principle that enforcement must stop at a certain point and fixes that point by reference to federal definitions of budget standards that are automatically adjusted for inflation and changes in living patterns. Significantly, the recommendation emphasizes the budget of the father's new family,[41] and

---

41. Note that cost of living increases since 1975 would require substantial updating of the 1975 figures used in this Guide.

TABLE I. FAMILY MAINTENANCE STANDARD

BASED ON COST OF LOWER BUDGET FOR A
FOUR-PERSON FAMILY URBAN UNITED
STATES, AUTUMN 1975*

Budget item	Annual cost	Monthly cost
Food at home	$2,563	$214
Food away from home	389	32
Shelter, rent**	1,391	116
Housefurnishings and operation	467	39
Transportation***	702	59
Clothing	771	64
Personal care	248	21
Medical care †	818	68
Other family consumption ††	447	37
Other items †††	436	36
Total, all goods and services	$8,232	$686
Cost adjustment for automobile owner	237	20
Total, including cost of automobile ownership	$8,469	$706

*U.S. Department of Labor, Bureau of Labor Statistics, *News,* Table I. Annual Costs of Lower Budget for a Four-Person Family, Autumn 1975, May 5, 1976.

437

would consider for collection for "old" family responsibilities only such amounts as exceed the new family's budget, plus allowable "deductions," which are classified as "mandatory" [42] and for "special

---

** Includes contract rent plus heating fuel, gas, electricity, water, specified equipment, and insurance on household contents.

*** Weighted proportion of average costs of automobile owners and nonowners.

† Weighted proportion of average costs of families paying full cost, families paying half cost and families covered by non-contributory insurance plans (paid by employer).

†† Includes reading, recreation, tobacco products, alcoholic beverages, education and miscellaneous expenditures.

††† Includes allowances for gifts and contributions, life insurance and occupational expenses.

42. *Allowable Mandatory Deductions.* Nearly all persons are subject to deductions from their earned or other income. Some are voluntary as, for example, savings bond withholdings. Others are mandatory as, for example, tax withholdings.

Allowable mandatory deductions from total funds are defined in this Guide as deductions over which the absent parent has no control. In determining funds available for child support payments, the total amount of all such deductions should be subtracted from total funds (income and prorated assets). The following allowable deductions are recommended (not all deductions are applicable in every state, nor to every person):

— Federal income tax (withholdings at an appropriate level) *
— Federal social security tax (FICA)
— State and other local income tax (withholdings at an appropriate level) *
— State unemployment insurance tax, where applicable
— State disability insurance
— Union dues, where required
— Retirement contributions (other than FICA) if required as a condition of employment
— Garnishment or similar proceedings as provided by state law, solely for the payment of support obligation and any arrearages

* Appropriate tax tables offer a guideline for approximating the reasonableness of the level of withholdings.

438

needs." [43] Multipliers redefine the precise amount of

Other regular deductions from earned or other income are presumed to be voluntary and under the control of the parent. These should *not* be deducted from total available funds in calculating the child support obligation:

— Savings bonds purchase
— Contributions to religious, charitable, or educational organizations
— Union dues, union initiation fees (except as described above)
— Credit union savings or loan payment **
— Premiums for medical and hospital insurance (unless coverage includes absent parent's children in custodial family)
— Deferred annuity payments
— Contributions to retirement programs that are not a condition of employment
— Payment for rent or board to an employer
— Garnishment,** other than for the payment of child support obligation as described above
— Voluntary wage assignment — an agreement negotiated generally as a condition of a loan **
— Repayment of a loan or payroll advances made by the employer **

** If the purpose of the garnishment, voluntary wage assignment, credit union or employer loan or payroll advance is to purchase or make payment for special needs such withholdings could qualify as allowable deductions for special needs from total funds available.

Since the Family Maintenance Standard includes allowances for hospital and medical insurance, life insurance, contributions and work related expenses, voluntary payroll withholdings for these purposes should not be deducted from total funds available to the absent parent for child support obligation.

43. *Allowable Deductions for Special Needs.* The Family Maintenance Standard includes allowances for necessary goods and services at a

439

money available to pay child support in terms of the

specified level of living. While there is merit to using a single standard — adjusted for family size — for all families, actual family situations may deviate from this standard to the point where family living costs are seriously affected. To avoid serious inequities that could result in individual cases, this Guide recommends allowances be made for special justifiable needs with specifically defined expenses that are continuing or fixed costs to the parent. The recommended deductions from total funds available to the absent parent for such special needs are:

— Medical expenses, when not reimbursed by insurance and when the cost exceeds the amount provided for medical care in the basic Family Maintenance Standard.
— Payment on debts contracted for large medical or dental expenses, not reimbursed by insurance.
— Educational expenses, or special child care arrangements, when related to a medical or health problem. Such expenses should be treated as an unusual medical expense and a deduction allowed for the special need.
— Child care costs for a child counted as a dependent in the absent parent's household, when necessary to enable the absent parent to be employed. Such an allowance can also be made to enable the absent parent's spouse to be employed, provided that spouse's income is included in the determination of total funds available to the absent parent.
— Cost of special clothing or equipment required for employment and not reimbursed by the employer.
— Car payments, when the car is necessary for employment. The car should be of "reasonable" value. Payments on a car used for pleasure are not to be included as a deduction for special needs.
— Employment expenses (unreimbursed by employer) of a dependent wage earner if the income of such a dependent is included in the total funds available to the absent parent and the dependent is included in the count of family size in determining the appropriate Family Maintenance Standard for that family. (The Family Maintenance Standard includes work related expenses for only one wage earner.)

440

size of the absent parent's new family.[44]

The trouble is that the proposed budget and allowances push the Community Council to an unrealistically high income level before there would be *any* payments to an "old" family. This is not surprising since the budget proposed for the father's new family is derived from actual income and consumption figures in "normal" (presumably undivorced)

44.

TABLE II. FAMILY MAINTENANCE STANDARD BY FAMILY SIZE

BASED ON COST OF LOWER BUDGET FOR A
FOUR-PERSON FAMILY URBAN UNITED
STATES, AUTUMN 1975

Family size	Equivalence weights*	Dollar amount for goods and services	
		Annual	Monthly
1	.52	$ 4,281	$357
2	.68	5,598	466
3	.84	6,915	576
4	1.00	8,232**	686**
5	1.16	9,549	796
6***	1.32***	10,866	906

* Equivalence weights devised for the Public Services Administration and used to determine income eligibility for service programs under Title XX of the Social Security Act. 40 Fed. Reg. No. 125, June 27, 1975.

** From Table I, Total, all goods and services, weighted proportion of average costs for automobile owners and nonowners.

*** Although the Public Services Administration adjustment for family size above six persons is the addition of 3 percentage points to the equivalence weight for a family of six for each additional family member, this Guide recommends 10 percent (.10) as a more equitable and realistic increase which, at the same time, takes account of the economy of providing for larger families.

U.S. households. In this manner, the study reaches a conclusion that would prevent significant amounts of child support from being collected from absent parents who earn less than solid middle class incomes.[45]

In Utopia, that might be the answer. Indeed, even in our world it might well be desirable to give the father's current family the overriding weight the New York study recommends — *if AFDC support for the "old family" were more adequate (and more uniform nationally).*[46] However, given the current state of affairs, application of the study's recommendations would produce potentially enormous differences between the standards of living of the father's first and second families. By excusing contributions from a father who enjoys the satisfactory standard of living proposed in the Community Council budget, the formula relegates "earlier" children to the relative squalor of inadequate AFDC support. Accordingly, the Guide's attempt to define the "bottom line" solely and so generously in terms of the father's current responsibilities and wholly at the expense of his "old" dependents, cannot be justified — not in terms of fairness nor perhaps in terms of constitutionality.

This discussion does not solve the basic dilemma, it only points toward a solution. It seems clear that, on the one hand, the pragmatic attraction of the New York Study's "overemphasis" on the needs of the second family must be resisted. On the other hand, it is equally clear that OCSE

---

45. In 1975, the median family income was $13,719. U.S. DEPT. OF COMMERCE, BUREAU OF THE CENSUS, STATISTICAL ABSTRACT OF THE UNITED STATES 1978 at 455. In 1978, the median family income stood at $17,640, up from $14,958 in 1976 and $12,051 in 1973. However, taking into account inflation and expressed in constant dollars, the 1973 figure actually was slightly *higher* than the 1978 figure. WALL STREET JOURNAL, November 26, 1979, p. 7.

46. *Infra* text at note 82.

must set "bottom line" enforcement standards to avoid the worst of all possible consequences of the enforcement program — to end up with two broken families where previously only one existed. The task is to find the formula that will assure a reasonable approximation of financial equality between all of the father's dependents, at a "livable" level for all.

Part of the problem is that this analysis has remained, so far, altogether on the "collection side" of the child support equation. The "disbursement side" is equally important. Part of the solution to the difficult task of providing the "equitable" apportionment of resources between the old and the new families that OCSE itself seeks, may (perhaps unexpectedly) lie there.

Specifically, while society's interest in the economic and social survival of the family that is currently functioning is great, it does not follow that this social interest should be asserted at the sole expense of the "earlier" children. Instead, *society* should stand ready to incur the public expense that would allow the "earlier" children to live under a budget similar to that allowed the current family. *And, some part of this goal may be realized by a new AFDC-related formula for applying the father's support payments: More would go to his children and less for reimbursement of the state.*[47] The resulting inequality between AFDC families with paying fathers and those without could be justified far more easily than the inequality threatened in the balance between the fathers' earlier and current dependents.

4. Enforcement of Alimony Obligations.

To state the principles relating to the rights of *children* more clearly, not considered in the preceding section were

---

47. *Infra* text at notes 74-96.

the complicating questions of a divorced or current *wife's* support claim, the possible priority of either claim, and the mother's duty and ability to help support her children. To the extent, however, that the payment made by the father supports the mother in her ability to care for the child, lines between alimony and child support become blurred. Accordingly, various proposals to bring the enforcement of alimony obligations under the federal act [48] are not without merit and should be considered.

A strong argument favors at least the ex-wife with children in her custody. At the AFDC level, public aid supplied to the mother is reimbursed by the collection of alimony. More importantly, at *any* level, support awards typically do not adequately or clearly distinguish between alimony and child support. Indeed, the income tax laws positively encourage "mislabelling" of child support as alimony, because it thereby becomes tax-deductible by the payor.[49] If as is often the case, the payor's marginal tax rate is higher than that of the recipient, a cash saving results, thus increasing the total resources available for division. Aside from this middle class tax "gimmick," there are other reasons not to distinguish very clearly between alimony and child support. After all, the mother needs the alimony to support herself so that she can provide care for the children. Worse, without the alimony payment, she may have to dip into child support to support herself. In a detailed survey of judges' attitudes in Illinois, the following

---

48. *E.g.,* HEW, LEGISLATIVE PROPOSALS FOR FISCAL YEAR 1980 BUDGET. A savings to the federal government of $18 million annually is expected. (Source: Senate Finance Committee Staff). *Cf.,* 1 CHILD SUPPORT REPORT, No. 3, March 1979, p. 4. It should be noted that 42 U.S.C.A. § 602(a)(26) *now* requires assignment of support rights accrued from "any other person," including spouses. What is not provided, is access to the collection mechanism. *Cf.,* SSA-AT-79-22 (June 18, 1979) p. 3.

49. Commissioner v. Lester, 366 U.S. 299, 81 S. Ct. 1343, 6 L. Ed. 2d 306 (1961). *See* H. KRAUSE, FAMILY LAW IN A NUTSHELL 358-60 (1977).

findings underscore the close relationship between alimony and child support:

> Pursuing the question of alimony the judges were asked if they utilized a "rule of thumb" in its determination where no children were involved. Seventy-nine percent answered that they had not developed any such guideline. The twenty-one percent that had, most often cited "need" as the principal factor in their decision. Those that had developed a "rule" often noted that there was minimal use of it since alimony was infrequently requested in divorces where children were not involved. Along this line, several justices said their "rule of thumb" was to not award alimony in the absence of children unless there were severely mitigating circumstances.
>
> Where children were involved, twenty-seven percent stated they had developed some guidelines or that their guidelines differed from situations without children. In these circumstances there was a tendency to approach alimony as one element in a financial package, which also contained support. Generally more emphasis was placed on the total amount provided than the division between the two.[50]

Some may argue that alimony enforcement under the program recommends itself simply because the mechanism is available. That, however, may not be a wholly satisfactory idea. So far, we have made the social value judgment that *child* support is so essential that "heroic" new measures are needed to facilitate enforcement. When alimony is wholly divorced from child support, however, when the ex-wife does not have children in her custody, a second value judgment may be required. While the bankruptcy laws (which treat child support and alimony

---

50. Johnson, *Divorce, Alimony, Support and Custody: A Survey of Judges' Attitudes in One State,* 3 F.L.R. 4001, 4003 (1976).

alike) [51] seem to furnish an analogy in favor of alimony enforcement, we must be aware that any extended use of the new enforcement mechanism will quickly generate all sorts of new demands on the system — especially regarding the parent-locator feature. Congress already is considering whether recourse to the parent-locator system should be allowed in child custody cases.[52] Can the commercial creditor be far behind? Or various agencies of the federal and state governments? Caution may be indicated, lest too great a price be paid in loss of privacy.[53] Moreover, a national trend is running against alimony, and alimony without child custody already may be quantitatively so unimportant as not to merit opening the door. A final consideration may be that, where there is long-term alimony without child custody, there typically is enough money in the picture so that traditional collection procedures are reasonably adequate. To summarize, current legislative proposals should be clarified to allow alimony enforcement at all levels (and not only for AFDC recipients), but only if and *for so long as it is combined with child support collection.*[54]

5. The Case for Blood Typing Evidence.

Serious consideration must be given to collateral enforcement costs that may produce *non*liability for support and thereby threaten a program's good-looking cost versus collection ratio. For instance, the administration of the

---

51. For the time being, however, *assignments* of support to the state are dischargeable in bankruptcy. *See* OCSE-AT-79-8 (October 9, 1978) and *supra* ch. I.3., text at notes 85-87.

52. *E.g.,* H.R. 1290, H.R. 3654, 96th Cong., 1st Sess. (1979).

53. *Supra* ch. VII.2., text at notes 12-17.

54. *See* H.R. 4904 § 401, 96th Cong., 1st Sess. (Nov. 9, 1979) which proposes to accomplish many of the objectives just stated.

"good cause" exception to the mother's duty to cooperate will make enforcement more expensive — all the more so if the exception is granted.[55] The provision of counsel to indigent men will cost money — both to pay the defense lawyer and (if he is successful) in terms of losing a potential "father." [56] Similarly, providing blood tests to men named as fathers of nonmarital children is costly not only because of the expense of the tests, but if the test *exclude* the accused as a potential father, the enforcer has lost a potential support obligor. Prosecutors (and support enforcement authorities generally) have been understandably reluctant to commit scarce funds to activities that seem to work against their own interests.

However, now that Washington is putting its resources and initiative behind the ascertainment of nonmarital paternity and support enforcement, it cannot in good conscience keep its hands off the means by which these obligations are defined and enforced. The program's concern with giving the child and the taxpayer their due must be matched with equal concern that the man accused of being the father be accorded due process. When providing counsel, the California Supreme Court has stated the case eloquently:

> Without the assistance of counsel, neither [man] was in a position to respond adequately to the district attorney's discovery requests nor to initiate discovery himself. Without the assistance of counsel, neither was able to procure the assistance of experts to perform blood group tests which might conclusively have exonerated him. . . .
>
> Appointment of counsel for indigent defendants will make the fact-finding process in paternity cases more accurate, thereby furthering the state's *legitimate*

55. *Supra* ch. IX. 2-5.
56. *Supra* ch. V. 7.

interests in securing support for dependent children. . . .

Appointment of counsel will not only advance substantial state interest, it should serve the child's interests as well. The child, to a large extent forgotten in such proceedings, has been termed the "principal plaintiff" in a paternity action. In a sense, it is the child's identity that is litigated in a proceeding to determine parentage. Any determination that a particular individual is a child's biological father may have profound sociological and psychological ramifications. Further, the child's rights of support and inheritance against the father are at issue, as well as his or her future obligation to support the father. *It is in the child's interest not only to have it adjudicated that some man is his or her father and thus liable for support, but to have some assurance that the correct person has been so identified. When the state initiates paternity proceedings, whether on behalf of the mother or the child, the state owes it to the child to ensure that an accurate determination of parentage will be made.*[57]

With the possible exception of effective legal representation, nothing is as urgently in need of attention — and as easily accessible to constructive federal involvement — as is the field of blood testing. Emphasis on blood typing is all the more urgent in the face of substantial evidence that indicates considerable willingness on the part of zealous prosecutors (whose superiors look for attractive dollar rations) to short-change the "justice ratio" by avoiding blood typing tests. True, blood typing tests will reduce the number of men now held liable for child support, but only by eliminating the possibly numerous *non*-fathers now ordered to support the children of other men. More-

---

57. Sales v. Cortez, 24 Cal. 3d 22, 30-34, 154 Cal. Rptr. 529, 535-37, 593 P.2d 226, 232-35 (1979) (some citations and footnotes omitted, emphasis added).

over, not all aspects of blood typing tests work against the child support enforcer. As discussed in detail earlier, probability calculations in many cases may provide circumstantial evidence that more or less positively indicates paternity.[58]

Judge Kenneth Turner of Tennessee's Shelby County explains that "ninety-five percent of the suspected fathers admit paternity even before the case comes to trial" and, in Forrest City, Arkansas, Samantha Fisher, a IV-D official, boasts that "seventy-five percent of the people I interview admit paternity and we have no problem getting payments from them." [59] Similar reports come informally from all over the country. But how many of these men are in truth the fathers? What is it that causes these men to admit paternity so freely and incur eighteen years of support liability? Is it what Judge Turner thinks — "most of these guys feel pretty good afterward about having done the right thing" — or do these men simply admit sexual access to the mother and feel uncomfortable with the idea that "their" girl may have had a concurrent relationship with another man at the probable time of conception? To identify the error rate, a most useful study — yet to be commissioned — would run full blood tests on a representative sample of these men who admit paternity for the asking. It is by no means inconceivable that the results of such a study would be sobering and compel the conclusion that voluntary admissions of paternity should be accepted only upon careful investigation and, if there is the slightest doubt, blood tests.

Before going on, it is worth reemphasizing here that courts are becoming increasingly concerned about

---

58. *Supra* ch. VI. 2. B.

59. U.S. NEWS AND WORLD REPORT at p. 50, Feb. 12, 1979; 1 OCSE CHILD SUPPORT REPORT at p. 4, (Sept. 1979).

"voluntary" admissions of paternity and corresponding assumptions of support obligations when circumstances make it appear that undue pressures have been brought to bear upon the man.[60]

Of course, costs *are* a problem. Even assuming performance at a specified level of quality (and getting away from the irresponsible practice of some enforcement agencies to assign paternity testing to the "lowest bidder" without effective quality control), reliable cost figures are difficult to isolate.[61] So much depends on allocation of overhead and the volume factor. Given a fixed overhead, however, it is safe to assume that the greater the volume of tests in any given laboratory, the lower will be the unit cost. If the laboratory in question exists primarily for other purposes, it may not be unfair to emphasize the direct

---

60. County of Ventura v. Castro, 93 Cal. App. 3d 402 (1979). *See supra* ch. 5.2, text at note 12.

61. An informal survey of 9 laboratories conducted by Dr. Richard H. Walker, chairman of the Committee on Parentage Testing of the American Association of Blood Banks in Jan. 1979, produced the following information:

SURVEY OF CHARGES FOR PATERNITY TESTING

JANUARY 1979

	Red Cell Systems	Enzyme & Protein Systems	HLA	Total Charge for Trio
1) West Coast	9	15	no	$ 750
2) West Coast	9	None	yes	600
3) North Central	9	3	yes	480
4) North Central	6	10	yes	420
5) North Central	5	None	yes	400
6) West Coast	1	0	yes	375
7) North Central	7	1	yes	325
8) North Central	8	6	no	275
9) Mid West	6	0	yes	450

additional costs of paternity tests and discount the general overhead. But *no matter what the precise cost of typing blood, there is no question that these costs are only a fraction of the staggering amounts potentially involved in eighteen years of child support obligation.*

Aside from the cost factor, which points toward large-volume laboratories, the stringent quality controls that must govern testing are in some respects impossible or impractical to maintain by small laboratories or individual testers. Nor could compliance by the latter be monitored effectively. Since geographic concentration of blood testing for paternity cases offers considerable economies of scale, centralization seems to be the most sensible long-term solution. Only laboratories that are involved routinely and continuously in paternity testing are in a position economically to assure themselves of the highest professional expertise. Only they can afford to maintain the expensive and extensive stocks of fresh testing sera that are needed to execute sophisticated blood tests.

In light of this, it is unfortunate that one of the most significant paternity-related features of the federal child support enforcement legislation — which had been passed by the Senate several times — was omitted by the Conference Committee in a final hour of compromise between the House and Senate versions of the Act. The latter had contained the following clause:

> *Regional Laboratories to Establish Paternity Through Analysis and Classification of Blood*
> Sec. 461. (a) The Secretary shall, after appropriate consultation and study of the use of blood typing as evidence in judicial proceedings to establish paternity, establish, or arrange for the establishment or designation of, in each region of the United States, a laboratory which he determines to be qualified to provide services in analyzing and classifying blood for the purpose of determining paternity, and which is

451

prepared to provide such services to courts and public agencies in the region to be served by it.

(b) Whenever a laboratory is established or designated for any region by the Secretary under this section, he shall take such measures as may be appropriate to notify appropriate courts and public agencies (including agencies administering any public welfare program within such region) that such laboratory has been so established or designated to provide services, in analyzing and classifying blood for the purpose of determining paternity, for courts and public agencies in such region.

(c) The facilities of any such laboratory shall be made available without cost to courts and public agencies in the region to be served by it.

(d) There is hereby authorized to be appropriated for each fiscal year such sums as may be necessary to carry out the provisions of this section.[62]

Centralized blood typing facilities such as those contemplated in the provision just quoted are not an untried idea. Indeed, the proposal here under discussion was inspired by the existence abroad, especially in Copenhagen, Oslo, and Stockholm, of blood typing laboratories serving the whole of their respective countries.[63] Nor would the procedure contemplated by the unsuccessful legislative proposal have been unduly cumbersome or complicated. Many American blood banks and other laboratories are presently able to conduct complex blood tests.[64]

Aside from the idea of centralized laboratories, we should

---

62. H.R. 17045 (Senate) 93rd Cong., 2d Sess. (Dec. 14, 1974).

63. *See* Appendix F *infra*.

64. Polesky & Krause, *Blood Typing in Disputed Paternity Cases: Capabilities of American Laboratories,* 10 Fam. L.Q. 287 (1976), 17 Transfusion 521 (1977), Appendix H; Using Blood Tests to Establish Paternity, Condensed Report, Center for Policy Research, Inc., Dept. of HEW, OCSE, IM-77-11 (1977). HHS (formerly HEW) has published two useful references through its National Child Support Reference Center: Tempo No. 4, *Blood Testing* and Tempo No. 9 *Blood Laboratories* (1980).

note the Senate's vote that *all* blood typing tests be performed at public expense. It certainly is cause for concern that the significant cost of blood tests and the prevailing practice under State law of charging these costs to the accused man [65] (even if the tests exonerate him) [66] are serious obstacles to having blood tests performed. Ironically, it is more often that the "backward" state which views paternity proceedings as criminal may provide blood tests at public expense.[67] Where the action is civil, the climate is only slowly changing in favor of the indigent accused.[68] One forward-looking case has held that "the right to have blood tests performed cannot be denied an indigent defendant without violating the equal protection clause of the Fourteenth Amendment. . . ." [69] Federal financial participation is now available, however, to defray the cost of blood typing in IV-D cases.

Despite the expenditure of hundreds of thousands of dollars in research funds and the expression of "good will," [70] OCSE has not effectively moved into this crucial

---

65. Typical provisions allow the court, "in its discretion" to require "the person requesting the blood grouping test to pay the cost thereof." VA. CODE ANN. § 20-61.2 (Cum. Supp. 1978); N.C. GEN. STAT. 49-7 (1975).

66. As one judge cynically put it, in such cases the defendant typically is more than happy to pay for the tests!

67. Supra ch. V.6. This may extend to states still viewing the paternity action as "quasi-criminal" in nature. *Cf.*, Lurry v. Mills, 152 N.J. Super. 127, 377 A.2d 804 (1977).

68. *See* Michael B. v. Superior Court, 86 Cal. App. 3d 1006, 150 Cal. Rptr. 586 (1978); *In re* Proceeding for Paternity Under Article 5 of Family Court Act, 82 Misc. 2d 1094, 371 N.Y.S.2d 611 (1975); Smith v. Walker, 138 N.J. Super. 187, 350 A.2d 319 (1975).

69. Franklin v. District Court of Jud. Dist., 571 P.2d 1072, 1074 (Colo., 1977).

70. OCSE strongly encourages the use of extended factor blood testing and HLA tissue typing in contested paternity cases. We also support any legislative or judicial awareness initiatives that permit the admission of blood tests as inclusionary as well as exclusionary

area. On the contrary, OCSE's occasional, unselective transmission of unevaluated information [71] may be a disservice to the need for better understanding in this area. Despite all disclaimers of responsibility,[72] these missives carry OCSE's persuasive authority to the recipient. Worse yet, they are too often the *only* information readily available to enforcement staffs. What is needed is precisely

---

> evidence. Each jurisdiction entering into agreements with paternity testing labs should specify precise quality control limits and verification procedures as an essential part of the agreement. The IV-D agency should seek appropriate medical consultation within the State in preparing the agreement. This office has always and will continue to provide Federal financial participation for blood typing costs if the tests have been requested by the IV-D agency or ordered by the judge.

Letter of December 26, 1979, from Louis B. Hays, Esq., Deputy Director, OCSE, to Harry D. Krause.

71. For instance, OCSE's CHILD SUPPORT REPORT, carried the following notice in an early 1979 issue:

> HLA BLOOD TESTING ARTICLE AVAILABLE. The National Child Support Enforcement Reference Center has acquired copies of an article by Paul I. Terasaki entitled "Resolution of HLA Testing of 1,000 Paternity Cases not Excluded by ABO Testing." The article, reprinted from the *Journal of Family Law,* describes the principles and uses of the HLA blood test, which is one of the most powerful tests available. Also included with the article are instructions for submitting samples to the laboratory at the University of California-Los Angeles for HLA testing. For copies of the article, contact the Reference Center.

In a similar vein, OCSE-IM-79-11 (June 4, 1979) transmitted to all state agencies administering child support enforcement plans a "simplified explanation of paternity testing" which had been prepared by what appeared to be a private blood typing clinic. The "explanation" begins with the following recommendation: "Call Dr. Galindo or Dr. Stroud at (512) 690-1010 and explain to them your need for paternity testing. Fees and method of payment will be discussed at this time."

72. "No official support or endorsement of the laboratory that developed these procedures by the Office of Child Support Enforcement, Department of Health, Education, and Welfare is intended or should be inferred." OCSE-IM-79-11 (June 4, 1979).

the opposite: OCSE's unequivocal endorsement of *reliable* information. The A.M.A.-A.B.A. Guidelines may be a promising starting point.

The enactment of the proposed federal legislation on this subject would have been very useful. On the other hand, in its assigned role as developer and supervisor of state plans for ascertainment of paternity, OCSE could and should face the question of blood tests even now. It should develop mandatory standards for judicial and judicious use of blood typing evidence, including the use of "probability calculations." Increasing prosecutorial and judicial utilization of doubtful calculations has made the latter an area in which responsible inquiry, resulting in the definition of scientifically valid standards, is very much needed. OCSE's involvement should further extend to recommendations concerning the "designation" and "accreditation" of qualified laboratories by an appropriate private or public agency.[73] OCSE also should give early priority to recommending or requiring (as part of state plans) adherence to standard procedures, including forms, which would facilitate the introduction of the blood typing evidence into the courts.[74] OCSE must remind the states that the federal program was designed to impose responsibility on the absent *parent,* not just anyone.

---

73. The regulations make a (too) modest beginning:

> The IV-D agency shall identify laboratories within the State which perform legally and medically acceptable tests, including blood tests, which tend to identify the father or exclude the alleged father from paternity. A list of such laboratories shall be available to appropriate courts and law enforcement officials, and to the public upon request. [45 CFR § 303.5(c) (1979).]

74. *Supra* ch. VI. 3-4.

6. AFDC Levels and Child Support Collections: Should Some of the Father's Money Go to His Children?

On thirty-seven pages detailed with numerous examples, OSCE valiantly (although not altogether successfully) [75] attempts to explain the labyrinthine complexity of the law and regulations covering the distribution of support collections. [76] This is not the place to dwell on calculations of detail. *Whatever* the state's method of determining AFDC benefits and applying the father's support dollar, the *federal* policy question is whether *all* of the father's support payment should be retained by the State as reimbursement for aid rendered or whether the children should be shown a tangible benefit from their father's contribution, even if his payment falls short of what would reimburse the State for aid rendered.

Despite complex technicalities, it is tolerable to generalize that current child support payments reduce current AFDC assistance dollar-for-dollar and even payments on arrears are withheld until past assistance is reimbursed. [77] This was not always so. For the first fifteen months of its operation, the new federal law allowed 40% of the first $50 of each monthly payment to be "disregarded," *i.e.*, a maximum of $20 per month was given to the children over and above their AFDC allowance. [78] This provision expired in 1976, and no serious new efforts are in sight to revive this or any similar program.

---

75. "The explanation given in example 20 of AT-76-5 (March 11, 1976) is an incorrect example of a 302.51(b)(3) payment." Letter of December 26, 1979, from Louis B. Hays, Deputy Director, OCSE, to Harry D. Krause.

76. OCSE-AT-76-5 (March 11, 1976), especially pp. 1-31.

77. 42 U.S.C. § 657(b)(2)(4); 45 C.F.R. § 302.51(b)(3), (4) (1979). *See supra* ch. VIII.3.e.

78. 42 U.S.C.A. § 657(a)(1).

The revival of a limited "support disregard" would have three important policy dimensions:

First, allowing the children a tangible benefit from the father's contribution may provide an incentive to the mother to cooperate in locating (and ascertaining) the father. By the same token, if fathers saw their payment putting their families into at least a somewhat better position than that of families for which no support is collected, there presumably would be a salutary effect on many fathers' willingness to pay. The idea of a "support collection disregard" is not new, nor foreign in principle, to existing AFDC policy. Such a "disregard" would be closely analogous to the "earnings disregard" current law allows the AFDC mother and students to encourage them to go to work. The latter apparently has worked well enough to have evoked recent proposals to increase the incentive.[79]

---

79. JOINT COMMITTEE PRINT, SOCIAL SECURITY FINANCING AMENDMENTS OF 1977, H.R. 9346, Comparison of House and Senate Bills with Existing Law at 44-45 (Nov. 28, 1977):

Under present law States are required, in determining need for Aid to Families with Dependent Children, to disregard:
1. All earned income of a child who is a full-time student, or a part-time student who is not a full-time employee; and
2. The first $30 earned monthly by an adult plus one-third of additional earnings. Costs related to work (such as transportation costs, uniforms, union dues, child care and other items) are also deducted from earnings in calculating the amount of welfare benefit. The $30 plus one-third disregard is based on total earnings and not on earnings net of work expense deductions. . . .
The Senate amendment would require States to disregard the first $60 earned monthly by an individual working full-time ($30 in the case of an individual working part-time — work under 40 hours weekly would be considered part-time unless it involved 35 hours per week and weekly wages of at least $92.) There would be no deduction for individual itemized work expenses except that reasonable child care expenses, subject to limitations prescribed by the Secretary would also be disregarded. The remaining earnings (net of the basic

Second, as discussed earlier, allocating some of the father's support contribution to the children over and above their AFDC allowance may help alleviate the serious problem of dealing equitably both with the father's current family and his "earlier" dependents.[80]

Finally, the question may fairly be raised whether the father's support payment should not be utilized to help reduce the most blatant inequity of the AFDC system — the widely different benefit levels provided in the several states under varying state formulas for determining "need," as accentuated further by each state's own choice as to what percentage of the state-defined need actually is paid to recipients.[81] The following table describes the national picture as of April, 1978:[82]

$60 or $30 disregard and child care expenses) would be disregarded according to the following formula: $1/3$ of up to $300 of additional earnings would be disregarded and $1/5$ of earnings above that.

Subsequent proposals have involved other variations. *See, e.g.,* SENATE COMM. ON FINANCE, ADOPTION ASSISTANCE AND CHILD WELFARE ACT OF 1979, REPORT NO. 96-336 at 88-89 (Oct. 2, 1979).

80. *Supra* text at notes 27-47.

81. 45 C.F.R. § 233.20 (1978). For a review and explanation of this technically complicated area, *see* JOINT ECONOMIC COMMITTEE, *Studies in Public Welfare, Paper No. 20,* HANDBOOK OF PUBLIC INCOME AND TRANSFER PROGRAMS: 1975, 93d Cong. 2d Sess., at 161-66 (1974). *Also see* Jefferson v. Hackney, 406 U.S. 535, 92 S. Ct. 1724, 32 L. Ed. 2d 285 (1972).

82. DEPT. of H.E.W., SOCIAL SECURITY ADMINISTRATION, FAMILY ASSISTANCE CHARACTERISTICS OF STATE PLANS FOR AID TO FAMILIES WITH DEPENDENT CHILDREN, pp. 236-37 (1978).

AMOUNT FOR ALL BASIC NEEDS, AS DEFINED BY
THE STATE IN ITS NEED STANDARD, AND
AMOUNT OF PAYMENT TO A FAMILY
WITH NO COUNTABLE INCOME
AFTER APPLICATION OF ANY
METHOD OF LIMITING PAY-
MENT USED BY STATE, AS
OF APRIL 1, 1978,
BY STATE

Family of 4 Persons
(1 Needy Adult and 3 Children)

State	Column 1: State Need Standard for All Basic Needs	Column 2: Amount of Assistance Payment to a Family With No Income
Alabama	$240.00	$148.00
Alaska	400.00	400.00
Arizona	282.00	197.00
Arkansas	273.00	188.00
California	444.00	423.00
Colorado	290.00	290.00
Connecticut	384.00	384.00
Delaware	287.00	287.00
D.C.	349.00	314.00
Florida	230.00	191.00
Georgia	227.00	148.00
Guam	306.00	306.00
Hawaii	533.00	533.00
Idaho	395.00	344.00
Illinois	300.00	300.00

Family of 4 Persons
(1 Needy Adult and 3 Children)

State	Column 1: State Need Standard for All Basic Needs	Column 2: Amount of Assistance Payment to a Family With No Income
Indiana	$363.00	$275.00
Iowa	369.00	369.00
Kansas	306.00	306.00
Kentucky	235.00	235.00
Louisiana	410.00	164.00
Maine	349.00	314.00
Maryland	314.00	251.00
Massachusetts	358.00	358.00
Michigan	459.00	459.00
Minnesota	404.00	404.00
Mississippi	252.00	60.00
Missouri	365.00	237.00
Montana	252.00	252.00
Nebraska	370.00	370.00
Nevada	341.00	276.00
New Hampshire	346.00	346.00
New Jersey	356.00	356.00
New Mexico	239.00	220.00
New York	476.00	476.00
North Carolina	200.00	200.00
North Dakota	389.00	389.00
Ohio	431.00	267.00
Oklahoma	309.00	309.00
Oregon	470.00	428.00

	Family of 4 Persons (1 Needy Adult and 3 Children)	
	Column 1: State Need Standard for All Basic Needs	Column 2: Amount of Assistance Payment to a Family With No
State		Income
Pennsylvania	$373.00	$373.00
Puerto Rico	126.00	54.00
Rhode Island	359.00	359.00
South Carolina	217.00	117.00
South Dakota	333.00	333.00
Tennessee	217.00	139.00
Texas	187.00	140.00
Utah	457.00	352.00
Vermont	560.00	423.00
Virgin Islands	166.00	166.00
Virginia	272.00	245.00
Washington	416.00	416.00
West Virginia	332.00	249.00
Wisconsin	520.00	442.00
Wyoming	270.00	270.00

Lest the reader be *too* shocked when these benefit levels are compared with the "official" poverty line in 1978 of $6,662 (or $555 per month) for a non-farm family of four,[83] it should be remembered that these payments are not the only public resources that are made available to aid recipients. For primarily historical reasons (although "paternalism" has played its role) our welfare system

---

83. WALL STREET JOURNAL, Nov. 26, 1979, p. 7. *See supra* note 36.

provides a patchwork of cash and in kind benefits of which the AFDC program is but one element, albeit a very important one. A variety of other resources supplement the AFDC income of the typical recipient. These benefits range from food stamps to subsidized housing, from medical care to school lunches, from day care to dental treatment, from private charity to a vast number of other programs in our so erratically redistributive social "system." [84]

As reported in Secretary Califano's 1977 welfare reform study for President Carter,

> In 22 States, AFDC benefits plus Food Stamps exceed the earnings of a full-time worker at the minimum wage. If the full-time worker is ineligible for any additional benefits like Medicaid, he will be even worse off than a similarly situated person on welfare. . . .
>
> In Wisconsin, a family of four, with the father working half-time at the minimum wage, has a total income of $8,628 (including earnings, the earned income tax credit, AFDC-UF, Food Stamps, and the insurance value of Medicaid, less FICA taxes). If the father works full-time his income will drop by some $3,000 to $5,691 (including earnings, earned income tax credit, Food Stamps, and less FICA taxes). He loses his AFDC-UF payments and his and his wife's Medicaid coverage. [85]

A clear assessment is lacking of precisely what impact

---

84. *See generally* Joint Economic Committee, *Studies in Public Welfare, Paper No. 20,* Handbook of Public Income Transfer Programs: 1975, 93d Cong., 2d Sess. (1974).

85. Report to the President, May 1, 1977, pp. 12-13, transmitted by letter dated May 3, 1977, from Secretary Joseph A. Califano to President Jimmy Carter (mimeograph).

these programs have on "poverty."[86] For reasons not susceptible to wholly rational analysis, the federal government itself reports not only AFDC benefit levels but defines "poverty" as a generalized economic indicator in

---

86. It has been estimated that

in fiscal 1977, the Federal government alone spent $31.4 billion for medicare and Medicaid, $5 billion for food stamps and $3 billion to subsidize public housing. When these and other in-kind payments are included in the statistics, says economist Morton Paglin of Portland State University, the number of Americans below the poverty line falls from the official figure of 25 million to 6.7 million. [NEWSWEEK, Oct. 9, 1978.]

See also Paper No. 3, p. 6-2, Table 22, attached to Report to the President, May 1, 1977, pp. 12-13, transmitted by letter dated May 3, 1977, from Secretary Joseph A. Califano to President Jimmy Carter (mimeograph):

DIFFERENCE BETWEEN BEFORE AND AFTER TRANSFER POOR

FY 1976

	Households w Before Tax Before-Trans. Income Below the Poverty Standard	Households w Before Tax After Soc. Insurance Income Below the Poverty Standard	Households w Before Tax After All Cash Trans Income Below the Poverty Standard	Households w Before Tax After In-Kind Transfer Income Below the Poverty Standard	Households with After Total Trans. and Tax Income Below the Poverty Standard
A. All Households					
1. Number (thousands)	20,237	11,179	9,073	5,336	5,445
2. % All Households	25	14	11	7	7
B. Unattached Individuals					
1. Number (thousands)	9,932	5,582	4,752	3,076	3,142
2. % All Unattached Individuals	46	26	22	14	15
C. Multiple Person Families					
1. Number (thousands)	10,305	5,597	4,321	2,260	2,303
2. % All Multiple Person Families	18	10	8	4	4

463

terms of *money* incomes, instead of "cashing out" and totalling all resources of the spending unit. Of course, it is debatable which of these programs yield benefits to the recipient that can fairly be deemed equivalent to cash (and if so, how much). In the case of food stamps, the answer obviously is "100 percent," in the case of public housing, it is partially "yes" and the answer is still positive in the case of medical care (if the cost of an insurance premium providing equivalent protection is counted), but the answer becomes progressively less clear as the inquiry goes on. Soon the cash value to the beneficiary of benefits provided in kind does not nearly equal their cost to the public. Another problem is that these in-kind benefits tend not to be distributed evenly.

Despite these uncertainties, it is clear that to count only the cash incomes of AFDC recipients is to misstate the "poverty situation" grossly. However, it is equally clear that there *is* a money problem at the lower levels of the "welfare class," and obviously this problem is more serious in the states that pay less aid than it is in the states that pay more (aside from appropriate adjustments for variations in the cost of living). This is not the place to resurrect the long and bitter debate regarding federal imposition of a uniform national aid standard. That debate, in recent years, has been lost to state autonomy and other pressures, along with the many welfare reform proposals of recent years.[87] Although the House passed H.R. 4904 in November, 1979, which, among other changes, would

---

87. *See, e.g.,* Demkovich, *Welfare Focus, A Preview of Coming Attractions,* NATIONAL JOURNAL, Sept. 23, 1978, p. 1519. For the full text of President Carter's welfare message to Congress *see Carter Asks New Welfare System,* NEW YORK TIMES, August 7, 1977, p. 1. *See also* D. MOYNIHAN, THE POLITICS OF A GUARANTEED INCOME: THE NIXON ADMINISTRATION AND THE FAMILY ASSISTANCE PLAN (1973), and Moynihan, *Income by Right,* THE NEW YORKER, Jan. 13, 20, 27 (1973).

require all states to pay at least 65 percent of the federally defined poverty level (counting food stamps but not other in-kind benefits) strong opposition persists in the Senate to what is seen by some as too much federal control over the program.[88]

This is the time to raise the recommendation that the absent father's support payment be used to bring his AFDC family up to a federally defined minimum standard (adjusted by regional cost of living factors), such as the "poverty level."[89]

If this sensible solution is not feasible in the political tug of war between state sovereignty and federal influence (and money), there is the intermediate position that the father's support payment should at least be used to bring his family up to state-defined "need standards" before it is applied to assistance reimbursement, in those twenty-eight states that pay less than their own standard of need.[90]

---

88. CONGRESSIONAL QUARTERLY, Nov. 10, 1979, p. 2534.

89. To illustrate, current AFDC benefits, including food stamps but no other in-kind benefits, amount to the following percentages of the poverty level: Hawaii (96%), Vermont (91%), New York (91%), Michigan (91%), Wisconsin (89%), Washington (87%), Oregon (85%), Minnesota (85%), Connecticut (85%), California (85%), Massachusetts (82%), Iowa (82%), Alaska (82%), New Jersey (79%), Utah (79%), North Dakota (79%), Nebraska (79%), Idaho (78%), Pennsylvania (78%), Rhode Island (77%), New Hampshire (76%), South Dakota (75%), Illinois (74%), Montana (74%), Maine (72%), Dist. of Col. (72%), Oklahoma (72%), Colorado (71%), Kansas (71%), Wyoming (71%), Ohio (70%), Delaware (69%), Virginia (69%), Nevada (68%), Indiana (68%), Maryland (67%), Missouri (65%), West Virginia (65%), Kentucky (63%), New Mexico (62%), Arizona (60%), North Carolina (59%), Florida (58%), Arkansas (57%), Louisiana (55%), Alabama (53%), Georgia (53%), Tennessee (53%), Texas (52%), South Carolina (50%), Mississippi (49%). House Committee on Ways and Means, 96th Cong., 1st Sess., H. Rep. 96-451, Part I at 92 (1979).

90. This clearly is the less desirable — if politically perhaps the more feasible — route. Twenty-two states pay "full need" so that nothing would change in those states, and only the twenty-eight states that pay

Under contract for the staff of the Senate Finance Committee as far back as 1972, this observer commented on

---

less than need would be affected by this compromise proposal. The trouble is that the problem of inadequacy of AFDC benefits is only more *obviously* serious in the states that pay less than their own definition of "need" than it is in those states that pay "full need." By employing a lower definition of need, some states that pay full need actually pay less aid than some states that pay less than full need! To illustrate, on October 1, 1978, Delaware paid all of a need of $287 and California paid $423 of a need of $444; Illinois paid $300 on a need of $300 and Idaho paid $344 on a need of $395. Further distortions result from the fact that some of the states that pay less than "need" apply their percentage reduction *after* deducting income and others *before*. Assuming a state-defined need of $250, a support payment of $100 and an 80% factor applied to the need standard, the first method would yield monthly aid of $120. ($250 minus $100 times .8). The second method would produce aid in the amount of only $100 ($250 times .8 minus $100). While the states in the first category thus give the family a greater benefit from the father's payment than do the states in the second category, the state-defined need standards and the percentage reductions in the states that pay less than need vary so widely that even a state with the less advantageous reduction formula may provide more total aid to a family than another state with a "better" formula. The various methods of calculating benefits are detailed, state by state, in DEPT. OF H.E.W., SOCIAL SECURITY ADMINISTRATION, FAMILY ASSISTANCE CHARACTERISTICS STATE OF PLANS FOR AID TO FAMILIES WITH DEPENDENT CHILDREN, pp. 234-35 (1978).

It is not that the problem caused by these varying state formulae has escaped federal attention entirely. OCSE emphasizes that the consideration of (and payment to the family of) child support collections as income, filling the gap between the assistance payment and the need standard is *not* permitted, except to prevent, in certain states under specific circumstances, a decrease in total disposable income available to a family due to retention of child support collections by the state that previously had been paid directly to the family. OCSE-AT-76-5 (1976) at p. 21. Tit. 42 U.S.C.A. § 602(a)(28), added in 1975, provides:

> A State plan for aid and services to needy families with children must — provide that, in determining the amount of aid to which an eligible family is entitled, any portion of the amounts collected in any particular month as child support pursuant to a plan approved under part D, and retained by the State under section 457, which (under the State plan approved under this part as in effect both

466

legislative proposals preceding the enactment of the support enforcement program:

> To deal first with the relationship of the disposition of the father's payment to state-defined levels of need: a dollar for dollar offset against AFDC payments of the father's contribution would be entirely justifiable, *if AFDC payments were adequate to meet reasonable minimum needs of the recipient families.* This, however, is not the case in many states.... In *Rosado v. Wyman,* 397 U.S. 397 (1970), the late Justice Harlan ... having the survival capability of AFDC recipients in mind, saw evidence that Congress *would prefer* state programs to meet at least state-defined levels of need. If funding problems and political considerations have

---

> during July 1975 and during that particular month) would not have caused a reduction in the amount of aid paid to the family if such amounts had been paid directly to the family, shall be added to the amount of aid otherwise payable to such family under the State plan approved under this part.

44 Fed. Reg. 29122 (May 18, 1979) explains:

> This rule will affect assistance payments in three groups of States: (1) Those which did not, in July 1975, and which do not now, discount child support payments "dollar-for-dollar" in computing the amount of a family's assistance; (2) those which permit recipients to retain $5 per month of income, under 45 C.F.R. 233.20(a)(4)(i), without any reduction in assistance; and (3) those which allow the conservation of certain kinds of income for the future identifiable needs of a child under section 402(a)(8)(B)(i) of the Act without any reduction in assistance.

OCSE explains further (letter of December 26, 1979, from Louis B. Hays, Esq., Deputy Director, OCSE, to Harry D. Krause):

> Section 402(a)(28) applies where the State uses (and used in July 1975) a method for determining the assistance payment in which all or part of the countable income does not effect an equal reduction in the assistance payment. [Following] is an explanation and examples from a draft, proposed regulation implementing Section 402(a)(28). This excerpt represents the Department's current thinking as to how Section 402(a)(28) should be implemented but has not yet been published as a Notice of Proposed Rulemaking:

> There were six methods for determining the amount of the assistance payment being implemented by States in July 1975, in which a

467

hitherto prevented many states from satisfying their own definitions of need, the influx of "new money" resulting from the proposed program of federally assisted support enforcement will provide an ideal opportunity to realize Congress' own preference. *This means that there should be no serious debate about imposing a federal requirement in connection with the support enforcement program that the absent parent's contributions should first be applied toward meeting the recipient family's state-defined level of need.* These

supplemental payment would have to be determined. These methods are illustrated below:

1. *Income is subtracted from the need standard. The payment is the deficit or the maximum by family size, whichever is less.*

Determine assistance payment:

	Column A Treat child support as income	Column B Do not treat child support as income
Need standard	$300	$300
Support payment	− 100	− 0
Deficit	$200	$300
Max. by family size	150	150
Assistance payment	$150	$150

Determine total disposable income:

Assistance payment	$150	$150
Support payment	+ 100	+ 0
	$250	$150

Determine supplemental payment using total disposable income:

Column A	$250
Column B	− 150
	$100 supplemental payment

Determine total assistance payment:

Current assistance payment	$150
Supplemental payment	+ 100
Total assistance payment	$250

considerations apply with equal force to the proposal that, if the father's payments exceed the AFDC level of benefits and welfare benefits have been received by his dependents in the past, any excess would not go to the family but would be used first to offset past welfare

---

2. *Income is subtracted from the need standard. The payment is a percent of the deficit.*

Determine assistance payment:

	Column A	Column B
	Treat child support as income	Do not treat child support as income
Need standard	$300	$300
Support payment	- 100	- 0
Deficit	$200	$300
Ratable reduction	x.70(%)	x.70(%)
Assistance payment	$140	$210

Determine total disposable income:

Assistance payment	$140	$210
Support payment	+100	+ 0
	$240	$210

Determine supplemental payment using total disposable income:

Column A	$240
Column B	-210
	$ 30 supplemental payment

Determine total assistance payment:

Current assistance payment	$210
Supplemental payment	+ 30
Total assistance payment	$240

469

payments to the family. In this case also, the father's payments should be applied to supporting his family at least until the AFDC need level is met.

3. Income is subtracted from the need standard. The payment is a percent of the deficit or the maximum by family size, whichever is less.

OR

4. Income is subtracted from the need standard. The payment is a percent of the deficit or the maximum on the total money payment, whichever is less.

Determine assistance payment:

	Column A Treat child support as income	Column B Do not treat child support as income
Need standard	$300	$300
Support payment	-100	- 0
Deficit	$200	$300
Ratable reduction	x.70(%)	x.70(%)
	$140	$210
Maximum*	$150	$150
Assistance payment	$140	$150

Determine total disposable income:

Assistance payment	$140	$150
Support payment	+100	+ 0
	$240	$150

Determine supplemental payment using total disposable income:

Column A	$240
Column B	-150
	$ 90 supplemental payment

Determine total assistance payment:

Current assistance payment	$150
Supplemental payment	+90
Total assistance payment	$240

*Maximum either by family size or on the total money payment.

SECOND THOUGHTS FOR THE SECOND FIVE YEARS

It is a further question whether, after the state-defined need level is reached, additional collections should be offset on a dollar for dollar basis or whether a partial offset system should be developed (perhaps patterned after the work incentive provisions applicable to AFDC recipients, 42 USCA § 602(a)(7)(8) (1969)). If the idea of our welfare system is to do more

---

5. *Income is subtracted from a reduced need standard. The payment is the deficit or the maximum by family size, whichever is less.*

Determine assistance payment:

	Column A	Column B
	Treat child support as income	Do not treat child support as income
Need standard	$300	$300
Ratable reduction	x.70(%)	x.70(%)
Reduced standard	$210	$210
Support payment	-100	- 0
Deficit	$110	$210
Assistance payment	110	150
Max. by family size	$150	$150

Determine total disposable income:

Assistance payment	$110	$150
Support payment	+100	+ 0
	$210	$150

Determine supplemental payment using total disposable income:

Column A	$210
Column B	-150
	$ 60 supplemental payment

Determine total assistance payment:

Current assistance payment	$150
Supplemental payment	+60
Total assistance payment	$210

471

than to preserve the *status quo* of poverty, it may well be wise to consider the provision of additional benefits to the family to lift recipients up to the *federally defined poverty standard,* before a full dollar for dollar offset is employed. The short-term loss of the taxpayer's dollars may well be more than offset by the long-run social gain from reducing extreme deprivation. . . .[91]

6. *Income is subtracted from a reduced need standard. The payment is the deficit or the maximum on the total money payment, whichever is less.*

Determine assistance payment:

	Column A Treat child support as income	Column B Do not treat child support as income
Need standard	$500	$500
Ratable reduction	x.70(%)	x.70(%)
Reduced standard	$350	$350
Support payment	−100	− 0
Deficit	$250	$350
Assistance payment	$250	$300
Max. on total money payment	$300	$300

Determine Total Disposable income:

Assistance Payment	$250	$300
Support payment	+100	+ 0
	$350	$300

Determine supplemental payment using total disposable income:

Column A	$350	
Column B	−300	
	$ 50	supplemental payment

Determine total assistance payment:

Current assistance payment	$300
Supplemental payment	+ 50
Total assistance payment	$350

91. H. Krause, Review of Part X, Child Support, 92d Cong., 2d Sess., Soc. Sec. Am. of 1972, Committee on Finance, U.S. Senate, H.R. 1 (unpublished consultant's paper).

A serious new initiative should point in the direction of "diverting" at least some of the father's support payments to their primary purpose — to assure a tolerable life for his children. Precisely what form this is to take must be left to political and economic realities, but the basic notion should not shock anyone. Unfortunately, OCSE writes that "there are no plans to reinstate the 'incentive disregard' or bonus that you [this author] spoke of. Occasionally, it has been proposed but has been met with non-acceptance because it is expensive to administer, complicates the distribution of collections, and does not assure better cooperation on the part of the custodial parent. No other method of giving the family a tangible benefit from the absent parent's support payment has been proposed." [92]

An afterthought should go to the more recently instituted reimbursement obligation for Medicaid.[93] There *is* a difference in principle between reimbursement for cash assistance and assistance in kind (which does not always lend itself to being converted into cash). Where do we propose to stop? Will we decide to add reimbursement for food stamps or public housing to the list? If that seems remote, how does it differ from Medicaid reimbursement? (Indeed, it would seem that food stamps are more clearly a cash-equivalent than is medical care). Ultimately, should those who can pay, be asked to reimburse subsidized mass transit systems used by their dependents? Should our schools be public or should we charge tuition?

The time seems ripe for a reassessment of what is public and what is private responsibility. As mentioned earlier, some Western European "social welfare states" which strictly insist on enforcement of the parental child support obligation, have reallocated what the parent owes and what

---

92. Letter of December 26, 1979, from Louis B. Hays, Esq., Deputy Director, OCSE, to Harry D. Krause.

93. *Supra* ch. VIII. 3.h.

society provides, to the point where the cost of medical care and education, including higher education, is borne by society at large. As also suggested above, it may soon be our turn to consider new definitions regarding the extent and mix of private and public child support obligations. In this light, enforcing reimbursement for the (all too frequently excessive) cost of Medicaid may be a step back, not forward.

True, there *is* the curious limitation in the regulations that limits Medicaid reimbursement to situations in which a court order specifically allocates amounts to medical support. This may indeed provide a measure of protection for those fathers who have an order outstanding against them. But not for others.[94] Nor does it seem to have been so intended.[95]

---

94. Some limitation, applicable in some or even many cases, may be found in court-ordered support amounts which may set an upper limit to the absent parent's responsibility. No such limit seems to apply, however, if there is no court order outstanding. *See supra* ch. VIII. 3.e, text after note 114.

95. Statement by S. Duval, Chief, Policy Branch, OCSE, *Child Support Enforcement in Action,* 4 NRFSEA NEWS, at 44 (Special issue, March, 1979).

> We took a defensive posture, generally. This may well be in statute and regulations an optional program, but we are very concerned it will not be optional. We heard pretty quickly from our side of the house, the state IV-D directors, that indeed whether they wanted it or not, they would be required to enter into these cooperative agreements. So, we thought we would do what we could to protect our program. We are very concerned that the capability to collect cash child support not be diminished by the existence of this program. This is our main problem with it. We believe we have a consensus within the department that that not occur, that cash child support increase and not be in any way damaged by the medical support enforcement. . . .
>
> There is another interesting little provision in 302.50. We have said that no portion of any amounts collected under the IV-A assignment may be used to satisfy medical support obligation unless the court or administrative order specifies an amount for medical support. *Again, that was part of our defensive posture.* (Emphasis added.)

True, it seems to be the consensus of those charged with the administration of the program that the Medicaid reimbursement provisions are concerned primarily with obtaining support orders that specify that the support obligor purchase health insurance for his dependents, as well as with the recovery of Medicaid expenditures from insurance carriers under existing policies that had been ignored in the past. Accordingly, the professional discussion so far has been concerned much more with the rebilling of Medicaid costs to insurance carriers or other responsible agencies than with the establishment of individual liability.[96] However, if that is the real thrust of Public Law 95-142,[97] surely that law brings forth a mountain where a molehill was all that was needed! Could OCSE not simply have required the state IV-D authorities to insist on health insurance coverage as part and parcel of support orders, where financially possible and could public aid offices not have been instructed first to rely on coverage by private carriers, where available, before providing Medicaid?

True, the director of child support enforcement of one important state characterizes the Medicaid provisions as a "bad thing" that "got federal administrators bogged down by titles" and suggests that the "natural jealousy between administrators has fomented this mess." Indeed, herein may lie the real explanation.

As a practical matter, finally, it may be expected that the support enforcement agencies will for some time be so busy with the overwhelming number of "normal" enforcement cases that they will not have time, funds or energy to turn to "fringe" areas, such as this one, involving not only a rather small number of fathers who would be capable of

---

96. *See, e.g., Child Support Enforcement in Action,* 4 NRFSEA NEWS, at 42-46 (Special issue, March, 1979).

97. October 25, 1977, 91 STAT. 1196-97. *See* 42 U.S.C.A. § 1396k (Supp. 1980).

paying, but involving also a somewhat complex — though seemingly inescapable — interpretation of law and the regulations that may well run counter to legislative intent.

7. The Pressing Need to Continue Funding for Non-ADFC Support Enforcement.

In these last paragraphs of this book, it is well worth reemphasizing the significance of the federal support enforcement legislation — above and beyond the welfare context. The legislation represents to date the most important federal legislative venture into *family law:* The provisions encouraging non-AFDC support enforcement under the program alleviate the all too common lot of the abandoned mother who has sufficient productive capacity and pride to keep herself and her children above the welfare-eligibility line, but whose earning capacity may have been impaired by a role-divided marriage and now is restricted by the custodial services she renders her children. The typical father's earnings enable him to make a reasonable contribution to child support, but he does not earn enough to do that without "pain." Unless "encouraged," many fathers thus are unwilling to make their proper contributions which, though significant in terms of their children's needs, too often are not large enough to make it economical to involve lawyers in repeated enforcement forays under the cumbersome and correspondingly expensive traditional child support enforcement procedures.

When it discussed the controversy over the continuation of federal funding for this important aspect of the program, the Senate Finance Committee summarized the case for non-AFDC enforcement:

> The purpose of the requirement on the States to provide services to nonrecipients is to assure that

476

abandoned families with children have access to child support services before they are forced to apply for welfare. Access to these services may mean the difference between a family's dependence on welfare for support or being supported by a legally responsible parent. The fact that these services are in demand and are benefiting families is evident from program statistics. Since the beginning of the program a total of $1.4 billion has been collected on behalf of non-AFDC families. The amount of collections grew from $308 million in fiscal year 1976 to $578 million in 1978. The number of non-AFDC families who received services grew from 268,000 in 1976 to 535,000 in 1978.[98]

The extension to the "private sector" of the parent locator, paternity establishment and enforcement and collection features may well be the most important single feature of the Act. Congressional reluctance to provide funds to the states has created uncertainty and discouraged progress in this area.[99] Fortunately, there is hope that Congress will soon resolve this issue by making permanent the federal-state reimbursement features for non-AFDC support enforcement. On December 20, 1979, Congress passed H.R. 3091 which makes federal financial participation available retroactively from October 1978 to March 1980. At this writing, legislation to provide permanent funding for non-AFDC collections again was pending.[100] A serious complication in the pending

---

98. SENATE COMM. ON FINANCE, STAFF DATA AND MATERIALS ON CHILD SUPPORT at 5-6 96th Cong., 1st Sess. (Comm. Print 96-7, 1979). *See* 45 C.F.R. § 304.20(a)(4) (1979) and U.S.C.A. Tit. 42 §§ 654(6), 655(a) for the authorizing legislation and regulations that expired October 1st, 1978.

99. *Supra* ch. VIII. 3.b. There is an element of unfairness in requiring the states to collect non-AFDC support and not only fail to help them with the cost, but to threaten to impose a financial penalty on matching for all expenditures. *See* SENATE COMM. ON FINANCE, REPORT NO. 95-573, PUBLIC ASSISTANCE AMENDMENTS of 1977 at 95, 95th Cong., 1st Sess. (1977).

100. H.R. 4904 § 402, 96th Cong., 1st Sess. (November 9, 1979).

legislation was the proposal to impose a ten percent charge on all non-AFDC collections, except where the deduction of that fee would make the recipient eligible for public aid.[101] The wisdom of a government imposing a fee of this magnitude is debatable when the "governmental service" at issue is nothing more exorbitant than provision of access to the legal system!

8. Postscript.

Congress enacted two major bills in June, 1980. Among other things, Public Law 96-265 (previously H.R. 3236) provided 75 percent federal matching for expenditures attributable to child support duties performed by court personnel (except judges), increased to 90 percent the federal share of the cost of automatic data processing and information retrieval systems and provided access to (Social Security) wage information and payments of retirement income for purposes of "establishing and collecting child support obligations." [102]

Public Law 96-272 (which had evolved from H.R. 3434) improved incentives for the states in their collection efforts. Much more importantly, the Act finally put an end to the protracted dispute about federal funding for non-AFDC collections.[103] At the end of March, 1980, temporary funding had expired, leading OCSE to inform the state agencies of the cut-off.[104] Federal funding now was made permanent, *retroactively to March 31, 1980,* so that, except for administrative confusion, no interruption actually occurred. Moreover, the final version dropped the proposed ten percent "contingent" fee feature (deplored just above),

---

101. *Id.,* § 402(b).
102. 96th Cong., P.L. 96-265, 94 STAT. 462-69, June 9, 1980.
103. 96th Cong., P.L. 96-272, 94 STAT. 527-28, 531-32, June 17, 1980.
104. OCSE-AT-80-6, March 31, 1980.

so that the non-AFDC claimant continues to obtain the same collection service as she or he did previously, by payment of a small fee.[105] Beyond that, Public Law 96-265 had, a week earlier, made available the Internal Revenue Service to collect child support for non-AFDC families where the states have been unable to so collect and the lack of payment is a non-compliance with a court order to support.

As emphasized in so much detail above,[106] this observer ranks non-AFDC collections one of the most important aspects of the national child support enforcement program. Indeed, permanent Congressional commitment on the funding issue (with IRS collection, if needed, thrown in as a bonus), provides an optimistic not on which to end — in the hope, of course, that as Congress becomes more accustomed to its new responsibility, further improvements in the program will follow.

---

105. *Supra* ch. VIII. 3.b, text at note 54.
106. *Supra* ch. VIII. 3.b, text at notes 60-65; ch. X.7.

Appendix A

REVISED UNIFORM RECIPROCAL ENFORCEMENT OF SUPPORT ACT (1968)

Drafted by the

NATIONAL CONFERENCE OF COMMISSIONERS ON UNIFORM STATE LAWS

and by it

APPROVED AND RECOMMENDED FOR ENACTMENT
IN ALL THE STATES

at its

ANNUAL CONFERENCE
MEETING IN ITS SEVENTY-SEVENTH YEAR
AT PHILADELPHIA, PENNSYLVANIA
JULY 22—AUGUST 1, 1968

APPROVED BY THE AMERICAN BAR ASSOCIATION AT ITS
MEETING AT PHILADELPHIA, PENNSYLVANIA
AUGUST 7, 1968

The Committee which acted for the National Conference of Commissioners on Uniform State Laws in preparing the Revised Uniform Reciprocal Enforcement of Support Act was as follows:

W. J. BROCKELBANK, 203 South Polk Street, Moscow, Idaho 83843, *Chairman*

BOYD M. BENSON, 76 Third Street, S.W., The National Bank of South Dakota Building, Huron, South Dakota 57350

WILLIAM S. BURRAGE, 3 Court Square, Middlebury, Vermont 05753

LOWRY N. COE, 8400 Wisconsin Avenue, Bethesda, Maryland 20014

FRED T. HANSON, 316 Norris Avenue, McCook, Nebraska 69001

EUGENE A. BURDICK, P.O. Box 757, Williston, North Dakota 58801, *Chairman of Section F*

PART I—*General Provisions*

SECTION 1. [*Purposes.*] The purposes of this Act are to improve and extend by reciprocal legislation the enforcement of duties of support.

SECTION 2. [*Definitions.*]

(a) "Court" means the [here insert name] court of this State and when the context requires means the court of any other state as defined in a substantially similar reciprocal law.

(b) "Duty of support" means a duty of support whether imposed or imposable by law or by order, decree, or judgment of any court, whether interlocutory or final or whether incidental to an action for divorce, separation, separate maintenance, or otherwise and includes the duty to pay arrearages of support past due and unpaid.

(c) "Governor" includes any person performing the functions of Governor or the executive authority of any state covered by this Act.

(d) "Initiating state" means a state in which a proceeding pursuant to this or a substantially similar reciprocal law is commenced. "Initiating court" means the court in which a proceeding is commenced.

(e) "Law" includes both common and statutory law.

(f) "Obligee" means a person including a state or political subdivision to whom a duty of support is owed or a person including a state or political subdivision that has commenced a proceeding for enforcement of an alleged duty of support or for registration of a support order. It is immaterial if the person to whom a duty of support is owed is a recipient of public assistance.

(g) "Obligor" means any person owing a duty of support or against whom a proceeding for the enforcement of a duty of support or registration of a support order is commenced.

(h) "Prosecuting attorney" means the public official in the appropriate place who has the duty to enforce criminal laws relating to the failure to provide for the support of any person.

(i) "Register" means to [record] [file] in the Registry of Foreign Support Orders.

(j) "Registering court" means any court of this State in which a support order of a rendering state is registered.

(k) "Rendering state" means a state in which the court has issued a support order for which registration is sought or granted in the court of another state.

(l) "Responding state" means a state in which any responsive proceeding pursuant to the proceeding in the initiating state is commenced. "Responding court" means the court in which the responsive proceeding is commenced.

(m) "State" includes a state, territory, or possession of the United States, the District of Columbia, the Commonwealth of Puerto Rico, and any foreign jurisdiction in which this or a substantially similar reciprocal law is in effect.

(n) "Support order" means any judgment, decree, or order of support in favor of an obligee whether temporary or final, or subject to modification, revocation, or remission, regardless of the kind of action or proceeding in which it is entered.

SECTION 3. [*Remedies Additional to Those Now Existing.*] The remedies herein provided are in addition to and not in substitution for any other remedies.

SECTION 4. [*Extent of Duties of Support.*] Duties of support arising under the law of this State, when applicable under section 7, bind the obligor present in this State regardless of the presence or residence of the obligee.

PART II—*Criminal Enforcement*

SECTION 5. [*Interstate Rendition.*] The Governor of this State may

(1) demand of the Governor of another state the surrender of a person found in that state who is charged criminally in this State with failing to provide for the support of any person; or

(2) surrender on demand by the Governor of another state a person found in this State who is charged criminally in that state with failing to provide for the support of any person. Provisions for extradition of criminals not inconsistent with this Act apply to the demand even if the person whose surrender is demanded was not in the demanding state at the time of the commission of the crime and has not fled therefrom. The demand, the oath, and any proceedings for extradition pursuant to this section need not state or show that the person whose surrender is demanded has fled from justice or at the time of the commission of the crime was in the demanding state.

SECTION 6. [*Conditions of Interstate Rendition.*]

(a) Before making the demand upon the Governor of another state for the surrender of a person charged criminally in this State with failing to provide for the support of a person, the Governor of this State may require any prosecuting attorney of this State to satisfy him that at least [60] days prior thereto the obligee initiated proceedings for support under this Act or that any proceeding would be of no avail.

(b) If, under a substantially similar Act, the Governor of another state makes a demand upon the Governor of this State for the surrender of a person charged criminally in that state with failure to provide for the support of a person, the Governor may require any prosecuting attorney to investigate the demand and to report to him whether proceedings for support have been initiated or would be effective. If it appears to the Governor that a proceeding would be effective but has not been initiated he may delay honoring the demand for a reasonable time to permit the initiation of a proceeding.

(c) If proceedings have been initiated and the person demanded has prevailed therein the Governor may decline to honor the demand. If the obligee prevailed and the person demanded is subject to a support order, the Governor may decline to honor the demand if the person demanded is complying with the support order.

PART III—*Civil Enforcement*

SECTION 7. [*Choice of Law.*] Duties of support applicable under this Act are those imposed under the laws of any state where the obligor was present for the period during which support is sought. The obligor is presumed to have been present in the responding state during the period for which support is sought until otherwise shown.

SECTION 8. [*Remedies of State or Political Subdivision Furnishing Support.*] If a state or a political subdivision furnishes support to an individual obligee it has the same right to initiate a proceeding under this Act as the individual obligee for the purpose of securing reimbursement for support furnished and of obtaining continuing support.

SECTION 9. [*How Duties of Support Enforced.*] All duties of support, including the duty to pay arrearages, are enforceable by a proceeding under this Act including a proceeding for civil contempt. The defense that the parties are immune to suit because of their relationship as husband and wife or parent and child is not available to the obligor.

485

SECTION 10. [*Jurisdiction.*] Jurisdiction of any proceeding under this Act is vested in the [here insert title of court desired].

SECTION 11. [*Contents and Filing of [Petition] for Support; Venue.*]

(a) The [petition] shall be verified and shall state the name and, so far as known to the obligee, the address and circumstances of the obligor and the persons for whom support is sought, and all other pertinent information. The obligee may include in or attach to the [petition] any information which may help in locating or identifying the obligor including a photograph of the obligor, a description of any distinguishing marks on his person, other names and aliases by which he has been or is known, the name of his employer, his fingerprints, and his Social Security number.

(b) The [petition] may be filed in the appropriate court of any state in which the obligee resides. The court shall not decline or refuse to accept and forward the [petition] on the ground that it should be filed with some other court of this or any other state where there is pending another action for divorce, separation, annulment, dissolution, habeas corpus, adoption, or custody between the same parties or where another court has already issued a support order in some other proceeding and has retained jurisdiction for its enforcement.

SECTION 12. [*Officials to Represent Obligee.*] If this State is acting as an initiating state the prosecuting attorney upon the request of the court [a state department of welfare, a county commissioner, an overseer of the poor, or other local welfare officer] shall represent the obligee in any proceeding under this Act. [If the prosecuting attorney neglects or refuses to represent the obligee the [Attorney General] may order him to comply with the request of the court or may undertake the representation.] [If the prosecuting attorney neglects or refuses to represent the obligee, the [Attorney General] [State Director of Public Welfare] may undertake the representation.]

SECTION 13. [*Petition for a Minor.*] A [petition] on behalf of a minor obligee may be executed and filed by a person having legal custody of the minor without appointment as guardian ad litem.

SECTION 14. [*Duty of Initiating Court.*] If the initiating court finds that the [petition] sets forth facts from which it may be determined that the obligor owes a duty of support and that a court of the responding state may obtain jurisdiction of the obligor or his property it shall so certify and cause 3 copies of the [petition] and its certificate and one copy of this Act to be sent to the responding court. Certification shall be in accordance with the requirements of the initiating state. If the name and address of the responding court is unknown and the responding state has an information agency comparable to that established in the initiating state it shall cause the copies to be sent to the state information agency or other proper official of the responding state, with a request that the agency or official forward them to the proper court and that the court of the responding state acknowledge their receipt to the initiating court.

SECTION 15. [*Costs and Fees.*] An initiating court shall not require payment of either a filing fee or other costs from the obligee but may request the responding court to collect fees and costs from the obligor. A responding court shall not require payment of a filing fee or other costs from the obligee but it may direct that all fees and costs requested by the initiating court and incurred in this State when acting as a responding state, including fees for filing of pleadings, service of process, seizure of property, stenographic or duplication service, or other service supplied to the obligor, be paid in whole or in part by the obligor or by the [state or political subdivision thereof]. These costs or fees do not have priority over amounts due to the obligee.

SECTION 16. [*Jurisdiction by Arrest.*] If the court of this State believes that the obligor may flee it may

(1) as an initiating court, request in its certificate that the responding court obtain the body of the obligor by appropriate process; or

(2) as a responding court, obtain the body of the obligor by appropriate process. Thereupon it may release him upon his own recognizance or upon his giving a bond in an amount set by the court to assure his appearance at the hearing.

SECTION 17. [*State Information Agency.*]

(a) The [Attorney General's Office, State Attorney's Office, Welfare Department or other Information Agency] is designated as the state information agency under this Act, it shall

(1) compile a list of the courts and their addresses in this State having jurisdiction under this Act and transmit it to the state information agency of every other state which has adopted this or a substantially similar Act. Upon the adjournment of each session of the [legislature] the agency shall distribute copies of any amendments to the Act and a statement of their effective date to all other state information agencies;

(2) maintain a register of lists of courts received from other states and transmit copies thereof promptly to every court in this state having jurisdiction under this Act; and

(3) forward to the court in this State which has jurisdiction over the obligor or his property petitions, certificates and copies of the Act it receives from courts or information agencies of other states.

(b) If the state information agency does not know the location of the obligor or his property in the state and no state location service is available it shall use all means at its disposal to obtain this information, including the examination of official records in the state and other sources such as telephone directories, real property records, vital statistics records, police records, requests for the name and address from employers who are able or willing to cooperate, records of motor vehicle license offices, requests made to the tax offices both state and federal where such offices are able to cooperate, and requests made to the Social Security Administration as permitted by the Social Security Act as amended.

(c) After the deposit of 3 copies of the [petition] and certificate and one copy of the Act of the initiating state with the clerk of the appropriate court, if the state information agency knows or believes that the prosecuting attorney is not prosecuting the case diligently it shall inform the [Attorney General] [State Director of Public Welfare], who may undertake the representation.

SECTION 18. [*Duty of the Court and Officials of This State as Responding State.*]

(a) After the responding court receives copies of the [petition], certificate, and Act from the initiating court the clerk of the court shall docket the case and notify the prosecuting attorney of his action.

(b) The prosecuting attorney shall prosecute the case diligently. He shall take all action necessary in accordance with the laws of this State to enable the court to obtain jurisdiction over the obligor or his property and shall request the court [clerk of the court] to set a time and place for a hearing and give notice thereof to the obligor in accordance with law.

(c) [If the prosecuting attorney neglects or refuses to represent the obligee the [Attorney General] may order him

489

to comply with the request of the court or may undertake the representation.] [If the prosecuting attorney neglects or refuses to represent the obligee, the [Attorney General] [State Director of Public Welfare] may undertake the representation.]

SECTION 19. [*Further Duties of Court and Officials in the Responding State.*]

(a) The prosecuting attorney on his own initiative shall use all means at his disposal to locate the obligor or his property, and if because of inaccuracies in the [petition] or otherwise the court cannot obtain jurisdiction the prosecuting attorney shall inform the court of what he has done and request the court to continue the case pending receipt of more accurate information or an amended [petition] from the initiating court.

(b) If the obligor or his property is not found in the [county], and the prosecuting attorney discovers that the obligor or his property may be found in another [county] of this State or in another state he shall so inform the court. Thereupon the clerk of the court shall forward the documents received from the court in the initiating state to a court in the other [county] or to a court in the other state or to the information agency or other proper official of the other state with a request that the documents be forwarded to the proper court. All powers and duties provided by this Act apply to the recipient of the documents so forwarded. If the clerk of a court of this State forwards documents to another court he shall forthwith notify the initiating court.

(c) If the prosecuting attorney has no information as to the location of the obligor or his property he shall so inform the initiating court.

SECTION 20. [*Hearing and Continuance.*] If the obligee is not present at the hearing and the obligor denies owing the duty of support alleged in the petition or offers evidence constituting a defense the court, upon request of either party, shall continue the hearing to permit evidence relative to the duty to be adduced by either party by deposition or by appearing in person before the court. The court may designate the judge of the initiating court as a person before whom a deposition may be taken.

SECTION 21. [*Immunity from Criminal Prosecution.*] If at the hearing the obligor is called for examination as an adverse party and he declines to answer upon the ground that his testimony may tend to incriminate him, the court may require him to answer, in which event he is immune from criminal prosecution with respect to matters revealed by his testimony, except for perjury committed in this testimony.

SECTION 22. [*Evidence of Husband and Wife.*] Laws attaching a privilege against the disclosure of communications between husband and wife are inapplicable to proceedings under this Act. Husband and wife are competent witnesses [and may be compelled] to testify to any relevant matter, including marriage and parentage.

SECTION 23. [*Rules of Evidence.*] In any hearing for the civil enforcement of this Act the court is governed by the rules of evidence applicable in a civil court action in the _____ Court. If the action is based on a support order issued by another court a certified copy of the order shall be received as evidence of the duty of support, subject only to any defenses available to an obligor with respect to paternity (Section 27) or to a defendant in an action or a proceeding to enforce a foreign money judgment. The determination or enforcement of a duty of support owed to one obligee is unaffected by any interference by another obligee with rights of custody or visitation granted by a court.

491

SECTION 24. [*Order of Support.*] If the responding court finds a duty of support it may order the obligor to furnish support or reimbursement therefor and subject the property of the obligor to the order. Support orders made pursuant to this Act shall require that payments be made to the [clerk] [bureau] [probation department] of the court of the responding state. [The court and prosecuting attorney of any [county] in which the obligor is present or has property have the same powers and duties to enforce the order as have those of the [county] in which it was first issued. If enforcement is impossible or cannot be completed in the [county] in which the order was issued, the prosecuting attorney shall send a certified copy of the order to the prosecuting attorney of any [county] in which it appears that proceedings to enforce the order would be effective. The prosecuting attorney to whom the certified copy of the order is forwarded shall proceed with enforcement and report the results of the proceedings to the court first issuing the order.]

SECTION 25. [*Responding Court to Transmit Copies to Initiating Court.*] The responding court shall cause a copy of all support orders to be sent to the initiating court.

SECTION 26. [*Additional Powers of Responding Court.*] In addition to the foregoing powers a responding court may subject the obligor to any terms and conditions proper to assure compliance with its orders and in particular to:

(1) require the obligor to furnish a cash deposit or a bond of a character and amount to assure payment of any amount due;

(2) require the obligor to report personally and to make payments at specified intervals to the [clerk] [bureau] [probation department] of the court; and

(3) punish under the power of contempt the obligor who violates any order of the court.

SECTION 27. [*Paternity.*] If the obligor asserts as a defense that he is not the father of the child for whom support is sought and it appears to the court that the defense is not frivolous, and if both of the parties are present at the hearing or the proof required in the case indicates that the presence of either or both of the parties is not necessary, the court may adjudicate the paternity issue. Otherwise the court may adjourn the hearing until the paternity issue has been adjudicated.

SECTION 28 [*Additional Duties of Responding Court.*] A responding court has the following duties which may be carried out through the [clerk] [bureau] [probation department] of the court:

(1) to transmit to the initiating court any payment made by the obligor pursuant to any order of the court or otherwise; and

(2) to furnish to the initiating court upon request a certified statement of all payments made by the obligor.

SECTION 29. [*Additional Duty of Initiating Court.*] An initiating court shall receive and disburse forthwith all payments made by the obligor or sent by the responding court. This duty may be carried out through the [clerk] [bureau] [probation department] of the court.

SECTION 30. [*Proceedings Not to be Stayed.*] A responding court shall not stay the proceeding or refuse a hearing under this Act because of any pending or prior action or proceeding for divorce, separation, annulment, dissolution, habeas corpus, adoption, or custody in this or any other state. The court shall hold a hearing and may issue a support order pendente lite. In aid thereof it may require the obligor to give a bond for the prompt prosecution of the pending proceeding. If the other action or proceeding is concluded before the hearing in the instant proceeding and the judgment therein provides for the support demanded in the [petition] being heard the court must conform its support order to the amount allowed in the other action or proceeding. Thereafter the court shall not stay enforcement of its support order because of the retention of jurisdiction for enforcement purposes by the court in the other action or proceeding.

SECTION 31. [*Application of Payments.*] A support order made by a court of this State pursuant to this Act does not nullify and is not nullified by a support order made by a court of this State pursuant to any other law or by a support order made by a court of any other state pursuant to a substantially similar act or any other law, regardless of priority of issuance, unless otherwise specifically provided by the court. Amounts paid for a particular period pursuant to any support order made by the court of another state shall be credited against the amounts accruing or accrued for the same period under any support order made by the court of this State.

[SECTION 32. [*Effect of Participation in Proceeding.*] Participation in any proceeding under this Act does not confer jurisdiction upon any court over any of the parties thereto in any other proceeding.]

[SECTION 33. [*Interstate Application.*] This Act applies if both the obligee and the obligor are in this State but in different [counties]. If the court of the [county] in which the [petition] is filed finds that the [petition] sets forth facts from which it may be determined that the obligor owes a duty of support and finds that a court of another [county] in this State may obtain jurisdiction over the obligor or his property, the clerk of the court shall send the [petition] and a certification of the findings to the court of the [county] in which the obligor or his property is found. The clerk of the court of the [county] receiving these documents shall notify the prosecuting attorney of their receipt. The prosecuting attorney and the court in the [county] to which the copies are forwarded then shall have duties corresponding to those

494

imposed upon them when acting for this State as a responding state.]

SECTION 34. [*Appeals.*] If the [Attorney General] [State Director of Public Welfare] is of the opinion that a support order is erroneous and presents a question of law warranting an appeal in the public interest, he may

(a) perfect an appeal to the proper appellate court if the support order was issued by a court of this State, or

(b) if the support order was issued in another state, cause the appeal to be taken in the other state. In either case expenses of appeal may be paid on his order from funds appropriated for his office.

PART IV—*Registration of Foreign Support Orders*

SECTION 35. [*Additional Remedies.*] If the duty of support is based on a foreign support order, the obligee has the additional remedies provided in the following sections.

SECTION 36. [*Registration.*] The obligee may register the foreign support order in a court of this State in the manner, with the effect, and for the purposes herein provided.

SECTION 37. [*Registry of Foreign Support Orders.*] The clerk of the court shall maintain a Registry of Foreign Support Orders in which he shall [file] foreign support orders.

SECTION 38. [*Official to Represent Obligee*]. If this State is acting either as a rendering or a registering state the prosecuting attorney upon the request of the court [a state department of welfare, a county commissioner, an overseer of the poor, or other local welfare official] shall represent the obligee in proceedings under this Part.

[If the prosecuting attorney neglects or refuses to represent the obligee, the [Attorney General] may order him to comply with the request of the court or may undertake the representation.] [If the prosecuting attorney

495

neglects or refuses to represent the obligee, the [Attorney General] [State Director of Public Welfare] may undertake the representation.]

SECTION 39. [*Registration Procedure; Notice.*]

(a) An obligee seeking to register a foreign support order in a court of this State shall transmit to the clerk of the court (1) three certified copies of the order with all modification thereof, (2) one copy of the reciprocal enforcement of support act of the state in which the order was made, and (3) a statement verified and signed by the obligee, showing the post office address of the obligee, the last known place of residence and post office address of the obligor, the amount of support remaining unpaid, a description and the location of any property of the obligor available upon execution, and a list of the states in which the order is registered. Upon receipt of these documents the clerk of the court, without payment of a filing fee or other cost to the obligee, shall file them in the Registry of Foreign Support Orders. The filing constitutes registration under this Act.

(b) Promptly upon registration the clerk of the court shall send by certified or registered mail to the obligor at the address given a notice of the registration with a copy of the registered support order and the post office address of the obligee. He shall also docket the case and notify the prosecuting attorney of his action. The prosecuting attorney shall proceed diligently to enforce the order.

SECTION 40. [*Effect of Registration; Enforcement Procedure.*]

(a) Upon registration the registered foreign support order shall be treated in the same manner as a support order issued by a court of this State. It has the same effect and is subject to the same procedures, defenses, and proceedings for reopening, vacating, or staying as a support order of this State and may be enforced and satisfied in like manner.

(b) The obligor has [20] days after the mailing of notice of the registration in which to petition the court to vacate the registration or for other relief. If he does not so petition the registered support order is confirmed.

(c) At the hearing to enforce the registered support order the obligor may present only matters that would be available to him as defenses in an action to enforce a foreign money judgment. If he shows to the court that an appeal from the order is pending or will be taken or that a stay of execution has been granted the court shall stay enforcement of the order until the appeal is concluded, the time for appeal has expired, or the order is vacated, upon satisfactory proof that the obligor has furnished security for payment of the support ordered as required by the rendering state. If he shows to the court any ground upon which enforcement of a support order of this State may be stayed the court shall stay enforcement of the order for an appropriate period if the obligor furnishes the same security for payment of the support ordered that is required for a support order of this State.

SECTION 41. [*Uniformity of Interpretation.*] This Act shall be so construed as to effectuate its general purpose to make uniform the law of those states which enact it.

SECTION 42. [*Short Title.*] This Act may be cited as the Revised Uniform Reciprocal Enforcement of Support Act (1968).

SECTION 43. [*Severability.*] If any provision of this Act or the application thereof to any person or circumstance is held invalid, the invalidity does not affect other provisions or applications of the Act which can be given effect without the invalid provision or application, and to this end the provisions of this Act are severable.

Appendix B

UNIFORM PARENTAGE ACT

Drafted by the

NATIONAL CONFERENCE OF COMMISSIONERS
ON UNIFORM STATE LAWS

and by it

APPROVED AND RECOMMENDED FOR ENACTMENT
IN ALL THE STATES

at its

ANNUAL CONFERENCE
MEETING IN ITS EIGHTY-SECOND YEAR
AT HYANNIS, MASSACHUSETTS
JULY 26-AUGUST 2, 1973

Approved by the American Bar Association at its Annual Meeting in 1974

The Committee which acted for the National Conference of Commissioners on Uniform State Laws in preparing the Uniform Parentage Act was as follows:

LEWIS C. GREEN, 1830 Boatmen's Bank Bldg., St. Louis, MO 63102, *Chairman*

LOREN M. BOBBITT, Room 112, State House, Springfield, IL 62706

ELWYN EVANS, 502 Market Tower Bldg., Wilmington, DE 19801

RICHARD E. FORD, 203 W. Randolph St., Lewisburg, WV 24901

WILLIAM C. GARDNER, 615 F. St., NW, Washington, DC 20004

CLARKE A. GRAVEL, 109 S. Winooski Ave., Burlington, VT 05401

W. L. MATTHEWS, JR., University of Kentucky College of Law, Lexington, KY 40506

DWIGHT A. HAMILTON, 900 Equitable Building, Denver, CO 80202 *Chairman, Division C, Ex Officio*

EUGENE A. BURDICK, P. O. Box 757, Williston, ND 58801, *President, Ex Officio*

Reporter-Draftsman

HARRY D. KRAUSE, University of Illinois College of Law, Champaign, IL 61820

SECTION 1. [*Parent and Child Relationship Defined.*]

As used in this Act, "parent and child relationship" means the legal relationship existing between a child and his natural or adoptive parents incident to which the law confers or imposes rights, privileges, duties, and obligations. It includes the mother and child relationship and the father and child relationship.

SECTION 2. [*Relationship Not Dependent on Marriage.*]

The parent and child relationship extends equally to every child and to every parent, regardless of the marital status of the parents.

SECTION 3. [*How Parent and Child Relationship Established.*] The parent and child relationship between a child and

(1) the natural mother may be established by proof of her having given birth to the child, or under this Act;

(2) the natural father may be established under this Act;

(3) an adoptive parent may be established by proof of adoption or under the [Revised Uniform Adoption Act].

500

SECTION 4. [*Presumption of Paternity.*]

(a) A man is presumed to be the natural father of a child if:

(1) he and the child's natural mother are or have been married to each other and the child is born during the marriage, or within 300 days after the marriage is terminated by death, annulment, declaration of invalidity, or divorce, or after a decree of separation is entered by a court;

(2) before the child's birth, he and the child's natural mother have attempted to marry each other by a marriage solemnized in apparent compliance with law, although the attempted marriage is or could be declared invalid, and,

(i) if the attempted marriage could be declared invalid only by a court, the child is born during the attempted marriage, or within 300 days after its termination by death, annulment, declaration of invalidity, or divorce; or

(ii) if the attempted marriage is invalid without a court order, the child is born within 300 days after the termination of cohabitation;

(3) after the child's birth, he and the child's natural mother have married, or attempted to marry, each other by a marriage solemnized in apparent compliance with law, although the attempted marriage is or could be declared invalid, and

(i) he has acknowledged his paternity of the child in writing filed with the [appropriate court or Vital Statistics Bureau],

(ii) with his consent, he is named as the child's father on the child's birth certificate, or

(iii) he is obligated to support the child under a written voluntary promise or by court order;

501

(4) while the child is under the age of majority, he receives the child into his home and openly holds out the child as his natural child; or

(5) he acknowledges his paternity of the child in a writing filed with the [appropriate court or Vital Statistics Bureau], which shall promptly inform the mother of the filing of the acknowledgment, and she does not dispute the acknowledgment within a reasonable time after being informed thereof, in a writing filed with the [appropriate court or Vital Statistics Bureau]. If another man is presumed under this section to be the child's father, acknowledgment may be effected only with the written consent of the presumed father or after the presumption has been rebutted.

(b) A presumption under this section may be rebutted in an appropriate action only by clear and convincing evidence. If two or more presumptions arise which conflict with each other, the presumption which on the facts is founded on the weightier considerations of policy and logic controls. The presumption is rebutted by a court decree establishing paternity of the child by another man.

SECTION 5. [*Artificial Insemination.*]

(a) If, under the supervision of a licensed physician and with the consent of her husband, a wife is inseminated artificially with semen donated by a man not her husband, the husband is treated in law as if he were the natural father of a child thereby conceived. The husband's consent must be in writing and signed by him and his wife. The physician shall certify their signatures and the date of the insemination, and file the husband's consent with the [State Department of Health], where it shall be kept confidential and in a sealed file. However, the physician's failure to do so does not affect the father and child relationship. All papers and records pertaining to the insemination, whether

502

part of the permanent record of a court or of a file held by the supervising physician or elsewhere, are subect to inspection only upon an order of the court for good cause shown.

(b) The donor of semen provided to a licensed physician for use in artificial insemination of a married woman other than the donor's wife is treated in law as if he were not the natural father of a child thereby conceived.

SECTION 6. [*Determination of Father and Child Relationship; Who May Bring Action; When Action May Be Brought.*]

(a) A child, his natural mother, or a man presumed to be his father under Paragraph (1), (2), or (3) of Section 4(a), may bring an action

(1) at any time for the purpose of declaring the existence of the father and child relationship presumed under Paragraph (1), (2), or (3) of Section 4(a); or

(2) for the purpose of declaring the non-existence of the father and child relationship presumed under Paragraph (1), (2), or (3) of Section 4(a) only if the action is brought within a reasonable time after obtaining knowledge of relevant facts, but in no event later than [5] years after the child's birth. After the presumption has been rebutted, paternity of the child by another man may be determined in the same action, if he has been made a party.

(b) Any interested party may bring an action at any time for the purpose of determining the existence or non-existence of the father and child relationship presumed under Paragraph (4) or (5) of Section 4(a).

(c) An action to determine the existence of the father and child relationship with respect to a child who has no presumed father under Section 4 may be brought by the child, the mother or personal representative of the child, the [appropriate state agency], the personal representative or a parent of the mother if the mother has died, a man alleged or alleging himself to be the father, or the personal representative or a parent of the alleged father if the alleged father has died or is a minor.

(d) Regardless of its terms, an agreement, other than an agreement approved by the court in accordance with Section 13(b), between an alleged or presumed father and the mother or child, does not bar an action under this section.

(e) If an action under this section is brought before the birth of the child, all proceedings shall be stayed until after the birth, except services of process and the taking of depositions to perpetuate testimony.

SECTION 7. [*Statute of Limitations.*] An action to determine the existence of the father and child relationship as to a child who has no presumed father under Section 4 may not be brought later than [3] years after the birth of the child, or later than [3] years after the effective date of this Act, whichever is later. However, an action brought by or on behalf of a child whose paternity has not been determined is not barred until [3] years after the child reaches the age of majority. Sections 6 and 7 do not extend the time within which a right of inheritance or a right to a succession may be asserted beyond the time provided by law relating to distribution and closing of decedents' estates or to the determination of heirship, or otherwise.

SECTION 8. [*Jurisdiction; Venue.*]

(a) [Without limiting the jurisdiction of any other court,] [The] [appropriate] court has jurisdiction of an action brought under this Act. [The action may be joined with an action for divorce, annulment, separate maintenance, or support.]

(b) A person who has sexual intercourse in this State thereby submits to the jurisdiction of the courts of this State as to an action brought under this Act with respect to a child who may have been conceived by that act of intercourse. In addition to any other method provided by [rule or] statute, including [cross reference to "long arm statute"], personal jurisdiction may be acquired by [personal service of summons outside this State or by registered mail with proof of actual receipt] [service in accordance with (citation to "long arm statute")].

(c) The action may be brought in the county in which the child or the alleged father resides or is found or, if the father is deceased, in which proceedings for probate of his estate have been or could be commenced.

SECTION 9. [*Parties.*] The child shall be made a party to the action. If he is a minor he shall be represented by his general guardian or a guardian ad litem appointed by the court. The child's mother or father may not represent the child as guardian or otherwise. The court may appoint the [appropriate state agency] as guardian ad litem for the child. The natural mother, each man presumed to be the father under Section 4, and each man alleged to be the natural father, shall be made parties or, if not subject to the jurisdiction of the court, shall be given notice of the action in a manner prescribed by the court and an opportunity to be heard. The court may align the parties.

SECTION 10. [*Pre-Trial Proceedings.*]

(a) As soon as practicable after an action to declare the existence or non-existence of the father and child relationship has been brought, an informal hearing shall be held. [The court may order that the hearing be held before a referee.] The public shall be barred from the hearing. A record of the proceeding or any portion thereof shall be kept if any party requests, or the court orders. Rules of evidence need not be observed.

(b) Upon refusal of any witness, including a party, to testify under oath or produce evidence, the court may order him to testify under oath and produce evidence concerning all relevant facts. If the refusal is upon the ground that his testimony or evidence might tend to incriminate him, the court may grant him immunity from all criminal liability on account of the testimony or evidence he is required to produce. An order granting immunity bars prosecution of the witness for any offense shown in whole or in part by testimony or evidence he is required to produce, except for perjury committed in his testimony. The refusal of a witness, who has been granted immunity, to obey an order to testify or produce evidence is a civil contempt of the court.

(c) Testimony of a physician concerning the medical circumstances of the pregnancy and the condition and characteristics of the child upon birth is not privileged.

SECTION 11. [*Blood Tests.*]

(a) The court may, and upon request of a party shall, require the child, mother, or alleged father to submit to blood tests. The tests shall be performed by an expert qualified as an examiner of blood types, appointed by the court.

(b) The court, upon reasonble request by a party, shall order that independent tests be performed by other experts qualified as examiner of blood types.

(c) In all cases, the court shall determine the number and qualifications of the experts.

SECTION 12. [*Evidence Relating to Paternity.*] Evidence relating to paternity may include:

(1) evidence of sexual intercourse between the mother and alleged father at any possible time of conception;

(2) an expert's opinion concerning the statistical

probability of the alleged father's paternity based upon the duration of the mother's pregnancy;

(3) blood test results, weighted in accordance with evidence, if available, of the statistical probability of the alleged father's paternity;

(4) medical or anthropological evidence relating to the alleged father's paternity of the child based on tests performed by experts. If a man has been identified as a possible father of the child, the court may, and upon request of a party shall, require the child, the mother, and the man to submit to appropriate tests; and

(5) all other evidence relevant to the issue of paternity of the child.

SECTION 13. [*Pre-Trial Recommendations.*]

(a) On the basis of the information produced at the pre-trial hearing, the judge [or referee] conducting the hearing shall evaluate the probability of determining the existence or non-existence of the father and child relationship in a trial and whether a judicial declaration of the relationship would be in the best interest of the child. On the basis of the evaluation, an appropriate recommendation for settlement shall be made to the parties, which may include any of the following:

(1) that the action be dismissed with or without prejudice;

(2) that the matter be compromised by an agreement among the alleged father, the mother, and the child, in which the father and child relationship is not determined but in which a defined economic obligation is undertaken by the alleged father in favor of the child and, if appropriate, in favor of the mother, subject to approval by the judge [or referee] conducting the hearing. In reviewing the obligation undertaken by the alleged father in a compromise agreement, the judge [or referee]

conducting the hearing shall consider the best interest of the child, in the light of the factors enumerated in Section 15(e), discounted by the improbability, as it appears to him, of establishing the alleged father's paternity or non-paternity of the child in a trial of the action. In the best interest of the child, the court may order that the alleged father's identity be kept confidential. In that case, the court may designate a person or agency to receive from the alleged father and disburse on behalf of the child all amounts paid by the alleged father in fulfillment of obligations imposed on him; and

(3) that the alleged father voluntarily acknowledge his paternity of the child.

(b) If the parties accept a recommendation made in accordance with Subsection (a), judgment shall be entered accordingly.

(c) If a party refuses to accept a recommendation made under Subsection (a) and blood tests have not been taken, the court shall require the parties to submit to blood tests, if practicable. Thereafter the judge [or referee] shall make an appropriate final recommendation. If a party refuses to accept the final recommendation, the action shall be set for trial.

(d) The guardian ad litem may accept or refuse to accept a recommendation under this Section.

(e) The informal hearing may be terminated and the action set for trial if the judge [or referee] conducting the hearing finds it unlikely that all parties would accept a recommendation he might make under Subsection (a) or (c).

SECTION 14. [*Civil Action; Jury.*]

(a) An action under this Act is a civil action governed by the rules of civil procedure. The mother of the child and the alleged father are competent to testify and may be compelled to testify. Subsections (b) and (c) of Section 10 and Sections 11 and 12 apply.

(b) Testimony relating to sexual access to the mother by an unidentified man at any time or by an identified man at a time other than the probable time of conception of the child is inadmissible in evidence, unless offered by the mother.

(c) In an action against an alleged father, evidence offered by him with respect to a man who is not subject to the jurisdiction of the court concerning his sexual intercourse with the mother at or about the probable time of conception of the child is admissible in evidence only if he has undergone and made available to the court blood tests the results of which do not exclude the possibility of his paternity of the child. A man who is identified and is subject to the jurisdiction of the court shall be made a defendant in the action.

[(d) The trial shall be by the court without a jury.]

SECTION 15. [*Judgment or Order.*]

(a) The judgment or order of the court determining the existence or non-existence of the parent and child relationship is determinative for all purposes.

(b) If the judgment or order of the court is at variance with the child's birth certificate, the court shall order that [an amended birth registration be made] [a new birth certificate be issued] under Section 23.

(c) The judgment or order may contain any other provision directed against the appropriate party to the proceeding, concerning the duty of support, the custody and guardianship of the child, visitation privileges with the child, the furnishing of bond or other security for the payment of the judgment, or any other matter in the best interest of the child. The judgment or order may direct the father to pay the reasonable expenses of the mother's pregnancy and confinement.

(d) Support judgments or orders ordinarily shall be for periodic payments which may vary in amount. In the best interest of the child, a lump sum payment or the purchase of an annuity may be ordered in lieu of periodic payments of support. The court may limit the father's liability for past support of the child to the proportion of the expenses already incurred that the court deems just.

(e) In determining the amount to be paid by a parent for support of the child and the period during which the duty of support is owed, a court enforcing the obligation of support shall consider all relevant facts, including

(1) the needs of the child;

(2) the standard of living and circumstances of the parents;

(3) the relative financial means of the parents;

(4) the earning ability of the parents;

(5) the need and capacity of the child for education, including higher education;

(6) the age of the child;

(7) the financial resources and the earning ability of the child;

(8) the responsibility of the parents for the support of others; and

(9) the value of services contributed by the custodial parent.

SECTION 16. [*Costs.*] The court may order reasonable fees of counsel, experts, and the child's guardian ad litem, and other costs of the action and pre-trial proceedings, including blood tests, to be paid by the parties in proportions and at times determined by the court. The court may order the proportion of any indigent party to be paid by [appropriate public authority].

SECTION 17. [*Enforcement of Judgment or Order.*]

(a) If existence of the father and child relationship is declared, or paternity or a duty of support has been acknowledged or adjudicated under this Act or under prior law, the obligation of the father may be enforced in the same or other proceedings by the mother, the child, the public authority that has furnished or may furnish the reasonable expenses of pregnancy, confinement, education, support, or funeral, or by any other person, including a private agency, to the extent he has furnished or is furnishing these expenses.

(b) The court may order support payments to be made to the mother, the clerk of the court, or a person, corporation, or agency designated to administer them for the benefit of the child under the supervision of the court.

(c) Willful failure to obey the judgment or order of the court is a civil contempt of the court. All remedies for the enforcement of judgments apply.

SECTION 18. [*Modification of Judgment or Order.*] The court has continuing jurisdiction to modify or revoke a judgment or order

(1) for future education and support, and

(2) with respect to matters listed in Subsections (c) and

(d) of Section 15 and Section 17(b), except that a court entering a judgment or order for the payment of a lump sum or the purchase of an annuity under Section 15(d) may specify that the judgment or order may not be modified or revoked.

SECTION 19. [*Right to Counsel; Free Transcript on Appeal.*]

(a) At the pre-trial hearing and in further proceedings, any party may be represented by counsel. The court shall appoint counsel for a party who is financially unable to obtain counsel.

(b) If a party is financially unable to pay the cost of a transcript, the court shall furnish on request a transcript for purposes of appeal.

SECTION 20. [*Hearings and Records; Confidentiality.*] Notwithstanding any other law concerning public hearings and records, any hearing or trial held under this Act shall be held in closed court without admittance of any person other than those necessary to the action or proceeding. All papers and records, other than the final judgment, pertaining to the action or proceeding, whether part of the permanent record of the court or of a file in the [appropriate state agency] or elsewhere, are subject to inspection only upon consent of the court and all interested persons, or in exceptional cases only upon an order of the court for good cause shown.

SECTION 21. [*Action to Declare Mother and Child Relationship.*] Any interested party may bring an action to determine the existence or non-existence of a mother and child relationship. Insofar as practicable, the provisions of this Act applicable to the father and child relationship apply.

SECTION 22. [*Promise to Render Support.*]

(a) Any promise in writing to furnish support for a child, growing out of a supposed or alleged father and child relationship, does not require consideration and is enforceable according to its terms, subject to Section 6(d).

(b) In the best interest of the child or the mother, the court may, and upon the promisor's request shall, order the promise to be kept in confidence and designate a person or agency to receive and disburse on behalf of the child all amounts paid in performance of the promise.

SECTION 23. [*Birth Records.*]

(a) Upon order of a court of this State or upon request of a court of another state, the [registrar of births] shall prepare [an amended birth registration] [a new certificate of birth] consistent with the findings of the court [and shall substitute the new certificate for the original certificate of birth].

(b) The fact that the father and child relationship was declared after the child's birth shall not be ascertainable from the [amended birth registration] [new certificate] but the actual place and date of birth shall be shown.

(c) The evidence upon which the [amended birth registration] [new certificate] was made and the original birth certificate shall be kept in a sealed and confidential file and be subject to inspection only upon consent of the court and all interested persons, or in exceptional cases only upon an order of the court for good cause shown.

SECTION 24. [*Custodial Proceedings.*]

(a) If a mother relinquishes or proposes to relinquish for adoption a child who has (1) a presumed father under Section 4(a), (2) a father whose relationship to the child has been determined by a court, or (3) a father as to whom the child is a legitimate child under prior law of this State or under the law of another jurisdiction, the father shall be given notice of the adoption proceeding and have the rights provided under [the appropriate State statute] [the Revised Uniform Adoption Act], unless the father's relationship to the child has been previously terminated or determined by a court not to exist.

(b) If a mother relinquishes or proposes to relinquish for adoption a child who does not have (1) a presumed father under Section 4(a), (2) a father whose relationship to the child has been determined by a court, or (3) a father as to whom the child is a legitimate child under prior law of this State or under the law of another jurisdiction, or if a child otherwise becomes the subject of an adoption proceeding, the agency or person to whom the child has been or is to be relinquished, or the mother or the person having custody of the child, shall file a petition in the [   ] court to terminate the parental rights of the father, unless the father's relationship to the child has been previously terminated or determined not to exist by a court.

513

(c) In an effort to identify the natural father, the court shall cause inquiry to be made of the mother and any other appropriate person. The inquiry shall include the following: whether the mother was married at the time of conception of the child or at any time thereafter; whether the mother was cohabiting with a man at the time of conception or birth of the child; whether the mother has received support payments or promises of support with respect to the child or in connection with her pregnancy; or whether any man has formally or informally acknowledged or declared his possible paternity of the child.

(d) If, after the inquiry, the natural father is identified to the satisfaction of the court, or if more than one man is identified as a possible father, each shall be given notice of the proceeding in accordance with Subsection (f). If any of them fails to appear or, if appearing, fails to claim custodial rights, his parental rights with reference to the child shall be terminated. If the natural father or a man representing himself to be the natural father, claims custodial rights, the court shall proceed to determine custodial rights.

(e) If, after the inquiry, the court is unable to identify the natural father or any possible natural father and no person has appeared claiming to be the natural father and claiming custodial rights, the court shall enter an order terminating the unknown natural father's parental rights with reference to the child. Subject to the disposition of an appeal, upon the expiration of [6 months] after an order terminating parental rights is issued under this subsection, the order cannot be questioned by any person, in any manner, or upon any ground, including fraud, misrepresentation, failure to give any required notice, or lack of jurisdiction of the parties or of the subject matter.

(f) Notice of the proceeding shall be given to every person identified as the natural father or a possible natural father [in the manner appropriate under rules of civil procedure

514

for the service of process in a civil action in this state, or] in any manner the court directs. Proof of giving the notice shall be filed with the court before the petition is heard. [If no person has been identified as the natural father or a possible father, the court, on the basis of all information available, shall determine whether publication or public posting of notice of the proceeding is likely to lead to identification and, if so, shall order publication or public posting at times and in places and manner it deems appropriate.]

SECTION 25. [*Uniformity of Application and Construction.*] This Act shall be applied and construed to effectuate its general purpose to make uniform the law with respect to the subject of this Act among states enacting it.

SECTION 26. [*Short Title.*] This Act may be cited as the Uniform Parentage Act.

SECTION 27. [*Severability.*] If any provision of this Act or the application thereof to any person or circumstance is held invalid, the invalidity does not affect other provisions or applications of the Act which can be given effect without the invalid provision or application, and to this end the provisions of this Act are severable.

SECTION 28. [*Repeal.*] The following acts and parts of acts are repealed:

(1) [Paternity Act]

(2)

(3)

SECTION 29. [*Time of Taking Effect.*] This Act shall take effect on [   ].

Appendix C

CITATIONS TO STATE STATUTES ON CHILD SUPPORT ENFORCE-MENT AND PATERNITY

GERD OTTE, LLM*

ABBREVIATIONS

Art.	— Article
C	— cumulative
CA	— Cumulative Annotations
CC	— Civil Code
CCP	— Code of Criminal Procedure
ch.	— Chapter
Civ. Proc.	— Civil Procedure
CPLR	— Civil Practice Law and Rules
CS	— Cumulative Supplement
evid.	— Evidence
F.C.	— Family Court
ill. ch.	— illegitimate child
IO	— implied obligation
leg.	— legitimate child
pen.	— penal
Rev. Act	— Revised Act
seq.	— sequence
SP	— Supplementary Pamphlet
ss	— Sections
tit.	— Title
+	— et seq.
§	— Section

---

* University of Illinois; Dr. jur. Bielefeld.

APPENDIX C

	Alabama, Ala. Code §	Alaska, Alaska Stat. §	Arkansas, Ark. Stat. Ann. §
1. Support Obligation	30-3-1	25.20.030	57-633 IO
a. Child support	30-2-31	25.20.030	57-633 IO
b. Illegitimate support	26-12-4		
c. States not allowing alimony			
d. Relative responsibility			
2. Amount of Support Obligation	26-12-4	47.23.060	
a. Fixed criteria		47.23.060	
b. Schedules or $ amounts	26-12-4		
3. Period of Obligation			
a. Majority			
b. Emancipation			
c. Higher education			
4. Paternity Statute	26-12-1 +		34-701 +
Blood test provision	26-12-5		34-705.1 +
5. Enforcement			
a. Criminal nonsupport	30-4-51, 30-4-63	11.51.120	41-2405
b. Contempt	30-4-58	09.50.010	
i. criminal	12-3-11	09.50.020	41-2452
ii. civil	12-3-11	09.50.020	34-1212
c. Civil enforcement	30-4-59		34-1212
i. garnishment (wage deduction)		47.23.070	34-1212
ii. bond, security, lien on land	30-4-59	47.23.230	34-1211
6. Uniform Acts, National Conference of Commissioners on Uniform State Laws			
a. Enforcement of Foreign Judgments Act		(1964 Rev. Act): §§ 09.30.200 to 09.30.270	(1948): §§ 29-801 to 29-818
b. Foreign Money-Judgment Recognition Act		§§ 09.30.100 to 09.30.180	
c. Parentage Act			
d. Act on Paternity (officially "withdrawn" by NCCUSL in 1979)			
e. URESA	§§ 30-4-80 to 30-4-98	§§ 25.25.010 to 25.25.270	§§ 34-2401 to 34-2442

	Arizona, Ariz. Rev. Stat. §	California, Cal. (subject) Code § (West)	Colorado, Colo. Rev. Stat. §
1. Support Obligation	12-2451 SP	CC § 196 + C	14-10-115
a. Child support	12-2451 SP	CC § 196 + C	14-10-115
		CC § 4700 C	
b. Illegitimate support	8-601 CS	CC § 196 + C	
c. States not allowing alimony			
d. Relative responsibility	46-295 CS		
2. Amount of Support Obligation			
a. Fixed criteria			
b. Schedules or $ amounts			
3. Period of Obligation			
a. Majority		CC 4700 C	
b. Emancipation			
c. Higher education			
4. Paternity Statute	12-841 + SP	Evid. § 895	
Blood test provision	12-847 SP	Evid. § 890 +	19-6-112
5. Enforcement			14-6-112
a. Criminal nonsupport			14-6-101
b. Contempt			19-6-118
i. criminal	12-861 +	Pen. § 166	
ii. civil		CC § 7012 C	
c. Civil enforcement			
i. garnishment (wage deduction)		CC § 4701 + & CCP § 723.030 C	
ii. bond, security, lien on land			14-6-109
6. Uniform Acts, National Conference of Commissioners on Uniform State Laws			
a. Enforcement of Foreign Judgments Act	(1964 Rev. Act): §§ 12-1701 to 12-1708		(1964 Rev. Act): §§ 13-53-101 to 13-53-108
b. Foreign Money-Judgment Recognition Act		Civ. Proc. §§ 1713 to 1713.8	§§ 13-62-101 to 13-62-109
c. Parentage Act		CC §§ 7000 to 7018	§§ 19-6-101 19-6-129
d. Act on Paternity (officially "withdrawn" by NCCUSL in 1979)			
e. URESA	(1968): §§ 12-1651 to 12-1691 SP	(1968): Civ. Proc. §§ 1650 to 1699	(1968): §§ 14-5-101 to 14-5-143

	Connecticut, Conn. Gen. Stat. Ann. §	Delaware, Del. Code Ann. tit. x, §	District of Columbia, D.C. Code Encycl. § (West)
1. Support Obligation	46b-37 C	13, § 501 & 701 CS	16-911 CA
a. Child support	46b-171 C	13, § 501 & 505 (Priority) CS	16-911 CA
b. Illegitimate support		13, § 501 CS	
c. States not allowing alimony			
d. Relative responsibility			
2. Amount of Support Obligation		13, § 514 CS	
a. Fixed criteria			
b. Schedules or $ amounts			
3. Period of Obligation			
a. Majority		13, § 501 CS	
b. Emancipation			
c. Higher education		13, § 501 CS	
4. Paternity Statute	46b-160 + C		16-909 CA
Blood test provision	46b-168 C		16-2343 CA
5. Enforcement	52-362 C		
a. Criminal nonsupport	53-304 C	13, § 521 CS	
b. Contempt			
i. criminal		13, § 516 CS	
ii. civil		13, § 516 CS	
c. Civil enforcement			16-2341 CA
i. garnishment (wage deduction)		13, § 516 CS	16-911 CA
ii. bond, security, lien on land			
6. Uniform Acts, National Conference of Commissioners on Uniform State Laws			
a. Enforcement of Foreign Judgments Act	(1964 Rev. Act): §§ 52-604 to 52-609		
b. Foreign Money-Judgment Recognition Act			
c. Parentage Act			
d. Act on Paternity (officially "withdrawn" by NCCUSL in 1979)			
e. URESA	(1950): §§ 46b-180 to 46b-211	(1950): 13 §§ 601 to 639	(1950) §§ 30-301 to 30-324

	Florida, Fla. Stat. Ann. § (West)	Georgia, GA Code Ann. §	Hawaii, Hawaii Rev. Stat. §
1. Support Obligation	39.11 IO	74-105 C	573-32
a. Child support	39.11	74-105 C	
b. Illegitimate support	39.11	74-202 C	577-14
c. States not allowing alimony			
d. Relative responsibility			
2. Amount of Support Obligation			
a. Fixed criteria			
b. Schedules or $ amounts	742.041		
3. Period of Obligation	742.041 & 743.07 C		
a. Majority			
b. Emancipation			
c. Higher education			
4. Paternity Statute	742.011 +		
Blood test provision		74-9902 C	
5. Enforcement	61.17 +		
a. Criminal nonsupport	827.06	74-9902 C	709-903
b. Contempt	61.18		
i. criminal			
ii. civil			
c. Civil enforcement			
i. garnishment (wage deduction)	61.12 C		571-52
ii. bond, security, lien on land			575-2
6. Uniform Acts, National Conference of Commissioners on Uniform State Laws			
a. Enforcement of Foreign Judgments Act			
b. Foreign Money-Judgment Recognition Act			
c. Parentage Act			584-1 to 584-26
d. Act on Paternity (officially "withdrawn" by NCCUSL in 1979)			
e. URESA	(1968): §§ 88.011 to 88.371	(1950): §§ 99-901a to 99-932a	(1950): §§ 576-1 to 576-41

APPENDIX C

	Idaho, Idaho Code §	Illinois, Ill. Rev. Stat. Ch. , §	Indiana, Ind. Code §
1. Support Obligation	32-1001 +	ch. 23 § 10-2	
a. Child support	32-1001 +	ch. 23 § 10-2 & ch. 40, § 505	31-1-9-10
b. Illegitimate support	7-1105	ch. 40 § 1352	31-6-6.1-10 & 13 CS
c. States not allowing alimony			§ 31-6-6-2
d. Relative responsibility		ch. 23 § 10-1	
2. Amount of Support Obligation			
a. Fixed criteria			
b. Schedules or $ amounts			
3. Period of Obligation	7-1121 (ill. ch.)	ch. 23 § 10-2	
a. Majority			
b. Emancipation		ch. 23 § 10-2	
c. Higher education	7-1121 (ill. ch.)		
4. Paternity Statute	7-1101 +	ch. 40 § 1351 +	31-6-6.1-1 + CS
Blood test provision	7-1115 +	ch. 40 § 1401 +	31-6-6.1-8 CS
5. Enforcement	56-203A	ch. 23 § 10-10 +	31-1-9-11 +
a. Criminal nonsupport	18-401	ch. 40 § 1101	35-46-1-5 CS
b. Contempt		ch. 37 § 707-4	31-2-8-1
i. criminal		ch. 37 § 707-4	
ii. civil		ch. 37 § 707-4	31-2-8-1
c. Civil enforcement			31-1-9-12
i. garnishment (wage deduction)	8-704	ch. 37 § 707-4	35-14-8-1
ii. bond, security, lien on land		ch. 40 § 706	31-1-9-12
6. Uniform Acts, National Conference of Commissioners on Uniform State Laws			
a. Enforcement of Foreign Judgments Act	(1964 Rev. Act): §§ 10-1301 to 10-1308	(1968): ch. 77 §§ 88 to 105	
b. Foreign Money-Judgment Recognition Act		ch. 77 §§ 121 to 129	
c. Parentage Act			
d. Act on Paternity (officially "withdrawn" by NCCUSL in 1979)			
e. URESA	(1968): §§ 7-1048 to 7-1089	(1968): ch. 40 §§ 1201 to 1242	(1950): §§ 31-2-1-1 to 31-2-1-39

522

	Iowa, Iowa Code Ann. § (West)	Kansas, Kan. Stat. Ann. §	Kentucky, Ky. Rev. Stat. §
1. Support Obligation	252.2		405.020 IO
a. Child support			
b. Illegitimate support	675.1	38-1106	406.011 CS
c. States not allowing alimony			
d. Relative responsibility	252.5		
2. Amount of Support Obligation			
a. Fixed criteria			
b. Schedules or $ amounts			
3. Period of Obligation			
a. Majority		60-1610	
b. Emancipation			
c. Higher education			
4. Paternity Statute	675.1 +	38-1101 +	406.021 + CS
Blood test provision		23-131	406.081
5. Enforcement	253.6 & 252 B.3 C		
a. Criminal nonsupport	726.5	21-3605	530.050 CS
b. Contempt	675.37 C		
i. criminal			
ii. civil			
c. Civil enforcement			
i. garnishment (wage deduction)		60-721 C	405.035 CS
ii. bond, security, lien on land			
6. Uniform Acts, National Conference of Commissioners on Uniform State Laws			
a. Enforcement of Foreign Judgments Act	(1964 Rev. Act): no. cit. (yet). Eff. 1-1-80	(1964 Rev. Act): §§ 60-3001 to 60-3008	
b. Foreign Money-Judgment Recognition Act			
c. Parentage Act			
d. Act on Paternity (officially "withdrawn" by NCCUSL in 1979)			§§ 406.011 to 406.180
e. URESA	(1950): §§ 252 A.1 to 252 A.12	(1968): §§ 23-451 to 23-491	(1968): §§ 407.010 to 407.440

523

	Louisiana, La. Rev. Stat. Ann. § (West) encl. La. Civ. Code (CC) Ann. Art. (West)	Maine, Me. Rev. Stat. Ann. tit. , §	Maryland, MD [subject (if therein)] Code Ann. § or MD. Ann. Code Art. , §
1. Support Obligation	CC Art. 227 CS	tit. 19 § 214 and 301 + CS	Art. 72A § 1
a. Child support	CC Art. 227 CS		
b. Illegitimate support	CC Art. 240 CS	tit. 19 § 271 CS	Art. 16 § 66H CS
c. States not allowing alimony			
d. Relative responsibility			
2. Amount of Support Obligation			
a. Fixed criteria			
b. Schedules or $ amounts			
3. Period of Obligation			
a. Majority			(Ill. ch. Art. 16 § 66H CS
b. Emancipation			
c. Higher education			
4. Paternity Statute		tit. 19 § 271 + CS	Art. 16 §§ 66A to 66P CS
Blood test provision	9.396 CS	tit. 19 § 277 CS	Art. 16 § 66G CS
5. Enforcement		tit. 19 § 502 + CS	Art. 27 § 88 & 97
a. Criminal nonsupport	14.74 C	tit. 19 § 481 CS	
b. Contempt		tit. 19 § 722 CS	
i. criminal	14.75 C		Art. 27 § 91
ii. civil			
c. Civil enforcement			
i. garnishment (wage deduction)	13:3928	tit. 19 § 511 CS	
ii. bond, security, lien on land		tit. 19 § 503 CS	Art. 27, § 88 & 101
6. Uniform Acts, National Conference of Commissioners on Uniform State Laws			
a. Enforcement of Foreign Judgments Act		(1964 Rev. Act): §§ 8001 to 8008	
b. Foreign Money-Judgment Recognition Act			Code, Courts & Judicial Proceedings §§ 10-701 to 10-709
c. Parentage Act			
d. Act on Paternity (officially "withdrawn" by NCCUSL in 1979)		tit. 19 §§ 271 to 287	
e. URESA	(1968): §§ 13.1641 to 13.1698	(1968): tit. 19 §§ 331 to 420	(1950): Art. 89C, §§ 1 to 39

	Massachusetts, Mass. Ann. (our ch. § (Michie Law Co-op)	Michigan, Mich. Stat. Ann. §	Minnesota, Minn. Stat. Ann. § (West)
1. Support Obligation		25.244(3)	518.17 & 518.57 CS
a. Child support		25.244(3)	
b. Illegitimate support		25.492	257.251 CS
c. States not allowing alimony			
d. Relative responsibility			
2. Amount of Support Obligation			
a. Fixed criteria			
b. Schedules or $ amounts			
3. Period of Obligation			
a. Majority			
b. Emancipation		25.244(3)	
c. Higher education			
4. Paternity Statute	ch. 273 § 11 + CS	25.491 — 25.510	257.251 + CS
Blood test provision	ch. 273 § 12A CS	25.496	Rule 35.01 + Dist. Ct. Rules
5. Enforcement	ch. 273 § 5 CS	25.244(3) (n. 2)	
a. Criminal nonsupport	ch. 273 § 1 & 15 CS	28.358	609.375 CS
b. Contempt	ch. 215 §§ 34A seq. CS		
i. criminal			588.02 +
ii. civil			257.262 CS
c. Civil enforcement			
i. garnishment (wage deduction)		25.504 27.3178 (519.18b) CS	518.611 CS
ii. bond, security, lien on land	ch. 208 § 12-14 CS	25.103; 25.499	518.57 CS
6. Uniform Acts, National Conference of Commissioners on Uniform State Laws			
a. Enforcement of Foreign Judgments Act			(1964 Rev. Act): §§ 548.26 to 548.33
b. Foreign Money-Judgment Recognition Act	ch. 235 § 23A	691.1151 to 691.1159	
c. Parentage Act			Minn. Laws 1980, ch. 589
d. Act on Paternity (officially "withdrawn" by NCCUSL in 1979)			
e. URESA	(1950): ch. 273A §§ 1 to 17	(1950): §§ 780.151 to 780.174	(1950): §§ 518.41 to 518.53

	Mississippi, Miss. Code Ann. §	Missouri, Mo. Ann. Stat. § (Vernon)	Montana, Mont. Rev. Codes Ann. §
1. Support Obligation	43-19-1 + CS	452.340	61-104 CS
a. Child support			61-104 CS
b. Illegitimate support	93-9-7		
c. States not allowing alimony			
d. Relative responsibility			
2. Amount of Support Obligation			
a. Fixed criteria			
b. Schedules or $ amounts			
3. Period of Obligation			
a. Majority			
b. Emancipation			
c. Higher education			
4. Paternity Statute	93-9-1 +		61-301 + CS
Blood test provision	93-9-21 +		61-312 CS
5. Enforcement			
a. Criminal nonsupport	97-5-33	568.040	94-304
b. Contempt	93-9-33		
i. criminal			
ii. civil			
c. Civil enforcement		452.130	61-126
i. garnishment (wage deduction)		452.140	
ii. bond, security, lien on land			94-9903
6. Uniform Acts, National Conference of Commissioners on Uniform State Laws			
a. Enforcement of Foreign Judgments Act		(1948): § 511.760	
b. Foreign Money-Judgment Recognition Act			
c. Parentage Act			§§ 61-301 to 61-334
d. Act on Paternity (officially "withdrawn" by NCCUSL in 1979)	§§ 93-9-1 to 93-9-75		
e. URESA	(1950): §§ 93-11-1 to 93-11-65	(1950): §§ 454.010 to 454.360	(1968): §§ 93-2601-41 to 93-2601-82

	Nebraska, Neb. Rev. Stat. §	Nevada, Nev. Rev. Stat. §	New Hampshire, N.H. Rev. Ann. §
1. Support Obligation	Indirect: 42-364 in conn. with 13-102		460:22†
a. Child support			
b. Illegitimate support	13-102	126.030	
c. States not allowing alimony			
d. Relative responsibility			165:19
2. Amount of Support Obligation			
a. Fixed criteria			
b. Schedules or $ amounts			
3. Period of Obligation			
a. Majority			
b. Emancipation			
c. Higher education			
4. Paternity Statute	13-112	126.325	
Blood test provision		56.010; 56.020	522:1 +
5. Enforcement			
a. Criminal nonsupport	28-449 and 13-116 (ill. ch.)	201.020; 126.300 (ill. ch.)	639:4 CS
b. Contempt			167:3
i. criminal			
ii. civil	42-358		
c. Civil enforcement			463:24
i. garnishment (wage deduction)	25-1558		161-C:21 + S
ii. bond, security, lien on land	42-371		161-C:10 + S
6. Uniform Acts, National Conference of Commis-sioners on Uniform State Laws			
a. Enforcement of Foreign Judgments Act	(1948): §§ 25-1587 to 25-15, 104	(1964 Rev. Act): — no cit. yet	
b. Foreign Money-Judgment Recognition Act			
c. Parentage Act		126.031-126.231	
d. Act on Paternity (officially "withdrawn" by NCCUSL in 1979)			§§ 168-A:1 to 168-A:12
e. URESA	(1968): §§ 42-762 to 42-7104	(1968): §§ 130.010 to 130.370	(1968): §§ 546:1 to 546:41

	New Jersey, N.J. Stat. Ann. (West) §	New Mexico, N.M. Stat. Ann. §	New York, N.Y. (Subject) Law McKinney §
1. Support Obligation			Jud. Fam. Ct. Act §§ 413 + IO
a. Child support			Jud. Fam. Ct. Act §§ 413 +
b. Illegitimate support	9:16-2	40-5-1	Jud. Fam. Ct. Act §§ 413 +
c. States not allowing alimony			
d. Relative responsibility	44:1-140 CS	40-5-2 (ill. ch.)	Soc. Serv. § 101
2. Amount of Support Obligation			
a. Fixed criteria			
b. Schedules or $ amounts			
3. Period of Obligation			
a. Majority			
b. Emancipation			
c. Higher education			
4. Paternity Statute	9:17-1 +		Jud. Fam. Ct. Act §§ 511 to 563
Blood test provision	2A:83-2		Jud. Fam. Ct. Act §§ 418 and 532 CS
5. Enforcement	2A:34-24	40-4-19 and 40-5-7 (ill. ch.)	
a. Criminal nonsupport		30-6-2 and 40-5-20 (ill. ch.)	Penal § 260.05
b. Contempt		40-4-19	Jud. Fam. Ct. Act § 440 CS
i. criminal			
ii. civil			
c. Civil enforcement			
i. garnishment (wage deduction)	44:4-105 CS	40-4-19	Jud. Fam. Ct. Act § 448 CS
ii. bond, security, lien on land	2A:17-56.1 CS	40-4-15 +	
6. Uniform Acts, National Conference of Commissioners on Uniform State Laws			
a. Enforcement of Foreign Judgments Act			(1964 Rev. Act): CPLR §§ 5401 to 5408 and Pers. Prop. § 496 IASS
b. Foreign Money-Judgment Recognition Act			CPLR §§ 5301 to 5309
c. Parentage Act			
d. Act on Paternity (officially "withdrawn" by NCCUSL in 1979)			
e. URESA	(1950): § 2A:4-30:1 to 2A:4-30.23	(1968) §§ 40-6-1 to 40-6-41	(1950): as Uniform Support of Dependents Law in: Dom. Rel. §§ 30-43

	North Carolina, N.C. Gen. Stat. §	North Dakota, N.D. Cent. Code §	Ohio, Ohio Rev. Code Ann. § (Page)
1. Support Obligation		14-09-08	3103.03
a. Child support		14-09-08	
b. Illegitimate support	49-1 +		3111.17
c. States not allowing alimony			
d. Relative responsibility		50-01-19	
2. Amount of Support Obligation			
a. Fixed criteria			
b. Schedules or $ amounts			
3. Period of Obligation			
a. Majority			
b. Emancipation			
c. Higher education			3103.03
4. Paternity Statute	49-14 CS	14-17-01 + S	3111.01 +
Blood test provision	8-50.1 CS	14-17-10 S	3111.16
5. Enforcement	50-13.4	14-08.1-02 S	
a. Criminal nonsupport	14-322 + & § 49-2 (ill. ch.)	14-07-15 S	
b. Contempt		14-08-07 S	
i. criminal			
ii. civil			
c. Civil enforcement	14-324		
i. garnishment (wage deduction)		14-08.1-03 S	
ii. bond, security, lien on land			
6. Uniform Acts, National Conference of Commissioners on Uniform State Laws			
a. Enforcement of Foreign Judgments Act		(1964 Rev. Act): §§ 28-20.1-01 to 28-20.1-08	
b. Foreign Money-Judgment Recognition Act			
c. Parentage Act		§§ 14-17-01 to 14-17-26	
d. Act on Paternity (officially "withdrawn" by NCCUSL in 1979)			
e. URESA	(1968): 52A-1 to 52A-32	(1968): §§ 14-12.1-01 to 14-12.1-43	(1968): §§ 3115.01 to 3115.34

529

	Oklahoma, Okla. Stat. Tit. §	Oregon, Or. Rev. Stat. §	Pennsylvania, Cons. Stat. Ann. § (Purdon)
1. Support Obligation	10 § 4 79S	109.010	
a. Child support	10 § 4 79S		
b. Illegitimate support	10 § 83		
c. States not allowing alimony			
d. Relative responsibility		416.010	
2. Amount of Support Obligation			
a. Fixed criteria			
b. Schedules or $ amounts		416.061	
3. Period of Obligation			
a. Majority			
b. Emancipation			
c. Higher education			
4. Paternity Statute	10 § 71 + 79S		
Blood test provision	10 § 501 +	109.250 +	28 § 307.1 + CS 48 § 131 CS
5. Enforcement			
a. Criminal nonsupport	21 § 852 79S	163.555	18 § 4322
b. Contempt		23.020	42 § 6705
i. criminal			
ii. civil			
c. Civil enforcement		419.515	42 § 6704
i. garnishment (wage deduction)	12 § 1276 79S	419.515	42 § 6709
ii. bond, security, lien on land	16 ch. 1 Appendix 12.1 79S		18 § 4322 and 62 § 1974
6. Uniform Acts, National Conference of Commissioners on Uniform State Laws			
a. Enforcement of Foreign Judgments Act	(1964 Rev. Act): 12 §§ 719 to 726	(1948): §§ 24.010 to 24.180	(1964 Rev. Act): 42 § 4306
b. Foreign Money-Judgment Recognition Act	12 §§ 710 to 718	§§ 24.200 to 24.255	
c. Parentage Act			
d. Act on Paternity (officially "withdrawn" by NCCUSL in 1979)			
e. URESA	(1968): 12 §§ 1600.1 to 1600.38	(1950): §§ 110.005 to 110.291	(1968): 42 §§ 6741 to 6780 (79 Pamphlet)

	Puerto Rico, P.R. Laws Ann. Tit. , §	Rhode Island, R.I. Gen. Laws §	South Carolina, S.C. Code §
1. Support Obligation	31 §§ 466 & 562	15-9-1 + IO	20-7-40 CS im.
a. Child support		15-9-1 + IO	20-7-40 CS im.
b. Illegitimate support	31 § 507		20-7-40 CS im.
c. States not allowing alimony			
d. Relative responsibility			
2. Amount of Support Obligation	31 § 565		
a. Fixed criteria			
b. Schedules or $ amounts			
3. Period of Obligation			
a. Majority			
b. Emancipation			
c. Higher education			
4. Paternity Statute	31 § 463	15-8-1 + S	
Blood test provision		15-8-11 S	
5. Enforcement			
a. Criminal nonsupport	33 § 4241 CS	11-2-1 S	20-7-40 CS
b. Contempt			
i. criminal			
ii. civil	33 § 4241 CS		
c. Civil enforcement		15-13-3.1 S	
i. garnishment (wage deduction)			
ii. bond, security, lien on land			
6. Uniform Acts, National Conference of Commissioners on Uniform State Laws			
a. Enforcement of Foreign Judgments Act			
b. Foreign Money-Judgment Recognition Act			
c. Parentage Act			
d. Act on Paternity (officially "withdrawn" by NCCUSL in 1979)			
e. URESA	(1950): 32 §§ 3311 to 3313v.	(1950): §§ 15-11-1 to 15-11-37	(1950): §§ 20-7-110 to 20-7-460

531

	South Dakota, S.D. Comp. Law Ann. §	Tennessee, Tenn. Code Ann. §	Texas, Tex. [subject] Code Ann. tit., § (Vernon)
1. Support Obligation	25-7-6 +	36-820 CS — IO	F.C. § 12.04 CS
a. Child support			
b. Illegitimate support	25-8-2	36-223	F.C. § 13.23 CS
c. States not allowing alimony			
d. Relative responsibility			
2. Amount of Support Obligation			
a. Fixed criteria			
b. Schedules or $ amounts			
3. Period of Obligation			
a. Majority			
b. Emancipation	25-5-20		
c. Higher education			
4. Paternity Statute		36-224 +	F.C. § 13.01 + CS
Blood test provision	15-6-35(a)	36-228	F.C. § 13.02 & 13.05 CS
5. Enforcement			F.C. § 14.09
a. Criminal nonsupport	25-7-16 +	39-202	PC § 25.05
b. Contempt		36-231 (ill.)	
i. criminal			
ii. civil			
c. Civil enforcement			
i. garnishment (wage deduction)		36-820 CS	
ii. bond, security, lien on land		36-225 & 231 (ill. ch.) 39-205 (leg.)	
6. Uniform Acts, National Conference of Commissioners on Uniform State Laws			
a. Enforcement of Foreign Judgments Act	(1964 Rev. Act): §§ 15-16A-1 to 15-16A-10	(1964 Rev. Act): §§ 26-801 to 26-807	
b. Foreign Money-Judgment Recognition Act			
c. Parentage Act			
d. Act on Paternity (officially "withdrawn" by NCCUSL in 1979)			
e. URESA	(1950): §§ 25-9-1 to 25-9-31	(1950): §§ 36-901 to 36-929	(1950): F.C. 21.01 to 21.66

	Utah, Utah Code Ann. §	Vermont, Vt. Stat. Ann. tit. §	Virgin Islands, V.I. Code Ann. tit. , §
1. Support Obligation	78-45-3 & 78-45-4		16 § 342
a. Child support	78-45-3 & 78-45-4		
b. Illegitimate support			16 § 297
c. States not allowing alimony			
d. Relative responsibility	17-14-2 S		16 § 345
2. Amount of Support Obligation			
a. Fixed criteria			
b. Schedules or $ amounts			16 § 342
3. Period of Obligation			
a. Majority			
b. Emancipation			
c. Higher education			
4. Paternity Statute	78-45a-1 +		16 § 291 +
Blood test provision	78-45a-7 & 78-25-18 78-45-9		
5. Enforcement			
a. Criminal nonsupport	76-7-201		16 § 371
b. Contempt			
i. criminal			
ii. civil			
c. Civil enforcement			
i. garnishment (wage deduction)		33 § 2726 S	16 § 352 CS
ii. bond, security, lien on land		33 § 2725 S	
6. Uniform Acts, National Conference of Commissioners on Uniform State Laws			
a. Enforcement of Foreign Judgments Act			
b. Foreign Money-Judgment Recognition Act			
c. Parentage Act			
d. Act on Paternity (officially "withdrawn" by NCCUSL in 1979)	§§ 78-45a-1 to 78-45a-17		
e. URESA	(1950): §§ 77-61a-1 to 77-61a-39	(1968): 15 §§ 385 to 428	(1950): 16 §§ 391 to 429

	Virginia, VA Code §	Washington, Wash. Rev. Code § (1979)	West Virginia, W.Va. Code §
1. Support Obligation		26.16.205 IO	48-8-1 IO
a. Child support		26.16.205 IO	
b. Illegitimate support	20-61.1 CS		48-7-4 IO
c. States not allowing alimony			
d. Relative responsibility			
2. Amount of Support Obligation			
a. Fixed criteria			
b. Schedules or $ amounts			
3. Period of Obligation			
a. Majority			
b. Emancipation			
c. Higher education			
4. Paternity Statute		26.26.060 +	48-7-1 +
Blood test provision	20.61.2 CS	26.26.100	48-7-8
5. Enforcement			
a. Criminal nonsupport	20-61 CS	26.20.030	48-8-1
b. Contempt			49-7-5
i. criminal			
ii. civil			
c. Civil enforcement		26.16.205	
i. garnishment (wage deduction)	20-78.1 CS	26.20.050	49-7-6
ii. bond, security, lien on land	8.01-460	74.20A.060	48-2-17
6. Uniform Acts, National Conference of Commissioners on Uniform State Laws			
a. Enforcement of Foreign Judgements Act		(1964 Rev. Act): §§ 6.36.010 to 6.36.910	
b. Foreign Money-Judgment Recognition Act		§§ 6.40.010 to 6.40.915	
c. Parentage Act		§§ 26.26.010 to 26.26.905	
d. Act on Paternity (officially "withdrawn" by NCCUSL in 1979)			
e. URESA	(1968): §§ 20-88.13 to 20-88.31	(1950): §§ 26.21.010 to 26.21.910	(1968): §§ 48-9-1 to 49-9-42

534

	Wisconsin, Wis. Stat. Ann. § (West)	Wyoming, Wyo. Stat. §
1. Support Obligation	52.01 CS	14-2-204
a. Child support		
b. Illegitimate support		
c. States not allowing alimony		
d. Relative responsibility	52.01 CS	
2. Amount of Support Obligation		
a. Fixed criteria		
b. Schedules or $ amounts		
3. Period of Obligation		
a. Majority		
b. Emancipation		
c. Higher education		
4. Paternity Statute		14-2-101 +
Blood test provision	52.36 CS & § 885.23	14-2-109
5. Enforcement	52.01 CS	14-2-204
a. Criminal nonsupport	52.055 CS	20-3-101
b. Contempt	52.01 CS	
i. criminal		14-2-204
ii. civil		
c. Civil enforcement	52.03 CS	
i. garnishment (wage deduction)	247.265 CS	
ii. bond, security, lien on land	247.30 CS	
6. Uniform Acts, National Conference of Commissioners on Uniform State Laws		
a. Enforcement of Foreign Judgments Act	(1964 Rev. Act): § 270.96	(1964 Rev. Act): 1-17-701 to 1-17-707
b. Foreign Money-Judgment Recognition Act		
c. Parentage Act		§§ 14-2-101 to 14-2-120
d. Act on Paternity (officially "withdrawn" by NCCUSL in 1979)		
e. URESA	(1968): § 52.10	(1968): §§ 20-4-101 to 20-4-138

Appendix D

JOINT AMA-ABA GUIDELINES:
PRESENT STATUS OF SEROLOGIC TESTING IN
PROBLEMS OF DISPUTED PARENTAGE*

American Medical Association, Committee on Transfusion and Transplantation, Drs. Jack P. Abbott and Kenneth W. Sell, Chairmen, and American Bar Association, Section on Family Law, Committee on Standards for the Judical Use of Scientific Evidence in the Ascertainment of Paternity, Harry D. Krause, Chairman, (Principal draftsmen: J. B. Miale, M.D., E. R. Jennings, M.D., W. A. H. Rettberg, M.D., K. W. Sell, M.D., and H. D. Krause).

Preface

In 1971, the American Bar Association's Section on Family Law approached the American Medical Association requesting that a joint committee be formed to study the implications of scientific advances in blood typing tests to determine (non)paternity and make appropriate recommendations.

This report brings to successful conclusion five years of close collaboration between members of the medical and legal professions.

It represents the first "official" statement concerning the science and art of blood typing in cases of disputed paternity since the reports of the AMA's Committee on Medicolegal Problems in 1952 and 1957 (Ref. 1,2). It also is the first such report that was developed jointly by individuals working

---

* Approved by the American Medical Association and by the Section on Family Law, American Bar Association. (In accordance with their policy against taking positions concerning technical reports involving non-legal subject matter, the House of Delegates of the American Bar Association has not taken a position on this report.)

with both professional associations. With the endorsement of the AMA and ABA, the report is intended to provide guidance to the legislator, the judge and the practicing lawyer as well as to medical personnel engaged in this specialty. The purpose throughout has been to provide an understandable, though not oversimplified, definition of the current state of capabilities. The report will provide a measure of certainty where rapid recent scientific developments have created uncertainty as to what has become scientific fact and what remains hypothesis, and as to what is practically possible and what remains performable only under highly specialized conditions.

While the report identifies certain systems as useful for routine testing, there is no intent to exclude anything that can be shown to produce useful results. Indeed, even while this report was being discussed, new developments, especially in the HLA sector, began to overshadow more traditional approaches, and further progress may be anticipated. On the legal side, it is expected that this report will lead to further work and specific legislative proposals, particularly regarding the law of evidence. In short, this report is intended as the beginning of a continuing process.

Many have helped bring us to this stage. Special thanks are due to John B. Miale, M.D., the principal draftsman on the medical side, as well as to Drs. Elmer R. Jennings, William Dolan and William Rettberg, subcommittee members and Dr. Herbert F. Polesky. On the legal side, thanks are due to Judge Orman Ketcham, Harry Fain, Esq., and Lawrence H. Stotter, Esq., who provided valuable comments on the numerous drafts through which this report was put. A great many thanks also go to the members of the original AMA's ad hoc committee consisting of Drs. Alexander S. Wiener, Chang Ling Lee and John B. Miale who originally undertook to study the medical side and who, after two years of fruitful and enlightening discussion greatly enhanced the depth and scope of this report. Much gratitude, finally, is due to Dr. Joseph B. Jerome of the AMA staff whose help and dedication were crucial to the successful completion of this report.

JACK P. ABBOTT
Chairman (1974-75)
Committee on Transfusion
and Transplantation
American Medical Association

KENNETH W. SELL
Chairman (1976-)
Committee on Transfusion
and Transplantation
American Medical Association

HARRY D. KRAUSE
Chairman, Ad Hoc
Committee on Standards for the
Judicial Use of Scientific Evidence in
the Ascertainment of Paternity and
Council Member, Section on Family Law,
American Bar Association

I. Introduction

* * *

B. *This report has been prepared with the following goals:*

1. To make available an authoritative guide to all parties who deal with the medicolegal problems of disputed parentage: physicians, attorneys, the courts, legislatures and federal and state health agencies. Accordingly, this report is concerned equally with medical and legal aspects.
2. To survey the total and potential role of serologic testing, as a guide to expanded application in the future.
3. To recommend the present-day application of a limited number of serologic systems which are believed to be cost-efficient, reliable and noncontroversial.

4. To present data indicating probabilities of exclusion of paternity given various combinations of test systems.

5. To recommend expanded application of serologic data in the estimation of probability of paternity and to discuss and provide guidance concerning the determination of "likelihood of paternity," a concept in common use in Germany and the Scandinavian countries but so far little used in the United States.

6. To recommend the adoption of standard procedures with regard to identification of the involved parties, the collection and identification of specimens, and acceptable laboratory quality control.

7. To make recommendations to the AMA and ABA as to goals to be achieved in the future.

8. To recommend legislation clarifying and simplifying the admissibility in evidence of test results and the effect thereof, including the evidentiary value of the estimation of "likelihood of paternity."

II. Systems Potentially Applicable in Disputed Parentage

As many as 62 immunologic and biochemical systems are potentially applicable (Table 1). The application of all known systems would establish nonpaternity for about 98 percent of falsely accused men. However, such extensive testing is neither feasible nor recommended, for the following reasons:

1. Antisera for all serologic systems are either not available or in some cases individual antisera are available only in one or very few laboratories.

2. The probability of exclusion in some of the serologic systems is very low, because there are "high frequency" factors found in a large portion of the population.

3. Biochemical systems are being applied to disputed parentage problems in other countries and by some

540

investigators in this country. Where available they can be used to supplement the blood group systems. The ones most useful are the protein systems (Gm, haptoglobin, Gc, Km), the red cell enzymes (AcP, PGM, ADA, EsD), and hemoglobin (beta-chain variants in Blacks).

4. The recommendation made in Section III affords a potentially very high chance of exclusion utilizing only seven tests systems at a reasonable cost, where the utilization of all known systems would cost disproportionately more with only a slight increase in probability of exclusion. No definite statement of cost of quality testing is possible since this may vary regionally. All parties should note that this is an area of special competence and the assignment of testing should not be based on the lowest price available.

5. It is not the intent to recommend in all medicolegal problems of disputed parentage that the entire set of tests is mandatory. It is often possible to establish exclusion with the basic blood group systems (ABO, Rh, and MNSs). When these basic tests do not allow exclusion, extended testing may be done (using Kell, Duffy, and Kidd systems) to increase the mean probability of exclusion to the 63-72 percent level. In the event no exclusion is produced at that stage, additonal testing using the HLA system (if necessary, by referral) may be done to raise the mean probability of exclusion to at least the 90 percent level. The discussion in this paragragh is in terms of the specific recommendations made in this report and is not intended to exclude the use of other systems (see III).

Table 1

Mean Probability of Exclusion of Non-Fathers for Potentially Useful Systems *

GENETIC MARKER OR SYSTEM	MEAN PROBABILITY OF EXCLUSION OF NON-FATHERS		
	BLACK	WHITE	JAPANESI
ABO	.1774	.1342	.1917
Auberger	.0105	.0186	. . .
Cartwright (Yt)	.0069	.0395	. . .
Colton	0	.0266	. . .
Cs	. . .	.0006	. . .
Diego	.0030	0	.0304
Dombrock	.0661	.0518	. . .
Duffy	.0420	.1844	.1159
Henshaw	.0151	0	. . .
Hunter	.0170	.0026	. . .
Kell	.0049	.0354	0
Kidd	.1545	.1869	.1573
Lewis¹	.0262	.0024	.0193
Lutheran	.0368	.0311	0
MNSs	.3206	.3095	.2531
P	.0026	.0266	.0809

* From reference 3, modified and with additions. Probabilities of exclusion of non-fathers are calculated from gene frequencies from various authors quoted in the reference, and are considered representatives.

1. Exclusion of paternity using Lewis cannot be made unless it is combined with secretor testing.

Table 1 (Continued)

GENETIC MARKER OR SYSTEM	MEAN PROBABILITY OF EXCLUSION OF NON-FATHERS		
	BLACK	WHITE	JAPANESE
Penney	0	.0109	0
Rh	.1859	.2746	.2050
Sd	. . .	.0052	. . .
Secretor	.0305	.0296	.0238
St	. . .	.0006	.0283
Sutter	.0667	0	. . .
U	.0001	0	. . .
Vel	0	.0184	0
Xg²	.1615	.0965	.1344
Acetylcholinesterase	. . .	.1153	. . .
Acid phosphatase	.1588	.2323	.1340
Adenosine deaminase	.0283	.0452	.0291
Adenylate kinase	.0059	.0428	0
Ag(x)	. . .	.0813	. . .
Alcohol dehydrogenase (locus 2)	. . .	.0452	. . .
Alcohol dehydrogenase (locus 3)	. . .	.1824	. . .
α-acid glycoprotein	.1834	.1773	.1583
α₁-antitrypsin	.0180	.0806	.0170

1. Exclusion of paternity using Lewis cannot be made unless it is combined with secretor testing.

2. These are sex-linked systems and are only useful in female children.

Table 1 (Continued)

GENETIC MARKER OR SYSTEM	MEAN PROBABILITY OF EXCLUSION OF NON-FATHERS		
	BLACK	WHITE	JAPANESE
Amylase (urinary)	.0411	.0399	. . .
Ceruloplasmin	.0504	.0059	.0214
Complement, third component	.0819	.1523	.0192
Diaphorase	. . .	.0085	. . .
Esterase D	. . .	.0913	. . .
Galactose-A-phosphate-uridyl-transferase	. . .	.0626	. . .
Glucose-6-phosphate dehydrogenase[2]	.0932	0	0
Glutamic oxaloacetic transaminase (soluble)	0	0	.0113
Glutamic pyruvic transaminase (soluble)	.1285	.1875	.1826
Glutathione reductase	.2071	.2016	. . .
Gm, serum groups	.2071	.2275	.1873
Group-specific component	.0731	.1661	.1560
Haptoglobin	.1873	.1834	.1596
Hemoglobin β	.0453	0	0
HLA	.78-.80	.78-.80	.78-.80

2. These are sex-linked systems and are only useful in female children.

Table 1 (Continued)

GENETIC MARKER OR SYSTEM	MEAN PROBABILITY OF EXCLUSION OF NON-FATHERS		
	BLACK	WHITE	JAPANESE
Km, serum group (Inv)	.2366	.0601	.1664
Malic enzyme (NADP) soluble	.1258	.1681	. . .
Parotid basic protein	.1163	.0050	0
Pepsinogen	.0126	.0126	0
Peptidase A	.0747	.1635	. . .
Peptidase C	.0665	.0102	. . .
Peptidase D	.0459	.0108	. . .
Phosphoglucomutase (locus 1)	.1344	.1457	.1476
Phosphoglucomutase (locus 3)	.1740	.1554	.1306
Properdin Factor B	. . .	.1443	. . .
Pseudocholinesterase (locus 1)	.0052	.0158	0
6-phosphogluconate dehydrogenase	.0335	.0229	.0586
Transferrin	.0410	.0064	.0079
Xm, serum group	.1757	.1625	. . .

III. Systems Recommended for Current Use in Exclusion of Paternity or Parentage

Seven serologic systems are recommended for routine investigations (Table 2).

This recommendation is based on the following considerations: (1) antisera for the six blood group systems are available and reliable, (2) each system provides a reasonably high probability of exclusion in relation to cost, (3) the six blood group systems provide a cumulative probability of exclusion of 63-72 percent, depending on race, (4) the addition of only one other system (HLA) increases the probability of exclusion to 91-93 percent as compared with a probability of exclusion of about 98 percent for 62 systems.

This recommendation is not intended to exclude the use of additional systems (i.e., haptoglobins, hemoglobin variants, etc.) when an investigator has special expertise in these systems. (See II, 3).

Table 2

The Seven Test Systems Recommended

SYSTEM	MEAN PROBABILITY OF EXCLUSION OF NON-FATHERS		
	Black	White	Japanese
1. ABO	.1774	.1342	.1917
2. Rh	.1859	.2746	.2050
3. MNSs	.3206	.3095	.2531
4. Kell	.0049	.0354	0
5. Duffy	.0420	.1844	.1159
6. Kidd	.1545	.1869	.1573
7. HLA	.78-.80	.78-.80	.78-.80

Table 2 gives the individual probabilities for each system. Cumulative probabilities when several systems are used are not simply the sum of each probability, since in many instances there might be exclusion in more than one system. Calculation of cumulative probabilities is based on the determination of non-exclusion for each system and then applying the formula:

Cumulative Probability $= 1 - (1-P_1) (1-P_2) \ldots (1-P_n)$, where P_1, P_2, and P_n are probabilities of individual exclusions. This formula is used to calculate cumulative probabilities for seven recommended systems (Table 3). It should be noted that this calculation gives the cumulative probability that at least one of these tests will exclude paternity of a falsely accused man.

APPENDIX D

Table 3

Cumulative Probability of Exclusion of Non-Fathers

Systems*	Cumulative Probability of Exclusion(%)		
	BLACKS	WHITES	JAPANESE
1	17.44	13.42	19.16
1 + 2	33.03	37.19	35.74
1 + 2 + 3	54.50	56.63	52.0
1 + 2 + 3 + 4	54.72	58.17	52.0
1 + 2 + 3 + 4 + 5	56.63	65.88	57.56
1 + 2 + 3 + 4 + 5 + 6	63.37	72.26	64.24
1 + 2 + 3 + 4 + 5 + 6 + 7	91.21	93.34	91.42

*1 = ABO; 2 = Rh; 3 = MNSs; 4 = Kell; 5 = Duffy; 6 = Kidd; 7 = HLA.

IV. Types of Exclusion

A. *Exclusion of Paternity*

Five types of equally acceptable and definite exclusion of a non-father are possible:

1. The classic type, in which the putative father is

548

lacking a specificity which is present in the child and is absent in the mother so that the specificity found in the child must have been inherited from another father (i.e., child is K +, mother and putative father are K-).

2. Exclusion when the child lacks both specificities found in the putative father (i.e., child is group O, putative father is group AB).

3. The child is homozygous with respect to a specificity not present in both parents (i.e., child is *KK*, mother is *Kk* or *KK*, father is *kk).*

4. The child lacks a specificity for which the putative father is homozygous (i.e., child is *kk*, putative father is *KK).*

5. Indirect exclusion where the study of the parents of the mother and putative father or the latters' siblings more clearly define their genetic makeup. For example, a person of phenotype (group) A_1 is either of genotype A_1A_1 or of genotype A_1O. The two genotypes cannot be distinguished by serologic studies on the given person. However, since the two genes are inherited one from each parent, parents of genotypes A_1A_1 and A_1A_1 cannot have a child of genotype A_1O.

B. *Exclusion of Maternity*

As noted in the following sections, it is possible to exclude maternity in certain serologic patterns involving a given mother-child-putative father set. For example, a woman of group A_2 cannot be the mother of a child of group A_1B, regardless of the group of the father.

In addition to situations involving disputed paternity, the question of excluding maternity arises in cases of alleged child exchange, when the exclusion of probability of maternity is of primary importance.

C. *Importance of Genetic Mutation*

The possibility of mutation, invalidating the normal inheritance pattern, is very small, estimated to occur once in 40,000 persons. This is so infrequent that it can be ignored in the interpretation of the serologic findings.

V. The Likelihood of Paternity

In order to increase the utility of serologic testing it is desirable to estimate the likelihood of paternity in cases when the putative father is not excluded. Such estimates are admissible evidence in many foreign countries.

In some special situations, as when there is genetic conformity between the child and putative father for an extremely rare specificity (not present in the mother), for example subgroup A_3 or the rare phenotype M^g, the likelihood of paternity is extremely high and obvious without resort to special calculations. Although such situations are not absolute proof of paternity the court can give this evidence due weight.

Usually the situation is not so simple. The serologist has to deal with various circumstances:

1. Calculation of likelihood of paternity in "one-man" cases, i.e., only one man has been named the putative father and he is not excluded. In this case the computation estimates the likelihood that the one man is in fact the father when compared to a random man.

2. Calculation of likelihood of paternity in "multiple men" cases, where more than one man is suspected or known to be involved, has been tested, and has not been excluded. In this case the computation estimates the likelihood of paternity for each of the involved men and the relative probabilities submitted in evidence. In multiple men cases when the man or men other than the accused are not available for testing there is no alternative at this time than to apply the random man formula.

The great majority of situations fall under the first category.

One simple but mathematically valid estimation of the likelihood of paternity is that when extended testing providing a very high probability of exclusion fails to exclude an accused man there is a high probability that he is in fact the father. The likelihood of paternity can be better estimated using gene frequencies.

In "one-man" cases Hummel (4, 5) has proposed the application of the equation of Essen-Möller (6). The plausibility of paternity, W, is calculated from:

$$W = \cfrac{1}{1 + \cfrac{(Y_1}{(X_1} \cdot \cfrac{Y_2}{X_2} \cdot \cfrac{Y_3}{X_3} \cdots \cfrac{)}{)}}$$

Where Y is the frequency of various blood group phenotypes of men among the normal male population and X is the frequency of corresponding phenotypes of true fathers in the given mother-child combination.

The calculation can be carried out from tables of genotype frequencies, but Hummel (5) has prepared tables based on logarithms which facilitate the estimation of probability of paternity.

Example: In a given child-mother-putative father combination the putative father is not excluded. The phenotypes are:

Child: A_1; Rh_0rh (cDe/cde); NN; K^+; Fy(a+)
Mother: A_1; Rh_i0rh (cDe/cde); MN; Kf⁻; Fy(a-)
Man: A_1; Rh_1rh (Cde/cde); MN; K^+, Fy(a+)

Calculation (using tables of Hummel (5))

1. $\Sigma \ \log \dfrac{y}{x} + 10$ for the blood group systems tested:

A-B-O	9.8739
Rh	9.9477
MN	9.9604
K	8.8865
Fy	9.8176
	48.4861

2. Subtract 10 (n-1), when n = number of systems used

$$
\begin{array}{r}
48.4861 \\
-40.0000 \\
\hline
8.4861
\end{array}
$$

3. Value for W = about 97 percent
4. Therefore, paternity is very likely (Table 4).

Table 4

Verbal Predicates, According to Hummel (5) for Different Likelihoods of Paternity (W), Comparing the Phenotype Frequency of the Putative Father to That of A Random Man With the Same Blood Group Phenotype

W	LIKELIHOOD OF PATERNITY
99.80 - 99.90	Practically proved
99.1 - 99.75	Extremely likely
95 - 99	Very likely
90 - 95	Likely
80 - 90	Undecided
< 80	Not useful

It must be noted that the calculations proposed by Hummel (5) are based on the comparison of the putative father to a random man, i.e., based on gene frequencies in a given population. This is open to criticisms which are however not serious. *First,* the comparison of the putative father with a "random" man may be criticized inasmuch as a comparison of the putative father with a non-random man might better approximate the true situation. However, it is just as unsound to choose a non-random man as it is to rely on general population frequencies. *Second,* the data of Hummel (5) are for gene frequencies for Caucasians in Germany. While it is predictable that gene frequencies can vary slightly for Caucasians in other areas the differences are so small that the estimates of likelihood of paternity would not vary significantly. Where there is in fact a marked difference in gene frequencies, as in some other racial groups, the tables worked out by Hummel (5) would not necessarily apply. In such situations the new gene frequencies should be substituted into the original formula. *Third,* the formula is based on a comparison of the putative father with one other non-excluded random man who is presumed to have had equal access to the mother. While this will not correspond to the facts in most cases of disputed paternity, it is a useful working hypothesis.

The difficulty judges, juries, and lawyers may experience in interpreting statistical evidence correctly, and possible due process issues under the Fourteenth Amendment of the U.S. Constitution arising in the light of the assumptions just discussed, raise questions regarding the indiscriminate use of such evidence. As indicated in the Recommendations, (See XI *infra),* the matter should be studied further and appropriate safeguards need be developed to guard against possible misinterpretation of calculations of "likelihood of paternity." It may also be noted that the relatively high exclusion rates that will be produced by the application of the recommended systems will reduce substantially the need for this type of evidence.

VI. Individual Systems

A. *ABO (A_1A_2BO) Blood Group System*

Tests performed on subjects' red blood cells and serum with appropriate antisera and lectins and cells of known blood group allow all subjects to be classified as belonging in one of the following categories: type O, type A_1, type A_2, type B, type A_1B, or type A_2B. The inheritance pattern is well established and allows a tabulation of phenotypes possible or not possible in children from a given mating (Table 5). In some combinations of serologic factors determined from the mother-child-father combination it is possible to exclude maternity (Table 5).

Table 5

Exclusion of Paternity and Maternity by the A_1A_2BO System

(If the phenotype of the putative father appears in the box corresponding to the child-mother pair the putative father is excluded. If ME appears in the box there is maternal exclusion.)

PHENOTYPE OF MOTHER	PHENOTYPE OF CHILD					
	O	A_1	A_2	B	A_1B	A_2B
O	A_1,B,A_2B	O,A_2,B,A_2B	O,B,A_1B	O,A_1,A_2	ME	ME
A_1	A_1,B,A_2B	None	A_1B	O,A_1,A_2	O,A_1,A_2	O,A_1,A_2
A_2	A_1,B,A_2B	O,A_2,B,A_2B	A_1B	O,A_1,A_2	ME	O,A_1,A_2
B	A_1,B,A_2B	O,A_1,B,A_2B	O,B,A_1B	None	O,A_2,B,A_2B	O,B,A_1B
A_1B	ME	None	ME	None	O,A_2	O,B,A_1B
A_2B	ME	O,A_2,B,A_2B	A_1B	None	O,A_2,B,A_2B	O

The following special serologic features of this system should be noted:

1. Subgroups of A are often incompletely developed at birth, may be adequately developed by three months of age and are usually fully developed by one year of age.

2. Subgroups of A give weak reactions with potent anti-**A** sera and stronger reactions with Anti-**AB,** and may be missed entirely if the antiserum is weak.

3. There is an extremely rare genetic type called cis-AB (Reviron and Salmon, Ref 8) or AB* (Salmon, Ref 9) where the transmissions of blood type AB appears to be by a single rather than two separate chromosomes, so that a cis-AB person can then be the parent of an O child and an O person can be the parent of a cis-AB child. Cis-AB reacts weakly with anti-**B,** and more strongly with anti-**B** from A_2 blood than with anti-**B** from A_1 blood. In cis-AB individuals who are secretors no B substance is demonstrable in their saliva, and the A substance may also be affected.

4. In the rare "Bombay" type the red cells contain no A, B, or H agglutinogens and may be typed as type O. However, the serum contains anti-**A,** anti-**B** and anti-**H.**

5. In an occasional leukemic or preleukemic subject there is a change in the reactivity of the red cells which simulates an actual change in blood type, i.e., red cells of a known type A or B person may simulate the reactions of type O cells. Acquired agammaglobulinemia, in leukemia and other diseases, may be characterized by the absence of isoagglutinins in the serum.

6. Change of red cell type has also been reported in subjects with colitis or carcinoma of the stomach, characterized by the red cells acquiring weak B characteristics, i.e., a person of type A_1 reacts as if the

group were A_1B. This is called "acquired B." Acquired B should be suspected clinically, from the weak reaction with anti-**B** and from the presence of anti-**B** isoagglutinin in the serum.

7. Failure to demonstrate the expected isoagglutinins in the serum may be due to: (1) acquired or congenital agammaglobulinemia, (2) a weak receptor as in persons of subtype A_4 or Ael, 3) the rare blood chimera situation.

B. *The Rh Blood Group System*

This system is more complicated than the ABO system and knowledge has progressed from the first basic distinction between Rh + and Rh- to the characterization of 40 phenotypes.

Because of its complexity the genetics and serologic principles of the system have come to be expressed by two quite dissimilar concepts, the CDE/cde nomenclature of Fisher and Race and the genetic and serologic principles expressed by the Rh-hr nomenclature of Wiener. A review of the differences between the two is given elsewhere (Miale, Ref. 10). Experts in this field use both interchangeably, though some prefer one or the other. As applied to disputed parentage, both lead to the same conclusion. A comparison of the two is given in Table 6.

Table 6

Comparison of CDE/cde and Rh-hr Nomenclatures

GENES		ANTISERA	
WIENER	FISHER-RACE	WIENER	FISHER-RACE
r	cde	Anti-rh'	Anti-C
r'	Cde	Anti-Rh	Anti-D
r^w	C^wde		
r''	cdE	Anti-rh	Anti-E
r^y	CdE	Anti-rh^w	Anti-C^w
R^o	cDe	Anti-hr'	Anti-c
R^1	CDe		
R^{1w}	C^wDe	Anti-hr''	Anti-e
R^2	cDE	Anti-hr	Anti-f
R^z	CDE		

When six antisera are used: anti-**Rh**$_0$ (anti-D), anti-**rh**' (anti-C), anti-**rh**" (anti-E), anti-**Rh**^{w} (anti-Cw), anti-**hr**' (anti-c), anti-**hr**" (anti-e), plus anti-**hr** (anti-f) to distinguish between a few selected phenotypes, 28 phenotypes can be distinguished corresponding to 55 genotypes. Having determined the phenotype and genotype, or possible genotypes (Miale, Ref. 11), of the child-mother-putative father situation, exclusion or non-exclusion of paternity or exclusion of maternity is decided by standard genetic diagrams.

Example: Child's genotype: $r'r$ (Cde/Cde)

Mother's genotype: R^1r' (CDe/Cde)

Putative father's genotype: rr (cde/cde)

Children of the given mother and putative father must have a genetic makeup which reflects the inheritance of one gene from each parent. Accordingly, the only children possible from this mating must have one of the following genotypes: R^1r (CDe/cde) or $r'r$ (Cde/cde). Since the child in this example is of genotype $r'r'$ (Cde/Cde) the putative father is excluded.

Tables of exclusion have been constructed based on the more common genotypes of the child-mother-putative father combination (see Wiener and Nieberg, Ref. 12; Miale, Ref. 13; Erskine, Ref. 14), but should not be used to the exclusion of the application of standard genetic diagrams as in the example above.

The following special serologic features of the Rh system should be noted:

1. Many commercial antisera labelled anti-**rh'** (anti-C) contain both anti-**rh'** (anti-C) and anti-**rh**$_i$ (anti-Ce) and may in fact contain a preponderance of anti-**rh**$_i$ (anti-Ce). Anti-**rh**$_i$ (anti-Ce) differs from anti-**rh'** (anti-C) in its inability to agglutinate cells having the rare agglutinogens rh$_y$ (CdE) and RH$_z$ (CDE) (very rare in Whites, less rare in Mongols). In the rare genotype *Rhzrh* (CDE/cde) the cells react with anti-**rh'** (anti-C) but not with anti-**rh**$_i$ (anti-Ce).

2. Many rare specificities exist in the system. These define extremely rare genotypes but do not affect the basic pattern.

3. In some individuals the D antigen may fail to react with saline anti-RH_0 though a positive reaction is found with incomplete anti-Rh_0 used in conjunction with an antiglobulin reagent or when slide or rapid

tube sera is used. This phenotype, known as D^u, can be caused by interactions with genes on the paired chromosome or in individuals lacking part of the D antigen mosaic. Before excluding parentage of an $Rh_0(D)$ positive child when both alleged parents are $Rh_0(D)$ negative, tests for a weak D or D^u must be done.

C. *The MNSs Blood Group System*

This system is superficially simple, based on two pairs of codominant allelic genes (*M* and *N*) and three phenotypes (M, MN, and N) associated with a second pair of codominant allelic genes (*S* and *s*) determining phenotypes S, Ss and s. Transmission is by gene couplets *MS, Ms, NS,* and *Ns*. In addition, the agglutinogen U, present in all Whites but absent in some Blacks, is associated with both S and s. Therefore 4 antisera (anti-**M**, anti-**N**, anti-**S**, and anti-**s**) determine nine phenotypes.

The combinations of phenotypes in the child-mother-putative father combination leading to exclusion of paternity or maternity are shown in Table 7. This is based on testing with all four antisera, which gives the highest possible chance of exclusion (about 30 percent). If only three antisera are used (anti-**M**, anti-**N**, and anti-**S**) the chance of exclusion drops to about 24 percent. Table 8 gives the children possible in a given mother-putative father combination when only three antisera are used. The possibilities of establishing maternal exclusion are limited to two situations: A MS woman cannot be the mother of a NS child and a NS woman cannot be the mother of a MS child.

Table 7

Exclusion of Paternity (and Maternity) by the NMSs System from Nine Phenotypes Determined by Four AntiSera

(If the number of the phenotype of the putative father appears in the box corresponding to the child-mother pair the putative father is excluded. If ME appears in the box there is maternal exclusion.)

PHENOTYPE OF MOTHER	PHENOTYPE OF CHILD								
	1 MS	2 Ms	3 MSs	4 NS	5 Ns	6 NSs	7 MNS	8 MNs	9 MNSs
1. MS	2, 4, 5 6, 8	ME	1, 4, 6 6, 7	ME	ME	ME	1, 2, 3 5, 8	ME	1, 2, 3 4, 7
2. Ms	ME	1, 4, 5 6, 7	2, 4, 5 6, 8	ME	ME	ME	ME	1, 2, 3 4, 7	1, 2, 3 5, 8
3. MSs	1, 4, 5 6, 7	2, 4, 5 6, 7	4, 5, 6	ME	ME	ME	1, 2, 3 5, 8	1, 2, 3 5, 8	1, 2, 3
4. NS	ME	ME	ME	1, 2, 3 5, 8	ME	1, 2, 3 4, 7	2, 4, 5 6, 8	ME	1, 4, 5 6, 7
5. Ns	ME	ME	ME	ME	1, 2, 3 4, 7	1, 2, 3 5, 7	ME	1, 4, 5 6, 7	2, 4, 5 6, 8
6. NSs	ME	ME	ME	1, 2, 3 4, 7	1, 2, 3 4, 7	1, 2, 3	2, 4, 5 6, 8	1, 4, 5 6, 7	4, 5, 6
7. MNS	2, 4, 5 6, 8	ME	1, 4, 5 6, 7	1, 2, 3 5, 8	ME	1, 2, 3 4, 7	2, 5, 8	ME	1, 4, 7
8. MNs	ME	1, 4, 5 6, 7	2, 4, 5 6, 8	ME	1, 2, 3 4, 7	1, 2, 3 5, 8	ME	1, 4, 7	1, 5, 8
9. MNSs	2, 4, 5 6, 8	1, 4, 5 6, 7	4, 5, 6	1, 2, 3 5, 8	1, 2, 3 4, 7	1, 2, 3	2, 5, 8	1, 4, 7	None

561

Table 8

Exclusion of Paternity by the MNSs System When Only Three Antisera Are Used (anti-M, and Anti-N, and anti-S)

MATING	CHILDREN POSSIBLE
MS X MS	MS, M
MS X M	MS, M
M X M	M
MS X MNS	MS, MNS, M, MN
MS X MN	MS, MNS, M, MN
M X MNS	MS, MNS, M, MN
M X MN	M, MN
MS X NS	MNS, MN
MS X N	MNS, MN
M X NS	MNS, MN
M X N	MN
MNS X MNS	MS, M, NS, N, MNS, MN
MNS X MN	MS, M, NS, N, MNS, MN
MN X MN	M, N, MN
MNS X NS	MNS, MN, NS, N
MNS X N	MNS, MN, NS, N
MN X NS	MNS, MN, NS, N
MN X N	MN, N
NS X NS	NS, N
NS X N	NS, N
N X N	N

The following special features should be noted:

1. An exception to the rules that M parents cannot have an N child, or that N parents cannot have an M child, occurs in the rare (about 1:40,000, not to be confused with the rate of spontaneous mutation) instances where one of the pair of genes is M^g. Gene M^g determines an agglutinogen lacking M specificity, so the apparent exclusion in case of a putative father who is N with a child who is M might not hold if the father were M^gN and the child MM^g. Anti-M^g serum is not always available, but where exclusion is based only on the MN system all efforts should be made to test for M^g. In fact, should gene M^g be present in both the father and the child, this would be very strong indication of paternity.

2. The rare allele M^k inhibits the expression of the MN as well as the Ss locus.

3. In Blacks, the He (Henshaw) factor should be taken into account. It is present in about 3 percent of Blacks and absent in Whites. Anti-He may be present in anti-M serum so that an N+ and He+ individual might mistakenly be typed as MN.

4. S^u, an allele that produces neither S nor s antigen, occurs in about 23 percent of Blacks. No antiserum defining a product of this gene has been found. S^u must be taken into consideration when there is an apparent exclusion of parentage of a Black individual who tests as homozygous S or s.

5. Agglutinogen U should also be considered in Blacks. It is present in all Whites but absent in a small percentage of Blacks. Blacks who are U negative also lack both S and s. Testing with anti-U serum can be helpful in interracial child-mother-putative father combinations, but only when one is U-negative.

D. *The Kell Blood Group System*

There are many specificities in this system, but only two are useful in disputed parentage, K and k. The use of two antisera, anti-**K** and anti-**k** defines three phenotypes, K, k, and Kk, corresponding to genotypes *KK, kk,* and *Kk.* This makes a simple system that needs no further elaboration, exclusion being along classic lines.

The following special features should be noted:

1. Use of both anti-**K** and anti-**k** when testing Whites provides a chance of exclusion of about 3.5 percent. Since very few people are *KK,* testing with only anti-**K** reduces the chance of exclusion by only a few tenths of one percent.

2. The incidence of agglutinogen K is extremely small in Blacks and is zero in Chinese and Japanese. In these racial groups no exclusion can be expected on the basis of this blood group system. On the other hand, in an interracial situation the detection of K positively could provide strong likelihood of paternity.

E. *The Duffy Blood Group System*

Two antisera, anti-**Fy^a** and anti-**Fy^b**, define four phenotypes, F^y(a+b-), F^y(a+b+), F^y(a-b+) and F^y(a-b-), determined by allelic genes *Fy^a, Fy^b,* and *F^y.* Gene *F^y* has a high incidence in Blacks (about 78 percent) but has only rarely been identified in Whites, so that in Whites only the first three phenotypes are possible. Exclusion is along classic lines.

The following special features should be noted:

If a person fails to react with either anti-**Fy^a** or anti-**Fy^b** (assuming no technical errors), this would be strong evidence that he or she is Black.

F. *The Kidd Blood Group System*

Two antisera, anti-**Jk^a** and anti-**Jk^b** define three phenotypes,

Jk (a+b-), Jk(a+b+), and Jk(a-b+), determined by the pair of genes Jk^a and Jk^b. Exclusion is along classic lines.

The following special features should be noted:

A third gene has been postulated, *Jk*, determining a fourth phenotype, Jk(a-b-). This phenotype has been found in only one family of European Whites, and only in single instances in a Filipino woman, a Chinese, and a Hawaiian-Chinese.

G. *The HLA System*

It has been known for some time that in man there exists a major histocompatability system (HLA) of great complexity, composed of a series of many closely linked genes. Originally the serologically defined specificities of the HLA system were assigned to two linked loci, each with multiple alleles. These two loci are now designated HLA-A and HLA-B. More recently a third locus, HLA-C, was identified although its individual specificities are not easily identified in typing laboratories in the United States. A fourth locus, HLA-D, has also been identified by mixed lymphocyte culture reactions but is not yet readily detected by serological means. The specificities (or the antigens) which are controlled by genes at each of these four loci are now identified by numbers. When the specificity is first recognized, this is indicated by placing a lower case w in front of the number. Later, when general consensus has been reached and the specificity firmly established by the World Health Organization Nomenclature Committee, the w is dropped and the number retained.

A "blank" in a genotype might indicate either homozygocity for a single specificity at a locus or, alternatively, it might indicate an inability to identify an antigen. This is usually clarified by family studies. At present, the majority of antigens in the HLA-A and the HLA-B series are known.

The HLA system is one of genetic dominance. Therefore, two antigens or specificities are possible for each segregating locus. At present, as many as eight tissue antigens can be identified in each individual. More practical limitations of tissue typing today, however, include only the specificities of HLA-A and HLA-B (see Tables 9 and 10). A total of thirty-nine specificities are now recognized within these two loci. Currently available tissue typing trays (for transplantation only) provided by the National Institutes of Health to each of over 120 typing laboratories in the United States allow for identification of 32 of the genotypic specificities. Using these trays, more than 255 haplotypes can be recognized with as many as 65,025 genotypes. The number of antigens in the system (Table 11) makes it apparent that the HLA typing system offers the single most potent method for exclusion.

Table 9

Gene Frequencies of HLA-A Antigens (18)

	CAUCASOID	MONGOLOID	AMERICAN INDIAN	AFRICAN BLACK
HLA-A1	.11	.02	.01	.05
A2	.24	.18	.48	.19
A3	.12	.01	.01	.08
A9	.13	.41	.25	.13
A10	.05	.07	.00	.08
A11	.09	.13	.01	.08
A28	.05	.02	.09	.09
A29	.02	.01	.00	.05
Aw23	.03	.02	.00	.08
Aw24	.10	.34	.25	.05
Aw25	.01	.03	.00	.01
Aw26	.05	.07	.00	.07
Aw30	.04	.02	.02	.16
Aw31	.01	.00	.09	.02
Aw32	.04	.00	.00	.04
Aw33	.04	.07	.04	.07
"Blank"	.04	.06	.02	.06
Aw34*				
Aw36*				
Aw43*				

* Included within frequencies calculated for "blank".

"NOTE: Gene frequencies for each racial group add to more than one because Aw23 and Aw24 are newly described splits or sub-components of A9, and Aw25 and Aw26 are splits or sub-components of A10. Therefore, the gene frequencies for each of these more recently described antigens are included twice in the Table; that is, both are represented with the individual genes and then represented in a combined total as the gene frequency for the A9 and A10 antigen. If the gene frequencies for A9 and A10 are subtracted from the total, then the sum of gene frequencies approach the theoretical value of 1.0 more closely."

Table 10

Gene Frequencies of HLA-B Antigens (18)

	CAUCASOID	MONGOLOID	AMERICAN INDIAN	AFRICAN BLACK
HLA-B5	.01	.09	.11	.08
B7	.11	.02	.01	.12
B8	.07	.01	.00	.04
B12	.11	.03	.01	.12
B13	.02	.04	.00	.01
B14	.03	.00	.01	.03
B18	.07	.01	.01	.03
B27	.04	.04	.03	.00
Bw15	.07	.16	.15	.04
Bw16	.03	.05	.12	.01
Bw17	.06	.03	.01	.21
Bw21	.03	.00	.04	.01
Bw22	.02	.13	.00	.01
Bw35	.10	.06	.23	.06
Bw40	.05	.24	.13	.06
"Blank"	.11	.12	.16	.15
Bw37*				
Bw38*				
Bw39*				
Bw41*				
Bw42*				

* These antigen frequencies are included within the figure given for "blank" for each of the ethnic groups

569

Table 11
Recognized HLA Specificities *

NEW	PREVIOUS	NEW	PREVIOUS
HLA-A1	HL-A1	HLA-B5	HL-A5
HLA-A2	HL-A2	HLA-B7	HL-A7
HLA-A3	HL-A3	HLA-B8	HL-A8
HLA-A9	HL-A9	HLA-B12	HL-A12
HLA-A10	HL-A10	HLA-B13	HL-A13
HLA-A11	HL-A11	HLA-B14	W14
HLA-A28	W28	HLA-B18	W18
HLA-A29	W29	HLA-B27	W27
HLA-Aw19	Li		
HLA-Aw23	W23	HLA-Bw15	W15
HLA-Aw24	W24	HLA-Bw16	W16
HLA-Aw25	W25	HLA-Bw17	W17
HLA-A26	W26	HLA-Bw21	W21
HLA-Aw30	W30	HLA-Bw22	W22
HLA-Aw31	W31	HLA-Bw35	W5
HLA-Aw32	W32	HLA-Bw37	TY
HLA-Aw33	W19.6	HLA-Bw38	W16.1
HLA-Aw34	Malay 2	HLA-Bw39	W16.2
HLA-Aw36	Mo*	HLA-Bw40	W10
HLA-Aw43	BK	HLA-Bw41	Sabell
		HLA-Bw42	MWA
HLA-Cw1	T1	HLA-Dw1	LD 101
HLA-Cw2	T2	HLA-Dw2	LD 102
HLA-Cw3	T3	HLA-Dw3	LD 103
HLA-Cw4	T4	HLA-Dw4	LD 104
HLA-Cw5	T5	HLA-Dw5	LD 105
		HLA-Dw6	LD 106

* The previously reserved specificities W4(4a) and W6(4b) remain w4 and w6. These specificities are closely associated with the B locus.

HLA typing is currently evolving so that the specificity of individual test sera must be considered in establishing the reliability of the test results. Tissue typing laboratories are widely distributed throughout the country and their facilities could be available for paternity testing. Bulk sera are currently available to qualified individuals upon application to NIAID. Selected antisera are also commercially available. HLA typing has already been used in Europe for paternity exclusion and has been successful in many cases where red cell typing has failed to exclude paternity (15, 16, 17).

As in other genetic systems, HLA sometimes shows an unusually high association between antigens which constitute a single haplotype. This is referred to as genetic dysequilibrium. Often such associations are very selective for certain ethnic groups or subpopulations within various geographic regions of the world. There is a considerable amount of data available on haplotype frequencies (Ref. 18, 19, 20). However, even larger numbers of special groups must be typed to provide the statistical basis for analysis of their HLA inheritance. Even when all haplotype frequencies are known, the HLA typing laboratory will still require a determination of the racial and geographic origin of the subjects in order to calculate the probability of exclusion of paternity.

EXCLUSION

The calculation of probabilities for either exclusion or identification of a putative father is complicated by our inability to assign a haplotype designation to the father, even when we have identified all four HLA (A and B) antigens. If a putative father is shown to have both HLA antigens which constitute the paternal haplotype inherited by the child, he still could be excluded if studies of the putative father's father and mother revealed that he had inherited the antigens singly; that is, one from each parent.

571

Using gene frequencies, it is possible to ascribe a general probability of exclusion by using the formula $(1-P)^4P$ (Ref. 17). The sum of these "probabilities of exclusion" then will give the total probability of exclusion. Using a smaller number of antigen specificities than are generally known today, it was possible to predict that HLA typing would exclude between 76 percent (Ref. 18) to 81 percent (Ref. 17) of men falsely accused of paternity.

LIKELIHOOD OF PATERNITY

The calculation of the statistical likelihood that an accused man is the real father is an even more complicated problem. Here we must calculate the possibility that a man who has both antigens of the suspected paternal haplotype of a child may have inherited these antigens independently, one from each parent (a "Trans" configuration). If they indeed have been inherited together as a true haplotype, they are said to be "Cis" in nature and could have been inherited by a child. If the exact haplotype of the child that has been inherited from the father can be determined, then only those men who have both antigens could possibly be the father. If they have both antigens, the probability that they are in Cis position is $2P-P^2$ (Ref. 16). The probability of Trans configuration of the antigens can also be calculated.

These calculations are made knowing that the two antigens in question have been detected in a putative father. However, they ignore the possibility that the other two antigens have also been identified. If all four HLA antigens are known, then a more precise calculation of Cis or Trans possibilities can be made using haplotype frequency tables. Unfortunately, haplotype frequencies are now known only for the common haplotypes. Until all haplotype frequencies have been identified, we probably must be satisfied with simple calculation of serotype frequencies of antigens to determine the likelihood of paternity. Fortunately, the current data commonly allows for the ready identification of antigen frequencies after serologic identification using lymphocytotoxicity tests. Using antigen frequencies, it is possible to determine the likelihood that a man in the random population would possess both antigens which have been identified as paternal HLA antigens of the child in question. In the case of the rarer antigens, this likelihood can be minimized (often less than 1 percent). However, with some common haplotypes, such as HLA-A3 HLA-B7, the general population demonstrates almost a 7.6 percent frequency. Family studies, of course, would be helpful in confirming that the putative father did indeed inherit the antigens in a Cis configuration and therefore would be the most likely to be the father. However, it is difficult to see how the cooperation of family members could be obtained to allow family testing which would result in identification of paternity as opposed to exclusion.

As for some of the very rare blood group subgroups there are very rare HLA specificities (i.e., HLA-Aw35 or HLA-B14) which, if present in both the child and putative father but absent in the mother would indicate a very high probability of paternity.

Example:

	HLA Antigens Present	Possible Haplotypes
Mother B12	A2,A9,B5,B12	A2 B 5 A 9 A2 B12 A 9 B 5
Child B12	A2,A11,B7,B12	A2 B 7 A11 A2 B12 A11 B 7

573

This child inherited the A2 B12 Haplotype from this mother. Therefore, the real father must have A11 B7 as one of his HLA Haplotypes.

Identification of Putative Father
A3 A11 B7 B5

This male could have the A11 B7 as one of his Haplotypes. So he is not excluded as a possible father. The frequency of B7 in Caucasions is .11 and A11 is .09. The likelihood of these two antigens occurring randomly in the population together is .0099, or about one in a hundred. This would suggest that a putative father who contained these two antigens, that is, A11 B7, would be wrongly identified as the father, approximately one time in a hundred.

Exclusion of Putative Father
A3 A11 B5 B^w15

This man cannot have A11 B7 haplotype and so is excluded as the father.

Finally, the possibility of recombination between antigens of the various allelic series of the HLA complex must be considered by the laboratory which performs the tissue typing. For instance, the recombination rate between antigens of the A and B loci is approximately 0.8 percent (Ref. 21).

H. *Serum Protein and Red Cell Enzyme Systems*

Numerous polymorphic serum protein and red cell enzyme systems (See Table 1) have been well defined by appropriate family studies (Ref. 22). The genetics of these systems makes it possible to use them in determining exclusions as outlined in Section IV. Many of these systems are stable in frozen samples. Thus, stored hemolysates or serum can be used when other tests fail to provide an exclusion (Ref. 23).

Group Specific Component

Electrophoresis on a single polyacrylamide gel can simultaneously distinguish the phenotypes of the Group Specific Component, Transferrin and Albumin systems (Ref. 24). Though only the Gc is routinely useful, the other systems can provide additional data on rare occasions.

Haptoglobin

Haptoglobin, a serum protein system with an exclusion probability of .18, can be determined simultaneously with ceruloplasmin on polyacrylamide gels stained with an ortho-dianisidine substrate (Ref. 24).

Gm and Km

Human immunoglobulins contain numerous allotypes which have varying racial distribution. These markers (Gm, Am and Km-formerly known as Inv) can be detected by serologic systems (Ref. 25). Their use is limited in children under six months of age whose markers may not be completely developed and in rare individuals with immunodeficiency states.

Acid Phosphatase

Overnight electrophoresis on starch gel followed by reaction with an appropriate substrate makes it possible to determine the phenotype of the red cell enzyme acid phosphatase which has an exclusion probability of .23 in Whites. Simultaneously the less useful isoenzymes of adenylate kinase, adenosine deaminase and 6-phosphogluconate dehydrogenase can be established from the same gel by reaction with other substrates (Ref. 23).

Phosphoglucomutase

This stable enzyme found in erythrocyte hemolysates like the previous systems is useful both in determining non-paternity and probabilities of paternity when gene frequencies for the test population are established. Isoenzyme patterns is this system, as in most of the other systems, can be recorded on photographs.

VII. Procedures and Forms Relating to the Introduction of Evidence

To satisfy the requirements of the law of evidence and to facilitate the introduction of evidence into the courts, it is recommended that standard procedures, including forms, be adopted. The full series of events relating to the testing procedures, beginning with the court's order (or other request) that samples be taken and tests made, covering the laboratory's procedures and ending with the expert's report to the court, must be documented.

It is recommended that only requests for tests from the court, an officer of the court, or an attorney be honored. All parties should appreciate and preserve the confidentiality of the test results. Test results should be provided only to the requesting agency, court, or party or parties unless there is written authorization from the court, or party or parties concerned, for other distribution.

While it may be desirable to develop and encourage universal adoption of standard forms which satisfy all applicable legal requirements, it is probably sufficient to agree on a standard content of forms, along the lines here expressed.

A. *The Initial Request*

The initial request that blood and other samples be obtained and tested should identify the court or other requesting party, the case, the parties involved in the case and the purpose of the tests (i.e., exclusion of paternity, exclusion of maternity, etc.). The request should direct the named parties to present themselves to the expert or to a laboratory at a designated place, date and time. Each person to be tested should receive a copy of the request. If the testing is to be done elsewhere than in the laboratory where the samples are obtained, the request should state the name and address of the expert to whom the samples should be shipped. The initial request should indicate the party or parties to whom the results of the tests and the opinion of the expert should be sent.

B. *Identification of Parties when Testing for Disputed Parentage*

It is essential that the persons to be tested in a case of disputed parentage be identified and the identification documented in such a way that there can be no question of identification in court. This can be achieved in various ways, but the following procedure is followed by most experts.

1. All the persons to be tested should be present at the same time if possible and identify each other. If one of the parties cannot be present at the same time he or she should be properly identified when he or she appears for the taking of the sample.
2. The following identification and documentation of identification should be made on an appropriate form or forms:
   a. Date blood samples are drawn.
   b. Name, address, social security number (if any), driver's license number (if any), and signature of each party, indicating which is the child (or children), which the mother, and which the putative father (or fathers).
   c. Permission of each person to be tested for blood and other samples to be obtained, including a statement that he or she understands the purpose of the tests. Typically, the mother or legal guardian will give permission for children or minors.

    d. Right thumb print of each party.* If the baby is less than one year old a properly prepared footprint or palm print is probably better than a thumbprint.†

    e. Separate Polaroid photographs of each party, dated and signed on the back and countersigned by a witness. The baby's photograph is signed by the mother.

    f. If blood samples are drawn elsewhere the above procedures should still be followed [if] at all possible, as the responsibility for identifying the party involved rests with the person who obtains the blood samples. It is recommended that the specimens be shipped by registered mail.

C. *Identification of Specimens*

1. Anticoagulated (sodium citrate or ACD solution) and clotted venous blood is obtained from each party. Five to ten ml. of each should be obtained from adults and older children. In infants and small babies capillary blood can be used, collected with micropipettes.

2. Each tube should be capped, labeled with the name of the donor and his or her relationship to the others (baby, mother, putative father) and initialed by the phlebotomist and the physician responsible for the taking of the sample.

3. Samples drawn elsewhere should be identified in the same way, then countersigned by the person receiving them and the physician responsible for the testing.

4. If saliva is collected the above rules of identification also apply.

---

* The Sirchie system (Sirchie Laboratories, P.O. Box 23845, Pleasant Hill, California 94523), is convenient.

† The Hollister Disposable Footprinter (Hollister, Inc., 211 E. Chicago Avenue, Chicago, Illinois 60611), is convenient.

VIII. Guidelines for the Expert

It is assumed that no specific technical instructions are necessary for an investigator who is qualified as an expert. Specific caveats are given in each section dealing with test systems. The following guidelines are designed to insure procedural uniformity.

1. Tests should be performed in duplicate, using a different source of blood grouping reagents for each, and each read independently by two observers.
2. An appropriate working form should be used to record the test results and appropriate controls. The form should show the date the tests were performed and the names of the technologists or physicians who performed the tests or read the results.

IX. The Report of the Expert

Based on the test data, the expert sends a written report of his findings and conclusions to the attorneys representing the parties, or to the court if the testing was ordered by the court. All original data and documentation remain in the expert's files. The report should be sufficiently detailed as to the findings and the expert's opinion based on the findings as to minimize questions. If the test shows a strong likelihood of paternity (as defined in Table 4) this evidence should be given to the court along with a description of the method used for calculating likelihood of paternity.

The report shall be received in evidence by stipulation of the parties or by order of the court.

X. Identification of Qualified Laboratories

It is the opinion of the committee that those laboratories which desire to be "accredited" for this purpose should be required to meet rigorous standards of performance. For the purpose of recognition and accrediting of qualified laboratories the committee believes that qualified accrediting agencies can follow past patterns which have proved effective. Standards should be established regarding personnel, space, equipment, reagents and records. A proficiency testing program should be developed that could be offered, through the Center for Disease Control, the College of American Pathologists or other accrediting agencies. It is the opinion of the Committee that all those laboratories which are capable of performing these tests in a satisfactory manner should be permitted to offer this service and be eligible for reimbursement under the several Federal and State programs.

XI. Recommendations

1. It is recommended that this report be adopted by the AMA Board of Trustees and by the American Bar Association.
2. It is recommended that this report be published jointly by the AMA and ABA, in the Journal of the American Medical Association and in the Family Law Quarterly or other journal designated by the ABA.
3. It is recommended that steps be taken to obtain such Federal, State, or other support as to enable widespread inclusion of HLA studies in the battery of tests used in cases of disputed parentage. This should include not only making available reliable HLA antisera but also provisions for education and continuing education.
4. It is recommended that the National Conference of Commissioners on Uniform State Laws develop new uniform legislation or amend the "Uniform Parentage Act" and the "Uniform Blood Test Act" to (1) clarify judicial authority to order blood tests and (2) simplify the admissibility in evidence of test results and the probative effect thereof, including the evidentiary value of estimations of "likelihood of paternity".

5. It is recommended that the Department of Health, Education and Welfare and the appropriate agencies on the state and local levels adopt and utilize the findings and recommendations of this report in the administration and implementation of P.L. 93-647 as it relates to the establishment of paternity.

6. It is recommended that the AMA and ABA establish procedures to monitor medical and legal developments in this field to facilitate continuing revision and updating of this report as may at any time appear necessary.

REFERENCES

1. *Medicolegal Application of Blood Grouping Tests,* Bureau of Legal Medicine and Legislation. JAMA *149:699-705,* 1952.

2. *Medicolegal Applications of Blood Grouping Tests,* Committee on Medicolegal Problems. JAMA 164:2036-2044, 1957.

3. Chakraborty R. Shaw M, Schull W J: *Exclusion of paternity: The Current State of the Art.* AM. J. HUM. GENET, *26:*477-488, 1974.

4. Hummel, K et al: *Biostatistical Opinion of Parentage, Based Upon the Results of Blood Group Tests,* Vol. 1, 1971; VOL. 2, 1972, Stuttgart, Gustav Fischer Verlag.

5. Hummel, K: Die medizinische Vaterschaftsbegutachtung mit biostatistischem Beweis, 1961, Stuttgart, Gustav Fischer Verlag.

6. Essen-Möller E: Die Beweiskraft der Aehnlichkeit im Vaterschaftsnachweis; theoretische Grundlagen. Mitt Anthrop Ges (Wien) *68:*368, 1938.

7. Mayr W.R: Grundlagen zur Berechnung der Vaterschafts-wahrscheinlichket im HL-A-System. Z Immunitaetsforsch *144:*18-27, 1972.

8. Reviron J, Jacquet A, Salmon C: Un exemple de chromosome "CIS A₁ B". Étude immunologique et génétiquè du phénotype induit. Nouv Rev Fr Hematol *8:*323-338, 1968.

9. Salmon C: Immunogenetique des antigénes ABH, Nouv Rev Fr Hematol *11:*850-862, 1971.

10. Miale J B: LABORATORY MEDICINE-HEMATOLOGY, 1972, (Fourth Ed.), St. Louis, C.V. Mosby Co., p 677-681.

APPENDIX D

11. Miale J B: LABORATORY MEDICINE-HEMATOLOGY, 1972, (Fourth Ed.), St. Louis, C.V. Mosby Co., Table 9-34, p 682.

12. Wiener A S and Nieberg K C: Exclusion of parentage by Rh-Hr blood tests: revised table including blood factors RH_0, rh^1, rh^{11}, hr^1, hr^{11}, and hr. J. Forensic Med 10:6, 1963.

13. Miale J B: LABORATORY MEDICINE-HEMATOLOGY, 1972, (Fourth Ed.), St. Louis, C.V. Mosby Co., p 686.

14. ERSKINE A G: THE PRINCIPLES AND PRACTICE OF BLOOD GROUPING, 1973, St. Louis, C.V. Mosby Co., p 174.

15. Speiser P: Das HL-A-System im Paternitätsprozess mit Berücksichtigung des Beweiswertes. Wien Klin Wochenschr 87:321-326, 1975.

16. Soulier J P, Prou-Wartelle O, Muller J Y: Paternity research using the HL-A system. Haematologia (Budapest) 8:249-265, 1974.

17. Jeannet M, Hässig A, Bernheim J: Use of the HL-A antigen system in disputed paternity cases. Vox Sang 23:197-200, 1972.

18. DAUSSET J AND COLOMBANI J: HISTOCOMPATIBILITY TESTING 1972, 1973, Baltimore, Williams and Wilkins Company.

19. Mayr W R: Die Genetik des HL-A Systems. Populations und Familienuntersuchungen unter besonderer Berucksichtigung der Paternitätsserologie. Humangenetik 12:195-243, 1971.

20. Dausset J, Colombani J, Legrand L and Fellows M: Genetics of the HL-A System: deduction of 480 haplotypes, p. 53 in Terasaki PI (ed) Histocompatibility Testing 1970, Baltimore, Williams and Wilkins Co.

21. Amos, D.B., Ward, F.E.: *Immunogenetics of the HL-A System*, PHYSIOL. REVIEWS, 55:206-246, 1975.

22. Dykes, Dale: *Serum Proteins and Erythrocyte Enzymes in Paternity Testing in a Seminar on Polymorphisms in Human Blood*, pp 27-42, AABB Washington D.C. 1975.

23. Dykes, Dale and Polesky, Herbert F.: *The Usefulness of Serum Proteins and Erythrocyte Enzyme Polymorphisms in Paternity Tests*, AJCP 65:816-820, 1976.

24. POLESKY, H.F., ROKALA, D., HOFF, T.: SERUM PROTEINS IN PATERNITY TESTING, Ed. H.F. Polesky, pp 30-44. ASCP, Chicago 1975.

25. Schanfield, M.S., Polesky, H.F. and Sebring, E.S.: *Gm and Inv Typing in Paternity Testing*, Ed. H.F. Polesky, pp 45-53. ASCP Chicago 1975.

26. Wiener, A.S. and Socha, W.W.: *Methods Available for Solving Medicolegal Problems of Disputed Parentage*. J. FORENSIC SCI. 21(1):42-64, 1976.

27. PATERNITY TESTING BY BLOOD GROUPING, Second Edition, Ed. L. Sussman, C. Thomas, Springfield, Illinois 1976.

Appendix E

PRINCIPLES OF PATERNITY TESTING*

CHANG LING LEE, M.D.†

Genetic Markers

DEFINITION

Blood tests for paternity problems are based on the existence of genetic markers which are personal characteristics inherited from the parents and controlled by genes on a pair of chromosomes. Personal characteristics can be physical, such as the color of hair, eyes and skin, or detectable properties of the blood components. While the former may occasionally be helpful in arriving at a decision, the latter exhibit a wide variety of differences which are scientifically identifiable and thus become the most useful tool for solving parentage problems.

BLOOD COMPONENTS

The blood consists of red and white blood cells, platelets, and liquid plasma. Each component contains a number of

* This paper was developed from presentations made at the Annual Meeting of the American Bar Association, August 1974, Honolulu, and at HEW-sponsored workshops in Chicago and San Francisco, March 1975. It was carefully reviewed and updated by the author in 1979. The author wishes to acknowledge the critical review of the manuscript by Professor Harry D. Krause and the editorial assistance of Ms. Ann Pearl Owen of the College of Law, University of Illinois. Edited by and reprinted with permission from FAMILY LAW QUARTERLY, vol. 9, pp. 615-33 (1975).

†Director, Charles Hymen Blood Center, Mount Sinai Hospital Medical Center, Scientific Director, Mid-America Regional Red Cross Blood Program, Professor of Medicine and Pathology, Rush Medical College, Chicago, Illinois.

genetic markers (See Table I). More than 260 genetic markers, known as isoantigens, and over 50 called isoenzymes for red blood cells have been reported. Nearly 100 markers are known for plasma protein. For white blood cells, 50 markers known as HLA isoantigens are well established and many more described. Platelets share many HLA isoantigens with leukocytes in addition to having their own specific antigens.

Genetic markers which are inherited as part of a group at the same location on a pair of chromosomes are designated as a system. The genetic markers A, B, and O are in the ABO system, as M, N, S, and s are in the MNSs system. In this way, more than 455 listed genetic markers of blood components have been grouped into 51 systems.

TABLE I

Blood Group Genetic Markers Used In Parentage Problems

Blood Components	Genetic Markers		Groups or Systems	
	#Known	#Used	#Known	≠Used
Red blood cell isoantigens	260+	24	24	10
Red blood cell isoenzymes	55+	15	13	7
Plasma protein	90+	16	13	7
White blood cell isoantigens (HLA)	50+	21	1	1
Total	455+	76	51	25

SELECTION OF GENETIC MARKERS

In theory, each person can be identified by the genetic markers in his blood just as by his fingerprints. In practice, it would become much too involved if tests were to be done for all these genetic markers. Not all genetic markers are equally useful. In selecting genetic markers for paternity testing, the following considerations are important:

1. Inheritance — Not all the reported genetic markers are well established, only those which have been well documented through careful study of family members and the general population should be used in paternity testing.

2. Frequency — The incidence of genetic markers in a given population varies widely. Genetic markers with frequencies between 20% and 50% provide a good chance for exclusion from paternity and are thus most useful. Those with low frequencies are useful for the estimation of likelihood of paternity. Those with high frequencies are only of limited value in paternity testing since they seldom allow a differentiation between the alleged father and other men.

3. Practicality — Reagents for testing must be readily available and reliable. The procedures should be reproducible and give clear-cut results. Cost is another consideration but should not be overemphasized when compared to the cost of supporting the child.

4. Reliability — Attention should be paid to the fact that genetic variants, wide ethnic differences, and variations under different physiologic and pathologic conditions are known to exist for certain genetic markers.

Inheritance

GENES

Many characteristics are controlled by two genes at the same location on a pair of chromosomes. Each human body cell has 23 pairs of chromosomes, while the mature sperms or ova contain only 23 single chromosomes; thus, only one of a pair of genes is present and transmitted from each parent to the offspring. For example, if *a* and *b* are a pair of genes, either *a* or *b* is transmitted to the offspring; it cannot be neither or both (figure I).

FIGURE 1

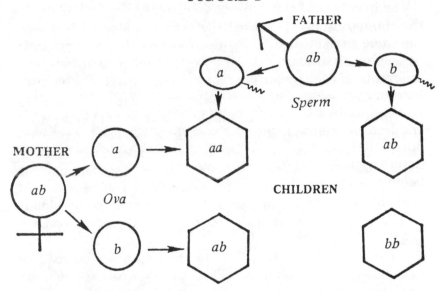

AN EXAMPLE OF INHERITANCE. Sperms and ova carry one of a pair of genes, either *a* or *b*. After fertilization the genes from a sperm and an ovum join to form three possible genotypes; *aa, ab,* and *bb.*

When an ovum is fertilized by a sperm, the 23 chromosomes in each combine to form again 23 pairs of chromosomes. One half of the genes or genetic markers are derived from the father and the other half from the mother. Using the same example as in Figure 1, the children can be only one of 3 types: *aa, bb* or *ab,* depending on whether the ovum and the sperm fertilizing it are carrying the *a* or *b* gene.

GENOTYPES

The gene combination on a pair of chromosomes, *aa, bb,* or *ab* is called genotype. Persons with genotype *aa* or *bb* are designated as homozygous (*i.e.,* with identical genes), persons with type *ab* as heterozygous (*i.e.,* with different genes).

The genotype of the parents determines the genotype of the children (Table II). If both parents are homozygous for the same gene (*aaxaa* or *bbxbb*), all of their children must be homozygous (*aa* or *bb*). If the parents are homozygous for different genes (*aaxbb*), all their children must be heterozygous *(ab).* If one parent is homozygous (*aa* or *bb*) and the other parent heterozygous (*ab*), one half of their children is expected to be homozygous (*aa* or *bb*) and the other half heterozygous (*ab*). If both parents are heterozygous (*abxab,* as in Figure 1), their children can belong to any of the three types (*aa, bb, ab*).

TABLE II

Expected Frequencies of Genotypes of Children of Different Matings

Genotype of Mother		Father	Genotypes of Children aa	Genotypes of Children ab	Genotypes of Children bb
aa	X	aa	100%		
bb	X	bb			100%
aa	X	bb		100%	
bb	X	aa		100%	
aa	X	ab	50%	50%	
ab	X	aa	50%	50%	
bb	X	ab		50%	50%
ab	X	bb		50%	50%
ab	X	ab	25%	50%	25%

The genotype *aa,* or *bb* is usually assumed by the absence of the *b* or *a* marker but can be established through the study of family members.

For some characteristics, a third gene may be an alternate at the same location on a pair of chromosomes. The ABO blood group is an example. Without considering the subgroups of A, there are three genes in the group, *A, B,* and *O.* Any two of them can be on a pair of chromosomes to form genotypes, while the mature sperm or ovum, having only one of each pair of chromosomes, has only one of the genes. Table III illustrates six possible genotypes, *AA, BB, OO, AB, AO, BO* and the frequency of each gene or genotype.

At the present time, differentiation of *AA* from *AO* is not possible except by studying the family members. Consequently, both types, *AA* and *AO,* are designated as group A (the phenotype or group to which the individual is assigned on the basis of visible characteristics or laboratory findings). Similarly, the phenotype B consists of *BB* and *BO* genotypes. This is why group A or B parents can have children of group O. In other words, a man of group A or B, who is heterozygous (*AO* or *BO*) may have a child that is neither group A nor group B.

TABLE III

ABO Genotypes of Children of Different Matings*

with their frequencies among whites

GENE ON MOTHER'S OVUM Frequency	GENE ON FATHER'S SPERM		Frequency
	A 0.285	B 0.079	O 0.636
A 0.285	AA 0.081	AB 0.023	AO 0.181
B 0.079	AB 0.023	BB 0.006	BO 0.050
O 0.636	AO 0.181	BO 0.050	OO 0.404

*Subgroups of A are not taken into consideration

RULES OF INHERITANCE

According to the principle discussed above, the following rules of inheritance can be stated:

1. A child cannot have a genetic marker which is absent in both parents.

2. A child must inherit one of a pair of genetic markers from each parent.

3. A child cannot have a pair of identical genetic markers (*aa*) unless both parents have the marker (*a*).

4. A child must have the genetic marker (*a* or *b*) which is present as an identical pair in one parent (*aa* or *bb*).

Parentage Problems

DISPUTED PATERNITY

Disputed paternity is by far the most important parentage problem. In this situation, the mother is always considered to be the true mother. The genetic markers which are found in the child but are absent in the mother must therefore come from the true father. Exclusion of paternity is normally the primary consideration. Based on the four rules of inheritance above, four types of exclusions from paternity are possible. (See Table IV)

1. The child has a genetic marker (such as blood group A) which is absent in the mother and cannot be demonstrated in the alleged father.

2. In a 3 alternate-genetic marker system (such as ABO), the child (type O) lacks both genetic markers (absence of both A and B in the child) which are demonstrated in the alleged father (type AB).

3. A child is homozygous for a genetic marker (such as *EE*) which is not present in both parents.

4. A child lacks a genetic marker (M-negative) while the alleged father is homozygous for it (*MM*).

The first two types of exclusions are based on the presence or absence of certain genetic markers demonstrable by direct examinations and are known as DIRECT EXCLUSIONS. With extremely rare exceptions (Table IV), these two types of exclusions can be accepted with great confidence.

TABLE IV

Exclusion of Paternity

Types of Exclusion		Mother	Child	Alleged Father	Very Rare Exceptions*
Direct	1	A–	A+	A–	"Bombay"
	2		O	AB	"Cis-AB"
Indirect	3	E+	*EE*	E–	"D--"
	4		M–	*MM*	"M^g"

*Examples for which tests can verify

The third and fourth types of exclusions which are based on the inference of homozygous genotypes determined by a negative reaction in a particular test are known as Indirect Exclusions, and should be accepted with caution. The particular test should be repeated with the same and different reagents or by a different technologist, or in a different laboratory. For some markers, zygosity may be determined by the use of the titration method. The use of other genetic markers may reveal additional exclusions.
* * *

Evaluation of Test Results

Customarily, the results of a paternity test are reported as "the alleged father is excluded from paternity" or "the alleged father is not excluded from paternity." This seems simple and straightforward and has been generally accepted. However, with progress in science and the increasing demands for better service, this type of reporting may be challenged in at least three aspects.

591

Reliability of Exclusion From Paternity

PITFALLS

Were blood specimens drawn from the right parties? Were the tests done properly with reliable reagents, suitable instruments, appropriate techniques and by experienced technologists? Were results of the tests correctly interpreted? Has the validity of an indirect exclusion been seriously and carefully examined? Have all the known genetic variations, ethnic differences, as well as physiologic and pathologic conditions been taken into consideration? If any of these aspects are neglected, a true father may be relieved from supporting his child, a true parent may be denied his child, or an immigrant child may be barred from reunion with its true parents. These considerations will become even more pertinent as soon as a variety of genetic markers not yet customarily used in many laboratories are included.

LIMITATIONS

The more tests that are made the more genetic variations are found in many systems; it can be expected that eventually even more will be found. Although some of these variants are rare, they should be taken into consideration before a conclusion is reached. Some variants can be verified by additional testing, others by studying the family members. In view of these new findings, an exclusion from paternity can no longer be considered 100% certain. This is not unexpected since practically all existing rules have exceptions, especially in biology. That is why statistics are often used. Any chance above 95% is considered to be significant. A similar philosophy may have to be applied in paternity exclusion cases, in which the change is usually above 99%. Thus, an appropriate report should read:

"According to the current knowledge and our test results, Mr. X is excluded from paternity of x."

CRITERIA

Direct exclusion by one genetic marker is usually sufficient for an exclusion judgment, provided that all the above pitfalls and limitations have been taken into consideration.

Indirect exclusion by one genetic marker should be verified by additional tests or substantiated by other genetic markers.

In case of any doubt, tests should be repeated by different technologists with different lots of reagents and, preferably, in different laboratories. Should there be any discrepancy in test results from two laboratories, a third laboratory may be asked to resolve the difference. In several European countries, centers for paternity studies have been established to assure the quality and reliability of the test results.

Confidence in a Non-Exclusion

What is the change of excluding a man wrongfully named as father through tests used in a particular laboratory? The confidence in a non-exclusion depends on the number and the type of genetic markers used in the tests (See Table VI), as well as on the genetic pattern of a mother-child combination (See Table VII).

TABLE VI

Chances for Exclusion of Paternity
In 25 Blood Group Systems*

Systems or Genetic Markers	Chances in %		Systems or Genetic Markers	Chances in %	
	Individual	Cumulative		Individual	Cumulative
1. HLA(21 markers)	76	76	14. C3(1,2)	13.8	98.69
2. M,N,S,s	32	84.7	15. EsD(1,2)	9.0	98.81
3. D,C,C^w,c,E,e	29	88.7	16. ADA(1,2)	5.8	98.88
4. AcP(A,B,C)	25	91.3	17. Km(1,3)	5.7	98.90
5. A$_1$.A$_2$,B,O	20	93	18. Xg^a	5	99.00
6. Glm^a,Glm^x,G3m^b	20	94.4	19. K,k	4	99.03
7. Jk^a,Jk^b	18.7	95.5	20. P$_1$	4	99.07
8. GPT(1,2)	18.6	96.3	21. Se	4	99.11
9. Fy^a,Fy^b	18.4	97	22. Lu^a,Lu^b	3.6	99.14
10. Hp(1,2)	18	97.5	23. AK(1,2)	3.3	99.17
11. Gc(1,2)	16	97.9	24. PGD(A,C)	2.1	99.19
12. PGM$_1$(1,2)	14.5	98.23	25. Tf(C,B$_2$,D$_1$)	1	99.27
13. Ag(x,y)	14.3	98.48			

* Based on gene frequencies of whites. For many genetic markers, only minor differences exist among various white populations.

594

TABLE VII

An Example of Chance of Exclusion for a
Given Mother-Child Combination
(Based on frequencies in the white population)

	Mother	Child	Chance of a Man Being	
			Not excluded	Excluded
	K–	K+	K+(8%)	K–(92%)
Genetic Markers	M–	M+	M+(80%)	M–(20%)
	B–	B+	B+(11%)	B–(89%)

Cumulative chance of NON-EXCLUSION = 8% X 80% X 11% = 0.7%

Cumulative chance of EXCLUSION = 100% − 0.7% = 99.3%

With this combination, 993 innocent men in 1,000 could be excluded

CHANCE OF EXCLUSION BY THE TYPE OF GENETIC MARKERS

Each genetic marker or system of genetic markers provides different chances of exclusion as listed in Table VI. The white blood cell isoantigen system alone provides a 76% chance of exclusion. The next 13 systems provide from 32% to 13.8% chance of exclusion. By using the first 4 systems, a cumulative chance of over 90% is reached; by the first 7 systems, a 95% chance; and by all systems, a chance of 99.27%. In practice, only a limited number of laboratories presently have the capability of testing nearly all these genetic markers. The amount of involvement may not be justified by the small increase in chance of exclusion. The selection of genetic markers by various countries as illustrated in Figure 3 may serve as a practical guide. In the United States, tests with a chance of 70% of exclusion can be carried out by a number of laboratories. If demand and interest increase, the capability of conducting tests with a

90% or higher chance of exclusion could be reached in a short time.

Cumulative Chance of Exclusion

The cumulative chance of exclusion is not equal to the sum of individual chances. Its calculation is given in the following example: The MNSs system provides a 32% chance of exclusion; the ABO system, 20%; thus, 32% x 20% = 6.4% of men in a given population will be excluded by both these systems. Since a person cannot be excluded more than once, the cumulative chance of exclusion by both systems is the sum of the exclusions in both systems minus their product, *i.e.,* 32% + 20% — 6.4% = 45.6%. An alternate method of computation would be to obtain the product of non-exclusions (100% — 32%) (100% — 20%) = 54.4% and deduct it from 100% (100% — 54.4%) = 45.6%. This method is simpler if more than two systems are involved.

Chance of Exclusion by the Number of Genetic Markers Used

The chance of exclusion from paternity varies with the number of genetic markers used with each system (Figure 4). In the MN system, the use of 2 markers (M and N), provides an 18.7% chance; of 3 markers (M, N and S), a 23.9%; of 4 markers (M, N, S and s), a 32% chance. In the ABO system, the use of 3 markers (A, B and O), provides a 16.5% chance; of 4 markers (A_1, A_2, B and O), a 20% chance. In the Rh system, the use of 1 marker (D) provides only a 1.8% chance; of 4 markers (D, C, E and c), a 25.6%; of 6 markers (D, C, E, c, e and C^w), a 29% chance. Consequently, there are three different chances for an innocent man to be excluded from paternity: Laboratory #1, using only 6 markers, provides a 33% chance; laboratory #2, using 11 markers, a 54.7%; laboratory #3, using 14 markers, a 61.4% chance.

FIGURE 4

Three Levels of Chance of Exclusion of Paternity
According to the number of genetic markers used in each system

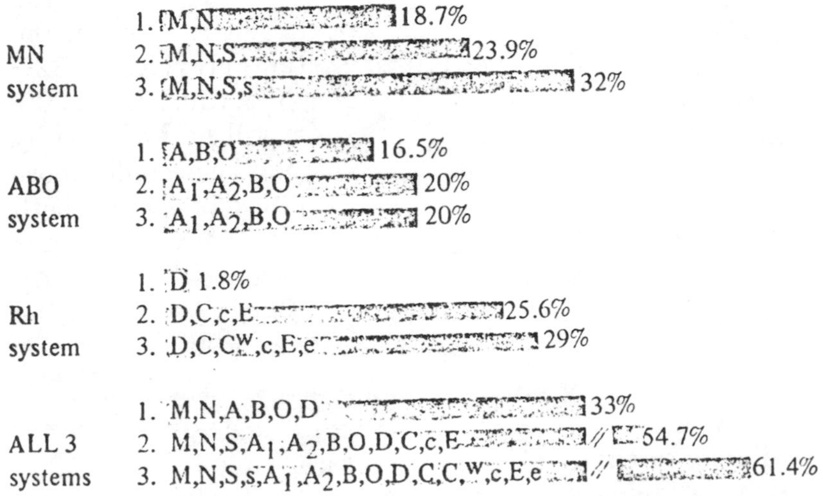

MN
system
1. M,N ▩ 18.7%
2. M,N,S ▩ 23.9%
3. M,N,S,s ▩ 32%

ABO
system
1. A,B,O ▩ 16.5%
2. A_1,A_2,B,O ▩ 20%
3. A_1,A_2,B,O ▩ 20%

Rh
system
1. D 1.8%
2. D,C,c,E ▩ 25.6%
3. D,C,C^w,c,E,e ▩ 29%

ALL 3
systems
1. M,N,A,B,O,D ▩ 33%
2. M,N,S,A_1,A_2,B,O,D,C,c,E ▩ 54.7%
3. M,N,S,s,A_1,A_2,B,O,D,C,C^w,c,E,e ▩ 61.4%

CHANCE OF EXCLUSION FOR A GIVEN MOTHER-CHILD
COMBINATION

The chance of exclusion may also depend on a given
mother-child combination. (See Table VII) In this example,
the mother is negative for 3 genetic markers (K, M, B), her
child is positive for all of them. If the alleged father is not
excluded, he must be positive for all 3 markers. The chance
of finding a random man with these 3 markers is 8% x 80%
x 11% = 0.7% or 7 out of 1000 persons. Thus, the
cumulative chance of exclusion is 100% — 0.7% = 99.3%.
This means that in this particular mother-child
combination there is 99.3% chance for the average innocent
man to be excluded from paternity by the use of only 3
genetic markers. This type of combination is uncommon,
but it does indicate the importance of genetic patterns of a
given mother-child combination.

597

A Practical Approach

In some cases, the alleged father can be excluded by a minimal number of tests and additional tests would serve no useful purpose. In case there is no exclusion, additional tests should be done to provide at least a 70 percent chance of exclusion in order to be fair. If the man named as father or the court is not satisfied with the results, further tests can be conducted. Thus, it may be practical to adopt the three step test system, a preliminary test, a standard test and an extended test.

Likelihood of Paternity

The Logic Behind the Likelihood of Paternity

It is true that one cannot be 100 percent sure of the true father, sometimes not even of the mother. However, the courts are seeking only a preponderance of evidence. In other words, while absolutely certain evidence is seldom available, calculated chances are acceptable in the courts.

If the child and the alleged father share one or several uncommon genetic markers, and the chance of such occurrence is less than one in one thousand or even in a million; if the man admits his involvement with the child's mother, and his brother, who may have the same genetic pattern, has an "alibi," a positive assignment of paternity may be made. In reality, the chances are usually greater than one in a thousand and can be evaluated in two ways:

1. *By The Genetic Pattern of a Given Mother-Child Combination (Table VII).* If the child has 3 genetic markers (K, M, B) which are absent in the mother, then the alleged father, in order not to be excluded from paternity, must have all 3 genetic markers. The chance of finding a person in the population with all 3 genetic markers is only 7 in a thousand or 1 in 143. Therefore, such an alleged father is likely to be the true father, provided there is no other stronger evidence against this assumption.

2. *By Comparison between the Alleged Father and a Random Man for Being the True Father.* A comparison is made between the chances of the sperms of the alleged father and a random man carrying the genetic markers required for being the true father in a given mother-child combination. For this type of calculation, one must know the frequencies of genes and genotypes of each genetic marker. (See Table III for an example of gene frequencies).

The term gene frequency means the chance of finding sperms or ova carrying a specific gene in a given population, such as 0.285, 0.079 and 0.636 for *A, B* and *O* genes, respectively, for Caucasians. That is, out of 100 random men in the population, sperms or ova of 28 carry *A,* 8 carry *B* and 64 carry O. The calculation of gene frequencies is beyond the scope of this report.

The genotype frequencies are derived from the gene frequencies. For instance, frequency of genotype *AA* is the product of 0.285 (*A*) x 0.285(*A*) = 0.081 (8.1%). The frequency of *AO* is the product of 0.285(*A*) x 0.636(*O*) 2 = 0.362 (36.2%). The phenotype frequency of A (determined by direct examination) is the sum of frequencies of *AA* and *AO* which is 0.088 + 0.362 = 0.443 (44.3%). Among the persons of group A, 0.081/0.443 = 18% are AA and 0.362/0.443 = 82% are AO.

By knowing the gene and genotype frequencies of A, the chance of a man's being the father of a child of group A can be estimated under two situations. The accused man could be either the true father who must have the genetic marker required for a given mother-child combination (A) or a random man who may happen to have the required genetic marker (A). Out of 100 random white men, the sperm of 28 would carry A and could be the father of a child of group A, *i.e.,* the gene frequency of A represents the chance of a random man. On the other hand, if the mother is *O,* 100% of the children must be group A if the father's genotype is

AA, whereas only 50% of his children would be group A if he is *AO.* Since 18% of group A persons are *AA* and 82% are *AO,* the chance of a group A person being the true father is 100% x 18% + 50% x 82% = 18% + 41% = 59%. Thus, an unexcluded man of group A has a chance of being the true father of a group A child in the ratio of 59%:28%, or approximately 2 times greater than the chance of a random man. A similar type of estimation can be applied to genetic markers other than A.

Figure 5 shows an example of the estimation of likelihood of paternity based on the same mother-child combination as shown in Table VII. The child has genetic markers K, M and B which are absent in the mother and must come from the true father. If the alleged father is not excluded, he must have all three genetic markers. The chance of a man who is positive for K, M and B to transmit them to a child is 18.7% while the chance of a random man of the same population is 0.176%. Thus, the chance of the alleged father is 18.7%:0.176% or 106 times greater than that of a random man. It is unlikely that during the conception period, another 105 men were involved with the mother of the child. Statistically, odds of 20 to 1 or 95% or better are considered to be significant. Again, other evidence should be taken into consideration.

FIGURE 5

Comparison Between

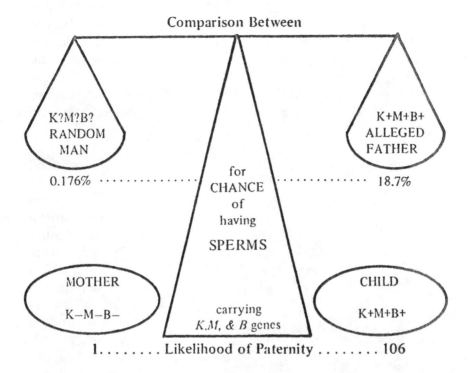

K?M?B? RANDOM MAN

K+M+B+ ALLEGED FATHER

0.176%

for CHANCE of having SPERMS

18.7%

MOTHER

K–M–B–

carrying K,M, & B genes

CHILD

K+M+B+

1 . . . . Likelihood of Paternity 106

The second type of estimation not only considers all three parties involved, but also uses the frequencies of genes which are obviously preferable to that of phenotypes as discussed earlier. When two or more men are involved, a similar estimation can be used.

* * *

Appendix F

THE USE OF BLOOD TYPING IN CASES OF DISPUTED PATERNITY IN DENMARK*
KLAUS HENNINGSEN, M.D.†

Legal Presumptions and Court Procedure.

The applicability of blood groups and other biological evidence to legal cases of disputed paternity is, to a large extent, dependent on the law. In Denmark, the bill of May, 1960, concerning the legal rights of children has the following provisions regarding the paternity of a child. For children born in lawful marriage, the husband is *a priori* presumed to be the father. That presumption does not have to be proved, but may be disproved, if hereditary characteristics of the child or other special circumstances obviously exclude his paternity. If the court is satisfied *in confesso,* or otherwise, that the wife has had sexual relations with other men during the period of conception, the *a priori* presumption regarding the husband's paternity may also be disregarded, and another man may be presumed to be the father.

For children born out of wedlock, the law distinguishes between cases in which only one man is involved and cases involving more men. The mother of a child born out of wedlock is required by law to notify the authorities as to who the father of the child may be. If she has had relations with more than one man during the period of conception, she is required to name them all.

---

* This paper was prepared by Dr. Henningsen at the request of Harry D. Krause and financed by the H.E.W. grant described under "Acknowledgments". It is a composite of Dr. Henningsen's original draft as well as his responses to more detailed and specific inquiries.

† Head of Serological Department. University Institute of Forensic Medicine, Copenhagen.

If one man is named, the man may officially acknowledge paternity, closing the case. If, however, he does not so acknowledge, a court case is necessary, and the man will be adjudged the father unless the court, according to the evidence in the case, including the results of a blood group examination, considers his paternity improbable.

In cases involving two or more men (which must always be court cases), the law provides that a man can only be determined to be the father of the child if his paternity is "considerably more probable" than the paternity of any of the other men involved. Only in cases which include one or more unidentified men, by admission or by reasonable suspicion, is objective, positive evidence of a man's paternity necessary to satisfy the law's provisions for determination of paternity.

In all disputed cases the court will order blood tests; the parties involved are required by law to permit the taking of blood samples. For the whole of Denmark, blood-grouping for forensic purposes has been centralized since 1927 at the blood-group department of the Institute of Forensic Medicine, Copenhagen University. Since then, more than 70,000 cases have been examined.

When the court has decided to require a blood test, a requisition stating the data of the parties involved is sent to the Institute. The parties are ordered to go to their physicians or, preferably, to the local public-health medical officer for the blood sampling. If the parties reside in Copenhagen, they are usually referred to the Institute for the blood sampling. For each person, the court partly fills out a form in duplicate and sends it to the doctor who is to take the blood. After taking the blood, the doctor mails the samples to the Institute, with Form D stating how the identity of the party was checked and certifying that the physician has asked if a blood transfusion has been received within the previous four months. The duplicate Form C is signed by the party and sent to the court to inform it that the blood sample has been taken.

Institute Laboratory Procedures.

The blood samples, which are either taken by the staff of the laboratory or sent to the laboratory by mail, are placed in a rack, labeled with a working number, and registered under this number in the daily record of experiments. The laboratory technicians prepare suspensions and start the actual typing procedure, *i.e.,* mix antibody and suspensions for incubation, insert serum samples in the gel for electrophoresis, etc. The actual reading of the results is performed by a member of the academic staff, together with a technician. The reactions are dictated by the academic assistant and recorded by the technician. The diagnosis in the record is then cross-checked by a second reading with the actual reactions. Further, all tests, including preparation of suspensions and sampling of serum and erythrocytes, are performed twice by two completely independent procedures. Before and after the examination the academic assistant compares the proper sequence of the samples in the rack to the sequence in the record and guarantees the sequence by his signature in the record. From the record of experiment, a member of the office staff transfers the results to the file of the case, and the correct transfer is checked by cross-checking with another member of the staff.

In exclusion cases and cases to be submitted to supplementary examination, new samples are requested from all parties of the case. When they arrive, they are dealt with in the manner as described above, with the exception that the over-all examination is not performed in duplicate. The examination is done blindly, but special tests (*e.g.,* absorptions, electrophoresis in special medium, etc.) are performed according to the character of the exclusion found by the first examination.

The samples for supplementary examinations are of course further subjected to grouping according to the systems used for this part of the examination. With regard to exclusions found by the supplementary examination, special tests (according to the exclusion found) are performed on aliquots of serum or erythrocytes which have been kept deep-frozen for this purpose until samples from all parties have been received. Of course, the results of any special procedures are also invariably read by an academic staff member together with the technician.

When all samples in a case have been received and tested as specified by the rules of the department, the results are evaluated and a member of the office staff writes out the statement to be sent to the court. This statement is signed by an academic staff member, preferably by the head, after cross-checking the reactions given in the statement with the original records of experiment.

Results of Testing.

The number of cases examined by the Institute had been nearly constant for many years at about 2,000 cases per year, but has decreased recently to about 1,500-1,600 cases per year. However, the ratio between one-man and more-than-one-man cases is unchanged, with one-man cases constituting about two-thirds of the total. The frequency of non-fathers in one-man cases, calculated from the actual percentage of exclusion compared to the theoretical percentage of exclusion, has been about 15-20 percent for many years. In two-man cases, one of the two named men is calculated to be the biological father in about 85 percent of the cases. However, the percentage of biological fathers decreases in cases involving three or more men.

The Three-Stage Examination.

Due partly to the gradual evolution of the knowledge of genetic systems applicable to the problem of disputed paternity, and partly to cost-benefit considerations regarding the relatively high number of true fathers in our one- and two-man cases, the Institute's examinations in paternity cases are conducted in three stages.

The first stage, or standard examination, which is performed on all cases, presently uses the following systems: A_1A_2B0, MN, Rh, Kell, Hp, Gc. (See Table 1.) The average theoretical percentgage of exclusion at this level is about 70. Considering that after the standard examination less than 5 percent of the non-excluded men are non-fathers in one-man cases and in two-man cases in which one of the men is excluded, only the standard examination is performed in such cases, unless the court specifically asks for further examination, or unless the result of the standard examination indicates that the man's paternity is improbable without actually excluding it.

TABLE 1

Three Stage Examination in Cases of Disputed Paternity

I. Standard Examination: Effectiveness (1974)
    A_1A_2BO - MN - Rh - K - Hp -Gc: 69%

II. Supplementary Examination:
    Ss - C^w - Fya - P - Gm - EAP   70%
    PGM - AK - PGD - ADA - GPT

                                             91%

III. "Anthropological" Examination
    C3 - HLA   › 90%
    Morphological Traits

All cases which involve two or more non-excluded men after the standard examination are automatically subjected to stage two, the supplementary examination which presently consists of the following factors and systems: Ss, CW, Fya, P, Lea (Secr.), Gm, PGM, EAP, AK, PGD, ADA, GPT. The theoretical exclusion of stage two is also about 70 percent. In addition to evidencing exclusions, this stage involves an evaluation of the blood-group statistical evidentiary value with regard to the paternity of non-excluded men.

The third stage, which in Denmark is termed the anthropological examination, is performed by a special department of the Institute. Rather few morphological characteristics are used: eye color, finger- and palm-print patterns, and some physiognomic characteristics and indices are all evaluated on the basis of a sample of some 200 families examined by the head of the department, Dr. Gürtler.

The serological systems employed at this stage are divisible into two groups: either they are systems which, due to scarcity of antisera or for other practical reasons, are best reserved for special cases; or they are newly discovered systems which, due to limited experimental experience, have not yet attained the formal reliability which is deemed necessary for exclusions in stage two. Presently, the third-stage examination involves these systems: red-cell factors (for instance, Lua, Jka, and Jkb), serum factors C3 and Inv, and, most important, the white-cell HLA factors. The results regarding non-excluded men are expressed in an index form, which makes it possible to make a final, comprehensive, biostatistical evaluation including all the blood-group results obtained earlier in the case, the blood-group results obtained at the third stage, and the result of the morphologic examination. Special features, as for instance racial characteristics, hereditary malformations, etc., are also taken into consideration at the third stage and evaluated in the final result.

The third stage is primarily used for cases in which more than one man remains after the supplementary examination. But it is also used for some cases with only one man left if the court wants further biological evidence comparing the paternity of the accused man to that of an acknowledged but unidentified one, or to an unacknowledged other man suspected by the court. It may here be mentioned that the court will ask the medico-legal council, an official board of experts serving as advisory board for the legal authorities in medico-legal matters, to perform any combined evaluation of these results and other biological evidence (*e.g.*, evidence regarding low fertility, time of cohabitation in relation to menstrual cycle, etc.).

The advantage of this division into three stages is that the effectiveness of the examination, as expressed by the actual exclusion rate, is higher if stages two and three are reserved for that fraction of the cases in which it is known (or at least highly probable) that non-fathers are involved, than if they are used indiscriminately for all cases.

The disadvantage is that about 5 percent non-fathers are left undetected in one-man cases and in two-man cases where one man has already been excluded. However, it is reasonable to believe, and is borne out to some degree by experience, that the court may be able to select those cases in which, despite the testimony of the mother, there is a high probability that an unnamed man has had sexual access to the mother. The court can then request supplementary examination.

Another disadvantage is that blood-group statistical evaluation cannot reasonably be performed if one takes into account only the relatively few systems used for the standard examination. In general, however, this is acceptable because of the high *a priori* probability of

609

paternity within the pertinent groups of cases, and the fact that positive blood-group evidence is not a prerequisite of the law for a determination of paternity.

The first and second stages may be performed shortly after the birth of the baby, although the development of certain factors such as P, Hp, and Gm may necessitate a new sample from the child when it is about a year old. As the third stage involves the examination of morphological traits which are not sufficiently developed until the child is at least two years old, this stage must of necessity be limited to the relatively few cases which cannot be solved satisfactorily by the first and second stages.

Determination of Examination Tests.

The selection of systems for the different stages is for the most part historically determined. In the 1930s and 1940s there was one purely serological blood-group examination (ABO, A_1A_2, MN) and one purely morphological anthropological examination.

With the adoption of the Rh-system after the war, it became the Institute's practice to start a new system as part of the anthropological examination. Later, when the experience was deemed sufficient, the Institute promoted the system to the purely serological stage.

The supplementary blood-group examination, which divides the serological part in first and second stages, was designed in the 1950s for two reasons. Primarily, we found it prudent to use the newer systems only in cases involving two or more men, in order to avoid the risk that an exclusion with a rather limited statistical reliability should be the only evidence for another man. In addition, the second stage was designed to limit the use of the new systems to cases which involved at least one non-father with certainty, in order to put the limited resources of rare sera and/or laboratory facilities to the best use. Later, when the experience regarding the reliability of exclusions within the system had grown sufficiently, the system could be promoted to the first stage, depending on availability of the necessary facilities.

Today it might be reasonable to include, for instance, acid phosphatase and PGM in our first stage, and to demote the rather inefficient Kell system. However, the problem is complicated by such factors as the frequency of non-fathers in the sample, the diminished effectiveness due to concomitant exclusions in several systems, and the legal, statistical, economic, and psychological considerations which must be taken into account when a new set-up is planned.

A solution might seem to be in some sort of individualization by fixing a certain limit of chance of exclusion, or a certain limit of blood-group statistical index to be obtained in every case. However, the actual effectiveness of such a system is again dependent on the ratio of fathers to non-fathers in the sample. The problem has not yet been satisfactorily solved; at the moment, the best approach seems to be to let the court decide if the circumstances of the case justify examinations beyond the reasonably efficient standard examination.

Scientific Basis for "New" Systems.

Generally speaking, the procedure in taking up "new" systems is the following:

1. The techniques are practiced in the laboratory until reproducible results are obtained;

2. A series of random samples and mother/child combinations is grouped and analyzed, and the results are compared to the results of other laboratories;

3. A limited number of persons are tested several times with varying intervals and under varying conditions in order to ascertain the constancy of the system. In addition,

samples from persons of various age groups are investigated;

4. With several systems, but not in all cases, a long series of samples is tested blindly by the Institute as well as by other laboratories in the field (for instance, in Norway and Sweden.)

When our experience with the system is estimated to be sufficient for reliable typing, the system is first used for practical purposes as part of the third-stage (anthropological) examination, with an intentionally underestimated reliability. Later, when the Institute's sample (especially mother-child samples together with foreign family- and mother-child samples) has attained sufficient size, the reliability of an exclusion is calculated as the inverse of the paternity index on the basis of the Institute's figures and published non-Danish study materials.

The principles used for estimating the reliability are, in my opinion, formally correct. Nevertheless, in systems with genes of low frequency they may lead to apparent non-biological underestimation of the reliability of exclusions according to the first rule, if one of the rare genes is involved. This is the case, for instance, in the HLA system, where so many genes are of low frequency. It does not matter too much if another, unexcluded man is involved, as the rarity of the factor in question will raise this man's blood-group statistical paternity index proportionately as the formal reliability of the exclusion is decreased. However, if only the excluded man is known, the strict and probably non-biological adherence to this method of calculation poses a problem which the Institute has not yet solved satisfactorily. It is probably biologically correct to analogize the different allelic factors within a system; but, on the other hand, such a procedure is not quite consistent with the Institute's claim that reliability estimates rest primarily on the quantitative figures of the study sample.

The following are examples of the order of magnitude of the samples, from the literature and from the Institute's experiments used for the first general reliability estimate of a system:

Acid phosphatase, March, 1971:	2000 mother/child combinations, 1,017 families
PGM, March, 1971:	2588 mother/child combinations, 1,082 families
AK, November, 1972:	2750 mother/child combinations, 1,010 families
ADA, October, 1972:	1175 mother/child combinations, 1,040 families
GPT, September, 1974:	2,987 mother/child combinations, 528 families

For each system the number of apparent incompatibilities with the accepted rules of heredity is taken into account by the calculation. If no instance of incompatibility is found in the sample, the calculation is based on one hypothetical exception.

Use of the Paternity Index.

The result of the blood-group examination may either be an exclusion of paternity by one or more systems or a non-exclusion by any of these systems. The fact that a man is not excluded in an individual case may to some extent indicate paternity by sufficiently high theoretical percentage of exclusion. But this does not exhaust the information of the blood-group results. As first described by Essen-Møller (Refs. 1, 2), the frequency of a given blood-group constellation between mother, child, and man in a sample of biological fathers, and in a sample of non-fathers, may be calculated from the gene frequencies of the population. Essen-Møller elaborated this ratio (called the $\frac{x}{y}$ ratio) to a probability expression presuming an *a priori* equal chance of paternity for the known, unexcluded man and an unknown man. This presumption, which evidently does not hold true in actual cases, has been much criticized. Nevertheless, the method is used extensively (*e.g.,* in Germany).

In Denmark, however, the Institute of Forensic Medicine abstains from the calculation of probability and gives only the above-mentioned $\frac{x}{y}$ ratio, which, in our opinion, expresses the evidentiary value of the blood-group results for or against paternity. This evidence may then be used by the court, together with other evidence of the case, in the court's final evaluation of the accused's probability of paternity. The $\frac{x}{y}$ ratio, which in the statement of the Institute is termed "blood group statistical paternity index," suggests paternity when higher than 1 and weighs against it when less than 1. But, in analogy to the statistical confidence limit of 95 percent, the Institute considers only indices higher than 19 or less than 0.05 significant by themselves.

It is evident that blood-group statistical considerations and the estimate of the reliability of an exclusion are critically dependent on the knowledge of representative gene frequencies of the population to which the parties belong. In Denmark there are few natural boundaries between the different parts of the country; the population is very homogeneous and well suited for such statistical, genetic analysis. The existence of an non-homogeneous population, and especially of isolates with vastly differing gene frequencies, may well invalidate blood-group statistical evaluation for paternity cases if such variables are not taken into consideration.

Guidance for the court regarding the evaluation is always enclosed with the Institute's statement of the result in exclusion cases and in cases involving blood-group statistical evaluation. This guidance, which was originally agreed upon in 1952 by the forensic blood-group workers in the Scandinavian countries, has since been revised several times and is approved in Denmark by the Medicolegal Council (Ref. 3).

If the paternity of the accused is not excluded by the standard examination, the Institute only states that, according to the systems used, the results do not preclude his paternity for the child in question. In the majority of one-man cases and two-man cases in which the other man is excluded, the circumstances are such that the accused acknowledges paternity or the court feels justified to render a verdict of paternity. In cases involving supplementary examination without exclusion, it is also stated that the results of the examination do not preclude paternity; however, the blood-group statistical index of the non-excluded man or men is also given.

The evidentiary value of the paternity index may, on request, be elaborated upon by stating that the blood-group results suggest the man's paternity, as compared to an unidentified man having an *a priori* equal chance of paternity, in the ratio of the numerical value of the index to 1. This ratio, which may also be expressed in percentages, equals the paternity probability of Essen-Møller.

If two or more men are left unexcluded, their indices are given and the ratio of those is expressed in percentages. These percentages are not equal to paternity probabilities, unless all other conditions are assumed to be equal and the possibility of an unidentified other man is neglected.

615

Assuming the existence of a further unidentified man and allowing all the men equal *a priori* chances of the paternity, the probability of paternity of the men examined may be calculated, for instance, according to a formula devised by Schulte-Mönting and Hummel (Ref. 4). This calculation is not performed by the Institute, unless the court explicitly requests it and states the non-serological circumstances for the calculation. However, the fact that the indices given are absolute values characteristic of the mother-child-man constellation in question is usually sufficient for the court to evaluate that result, together with the other circumstances of the case.

The result of the third-stage examination is expressed according to the same principles as that of the second-stage examination with regard to both serological and morphological characteristics.

The System at Work—1972.

An analysis of cases registered at the Institute during 1972 has been prepared. The sample includes 1,565 cases, of which, 1,046 ($^2/_3$) are one-man cases. (See Table 2.) The theoretical percentage of exclusion by the standard examination was 69 percent. In one-man cases 10.4 percent of the men were excluded, corresponding to about 85 percent fathers in this group.

Table 2

1972 Material

One-man cases	1046	67%
Two-man cases	428	27%
More than two-man cases	91	6%
Total	1565	100%

RESULT OF STANDARD EXAMINATION IN ONE- AND TWO-MAN CASES

One-Man Cases:

Non-exclusion	937	89.6%
Exclusion	109	10.4%

Two-Man Cases:

Non-exclusion	107	25%
Exclusion (1 man)	306	71.5%
Exclusion (2 men)	15	3.5%

Two-man cases numbered 428. They involved 856 men, of which 336 were excluded (*i.e.,* 57 percent non-fathers). In other words, the biological father was one of the alleged possibilities in about 85 percent of the two-man cases also.

In 91 cases (6%) from three to seven men were involved. The total number of men in this group was 320, of which 227 were excluded by standard and supplementary examination (Table 3). Due to the heterogeneity of this small group of cases, a calculation of the number of real fathers within this group is difficult. However, the experience of the Institute is that the percentage of cases involving actual fathers is lower here than in the other two groups.

Table 3

Result of One- and Two-Stage Examination of Cases Involving More Than Two Men in 1972 Material

Number of men involved	Number excluded								Total no. cases
	0	1	2	3	4	5	6	7	
3	2	6	42	8					58
4	0	0	1	21	3				25
5	0	0	0	0	4	0			4
6	0	0	0	0	0	2	0		2
7	0	0	0	0	0	2	0	0	2
No. of men excluded	6	86	87	28	20				91

$227 = 71\%$ of 320 men

Number of Cases

With No Man Left   11 = 12%
With One Man Left   69 = 76%
With More Than One Man Left   11 = 12%

Of the 937 one-man cases which did not result in exclusion by the standard examination, supplementary examination was requested by the court in 65 cases. Remembering that a total of about 50 non-fathers were left undetected in these 937 cases, it is interesting to note that 14 of the 65 men were excluded — that is, about $^1/_3$ of the unrecognized non-fathers were disclosed by the court's selection of cases for supplementary examination. Considering that the theoretical percentage of exclusion of stage two in 1972 was about 60 percent, the court's selection may be calculated to have included almost half of the total number of non-fathers who were not excluded by the standard examination.

Supplementary examination of the 107 two-man cases which did not result in exclusion by standard examination brought the following results. In 66 cases (62%), one of the two men was excluded; in three cases both were excluded. Only 38 (9%) of the original 428 two-man cases had to be referred to the third-stage examination.

In order to elucidate the value of the index calculation, we have analyzed a group of 109 one-man cases and 392 two-man cases which were subjected to supplementary examination during 1970-72. The scope of examination has not been completely consistent during the entire period; some of the enzyme systems (e.g., GPT) have been used only recently, and some blood factors (e.g., Fy^a and s) periodically have been used only for selected cases. The indices may consequently be slightly distorted toward lower values, but their general distribution is little affected by this inconsistency.

Figures 1, 2, and 3 give the distribution of indices of non-excluded men from a) 109 one-man cases, b) 158 two-man cases in which the other man is excluded, and finally c) the distribution in 117 two-man cases in which neither man was excluded. The distribution within the two first classes, in which the vast majority of men (according to the *a priori* expectation and the selection performed by the examination), can be assumed to be the real fathers, does not differ significantly. Only about half of the men have an index above 19 at this level of examination. On the other hand, the difference between the distribution in these two classes and the distribution in the third class is highly significant — partly because at least half of the men in the third class are non-fathers, but also partly because of the correlation of the index with the theoretical percentage of exclusion characteristic for the mother-child constellations. Of course, this has a bearing upon the distribution of the index in a class which is selected by non-exclusion of non-fathers. Thirty-five of the 234 men had an index above 19, but an analysis of the indices in each case disclosed that in 6 of the 117 cases the indices of both men exceeded 19, showing that in at least 5 percent of these selected cases a non-father attained an index of 19 or more. The high indices of non-fathers are in most cases due to the fact that both men have a rare factor, such as the Kell factor, indispensable in the type of the real father.

Figure 1

Distribution of Index in Nonexcluded Men of 109 Originally One-Man Cases (1970-72 Material)

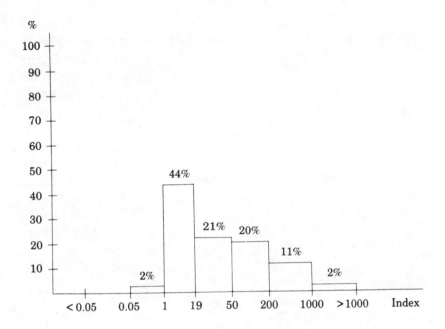

Figure 2

Distribution of Index of Non Excluded Men in 158 Two-Man Cases in Which the Other Man Is Excluded (1970-72 Material)

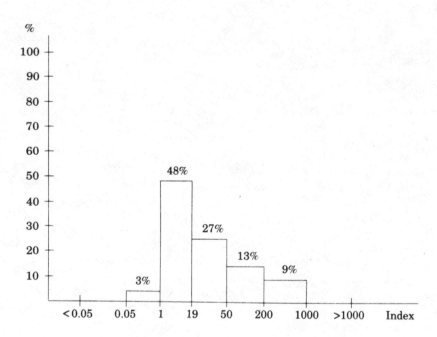

Figure 3

Distribution of Index in Non-Excluded Men of 117 Two-Man Cases in Which Neither Is Excluded (1970-72 Material)

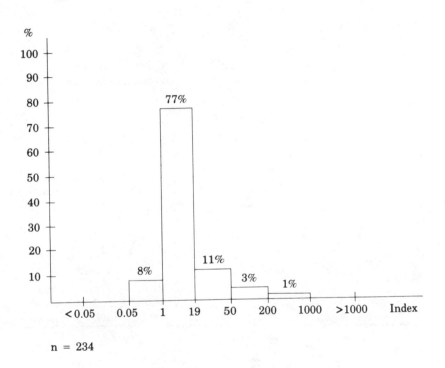

n = 234

In only 3 of the 117 cases, the difference between the indices of the two men exceeded 19 to 1 (or the 95 percent to 5 percent) limit (Figure 4).

Figure 4

Relation $\dfrac{\text{Index man 1}}{\text{Index man 2}}$ In Non-Excluded Men of 117

Two-Man Cases In Which Neither Is
Excluded (1970-72 Material)

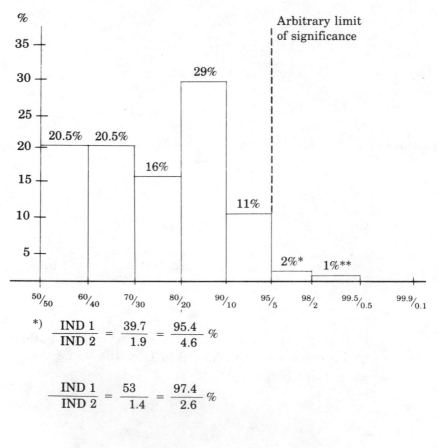

$$\text{*)} \quad \frac{\text{IND 1}}{\text{IND 2}} = \frac{39.7}{1.9} = \frac{95.4}{4.6} \ \%$$

$$\frac{\text{IND 1}}{\text{IND 2}} = \frac{53}{1.4} = \frac{97.4}{2.6} \ \%$$

$$\text{**)} \quad \frac{\text{IND 1}}{\text{IND 2}} = \frac{12.45}{0.116} = \frac{99}{1} \ \%$$

Table 4

Result of HLA Grouping at Three-Stage Examination in a
Series of One-Man Cases

Index Prior to HLA Grouping	No.	HLA Exclusion	Index After HLA Grouping					
			0.1 / 1	1 / 19	19 / 50	50 / 200	200 / 1000	>1000
0.005 - 0.01	1	1						
0.01 - 0.05	1	1						
0.05 - 0.1	3	3						
0.1 - 1	3	1	1		1			
1 - 10	4					2	1	1
10 - 19	7	1				2	1	3
19 - 50	10					2	7	1
50 - 200	10					1	4	5
200 - 1000	2							2
1000	3							3
	44	7	1		1	7	13	15

In a number of cases (which are designated "statistical exclusions" and which are not included in the sample in Figure 3), the prerequisite to a man's paternity is the assumption that his phenotype within one or more systems is characterized by a very rare genotype. As a result, his index is extremely low. Apart from such cases, the amount of information obtained by index calculation is rather slight in two-man cases without exclusion.

In order to demonstrate the effectiveness of the HLA system, which has been included in the serological part of the third-stage examination for about a year, an analysis of the one- and two-man cases examined during this period is given. At present, the HLA system is by far the most polymorphic and informative of the genetic marker systems which can be used as a means of demonstrating non-paternity — or, conversely, by non-exclusion, as evidence for paternity. At the level of examination which presently can be performed by the Institute, the theoretical percentage of exclusion of the HLA system is about 90. If used indiscriminately for all cases, this high efficiency would be reduced by about 90 percent due to concomitant exclusions by other systems. For practical as well as for scientific considerations regarding the reliability of HLA exclusions, it has until now been used only for the third-stage examination. Consequently, almost the whole efficiency of the system is obtained in this highly select group of cases.

In Table 4, the sample consists of one-man cases in which the results of the first two stages for some reason or other are not found sufficiently informative by the court. Forty-four such cases are presented correlating the men's indices prior to and after HLA determination. In only one of thirty-six cases in which the man's index exceeded 1 was the man excluded. None of the men with indices over 19 were excluded. The indices of ten non-excluded men with indices between 1 and 19 have risen to more than 50 — or, expressed in percentages, had passed the 98 percent confidence limit. Of course the series represents a selected and non-homogeneous group of cases, and the table only shows how the HLA system in the third-stage examination solves practically all the cases selected by the court for this stage.

Table 5 gives the results of HLA determination in thirty two-man cases divided into classes according to the ratio of the indices of the two men in each case. In every case one man is excluded. It must be stressed that this series represents a selection by the court. But the series has not been subjected to selection by the Institute and is consecutive, excepting the omission of six cases in which other systems excluded one of the men, four of which exclusions were corroborated by the HLA system.

Table 5

Two-Man Cases in Which One Man is Excluded by HLA Grouping at Three-Stage Examination

Ind. 1 / Ind. 2 Prior to HLA Grouping	No.	HLA Exclusion	Index of Non-Excluded Man After HLA Grouping					
			10-19	19-50	50-200	200-1000	>1000	
$\frac{50\%}{50} - \frac{60\%}{40}$	8	8	1	1	1	4	1
$\frac{60\%}{40} - \frac{70\%}{30}$	1	1	1				
$\frac{70\%}{30} - \frac{80\%}{20}$	2	2			2		
$\frac{80\%}{20} - \frac{90\%}{10}$	7	7		2	1	4	
$\frac{90\%}{10} - \frac{95\%}{5}$	5	5				2	3
$> \frac{95\%}{5}$	7	7			3		4
	30	30	2	3	7	10	8

628

In every case in which the ratio between the two men's indices exceeded 95 percent to 5 percent prior to HLA examination, the man with the lower index was excluded by the HLA system. Eight men with an index below 1 before HLA determination were all excluded by the HLA system. Eighteen of the excluded men had an index between 1 and 19, and four had an index exceeding 19 (cases no. 3, 9, 20 and 30). In none of these four cases did the ratio between the indices of the two men prior to HLA determination exceed 19 to 1 (see Table 6). In only two cases was the index of the non-excluded man after HLA determination below 19 (cases no. 5 and 16). The indices before and after HLA determination of these two cases are also given in Table 6.

Table 6

Case No.	Index Prior to HLA		Relation, Ind. 1/Ind. 2	Index of Man Not Excl. by HLA
	Non-excl. by HLA	Excluded by HLA		
3	38	150	20%/80%	338
9	32	30	51%/49%	510
20	962	737	57%/43%	18800
30	55	70	44%/56%	768
5	2.2	2.2	50%/50%	15
16	1.2	0.6	67%/33%	11

APPENDIX F

Summary

Under the conditions stated above, the results of the Danish three-stage system may be summarized as follows:

First Stage: Standard Examination.

In one-man cases, about 70 percent of the non-fathers are excluded, leaving unrecognized non-fathers in about 5 percent of the cases. The court has the discretion to select the cases for further examination according to other circumstances of each case.

In two-man cases, one of the men is excluded in about 70 percent of the cases. The remaining 30 percent automatically are recalled for supplementary examination.

In three-or-more-man cases about 70 percent of non-fathers are excluded. In most cases the supplementary examination is performed for non-excluded men before the case is closed.

Second Stage: Supplementary Examination.

About 70 percent of remaining non-fathers are excluded. Positive blood-group statistical evidence for the paternity of non-excluded men results in about half of the cases. The combined theoretical percentage of exclusion of the first and second stages is about 90 percent.

Third Stage: Anthropological Examination.

More than 90 percent of the remaining non-fathers are excluded. The Institute furnishes significant blood-group statistical evidence for paternity for the vast majority of non-excluded men. The combined theoretical percentage of exclusion of all three stages thus exceeds 99 percent.

The principle of an examination by stages may well be criticized but is justified, in my opinion, by the relatively high incidence of fathers in the majority of cases, and by the fact that in a one-stage examination the practical yield of each system is greatly diminished by concomitant exclusions through different systems. However, the conditions for selection cases and the choice of systems for the different stages may well be discussed and must be reconsidered periodically according to the character of the cases, the costs involved, and the efficiency of the systems at our disposal.

Present knowledge of genetic markers of human blood makes it possible to exclude almost all non-fathers in cases of disputed paternity and, under certain conditions (*e.g.*, homogeneity of population and knowledge of the pertinent gene frequencies), to obtain significant blood-group statistical evidence for paternity in most real fathers. However, full-scale exploitation of these possibilities raises several practical as well as scientific problems. In establishing a general system for the investigation of paternity cases, one must be aware of these problems and must consider the many factors which determine the practical return of the scientific possibilities.

Appendix: Costs of the Institute

The question of costs is difficult. On the one hand, a high volume of samples tends to produce more rational and economic procedures. On the other hand, the administration will be more complicated and may tend to counteract this effect. It all depends on the organization. However, I think that a laboratory handling fewer than about 2,000 cases a year must be either scientifically understaffed or less economical.

The main factors deciding the actual costs are of course:

(a) *Wages for Scientific and Technical Staff.* In this connection it is most important, for the quality of the work, that the staff be sufficient to allow time for scientific work besides the daily routine.

(b) *Test Sera and Chemicals.* Of course, costs are highly variable depending on the requirements with regard to extent and reliability, the source of reagents, technique, etc. To illustrate, in our routine we test each sample with five separate anti-M and five separate N-sera. On the other hand, for Rh determination our laboratory obtains about 100-200 tests per millilitre anti-serum.

(c) *Instruments and Other Laboratory Facilities.* Hitherto the price of laboratory equipment for blood-grouping has been low compared to other biological equipment. With the growing need for more refined serological and biochemical analysis, however, more and more expensive equipment has become necessary. It appears that this trend will continue.

(d) *Paper, postage, etc.*

(e) *Rent and utilities.*

Staff:

Serologic dept.:

4 scientists

12 technicians
3 secretaries
Anthropological dept.:
  2 scientists
  2 technicians
  1 secretary

Laboratory and office space: about 600 m^2 excluding the small anthropological department. When we move to a new building in 1976, this area will be almost doubled.

Capacity: about 2,000 cases per year standard examination; 400 cases supplementary examination; 200 cases anthropological examination.

To this must be added the rather moderate capacity of our small trace-department for stains in criminal cases.

REFERENCES

1. E. Essen-Møller, 68 MITT. ANTHROP. GES. (Wein) 368 (1938).
2. E. Essen-Møller & C.E. Quensel, 31 DEUTSCH Z. GES. GER. MED. 70 (1939).
3. K. HENNINGSEN, 2 METHODS OF FORENSIC SCIENCE 209-28 (1963).
4. J. Schulte-Mönting & K. Hummel, 138 Z. IMMUN. FORSCH. 295 (1969).

Appendix G

THE USE OF BLOOD TYPING IN CASES OF DISPUTED PATERNITY IN ENGLAND

WILLIAM D. SNAPP* WITH HARRY D. KRAUSE AND PAUL HAVEMAN**

I. HISTORICAL BACKGROUND

Blood test evidence [1] was first used in an English case involving a paternity dispute in 1938.[2] Several reasons explain why blood test evidence was not used much between 1938 and 1972: no party could compel any other person to provide a blood sample in the absence of a court order.[3] Worse, the courts had no power to order anyone to undergo blood tests in order to resolve an issue of paternity.[4] In the late 1960s, the courts carved an exception into this rule: the the Court of Appeals upheld a decision that the lower courts could order blood tests on an infant in a case involving the custody of that infant.[5] In a subsequent decision involving a husband accusing his wife of committing adultery, the Court of Appeals extended the judicial power to order blood tests on infants by holding that judges could order a blood test whenever it was in the best interests of the child to do so.[6] These decisions, however, did not provide judges with the power to order *adults* to undergo blood tests.

Another factor which has limited the use of blood test evidence to resolve paternity disputes is the presumption of legitimacy.[7] In divorce and nullity proceedings, that presumption was at one time so strong that blood test results were irrelevant to the outcome of the case.[8] In the early nineteenth century a husband had to prove that he was abroad during the entire possible period of conception in order to overcome the presumption that he had fathered his wife's child.[9] Later this burden was reduced so that the husband merely had to prove beyond all reasonable doubt that he was not the father of the child.[10] Although a blood test

* J.D., University of Illinois.
** University of Regina, Saskatchewan.

could prove non-paternity beyond a reasonable doubt,[11] a wife could avoid this result by simply refusing a request that she submit herself and her child to blood tests.[12] More recently, dicta in *Blyth v. Blyth*[13] implied that the presumption of legitimacy is rebuttable on the balance of probabilities.

In 1966 the judges of the Probate, Divorce and Admiralty Division of the High Court asked that the Law Commission consider whether the law should be changed so that the courts could order parties to undergo blood tests when the issue of paternity arises in a case.[14] After researching the issue thoroughly, the Law Commission published a report proposing that the courts be able to direct the alleged father(s), the mother and the child to submit to blood tests and that the presumption of legitimacy be rebuttable by proof on a balance of probabilities.[15] The draft clauses propounded by the Law Commission formed the basis for Part III and section 26 of Part IV of the Family Law Reform Act 1969.[16]

II. The Operation of the New Statutory Provisions

Obtaining a Court Direction.

Any party to a civil proceeding in which the paternity of a person is an issue may ask the court to direct that blood tests be performed on that person, the mother of that person and/or any party alleged to be the father of that person.[17] The court may not direct the performance of blood tests on its own motion,[18] but may entertain applications by the parties at any time after the plaintiff has made the complaint.[19] In order to encourage applications, the courts must provide each party to cases involving paternity disputes with a form that explains the nature of blood tests, the usefulness of blood test evidence and the procedure for applying to the court for a direction ordering the tests.[20] Although no rule specifies the precise time when the court clerk is to transmit the information form to each party, it is expected that the form will be given to the plaintiff as soon as the complaint is filed and that it will be served with the summons on the defendant.[21]

If one party requests a direction ordering blood tests, the court clerk must inform the other party about the request.[22] The non-requesting party may consent to the giving of the direction. If not, the court cannot give a direction calling for the tests unless all parties are present.[23] Presumably, this requirement allows the judge to hear arguments supporting and opposing the request before a direction is granted or denied. If the court grants the direction, the court must provide a copy of the direction to every person who is to be tested.[24] If the person to be tested is mentally incompetent or is under the age of sixteen, the copy of the direction must be given to the person who has the incompetent's care and control.

Preparation for the Testing Process.

After the court directs that one or more persons take a blood test, the person who originally applied for the direction must pay for the tests and for any expenses incurred by any person as a result of the tests.[25] The fees for the actual taking of blood samples and the performance of the blood typing tests are nominal.[26] The court clerks have been warned to expect the possible need for a second drawing of blood samples from the subjects. Therefore, clerks normally charge the applicant an amount sufficiently large (£36 in 1971) to cover a second run.[27] If the fees of the sampler and tester are less than the amount deposited, the remainder is refunded. If the applicant ultimately wins the case, the judge may order the losing party to reimburse the applicant for the expense of the blood testing process.[28]

Each person who is to undergo a blood test must furnish the court clerk his or her photograph.[29] If the subject is under a disability, the person having his or her care and custody must supply the photograph. This requirement is waived if the child is less than one year old at the time the blood tests are ordered, or if the physician of a subject who suffers from a mental disorder certifies that a photograph cannot or should not be taken.

The parties are given at least fourteen days to make the necessary payments and supply identification photographs.[30] If any one fails to meet the time limit set by the court, the court clerk informs the judge. At that point, the judge has discretion to vary or revoke his direction.[31] If the designated persons have given the required payments and photographs to the court clerk, the clerk must arrange for appropriate medical practitioners to take the blood samples and for an approved testing facility to type the blood samples.[32]

After making these arrangements, the court clerk notifies each subject (or, where a subject is under a disability, to the person having his or her care and control) when and where the sample is to be drawn.[33] The notice states, "Any traveling or other expenses reasonably incurred in complying with this requirement are payable in the first instance by the person who applied to the court for the direction . . . ." This requirement can raise some problems,[34] because the court clerk does not collect money from the applicant to cover travel expenses. This leaves the adverse parties to arrange a mutually acceptable scheme for handling the expenses.

The court clerk must fill in the first two sections of a direction form which will be sent to the sampler and affix the subject's photograph.[35] The form indicates the name of the subject and, if the subject is under sixteen years old or suffering from certain mental disorders, the name of the person who has his or her care and control. The form also lists the names of the other persons from whom samples will be taken as well as the names, addresses and telephone numbers of the other samplers involved. This information is included so that one sampler can inform other samplers if one of the subjects has refused to give a sample.[36] This communication might prevent the needless taking of samples from the other subjects.

The Taking and Testing of the Blood Sample.

The duties of the blood samplers are prescribed by the Secretary of State in detailed regulations.[37] Blood tests ordered by a court direction may be performed only at a testing center approved by the Secretary of State.[38] In order to gain approval, an individual or an institution must apply for an appointment.[39] In this application the applicant must indicate the number of typing processes he, she or it is capable of performing. On that basis, the Secretary of State will accept or reject the request for appointment. As a result of this process, the accredited testers do not perform precisely the same tests. However, despite this limited degree of variability, the accredited testers uniformly use enough typing systems to achieve a 90 percent exclusion rate.[40] For example, the London Hospital Medical College routinely uses thirteen typing systems to classify blood in paternity disputes.[41]

After typing the blood samples, the tester is required to complete a report which states:

(a) the results of the tests;

(b) whether the party to whom the report relates is or is not excluded by the results from being the father of the person whose paternity is to be determined; and

(c) if the party is not so excluded, the value, if any, of the results in determining whether that party is that person's father. . . .[42]

If there is an exclusion, the tester explains which test(s) establish the exclusion. If the putative father is not excluded, the tester indicates the percentage of unrelated men of a specified ethnic origin that would be expected to have a non-excludable blood type. The tester does not express an opinion as to whether the putative father is, in fact, the father of the child. The court must use the percentage figure in conjunction with other facts to arrive at its determination of the case.

The Use of the Blood Test Report.

After the tester submits a report to the court, the court clerk must send a copy of the report to all the parties involved in the litigation.[43] A party may ask the court for leave to obtain a written statement from the tester to explain or amplify an assertion or conclusion noted in the report.[44] That written statement becomes a part of the report which the court will consider in reaching a decision in the case. For example, a report might state that only 2 percent of unrelated men of East Indian origin would be expected to have non-excludable blood types. A putative father might wish to present evidence that the mother had sexual relations with men from other ethnic groups. At this juncture the tester may be asked to calculate the percentage estimate using a broader, more universal group.[45]

If a party wishes to call the sampler or the tester as a witness, he must notify the other parties of this intention within fourteen days after receiving the blood test report.[46] A sampler or tester called as a witness may be subjected to cross-examination by the party calling him. In practice, however, samplers and testers are seldom, if ever, called as witnesses.[47]

Cooperation of the Subjects.

Even if the court directs a person to undergo a blood test, a sampler may not take a blood sample from that person without his consent.[48] A minor who has attained the age of sixteen may consent for himself,[49] but no blood sample may be taken from a younger minor without the consent of the person who has his or her care and custody.[50] In order to take a blood sample from a person who is suffering from a mental disorder and is incapable of understanding the nature and purpose of blood tests, the person who has the incompetent's care and custody must consent, and the incompetent's doctor must certify that the sampling process will not prejudice proper care and treatment.[51]

The drafters of the new English legislation included the provisions requiring that the subject consent to the sampling process because they felt that the general public and medical practitioners would oppose any form of physical compulsion in the sampling process.[52] The statute, however, does not prohibit the use of force if the subject is under sixteen years old or suffers from a mental disorder. In these cases the person having the care and control of the subject might give consent even though the subject objects to the sampling process. One commentator has implied that samplers should use force in these cases only if its use would not be "unseemly".[53]

If the court direction is to have any significance, the court must have some means of persuading the subjects to submit to blood tests. The drafters of the English statute believed, however, that more harm than good would result if the courts were given the power to fine, or to apply any similar sanction, to any person who refused to comply with the court's direction.[54] Therefore, the English statute provides that a court may draw any inferences that seem proper from any person's failure to take any step required of him by the court's direction.[55] For example, if the man accused of fathering the child refuses to submit to a blood test, the court could infer that he had reason to believe that the test results would not exclude him. Moreover, the statute effectively allows the court to deny the benefits of the presumption of legitimacy to any party who refuses to comply with a court direction.[56]

The Problem of Impersonation.

Mistaken identification of subjects can totally destroy the usefulness of blood tests. A party who has reason to believe that accurate blood test results would harm his or her case might ask a friend to take his or her or the child's place. As noted above, the form sent to the sampler makes such deception difficult because a picture of the subject is included. The statute includes a further provision intended to discourage this practice: any person impersonating a subject or intentionally proffering the wrong child for the purpose of providing a court directed blood sample may be imprisoned for two years or fined £400.[57]

Non-Directed Blood Tests.

The statutory power of courts to direct blood tests was not intended to make voluntary blood test results inadmissible.[58] No statutory provision requires that these non-directed tests be performed in accordance with the procedures established for directed tests. An informal survey of accredited testers revealed in 1974 that the testers prefer to perform directed rather than non-directed blood tests.[59] A joint statement by two testers lists some of the major reasons for that preference:

1. In the absence of a Court direction, no direction forms are issued, and although none of us are addicted to form filling, these forms are of considerable value.

(a) Correct identification of the individuals is made easy because the forms have photographs attached.

(b) They ensure that the sampler remembers to enquire about recent blood transfusions.

(c) They require signatures from the individuals confirming their identity and indicating appreciation of the penalties involved in giving false information.

The signature is also written evidence that the blood sample has been given voluntarily and in the case of the mother or other person in control of the child it includes permission to sample the child.

2. Without a Court direction, there is no legal compulsion to seek the services of an accredited blood group specialist who is a member of the Home Office panel of testers.

3. On the rare occasions that the blood group specialist requires further samples from the individuals, it facilitates matters if the arrangements can be made by an impartial body i.e. the Court rather than by application to the solicitors representing the parties.

Despite the preference of the accredited testers, only about one-third of the blood tests they perform in connection with paternity disputes involve a court direction.[60]

III. CONCLUSION

An efficient and thorough procedure for dealing with blood tests in paternity disputes has been established in England. The English have dealt effectively with the problems of identifying reliable testing facilities, guaranteeing the payment of professional fees, obtaining the consent of the subject and properly identifying the subject. The procedures there developed may well lend themselves to adaptation in the United States, a sister (daughter) common law country, and have therefore been described in this detail.

REFERENCES

1. *See generally* The Family Law Reform Act 1969, Ch. 46, Part III, §§ 20-25; HOME OFFICE CIRCULAR 248/1971 (Dec. 10, 1971); [1971] STAT. INSTR. (No. 1861); [1971] STAT. INSTR. (No. 1991).

2. Bartholomew, *The Nature and Use of Blood Group Evidence,* 24 MOD. L. REV. 313, n. 3 (1961).

3. "The lightest exercise of physical violence to the person, even though beneficial (e.g. a surgical operation), is an assault in law unless it has been consented to or unless there is some other lawful justification. In this technical sense the taking of a sample of blood for testing constitutes an assault in the absence of consent or lawful authority such as a court order." LAW COM. NO. 16, 8 (1968).

4. W. v. W. (No. 4), [1963] P. 67; 234 THE LAW TIMES (London) 365 (July 5, 1963).

5. *In re* L. [1968] P. 119; Law Com. No. 16, 11 (1968).

6. B.R.B. v. J.B. [1968] 2 All E.R. 1023, 1025; Law Com. No. 16, 11-12 (1968).

7. Law Com. No. 16, 12 (1968).

8. *Id.,* 5-8.

9. Head v. Head, (1823) 1 Sim. & St. 150.

10. Law Com. No. 61, 5 (1968).

11. *Id.,* 34-38.

12. Watson v. Watson, [1954] p. 48.

13. [1966] A.C. 643 per Lord Denning at 669 and per Lord Pearce at 673.

14. Law Com. No. 16, 1 (1968).

15. *Id.,* 29-30.

16. *Cf.,* Law Com. No. 16, 31-33 n.3 (1968), with The Family Law Reform Act 1969, Ch. 46, Part III, §§ 20-25 and Part IV, § 26.

17. The Family Law Reform Act 1969, Ch. 46, Part III, § 20(1).

18. B. Harris, The Use of Blood Tests in Determining Paternity 2 (1972).

19. [1971] Stat. Instr. 2 (No. 1991).

20. *Id.,* 2, 4.

21. B. Harris, The Use of Blood Tests in Determining Paternity 1 (1972).

22. [1971] Stat. Instr. 2 (No. 1991).

23. *Id.,* 2.

24. *Id.*

25. The Family Law Reform Act 1969, Ch. 46, Part III, § 20(6).

26. B. Harris, The Use of Blood Tests in Determining Paternity 28 (1972).

27. Home Office Circular 248/1971, 5 (Dec. 10, 1971).

28. The Family Law Reform Act 1969, Ch. 46, Part III, § 20(6):

Fees

Samplers

The fees which may be charged by a sampler in respect of one direction requesting him to take samples shall be as follows:

For making all necessary arrangements (whether or not samples are taken): £2

For making further arrangements (whether or not samples are taken) to give effect to a variation by the court of a direction: £2

For taking sample	
from first subject:	£2
from each subject after the first:	£1
For taking second or subsequent samples from one or more subjects	
if one such sample:	£2
if two such samples:	£3
if three or more such samples:	£5

Testers

The fees which may be charged by a tester in respect of tests for the purpose of giving effect to one direction shall be as follows:

For making a report in accordance with the direction and testing four or less samples:	£25
For testing each sample after the fourth covered by a report	£5
For testing samples where no report is made	
in respect of the first sample:	£10
in respect of each subsequent sample:	£5

29. [1971] STAT. INSTR. 2 (No. 1991).

30. *Id.*

31. *Id.*, 3.

32. *Id.*

33. *Id.*, 3, 6.

34. B. HARRIS, THE USE OF BLOOD TESTS IN DETERMINING PATERNITY 4, 5 (1972).

35. [1971] STAT. INSTR. 3 (No. 1991).

36. HOME OFFICE CIRCULAR 248/1971, 8 (Dec. 10, 1971). *See* text at note 50.

37. The Blood Tests (Evidence of Paternity) Regulations [1971] STAT. INSTR. 1-4 (No. 1861):

> In pursuance of section 22 of the Family Law Reform Act 1969, I hereby make the following Regulations:
> Citation and commencement
> 1. These Regulations may be cited as the Blood Tests (Evidence of Paternity) Regulations 1971 and shall come into operation on 1st March 1972.
> Interpretation
> 2. (1) In these Regulations, unless the context otherwise requires, — 'the Act' means the Family Law Reform Act 1969;
> "court" means a court which gives a direction for the use of blood tests in pursuance of section 20(1) of the Act;
> 'direction' means a direction given as aforesaid;
> 'direction form' means Form 1 in Schedule 1 to these Regulations;

'photograph' means a recent photograph, taken full face without a hat, of the size required for insertion in a passport;

'sample' means blood taken for the purpose of tests;

'sampler' means a registered medical practitioner or tester nominated in a direction form to take blood samples for the purposes of the direction;

'subject' means a person from whom a court directs that blood samples shall be taken;

'tester' means a person appointed by the Secretary of State to carry out blood tests;

'tests' means blood tests carried out under Part III of the Act and includes any test made with the object of ascertaining the inheritable characteristics of blood.

(2) A reference in these Regulations to a person who is under a disability is a reference to a person who has not attained the age of 16 years or who is suffering from a mental disorder within the meaning of the Mental Health Act 1959 and is incapable of understanding the nature and purpose of blood tests.

(3) The Interpretation Act 1889 shall apply to the interpretation of these Regulations as it applies to the interpretation of an Act of Parliament.

Direction form

3. A sampler shall not take a sample from a subject unless Parts I and II of the direction form have been completed and the direction form purports to be signed by the proper officer of the court or some person on his behalf.

Subjects under disability to be accompanied to sampler

4. A subject who is under a disability who attends a sampler for the taking of a sample shall be accompanied by a person of full age who shall identify him to the sampler.

Taking of samples

5. (1) Without prejudice to the provisions of rules of court, a sampler may make arrangements for the taking of samples from the subjects or may change any arrangements already made and make other arrangements.

(2) Subject to the provisions of these Regulations, where a subject attends a sampler in accordance with arrangements made under a direction, the sampler shall take a sample from him on that occasion.

(3) A sampler shall not take a sample from a subject if —
(i) he has reason to believe that the subject has been transfused with blood within the three months immediately preceding the day on which the sample is to be taken; or
(ii) in his opinion, tests on a sample taken at that time from that subject could not effectively be carried out for the purposes of and in accordance with the direction; or

646

      (iii) in his opinion, the taking of a sample might have an adverse effect on the health of the subject.

(4) A sampler may take a sample from a subject who has been injected with a blood product or blood plasma if, in his opinion, the value of any tests done on that sample would not be thereby affected, but shall inform the tester that the subject was so injected.

(5) Where a sampler does not take a sample from a subject in accordance with arrangements made for the taking of that sample and no other arrangements are made, he shall return the direction form relating to that subject to the court, having stated on the form his reason for not taking the sample and any reason given by the subject (or the person having the care and control of the subject) for any failure to attend in accordance with those arrangements.

(6) A subject who attends a sampler for the taking of a sample may be accompanied by his legal representative.

Sampling procedure

6. (1) A sampler shall comply with the provisions of this Regulation, all of which shall be complied with in respect of one subject before any are complied with in respect of any other subject; so however that a report made in accordance with the provisions of section 20(2) of the Act or any other evidence relating to the samples or the tests made on the samples shall not be challenged solely on the grounds that a sampler has not acted in accordance with the provisions of this Regulation.

(2) Before a sample is taken from any subject who has attained the age of 12 months by the date of the direction, the sampler shall ensure that a photograph of that subject is affixed to the direction form relating to that subject unless the direction form is accompanied by a certificate from a medical practitioner that the subject is suffering from a mental disorder and that a photograph of him cannot or should not be taken.

(3) Before a sample is taken from a subject, he, or where he is under a disability the person of full age accompanying him, shall complete the declaration in Part V of the direction form (that that subject is the subject to whom the direction form relates and, where a photograph is affixed to the direction form, that the photograph is a photograph of that subject) which shall be signed to in the presence of and witnessed by the sampler.

(4) Where a subject is suffering from a mental disorder, the sampler shall not take a sample from him unless the sampler is in possession of a certificate from a medical practitioner that the taking of a blood sample from the subject will not be prejudicial to his proper care and treatment.

647

(5) A sample shall not be taken from any subject unless —
  (a) he or, where he is under a disability, the person having the care and control of him, has signed a statement on the direction form that he consents to the sample being taken; or
  (b) where he is under a disability and is not accompanied by the person having the care and control of him, the sampler is in possession of a statement in writing, purporting to be signed by that person that he consents to the sample being taken.

(6) The sampler shall affix to the direction form any statement referred to in sub-paragraph (b) of the preceding paragraph.

(7) If a subject or, where he is under a disability, the person having the care and control of him, does not consent to the taking of a sample, he may record on the direction form his reasons for withholding his consent.

(8) When the sampler has taken a sample he shall place it in a suitable container and shall affix to the container a label giving the full name, age and sex of the subject from whom it was taken and the label shall be signed by the sampler and by that subject or, if he is under a disability, the person accompanying him.

(9) The sampler shall state in Part VII of the direction form that he has taken the sample and the date on which he did so.

Despatch of samples to tester

7. (1) When a sampler has taken samples, he shall, where he is not himself the tester, pack the containers together with the relevant direction forms and shall despatch them forthwith to the tester by post by special delivery service or shall deliver them or cause them to be delivered to the tester by some person other than a subject or a person who has accompanied a subject to the sampler.

  (2) If at any time a sampler despatches to a tester samples from some only of the subjects and has not previously despatched samples taken from the other subjects, he shall inform the tester whether he is expecting to take any samples from those other subjects and, if so, from whom and on what date.

Procedures where sampler nominated is unable to take the samples

8. (1) Where a sampler is unable himself to take samples from all or any of the subjects, he may nominate another medical practitioner or tester to take the samples which he is unable to take.

  (2) The sampler shall record the nomination of the other sampler on the relevant direction forms and shall forward them to the sampler nominated by him.

648

38. *Id.,* 1.

39. Interview with Drs. Barbara E. Dodd and Patrick J. Lincoln, lecturers with the Department of Forensic Medicine, London Hospital Medical College, London, Apr. 11, 1973.

40. *Id.*

41. The thirteen typing systems in routine use are: ABO, MNSs, Rh (including tests with antisera for the following antigens: D, C, C^w, C^x, c, E, e), Kell, Duffy, Lutheran, Kidd, Gm 1, P 1, Haptoglobins, Phospho-gluco-mutase (PGM), Red cell Acid Phosphotase (E.A.P.), and Gluco-pyruvate transaminase (GPT). *Id.*

42. The Family Law Reform Act 1969, Ch. 46, Part III, § 20(2).

43. [1971] STAT. INSTR. 3 (No. 1991).

44. The Family Law Reform Act 1969, Ch. 46, Part III, § 20(4).

45. Interviews with Drs. Barbara E. Dodd and Patrick J. Lincoln.

46. The Family Law Reform Act 1969, Ch. 46, Part III, § 20(5).

47. Interviews with Drs. Barbara E. Dodd and Patrick J. Lincoln.

48. The Family Law Reform Act 1969, Ch. 46, Part III, § 21(1).

49. *Id.,* § 21(2).

50. *Id.,* § 21(3).

51. *Id.,* § 21(4).

52. LAW COM. NO. 16, 17 (1968).

53. Lanham, *Reforms in Blood Test Law,* 9 MED. SCIENCE AND THE LAW 172, 173 (1969).

54. LAW COM. NO. 16, 17 (1968).

55. The Family Law Reform Act 1969, Ch. 46, Part III, § 23(1), (3).

56. *Id.,* § 23(2).

57. *Id.,* § 24.

58. LAW COM. NO. 16, 14 (1968).

59. P. Havemann, Medico-Legal Cooperation in the Ascertainment of Paternity, January 1, 1975 (unpublished memorandum prepared for Harry D. Krause).

60. *Id.*

Appendix H

BLOOD TYPING FOR PATERNITY, CURRENT CAPACITIES AND POTENTIAL OF AMERICAN LABORATORIES—A SURVEY*

HERBERT F. POLESKY** AND HARRY D. KRAUSE

Table 1

Characteristics of Surveyed Population

Classification	Number Surveyed	Number Responded (%)	Number Doing Paternity Testing
AABB Reference Laboratories	31	30 (96.8)	19
Workshop participants	138	53 (38.4)	40
Blood groupers	8	7 (87.5)	6
Totals	177	90 (50.8)	65

Materials and Methods.

A questionnaire was sent to 31 laboratories designated as Reference Laboratories by the American Association of Blood Banks (AABB), to 138 participants attending a series of workshops on paternity testing offered at the biannual national meetings of the American Society of Clinical Pathologists (ASCP) and a group of eight laboratories known to the authors as centers doing or consulting on paternity testing problems. Respondents were asked to provide data on the extent of routine testing done at the

* Edited by the authors and reprinted with permission from FAMILY LAW QUARTERLY, vol. 10, pp. 287-94 (1976) and TRANSFUSION, Vol. 17, pp. 521-24. (Footnotes omitted.) Funds for clerical work, postage, computer tabulations and research assistance were provided by the HEW grant, Office of Child Development, OCD-CB-452.

** Director, Minneapolis War Memorial Blood Bank.

651

time of the survey (late 1974). Inquiry was made concerning the volume of testing between January 1 and December 31, 1973, current charges, who did the testing and how individuals tested were identified. Each laboratory's potential for providing additional tests beyond those now applied in paternity matters was ascertained by questions on current availability of specific additional tests (now applied to other uses).

The responses were tabulated and compared by the type of institution (hospital, community blood bank, private laboratory), location (metropolitan *vs.* nonmetropolitan, the latter covering locations with a population of less than 250,000), and annual volume of activity (high: more than 5,000 units of blood, intermediate: 1,000 to 5,000 units, low: less than 1,000 units).

Results.

Responses were obtained from 90 (51 percent) of the 177 laboratories surveyed. All but one of the AABB Reference Laboratories responded. Sixty-five (72 percent) of those responding (see Table 1) routinely did paternity testing. During 1973, these laboratories had tested 2,175 groups of three or more individuals in cases of disputed parentage. More than half (52 percent) of the laboratories had done less than ten studies and only 11 (19%) reported doing more than 50 studies during the year (see Table 2).

All respondents included ABO, Rh [Rh_o (D), rh'(C), rh"(E), hr'(c) and hr"(e)] and M in their routine testing. Table 3 shows that a wide variety of other blood group antigens, serum proteins and erythrocyte enzymes were used by one or more laboratories. Specifically, at the time of the survey, 16 per cent of AABB Reference Laboratories were doing some erythrocyte enzyme testing compared to only 2 percent of the rest of the sample. Similarly, 16 percent of the AABB Reference Laboratories had capacity for HLA typing compared to only 2 percent of the other respondents.

Table 2

Volume of Paternity Testing Reported by Respondents for 1973

Type of Laboratory	Number of Laboratories Grouped by Work Load				
	< 10*	10–20	21–50	50–100	> 100
AABB	8	1	3	2	2
Other	22	9	4	4	3
Metropolitan	15	4	5	6	5
Nonmetropolitan	15	6	2	0	0
Community blood bank	2	1	2	0	1
Hospital	21	6	4	2	2
Other**	7	3	1	4	2

* Based on groups of three or more individuals.
** Private laboratories and nonhospital government facilities.

Table 3

Comparison of Tests Available and Those Routinely Used in Paternity Testing (PT)

Test System	AABB Reference Labs		Number of Labs Available (60)	All Other Labs Routine in PT (46)
	Available (30)	Routine in PT (19)		
A$_1$	100*	84.2	96.7	78.3
C^w	96.7	36.8	51.7	15.2
N	100	100	90.0	97.8
S	96.7	63.2	76.7	63.0
s	93.3	57.9	68.3	52.2
K	100	57.9	78.3	58.9
k	96.7	36.8	60.0	37.0
Kp^a	79.3	21.1	26.7	4.3
Kp^b	79.3	21.1	24.9	2.2
Fy^a	100	47.4	63.3	37.0
Fy^b	86.7	31.6	53.3	21.7
Jk^a	96.7	36.8	51.7	23.2
Jk^b	73.3	15.8	38.3	13.0
Lu^a	83.3	15.8	39.8	10.9
P	76.6	21.1	20.0	6.5
Xg^a	73.3	5.3	15.0	2.2
Le^a	83.3	15.8	51.7	6.5
Le^b	76.6	15.8	48.3	4.3
Se	86.7	5.3	28.3	2.2
Gm	20.0	21.1	6.6	0
Km	6.6	5.3	0	0
Hp	34.0	15.8	20.0	3.3
Gc	16.6	15.8	5.0	0
AcP	13.3	15.8	1.7	0
PGM	16.6	15.8	0	0
Hb	26.6	21.1	16.6	1.7
HLA	16.6	0	1.7	0

* Percentage of respondents.

The extent of testing by AABB Reference Laboratories was significantly greater than that done by others. More testing was also routine in laboratories classified as metropolitan compared to those in nonmetropolitan areas. Moreover, institutions located in metropolitan areas and those handling larger numbers of units of blood (more than 5,000/year) were shown to have a greater testing *potential* *i.e.,* the capacity to do informative tests not now routinely used in cases of disputed parentage than was possessed by laboratories in nonmetropolitan areas or those engaged in less blood banking activity.

Table 4

Charges for Testing a Group of Three Individuals

	Charges ($)	
Type of Laboratory	Range	Mean
AABB reference		
Laboratories	10–150	45
Others	16–82	39
Community blood		
banks	25–50	34
Hospitals	16–150	42
Others	10–82	44

The mean charge for testing three individuals was $42. Charges ranged from $10 to $150 (see Table 4) and did *not* correlate with the extent or volume of testing or the location or type of institution.

In most of the laboratories surveyed (and in all of the AABB Reference Laboratories), samples submitted for determination of parentage were tested in duplicate. Only 10 percent responded that tests were done singly. A few laboratories tested in triplicate. Twenty-two percent of respondents reported that repeat samples were drawn if an exclusion was found.

Testing usually was done by a medical technologist (92.3 percent of respondents) although in some cases samples also were tested by a physician (26.2 percent). Physicians do the procedure in only 5 percent of the AABB Reference Laboratories and in 20 percent of the nonmetropolitan laboratories, as compared to about 30 percent in all other categories.

While most laboratories prefer to draw blood themselves from the persons to be tested, 60 percent of the AABB

Reference Laboratories stated that they accepted mailed samples in contrast to only 11 percent of the low (or unknown) volume group and only 23 percent of the nonmetropolitan laboratories. Of the total sample, 43 percent stated that mailed specimens would be accepted.

Individuals appearing for paternity tests were identified as follows: Children by a heel or hand print: 42 percent of the total sample obtained fingerprints, 39 percent photographed the individuals and 35 percent relied on drivers licenses for identification. Another method (used by approximately 10 percent of the respondents) is mutual identification by the involved persons. No single method was used by a majority of the respondents.

Because of increasing interest, especially in Europe, in using statistical calculations to determine the "probability" of paternity of alleged fathers in cases which produce no exclusion, it was asked how many laboratories routinely perform these calculations (paternity index = PI): Forty percent of the laboratories surveyed stated their capability of making such calculations, but only 12 percent do them routinely. The AABB Reference Laboratories reported that they calculate PI only on request.

Conclusion.

This survey of paternity testing practices in the USA for the year 1973 indicates that a diverse group of laboratories, many with a relatively small volume of cases, are providing paternity testing services of greatly varying sophistication and detail. This contrasts with the practice in Europe, especially in Scandinavia, where rather extensive testing is done in few centralized institutions many of which specialize in forensic medicine. As a group, the AABB Reference Laboratories (which are so designated because of their expertise in handling transfusion problems), do substantially more paternity testing than any of the other laboratories surveyed. This group of laboratories also reported the greatest capacity for adding further genetic systems to their routine testing of paternity samples.

Appendix I

STATE AGENCIES ADMINISTERING CHILD SUPPORT PROGRAMS UNDER TITLE IV-D OF THE SOCIAL SECURITY ACT

ALABAMA

Mr. Lamar Lott
Acting Director
Division of Child Support Activities
Bureau of Financial Assistance
State Department of Pensions and Security
64 North Union Street
Montgomery, Alabama 36130
(205) 832-6561

ALASKA

Mr. Dan Copeland
Administrator
Child Support Enforcement Agency
Department of Revenue
201 East 9th Avenue, Room 202
Anchorage, Alaska 99501
(907) 276-8148

ARIZONA

Mr. John Ahl
Program Administrator
Child Support Enforcement Administration
Department of Economic Security
Post Office Box 6123
Phoenix, Arizona 85005
(602) 271-4759

ARKANSAS

Mr. Alfred Garrett
Manager

Office of Child Support Enforcement
Arkansas Social Services
Post Office Box 3358
Little Rock, Arkansas 72203
(501) 371-1614

CALIFORNIA
Mr. Robert A. Barton
Chief
Child Support Program Management Branch
Department of Social Services
744 P. Street
Sacramento, California 95814
(916) 322-6384

COLORADO
Mr. Kenneth Muroya
Director
Division of Child Support Enforcement
Department of Social Services
1575 Sherman Street
Denver, Colorado 80203
(303) 839-2422

CONNECTICUT
Mr. Anthony DiNallo
Chief
Bureau of Child Support
Department of Human Resources
110 Bartholemew Avenue
Hartford, Connecticut 06105
(203) 566-3053

DELAWARE
Mr. Charles S. Willis
Chief

Bureau of Child Support Enforcement
Department of Health and Social Services
920 Church Street
Wilmington, Delaware 19801
(302) 571-3620

DISTRICT OF COLUMBIA
Mr. Eugene Brown
Chief
Office of Paternity and Child Support Enforcement
Department of Human Resources
601 Indiana Avenue, N.W., Room 1008
Washington, D.C. 20011
(202) 724-8820

FLORIDA
Mr. Samuel G. Ashdown, Jr.
Director
Office of Child Support Enforcement
Department of Health and Rehabilitative Services
1317 Winewood Boulevard
Tallahassee, Florida 32301
(904) 488-9900

GEORGIA
Mr. Tracy Teal
Chief
Child Support Recovery Unit
State Department of Human Resources
618 Ponce de Leon Avenue, N.E.
Atlanta, Georgia 30334
(404) 894-4118

GUAM
Ms. Julia Perez
Supervisor

Child Support Enforcement Unit
Division of Social Services
Department of Public Health and Social Services
Government of Guam
Post Office Box 2816
Agana, Guam 96910

HAWAII
Mr. James O'Brien
IV-D Director
Child Support Enforcement Services
770 Kapiolani Boulevard
Honolulu, Hawaii 96809
(808) 548-5779

IDAHO
Mrs. Pat Barrell
Chief
Bureau of Child Support Enforcement
Department of Health and Welfare
Statehouse Mail
Boise, Idaho 83720
(208) 384-2480

ILLINOIS
Mr. Dale Johnson
Chief
Bureau of Child Support
Department of Public Aid
316 South Second Street
Springfield, Illinois 62762
(217) 782-1383

INDIANA
Mr. Thomas W. McKean
Director

Child Support Enforcement Division
State Department of Public Welfare
141 S. Merridian Street, 4th Floor
Indianapolis, Indiana 46225
(317) 232-4903

IOWA
Mr. John Terrell
Director
Child Support Recovery Unit
Iowa Department of Social Services
Hoover Building — 1st Floor
Des Moines, Iowa 50319
(515) 281-6015

KANSAS
Ms. Betty Hummel
Director
Location and Support
Department of Social and Rehabilitation Services
2700 West 6th — Biddle Building
Topeka, Kansas 66606
(913) 296-4188

KENTUCKY
Mr. Harry G. Dickerson, Jr.
Director
Division of Child Support Enforcement
Bureau of Social Insurance
Department of Human Resources
275 East Main Street, 6th Floor
Frankfort, Kentucky 40601
(502) 564-2285

LOUISIANA
Mr. O. J. White

Director
Support Enforcement Services Program
Office of Family Services
Department of Health and Human Resources
Post Office Box 44276
Baton Rouge, Louisiana 70804
(504) 689-4780

MAINE

Mr. Colburn Jackson
Director
Support Enforcement Locator Unit
Bureau of Social Welfare
Department of Health and Welfare
State House
Augusta, Maine 04330
(207) 289-2886

MARYLAND

Mr. John Williams
Chief
Bureau of Support Enforcement
Department of Human Resources
11 South Street
Baltimore, Maryland 21202
(301) 383-3501

MASSACHUSETTS

Miss Gertude Linehan
Director
Child Support Enforcement Unit
Department of Public Welfare
600 Washington Street
Boston, Massachusetts 02111
(617) 727-7820

MICHIGAN
Mr. David L. Bailey
Director
Office of Child Support
Department of Social Services
300 South Capitol Avenue
Lansing, Michigan 48926
(517) 373-7570

MINNESOTA
Mrs. Bonnie Becker
Acting Director
Office of Child Support
Department of Public Welfare
Centennial Office Building
St. Paul, Minnesota 55155
(612) 296-2499

MISSISSIPPI
Mr. Monte L. Barton
Director
Child Support Division
State Department of Public Welfare
Post Office Box 4321 - Fondren Station
Jackson, Mississippi 39216
(601) 956-8713, ext. 6716

MISSOURI
Mr. Paul Nelson
Administrator
Child Support Enforcement Unit
Division of Family Services
Department of Social Services
Post Office Box 88
Jefferson City, Missouri 65103
(314) 751-4301

MONTANA
  Mr. Ray Linder
  Bureau Chief
  Child Support Enforcement Bureau
  Montana Department of Revenue
  323 Sam Mitchell Building
  Helena, Montana 59601
  (406) 449-2846

NEBRASKA
  Mr. David C. Rasmussen
  Administrator
  Child Support Enforcement Office
  Department of Public Welfare
  Post Office Box 95026
  Lincoln, Nebraska 68509
  (402) 471-3121, ext. 140

NEVADA
  Mr. William Furlong
  Chief
  Child Support Enforcement
  Nevada State Welfare Division
  Department of Human Resources
  251 Jeanell Drive
  Carson City, Nevada 89701
  (702) 885-4744

NEW HAMPSHIRE
  Mr. George Sinclair
  Support Unit Supervisor
  Division of Welfare
  State Department of Health and Welfare
  Hazen Drive
  Concord, New Hampshire 03301
  (603) 271-4426

NEW JERSEY
Mr. G. Thomas Riti
Director
Child Support and Paternity Unit
Department of Human Services
Post Office Box 1627
Trenton, New Jersey 08625
(609) 890-9500, ext. 419

NEW MEXICO
Mr. Ben Silva
Chief
Child Support Enforcement Bureau
Department of Human Services
Post Office Box 2348 - Crown Building
Santa Fe, New Mexico 87502
(505) 827-5591

NEW YORK
Mr. Meldon F. Kelsey
Director
Office of Child Support Enforcement
New York State Department of Social Services
40 North Pearl - Seventh Floor
Albany, New York 12243
(518) 474-9081

NORTH CAROLINA
Mr. George W. Flemming
Chief
Child Support Enforcement Section
Division of Social Services
Department of Human Resources
Albemarle Building - Room 1017
325 N. Salisbury Street
Raleigh, North Carolina 27611
(919) 733-4120

NORTH DAKOTA
Mr. Thomas C. Tupa
Administrator
Child Support Enforcement Agency
Social Service Board of North Dakota
Russell Building — Highway 83 North
Bismarck, North Dakota 58505
(701) 224-3582

OHIO
Mr. Michael Seidemann
Chief
Bureau of Child Support
Department of Public Welfare
State Office Tower
30 East Broad Street
Columbus, Ohio 43215
(614) 466-3233

OKLAHOMA
Mr. Tom Wood
Program Administrator
Child Support Enforcement Unit
Department of Institutions, Social and
    Rehabilitative Services
Post Office Box 25352
Oklahoma City, Oklahoma 73125
(405) 521-3641

OREGON
Mr. Leonard T. Sytsma
Manager
Support Services
Department of Human Resources

Post Office Box 14506
Salem, Oregon 97310
(503) 378-6093

PENNSYLVANIA
Miss Linda M. Gunn
Director
Child Support Programs
Office of Program Accountability
Department of Public Welfare
Post Office Box 2675
Harrisburg, Pennsylvania 17120
(717) 787-3660

PUERTO RICO
Mr. Pedro Martin Maleonado
Director
Child Support Enforcement Program
Department of Social Services
Post Office Box 11398, Fernandez Juncos Station
Santurce, Puerto Rico 00908
(809) 722-4731

RHODE ISLAND
Mr. George Moriarty
Chief Supervisor
Bureau of Family Support
Department of Social and Rehabilitative Services
77 Dorrance Street
Providence, Rhode Island 02903
(401) 277-2409

SOUTH CAROLINA
Mr. T. Vernon Drew, Jr.
Director

Child Support Unit
Public Assistance Division
Bureau of Public Assistance and Field Operations
Department of Social Services
Post Office Box 1520
Columbia, South Carolina 29202
(803) 758-8860

SOUTH DAKOTA
Mr. Leland E. Swann
Program Administrator
Office of Child Support Enforcement
State Office Building #3 — Illinois Street
Pierre, South Dakota 57501
(605) 773-3641

TENNESSEE
Mr. Michael D. O'Hara
Director
Child Support Services
Legal Services Division
Department of Human Services
111-19 7th Avenue N. — Sixth Floor
Nashville, Tennessee 37203
(615) 741-3288

TEXAS
Mr. Edwin N. Horne
Chief
Support Enforcement Branch
Department of Human Resources
John H. Reagan Building
Austin, Texas 78701
(512) 835-0440, ext. 2036

UTAH
Mr. James Kidder
Director
Bureau of Child Support Enforcement
Office of Recovery Services
Department of Social Services
Post Office Box 2500
Salt Lake City, Utah 84110
(801) 533-7438

VERMONT
Mr. Bert N. Smith
Director
Support and Fraud Division
Department of Social Welfare
State Office Building
Montpelier, Vermont 05602
(802) 241-2866

VIRGIN ISLANDS
Mr. Harry Biske
Director
Division of Paternity and Child Support
Insular Department of Social Welfare
Post Office Box 539
Charlotte Amalie
St. Thomas, Virgin Islands 00801
(809) 774-0930, ext. 279

VIRGINIA
Ms. Jean White
Acting Chief
Bureau of Support Enforcement
Department of Welfare
8004 Franklin Farms Drive
Richmond, Virginia 23288
(804) 281-9154

WASHINGTON
Mr. Robert Querry
Chief
Office of Support Enforcement
Department of Social and Health Services
Post Office Box 9162-FU-11
Olympia, Washington 98504
(206) 753-1431

WEST VIRGINIA
Mr. Thomas Gunnoe
Assistant Commissioner
Office of Child Support Enforcement
Department of Welfare
1900 Washington Street, East
Charleston, West Virginia 25305
(304) 348-3780

WISCONSIN
Mr. Duane Campbell
Director
Bureau of Child Support
Division of Economic Assistance
18 South Thornton Avenue
Madison, Wisconsin 53708
(608) 266-0528

WYOMING
Mrs. Shirley Kingston
Director
Child Support Enforcement Section
Division of Public Assistance and Social Services
State Department of Health and Social Services
Hathaway Building
Cheyenne, Wyoming 82001
(307) 777-7561

INDEX

A

AGENCIES.
See FEDERAL GOVERNMENT; STATE
DEPARTMENTS AND AGENCIES.

**AID TO FAMILIES WITH DEPENDENT CHILDREN
(AFDC).**
Benefit levels, pp. 458-461.
Collection of child support.
Collection for non-AFDC claimants, pp. 323-330,
476-478.
Collections of child support, p. 318.
Distribution of support collections, pp. 340, 456.
Retention of support payments by state as
reimbursement for aid rendered, pp. 456-476.
"Need" standards, pp. 458-461.
Poverty level, p. 461.
Statistics, pp. x-xi, 117.

ALIMONY.
Enforcement under federal program, pp. 443-446.

AMERICAN BAR ASSOCIATION (ABA).
Blood tests for paternity.
Joint AMA-ABA guidelines, pp. 537-582.
Position on child support enforcement.
Mother's duty to cooperate, p. 369.

AMERICAN MEDICAL ASSOCIATION (AMA).
Blood tests.
Joint AMA-ABA guidelines.
Present status of serologic testing in problems of
disputed parentage, pp. 537-582.

L

LABORATORIES.

Blood tests.

Costs of typing blood, pp. 450-455.

Paternity.

Survey of American laboratories.

Current capacities and potentials, Appx. H, pp. 651 to 657.

Procedures and safeguards, pp. 272-280.

Reliability, pp. 243-246.

LEGITIMACY, pp. 103-113.

See ILLEGITIMACY.

LIENS, pp. 74-81.

LIMITATION OF ACTIONS.

Paternity.

Ascertaining father of nonmarital child, pp. 184-188.

M

MAINTENANCE.

Support and maintenance.

See SUPPORT AND MAINTENANCE.

MARRIAGE.

Uniform Marriage and Divorce Act.

See UNIFORM MARRIAGE AND DIVORCE ACT.

MODIFIED SUPPORT OBLIGATIONS.

Separation agreements.

Response to significant change in circumstances, pp. 18, 19.

Support and maintenance.

General provisions.

See SUPPORT AND MAINTENANCE.

MOTHERS.
  Ascertaining and locating absent father.
    Cooperation of mother.
      Aid.
        Good cause exception.

UNIFORM RECIPROCAL ENFORCEMENT OF SUPPORT ACT (URESA).